Gurus and Media

Gurus and Media

Sound, image, machine, text and the digital

Edited by

Jacob Copeman, Arkotong Longkumer
and Koonal Duggal

First published in 2023 by
UCL Press
University College London
Gower Street
London WC1E 6BT

Available to download free: www.uclpress.co.uk

Collection © Editors, 2023
Text © Contributors, 2023
Images © Contributors and copyright holders named in captions, 2023

Cover image credits:
Vivekananda. Wikimedia Commons. CC BY-SA 4.0.
Guru Rewben Mashangva. Photo courtesy of Vidura Jang Bahadur.
Business Guru. Shutterstock.
Ganesh and Robot. Courtesy of Emmanuel Grimaud.
Anandamayi Maa. Wikimedia Commons. CC BY-SA 4.0.
Christ the Guru. Courtesy of Christian Musicological Society of India.

The authors have asserted their rights under the Copyright, Designs and Patents Act 1988 to be identified as the authors of this work.

A CIP catalogue record for this book is available from The British Library.

Any third-party material in this book is not covered by the book's Creative Commons licence. Details of the copyright ownership and permitted use of third-party material are given in the image (or extract) credit lines. If you would like to reuse any third-party material not covered by the book's Creative Commons licence, you will need to obtain permission directly from the copyright owner.

This book is published under a Creative Commons Attribution-Non-Commercial 4.0 International licence (CC BY-NC 4.0), https://creativecommons.org/licenses/by-nc/4.0/. This licence allows you to share and adapt the work for non-commercial use provided attribution is made to the author and publisher (but not in any way that suggests that they endorse you or your use of the work) and any changes are indicated. Attribution should include the following information:

Copeman, J., Longkumer, A. and Duggal, K. (eds). 2023. *Gurus and Media: Sound, image, machine, text and the digital*. London: UCL Press. https://doi.org/10.14324/111.9781800085541

Further details about Creative Commons licences are available at https://creativecommons.org/licenses/

ISBN: 978-1-80008-556-5 (Hbk.)
ISBN: 978-1-80008-555-8 (Pbk.)
ISBN: 978-1-80008-554-1 (PDF)
ISBN: 978-1-80008-557-2 (epub)
DOI: https://doi.org/10.14324/111.9781800085541

Contents

List of figures	vii
Notes on contributors	xi
Acknowledgements	xvii

	Gurus and media: an introduction *Jacob Copeman, Koonal Duggal and Arkotong Longkumer*	1
1	The sonic guru: Rewben Mashangva, folk, roots and the blues *Arkotong Longkumer*	61
2	'Non-human gurus': yoga dolls, online avatars and meaningful narratives *Patrick S. D. McCartney and Diego Lourenço*	95
3	Governing with a lockdown beard: the COVID-19 crisis as a laboratory for Narendra Modi's Hindutva *David Landau and Nina Rageth*	125
4	'Immortal gurus of *Bhārata*': the social biography of a contemporary image *Raphaël Voix*	149
5	Languages of longing: Indian gurus, Western disciples, and practices of letter writing *Somak Biswas*	183
6	*Śabda-guru*: conflicts of guruship, mediational phenomenology and *Śabda*-philosophy in Sikhism *Arvind-Pal Singh Mandair*	211
7	Hacking God: Ganesh Yourself, an incarnation experiment in human divine circuitry *Emmanuel Grimaud*	235

8 Flooding the Web: absence-presence and the media
   strategies of Nithyananda's digital empire   271
   Amanda Lucia

9 When God dies: multi-mediation, the elsewhere and
   crypto-futurity in a global guru movement   299
   Tulasi Srinivas

10 Envisioning silence: Ramana Maharshi and the rise of
   Advaitic photography   325
   Yagna Nag Chowdhuri

11 'Christ the guru': artistic representations of Jesus Christ
   in South India and their mediated notions of guru-ness   349
   E. Dawson Varughese

12 The total guru: film star guruship in the time of Hindutva   375
   Jacob Copeman and Koonal Duggal

13 Doing seeing: televised yoga, consumption and religious
   nationalism in neoliberal India   419
   Srirupa Bhattacharya

Index   445

List of figures

0.1	'Save Hindu saints.' https://www.trendsmap.com/twitter/tweet/1540889774982062082.	8
0.2	'There is no culture without saints. But … why such atrocities on the community of saints?' https://www.trendsmap.com/twitter/tweet/1540889774982062082.	9
0.3	'Shouldn't the godmen be booked for mimicking us?' Cartoon by Satish Acharya.	12
0.4	Rohith Vemula case: Dalit students protest in 'Eklavya' avatar.	17
1.1	Guru in concert.	65
1.2	Guru in concert.	65
1.3	Issued by the Ministry of Culture when guru Mashangva received the Padma Shri. https://twitter.com/MinOfCultureGoI/status/1354753591622291457/photo/1.	67
1.4a	'No more killings', a song written by a guru.	68
1.4b	'Winning peace together', a song written by a guru.	68
1.5a	Front cover of the Bob Dylan lyric book.	75
1.5b	Back cover of the Bob Dylan lyric book.	75
2.1	'Barbie movimientos made to move opinion'.	101
2.2	Hybrid 'yoga' doll.	108
2.3	'Made to move Barbie DHL84 (2015)'.	108
4.1	*The sons of ambrosia*. The forty-two monks of India.	151
4.2	*The great incarnations of eternal India*. Fifty immortal gurus of Bharat.	151
4.3	*Saints of India*.	152
4.4	*A group of thirty religious men of India*.	156
4.5	Potpourri of divine figures.	160
4.6	*The forty-three monks of India*.	162
4.7	Portrait of Sri Sri NitaiChaitanya Paramhansadev.	162
4.8	*The fifty-one monks of India*.	163
4.9	*The forty-two monks of India*.	164

4.10	*The family of ambrosia*. The group of 60 great spirits of Bhāratavarṣa.	166
4.11	Vivekananda, Calcutta.	167
4.12	Brahmananda, Calcutta.	167
4.13	False brahmananda.	168
4.14	*The extraordinary children of ambrosia*.	169
5.1	Tagore's letter to Pearson, 15 January 1913.	188
5.2	Pearson asking to refer to Tagore as guru, 17 December 1912.	189
5.3	C. F. Andrews fundraising for Shantiniketan, 20 November 1931.	198
5.4	Envelope (in Tagore's hand) addressed to Andrews, then residing with Gandhi at Sabarmati, 1918.	206
7.1	*Ganesh Yourself*, film, 2016.	236
7.2	*Ganesh Yourself*, film, 2016.	238
7.3	*Ganesh Yourself*, film, 2016.	245
7.4	*Ganesh Yourself*, film, 2016.	267
10.1	Still from *The Razor's Edge*, 1946.	331
10.2	'Welling Bust' (1946).	333
10.3	'Mani Bust' (1930s).	335
10.4	Ramana reading (date and photographer unknown).	339
10.5	'"Last day" of Ramana' (1950). Taken by Henri Cartier-Bresson.	341
10.6	Photographer T. N. Krishnaswami with Ramana (date and photographer unknown).	345
11.1	Façade of Dharmaram College, Bengaluru.	358
11.2	Oil painting: *Christ the Guru* by M. P. Manoj (1993).	358
11.3	*St Anthony's Shrine*, a painted, concrete-moulded tableau installed in 2003 at St Anthony's Friary Church, Bengaluru by the Keralite artist, Fr Saji Mathew.	361
11.4	'In *padmasana* posture': *St Anthony's Shrine*, a painted, concrete-moulded tableau installed in 2003 at St Anthony's Friary Church, Bengaluru by the Keralite artist, Fr Saji Mathew (detail).	363
11.5	*Missio I*, 1986, by Jyoti Sahi ('Missio': International Catholic Mission Society, Germany).	365
11.6	*Missio II*, 1986, by Jyoti Sahi ('Missio': International Catholic Mission Society, Germany).	369
12.1	Still from *MSG: The Messenger* official trailer.	388
12.2	Still from *MSG 2*.	397

12.3	Still from *MSG 2*.	397
12.4	Still from *MSG 2*.	397
12.5	Guru as 'saviour' of Rajput women held captive by Muslim ruler Zalim Khan in *MSG: Warrior Lion Heart*.	402
12.6	Guru as 'cow vigilante' confronting Muslim men depicted as cow smugglers in *MSG: Warrior Lion Heart*.	403

Notes on contributors

Srirupa Bhattacharya completed her PhD in sociology from Jawaharlal Nehru University in 2016 with a doctoral fellowship from the Indian Council for Social Science Research (2013–15). She has taught undergraduate sociology at Delhi University (2016–21) and was a postdoctoral fellow at the International Institute for Asian Studies, Leiden University (2021–2). She is working on converting her thesis into a book. Her research explores the relationship between Hindu religious organisations and liberalisation in India. She currently teaches Sociology in GITAM School of Humanities and Social Sciences, Visakhapatnam.

Somak Biswas is *Past and Present* Fellow at the Institute of Historical Research, London. A social and cultural historian of modern South Asia, Britain and empire, he was educated at Jawaharlal Nehru University and the University of Warwick. His first book, *Passages through India: Indian gurus, Western disciples and the politics of Indophilia, 1890–1940* (Cambridge University Press), is published in 2023.

Yagna Nag Chowdhuri received her doctorate in the field of Asian literature, religion and culture from Cornell University in 2020. She is a Senior Consultant at ORS Impact, where she supports social justice organisations in their journey to create more impact. Her research focuses on the concept of the guru, media studies, utopia and practices of self-transformation, and transnational spiritual communities.

Jacob Copeman is Research Professor, University of Santiago de Compostela, Distinguished Researcher (Oportunius) and Senior Researcher (CISPAC). He co-edited *The Guru in South Asia: New interdisciplinary perspectives* (Routledge, 2012). He is also co-editor of *Global Sceptical Publics: From non-religious print media to 'digital atheism'* (UCL Press, 2022) and *An Anthropology of Intellectual Exchange: Interactions, transactions and ethics in Asia and beyond* (Berghahn, 2023) and co-author of *Hematologies: The political life of blood in India* (Cornell University Press,

2019). He is Principal Investigator of the ERC-funded project 'Religion and its others in South Asia and the world: Communities, debates, freedoms'.

E. Dawson Varughese works at the intersection of world literature, visual studies and cultural studies, drawing on ethnographic research paradigms to conduct her fieldwork. She is the author of *Beyond the Postcolonial: World Englishes literature* (Palgrave Macmillan, 2012), *Reading New India: Post-millennial Indian fiction in English* (Bloomsbury Academic, 2013), *Indian Writing in English and Issues of Visual Representation* (with Lisa Lau, Palgrave Macmillan, 2015), *Genre Fiction of New India: Post-millennial receptions of 'weird' narratives* (Routledge, 2016) and *Visuality and Identity in Post-millennial Indian Graphic Narratives* (Palgrave Macmillan, 2017).

Koonal Duggal is Research Fellow in Social Anthropology at the University of Edinburgh. He is currently working on a research project titled 'Gurus, anti-gurus and media in North India', funded by a Leverhulme Research Project Grant. He completed his MA in Art History and Aesthetics at the Maharaja Sayajirao University of Baroda, and has a PhD in cultural studies from the English and Foreign Languages University, Hyderabad. His work has been published in the journal *South Asian Popular Culture*. He is the first recipient of the Sher-Gil Sundaram Arts Foundation (SSAF) and Asia Art Archive in India (AAA) Research Grant for *Histories of Ideas, Art Writing, and Visual Culture* (2018). His research interests revolve around the politics of caste, religion, media studies and popular visual culture.

Emmanuel Grimaud is a Director of Research at CNRS (LESC-UMR7186, Nanterre University) and a filmmaker. He was awarded the bronze medal of the CNRS in 2011. He is the author of the first ethnography of the Bombay film studios (*Bollywood Film Studio*, 2003), a monograph on a Gandhi lookalike (*Le Sosie de Gandhi*, 2004), an ethnography of religious automata in India (*Gods and Robots*, 2007), and a film about the making of a robot of Ganesha to allow anyone to incarnate God and have a conversation (*Ganesh Yourself*, 2016). His latest film, *Black Hole: Why I have never been a rose* (2019), was awarded the Jury Special Prize at the Jean Rouch festival 2020. He curated the exhibition *Persona: Strangely human* (2016) in the Quai Branly Museum (Paris) with Anne-Christine Taylor and Denis Vidal.

David Landau received his PhD from SOAS, University of London and is a postdoctoral researcher at the University of Zurich. His research interests include Hindi literature, nationalism and minor literature.

Arkotong Longkumer is Senior Lecturer in Modern Asia at the University of Edinburgh. He is the author of *The Greater India Experiment: Hindutva and the northeast* (Stanford University Press, 2020; Indian edition Navayana, 2022), which was long-listed for the Kamaladevi Chattopadhyay New India Foundation Book Prize 2021. He is also the author of *The Poetry of Resistance: The Heraka movement of Northeast India* (North-Eastern Social Research Centre, 2016) and co-author of an Open Access book, *Indigenous Religion(s): Local grounds, global networks* (Routledge, 2020). He co-edited a special issue of *Contemporary South Asia* on Neo-Hindutva (2018). He is the recipient of the British Academy Mid-Career Fellowship (2017–18), and visiting fellowships at the Arctic University of Norway. He was the co-Principal Investigator (with Jacob Copeman) of a three-year project funded by the Leverhulme Trust on 'Gurus and media', and from November 2022 has been the Principal Investigator on a four-year project funded by the Arts and Humanities Research Council, 'Decolonising the museum: Digital repatriation of the Gaidinliu collection from the UK to India'.

Diego Lourenço is a historian, a playwright, and a PhD candidate at the Humboldt University of Berlin. He investigates contemporary yoga's historiography and social dimensions in eight countries with imperial or colonial histories: Brazil, Portugal, Mexico, Spain, India, the UK, the USA and Germany. His research combines history, psychology and sociology in the global study of yoga and inequality.

Amanda Lucia is Professor of Religious Studies at the University of California, Riverside. She is the author of *White Utopias: The religious exoticism of transformational festivals* (University of California Press, 2020), which explores the intersection of whiteness, religious exoticism and contemporary yoga spirituality. Her previous publications include *Reflections of Amma: Devotees in a global embrace* (University of California Press, 2014), and numerous articles. She is also the Principal Investigator for the Religion and Sexual Abuse Project, www.religionandsexualabuse project.org. Her current research focuses on celebrity gurus, and negotiations between religious authority and secular law.

Arvind-Pal S. Mandair holds the Tara Singh and Balwant Kaur Chattha, Gurbax Singh and Kirpal Kaur Brar Professorship in Sikh Studies at the University of Michigan. He is the Director of Graduate Studies for the Department of Asian Languages and Cultures and has a Faculty Associate appointment in the Department of American Studies. His recent publications include *Violence and the Sikhs* (Cambridge University Press,

2022) and *Sikh Philosophy: Exploring Gurmat concepts in a decolonizing world* (Bloomsbury Academic, 2022). Earlier books include *Religion and the Specter of the West* (Columbia University Press, 2009), *Secularism and Religion-Making* (with Markus Dressler, Oxford University Press, 2011), *Sikhism: A guide for the perplexed* (Bloomsbury, 2013) and *Teachings of the Sikh Gurus* (with Christopher Shackle, Routledge, 2005). He is the founding editor of the Routledge journal *Sikh Formations: Religion, Culture and Theory* and co-edits two new book series: *Routledge Critical Sikh Studies* and *Routledge Studies in Translation and Religion*. Details about his work can be found on his website arvindpalmandair.com.

Patrick S. D. McCartney, PhD is based in Japan as a Phoenix Fellow at Hiroshima University. His other affiliations include being a Research Associate at Nanzan University's Anthropological Institute, an ISRF Research Fellow at the University of Santiago-Compostela, Spain, and a Visiting Fellow at the Australian National University. He is a socio-cultural anthropologist/archaeologist-philologist who works at the boundaries of the politics of imagination and the economics of desire, exploring the biographies of Sanskrit and yoga and their relations to political theology, competitive diplomacy and faith-based development. His new research project, *Impaling the Yogi*, explores the complex and dynamic archaeological, philological, historical and anthropological transmission of rope- and pole-dancing wrestler-acrobats across the ancient, medieval and contemporary worlds. It focuses on street-performing guilds and their engagement with merchant and mercenary guilds between Europe and Asia.

Nina Rageth is Senior Assistant and Lecturer at the University of Zurich. She is trained as a scholar in the study of religion with a social-scientific approach. Her recent research has focused on the promotion of Siddha medicine by Hindu gurus and she has worked more broadly on New Religious Movements, discourses and practices related to spirituality and the interplay of religion and medicine.

Tulasi Srinivas is Professor of Anthropology, Religion and Transnational Studies in the Marlboro Institute of Interdisciplinary Studies at Emerson College. She is the author of the award-winning *Winged Faith: Rethinking globalization and religious pluralism through the Sathya Sai Movement* (Columbia University Press, 2010), *Curried Cultures: Globalization, food, and South Asia* (University of California Press, 2012) and more recently *The Cow in the Elevator: An anthropology of wonder* (Duke University Press, 2018), and of numerous other co-authored and edited books and papers. Srinivas has appeared on NPR and WNYC, and is the winner of several teaching awards and prestigious fellowships at the Radcliffe Institute of Advanced Study at Harvard University, the Rockefeller Foundation, the Berkley Center for Religion, Peace and World Affairs at Georgetown University, and the American Council of Learned Societies.

Raphaël Voix is a social anthropologist, research fellow at the French National Centre for Scientific Research (CNRS) and member of the Centre for South Asian and Himalayan Studies (CESAH), Paris. His research focuses on sectarian Hinduism in West Bengal. He has co-edited *Filing Religion: State, Hinduism and courts of law* (with Gilles Tarabout and Daniela Berti, Oxford University Press, 2016) and published in different academic journals and edited books.

Acknowledgements

This volume was made possible through the support of the Leverhulme Trust under its Research Project Grant programme ('Gurus, anti-gurus, and media in North India'; RPG-2018-145). Its electronic open-access publication has been made possible through the generous financial support of the Consellería de Cultura, Educación e Universidade, Galicia, in collaboration with the Universidade de Santiago de Compostela (USC). At USC, the support of Paula Solla has been simply indispensable. Sincere thanks are due to Daniel Gold, Bhuvi Gupta, Aya Ikegame, William Mazzarella, Arjun Appadurai, Nandini Gooptu, Neelabh Gupta, Sanjay Srivastava and Tulasi Srinivas for their support and comradeship. The importance to the volume of the special combination of generosity, inspiration and expertise offered by Lindsay Graham, Amanda Lucia and Patrick McCartney is difficult to overstate: we are extremely grateful. Our thanks to Vidura Jang Bahadur for allowing us to use his photograph of Rewben Mashangva to grace the front cover, to Salman Baba for designing the cover, and to Glynis Baguley for superlative copy-editing. Thanks also to the contributors for the provocation and stimulation of their chapters and to the UCL Press team for its encouragement, patience and professionalism.

The pervasive presence of gurus has had many incarnations across time and space. As pedagogues, gurus mediate between the past, the present and the future, carrying ancient knowledge of various kinds – not only sacred but also pertaining to the visual and performing arts, though the latter also are often sacredly derived – ideally conveying it to disciples and devotees, or, better, imbuing them with it through embodied interactions (subject of course to an array of restrictions on who might form appropriate – for instance, sufficiently pure – mediators and recipients).[2] The present volume explores manifestations of, and changes to, what we call the guru's methodologies of presence, as media forms and guru embodiments ebb, flow and come to nest within one another. The book is as interested in continuity as in innovation and innovations that occur in the cause of continuity, since novelty can only be gauged in the light of an understanding of the variety of long-standing and non-novel – but still under-theorised – ways in which gurus have operated as mediating subjects who are also subjects of mediation. Technologies of mediation that carry forth and sometimes compromise the guru mix performative and spiritual registers in ways that can allow us to see the guru afresh, and this is as true of historical as of contemporary mediations.

Nick Cave's song 'Red Right Hand' (1994) contains the lyrics:

He'll wrap you in his arms
Tell you that you've been a good boy
He'll rekindle all the dreams
It took you a lifetime to destroy
He'll reach deep into the hole
Heal your shrinking soul
But there won't be a single thing that you can do
He's a god, he's a man
He's a ghost, he's a guru

> (Nick Cave and the Bad Seeds, 'Red Right Hand')

Underscoring the global media dispersion of the guru concept by its very presence in a song by an Australia-born singer-songwriter based in the UK, the lyrics point to the profound comfort and depth, but also the terror and exploitation, that can lie within guru–devotee relationships, a kind of devotion that lies on the edge of the precipice: 'there won't be a single thing that you can do' in the face of the god who is a man, a ghost, a guru. They hint at the abuse that can result from the 'extreme authoritarianism' (McCartney 2018) that structures many if not all guru–disciple relationships, abuse that is liable not only to be reported and spread *in* the media, but also to be discovered and brought to light *by* media in the form of new media technologies such as hidden cameras.[3] Significantly, the profound hierarchy that creates the conditions for the abuse that generates such mediatisation results partly from gurus' own mediating function (specifically as the embodied mediators of forebears, gods and other natural and supernatural entities, and spiritual and other knowledge, including dance and musicianship). As early as the turn of the first millennium, writes Amanda Lucia (2021, 414), 'Gurus became understood as a special class of people who were deemed especially qualified to mediate, access, and embody the divine.'

This volume considers the diverse ways in which diverse kinds of gurus act as and engage with diverse forms of media. Of course, their presence is found in numerous forms of media, ranging from statuary to print publications, films, and social media with its attendant array of 'networked devotional public[s]' (Lazar 2019). Their presence manifests in bodies, words, texts, graffiti, dolls, sound, music, verse, samadhis (tombs) and visual images (e.g. reproductions in or on calendars, photographs, idols, stickers, lockets, TV, cinema, computers and phone screens). Different media forms and choices can have determining impacts on devotional practices and community building among followers. Well-known contemporary examples of highly mediatised guru–media engagements include the TV yoga guru and entrepreneur Baba Ramdev (Bhattacharya, this volume), the *Messenger of God* feature films starring the Dera Sacha Sauda (DSS) guru as versions of himself (Copeman and Duggal, this volume) and the use of digital media to take a guru's darshan[4] (a visual form of worship) (Warrier 2014).

However, we do not seek to imply that gurus are uniquely adept at employing media for their own ends. Media is frequently a guru's principal point of vulnerability: from the print media's amplification of the *pushtimarg* guru sex scandal of the 1860s, to more recent use of video slow motion and replay by Indian rationalists to expose malfeasance (Copeman and Hagström 2022). Indeed, a key media engagement of the guru has been on occasion to seek to silence it, whether through intimidation (see discussion below of the case of Mohammed Zubair) or through actual physical attacks on investigative journalists as seen in the case of followers of Asaram Bapu.[5] The spate of killings between 2013 and 2015 of rationalists who had creatively used a variety of media forms to criticise and debunk the claims of high-profile gurus also suggests that we should be wary of endorsing too readily the notion of a 'special' or mutually amplificatory guru–media relationship. Also significant is the ambivalence towards mass media of some guru-founded organisations, for instance the Madhvas (Okita 2012, 233), who traditionally have revealed their knowledge only to male Brahmans. As Madhva stated in his *Brahmasutrabhasya* 3.4.49, 'one should not think that this [the teachings imparted by a guru] is for mass distribution. Because there is a reason. When it is revealed in public, it would undesirably result that even those who are unqualified would receive [it].'[6] A positive relationship between media developments and gurus and their organisations is therefore not axiomatic. Rather, guru–media ecologies are 'a matter of obstacles, roadblocks, and traffic jams' as well as connectivity and circulation (Appadurai 2013, 69).

While there now exists an extremely rich body of literature on gurus and media, both historically and in the present, to date there has been no book-length work whose sole focus is on guru–media imbrications or that seeks to bridge the gap between scholarship on gurus and media and visual culture studies. In view of the centrality of media and mediation in domains of guruship, this chapter attempts to be both summative in reflecting on recent extremely productive guru–media scholarship and programmatic in identifying emergent themes and instances of these imbrications and exchanges that require more detailed analysis at present and in the future. In doing so the chapter provides a novel attempt to investigate guru iconographies across various time periods from the perspective of art history and visual culture and seeks to further existing important work on caste and gurus by considering this troubled relationship in the context of media and material culture.

First, recognising how the paradoxical simultaneity of the guru as a 'meta-person' (Graeber and Sahlins 2017) who is at once 'more than human' and 'all too human' couples with the extreme inequality of guru–devotee relationships to create the conditions for abuse and consequent media scrutiny, the chapter considers guru–media interactions centring on controversy and contested claims to legitimacy. Our particular focus here is on the role of the guru at a time of Hindutva supremacy in which taking offence has become 'a common condition for the organization of mass publics' (Cohen 2012, 106), and also on how such figures seem to provoke a particularly intensive intermediality and series of mimetic currents, even as they themselves mediate between earthly and spiritual planes. Next the chapter seeks to historicise the theme of guru domination, caste politics and Hindutva via the optics of matter and media, exploring both the mass remediation of Brahmanical guruship models that attended Hindutva's rise in the 1990s and the oppositional response it provoked, which we term 'the subaltern counter-publicity of the guru'. It becomes apparent that Hindutva is itself structurally composed of guru logics at different scales; it embodies a kind of 'fractal guruship'.[7] However, if Hindutva mediates principles of guruship, we see how a multitude of public gurus mediate principles of Hindutva. We suggest, in light of this relationship of mutual mediation, that continued investment by devotees and commentators in gurus as figures embodying hope and the promise of post-communal amity can aptly be described in terms of what Lauren Berlant (2011) has called 'cruel optimism'.

Then, under a broad conceptual schema of 'methodologies of presence', the chapter attempts to advance our understanding of the function of media in the dramatic production of guruship. Following Ilana Silber's (2019) work on the 'deep play' of public gifting which is 'suffused … with elements of play and symbolic recognition not unlike those attached to theatre' (p. 130), we position the performative dimension of guruship in the framework of guru repertoires, 'themselves shaping as well as shaped by dynamics of power, display and recognition on a public stage' (p. 125). The chapter proceeds to develop a concept of 'Guru, Inc.' as a means of reflecting upon the experimental, media-mobilising branding exercises of gurus. It also explores (after Gell 1998 and Corsín Jiménez 2018) the role of media and matter in enabling forms of 'distributed guruship' (guruship beyond the bounds of the biological organism) and 'spiderweb guruship' (guruship as a series of media-assisted affective and aesthetic traps for the captivation of devotees and other entities). Throughout, it foregrounds contested visions of the guru in the development of guru-centred publics and pluriform guruship more generally. In so doing, the chapter seeks both to recognise the importance of darshan and to avoid reducing visions of the guru to this paradigm alone.

Before we proceed further, a brief note is required on terminology. This Introduction employs the term 'guru' flexibly for a religious teacher or perceptor with connections, not necessarily formal ones, to the Hindu or the Sikh tradition. Apart from strictly religious understandings, the term is also used in traditional music and performance circles. There is a strong overlap between the figures of the ascetic and the guru – classically, the guru is an ascetic, though myriad exceptions exist – but, as Karen Pechilis (2015, 403) explains, there is a key 'difference between the categories of ascetic and devotee or saint on the one hand, and guru on the other. In the main, an ascetic or a devotee can perform that role by adopting established cultural ways of behaviour, but a guru needs the recognition of an audience in order to be a guru.' At the same time, not all gurus seek that status; some have it thrust upon them (as we discuss further below). Further, we employ the term 'public guru' to refer not only to globalising middle-class gurus who appear on television and possess millions of devotees but to any of the myriad, public-facing gurus who hold some sort of media presence and seek to engage with politics or social service activities beyond the confines of the ashram. The volume as a whole covers different sorts of guru and different sorts of media, and for different purposes. These differences are important, and the book does not aim to level out this diversity by putting rishis and sants in the same basket or by equating guruship as embodied, for instance, in yoga dolls, with the guru as embodied in Sikh scripture.[8] By juxtaposing such instances, however, the book proposes a kind of 'lateral comparison' – comparisons that 'travel sideways' – between different media contexts of guruship (Candea 2017). These contexts differ in highly significant ways, yet are at the same time culturally and historically profoundly intertwined.

Mediated guruship, Hindutva and the state

Outrage politics, media and the mimetic construction of the guru

Mediatisation of guru-centred controversies is not a new occurrence. The Maharaj libel case of the 1860s, for instance, hinged on allegations of adulterous behaviour among *gosains* of the *pushtimarg* (Gold 1988, 90–1; see also Malhotra 2022). Maya Warrier (2003, 233) suggests that much of this coverage relates to prevalent fears concerning the genuineness or otherwise of one's chosen master.[9] Such fears are 'fanned by the numerous stories ... prominently publicized in the mass media, about gurus being exposed as conmen (and women) with criminal connections, using their spirituality as a facade for making money, or sexual predators using the mask of their celibacy to run clandestine sex rackets'. However, if sensationalisation and moral panics have long comprised a key variety of media representation of guruship (McCartney 2018; Lucia 2018, and this volume), the present era of Hindutva supremacy and outrage politics features a further *meta-media* mode of representation in which criminality has come to lie in the act of pointing out actual criminal behaviour by gurus. This is because doing so 'hurts' Hindus' religious sentiments, the former (the pointing out) displacing actual guru criminality.[10] Consider how in June 2022, Alt News co-founder Mohammed Zubair was arrested under section 295A of the Indian Penal Code, which deems 'deliberate and malicious acts, intended to outrage religious feelings of any class by insulting its religion or religious beliefs' punishable by law, for describing three militant Hindutva gurus and priests – who had variously called for the eradication of Islam and the rape of Muslim women – 'hatemongers'.[11] Such effacement of guru criminality via attacks on those who call attention to it forms part of a wider well-known Hindutva agenda of intimidating its critics (especially media figures such as Zubair), which now frequently involves the 'weaponization of social media platforms' (Klein 2021) alongside 'intrusive levels of media surveillance' (Hamilton 2022, 392) that significantly restrain the activities of movements that dare to criticise the regime.

Unsurprisingly it is in part for electoral reasons that criticism of gurus is subject to legal and vigilante forms of Hindutva-instigated censorship, the assumption being that the political recruitment of consummate 'inclusive singularity' gurus constitutes simultaneously the recruitment of their followers.[12] Such 'ballot baba' gurus usually, though not always, direct their followers to vote for Hindutva political parties. In return, gurus may receive large-scale government funding (Ikegame 2012, 52), tax breaks (Copeman and Duggal, this volume) or – in the case of criminal gurus – protection from the law, their ashrams thus able to continue operating as something between a 'little fiefdom' (Singh 2017) and a 'temple racket' (Michelutti et al. 2019, 158).

However, the particular – highly possessive – Hindutva attitude towards the institution of guruship as a valued Hindu cultural good is a further key reason why Hindutva actors seek both to defend demonstrably corrupt and exploitative gurus and to censor and punish even mild media satire of the institution, with criticism of gurus coming to form yet another proof of a conspiracy to victimise Hindus, as in Christophe Jaffrelot's (1996, 76) famous description of Hindu nationalists as forming part of a majority with a minority complex. Figure 0.1, a popular meme that displays the photos of six gurus who have been the subject of multiple and varied criminal allegations ranging from corruption to child sexual abuse, murder and more, several of whom have served prison sentences for the offences, demonstrates well the enrolment of gurus into Hindutva's minority complex, with criminal gurus and their supporters exemplifying Amrita Basu's (2022, 61) wider point concerning how '[a]ggressors who think of themselves as victims are apt to deny and thus normalize the violence they engage in' (see also Figure 0.2). Indeed, an especially extreme and virulent Hindu nationalist organisation was established in 2007 for the express purpose of defending 'victimised' Hindu *sadhus* and

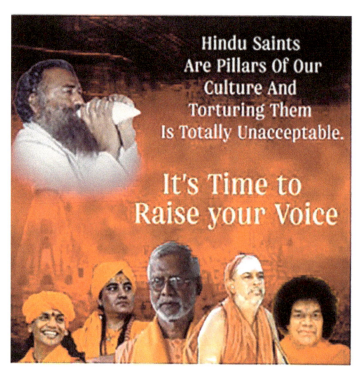

Figure 0.1 'Save Hindu saints.' https://www.trendsmap.com/twitter/tweet/ 1540889774982062082. Source: TrendsMap.com. Original source: Twitter.

gurus against their supposed large-scale persecution (Basu 2015, 185). In a tweet featuring the composite image depicted in Figure 0.1 and the hashtag '#AtrocitiesOnHinduSaints', BJP leader Subramaniam Swamy defends one particularly notorious criminal guru figure – Vishva Hindu Parishad[13] (VHP) ally Asaram Bapu[14] – for having 'brought several Hindus back "home" [i.e. 'reconverting' them] to *sanatan dharam* ['the eternal religion'; i.e. orthodox Hinduism]. That is why Vatican City asked Sonia Gandhi to get him trapped in a fake case. Hindus Must Unite. Raise Your Voice.'[15] Swami Nithyananda, the subject of Lucia's chapter in this volume, is one of the gurus featured in the composite 'persecuted gurus' image. As he faces numerous criminal charges, including large-scale financial fraud, it is the above-described 'crucial tropes [of] Hindutva' – that is, 'vocalised feelings of victimhood and a "siege mentality"' (Anderson 2015, 55) – that Nithyananda's followers drew on in mounting a global campaign that sought to 'recode Nithyananda and his followers not as criminals or frauds, but rather as persecuted and innocent victims of Hinduphobia' (Lucia, this volume).

Figure 0.2 'There is no culture without saints. But … why such atrocities on the community of saints?' https://www.trendsmap.com/twitter/tweet/154088977498206 2082. Source: TrendsMap.com. Original source: Twitter.

Gurus, then, are at the centre of the recently emerged 'more politically "voicy" Hindutva concerned with regulating and disciplining public representations of Hinduism' (Reddy 2012, 313). It is not only representations of gurus as abusers and criminals that it seeks to discipline but also more light-hearted, comedic ones. For instance, in 2008 several Hindutva organisations sought a ban on the Hollywood film *The Love Guru*, which satirised the commercialisation of guruship.[16] For these groups, however, the film offensively mocked Hindus and 'the sanctity of the Guru-disciple tradition' (Chaudhry 2012, 332). Meanwhile, if 'the 1980s saw the beginning of films of self-mockery of the public sphere', with savage satire of religious practices and forms of 'comic disrobing … all the more powerful as its targets were powerful godmen like the Saibaba of Puttaparti' (Nagaraj 2006, 103), there is now a Hindutva-led attempt to bring this era to a halt.

Despite this, and for the reasons discussed earlier, satire and exposés of gurus remain popular among the viewing public. Pavan Kumar Malreddy (2022), for instance, discusses three recent filmic 'unravellings' of discreditable gurus. In one such film, *PK*, the Islamophobic guru Tapasvi 'challenges PK to a live debate on television, where PK speaks about the need for people to remember to worship the God who made us, not the God we made and Tapasvi is exposed as a fraud' (Dwyer 2017, 260), while an episode of the hit TV police comedy *F.I.R.* in 2013 featured a sting operation against a guru who is secretly recorded admitting to money laundering.[17] Referencing the role of the hidden camera in an exposé of Swami Nithyananda, and especially the capturing on tape of Vedanti Maharaj, Pilot Baba and Guruvayur Surya Nambudiri offering the same money-laundering service,[18] the episode satirises both the corruption of holy men and the 'epistemophilic' excesses of the exposers, whose methods have been turned into a live-streamed spectacle.[19] Foucault famously argued that the modern disciplinary society arose out of a key shift from spectacle to surveillance: 'The spectacle turned into surveillance, the circle that citizens formed around the spectacle – all that is reversed. We have here a completely different structure where men who are placed next to each other on a flat surface will be surveilled from above by someone who will become a kind of universal eye' ([1973] 2013). But of course what we have in the case of live-streamed surveillance footage of Tiwari's confession – and also the hidden camera footage of Nithyananda's indiscretions as replayed on TV news and YouTube – is precisely both: surveillance as spectacle. In light of the *F.I.R.* satire, the filmic formatting of exposé and how gurus are seeking new methods of exposure to increase market share (with at least two saints now having made appearances on the Indian version of *Celebrity Big Brother* in which surveillance cameras cause contestants to become 24/7 voyeuristic objects of the viewing public), we might expand the point to suggest that a key way of seeing the guru in present times is at the 'intersection of surveillance, spectacle and exhibition' (Harcourt 2014, 23) – as 'exposing subjects' in an 'expository society' (p. 17).[20] For public gurus who 'blend … divinity and stardom' (Shearer 2000, 221), allegations of wrongdoing that generate media publicity might be welcomed as further conduits for spreading their message; certainly, public controversies and even a guru's imprisonment have been interpreted by devotees as necessary unfoldings for realising the guru's larger plan (see Copeman and Duggal, this volume; Goldberg 2015). Further, and to paraphrase William Mazzarella (2022), devotees' charismatic attraction to their gurus frequently has little to do, at root, with moral approval.

Dera Sacha Sauda (DSS) guru Gurmeet Ram Rahim Insan, a particularly vigorous exponent of what Copeman and Duggal in their chapter call (after Harcourt) a 'guruship of the exhibition', was the subject of a further meta-media controversy in 2016 when the comedian Kiku Sharda was arrested (once more under section 295A of the Indian Penal Code) following a TV sketch in which he mimicked the guru serving liquor and dancing with girls. Once more the criminal behaviour that seemed to matter most was not so much the guru's serial rape of his female devotees, murder of a critical journalist and castration of his close male associates (Tripathi 2018) – though the guru was eventually convicted of the first two of these and is currently serving a life sentence – as a comic's mocking reference to some of this behaviour.

Twitter commentators called attention to the mimetic irony. Figure 0.3, a cartoon by Satish Acharya in which Hindu deities observe Sharda in handcuffs and ask, 'Shouldn't the godmen be booked for mimicking us?', is a particularly good example. Astute though the commentary is, it barely begins to register the densely mimetic world of the guru and its media amplifications. Consider how the offensively represented guru had himself been the subject nine years earlier of an outcry centring on his own mimetic propensities. On that occasion, however, it was not a Hindu deity that the DSS guru had mimicked (though see Copeman and Duggal, this volume, on his imitation of gods as portrayed in devotional calendar art in his *MSG* film franchise). Rather, he had been photographed dressed up as, and conducting rituals extremely similar to those originated by, the revered final living Sikh guru, Guru Gobind Singh. Sikhs asserted that the DSS guru was claiming a deeply insulting equivalence between himself and their own (copied) guru, and this in a religion that expressly forbids further human gurus.[21] Here, intensive intermediality[22] had acted as a propellant for the mimetic capacities of media technologies, radically advancing what might otherwise have remained a local controversy: first arousing comment after a photograph of the event modelled on an iconic painting of the Sikh guru by portrait artist Sobha Singh (1901–86) was featured in a local newspaper, the image was quickly digitalised, spreading on the internet (on Sikh Facebook pages in particular) before featuring prominently, after the outbreak of serious unrest, in TV news reports. In this hall of mirrors Kiku had mimicked a particularly notorious mimic whose mimicry had itself been mimetically amplified by multiple media technologies.

Copeman and Duggal's chapter explores how cinema became yet another amplificatory means for the DSS guru to claim mimetic connection with iconic authority figures, from the 'Adi-guru' of indigenous tribal communities to Narendra Modi and beyond. The mimetic chain is extended still further in the chapter by David Landau and Nina Rageth, which describes the full blossoming of Modi's own guruship during the

Figure 0.3 'Shouldn't the godmen be booked for mimicking us?' Cartoon by Satish Acharya. Source: Twitter.

COVID-19 lockdowns of 2020–2. The move, which was perfectly in tune with his already existing authoritarianism and cult-leader status, once more was accomplished via intensely mediatised imitative sartorial and other aesthetic shifts that brought him closer into imagistic alignment with both guru image stereotypes and the historical 'guru-like' personages of M. K. Gandhi and Rabindranath Tagore, who are also the pivotal 'holy men' figures of Somak Biswas's chapter in this volume, which presents a detailed exposition of the letters exchanged between them and their

Western devotees. The mimetic faculty has been aptly defined as 'the competence of an agent to create authority and selfhood by means of imitation and alteration' (Brosius 2005, 99). What is important to observe here is just how central the mimetic faculty is to the circulation, authorisation and reproduction of the mediatised guru image.

The career of the famous Chola bronzes forms a revealing parallel with contemporary controversies centring on the mimetic reproduction of guru images. In medieval Tamil Nadu, where Jain and Buddhist traditions predominated before the emergence of Tamil Shaiva and Vaishnavite cults, popular poet-saints proliferated and converted local rulers. For instance, the Pallava ruler Mahendravarman I, a Jain, was later converted to Saivism by the saint Appar. Legitimation of such saint-influenced shifts was confirmed through the presence of these saints 'placed beside the shrine of their deity, either Shiva or Vishnu' in temples commissioned by rulers from Pallava, and also the Chola dynasty (Dehejia 1995, 141). Deification of the poet-saints took place through recitation of their poetry, worship of their images and ceremonial gatherings upon their deaths (Dehejia 1995, 141), with their presence famously embodied in the form of bronze sculptures (the Chola bronzes) prepared through an ancient wax technique of metal casting.

The parallel lies not only in how representation of the poet-saints forms a key prior instance of the intermediality of guru images (human-mediated deity, image, bronze sculpture), but also in the bronzes' intentional iconographic ambiguity causing them repeatedly to be misidentified as gods in various museums, exhibitions and auction catalogues. For instance, the elongated standing idol of 'Andal[,] who is depicted as a beautiful young woman holding a parrot, has been confused with Madurai's goddess Minakshi, while Shaiva saint Karaikkal Ammaiyar is an emaciated skeletal hag who has been mistaken for the fearsome goddess Kali' (Dehejia 1995, 142). Elucidating the phenomenon of iconographic transference, Dehejia shows how the iconography of Shaivite Nayanmar saints was modelled on Krishna, the difference (easy to miss) lying in how the right hand of Krishna in the *abhaya mudra* (gesture of protection) is replaced with Sambandar's hand, with its upward-pointing finger (p. 144). That is to say, the sculptors borrowed already established iconographic conventions almost in their entirety, with only very subtle variations, in order to deify and elevate Shaiva saints, who hitherto had not been regarded as incarnations of the godhead, thereby seeking to popularise the religion of Shiva via 'the familiar iconography of Krishna' (p. 149).

But the mimetic chain of guru representations did not end there, as can be seen in the case of a fresco depicting the close relationship between

King Rajaraja I and his guru Karuvar Devar inside the famous eleventh-century Brihadeshwara temple in Thanjavur. Frontally depicted in white with a white beard, the guru stands before the youthful disciple-king. The intimacy of the two figures is underscored through their close proximity (as also seen in later representations of the guru Dronacharya and Arjuna), almost like a couple. Signalling once more the mimetic intermediality of these images, the rendering of the figures discloses 'a great relationship to sculptural idioms of the time', with the 'almond-shaped eyes, the straight noses, and even the shapes of the faces [and jewellery detailed in dark outline] ... creat[ing] a configuration quite similar to what one might expect if a drawing was made of a typical Chola sculpture of this date' (Huntington 1985, 528).

Such examples, taken together with cases such as that of the DSS controversy but also the extraordinary *bhava* photographs of Anandamayi Ma manifesting as Durga, Shiva, Kali and Krishna, and Mata Amritanandamayi's performances of the goddess in sari-dress (Lucia 2014a, chapter 2) in which gurus actively present themselves as gods and such images are circulated and revered, demonstrate how the mimetic construction of the guru relies on specific techniques of artisanal mimesis (Sengupta 2021) in combination with the mimetic properties of new media technologies (Brosius 2005, 258), including their capacity to propel 'mimetic waves of sentiment ... more and more rapidly through populations' (Thrift 2009, 122), and *also* (as the DSS example shows particularly well) the role of what René Girard (2001, 11) termed 'mimetic rivalry', 'the rivalry resulting from the imitation of a model who becomes a rival or of a rival who becomes a model', with claims to authority and resultant contestations consequent on '[s]hared, copied, acquisitive mimetic desire' (Reyburn 2019, 74). Mimetic threads such as these often appear in overlapping or combinatory patterns of mutual extension within projects and processes of 'building a guru'. By themselves they might remain unconvincing; what matters (for building a guru) is the synergistic potency of the different mimetic currents in relation to one another, termed in other contexts the 'entourage effect' (Sobo 2016).

Brahmanical remediations and the subaltern counter-publicity of the guru

As many scholars have pointed out (e.g. Farmer 1996), the serial version of the epic *Ramayana*, telecast on the state-run channel Doordarshan (1987–8), was crucial for fashioning a Hindu public that enabled the rise of Hindu nationalism in India in the 1990s. The series 'not only aroused popular excitement around Hindu nationalism as a political sensibility but also, less conspicuously, wove Hindutva into the everyday lives of television viewers' (Udupa 2018, 454). Also less conspicuous, though forming part of the same political-symbolic complex, was how Brahmanical models of guruship – with their strict precepts concerning caste and gender – were showcased in the series. In the first episode, the sage Vasishtha (addressed as *Gurudev*) advises King Dasharatha to seek the blessing of rishi[23] Rishyasringara through the performance of *yajna* (fire sacrifice).[24] Vasishtha performs the Brahmanical ritual of naming, giving names – and identities – to the infants Ram, Laxman, Bharat and Shatrughan. The tradition of *guru-shishya* is further elaborated in the second and third episodes, in which guru Vasishtha takes Ram and his brothers, as *shishyas* (disciples/students), away from luxury and maternal love to the austerity of his gurukul (an ancient system of education), where he teaches them self-discipline, yoga and moral values. Ultimately, the figure of the rival guru, sage Vishwamitra, comes to overshadow that of Vasishtha. Vishwamitra teaches Ram how to navigate the material world, for instance training him in warfare against demons or antigods (*asuras*) and other agents capable of disrupting the lifeworld of Aryas (or Aryans). Vishwamitra also takes Ram to Janakpuri to marry Sita. The deep involvement of Vasishtha and Vishwamitra in running the dynasty as spiritual and political guides to the king reasserts to viewers the importance of the role played by the guru as a pivotal authority in the structures of power.

Let us also consider the guru Dronacharya, depicted in the Mahabharata teaching archery, another art of warfare, to the princes of the Kaurava and Pandava clans. Dronacharya, or Guru Drona, is instilled in Hindu-Indian consciousness as the ideal guru figure, his most famous student of course being Arjuna. In one iconic painting in the style of the Ajanta frescoes by the famous Bengal school artist Nandalal Bose, which featured in the book *Myths of the Hindus and Buddhists* ([1914] 1967) by revivalists Ananda Coomaraswamy and Sister Nivedita, Dronacharya is the central figure surrounded by disciples. The only figure emerging to prominence is the standing figure of Arjuna aiming his bow and arrow at a target, as Dronacharya, beside him, instructs.

Scholars have shown how state and government institutions mediate guruship and *guru-shishya* relationships in numerous ways. Aya Ikegame (2012), for instance, has explored the history of complex guru–state relations in the Princely State of Mysore, while Arkotong Longkumer (this volume) discusses the implications of the North East Zone Cultural Centre's (NEZCC) bestowal of the status of 'guru' on the Northeast cultural icon Guru Rewben Mashengwa (the NDA government also recently honoured Sadhguru Jaggi Vasudev with the Padma Vibhushan[25] for 'exceptional and distinguished service'[26]). However, it is representations of Guru Drona, as the ideal guru, that are most frequently at the heart of state remediations of guruship. One example is the state-sponsored Dronacharya Award for outstanding coaches in sports and games, which 'honour[s] the teacher who moulds an athlete into a star'.[27] The trophy features two male figures standing beside each other. While bearing a mimetic relationship to Nandalal Bose's illustration, the intimate bond between master and disciple is more prominent on the trophy: they hold the bow together, the guru's hand placed on Arjuna's arm as the arrow is aimed at the target. The two almost become one, as if the figure of the disciple is emerging from the guru.

State remediation of Dronacharya was also evidenced in April 2016 when the government of Haryana, under the leadership of former RSS *pracharak*[28] Manohar Lal Khattar, renamed Gurgaon[29] Gurugram, 'village of the guru'.[30] State publicity proclaimed that 'Haryana was a historic land mentioned in the *Bhagwat Gita* and Gurgaon had been a great centre of learning, where Guru Dronacharya used to provide education to the Pandavas and Kauravas. … [T]he village was given as "*gurudakshina*" [fee offered to the guru] to him by his students, the Pandavas.'[31] The guru is thus remediated into a 'state narrative of exemplarity' (Gayer and Therwath 2010) via award statuettes, government-sourced news stories, websites and other publicity, including one state's high-profile renaming of a global city. However, not mentioned in state publicity extolling Dronacharya as the ideal guru is the dark fate of one of his pupils, the tribal subject Ekalavya. Consideration of Ekalavya's fate positions Dronacharya as a very different sort of exemplar to the romanticised one envisioned by the state. From this angle Dronacharya comes to exemplify – or form the prototype of – the kind of guru who sees in his undisputed authority a licence to abuse the bodies of his disciples. Let us consider now a kind of subaltern counter-publicity of the (Brahmanical) guru.

Nandalal Bose also illustrated Ekalavya's story, but in contrast with his depiction of Dronacharya and Arjuna, surrounded by other disciples, we see in this illustration Ekalavya's solitary seated figure as an outcaste, untouchable subject who was denied the privilege of learning directly under the guru. For, despite his skill surpassing even that of Arjuna, he was rejected as a disciple by the guru: low-status Nishada princes like Ekalavya cannot reside with Ksatriyas and Brahmans in a gurukul (Cohen 2012, 103). For this reason, it was necessary for Ekalavya to find a way of making the guru present otherwise. Hence, Bose portrays the solitary figure learning archery beside an idol of his guru which he has made himself, Dronacharya, carved out of rock, an instance of 'distributed guruship'. According to Jaffrelot's compelling interpretation, since Ekalavya's aptitude greatly increased in spite of this, the story presents 'a sign that the value of the relation with the master stems first and foremost from the subjectivity of the disciple' (2012, 89). The necessary remediation of the guru, in another telling, is enacted slightly differently: 'the Nishada prince, touching Drona's feet with bent head, wended his way into the forest, and there he made a clay-image of Drona, and began to worship it respectfully, as if it was his real preceptor' (Mahabharata 1: 134, from Ganguli 1884, 280). Yet, upon hearing that he remained the guru of the low-status prince, even at one remove, Drona demanded Ekalavya's right thumb – vital, of course, for the practice of archery – as *guru dakshina*. The rejected disciple obeyed the command to self-mutilate as an act of devotion towards the guru.

Following this, we consider first a further critical visual remediation of the Guru Drona story, namely graffiti images on the walls of Hyderabad Central University of Ekalavya's severed hand alongside portraits of Rohith Vemula, a 26-year-old Dalit PhD student who had recently taken his own life, and then activism in which students re-enact and re-present Ekalavya's ordeal by lacerating their thumbs (Figure 0.4). Dalit activist criticism of Guru Drona and reverence for Ekalavya are not new: take the

Figure 0.4 Rohith Vemula case: Dalit students protest in 'Eklavya' avatar. Source: YouTube channel ABP News. https://www.youtube.com/watch?v=33hMHv3s5JM.

GURUS AND MEDIA: AN INTRODUCTION   17

famous activist Phoolan Devi's 'Ekalavya Sena' (army of Ekalavya), which taught self-defence to marginalised community members in the 1990s (Doron 2014) and a mock trial of Guru Drona conducted by Dalit activists in which he was sentenced to be hanged for not accepting Ekalavya as his student (Narayan 2006). Yet the graffiti images indicate how, in the wake of a number of suicides of students from historically marginalised communities facing discrimination in institutions of higher education, the figure of Ekalavya has taken on renewed significance as a symbol of the denial of access to learning in modern universities. For instance, soon after Vemula's suicide, protesting students organised public talks in a series called 'Ekalavya Speaks', in which students and academics from historically marginalised communities narrated their experiences of discrimination and exclusion in higher education.[32] Clearly, Dalit, Adivasi and Bahujan students' identification of and with Ekalavya as a historically oppressed subject features a conception of Guru Drona that is very different from state narratives of exemplarity, disturbing not only the politics of reverence attached to him but also dominant celebratory depictions of gurukuls, *guru–shishya* relations and *guru dakshina* as glories of Hindu civilisation. Dronacharya now comes to light as a conspicuous representative and advocate of a Brahmanical tradition that mythologically and materially justifies the system of untouchability and denial of access to those outside the Varna hierarchy – a tradition that remains alive and well – and as a kind of prototype for those gurus that claim custody and use-rights over the bodies of their disciples. We refer here both to the sexual exploitation of devotees, already mentioned, and to how gurus have enacted other forms of violence on their devotees, including castration and sterilisation (Voix 2008; Lucia 2021). The involvement of gurus in less overtly violent practices, such as mass blood donation campaigns, also often rests on expectations and assumptions of the guru's corporeal control over devotees and their automatic assent.[33]

Guru Drona was split into two via a practice of mediation from the start – the complex tyrant who first rejected and then demanded the mutilation of Ekalavya versus the idealised copy of the clay idol (Cohen 2012) – and there continue to be two Dronas, the one glorified in particular by Hindutva organisations and that of a figure considered to be fit for hanging. Famously, another Brahmanical guru-like figure resisted by Ambedkarite Dalits, but defended by Hindutva organisations, is the sage Manu. Ever since Dr Ambedkar's original Mahad Satyagraha agitation of 1927, resisting the Brahmanical guru has taken the form of annually burning the *Manusmriti* (Laws of Manu), the corpus of Hindu religious laws that prescribes Dalits' subordination. But not only texts.

When, in 1989, a 10-foot-tall statue of Manu holding the book was installed inside the compound of the Rajasthan High Court in Jaipur, a huge state-wide Dalit agitation demanded its removal, which was met by large-scale opposition from the Hindutva organisation the VHP. The statue, which is still standing, most recently was smeared with black paint by Adivasi and Dalit activists from Aurangabad, an event that was linked with global media circuits, activists claiming inspiration from the toppling of the statue of the benefactor of Bristol and slave trader Edward Colston following Black Lives Matter protests in 2020.[34]

We have considered, then, how mass remediations of the guru on state television have showcased and endorsed the figure of the Brahman guru as a pivotal authority to be submitted to, and other state remediations that include awards, renamings and statues. We have seen how Hindutva forces have been entwined with these remediations at every step, but also how such remediations have been strongly contested in practices of counter-mediation of the guru. The material media of guruship can form potent objects of controversy, from the bow and arrows, clay idol and bodily severing featured in the Mahabharata, right up to the present day. Such media have been vital for both perpetuating and stymieing particular conceptions of the guru. If Manu as guru/rishi is embodied as scriptural authority in the *Manusmriti*, the burning of this text by Ambedkar and then annually on Manusmriti Dahan Divas, as well as attacks on his statue, are acts of resistance against the figure of the Brahmanical guru more broadly.[35] Valuable though recent scholarship on gurus as figures of controversy and exploitation is, its focus on recent cases runs the risk of entrenching the perception that the phenomenon is *only* a recent one. In contrast, we have engaged various guru iconographies and material and visual culture resources to convey how the guru has always been a figure not only of reverence but also of oppression, his relationship with his disciples profoundly unequal and prone to abuse based on differences of caste, class, gender and sexuality.

Hindutva, gurus and mediation

The triangular interactive relationship between Hindutva, gurus and media should already be clear.[36] Many studies now exist on the supportive relationship between Hindutva agendas and some gurus, which is uneven but in some cases undeniably extremely powerful. As Véronique Bouillier (2012, 373) explains, 'new religious movements and *gurus* who situate themselves outside the main traditional sectarian organisations', and possess largely urban middle-class devotees with access to and at ease in global media circuits, hold an 'affirmative assertion of Hindu identity [that] may lead to an ideological proximity with Hindutva'. Notably, the VHP has been supported by a variety of 'modern gurus' from its inception in 1964 onwards (Jaffrelot 1996, 194). Indeed, Lise McKean (1996), in her ground-breaking work on north Indian guru organisations and Hindutva in the 1980s and 1990s, underscored how gurus' adeptness at exploiting media technologies has made them particularly well equipped to 'assist in propagating Hindu nationalism'. Since Hindutva 'relies on referents to Hindu India's unparalleled spiritual prowess and moral authority' (McKean 1996, 1), and its proponents (as already noted) consider guruship a valued Hindu cultural good to the point of maintaining the fiction of the infallibility of individual gurus even where there is incontrovertible evidence of wrongdoing, it is not hard to understand why gurus and Hindutva might frequently instantiate relations of mutual mediation and support.[37] Here we seek not to cover the entirety of the relevant literature on guru–Hindutva entwinement, but rather to expand on McKean's work in exploring how media and mediation have played significant roles in finessing these connections.

Guru logics are clearly mediated by Hindutva organisations in numerous ways. The RSS is frequently framed as guru to the BJP and other constituents of the Sangh Parivar. Golwalkar, the second RSS leader, was known as Guruji. Meanwhile, 'a *pracharak* takes oath before the guru of the Sangh, the *bhagwa dhwaj* (saffron flag), which is recognised as the victory flag of Shivaji' (Kanungo 2012, 150), and found in the chariots of the wars of the Mahabharata, symbolising 'sacrifice, power. It is the color of fire' (Longkumer 2021, 18). Further, the Vivekananda Kendra, a Hindu nationalist 'spiritually oriented service mission', takes the Vedic syllable Om for its guru (Kanungo 2012, 150), demonstrating the shape-shifting quality of the guru beyond the human, the ready capacity of the originary template of the living person as a manifestation of the divine (Gold 1987, 3) to be transferred into other objects or concepts, some retaining a human trace or morphology as in our earlier discussions of Ekalavya's clay model and the chola bronzes (see also McCartney and Lourenço, this volume; Srinivas, this volume) and others abstracted from the human entirely (Mandair, this volume; Grimaud, this volume).

A further important Hindutva mediation of guruship concerns its ideological importance in Hindutva discourses concerning the Indian Constitution. Written by a Constituent Assembly dominated by the Congress Party, and serving as a key public resource for numerous marginalised groups (De 2018), the Constitution is almost always disparaged by Hindutva writers, with guruship proposed as the institution that ideally would replace it. Recalling the earlier discussion of Hindutva endorsement of Brahmanical guru forms that are deeply implicated in central structures of power, Anustup Basu explains that in the ideal Hindutva scenario, 'the president with authoritarian powers should be guided spiritually by a council of sages operating as the Raj Guru (the Brahmin advisor to the king)' (2020, 26). Basu considers such 'Brahmanical stewardship' to be already present in the form of the VHP's College of Holy Men: 'It is this assembly of god-men – now imagined along the lines of an ecumenical council with papal infallibility – that must incarnate the revived authority of the Raj Guru' (p. 27). Meanwhile, Jaffrelot (2012) has written of the RSS itself, made up of worldly abstainers, as a new kind of Raj Guru or moral counsellor – at least, that was Golwalkar's aim for it.

Hindutva's mediations of guru principles as structuring elements of the relations that comprise it suggest something almost akin to a 'fractal guruship', a recurrent self-similar organising principle at every scale (Lebner 2017, 13). But that is not all. The Hindutva organisation Hindu Janajagruti Samiti (Society for Hindu Awakening), in its literature, declares 'Bharat the "Spiritual Master (Guru)" of the World'.[38] Basu (2020, 161) describes the Sangh Parivar's relationship to the 'Vishwa Guru', or world teacher concept, in terms of 'providential yearning' for 'global spiritual dominance'. For the BJP, meanwhile, the concept forms part of a branding strategy for showcasing national glories, a means of increasing the country's '"magnetic power" by returning [it] to the *visva-guru* status it apparently once enjoyed' (McCartney and Lourenço, this volume). This brings us back to the convergence of gurus, Hindutva and commerce first analysed by McKean. Below we discuss the brand strategies of various gurus. Here we find something related but different: Hindutva 'world guru' appropriations enact the branding of the *country* via guruship models. In his important work on yoga guruship Patrick McCartney (2021, 62) goes further still to suggest that in harnessing yoga to cure the ills of the world – for instance in initiating International Yoga Day – 'Modi, as the representative of the Indian state, reflexively frames the nation as the paragon of moral virtue and, by default, *he* is the *visvaguru* (world teacher) who can guide humanity toward a greener, more sustainable form of development' (our emphasis).

This point is picked up in David Landau and Nina Rageth's chapter in this volume, which explores a novel 'guru twist' to what was already the unprecedented media phenomenon of Narendra Modi's ascent. The media's role in promoting Modi has received considerable scholarly attention (Srivastava 2015; Chakravartty and Roy 2015). In the years following the organised killings of Muslims that took place in Gujarat in 2002, during his tenure as Chief Minister, he came to be rebranded as a developmental 'strongman', relentless in the pursuit of development and industry (Cohen 2008). He was soon further transformed into an icon of yoga and fashion by the media, 'pampered, choreographed, and fawningly advertised in media engagements' (Basu 2020, 168). During the 2014 general election campaign, in addition to the hyperactivity of the famed BJP IT Cell that amplified his image at every step, 3D hologram technology was employed to extend Modi's presence even in his absence: 'If the sheer number of rallies at which Modi spoke was impressive, what was more impressive was the fact that millions of people in more than a thousand other locations were "touched" by the magical projection of his three-dimensional electronic image, like the coming down to earth of a distant god' (p. 169).

Yet Landau and Rageth register a significant departure from this mode of media self-presentation that took place during the COVID-19 lockdowns of 2020–1, a striking shift towards guru aesthetics. Adopting a new visual grammar, Modi now appeared with long hair and unkempt beard and in simpler, earthy-coloured clothes made from traditional fabrics that were symbolically coded as Hindu in various ways. His comportment, too, registered subtle changes. Landau and Rageth are careful to point out that varied ascetic traits – kinlessness, abstinence, celibacy – formed part of the Modi image even before his more full-throated 'guru turn'; the point is that 'it is a recent and notable phenomenon that the guru appearance is overriding other aspects of the previously multifarious Modi'. Following this, the authors conduct a rich exploration of this overriding, foregrounding the experimental nature of the guru performance as different combinations of worldliness and asceticism are tried out so that Modi can be positioned as 'in the world, but not of the world', with no single guru mimetically embodied but rather traits and accoutrements associated with varied guru personas, the better to evoke 'a multitude of references' and so tap a wider set of constituencies. The chapter by McCartney and Lourenço forms a fascinating counterpoint here, for it describes yet another manifestation of Modi as guru, this time as an animated character with whom one can learn yoga. In the BJP's 'Yoga with Modi' initiative, participants can enter a specially designed room where they are met by an 'anthropomorphically animated version of Modi' ready to dispense yoga classes in a variety of languages, with 'the claims of India be(com)ing the world guru [thereby] compressed into Modi's yoga guru avatar'.

In sum, Landau and Rageth marshal an array of recent instances of the guru turned politician to show that 'what we are witnessing is the merging of a Hindu guru and politician in one and the same person', with Modi's guru persona 'the epitome of this development' (see also Bouillier

2015, 2020). Harking back to the Raj Guru concept discussed earlier, we begin to see how Modi's 'guru turn' embodies a new totalism in which he unites the kingly and Raj Guru spheres, drawing on the reservoirs of authority associated with each figure to create 'a new and all-powerful position' (Landau and Rageth) – a guru beyond guruship and a politician beyond the political. Moreover, if Modi's intention was to embody a figure who often operates beyond democracy and accountability, then the guru was of course an appropriate choice for this.

One such guru figure is the DSS head, introduced earlier, who ruled as a kind of 'localised sovereign' (Humphrey 2004; Ikegame 2019) over a *dera* which operated as an extra-legal 'little fiefdom' with its own army and, reportedly, its own currency (Singh 2017).[39] The *MSG: Messenger of God* series of films he released from 2015 to 2017 – the subject of Copeman and Duggal's chapter in this book – showcase a kind of 'spillover' guruship that witnesses the guru translate himself into more and more spheres of operation and publicity. Since public guruship, 'channeled via recurrent, intent, dramatic forms of *deep play*' (Silber 2019, 135), already borrowed from theatre and other performance arts, the DSS guru's Bollywood performances were not entirely novel but rather made explicit existing latencies within the public guru operation. The films foreground in particular the guru's shift from promoting a 'banal, distanced, and -lite' form of Hindu nationalism (McCartney 2021, 36) to a more strident variety that explicitly endorses Modi's agenda. The films depict the heroic guru playing different versions of himself as he runs through a host of neo-Hindutva clichés: cow protection, *shuddhi*, strong-arm development and anti-Pakistan rhetoric complete with 'surgical strikes'. Reflecting the long-standing arrangement in which politicians and gurus cooperate in exacting dominion (Jaffrelot 2012) and mutually legitimate one another (Bouillier 2015), the *MSG* films' compliant transmission of various Hindutva priorities shows how gurus may mediate Hindutva principles just as Hindutva organisations mediate principles of guruship. Part of the shift was due to what we have called elsewhere the propensity of the guru to key into the momentum of a situation.[40] After all, with Modi recently installed as prime minister, Hindutva was now firmly in the ascendancy and a key association for the guru to 'harvest'. But the essay also suggests that the films' composition and narrative structure disclose a certain prophylactic intention on the part of the DSS. Significant here is that during the period in which the films were made and released, the guru was facing numerous serious criminal allegations that could – and ultimately did – result in lengthy prison sentences. The films' immunological strategy, the chapter suggests, was two-pronged: first (the carrot), they sought to position the guru as absolutely indispensable to the Hindutva project, and second (the stick), the notable presence within them of a million plus devotee extras evidently willing to defend their guru at all costs formed a warning to state authorities: stay back from the fiefdom.

Since Modi was in place as PM at the time of each film's release, to mediate in docile fashion Hindutva principles and talking points was simultaneously to transmit the priorities of the central government, and we have already seen how the state and gurus find ways of borrowing from each other's status and power at their convenience. This was also visible during the 2020–2 phase of the COVID-19 pandemic, when several well-known gurus were tasked with mediating key state and indeed global health authority communications as trusted vehicles for conveying to their followers key messages concerning social distancing, the need to obey state guidelines, etc. Thereby instantiated was a form of what elsewhere we have called 'bi-instrumentalism' (Copeman and Quack 2018): global and state health institutions tap into public gurus' authoritative status and the 'dense network of mediation strategies and technologies' (Zavos 2012, 3) they have at their disposal, but, equally, public gurus tap into the momentum of the situation as an opportunity to 'extend their range'. The different constituencies 'interoperate' one another: the relationship is bi-instrumental.

In an echo of how the British colonial government came to rely on Indian intermediaries to promote sanitary science and inoculation campaigns – seeking, as David Arnold (1993, 233) put it, 'to annex to their own cause the authority which "natural leaders" had over their coreligionists, caste-followers, and dependents' – Modi convened a videoconference call with Indian religious leaders to seek their assistance. Though ecumenical, with representatives from Islamic, Christian and Sikh organisations, it featured a heavy concentration of Modi's 'chosen gurus'[41] and guru organisations: Baba Ramdev, Sri Sri Ravi Shankar, Bhaiyyaji Joshi of the RSS, Sadhguru and representatives of BAPS, the Brahma Kumaris, Gayatri Parivar, Ramkrishna Mission, Vardhman Seva Kendra, Kalyanji Anandji and the Shri Sathya Sai Foundation. During the call, 'Brahmavihari Swami described to the PM the BAPS's steps to ensure not just resource support to the poor, but emotional and spiritual support to everyone to ensure the mental peace of citizens. He highlighted that adherence to the lockdown will be sustained only if everyone sees it as a religious and moral duty. Everyone pledged their support to the government's measures for the wellbeing of the citizens of India.'[42] With their business models already focused on well-being, soothing emotions and promotion of healthy living (Gooptu 2016), gurus were certainly well positioned to intervene in ways that might be beneficial for both citizens and themselves. At a time when 'the social dynamics of ventilation' (Solomon 2021, 105) could not have been more urgent, this was especially true of those gurus who specialise in breathing techniques. The 'breathing gurus', indeed, did not hold back in offering their own brand of 'breathing support' at a time when ventilators were in even shorter supply than usual.[43]

However, though public gurus need to be needed, and seek out opportunities for 'charismatic transfers' (Cohen 1998) between themselves and resonant political figures, such as the videoconference call with Modi, they are not necessarily amenable to controlled deployment.[44] Numerous gurus went 'off message': 'When a (vegetarian) Hindu leader gathered a number of followers for a *gaumutra* [cow urine] drinking session, he explained that the virus is an *avatara* descended to restore the universal balance which deteriorated because of the increasing numbers of meat-eaters. Several Indic gurus stated that the virus is the result of collective negative karma and urged for a return to a more holistic and *sattvik* [pure] lifestyle' (Lorea 2020, 308). India's rationalists claimed an upsurge in membership during the time of the pandemic because it brought home to '[m]any, especially the young, ... the futility of the teachings of godmen and practitioners of pseudoscience'.[45] Early in the pandemic doctors and rationalists were vexed by the 'dangerous claim' Baba Ramdev made about his newly developed Coronil tablets, namely that they effected a 100 per cent cure in seven days and a 69 per cent cure in three.[46] Later on in the pandemic doctors wore black armbands 'to protest against a guru ... who claims that yoga and traditional medicine offer stronger protection against Covid-19 than vaccines. Doctors accuse Baba Ramdev ... of deliberately stoking vaccine hesitancy and suspicions about modern medicine to promote his own ayurvedic medicine company, Patanjali Ayurved.'[47] Such cases are ambiguous. Insofar as they deviate from government scripts, we apparently observe the intercessory limits of the guru vis-à-vis state information distribution. Yet, if 'Modi's affirmation in 2014 that the transplantation of the elephant head of the god Ganesha to a human body was a great achievement of Indian surgery reflects an attempt to recover the "lost glory" of the Vishwa guru Bharat' (Kinnvall and Singh 2022, 11), Ramdev's agenda is consistent with this, even if it is also firmly focused on his own commercial interests.

Baba Ramdev and his embrace of television is the focus of Srirupa Bhattacharya's chapter in this volume, which shows how his success in spreading his message of health and religious nationalism on TV is enacted via the multiple ways in which audience, viewer and screen interact. She shows us how 'doing seeing' as a method allows television viewers to see a whole army of followers being recorded live with Baba Ramdev, all doing yoga at the same time. Meanwhile, television is also the medium through which a large range of consumer products, associated with the guru's company, Patanjali, are advertised. The act of watching becomes a collective activity, whereby a person's healing is connected to the healing of the nation. Drawing on, but moving beyond, studies such as that by Rajagopal (2001) on TV and Hindutva, the chapter shows how novel forms of community and vision are able to form around the performance of yoga live on TV in ways that 'expand the horizon of religious nationalism'.

Bhattacharya's chapter reflects on the (in)significance of darshan for many devotees. As has been well documented, the age of 'industrial gurus'[48] has produced many modes of de-territorialised darshanic exchange that show darshan's 'protean power to adapt to new technologies' (Dinkar 2021, 77). Omnipresent multimedia photographic depictions of gurus not only reinforce a sense of their omniscience for devotees, but enable darshan across time and space (Jacobs 2012). However, as Niharika Dinkar (2021) persuasively argues, the privileged position of darshan as an analytic frame for understanding varied South Asian optical regimes can lead scholars to overlook or flatten out other important visual genres. Dinkar suggests other forms of gaze that are deserving of further scrutiny, for instance the *tirchhi nazar* (slanted gaze) and non-reciprocal modes of bedazzlement that confound the eye. Bhattacharya, in her chapter, maintains a Foucauldian analytic of power-vision, while foregrounding non-darshanic ways of seeing and being seen by the guru. Unlike the devotees of other prominent public gurus, Ramdev's followers tend not to carry his image around with them. His image is certainly prominent in advertisements and well known from television, but his eyes are frequently closed in meditation: he is not giving darshan. Seeing operates differently here: the mode of visuality at stake – one that ideally operates to foster a particular knowledge system among viewers and disciplined techniques of the body in the service of national reform – is one in which 'seeing acquire[s] meaning only in praxis, or in doing; and doing acquire[s] meaning in being seen'. Further, and all-important in a context of long-standing state neglect of their concerns, Ramdev's followers, who ask him questions about health and yoga and gain answers, feel empoweringly seen, finally, by him.

Raphaël Voix's chapter provides a social biography of the career of a renowned religious image composed of portraits of 42 'Immortal Gurus of *Bhārata*'. The chapter does not explicitly draw Hindutva into its analytical compass, but it is noticeable how congruent the technical composition of the image is with the VHP's vision of 'a simplified, easily comprehensible, and commonly accessible Hinduism, understood as a … set of common symbolic denominators acceptable across sects' (Hansen 1999, 101). If 'the "modern gurus" [of the VHP] do not emphasise their sectarian affiliation but rather their "Hindu" allegiance' (Jaffrelot 1996, 196), it is fascinating to witness how such a flattening can be accomplished artistically, that is, the original portraits are extracted from their socio-religious contexts of origin via the removal of visual marks and gestures that reveal sectarian affiliation. Such visual decontextualisation – 'suppress[ing] an ornament, a necklace, a staff or a sectarian insignia' – removes much of what gave the original portraits their meaning, rendering the composite image 'mono-iconic'.

Yet a synergistic reading of the relationship between the 'Immortal Gurus' image and the agenda of national Hinduism is only one possible interpretation of a composition marked by striking 'semiotic virtuosity'. Understood by diverse constituencies in different ways, the image can also stand for a tolerant 'Hindu humanism' and egalitarianism: for instance, it features both the iconoclastic weaver Kabir and Shankaracharya, the archetypal symbol of Brahmanical hegemony, placing them on an equivalent footing. What we earlier called the triangular interactive relationship between Hindutva, media and guruship (as a set of concepts and logics as well as of specific persons) is evidently multilayered and multi-scalar. A further significance of Voix's chapter, then, is that it reminds us that there is no essential or inevitable relationship between Hindutva and guruship. Dalit gurus have sought to dismantle Hindutva and Brahmanical Hinduism entirely (Ikegame 2022); numerous radical bhakti saints have put forth powerful visions of community beyond conventional hierarchical norms (Omvedt 2008); various modern guru organisations and philosophies provide critiques of Hindutva reason (Warrier 2005, chapter 8; McLain 2012); and novelists (Gupta 2011), artists (e.g. Gulammohammed Sheikh[49]) and others have sought to rebuild a vision of composite religiosity after episodes of communal violence by invoking the figure of the guru as 'an example of identity in reverse' (Ramnath 2022) or as a 'crowd of narratives' capable of counteracting Hindutva dreams of singularity.[50] Can gurus, despite everything, prototype a coming disidentity politics?[51]

The south Indian portraits of Christ as guru explored in E. Dawson Varughese's chapter, which raise poignant questions about the translation and transposition of guruship idioms, are pertinent in this respect. What visual styles and gestures make a guru figure manifest? What colour palettes and artistic media are appropriate for bringing the entities of Christ and guru into complex imagistic relation? The images examined by Dawson Varughese – an oil painting (1993), a concrete-moulded tableau (2003), a mosaic installation (1974), and two additional paintings in different styles – instantiate, she suggests, 'encounters of inculturation'. Typically picturing Christ the guru as a seated figure, either meditating or teaching, they mediate between Christian, Hindu and Buddhist religious traditions. The powerful confluences communicated in these resonant images suggest to Dawson Varughese Voss Roberts's evocation of 'a place of silence', a place 'beyond doctrines, where the traditions meet' (2021, 347). On one level concepts of guruship seem readily, even glibly, transposable, from business gurus (Rhodes and Pitsis 2008) to beauty gurus (Lewis et al. 2016) and beyond. But given the frequently contentious colonial and postcolonial history of Hindu-Christian relations in South Asia, sensitive questions are raised here. If the recent commission of 'translation images' featuring Christ as guru is apparently straightforward evidence of attempts to build bridges between different religious groups, such images might be conceived differently for other historical moments as semiotic appropriation.[52]

Alexander Henn's (2015) analysis of Christian Purana literature in early modern Goa documents Jesuit attempts to make Christian concepts intelligible by using Hindu names. Central here was the relaying of biblical stories in Konkani-Marathi in a manner stylistically borrowed from the Hindu bhakti poet saints, Sri Sant Ekanatha (1533–99) in particular. However, though on one level this was indeed a mode of translation-cum-dialogue, it also aimed at displacement. On a popular level, however, it is true that non-superficial correspondences and borrowings did develop in south India between Hindu saints, Christian saints and martyrs and Muslim *pirs* (Bayly 1989); the Jesuits in Tamil Nadu, for instance, were able quite successfully to position Catholicism as 'a devotional *bhakti* order based on the teachings of Jesuit renouncer-gurus' (Mosse 2012, 18). One way in which we can see the images of Christ the guru analysed by Dawson Varughese, then, is as figures of translation that help us move beyond tenacious conceptions of religious traditions as fully constituted self-enclosed universes and intercultural exchange as mere encounter.

Martin Fuchs (2022, 172) rightly points to the hollowness of many gurus' claims of ecumenism and universal humanness, which are rarely matched by practice. Even in the case of egalitarian bhakti gurus, what is offered to the marginalised would-be devotee is frequently what Fuchs aptly terms a 'confined universalism' that is incapable of sustaining wider Dalit recognition or hopes for advancement (p. 175). Jeffery Long (2019), on the other hand, questions 'the tendency of some authors to identify Hindu pluralism, paradoxically, with a kind of Hindu triumphalism' (p. 8), finding in the Bengal saint Ramakrishna's multireligious mysticism evidence of a genuine, deep-rooted Hindu ecumenism – neither 'neo-Hindu' nor a mere product of colonialism – that can stand as a promising alternative to communalism and for the promotion of interreligious understanding (pp. 8, 21). What is more, Ikegame asks searching questions concerning whether ecumenism has any value at all for certain gurus and their followers. Responding to Orianne Aymard's (2014, 257) argument that 'openness, inclusiveness and moving away from narrowly defined caste rules is the key to cult survival following the death of the guru', Ikegame (2016, 117) states that lower-caste devotional movements 'for centuries remained strong [precisely] because their gurus – dead or alive – speak for their caste communities'.

It is a testament to the complex plurality of guruship that in spite of gurus' central position within systems of Brahmanical domination, multiple entanglements with Hindutva and the often fictional nature of their ecumenical universalism (Fuchs 2022) they are still capable of emerging in the ways we have discussed as figures of hope and promise. Discussing a Shaiva sect in Uttar Pradesh, Bouillier (2020, 31–2) shows how such hope and its failure can be extremely closely entwined, since it was the sect's very openness to Dalits and other marginalised communities that led – when its leaders embraced Hindutva – to the creation of a large, caste-transcending voter constituency for the BJP in the state. Indeed, the kind of hope that remains invested in gurus perhaps recalls Hirokazu Miyazaki's (2004) argument about the intimate relation between promise and failure: 'a promise, if it were to be fulfilled, would not be a promise' (Cohen 2013, 325). Arjun Appadurai (2007, 30) writes that 'the address of hope as a collective sentiment' engages 'the space between *is* and *ought*'. Deeply entangled with Hindutva and other forms of domination yet irreducible to them, there remains embedded within the guru a 'cluster of promises' (Berlant 2011, 23) that enable it productively to engage precisely the space identified by Appadurai and so to maintain a relation to the future as possible mediator between the (communal) environment one is in and the (unconditionally plural) environment one would wish to create. In this they form the object of what Lauren Berlant terms 'cruel optimism', the 'condition of maintaining an attachment to a significantly problematic object [and] compromised conditions of possibility' (p. 24).

Methodologies of presence

Absent-present guruship

Several chapters in this book are concerned with the different roles played by mediation when, for a variety of reasons, a guru cannot be physically present with devotees. These chapters disclose the particular ability of some gurus to be 'not just where their bodies are but in many different places simultaneously' (Empson 2007, 117). Following this, we draw on Alfred Gell's (1998) influential formulation of 'the distributed person' in developing the idea of distributed guruship. In Gell's schema, persons are to be treated 'not as bounded biological organisms, but … [as] all the objects and/or events in the milieu from which agency or personhood can be abducted' (p. 222).[53] However, while Gell is indeed our main stimulus here, his privileging of cognition and the intentionality of particular people 'behind the world of artifacts' (Miller 2005, 13; Chua and Elliott 2013, 10) means that his theory does not map exactly onto what we mean by distributed guruship. In many instances, distribution of guruship indeed takes place through the medium of all the objects and/or events, diffused in space and time, from which an originating guru's agency or personhood can be abducted (Gell 1998, 222, 232). We suggest, simply, that such indexes may mediate and extend the capacities not only of particular historically embodied gurus, but also schemas, values and principles of a larger, more diffuse and impersonal entity that for the sake of convenience we call guruship. Of course, the guru as person, thing or principle is far from unique in its capacity to set in train events caused by acts of mind, will or intention rather than the mere concatenation of physical events. But the guru's propensity via diverse mediations, from clay models, to dolls (Lucia 2014a; McCartney and Lourenço[54]), robots (Grimaud), tombs (Srinivas), texts and sayings (Biswas, Mandair), screen presences (Bhattacharya, Copeman and Duggal), photographic images (Chowdhuri, Voix) and more, to move their person, mind, presence and agentive capacities beyond the confines of particular spatio-temporal coordinates and so attain agentive presences is nevertheless striking and particularly meaningful in light of the intensity of attachments frequently at stake.

It is important to insist on this point in light of approaches that would restrict analysis to particular gurus in the sense of bounded biological organisms.[55] This section, and the volume more broadly, show how analyses that focus on specific guru figures, and those that demonstrate how traces and principles of guruship are not located in bounded individuals alone, but are distributable and so capable of inhabiting other forms of matter and relationship, are not only compatible modalities of analysis but vitally complementary ones (as in our discussion above of the doubled guru in the story of Ekalavya and also Hindutva as both fractally structured via self-similar guru principles at different scales and mediated by particular human gurus). To restrict analysis to specific human gurus and their histories would be to restrict apprehension of the full vibrancy and mutating import of guruship and foreclose the sorts of revelatory analyses presented in this book on experimental guruship inhabitations and guru performativities (for example Landau and Rageth on Modi performing the guru, Lucia on absent-present guruship, Mandair on guruship and Sikh scripture and guruship *as* Sikh scripture, Grimaud on machinic guru 'testing grounds' and McCartney and Lourenço on yoga doll guruship), all of which shed light on the ever-evolving means by which gurus may be generated.

Recognition of such boundary crossing does not imply a lack of specificity and historical exactitude, since the different aesthetic-devotional means by which splitting, doubling and proliferation of individual guru figures take place and the sometimes surprising and unpredictable motion of guru forms and principles (e.g. Longkumer, this volume) are themselves historically significant processes, as demonstrated for instance in our earlier discussion of the chola bronzes. On one level such bronzes, or Ekalavya's clay model, are signs in the sense that they can be taken as 'significantly substituting' for the guru's physical person (Eco 1976). But material signs do not merely encode and convey meanings. Like Gell we view objectified modes of guruship as systems of action intended to transform the world rather than to encode symbolic propositions about it (Gell 1998, 6). Capable of presentifying (Domasńka 2006) and making efficacious their subjects, the bronzes, Ekalavya's model and other guru traces are not mere substitutions for but significant extensions of the guru. 'Causality made visible' (Gell 1998, 44), they form instances, not representations, of guruship. Transferences between material, virtual and bounded (biological) forms of guruship are historically variegated. They emerge from particular local configurations of devotional, artisanal, iconographic, commercial and institutional practices and conventions that are not timeless but rather require careful historical appraisal.

Gurus' deaths can of course result in particularly stark absences for devotees and on occasion lead to controversy and even violence over the question of whether the guru is really dead or is in a deep state of samadhi, as in the case of Santan Dal leader Balak Brahmachari in 1993 (Chatterjee 1999) and more recently the Punjab-based guru Ashutosh Maharaj, who was certified dead in 2014 but whose devotees resisted attempts to cremate his body, placing it instead in a commercial freezer 'until such time as its owner decided to wake up' (Shearer 2020, 221). Despite such refusals to countenance a guru's death, the ability of spatio-temporally detached fragments of the guru's person to convey the guru beyond his or her bounded physical self is capable of making the guru present otherwise to devotees, to considerable ameliorative effect. Indeed, the spread of biographical events, memories of events, and a dispersed category of material objects, traces and leavings which can be attributed to the guru and which, in aggregate, testify to agency and patienthood during a biographical career, may prolong itself long after biological death and so cause the deceased guru to continue to be both present and effective, a point that is particularly telling in reference to Tulasi Srinivas's chapter in this book on Sathya Sai Baba, his death, and the 'crypto-futurity' of his movement, since all these saintly indexes hold the potential to make an absent guru present.[56]

Srinivas presents a deepening of conventional understandings of multimedia. While the guru's death was relayed on different media platforms, it was also a multimedia event in a second sense, in 'mediat[ing] different temporal, geographic and affective worlds'. The guru's hitherto 'nomadic charisma' (Srinivas 2010) was now transferred into the 'enclosing' space of a mausoleum that it supercharges with his presence. However, the mausoleum is not only an enclosing entity but one capable simultaneously of thrusting the guru's charisma into a cosmological Elsewhere in which his presence transcends past, present and future. The marble, body-enclosing mausoleum operates as a medium through which one can access the 'encrypted guru-self' even as the structure gestures to an Elsewhere in which the guru lives and remains unambiguously present across space and time, a kind of presence that, for the mourning devotee, is at once ameliorative and sublime. Thus, if biological death on one level contains or limits a guru's aura, on another it can, in some cases at least, extend and spill over the prior confines of its *praesentia*, now distributed with renewed power. Indeed, tombs, Jeremy Tanner (2013) has argued, have the capacity to extend personhood 'beyond the confines of biological life by means of a sometimes very elaborate index distributed in the causal milieu', with a series of 'protentions' and 'retentions' stretching their agentive capacities and achievements back and forth across time. The material means by which historical rulers, in particular, have enacted 'post mortem personhood' to facilitate their ongoing agentive sovereignty as 'distributed rulers' might help us reflect on the modes and means of distributed guruship, which of course becomes a particular matter of concern after a guru's biological death.

Amanda Lucia employs ideas of 'absence-presence' in reference to the digital afterlives of disappeared guru Swami Nithyananda's persona and movement. He is physically absent (on the run from various court cases), yet omnipresent in the mediascape of popular discourse, or, as Lucia puts it, the 'guru's assemblage of media representations creates a presence that replaces, alleviates, and even erases his conspicuous absence'. If there is a tension between media's ability to distribute a guru's presence and devotees' frequently felt desire for direct physical connection with them, it is also the case that media's ability to 'store' and distribute a guru's presence can attenuate a guru's physical absence.[57] Whether or not a guru's physical absence is a problem depends of course on the extent to which the guru's biological form is essential to the guru–disciple relationship. Lucia's chapter examines how one guru's hyper-mediation might disrupt altogether the conventional devotional necessity for actual embodied guruship, given that virtual interactions alone can generate millions of devoted followers at least as easily as the guru's actual physical presence. '[T]he more the guru has been persecuted and pursued – and the more he absconded –', writes Lucia, 'the less physically present he can be, and, as a result, the more his media representations effectively replace any semblance of the "real" guru's presence.' If this 'disrupt[s] the appositional relationship of absence and presence', his devotees' tactic of 'media flooding', which involves prolific cross-platform dissemination of counter-narratives to those describing his criminality, likewise blurs the boundary between the real and the fictional. For instance, what are labelled 'live' YouTube videos of the guru's image and words are in fact made up of spliced-together old footage. Such 'splitting, implosion and proliferation of the guru' (Lucia) showcase the media's capacity simultaneously to distribute and change the very nature of guruship.

Arvind Mandair's chapter in this book also explores the relations between absence and presence, the body and disembodiment, the guru in the form of the 'Word', or *sabda-guru*, lying at the centre of a tension between mediation and immediacy. Sikh tradition is undoubtedly characterised by the centrality of gurus. From the 10 living or personal gurus to the Sikh scripture, the Guru Granth Sahib, the tradition of gurus is deeply embedded within Sikhism. But the distribution of Sikh guruship across texts, community and other media highlights the tension between physical mediation (text, sound and embodiment) and the devotee's goal of absolute immediacy, or, as Mandair puts it, 'the incorporeal word, soundless sound, unpulsed vibration'. If such tension-filled striving encapsulates the paradoxes of mediation as discussed by scholars such as Mattijs van de Port (2011) and W. J. T. Mitchell (2005) – most prominently, a constant felt need to escape it coupled with its inescapability – it brings to the fore a further paradox, namely that, if guruship is distributed in the way described above, it is so in a highly impersonal form that breaks strikingly with dominant understandings of the guru as the epitome of person-centred worship, for 'the Word's incorporeal nature […] pushes the relation between Guru and Sikh towards a state of absolute depersonalised, formless, non-mediation (or immediacy), characteristic of pure consciousness'. But, of course, an emotional link with the personal gurus who founded the religion persists, indeed thrives. To reframe Domasńka's (2006, 346) approach to materialisation, the personal guru here might be described as 'non-absent': the *non-absent (personal) guru* (the absent personal guru whose absence is manifest) is based on double negation, it acquires positive meaning (two minuses equal a plus). The notion helps us to avoid presentifying an entity that is manifestly not physically (or theologically) present, and instead to acknowledge an absence that will not go away or, rather, of which we cannot rid ourselves.

Mandair's chapter also raises distinctive questions about the guru's authority and sovereignty. Depersonalisation of guruship, he notes, has the capacity to democratise spirituality by removing its accumulation within a single person, a particularly poignant observation in light of our earlier discussion of the rigid hierarchies and authoritarianism of other (particularly Brahmanical) modes of guruship. Indeed, Mandair contrasts the Sikh tradition's textual distribution of an impersonal guru with the anti-democratic 'exploitable proto-fascist tendencies' of devotional modalities centred on living gurus. Tracing the emergence of the impersonal, radically distributed guru form within Sikhism, he shows how the succession of the living guru became a recurring problem, with competing claims following several gurus' deaths causing schism and diffraction of authority among claimants. Recognising this, the fifth Guru, Arjan, began a consequential process of materially depersonalising the guru by employing a common name for the former gurus whose compositions he compiled into Adi Granth scripture.[58] Marco Deseriis (2015) calls such collective pseudonyms *improper names*, noting, like Mandair, their profound implications for sovereignty. While the authors of the different compositions could still be identified via a numeric code, the principle had nonetheless been established that spiritual authority was now to be located first of all in the incorporeal teachings of the Adi Granth, later renamed the Guru Granth Sahib when the tenth Guru, Gobind Singh, finally brought an end to the line of living gurus. The final paradox, however, is that the very success of Gurus Arjan and Gobind Singh in depersonalising guruship by transferring it into scripture (and the wider Sikh community) extends their own agentive capacities as personal gurus, objectified, as they are, in a text that expresses and further distributes their social efficacy in its every iteration.

Somak Biswas explores a further means of textually mediating a guru's absence in his chapter on letters sent between three guru figures – Swami Vivekananda, Rabindranath Tagore and M. K. Gandhi – and their Western disciples. Indeed, the imperial development of postal networks as a governmental technology for bridging time and distance in the mid-nineteenth century soon became also a material technology for distributing guruship and mediation of mentor–disciple relations. If these 'love letters' frequently evinced an almost erotic longing, they also safely contained it via a technology that is a function of distance even as it connects and makes present: indeed, letters are particularly well suited to establishing the 'intriguing combination of intimacy and distance' (Laidlaw 1995, 63) that marks so many guru–devotee relationships; meanwhile, a further notable way in which illicit longing was contained was through its reframing in maternal terms or subsumption into a professed love for India itself. Amidst the 'dense archipelago of affect' enabled by the letters, Vivekananda and Gandhi warned their partners in epistolary exchange against developing too strong a personal love for them, particularly in the case of their female disciples. Yet Biswas shows how, compensating for the physical separation between mentor and disciple, letters formed material artefacts of the guru's intimate personal presence: 'Letters became embodiments of gurus, evidencing their touch and self-presence.' In this way the letter as an 'embodied text' established a form of physical intimacy, handwriting and signature being particular important for achieving this. The performative force of the letters, then – especially those received by devotees from their gurus – stems from the 'writing acts' (Fraenkel 2007) that crafted them at least as much as from the substance of what they conveyed.

Yagna Nag Chowdhuri's chapter in this volume, which explores the multifaceted significance of photographs of Ramana Maharshi (1879–1950) among his devotees, also bears on the guru's absent-presence. Just as powerful photographs of Anandamayi Ma – which she is said to have 'breathed force' into and which are experienced by devotees in three dimensions – are an important means of mobilising new devotees, especially since her death (Aymard 2014, 58–60), the magnetic power of Ramana's photographed image is such that many people, in different parts of the world, upon seeing it on book covers or posters have felt compelled to journey to his ashram in Tamil Nadu. Devotees compare seeing his photo to falling in love. His ashram is an ashram of photographs: 'This enduring quality of Ramana, the sense of here and now conveyed through the photographs, structures the space of the ashram. All the halls and buildings of the ashram display photographs' (Chowdhuri). The timelessness of the images, which excise context, bears comparison with the chapter by Voix. Chowdhuri cites Susan Visvanathan on how Ramana's photos function as living images in the ashram: 'Devotees plead with Ramana's pictures – understand us, remember us, give us light, salvation, freedom from fear – and the curious miracle of Ramana's presence is that there are visible signs of his hearing prayers' (Visvanathan 2010, 115).

Chowdhuri argues that photographing the guru during his lifetime created intimations of his death, given what was to be their pivotal importance in preserving him after his passing. In the densely photographic world of Ramana, taking his photo was itself an act of devotion. Crucially, in actively participating in the process of being photographed – fulfilling the devotee-photographer's desire to photograph him, surrendering to the photographer as an act of self-denial – the distance between the revered photographic subject and the photographer (and subsequently the image viewer) is effaced, the camera now a space of unification of guru and devotee. Thus, in the context of the pluriform media guruships explored here, Chowdhuri's chapter contributes to building up a picture of gurus' expansive reach towards media as both a 'technology of the imagination' (Sneath et al. 2009) – that is, a concrete set of social and material means engendering 'the ability to bring to mind that which is not entirely present to the senses' (p. 12) – and as something that surpasses this in allowing physically absent gurus nonetheless to suffuse the devotee's body, senses and passions.

Emmanuel Grimaud's chapter examines a very different form of absent guruship. As will be evident, this book not only explores traditional modes of guruship – based on the Indic model of teacher–student relationships within the space of religious institutions – but moves beyond this binary to consider a very wide range of 'guru affects'. While McCartney and Lourenço's chapter examines animated guru dolls, Grimaud's addresses the problem of media animacy quite differently. Here, God is a robot, a gaming robot called Bappa 1.0 with the potential to remediate and create new ways of thinking about 'incarnation', guruship, and the possible capacity of the robot to take the place of God. From this proceeds the question: how do we consider notions of media upgrades (like software updates) to a God-image-subject, or hacking that might destabilise or corrupt it (like a corrupt file)? These are questions that are skilfully deployed, though not fully resolved, in Grimaud's experiment in the 'deconstruction of guruship'. In a novel instance of ethnographic conceptualism – 'ethnography conducted as conceptual art' (Ssorin-Chaikov 2013) – Grimaud and the artist Zaven Paré 'grope into the empirically adjacent in order to provoke the social into happening' (Corsín Jiménez and Estalella 2017, 864) through developing an interactive game in which passers-by in a street in Mumbai were invited to project themselves into a 'guru position', or something between a guru and an avatar of the deity Ganesh, the god-figure they were now able machinically to embody. Fascinatingly, this experiment in 'entrapment to guruship' mostly failed, the guru remaining absent or uninhabitable, with the game's embodiers, instead, having recourse to a voice that remained inimitably their own very human one. What might have been a means to detect 'gurus in the making' – for instance through taking up the rhetorical affordances of the device, rhetoric being indispensable for guru becoming in most instances (Frøystad 2012) – did not reveal a single one, to the extent, Grimaud concludes, that the device came to foreground the 'fragility of incarnation' and the possibility of *guru-retrogradation* as much as *guruisation*. The possibilities and pitfalls of performing guruship as a kind of aesthetic creation lead us directly to the question of guru branding.

Guru, Inc., guru readymades and guru performatives

Peter Sloterdijk (2013, 280) notes how 'the world of enlightenment games … has been affected by mediatization', reflecting that 'the appearance of performance talents among the teachers of well-tempered impossibility was only a matter of time'. Having adopted 'Western performance techniques among the forms of spiritual instruction', the controversial spiritual master Osho né Rajneesh (1931–90) is his case in point. 'Like a Duchamp of the spiritual field,' writes Sloterdijk (p. 281), Osho 'transformed all the relevant traditions into religious playthings and mystical ready-mades'. Later, at the height of his fame, he went further and 'turned himself into a ready-made': 'In assuming the Japanese-tinged name Osho in 1989 – "the joke is over" – he quick-wittedly connected to the recently developed neo-liberal, Buddhophile mood in the West and invented a label for himself with a promising future. This gesture announced that in the field of guru-centred anthropotechnics too, the age of re-branding had begun' (pp. 279–80). Sloterdijk's discernment of telling interdependencies between gurus, media, performance and branding defines the space in which we dwell in this section.

The parallel Sloterdijk draws between Duchamp and Osho invites particular reflection. Duchamp is widely regarded as having paved the way for conceptual art, and a case can indeed be made for some forms of guruship as a kind of conceptual art. Our discussion of Grimaud's work already implies this. If 'conceptual art experiments with the reduction of art objects to concepts' (Ssorin-Chaikov 2013, 7), certain forms of guruship experiment with the reduction of guruship to performance – undoubtedly a long-standing feature of the guru field, in which the content of instruction is frequently less important than cultivation of and engagement with the guru persona.[59] For Duchamp, the prefabricated readymade, detached from its intended use, showed how 'an ordinary object [could be] elevated to the dignity of a work of art by the mere choice of an artist'.[60] For instance, Modi, as discussed earlier, in essence detached and adopted the readymade persona of a Hindu guru via performing it (Landau and Rageth, this volume). Clothing, along with modes of comportment including speech, is frequently key to the mimetic and performative generation of guruship.[61] Following this, the Bollywood classic *Guide* (1965), based on R. K. Narayan's 1958 novel, features two varieties of what could be called 'guru performatives': in the first, we see the primary protagonist, Raju, become a Swami Ji quite accidentally after a *sadhu* lays an orange shawl over his sleeping body. A local villager, and soon the whole village, take him to be what he appears to be, a holy man, an identity Raju embraces and finesses dramaturgically. When, later, he seeks to disclose the performance and renounce his status, his devotees simply become more convinced of it. The second guru performative is that whatever the *maya* of his initial foray into guruship, he later on in fact does become 'great', fasting till death to bring a local drought to an end and save the villagers, which again suggests that artifice and depth in the guru field are not in a zero-sum game but form a complex whole.

The novel underlines the theatricality of Raju's adoption of the guru persona: 'realizing that he is trapped – "I have to play the part expected of me; there is no escape" (37) – Raju suspects "that his spiritual status would be enhanced if he grew a beard and long hair to fall on his nape. ... He bore the various stages of his make-up with fortitude" (39). Supplementing the physical guise, Raju uses cryptic spiritual statements and clichéd proverbs to complete his performance' (Bar-Yosef 2020, 4). Even the fast was a mistake. Having told villagers a story from his childhood of a holy man who fasted to end a drought, he found he was expected to do the same when there was a local drought. This does not disqualify his action or holy-man status as counterfeit but rather forms an example of how such guru performatives can operate as techniques for bringing into existence the entities they perform. Like the doubled form of ethnicity in John Comaroff and Jean Comaroff's account, guruship comes to appear as both 'innate and constructed' (2009, 40). To borrow a phrase from Wendy Doniger (2006), he had been masquerading as himself all along. In disclosing the deep play of guru becoming, *Guide* forms a parallel with Grimaud's experimental deconstruction of the guru form. Both enact a mode of conceptualism that makes 'the fragility of incarnation' (Grimaud) and the social reality of guruship more broadly 'conceivable' through depiction of its 'operational infrastructure' (Ssorin-Chaikov 2013, 5).

Narayan's work thus develops a helpful perspective on the relation between artifice and the devotional real that might be borne in mind in considering the controversy that followed the publication of Peter Heehs's *The Lives of Sri Aurobindo* in 2008. The biography triggered diverse complaints from devotees. Among them was Heehs's blunt treatment of the photographic retouching of the standard portrait of Aurobindo, which he first encountered on the wall of a yoga centre in 1968: 'I was struck by the peaceful expanse of his brow, his trouble-free face, and fathomless eyes. It would be years before I learned that all of these features owed their distinctiveness to the retoucher's art' (2008, x), an art he sees as the visual equivalent of hagiographic writings on Hindu saints (p. xiv), a germane comparison.[62] In stark contrast with the present-day 'triumph of the aesthetics of the imperfect', in which mythologising effects are produced through the intentional ageing of photographic images courtesy of digital apps (Bartholeyns 2014, 54–5), Heehs proceeds to describe the artifice of the portrait as follows: 'The sparkling eyes have been painted in; even the hair has been given a gloss. As a historical document it is false. As a photograph it is a botched piece of work' (Heehs 2008, x). Following our discussion of *Guide*, however, it is clear that the image can only be described in terms of 'falsification' if one holds that its only purpose is to stand transparently as a record of an event. For the devotee, however, it holds a very different evidential value as evidence of a *mentalité* (Pinney 2008a, S34). That is to say, the retouched portrait may be a fabrication, but not of something that doesn't exist.[63]

An 'assisted readymade' is a prefabricated object that is modified or assembled by the artist, a definition that is suggestive of the modes of associational labour engaged in by some gurus, which frequently function as forms of branding. Sloterdijk suggests something similar in describing Osho's adoption of hitherto absent or hidden Buddhist elements in terms of 'rebranding'. Such modification and assembly of what we term 'guru readymades' makes for a guru who is a meaningfully curated 'crowd of narratives'. If Osho was artist and artwork in one, a self-composed assisted readymade, guru Rewben Mashangva, the subject of Arkotong Longkumer's chapter, is a performing artist in the more conventional meaning of the term, one who, like Osho, is a master of assembly. The influences of Bob Dylan, Bob Marley and the sounds of nature are ever present in Mashangva's folk music. Blending various sounds from his homeland of Manipur with others from folk, jazz and blues, Mashangva has fashioned a unique career. Granted the title 'guru' in recognition of his contribution to music and cultural preservation by a regional institution that forms part of the Indian Ministry of Culture, he constitutes a very particular kind of guru in a region with no civilisational links to the concept (to wit, he is a Christian). A guru by virtue of his artistic craft, his title might seem to connect him to the guru traditions of the performing arts. But of course no such tradition exists for the unique folk–pop hybrid form created by Mashangva. While he does teach his craft to *shishya* students as a means of seeking to preserve and revive Tangkhul culture, he did this before receiving the award. Mashangva's guru status from this angle might seem entirely synthetic. While the case of Mashangva calls to mind the chapters by Dawson Varughese and McCartney and Lourenço as a further instance of transposition of guru principles into 'other' terrain, it also seems to underscore the incapacity of mainstream Hindu agencies to see excellence and its tuition outside a 'guru' frame of reference, as when a VHP volunteer considered the Naga Heraka icon Rani Gaidinliu a guru, conceptualising her tradition and its transmission in *parampara* terms (Longkumer 2010, 130, 220).

However, this is more than a story of cultural imposition. Having come to embrace the authority the title bestows on him as a further tool for cultural preservation, Mashangva reimagines what it means to be a guru in the same way he reimagines musical possibility. His music and guruship are both made in the form of an 'open enquiry' (Ingold 2013). He crosses cultural boundaries not only to create something new in his music, but also in accepting the ('Hindu') guru title (as a Tangkhul Christian), thereby taking the concept to new places and adding new layers of significance to it. His surprising assembly of cultural readymades makes him 'a guru in many keys' (Longkumer), and it is here that he does connect strongly with those currents of guruship which innovate (Lucia 2014b), cross boundaries, and prolifically engage in practices of spiritual bricolage. Further, his clear embrace of the guru as a figure of *doing* who takes pride in his work finds a reflection in radical bhakti saints such as Kabir and Sant Ravidas, whose poetry was 'marked with imagery drawn from their work, from the life of production – weaving, spinning, dyeing, farming, trading' (Omvedt 2008, 35). At the same time, congruent with the 'Faustian bargain' discussed by Comaroff and Comaroff that 'requires "natives" to perform themselves in such a way as to make their indigeneity legible to the consumer of otherness' (2009, 142), Mashangva understands the need to package himself and his indigeneity in appealing, domesticated ways and is well capable of branding himself differently for different audiences. Further, as an established national figure he is called upon by the state to represent India (and 'the Idea of India') internationally at various functions where, once more, the guru participates in the branding of the nation.

The CEO-function (Nanda 2009) and lively participation of public gurus in the 'spiritual marketplace' (Warrier 2003) as 'producers and purveyors of spiritual commodities' (McKean 1996, 1) and the connection between these developments and the progressive liberalisation of the Indian economy since the 1980s (Zavos 2012) has been much noted. Linked to this is a broad range of media branding techniques employed by gurus and their organisations which have been less fully addressed, with some significant exceptions.[64] It is these techniques that we point to and explore under the term 'Guru, Inc.'.[65] Adapted from the Comaroffs' (2009) *Ethnicity, Inc.*, it points to how certain gurus adapt themselves to – and take forward in distinct ways – the pervasive branding and selling of culture as a repository of tradition and allurement, and, conversely, to how other entities employ representations of guruship as part of their own branding. We mentioned earlier the BJP's employment of guru concepts in national branding strategies (McCartney and Lourenço); meanwhile, Koushiki Dasgupta (2021) describes the current cohort of global gurus as soft Hindutva's 'brand ambassadors'. Consider also the branding significance of the striking photographic portraits of Ramakrishna and Swami Vivekananda that played such an important role in popularising the Ramakrishna Mission. Early members of the Mission carried the popular 'Worshipped Pose' photograph of Ramakrishna with them on pilgrimages; it also formed the template for the marble statue of the Swami at Belur Math. Meanwhile, 'Vivekananda ordered more than a hundred copies of the "Chicago Pose" photograph for distribution, indicative of the keen interest he took in the outcomes of photographic sessions' (Beckerlegge 2012, 401).

Gandhi too was an 'innovative technician of mass publicity' (Mazzarella 2010, 31), skilled in the use of radio and print media in particular as means of 'self-branding in the national cause'. The mass mediatisation of the performative austerity of his political leadership – restrictive dietary habits including hunger strikes, celibacy, sartorial style – 'established on a visceral level … the paradigm of the modern political ascetic in India' (Chaudhury 2021, 8). 'Hundreds of monks attended the Indian National Congress' meeting in Nagpur in 1920', notes Mehta (2017, 503), 'out of curiosity to see how Gandhi was organising mass politics using their own political idiom.' One modern-day Indian marketing consultant describes Gandhi as 'the only superbrand that India has produced. … [H]e was a brand who was related to the pulse of the rural masses of India ...[,] a guy who believed in all the great things that brands believe in. Be different. Swim against the tide. Do things differently. Establish icons. Establish imagery. Strengthen imagery by persistent, focused segmentation of the market' (Mazzarella 2010, 19). Gandhi has come to form a marketing exemplar for commercial brand logics.

The guru-figure inspires marketers, who in turn inspire gurus. Given this circularity, it should not be a surprise that the necessity of sophisticated branding campaigns is now taken for granted across the world of public gurus. Upadhyay (2022) explains that 'tele-gurus' such as Ramdev, Sadhguru and Sri Sri Ravi Shankar convey a Hinduism that is 'fuzzy, unstructured, colourful, ... upbeat, fashionable and urban'.[66] But such (would-be) public gurus have varying degrees of success: 'Not-so-popular gurus or a guru-in-making ... might initially have to pay channels for air slots' (Upadhyay 2022). The 'hyper-mediated, branded charisma' (Mazzarella 2022) of those who succeed, however, allows them to occupy multiple spaces and fulfil multiple agendas. Consonant with our focus on how the guru 'can be depersonalized and become a kind of principle' (Jaffrelot 2012, 88), not all guru-linked branding is so keyed into personal referents, as Nicole Karapanagiotis (2021) shows in her study of the rebranding of Krishna Consciousness, which is more focused on programmes and centres and the creation of distinct 'intra-brands' within the movement. For instance, one brand removes all traces of 'Indian culture', the better to appeal to a wider constituency of practitioner, while another re-presents ISKCON as the theological fountainhead of postural yoga, and so on. Impersonal guru branding is also a key theme of McCartney and Lourenço's chapter, which argues that children's 'fashion' and 'action' yoga dolls mediate guru principles, and indeed can act as non-human gurus for the intergenerational transmission of yoga knowledge to children. Central to this consumptive spirituality model is an alternative architecture of authority and tradition. These do not flow from a teacher and neither are they legitimated by an established tradition; rather the toy industry enters the arena of 'yoga articulations', with the healthy 'yoga lifestyle' now transmitted through 'gift-giving from adults to children'. This very distinct manifestation of the guru-sphere is connected by Hindutva politicians to aspirations for a *swadeshi* toy industry' as a feature of 'New India' branding, a vision that is in tune with their 'world guru' ambitions, which these toys can be imagined as realising – doll by doll – via their global distribution. This of course is exactly the kind of 'triangulation of culture, identity, and the market' (Comaroff and Comaroff 2009, 20) that we are seeking to highlight under the rubric of

'Guru, Inc.'. The chapter also introduces Fisher-Price's 'meditation mouse', a 'fluffy guru' that relays guided meditations for over-excited toddlers: 'This soothing plush mouse is the go-to calming cuddle buddy to help your little one learn how to nama-stay relaxed', says the publicity. The themes of transposition and translation of guru principles are again salient, as they find a presence in product ranges. In curious resonance with Mandair's discussion of the depersonalized guru principle in Sikhism, and Lucia's of the splitting and proliferation of Nithyananda, but with a techno-branding twist, McCartney and Lourenço note: 'Unlike human gurus, who are limited by their historical context, charisma and mortality, non-human gurus can capture ideas and ideals that, if not atemporal, are temporally meaningful, seamlessly moving between the material and the virtual and from one generation to the next, with the potential benefit of remaining culturally relevant through unlimited updates.'

Spiderweb guruship

'[T]he purchasing act', write McCartney and Lourenço (this volume), 'entails a commitment to what the guru envisions or represents.' The suggestive notion of the purchasing act as commitment/devotion is unremarkable insofar as devotion to brands is exactly what marketing theory seeks to produce; in this sense, what we term spiderweb guruship – i.e., guruship as a series of media-assisted aesthetic and affective traps, principally for the captivation of devotees but also for that of further entities such as gurus, including the guru's own self – simply reflects standard branding priorities. But of course, as skilled devotional and affective technicians, gurus can be particularly well placed to convert devotion into purchasing acts. In the case of several public gurus, devotion is being recast in terms of what might be called a 'subscribe to the guru' model, with the guru-commodity leased out to devotee-users for time-limited experiences.[67] For instance, Sadhguru's online video platform offers various subscription plans to access exclusive Sadhguru 'content' in numerous languages and on 'any device'.[68] User testimonials register the enterprise's success in finessing the affective grip of the guru commodity, testifying that 'Sadhguru content is more powerful and impactful than I could have imagined. There hasn't been a video yet where tears haven't dropped. I feel like whatever is transmitted through this platform is somehow alive and touches me very profoundly.'[69] Sadhguru and his Isha Foundation have engineered a digital architecture of intimacy that enables the guru to seem individually present to every devotee-user through video replay 'as though this were the only interaction that mattered' (Thrift 2012, 19).

Sadhguru's subscription model is emblematic of how public guru organisations have engaged quite successfully in the development of 'enchanted digital ecosystems', consisting of online blessing tools, hashtags and social media metrics, 'to understand where one's known following is', and thereby to assist in 'targeted marketing of their practices-as-commodities' (Meena et al. 2020, 6). The mediatisation of guruship and the guru-isation of media provide further diverse means for the affective captivation of devotees. However, if the case of Sadhguru shows well how digital curation of guruship can extend the captivating capacities of already existing gurus, it is important to note that there now exist gurus who have become objects of devotion almost solely through digital media. That is to say, social media can go beyond simply providing new tools of devotional recruitment and interaction for prevailing gurus; they assist in actively producing new gurus from within those very spaces.[70] Ronie Parciack (2023) presents a particularly vivid case study in which Islamic and Hindu teacher–disciple traditions overlap, and we see how the digital turn can offer low-cost means of guru-*pir* creation 'in hyperlocal spheres'.

While we emphasise that a spiderweb guruship heuristic is far from universally applicable, we may note that even gurus who have no wish to captivate may do so anyway. For instance, ascetics with no desire to attain the status of guru may teach by example; hence, in many cases unwilling teachers are followed and watched, and build communities, on the basis of little will or intention (in the manner of the Buddha after his enlightenment and indeed Ramana). Such 'accidental guruship' specifically as a media phenomenon features in the chapters by Chowdhuri, Longkumer, Grimaud and Dawson Varughese, for of course accidental gurus are no less mediatised for the absence of intention.[71] As Chowdhuri explains, submitting to the camera was transformed into a spiritual exercise of self-surrender by Ramana. Arresting material and digital images of him and other gurus circulate and captivate regardless of will. Otherwise very local figures are subject to '"accidental" dissemination' (Pinney 2008b, 2) through media flows consequent on their devotees' and organisations' wish to capture their image or teachings, and thereby become accidental figures of mass culture and mass veneration.

On the other hand, in the arena of public gurus, which foregrounds and relies on increasingly sophisticated guru branding, captivation frequently *is* consequent on will and intention. It is here, where even seeking to differentiate between the highly mediatised religious guru and the proverbial management or marketing guru can become treacherous, that a vocabulary of captivation which pays heed not only to the word's connotations of 'attraction' and 'holding interest' but also to its origin in the Latin *captivat-*, 'taken captive', is particularly apt. We seek to show that the captivation of disciples via branding techniques to extend appeal may involve (and even depend on) a guru's own captivation by both the conceits of guruship and other gurus.

The captivating visual spectacles inaugurated by the Mumbai-based guru Radhe Maa, who reportedly lives in the house of a high-profile advertising executive who choreographs her appearances and 'make[s] it a point to put hoarding of Radhe Maa whenever my hoardings are empty in off season in Mumbai' are exemplary here.[72] At gatherings where she and her followers dance to Bollywood music, her red lipstick, other scarlet finery and shiny hairdo connote not only 'a conscious attempt to invoke the long-haired Shiva figurine in a female form but also purvey standardised images that calendar art makes so popular' (Gavaskar 2015, 9).[73] Like other gurus' dazzling production of 'wondertraps' (Copeman and Duggal 2023), images of the guru once more compel and captivate, but not necessarily through darshan, with the guru presenting herself in such a way as to affect and therefore exercise a certain captivating power over actual and potential devotees. Indeed, rather than power coming from the enactment of an authoritative gaze, we see how it results from a guru making herself visible in an aesthetically and affectively captivating form. If gurus use varieties of expressive infrastructure to affectively bind devotee-customers to guru products through effective identification of emotional pressure points (Thrift 2008, 37), Radhe Maa accomplishes something similar by '[d]ressing up as a "bride" in "new expensive lehngas [elaborately embroidered skirts]" every time she meets her *bhakts*', with '*sindoor* [vermilion powder worn by married Hindu women along the hair parting], *chooda* bangles [worn by recently married Hindu women], red lipstick, red velvet bedcovers …, [and] dripping jewellery' evoking powerful '[n]uptial fantasies' and themes of 'virginity, fertility, wifehood and wealth'.[74] The belittling 'anti-guruism' of academic discourse on marketing and management gurus has been criticised on account of its 'troublesome and all-too-easy colonial discourse of superiority' and its 'trace of a deprecated Hinduism' vis-à-vis the guru as classically understood, who is tainted by association (Rhodes and Pitsis 2008, 77–8). However, the critique depends on a distinction between the marketing and the spiritual guru that is often no longer tenable. Not only does there often exist a reciprocal flow of specialised knowledge between the two forms (as can be seen in our earlier discussion of Gandhi), but Radhe Maa's 'devotion of attractions' (Copeman and Duggal 2023), in which 'divinity goes pop' (Gavaskar 2015; Srivastava 2009), apparently occupies a space between, or even completely folds together, spiritual and marketing guruship modes (on the other hand, the aforementioned advertising executive declares that 'his advertising company Global Advertisers cannot propagate Radhe Maa because she is beyond everything').[75]

While it may be that 'Radhe Maa "does" religion the way Rakhi Sawant does item numbers', and her credentials have been questioned by naysayers who state that 'by calling this woman #RadheMaa we are disrespecting Radhe and Maa both',[76] it is not clear that publicity even such as this is not planned. The guru as a marketing creation is not completely new, but we do find perhaps its fullest expression here. Criticised by the Akhil Bhartiya Akhara Parishad (ABAP) for having 'no knowledge about religion or religious scriptures' and for being 'only well-versed in "singing and dancing"',[77] the readymade guru presides over captivating spectacles beyond which there is nothing else. Consequently, her guruship carries an air both of performative experiment and of a joke that went too far, capturing not only devotees but the guru herself in its web. (Osho was interested in performance and jokes but no one can say he had 'no knowledge about religion or religious scriptures'.) Her case bears comparison with the US documentary film *Kumaré* (2011), which more transparently enacts guruship as a hoax in the sense of something that 'lies in order to tell the truth' (Fleming and O'Carroll 2010, 58). Recounting its maker Vikram Gandhi's impersonation of an Indian guru by donning an appropriate costume and curating a selection of mantras, yoga poses and New Age-tinged 'Hindu teachings', the film effectively discloses the deep play of guru becoming – that is, the performative dimensions and operational infrastructure of guru generation qua devotee captivation – with the aesthetic trap he set captivating real followers. Recalling the indeterminate reality status of the guru depicted in *Guide*, however, Gandhi claimed he had not engaged in outright deception, since Kumaré was the person he now wished sincerely to be. In other words, he had himself become trapped by the institutional-performative complex he had sought to throw light on.[78]

A further modality of the spiderweb guru is to undertake captivation work that entangles multiple entities in its own self-image (Corsín Jiménez 2018). Just as brand strategists seek to increase a commodity's 'stickiness' by causing it to resonate across many different affective, sensory and semiotic registers at once (Thrift 2008, 39), spiderweb guruship can seek to enlarge the spiderweb precisely through modes of semiotic and affective diversification that seek to entangle multiple entities (e.g. forebear gurus) in the guru-image, the better to entangle devotees within that image, too. In the scenarios ethnographically conceptualised by Grimaud, there existed the enticing possibility that 'a follower could entrap a god and reverse the transfer of power', becoming – through inhabitations of the robot Bappa – a kind of guru. What resulted, however, was the apparent failure of those inhabiting the Bappa machine to capture adequately guruship's performative registers and therefore to captivate as a guru. Nevertheless, one technique of guru becoming is precisely to seek to entrap forebears or deities and reverse the transfer of power. This operates through the sorts of mimetic authority transfers discussed earlier. Gurus employ and evoke appropriate accoutrements, turns of phrase, comportment, imagery and media devices to prompt and circulate 'semiotic arousal' (Landes 2011, 14) and 'ancestry effects' (Albert 2001) as means of inscribing themselves into the histories and moral landscapes of given communities (Gayer and Therwath 2010).[79] Semiotic abduction in Batesonian terms as 'the lateral extension of recognising similarity between two discrete units (objects, behaviours, etc.) which proposes the possibility of further similarity' (Küchler and Carroll 2021, 8) operates as a method for the (more literal) abduction of 'others' into the concentrated 'entity cluster' (Grimaud) of the guru. After comedian Kiku Sharda's arrest in 2016 for sending up the DSS guru, discussed earlier, devotee tweets such as the following underscored their guru's abductive capacities: 'By mimicking him, Kiku Sharda has insulted Ram, Rahim, Jesus, Gurunanak, Mother Mary and Insaan [humankind]. Serves him right!'[80] Sathya Sai Baba enacted particularly prolific and high-profile associational additions.[81] But the 'incarnation games' (Grimaud) do not end there: other gurus – Prem Sai, for instance – claim or seek to prompt claims that they are Sathya Sai Baba.[82] The trapper is trapped in turn, the guru's power and authority abducted by would-be successors courtesy of mediated aesthetic techniques.

The ability of guru images to capture, and their susceptibility to being captured, are of course two sides of the same coin. Indeed, gurus' capture of other gurus and associations can exist in dynamic interaction with their own attempts to evade incorporative capture. Indra Devi's ungraspability is signalled by the frequent name changes that marked her many rebirths, which show how 'for her, constant openness to change was a spiritual precept' (Goldberg 2015, 9). The DSS guru's ever-changing name (which is currently Dr Saint Gurmeet Ram Rahim Singh Ji Insan) also builds up an ecology of associations with elements from Sikhism, Hinduism and Islam. If such additions 'brighten the halo around his syncretic claims, with an eye at perhaps broadening the base of his clientele from varied religious affiliations' (Singh 2017, 21), they also augment a cultivated semiotic instability beyond limiting capture.

In some cases, the terms capture/captivate will undoubtedly be too emphatic: in Rewben Mashangva's case, for instance, his own relationship to the guru category might be better described as one of curiosity about the possibilities that guruship and its cultural capital might afford him. Largely, however, the terms do, so to speak, capture the polyvalent, multidirectional appropriations at stake in mediated guru-devotee contexts. The chapters of this book disclose the multilayered captivation work of gurus, devotees and guru organisations as enacted across various media in which gurus and devotees feature as both subjects and objects of capture. The chapters by Lucia, Biswas, Bhattacharya, Srinivas, Mandair, Chowdhuri, and Copeman and Duggal, in particular, outline the ability of gurus to generate (sometimes paradoxical) captivating presences across a diverse range of media. To take the case of Sathya Sai Baba in Srinivas's chapter, here the guru both is captured in the tomb-space and exists dramatically beyond it, uncapturable. If, as we see in Chowdhuri's chapter, Ramana surrenders to photographic captivation, the captivating power of the resulting images (in which, to use a phrase from Voix, his presence is 'impregnated') continues to bring devotees to his 'ashram of photographs' from all over the world. Meanwhile, the material embodiment of letters between Gandhi and Tagore and their Western disciples left 'thick affective trail[s]' (Biswas) that were mutually entangling. On the other hand, the chapters by Longkumer and Dawson Varughese disclose the almost viral-like propensity of guru logics to cross-fertilise, inhabit, and indeed capture, 'other' lifeworlds. Yet, if to some degree the Northeast cultural icon Rewben Mashangva and Jesus himself are trapped into guruship or involuntarily subjected to guru formatting, such formatting potentially takes the form of what Deleuze calls 'double capture' (2006, 2), the 'becoming' that exists between two contrasting matters: a becoming-guru on the part of Rewben and Jesus is in the same instant a becoming-Rewben and becoming-Jesus on the part of guru logics. We see, then, how toys (McCartney and Lourenço), robots (Grimaud), photographs (Voix, Chowdhuri), digitalia (Lucia), tombs (Srinivas), singer-activists (Longkumer), paintings (Dawson Varughese), screens (Bhattacharya, Copeman and Duggal), religious and political leaders (Dawson Varughese, Landau and Rageth), letters (Biswas) and other textual forms (Mandair) are all capable of capturing, conveying and transforming different facets of guruship.

Acknowledgements

We are grateful to Amanda Lucia, Aya Ikegame, Patrick McCartney, Bhuvi Gupta and Lindsay Graham for stimulating and insightful feedback on earlier drafts of this chapter.

Notes

1 See also Morse (2012) and Myrvold (2007) on texts as gurus, Murphy (2022) on late nineteenth- and early twentieth-century vernacular print culture in Punjab as a key space for reimagining the Sikh Guru, Cerulli (2022) on textual practices among Ayurvedic gurus, and Biswas (this volume) on 'epistolary guruship'.
2 See Parry (1985).
3 See Copeman and Ikegame (2012) on the dramatic exposé of Swami Nithyanand, the subject of Lucia's chapter in this volume, via a hidden camera, and Copeman and Hagström (2022) on the use of video slow motion and other media technologies by Indian rationalists to expose gurus' miraculous claims. See also the important discussion of guru movements and sexual assault in Jain (2020, 124), where it is argued that 'we should avoid falling into dichotomous traps by too simplistically subsuming gurus and their sex scandals into "guru scandals" as if sexual violence is simply a result of an essentialized "guru model" or, more generally, of religious authoritarianism. The appeal to the dangers of guru charisma and devotion as an explanation for sexual violence pulls our attention away from larger social structures and norms that cultivate a dominant global culture of sexual violence.'
4 Darshan is the exchange of vision between worshipper and worshipped and is an important feature in the worship not only of temple gods but also of guru puja (Copeman 2009, 88, 120–2, 198).
5 Priyanka Dubey, 'Crisis of faith: The nightmarish struggle to bring Asaram to justice', *The Caravan*, 1 April 2017. https://caravanmagazine.in/reportage/asaram-nightmarish-struggle-bring-justice (accessed 28 April 2023).
6 Okita (2012) explains that some compromises are now made.
7 Fractal: 'a figure which demonstrates the property of *self-similarity* at different scales of magnification/minification' (Gell 1998, 137).
8 The point follows Klen and Sukyens (2018).
9 See Khandelwal (2004, 173), Copeman and Ikegame (2012, 297–8) and Copeman (2012).
10 See Rollier, Frøystad and Ruud 2019 on South Asian outrage politics.
11 'A telecoms engineer based in the southern city of Bangalore, Mr Zubair co-founded Alt News in 2017 with former software engineer Pratik Sinha to combat fake news. Over the past five years, the website has played a key role in debunking claims that spread disinformation about religion and caste and unscientific myths.' https://www.bbc.com/news/world-asia-india-62093974 (accessed 9 February 2023).
    See also: 'Zubair gets 14 more days in custody for calling Hindutva leaders facing hate charges "hatemongers"', *The Wire*, 5 July 2022, https://thewire.in/law/zubair-remanded-for-14-more-days-for-calling-hindutva-leaders-facing-hate-charges-hatemongers, and 'Mahant Bajrang Muni Das arrested days after giving rape threats to Muslim women in UP's Sitapur', *First Post*, 13 April 2022. https://www.firstpost.com/india/mahant-bajrang-muni-das-arrested-days-after-giving-rape-threats-to-muslim-women-in-ups-sitapur-10553531.html (both accessed 9 February 2023).
12 See Copeman and Ikegame (2012, 307–8).
13 'World Hindu Council', founded in 1964. It pursues a staunchly Hindutva-based agenda.
14 See Basu (2015, 185) on Asaram Bapu's participation in Hindutva politics and some of the charges against him. He currently resides in prison in Rajasthan (Lucia, this volume). See also Copeman and Ikegame (2012, 292).
15 See https://www.trendsmap.com/twitter/tweet/1540889774982062082 (accessed 28 March 2023).

16 Contrasting attitudes to gurus mark boundaries between the strikingly differentiated sets of groups and alliances that cohere under the banner of Hindutva. Representing a more austere version of Hindutva, Arun Shourie has criticised the crass commercialisation of present-day public guruship (Lucia 2022, 12).

17 SAB TV, 31 July 2013.

18 *Hindustan Times*, 11 May 2007. See also Shearer (2020). Our thanks to Amanda Lucia for alerting us to these cases.

19 See Copeman (2018) on epistemophilia as an almost erotic drive for 'unveiling'.

20 The saints who have appeared on *Big Boss* are Radhe Maa, on whom see Mannila and Zeiler (2020), and the Arya Samaj leader and social activist Swami Agnivesh (see Copeman and Ikegame 2012, 315).

21 For further details, see Copeman and Banerjee (2019, 193–201) and K. Duggal (2022).

22 Intermediality is (1) 'crossings between two or more media forms[, for example] ... the movement of narrative from one medium to another, ... in the form of filmic adaptations of novels', and (2) how one kind of media can be present in and through another (V. Duggal 2021, 113).

23 A Hindu sage or saint.

24 Vasishtha and Vishvamitra form part of the *Saptarishi* group of 'seven sages' in Vedic texts and the Upanishads. Valmiki's Ramayana describes Vasishtha as the family priest of the Ikshvaku dynasty who taught Ram and his brothers royal family duties.

25 The second-highest civilian award of the Republic of India.

26 *New Indian Express*, 27 August 2017.

27 Inaugurated in 1985, the Ministry of Youth Affairs and Sports bestows the award annually 'to the person who not only works as a mentor but chalks out the path a prodigy traverses on his way to stardom' (https://olympics.com/en/featured-news/dronacharya-award-given-india-coaches-excellence-first-recipient, accessed 9 February 2023).

28 Rashtriya Swayamsevak Sangh (RSS), Association of National Volunteers: a militant, highly disciplined Hindu nationalist organisation that is treated as a moral authority by other Hindutva groups. A *pracharak* is a full-time worker of the RSS.

29 A Delhi satellite but also a global centre in its own right that is 'home to the local offices of half the Fortune 500 companies'.

30 *Mint*, 16 April 2016.

31 *The Hindu*, 12 April 2016. This rationale has been challenged by another widely held view, namely 'that nomads used to hoard jaggery [*gur*] in the village in order to survive hard times during floods in the adjoining Yamuna river' (*Mint*, 16 April 2016).

32 Facebook 2016, 'Ekalavya Speaks'. https://www.facebook.com/EkalavyaNarratives/?ref=page_internal (accessed 9 February 2023).

33 See Copeman (2009).

34 Sukanya Shantha, 'As symbols of discrimination fall worldwide, meet the women who blackened Manu's statue', *The Wire*, 14 June 2020 (https://thewire.in/rights/kantabai-ahire-sheela-pawar-manu-statue-blackened-protest, accessed 9 February 2023).

35 By burning the Manusmriti, anti-caste and Ambedkarite activists resist the hegemony of Brahmanism which includes both caste-Hindu domination and Hindutva. Unlike secular and left-liberal opposition, which sees Hinduism as different from Hindutva, Ambedkarites see both Hinduism and Hindutva as part of Brahmanism. See also Fuchs (2022) on Dalit resistance towards Brahmanical guru figures.

36 The phrasing borrows from Fuchs's (2022, 175) stimulating discussion of the triangular relationship between God the Divine, layperson and guru/saint-poet.

37 See the insightful related discussion by John Zavos (2012).

38 Copeman and Ikegame (2012, 11).

39 *Dera* – the extended residential site of an influential figure – usually has similar connotations to 'ashram'.

40 Copeman and Ikegame (2012, 291).

41 'The victors in India's modern spiritual market', notes Prabhu Chawla in 'Spiritual caste divisions create gurus with Moolah, Hooplah and violent followers', *New Indian Express* (27 August 2017), '[d]espite variations in style and substance' have in common their great admiration for Narendra Modi, 'who reciprocates their admiration by gracing their public events with his presence'.

42 'BAPS participates in video conference of spiritual leaders with Prime Minister Modi, India', 30 March 2020. https://www.baps.org/News/2020/BAPS-Participates-in-Video-Conference-of-Spiritual-Leaders-with-Prime-Minister-Modi-18657.aspx (accessed 10 February 2023).

43 See for example 'Sadhguru offers simple yogic practices to increase oxygen levels and boost immunity in Covid times', *Free Press Journal*, 29 April 2021, https://www.freepressjournal.in/india/sadhguru-offers-simple-yogic-practices-to-increase-oxygen-levels-and-boost-immunity-in-covid-times (accessed 10 February 2023). Solomon (2021) explains that, in the hospital where he conducted fieldwork in Mumbai, even before COVID-19 'rationing ventilators [was] the norm and not the exception'. See Frøystad (2021) on gurus and Hindu rituals during the pandemic, and McCartney (2021).

44 See Copeman and Ikegame (2012).

45 Jinoy Jose P., 'Circles of reason: The growing rationalist movements in India', *The Hindu*, 25 September 2020.

46 Narendra Nayak, 'Don't believe claims of 100% cure for Covid-19', *Mangalore Today*, 23 June 2020, https://www.mangaloretoday.com/mainnewsprint/Don-rsquo-t-believe-claims-of-100-cure-for-Covid-19-Narendra-Nayak.html (accessed 10 February).

47 Amy Kazmin and Jyotsna Singh, 'Indian doctors protest against guru who claims yoga can defeat Covid', *Financial Times*, 1 June 2021.

48 After Pinney's 'industrial gods' (2008b).

49 'Essence of my art: Gulammohammed Sheikh in conversation with Vasudevan Akkitham', *Sahapedia*, 18 March 2020, https://www.sahapedia.org/essence-my-art-gulammohammed-sheikh-conversation-vasudevan-akkitham (accessed 10 February 2023).

50 'Crowd of narratives' is borrowed from Salman Rushdie's usage in the BBC radio programme 'Free Thinking' (14 October 2015).

51 See Copeman (2023) on Sikh names and disidentity politics.

52 See Das and Copeman (2015).

53 Georgina Born (2013, 132) explains that 'a material index elicits a certain cognitive operation, which Gell defines, after Peirce, as the "abduction" of social agency: the inference that the object is the outcome of social agency'. As Gell (1998, 21) puts it, 'objectification in artefact-form is how social agency manifests and realizes itself, via the proliferation of fragments of "primary" intentional agents in their "secondary" artefactual forms'.

54 This and the other references in this sentence are to chapters in this volume.

55 See Keul and Raman (2022, 3).

56 This paragraph paraphrases Gell (1998, 16, 222). See Orianne Aymard's (2014) exploration of the community of worship centring on Ma Anandamayi following her death in 1982. Though maintaining this community after her death has been a challenge for devotees, the guru's ability to live otherwise and 'presentify' via key 'mediums of guruship' (Aymard 2014, 9) – namely, powerful relics such as her tomb, photographs and items worn or used by her – has driven the continued distribution of her guruship.

57 See also Copeman and Duggal (this volume).

58 Mandair notes that Nanak had himself started this process.

59 For example, see Chowdhuri (this volume).

60 'Marcel Duchamp and the readymade', *MoMALearning*, https://www.moma.org/learn/moma_learning/themes/dada/marcel-duchamp-and-the-readymade/ (accessed 11 February 2023).

61 See earlier discussion of mimesis; also Copeman and Ikegame (2012), Malhotra (2022), and Landau and Rageth (this volume).

62 See Gleig (2012) for a sensitive account of this complex controversy.

63 We take inspiration here from Grimaud's (2011) work on special effect-assisted miracles performed by robotic Hindu deities which, evidently fabricated, nonetheless 'crystallize a hidden existence or unexploited potentiality'.

64 See in particular Patrick McCartney's ongoing work on yoga branding (e.g. 2021); also Karapanagiotis (2021).

65 We acknowledge that Rama Lakshmi employs the term in a 2016 (27 February) piece in the *Washington Post* titled 'Guru Inc.: India's holy men enter the world of big business', an article we came across well after the drafting of this introductory chapter, as this volume was going to press (https://www.washingtonpost.com/world/asia_pacific/guru-inc-indias-holy-men-enter-the-world-of-big-business/2016/02/26/6ee7a542-d596-11e5-a65b-587e721fb231_story.html, accessed 27 April 2023).

66 This was the case for Ram Rahim when he was promoting *MSG 2*. The first *MSG* film, having novelty value, saw journalists lining up for 'on[e]-on-one chats with the luridly dressed religious leader, even travelling to his headquarters in Sirsa in Haryana to seek an audience. ... Critics too ensured that *MSG* was added to their weekly quota of assignments, just in case the movie turned out to be so terrible that it was actually fun. The second time around, finding that

his novelty appeal has vanished, Singh has resorted to buying media space and putting out paid interviews.' Nandini Ramnath, *MSG 2: The Messenger* sees the return of the guru of bad cinema', Scroll.in, 18 September 2015, https://scroll.in/article/756336/msg-2-the-messenger-sees-the-return-of-the-guru-of-bad-cinema (accessed 11 February 2023).

67 See Thrift (2012, 143).

68 Isha Foundation, 'Of yoga, yogi and mysticism', https://isha.sadhguru.org/global/en/sadhguru-exclusive (accessed 11 February 2023).

69 Testimonial of Omar, student, Spain, at the Isha Foundation website. See Thrift (2008, 39) on 'affective grip'.

70 On (non-Indic) internet gurus more broadly, see Helen Lewis, 'Russell Brand's big rebrand: Conspiracy guru with 6 million followers', *The Times*, 17 December 2022, https://www.thetimes.co.uk/article/beaee026-7d79-11ed-a3d2-203363978915 (accessed 20 April 2023) and Lewis's BBC Radio 4 series *The New Gurus* (2022).

71 See also the earlier discussion of *Guide*.

72 Cine Buster, 'Sanjeev Gupta: "Sky is the limit"', 4 August 2017, https://www.cinebuster.in/sanjeev-gupta-sky-is-the-limit/ (accessed 11 February 2023).

73 See also Copeman and Duggal in this volume.

74 Shefalee Vasudev, 'Radhe Maa's outlandish red', *Mint*, 19 August 2015, https://www.livemint.com/Opinion/dJOojXO0qiGIDufA5vUIzK/Radhe-Mas-outlandish-red.html (accessed 11 February 2023). See Thrift (2012, 4) on 'expressive infrastructure'.

75 Cine Buster, 'Sanjeev Gupta: "Sky is the limit"'.

76 Rahul Mahajan, quoted in Nishita Karun, 'Hardships of becoming a guru: Radhe Maa talks', *ED Times*, 10 August 2015, https://edtimes.in/hardships-of-becoming-a-guru-radhe-maa-talks/ (accessed 11 February 2023).

77 *India Today*, 13 October 2020. The ABAP is an organisation of gurus, saints and ascetics. Though independent, 'in the recent past, it has openly supported the BJP' (*Indian Express*, 4 November 2021).

78 *Washington Post*, 16 March 2012.

79 This is as true for local as for global gurus (Srinivas 2010; Gold 2012).

80 *Indian Express*, 14 January 2016.

81 See Copeman and Ikegame (2012).

82 Sathya Sai Baba prophesied a coming Prema Sai. An official Sai Baba video notes the present existence of claimants, but asks: 'Why do we need to go anywhere else other than Swami [Sathya Sai Baba]? … There are so many people taking advantage and claiming themselves as Prema Sai. … For us, we have Swami who is the embodiment of love. … And we are so fortunate. He has given more than 1,500 discourses, which are all recorded. We have them available in audio and video' (Narendranath Reddy, 'What information do we have about Prema Sai?', https://www.sathyasai.org/video/faq-prema-sai, accessed 11 February 2023). The official Sathya Sai organisation has a strong commercial incentive to seek to prevent devotional attrition after the guru's death; it is interesting to note how media (recordings, videos) are invoked as adequate archive-based substitutions for, or extensions of, him. See Srinivas on the swami's funeral as a key moment in his 'encryption' in an archive (this volume).

References

Albert, Jean-Pierre. 2001. 'Sens et enjeux du martyre: De la religion à la politique', in *Saints, sainteté et martyre: La fabrication de l'exemplarité*, edited by Pierre Centlivres, 17–25. Neuchâtel/Paris: Editions de l'Institut d'ethnologie/Editions de la Maison des sciences de l'homme.

Anderson, Edward. 2015. '"Neo-Hindutva": The Asia House M. F. Husain campaign and the mainstreaming of Hindu nationalist rhetoric in Britain', *Contemporary South Asia* 23 (1): 45–66. https://doi.org/10.1080/09584935.2014.1001721.

Appadurai, Arjun. 2007. 'Hope and democracy', *Public Culture* 19 (1): 29–34. https://doi.org/10.1215/08992363-2006-023.

Appadurai, Arjun. 2013. *The Future as Cultural Fact: Essays on the global condition*. London: Verso.

Arnold, David. 1993. *Colonizing the Body: State medicine and epidemic disease in nineteenth-century India*. Berkeley: University of California Press.

Aymard, Orianne. 2014. *When a Goddess Dies: Worshipping Mā Ānandamayī after her death*. New York: Oxford University Press.

Banerjee, Dwaipayan and Jacob Copeman. 2020. 'Hindutva's blood', *South Asia Multidisciplinary Academic Journal* 24/25. https://doi.org/10.4000/samaj.6657.

Bartholeyns, Gil. 2014. 'The instant past: Nostalgia and digital retro photography', in *Media and Nostalgia: Yearning for the past, present and future*, edited by Katharina Niemeyer, 51–69. Basingstoke: Palgrave Macmillan.

Bar-Yosef, Eitan. 2020. 'A guide to performance: Role-playing, theatricality, and celebrity in R. K. Narayan's *The Guide* and *My Dateless Diary*', *Journal of Commonwealth Literature*. https://doi.org/10.1177/0021989420918654.

Basu, Amrita. 2015. *Violent Conjunctures in Democratic India*. Cambridge: Cambridge University Press.

Basu, Amrita. 2022. 'Normalizing violence: Lessons from Hindu nationalist India', in *Saffron Republic: Hindu nationalism and state power in India*, edited by Thomas Blom Hasen and Srirupa Roy, 59–71. Cambridge: Cambridge University Press.

Basu, Anustup. 2020. *Hindutva as Political Monotheism*. Durham, NC: Duke University Press.

Bayly, Susan. 1989. *Saints, Goddesses and Kings: Muslims and Christians in south Indian society, 1700–1900*. Cambridge: Cambridge University Press.

Beckerlegge, Gwilym. 2012. 'Media savvy or media averse? The Ramakrishna Math and Mission's use of the media in representing itself and a religion called "Hinduism"', in *Public Hinduisms*, edited by John Zavos, Pralay Kanungo, Deepa S. Reddy, Maya Warrier and Raymond Brady Williams, 398–416. New Delhi: Sage.

Berlant, Lauren. 2011. *Cruel Optimism*. Durham, NC: Duke University Press.

Born, Georgina. 2013. 'Music: Ontology, agency, creativity', in *Distributed Objects: Meaning and mattering after Alfred Gell*, edited by Liana Chua and Mark Elliot, 130–54. Oxford and New York: Berghahn Books.

Bouillier, Véronique. 2012. 'Modern *Guru* and old *Sampradaya*: How a Nath Yogi anniversary festival became a performance on Hinduism', in *Public Hinduisms*, edited by John Zavos, Pralay Kanungo, Deepa S. Reddy, Maya Warrier and Raymond Brady Williams, 373–91. New Delhi: Sage.

Bouillier, Véronique. 2015. 'Nāth yogīs' encounters with Islam', *South Asia Multidisciplinary Academic Journal*. https://doi.org/10.4000/samaj.3878.

Bouillier, Véronique. 2020. 'Yogi Adityanath's background and rise to power', *South Asia Multidisciplinary Academic Journal* 24/25. https://doi.org/10.4000/samaj.6778.

Brosius, Christiane. 2005. *Empowering Visions: The politics of representation in Hindu nationalism*. London: Anthem Press.

Candea, Matei. 2017. 'This is (not) like that', *HAU: Journal of Ethnographic Theory* 7 (1): 517–21. https://doi.org/10.14318/hau7.1.036.

Cerulli, Anthony. 2022. *The Practice of Texts: Education and healing in south India*. Oakland: University of California Press.

Chakravartty, Paula and Srirupa Roy. 2015. 'Mr. Modi goes to Delhi: Mediated populism and the 2014 Indian elections', *Television and New Media* 16 (4): 311–22. https://doi.org/10.1177/1527476415573957.

Chatterjee, Partha. 1999. 'Modernity, democracy and a political negotiation of death', *South Asia Research* 19 (2): 103–19. https://doi.org/10.1177/026272809901900201.

Chaudhry, Arun. 2012. 'American Hindu activism and the politics of anxiety', in *Public Hinduisms*, edited by John Zavos, Pralay Kanungo, Deepa S. Reddy, Maya Warrier and Raymond Brady Williams, 324–47. New Delhi: Sage.

Chaudhury, Proma Ray. 2021. 'The political asceticism of Mamata Banerjee: Female populist leadership in contemporary India', *Politics and Gender* 18 (4): 942–77. https://doi.org/10.1017/S1743923X21000209.

Chua, Liana and Mark Elliott. 2013. 'Introduction: Adventures in the art nexus', in *Distributed Objects: Meaning and mattering after Alfred Gell*, edited by Liana Chua and Mark Elliot, 1–24. Oxford and New York: Berghahn Books.

Cohen, Lawrence. 1998. *No Aging in India: Modernity, senility and the family*. Delhi: Oxford University Press.

Cohen, Lawrence. 2008. 'Science, politics, and dancing boys: Propositions and accounts', *Parallax* 14 (3): 35–47. https://doi.org/10.1080/13534640802159112.

Cohen, Lawrence. 2012. 'The gay guru: Fallibility, unworldliness, and the scene of instruction', in *The Guru in South Asia: New interdisciplinary perspectives*, edited by Jacob Copeman and Aya Ikegame, 97–112. Abingdon: Routledge.

Cohen, Lawrence. 2013. 'Given over to demand: Excorporation as commitment', *Contemporary South Asia* 21 (3): 318–32. https://doi.org/10.1080/09584935.2013.826630.

Comaroff, John L. and Jean Comaroff. 2009. *Ethnicity, Inc.* Chicago, IL: University of Chicago Press.

Coomaraswamy, Ananda K. and Sister Nivedita. [1914] 1967. *Myths of the Hindus & Buddhists*. New York: Dover Publications.

Copeman, Jacob. 2009. *Veins of Devotion: Blood donation and religious experience in north India*. New Brunswick, NJ: Rutgers University Press.

Copeman, Jacob. 2012. 'The mimetic guru: Tracing the real in Sikh–Dera Sacha Sauda relations', in *The Guru in South Asia: New interdisciplinary perspectives*, edited by Jacob Copeman and Aya Ikegame, 156–80. Abingdon: Routledge.

Copeman, Jacob. 2018. 'Exposing fakes', in *Fake: Anthropological keywords*, edited by Jacob Copeman and Giovanni da Col, 63–90. Chicago, IL: HAU Books.

Copeman, Jacob. 2023. 'Super Singhs and Kaurageous Kaurs: Sikh names, caste and disidentity politics', in *An Anthropology of Intellectual Exchange: Interactions, transactions and ethics in Asia and beyond*, edited by Jacob Copeman, Nicholas J. Long, Lam Minh Chau, Joanna Cook and Magnus Marsden. Oxford: Berghahn.

Copeman, Jacob and Dwaipayan Banerjee. 2019. *Hematologies: The political life of blood in India*. Ithaca, NY: Cornell University Press.

Copeman, Jacob and Koonal Duggal. 2023. '"Guruji rocked … Duniya shocked": Wondertraps and the full-palette guruship of Dera Sacha Sauda guru Dr Saint Gurmeet Ram Rahim Singh Ji Insan', in *Wonder in South Asia: Politics, aesthetics, ethics*, edited by Tulasi Srinivas. New York: SUNY Press.

Copeman, Jacob and John Hagström. 2022. 'Rationalist camera: Non-religious techniques of vision in India', in *Global Sceptical Publics: From non-religious print media to 'digital atheism'*, edited by Jacob Copeman and Mascha Schulz, 39–70. London: UCL Press.

Copeman, Jacob and Aya Ikegame. 2012. 'Guru logics', *HAU: Journal of Ethnographic Theory* 2 (1): 289–336. https://doi.org/10.14318/hau2.1.014.

Copeman, Jacob and Johannes Quack. 2018. 'Contemporary religiosities', in *Critical Themes in Indian Sociology*, edited by Sanjay Srivastava, Yasmeen Arif and Janaki Abraham, 44–61. New Delhi: Sage.

Corsín Jiménez, Alberto. 2018. 'Spiderweb anthropologies: Ecologies, infrastructures, entanglements', in *A World of Many Worlds*, edited by Marisol de la Cadena and Mario Blaser, 53–82. Durham, NC: Duke University Press.

Corsín Jiménez, Alberto and Adolfo Estalella. 2017. 'Ethnography: A prototype', *Ethnos* 82 (5): 846–66. https://doi.org/10.1080/00141844.2015.1133688.

Das, Veena and Jacob Copeman. 2015. 'Introduction. On names in South Asia: Iteration, (im)propriety and dissimulation', *South Asia Multidisciplinary Academic Journal* 12. https://doi.org/10.4000/samaj.4063.

Dasgupta, Koushiki. 2021. *Sadhus in Indian Politics: Dynamics of Hindutva*. New Delhi: Sage.

De, Rohit. 2018. *A People's Constitution: The everyday life of law in the Indian republic*. Princeton, NJ: Princeton University Press.

Dehejia, Vidya. 1995. 'Iconographic transference between Krsna and three Saiva saints', in *Indian Art and Connoisseurship: Essays in honour of Douglas Barrett*, edited by John Guy, 140–9. Ahmedabad: Mapin Publishing.

Deleuze, Gilles and Claire Parnet. 2006. *Dialogues II* (trans. Hugh Tomlinson and Barbara Habberjam), 2nd edn. London: Continuum.

Deseriis, Marco. 2015. *Improper Names: Collective pseudonyms from the Luddites to anonymous*. Minneapolis: University of Minnesota Press.

Dinkar, Niharika. 2021. '*Tirchhi Nazar*: The gaze in South Asia beyond *Darshan*', *South Asian Studies* 37 (2): 77–88. https://doi.org/10.1080/02666030.2021.2019409.

Domańska, Ewa. 2006. 'The material presence of the past', *History and Theory* 45 (3): 337–48.

Doniger, Wendy. 2006. *The Woman Who Pretended To Be Who She Was: Myths of self-imitation*. Oxford: Oxford University Press.

Doron, Assa. 2014. 'The politics of identity and the people left behind: The Mallah community of Uttar Pradesh', in *Development Failure and Identity Politics in Uttar Pradesh*, edited by Roger Jeffery, Craig Jeffrey and Jens Lerche, 188–210. New Delhi: Sage.

Duggal, Koonal. 2022. 'The "vexed" status of guru images: Visuality, circulation and iconographic conflicts', *South Asian Popular Culture* 20 (1): 97–117. https://doi.org/10.1080/14746689.2022.2047457.

Duggal, Vebhuti. 2021. 'Intermediality', *BioScope: South Asian Screen Studies* 12 (1–2): 113–16. https://doi.org/10.1177/09749276211026085.

Dwyer, Rachel. 2017. 'Calling God on the wrong number: Hindu–Muslim relations in *PK* (2014) and *Bajrangi Bhaijaan* (2015)', *Muslim World* 107 (2): 256–70. https://doi.org/10.1111/muwo.12189.

Eco, Umberto. 1976. *A Theory of Semiotics*. Bloomington: Indiana University Press.

Empson, Rebecca. 2007. 'Separating and containing persons and things in Mongolia', in *Thinking through Things: Theorising artefacts ethnographically*, edited by Amiria J. M. Henare, Martin Holbraad and Sari Wastell, 113–40. Abingdon: Routledge.

Farmer, Victoria L. 1996. 'Mass media: Images, mobilization, and communalism', in *Contesting the Nation: Religion, community, and the politics of democracy in India*, edited by David Ludden, 98–118. Philadelphia: University of Pennsylvania Press.

Fleming, Chris and John O'Carroll. 2010. 'The art of the hoax', *Parallax* 16 (4): 45–59. https://doi.org/10.1080/13534645.2010.508648.

Foucault, Michel. [1973] 2013. *La Société punitive: Cours au Collège de France, 1972–1973*. Paris: Gallimard.

Fraenkel, Béatrice. 2007. 'Actes d'écriture: Quand écrire c'est faire', *Langage et société* 121–2: 101–12. http://dx.doi.org/10.3917/ls.121.0101.

Frøystad, Kathinka. 2012. 'The mediated guru: Simplicity, instantaneity and change in middle-class religious seeking', in *The Guru in South Asia: New interdisciplinary perspectives*, edited by Jacob Copeman and Aya Ikegame, 181–201. Abingdon: Routledge.

Frøystad, Kathinka. 2021. 'Worship and the virus in Hindu India: Contested innovation, polarization, uneven digital acceleration', *Approaching Religion* 11 (2): 5–22. https://doi.org/10.30664/AR.107671.

Fuchs, Martin. 2022. 'The fiction of ecumenical universalism: Where gurus do not matter', in *Religious Authority in South Asia: Generating the guru*, edited by István Keul and Srilata Raman, 68–81. Abingdon: Routledge.

Ganguli, Kisari Mohan (trans.). 1884. *The Mahabharata*, vol. 1. Calcutta: Bharata Press.

Gavaskar, Mahesh. 2015. 'Divinity goes pop: Seamlessly weaving glamour, sensuousness and spirituality, Radhe Maa has redefined the spirituality market', *Economic & Political Weekly* 50 (34): 9.

Gayer, Laurent and Ingrid Therwath. 2010. 'Introduction: Modelling exemplarity in South Asia', *South Asia Multidisciplinary Academic Journal* 4. https://doi.org/10.4000/samaj.3011.

Geertz, Clifford. 1973. *The Interpretation of Cultures*. New York: Basic Books.

Gell, Alfred. 1998. *Art and Agency: An anthropological theory*. Oxford: Clarendon Press.

Girard, René. 2001. *I See Satan Fall Like Lightning* (trans. James G. Williams). Maryknoll, NY: Orbis.

Gleig, Ann. 2012. 'Researching new religious movements from the inside out and the outside in: Methodological reflections from collaborative and participatory perspectives', *Nova Religio* 16 (1): 88–103. https://doi.org/10.1525/nr.2012.16.1.88.

Gold, Daniel. 1987. *The Lord as Guru: Hindi sants in North Indian tradition*. Oxford: Oxford University Press.

Gold, Daniel. 1988. *Comprehending the Guru: Toward a grammar of religious perception*. Atlanta, GA: Scholars Press.

Gold, Daniel. 2012. 'Continuities as gurus change', in *The Guru in South Asia: New interdisciplinary perspectives*, edited by Jacob Copeman and Aya Ikegame, 241–54. Abingdon: Routledge.

Goldberg, Michelle. 2015. *The Goddess Pose: The audacious life of Indra Devi, the woman who helped bring yoga to the West*. New York: Vintage.

Gooptu, Nandini. 2016. 'New spirituality, politics of self-empowerment, citizenship, and democracy in contemporary India', *Modern Asian Studies* 50 (3): 934–74.

Graeber, David and Marshall Sahlins. 2017. *On Kings*. Chicago, IL: HAU Books.

Grimaud, Emmanuel. 2011. 'Gods and robots' (unpublished manuscript).

Gupta, Sukanya. 2011. 'Constructing Hindu religioscapes: Guruism and identity in South Asian diasporic fiction'. PhD dissertation, Louisiana State University.

Hamilton, Michael. 2022. 'The management of protest and dissent', in *Routledge Handbook of Illiberalism*, edited by András Sajó, Renáta Uitz and Stephen Holmes, 384–402. Abingdon: Routledge.

Hansen, Thomas Blom. 1999. *The Saffron Wave: Democracy and Hindu nationalism in modern India*. New Delhi: Oxford University Press.

Harcourt, Bernard E. 2014. 'Digital security in the expository society: Spectacle, surveillance, and exhibition in the neoliberal age of *big data*'/'Spectacle, surveillance, exposition: Relire Foucault à l'ère numérique.' Columbia Public Law Research Paper no. 14-404: 1–23/1–21. https://scholarship.law.columbia.edu/faculty_scholarship/1865/ (accessed 12 March 2023).

Heehs, Peter. 2008. *The Lives of Sri Aurobindo*. New York: Columbia University Press.

Henn, Alexander. 2015. 'Kristapurāṇa: Translating the name of God in early modern Goa', *South Asia Multidisciplinary Academic Journal* 12. https://doi.org/10.4000/samaj.4038.

Humphrey, Caroline. 2004. 'Sovereignty', in *A Companion to the Anthropology of Politics*, edited by David Nugent and Joan Vincent, 418–36. Malden, MA: Blackwell Publishing.

Huntington, Susan L. 1985. *The Art of Ancient India: Buddhist, Hindu, Jain*. New York: Weatherhill.

Ikegame, Aya. 2012. *Princely India Re-imagined: A historical anthropology of Mysore from 1799 to the present*. Abingdon: Routledge.

Ikegame, Aya. 2016. 'Review: *When a Goddess Dies: Worshipping Mā Ānandamayī after Her Death*. By Orianne Aymard. Oxford: Oxford University Press', *International Journal of Asian Studies* 13 (1): 116–17. https://doi.org/10.1017/S1479591415000248.

Ikegame, Aya. 2019. 'The guru as legislator: Religious leadership and informal legal space in rural South India', in *South Asian Sovereignty: The conundrum of worldly power*, edited by David Gilmartin, Pamela Price and Arild Engelsen Ruud, 58–77. Delhi: Routledge.

Ikegame, Aya. 2022. 'New Dalit assertion and the rejection of buffalo sacrifice in South India', *South Asia Multidisciplinary Academic Journal* 28. https://doi.org/10.4000/samaj.7944.

Ingold, Tim. 2013. *Making: Anthropology, archaeology, art and architecture*. Abingdon: Routledge.

Jacobs, Stephen. 2012. 'Communicating Hinduism in a changing media context', *Religion Compass* 6 (2): 136–51. https://doi.org/10.1111/j.1749-8171.2011.00333.x.

Jaffrelot, Christophe. 1996. *The Hindu Nationalist Movement and Indian Politics: 1925 to the 1990s*. New Delhi: Penguin.

Jaffrelot, Christophe. 2012. 'The political guru: The guru as éminence grise', in *The Guru in South Asia: New interdisciplinary perspectives*, edited by Jacob Copeman and Aya Ikegame, 80–96. Abingdon: Routledge.

Jain, Andrea R. 2020. *Peace Love Yoga: The politics of global spirituality*. New York: Oxford University Press.

Kanungo, Pralay. 2012. 'Fusing the ideals of the Math with the ideology of the Sangh? Vivekananda Kendra, ecumenical Hinduism and Hindu nationalism', in *Public Hinduisms*, edited by John Zavos, Pralay Kanungo, Deepa S. Reddy, Maya Warrier and Raymond Brady Williams, 119–40. New Delhi: Sage.

Karapanagiotis, Nicole. 2021. *Branding Bhakti: Krishna consciousness and the makeover of a movement*. Bloomington: Indiana University Press.

Keul, István and Srilata Raman. 2022. 'Gurus and their contexts in South Asia: An introduction', in *Religious Authority in South Asia: Generating the guru*, edited by István Keul and Srilata Raman, 1–7. Abingdon: Routledge.

Khandelwal, Meena. 2004. *Women in Ochre Robes: Gendering Hindu renunciation*. Albany, NY: SUNY Press.

Kinnvall, Catarina and Amit Singh. 2022. 'Enforcing and resisting Hindutva: Popular culture, the COVID-19 crisis and fantasy narratives of motherhood and pseudoscience in India', *Social Sciences* 11 (12): art. no. 550. https://doi.org/10.3390/socsci11120550.

Klein, Naomi. 2021. 'India targets climate activists with the help of Big Tech', *The Intercept*, 27 February. https://theintercept.com/2021/02/27/india-climate-activists-twitter-google-facebook/ (accessed 25 April 2023).

Klem, Bart and Bert Suykens. 2018. 'The politics of order and disturbance: Public authority, sovereignty, and violent contestation in South Asia', *Modern Asian Studies* 52 (3): 753–83. https://doi.org/10.1017/S0026749X17000270.

Küchler, Susanne and Timothy Carroll. 2021. *A Return to the Object: Alfred Gell, art, and social theory*. Abingdon: Routledge.

Laidlaw, James. 1995. *Riches and Renunciation: Religion, economy, and society among the Jains*. Oxford: Clarendon Press.

Landes, Richard. 2011. *Heaven on Earth: The varieties of the millennial experience*. New York: Oxford University Press.

Lazar, Yael. 2019. 'Intimacy 2.0: Guru–disciple relationship in a networked world'. *The Jugaad Project*, 8 July 2019. thejugaadproject.pub/home/intimacy-20-guru-disciple-relationship-in-a-networked-world (accessed 28 March 2023).

Lebner, Ashley. 2017. 'Introduction: Strathern's redescription of anthropology', in *Redescribing Relations: Strathernian conversations on ethnography, knowledge and politics*, edited by Ashley Lebner, 1–38. New York: Berghahn.

Lewis, Tania, Fran Martin and Wanning Sun. 2016. *Telemodernities: Television and transforming lives in Asia*. Durham, NC: Duke University Press.

Long, Jeffery D. 2019. 'Religious experience, Hindu pluralism, and hope: Anubhava in the tradition of Sri Ramakrishna', *Religions* 10 (3): art. no. 210, 7–23. https://doi.org/10.3390/rel10030210.

Longkumer, Arkotong. 2010. *Reform, Identity and Narratives of Belonging: The Heraka movement in Northeast India*. London: Continuum.

Longkumer, Arkotong. 2021. *The Greater India Experiment: Hindutva and the northeast*. Stanford, CA: Stanford University Press.

Lorea, Carola Erika. 2020. 'Religious returns, ritual changes and divinations on COVID-19', *Social Anthropology* 28 (2): 307–8. https://doi.org/10.1111/1469-8676.12865.

Lucia, Amanda. 2014a. *Reflections of Amma: Devotees in a global embrace*. Berkeley: University of California Press.

Lucia, Amanda. 2014b. 'Innovative gurus: Tradition and change in contemporary Hinduism', *International Journal of Hindu Studies* 18 (2): 221–63. https://doi.org/10.1007/s11407-014-9159-5.

Lucia, Amanda. 2018. 'Guru sex: Charisma, proxemic desire, and the haptic logics of the guru–disciple relationship', *Journal of the American Academy of Religion*, 86 (4): 953–88. https://doi.org/10.1093/jaarel/lfy025.

Lucia, Amanda. 2021. 'The global manifestation of the Hindu guru phenomenon', in *The Routledge Handbook of South Asian Religions*, edited by Knut A. Jacobsen, 413–27. New York: Routledge.

Lucia, Amanda. 2022. 'The contemporary guru field', *Religion Compass* 16 (2): art. no. e12427, 1–15. https://doi.org/10.1111/rec3.12427.

Malhotra, Anshu. 2022. 'Between sagacity and scandal: Celibacy, sexuality and a guru in nineteenth-century Punjab', in *Religious Authority in South Asia: Generating the guru*, edited by István Keul and Srilata Raman, 107–25. Abingdon: Routledge.

Malreddy, Pavan Kumar. 2022. 'Postsecular longings? Religious dissent, faith, and gurus in Indian cinema', *Third Text* 36 (2): 176–91. https://doi:10.1080/09528822.2022.2049159.

Mannila, Hanna and Xenia Zeiler. 2020. 'Mediatized gurus: Hindu religious and artistic authority and digital culture', in *Digital Hinduism*, edited by Xenia Zeiler, 145–62. Abingdon: Routledge.

Mazzarella, William. 2010. 'Branding the Mahatma: The untimely provocation of Gandhian publicity', *Cultural Anthropology* 25 (1): 1–39. https://doi.org/10.1111/j.1548-1360.2009.01050.x.

Mazzarella, William. 2022. 'Charisma in the age of Trumpism', *E-flux* (22 September). https://www.e-flux.com/notes/492472/charisma-in-the-age-of-trumpism (accessed 13 February 2023).

McCartney, Patrick. 2018. 'Downward facing dogs, core Indian values and institutionalised rape of children', *Sociology International Journal* 2 (6): 748–53. https://doi.org/10.15406/sij.2018.02.00133.

McCartney, Patrick. 2021. 'The not so united states of Yogaland: Post-nationalism, environmentalism, and applied + yoga's sustainable development', in *Nationalism: Past, present and future*, edited by Thomas J. Keaney, 1–122. Hauppauge, NY: Nova Science.

McKean, Lise. 1996. *Divine Enterprise: Gurus and the Hindu nationalist movement*. Chicago, IL: University of Chicago Press.

McLain, Karline. 2012. 'Praying for peace and amity: The Shri Shirdi Sai Heritage Foundation Trust', in *Public Hinduisms*, edited by John Zavos, Pralay Kanungo, Deepa S. Reddy, Maya Warrier and Raymond Brady Williams, 190–209. New Delhi: Sage.

Meena, Azhagu, Varuni Bhatia and Joyojeet Pal. 2020. 'Digital divine: Technology use by Indian spiritual sects', in *Proceedings of the 2020 International Conference on Information and Communication Technologies and Development*, art. no. 22, 1–11. New York: Association for Computing Machinery. https://doi.org/10.1145/3392561.3394650.

Mehta, Mona G. 2017. 'From Gandhi to gurus: The rise of the "guru-sphere"', *South Asia: Journal of South Asian Studies* 40 (3): 500–16. https://doi.org/10.1080/00856401.2017.1302047.

Michelutti, Lucia, Ashraf Hoque, Nicolas Martin, David Picherit, Paul Rollier, Arild E. Ruud and Clarinda Still. 2019. *Mafia Raj: The rule of bosses in South Asia*. Stanford, CA: Stanford University Press.

Miller, Daniel. 2005. 'Materiality: An introduction', in *Materiality*, edited by Daniel Miller, 1–50. Durham, NC: Duke University Press.

Mitchell, W. J. T. 2005. *What do Pictures Want? The lives and loves of images*. Chicago, IL: University of Chicago Press.

Miyazaki, Hirokazu. 2004. *The Method of Hope: Anthropology, philosophy, and Fijian knowledge*. Stanford, CA: Stanford University Press.

Morse, Jeremy G. 2012. 'The literary guru: The dual emphasis on bhakti and *vidhi* in western Indian guru-devotion', in *The Guru in South Asia: New interdisciplinary perspectives*, edited by Jacob Copeman and Aya Ikegame, 222–40. Abingdon: Routledge.

Mosse, David. 2012. *The Saint in the Banyan Tree: Christianity and caste society in India*. Berkeley: University of California Press.

Murphy, Anne. 2009. 'The Guru's weapons', *Journal of the American Academy of Religion* 77 (2): 303–32. https://doi.org/10.1093/jaarel/lfp035.

Murphy, Anne. 2022. 'The emergence of the social in the service of the Guru', in *Religious Authority in South Asia: Generating the guru*, edited by István Keul and Srilata Raman, 84–106. Abingdon: Routledge.

Myrvold, Kristina. 2007. *Inside the Guru's Gate: Ritual uses of texts among the Sikhs in Varanasi*. Lund: Centre for Theology and Religious Studies, Lund University.

Nagaraj, D. R. 2006. 'The comic collapse of authority: An essay on the fears of the public spectator', in *Fingerprinting Popular Culture: The mythic and the iconic in Indian cinema*, edited by Vinay Lal and Ashis Nandy, 87–121. New Delhi: Oxford University Press.

Nanda, Meera. 2009. *The God Market: How globalization is making India more Hindu*. New Delhi: Random House.

Narayan, Badri. 2006. *Women Heroes and Dalit Assertion in North India: Culture, identity and politics*. New Delhi: Sage.

Okita, Kiyokazu. 2012. 'Who are the Mādhvas? A controversy over the public representation of the Mādhva *Sampradāya*', in *Public Hinduisms*, edited by John Zavos, Pralay Kanungo, Deepa S. Reddy, Maya Warrier and Raymond Brady Williams, 210–23. New Delhi: Sage.

Omvedt, Gail. 2008. *Seeking Begumpura: The social vision of anticaste intellectuals*. New Delhi: Navayana.

Padoux, André. 2001. 'The Tantric guru', in *Tantra in Practice*, edited by David Gordon White, 41–51. Delhi: Motilal Banarsidass.

Parciack, Ronie. 2023. 'Defeat and glory: Social media, neoliberalism and the transnational tragedy of a divinized *baba*', *Religions* 14 (1): art. no. 123, 1–15. https://doi.org/10.3390/rel14010123.

Parry, Jonathan. 1985. 'The Brahmanical tradition and the technology of the intellect', in *Reason and Morality*, edited by Joanna Overing, 200–25. London: Tavistock Publications.

Pechilis, Karen. 2015. 'Women gurus in Hinduism', *Prabuddha Bharata* 120 (6): 401–9.

Pinney, Christopher. 2008a. 'The prosthetic eye: Photography as cure and poison', *Journal of the Royal Anthropological Institute* 14: S33–S46. https://doi.org/10.1111/j.1467-9655.2008.00491.x.

Pinney, Christopher. 2008b. 'The accidental Ramdevji', in *India's Popular Culture: Iconic spaces and fluid images*, edited by Jyotindra Jain. Mumbai: Marg Foundation. http://cscs.res.in/dataarchive/textfiles/textfile.2008-09-18.3427893094/file (accessed 13 February 2023).

Rajagopal, Arvind. 2001. *Politics after Television: Hindu nationalism and the reshaping of the Indian public*. Cambridge: Cambridge University Press.

Ramnath, Dhruv. 2022. 'Performance in guru–devotee identity in Hinduism', blog at *#gurumedia: film, image, art, sound, and beyond.* https://blogs.ed.ac.uk/gurusandmedia/2022/02/17/performance-in-guru-devotee-identity-in-hinduism (accessed 13 February).

Reddy, Deepa S. 2012. 'Hindu transnationalisms: Organisations, ideologies, networks', in *Public Hinduisms*, edited by John Zavos, Pralay Kanungo, Deepa S. Reddy, Maya Warrier and Raymond Brady Williams, 309–23. New Delhi: Sage.

Reyburn, Duncan B. 2019. 'Mimetic failure and the possibility of forgiveness', in *Theologies of Failure*, edited by Roberto Sirvent and Duncan B. Reyburn, 71–83. Eugene, OR: Cascade Books.

Rhodes, Carl and Alexandra Pitsis. 2008. 'Organization and mimetic excess: Magic, critique, and style', *International Studies of Management and Organization* 38 (1): 71–91. https://doi.org/10.2753/IMO0020-8825380104.

Rollier, Paul, Kathinka Frøystad and Arild Engelsen Ruud (eds). 2019. *Outrage: The rise of religious offence in contemporary South Asia.* London: UCL Press.

Sengupta, Rajarshi. 2021. 'From reference to knowledge repositories: On mimetic aspects of *kalamkari* making', *South Asian Studies* 37 (1): 51–71. https://doi.org/10.1080/02666030.2021.1969807.

Shearer, Alistair. 2020. *The Story of Yoga: From ancient India to the modern West.* London: Hurst & Company.

Silber, Ilana F. 2019. 'The gift as "deep play": A "note" on performance and paradox in the theatrics of public giving', in *Die Kunst der Gabe: Theater zwischen Autonomie und sozialer Praxis*, edited by Ingrid Hentschel, 125–45. Bielefeld: transcript Verlag.

Singh, Santosh K. 2017. '*Deras* as "little fiefdoms": Understanding the Dera Sacha Sauda phenomenon', *Economic and Political Weekly* 52 (37): 20–3.

Sloterdijk, Peter. 2013. *You Must Change Your Life: On anthropotechnics.* Cambridge: Polity.

Sneath, David, Martin Holbraad and Morten Axel Pedersen. 2009. 'Technologies of the imagination: An introduction', *Ethnos* 74 (1): 5–30. https://doi.org/10.1080/001418409 02751147.

Sobo, Elisa. 2016. 'Language, power, and pot: Speaking of cannabis as medicine', *Savage Minds*, 1 September. http://savageminds.org/2016/09/01/language-power-and-pot-speaking-of-cannabis-as-medicine/ (accessed 13 February 2023).

Solomon, Harris. 2021. 'Living on borrowed breath: Respiratory distress, social breathing, and the vital movement of ventilators', *Medical Anthropology Quarterly* 35 (1): 102–19. https://doi.org/10.1111/maq.12603.

Srinivas, Tulasi. 2010. *Winged Faith: Rethinking globalization and religious pluralism through the Sathya Sai movement.* New York: Columbia University Press.

Srivastava, Sanjay. 2009. 'Urban spaces, Disney-divinity and moral middle classes in Delhi', *Economic and Political Weekly* 44 (26/27): 338–45. https://doi.org/10.2307/40279794.

Srivastava, Sanjay. 2015. 'Modi-masculinity: Media, manhood, and "traditions" in a time of consumerism', *Television and New Media* 16 (4): 331–8. https://doi.org/10.1177/152747641 5575498.

Ssorin-Chaikov, Nikolai. 2013. 'Ethnographic conceptualism: An introduction', *Laboratorium* 5 (2): 5–18.

Tanner, Jeremy. 2013. 'Figuring out death: Sculpture and agency at the Mausoleum of Halicarnassus and the tomb of the First Emperor of China', in *Distributed Objects: Meaning and mattering after Alfred Gell*, edited by Liana Chua and Mark Elliott, 58–87. New York: Berghahn Books.

Thrift, Nigel. 2008. *Non-representational Theory: Space, politics, affect.* Abingdon: Routledge.

Thrift, Nigel. 2009. 'Different atmospheres: Of Sloterdijk, China, and site', *Environment and Planning D: Society and Space* 27 (1): 119–38. https://doi.org/10.1068/d6808.

Thrift, Nigel. 2012. 'The insubstantial pageant: Producing an untoward land', *Cultural Geographies* 19 (2): 141–68. https://doi.org/10.1177/1474474011427268.

Tripathi, Anurag. 2018. *Dera Sacha Sauda and Gurmeet Ram Rahim: A decade-long investigation.* Gurgaon: Penguin Books.

Udupa, Sahana. 2018. 'Enterprise Hindutva and social media in urban India', *Contemporary South Asia* 26 (4): 453–67. https://doi.org/10.1080/09584935.2018.1545007.

Upadhyay, Surya Prakash. 2022. 'Hindu spiritualism for a neoliberal age', *The India Forum*, 4 May. https://www.theindiaforum.in/article/hindu-spiritualism-neoliberal-age (accessed 13 February 2023).

Urban, Hugh B. 2015. *Zorba the Buddha: Sex, spirituality, and capitalism in the global Osho movement*. Oakland: University of California Press.

van de Port, Mattijs. 2011. '(Not) made by the human hand: Media consciousness and immediacy in the cultural production of the real', *Social Anthropology* 19 (1): 74–89. https://doi.org/10.1111/j.1469-8676.2010.00139.x.

Visvanathan, Susan. 2010. *The Children of Nature: The life and legacy of Ramana Maharshi*. New Delhi: Roli Books.

Voix, Raphaël. 2008. 'Denied violence, glorified fighting: Spiritual discipline and controversy in Ananda Marga', *Nova Religio* 12 (1): 3–25. https://doi.org/10.1525/nr.2008.12.1.3.

Voss Roberts, Michelle. 2021. 'A theology of Hindu–Christian relations', in *The Routledge Handbook of Hindu–Christian Relations*, edited by Chad M. Bauman and Michelle Voss Roberts, 345–54. Abingdon: Routledge.

Warrier, Maya. 2003. 'Processes of secularization in contemporary India: Guru faith in the Mata Amritanandamayi Mission', *Modern Asian Studies* 37 (1): 213–53. https://doi.org/10.1017/S0026749X03001070.

Warrier, Maya. 2005. *Hindu Selves in a Modern World: Guru faith in the Mata Amritanandamayi Mission*. Abingdon: RoutledgeCurzon.

Warrier, Maya. 2014. 'Online *bhakti* in a modern guru organization', in *Gurus of Modern Yoga*, edited by Mark Singleton and Ellen Goldberg, 308–23. Oxford: Oxford University Press.

Zavos, John. 2012. 'Researching public Hinduisms: An introduction', in *Public Hinduisms*, edited by John Zavos, Pralay Kanungo, Deepa S. Reddy, Maya Warrier and Raymond Brady Williams, 3–21. New Delhi: Sage.

1
The sonic guru: Rewben Mashangva, folk, roots and the blues

Arkotong Longkumer

I first discovered guru Rewben Mashangva through a video link on WhatsApp. It read *Songlines: An exploration of blues notes in folk music across India*. The roll of the camera shows the familiar, resounding geography of Northeast India. I hear the drone of the blues guitar.

'This is folk. The blues also same thing. For example, this is pure folk, our folk.' The camera pans across a room. A guitar slide creates a gliding effect (or a glissando) resembling the human voice. The deep vibratos of the blues and slight changes to the voicing texture the singing. An impromptu lyric of the film director accompanies the song, 'Oh, Vasudha, angel of my eyes, I love you ...' The music ends. The camera focuses on guru Rewben Mashangva: 'Now, the Western people say, the blues is coming originally from America, and not from Africa. Actually, the blues is started by black man, but started from America.' A black-and-white scene shifts to the American South, with Leadbelly singing a traditional cotton pickin' song. Guru then makes the point that the Naga people sang the blues even before American independence, even before the African slaves went to America. To emphasise this, he starts singing a traditional Tangkhul Naga work song, *hopi p*, with his son Saka Mashangva providing the refrain: *hopi p* (guru), *le ho le* (Saka) ....[1]

He tells me that blues and folk are different terms in the English language but in the Tangkhul language there is no difference: both blues and folk are 'haula'. This is perhaps not the place to tease out the fine-grained distinction between blues and folk,[2] but guru's emphasis is on the fact that the oral tradition of singing the blues based on 'work songs' and 'field hollers' (Eastman 1988) – whether it is in the American South or in his village of Choithar – is a universal, shared experience.

This chapter is about the sonic guru. It is my attempt to understand sonicity, and guru-charisma, in the context of sound, or what Jonathan Sterne calls 'a little piece of the vibrating world' (2003, 11). It brings to mind what Jacob Copeman and Aya Ikegame, in their ground-breaking work on gurus, call the gurus' 'uncontainability', their expansibility and 'unusual capacity to accrue resonances' (2012a, 3). From a village singer to, now, a national icon and global presence, guru Mashangva is upscaled. He is more than a musician; he is a reviver of tradition, an activist, a reformer and the leader of a movement that is reverberating. What are his influences, the making of his craft, and the affective resonances of his music? Steven Feld's (1996, 105) notion of 'acoustemology' as 'a sonic epistemology of emplacement' is helpful to highlight how guru is also texturing the contours of sound as *ecologies of creation*, a creative process that is charged with energy, knowledge, place-making and imagination.

Not only does this chapter present a unique picture of an Indigenous Christian guru (see Dawson, this volume) on the fringes of the Indian state and the manner in which he has been able to carve out a musical career against the odds, it also pursues the vexed process of translating 'guru' in the context of Northeast India. How might we think of 'guru', particularly when this Indic term is largely unfamiliar there? The tradition of 'guru', while largely understood as a model for the transmission of knowledge from a teacher to a student (whether spiritual or secular; see Copeman and Ikegame 2012a; Gold 1987; Openshaw 1998; Ranade 1998), requires that we ask how this term is reimagined when applied in a setting where the cultural and structural architecture of guruship is largely absent. Unlike its long-established tradition in many parts of India, where the guru is an individual within the community they serve and is well entrenched in the social, political and religious landscapes, guru Mashangva in many ways is a trailblazer. He is an individual guru, one who is reimagining what guruship means in a place where this tradition is largely non-existent and where it is strongly resisted. Therefore, Mashangva may not be recognisable as a 'guru' in the conventional Indic sense. What he is doing is translating what it means in the local idiom – bringing light to the roots slowly losing their steel – thereby creating a practical way in which the sonic experience of singing and listening connects to what Charles Hirschkind calls developing the 'body as an auditory instrument' (2006, 79). This chapter examines the manner in which Mashangva makes 'guru' his own, partly through state patronage and the enormous cultural and economic capital this brings in terms of recognition, but also as a cultural reviver who thinks about loss in innovative ways through the body as a receptor and transmitter of sound.

The nature of guruship is distinct when music is involved. While there is an absence of a canon in the sense of an established body of work (musical scores, for instance) in Indian music, the 'guru embodies the tradition' (Schippers 2007, 124), and students cannot access knowledge independently of their guru because it is largely transmitted orally (Ranade 1998). Guru Mashangva's case is slightly different. He certainly embodies this oral tradition, and, while his knowledge is transmitted through training some students, long-term patronage in one place – an important feature of guruship in the past – has largely been replaced by digital transmissions that produce mass mobilisation and following. In other words, one must rethink the place, status and techniques of gurus through music as a creative process of fusion, and understand that it is the guruship that sustains the media.

To describe what I mean by this process, I develop this notion of *ecologies of creation* that constitute what fusion is. It is about 'making' as an open enquiry that is about engagement, related to place and rooted in the land. A central idea is that it leads to growth and establishes a new way of doing and thinking (Ingold 2013). This idea of fusion brings me to my first point. Drawing on music, fusion often contests and troubles the uneven terrain in which it sits (is it jazz-rock, jazz-funk, jazz-soul?). It is not simply a combination of different genres but it has the ability to transform and establish its own idiom. Fusion thus represents the 'plurality and hybridity of the phenomenon' in its ability to exceed the hyphenated form (Holt 2007, 100; see also Fellezs 2011). A similar idea could be applied to gurus who are specialists in fusion.

Like fusion music that establishes a new idiom that does not simply replace or mimic a given tradition, gurus are involved in combining different practices and ideas to make something of their own, particularly when media is involved (see Copeman and Duggal, this volume). The fusion of different practices makes possible the kind of 'intentional hybridity' (Werbner 2001; see also Bakhtin 1981) that gurus participate in, allowing them to find complementary components to replace missing links in the chain of memory. According to Rogers, Claude Lévi-Strauss (1966), who originally used bricolage in the context of myth, where lost meanings were repaired by finding compatible resources, argues that bricoleurs 'combine their imagination with whatever knowledge tools they have at-hand in their repertoire (e.g., ritual, observation, social practices) and with whatever artifacts are available in their given context (i.e., discourses, institutions, and dominant knowledges) to meet diverse knowledge-production tasks' (Rogers 2012, 3). I will illustrate how guru Mashangva utilises the tools and knowledge that he has cultivated and now possesses through his relationship to the land, and the resources – musical tones, words and instruments – he has learnt to deploy in his music. He also innovates, and brings together different musical forms, to create a unique experience of sound that undergirds his guruship. From early influences of Bob Marley and Bob Dylan to the lasting impression of blues in his musical landscape, fusion is constitutive of many worlds, both human and non-human, and enables guru to be open to resonant encounters, and in the process fashion a distinct musical and cultural journey. This ability to innovate and to draw on different knowledge systems is not uncommon in many South Asian traditions and with many gurus: the ability to utilise one's agency and knowledge skilfully in a globalised world is one of the characteristics of adapting to the times and indeed of their survival (Aravamudan 2005; Srinivas 2010; Altglas 2014; Urban 2016).

The sonic guru

Sound for guru is more than just recognising a certain musical pattern; it encompasses culture, ritual, politics, tradition, geography, and the identity of a people (see also Holt 2007, 19). When guru performs, he wears the Raivat Kachon, a traditional Tangkhul body cloth. With it, he wears various necklaces, sometimes a bird feather, but always with a traditional Naga haircut (that is, kept long at the back and shaved at the sides), and a pair of leather boots, an acoustic guitar and a harmonica: this is the brand, the persona that identifies guru. This persona seen on stage defines his music, and through his appearance, his identity; people know that he is Naga through his music. He sings primarily in Tangkhul, though there are instances when he sings in English. 'It's not just his music, but it's his lifestyle', Alobo Naga, a musician from Nagaland, told me. 'Rewben is Rewben. I don't think I know anybody who sounds and sings like that' (see Figures 1.1 and 1.2).

Most musicians in the Northeast of India know or have heard of guru Mashangva and his music.[3] A Google search for 'guru Rewben Mashangva' yields around 10,000 results.[4] Most of the regional and national newspapers have covered aspects of his life and music – *East Mojo*, *Ukhrul Times*, the *Times of India* and *The Hindu* – while the *New York Times* has also explored guru's contribution to Bob Dylan's songs through the annual homespun celebration of Dylan's birthday in Shillong, the

Figure 1.1 Guru in concert; used with permission from guru Rewben Mashangva.

Figure 1.2 Guru in concert; used with permission from guru Rewben Mashangva.

capital of the north-eastern Indian state Meghalaya.[5] With more than 200 YouTube videos, comprising music videos, interviews, live concerts and community messages (about social distancing and COVID-19 facts; indeed he wrote a song about COVID-19, showing solidarity with Wuhan, called 'On the empty streets of Wuhan'[6]), getting anywhere between 900,000 views and a few hundred (with numerous comments), guru's presence online is definitely far-reaching, particularly compared with other artists from the region. He was awarded the fourth-highest civilian award, the Padma Shri, in November 2021, by the Government of India, demonstrating his contribution and indeed the capital that he has accrued on the national stage.[7]

Over a period of a few months, guru, his long-time collaborator Ngachonmi Chamroy and I spent a considerable time on the phone unpicking guru's life, his music and influences, and what it means to be a reviver of folk traditions.[8] He shared with me WhatsApp and YouTube clips of his songs, audio files of his music and film documentaries that were didactic but also provided a comprehensive picture of guru's music and the philosophy behind his ecologies of creation.[9] Our conversations were interspersed with guru and Ngachonmi breaking into song, humming a tune, or mimicking the sound of nature, to illustrate what they meant. Guru would send me audio files of his songs after our conversation to provide me with context, sometimes accompanied by a WhatsApp message saying that if some of his words were lost on me, hopefully the music would illuminate.

I received different interpretations of the idea of 'guru' in the broader cultural matrix of Northeast India. Grace Jajo, a journalist and friend who first introduced me to guru, told me that everyone in the colony in Imphal, the capital city of Manipur, where she and Rewben live, calls him 'guru'. It is colloquial, and informal, but also a widespread association. Guru is a formal title – a prefix like Dr or Reverend – that is tied to his identity. Some refer to him as Awo ('elder' in Tangkhul), though that seems less frequent and 'guru' is more common. This is how guru Mashangva explained his guru status to me: 'We have lost our culture and tradition and now it has become dark. So to bring light, a teacher is needed to light a candle, a lamp. Even if it's a small light, a thin light, the dark room can now see a little better.' 'Guru', in his words, means someone who is attempting to bring light to a world that has forgotten its roots. This explanation is in line with traditional understandings of gurus in India, though he also domesticates its meaning by interpreting it for the Naga audience with music. While he accommodates a variety of musical genres from folk, blues, reggae and rock, he is firm that he will not compromise on the tradition that he carries,

Figure 1.3 Issued by the Ministry of Culture when guru Mashangva received the Padma Shri. https://twitter.com/MinOfCultureGoI/status/1354753591622291457/photo/1. Source: Twitter.

both in the music he sings and in the culture he wears with pride. And it is for this commitment to a particular philosophy of music that the Government of India, Ministry of Culture, called him the 'father of Naga folk blues' when they awarded him the Padma Shri.

Guru Rewben Mashangva is from Choithar, a small village on the eastern side of Ukhrul district, in the Indian state of Manipur, close to Myanmar. Growing up in Choithar in the 1960s and 1970s was very difficult, particularly because of the ongoing Indo-Naga conflict in Ukhrul, which led to militarisation and violence between the Naga National Council (NNC), the Manipur Rifles, and the Volunteer Village Force (VVF). The conflict, and the toll it took on various Naga communities, created a scar that is etched onto the memory of the landscape. It is no surprise, then, that guru is a firm believer in peace building between different communities – whether Naga or not – and that this is reflected in his music, particularly in two songs, 'No more killings' and 'Winning peace together'.

As a child growing up in rural Choithar, guru remembers a hillock in the village that was taken over by the Manipur Rifles and later the VVF, who were tasked to fight Naga insurgency. A large Baptist church dominated the village. It was constructed on elevated ground, a vantage point that symbolised both its significance and its growing power over the Naga landscape (Chophy 2021; Thomas 2016; Longkumer 2019). The church was not only a place for solace, religious observation and calm, it was one of the few stable institutions in the village that provided succour in the midst of the tumultuous political situation of that period. Singing songs in

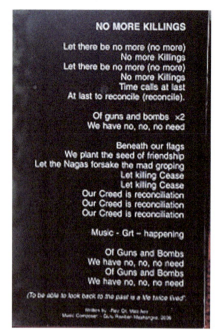 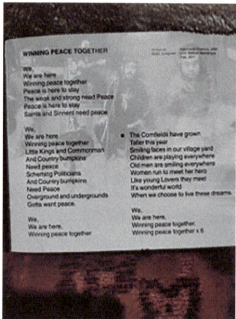

Figure 1.4a 'No more killings', a song written by a guru; used with permission from guru Rewben Mashangva.

Figure 1.4b 'Winning peace together', a song written by a guru; used with permission from guru Rewben Mashangva.

the church was an opportunity for him to meet with friends and to indulge in eating sweets, given to the children by the Sunday School teachers. He remembers singing 'Kumbaya' and 'Jesus loves me', familiar songs that are sung in many churches in the region. While these activities were writ large in a region that was increasingly becoming Christianised, guru was apprehensive of their growing power over Naga tradition, which was quickly being eviscerated by the encounter with outside forces. In fact (and he claims this is not a sign of protest), he changed his spelling from Reuben (biblical name) to Rewben, because he wanted a different spelling.

He remembers his schooling, first in Choithar, and then in Ukhrul, where he studied with Roman Catholic nuns who were mostly from south India. The biblical narratives and the education he received were alien and had no resonance with village life. For example, he recalls how travelling evangelists would carry pictures of Jesus, Moses and Abraham wrapped up in a scroll made of bamboo. The blue-eyed Jesus and his golden beard and hair were not a cynosure for him or his friends, but the sheep they were pictured herding appealed to them. During our talks, guru finds these events hard to recall, almost like passing memories,

memories that have to be teased out from the archives of personal history. But his first encounter with the guitar is effortlessly recalled and vividly narrated.

Around 1974–5, buffalo traders from Burma (now Myanmar) came to the village. They would bring their guitars, sometimes to play around the campfire, and sometimes to sell: in those days 80–90 rupees for a guitar was an impossible sum of money for poor farm hands like the Mashangva family. Most of the songs he heard were in Burmese, as these traders were from ethnic groups belonging to the Kuki, Zomi, Thadou, Naga and Lushai from across the Myanmar border in places like Somra. He says:

> I have very fond memories of those days; they would make camp, tie their buffaloes and sing songs near the fire. I particularly remember how each song they'd sing would start with the D chord and then sometimes C chord. And that's how I learnt the D chord from them.

The D chord is the tone that would influence much of guru's music. These Burmese songs were heavily influenced by Christian hymns; as he talks, he pauses, takes a breath, and begins to sing *la, la, la*. To appease the young Mashangva, his father attempted to make a guitar (he was a carpenter) crafted with pine from the forest, old telephone wires left by the Manipur Rifles for the strings, and wooden pegs for the machine head.[10] While it was a good attempt at guitar making, guru began to borrow a guitar from friends who had bought one from the Burmese traders. Practice makes perfect, was the mantra. The D chord was so overplayed on this shared guitar that it eventually wore down the fret. As his repertoire expanded, he slowly started to understand the structure of music and began to experiment, with the sense of an open enquiry leading to something (Ingold 2013, 6–7). The first song he started playing in earnest – and the song that made him famous – was called 'Changkhom philava' (princess shawl, a shawl then worn by men but now mostly by women). Increasingly familiar with other musicians all over the region, he travelled to places like Ukhrul and Imphal where he met guitarists like Apen Rungsung and rock bands such as National Highway 39. Apen became central to his development as a guitarist, as he helped guru understand the structure of chord progression beyond the scales he knew (A, E and D).

'Changkhom philava' is an interesting fusion of folk with blues (Eric Clapton and Roy Buchanan), the 'Tulsa sound' (blues, rockabilly, country and jazz) popularised by J. J. Cale, and hints of Bob Dylan's bracing, unvarnished tone, and has the chirping of cicadas in the background. In many ways, 'Changkhom philava' and his next song, 'Ngahuirot haoki kachi thali' (You seem to wither away) would set the standard, the kind of approach guru was keen on exploring, a kind of musical journey that would define him.

Ecologies of creation: sound and the mana of folk

Oral traditions play a vital role in how folk songs are passed down. There are no written musical notations. It is the spoken word, the songs, that tell the history of the people. According to Stephen Angkang, a Tangkhul elder, 'The folksongs of Tangkhul are basically an emulation of nature. The harmony produced by the sound of birds, insects, etc. were the foundation of their songs.'[11] Guru's music imitates nature. The sound of the cicada is present in his music: *ching, ching, ching*. In an interview with the *Hindu* newspaper, he discusses one of his own compositions, which he calls 'The cicada song'.[12] He says: 'Each season sounds different, have you noticed? In winters grass has dried, in the spring the new leaves blow with the wind, in the rains the water trickles at different speeds, it's all music.'[13]

He uses the horn of the Indian bison, or mithun, and cuts it to produce certain sounds: if the horn is long, it produces the A scale, if shorter, it's the C scale. Even when he creates his Indigenous instruments, such as the tingteila (a fiddle) or the yangkahui (a flute), the wood comes from the forests his ancestors used, especially wood that was used for building a log drum, a drum traditionally at the centre of a village, which averaged 10 metres in length and 4 metres in width, is hewn from a single, carefully selected tree, and has a head in the form of an animal or human figurine. These drums were used for celebrating victories and the taking of human heads, and marked village feasts and the funerals of the famous, each occasion having its own special rhythm (Alemchiba 1968, 66; Longkumer 2018a).

There is also the jaw harp (in Tangkhul 'mazui') that produces a particular sound (like *wah-wah*), and is made of bamboo skin. Other artists incorporate the sound of nature in their music. One musician, who counts guru as an inspiration, told me how her entire way of looking at music changed when she learnt to appreciate her Naga roots. She wanted to return to the sound of nature, an uncomplicated pattern, bereft of 'noise', that is, a certain kind of noise she associates with modern, Western instruments. Her music involved dried bamboo leaves, a clay pot and seeds in a pot as percussion instruments, with the human voice: 'just to have the voice, just to have these kinds of sounds'. She was not keen on recording her songs with any 'instrument or electronic stuff, whether acoustic or electronic, not having it come out from anything that was man-made, but rather textures, like natural textures and things like leaves and seed pods'. Songs are open, direct and straightforward. Whether they are erotic, or about war, when they are sung the melody mollifies the message and they do not create offence or anger.

Alobo Naga, a musician based in Dimapur, talks about how folk is rooted in the land and in traditions. Folk is more than just music; it is history. Alobo tells me: 'We learn the stories, the folktales about our ancestors, lifestyle, government, economy and culture, through our music. Only music, folk music, traditional clothes – those are the original documents that we have, since we have no original written manuscript.' There are different kinds of chants – khamahon – that are an intrinsic part of everyday life amongst the Tangkhuls. In work, in the fields, and in marriage ceremonies, these chants are non-lyrical tunes that are sung by groups of people. One of the best examples of this kind of singing – which combines the khamahon tradition with storytelling – is a traditional haunting melody, 'Matek chim', captured on camera atop a hill overlooking Jodhpur, in the north-western Indian state of Rajasthan. Guru Mashangva sings as a light breeze dances with the orange glow of the evening sun, during the Rajasthan International Folk Festival.

> The most beautiful belle
> Participating in the virgin dance, virgin dance
> Was made to sit on the high pedestal
> Was made to sit on the high pedestal of a princess.
> Grandpa and Grandma
> They were a society schooled in toiling on the earth
> Oh hey oh hey, oh hey oh hey
> Oh it's our wealth
> Let's learn and rehearse
> Ye to find a strong foundation
> Lo let's find a strong foundation
> And lace it up together
> The good tradition of Hao festivals
> Are gifts bestowed upon us by our forefathers
> The good tradition of Hao festivals
> Are gifts bestowed upon us by our forefathers
> Oh hey oh hey...[14]

Another song, 'Sapsa runglo sapsa' (literally, pounding of rice using a mortar and pestle), captures the village dynamic of work songs, the sound of animals, accompanied by slide guitar, the blues and the tingteila. The song represents the rhythmic pounding of village life, evoking movement, and a melody that naturally repeats. The lyrics go something like this:

> sapsa runglo sapsa
> The girls are pounding rice
> The boys are trapping the chicken
> The chicken cries keo-keo
> Like mushroom it is tasty
> I will tell, I will tell
> Don't disclose it
> We shall eat together
> sapsa runglo sapsa[15]

Guru has researched the folk traditions of his village and the region. He sought out elders, those who recalled the songs sung during the pre-Christian days. Initially, as his musical sensibilities were still quite undeveloped, he would only seek out songs that had good rhythms. Soon he began to find the songs monotonous, hearing the same tunes again and again, unable to distinguish the subtle tonal changes. Then he searched for songs with deeper meanings. 'At last', he says, 'the folk songs became food for my soul and run in my blood.'[16] One of the instruments he started to use was the tingteila (fiddle). He modified it to suit the modern tonal scale, and introduced it into his musical repertoire. Similarly, he popularised the yangkahui (flute) – it took him a year and a half to make and learn the instrument – made from a particular variety of thin bamboo available near the Indo-Burmese border, which produces, he says, three sounds at one blow and a pentatonic, not a chromatic, scale. He revived this tradition by modifying the structure of the flute to make it more appealing to modern tastes. He compares his flute playing to the likes of Ian Anderson from the British rock band Jethro Tull, and Hariprasad Chaurasia, the Indian classical flautist.

Marley, roots; Dylan, folk

It was only by listening to Bob Dylan and Bob Marley that guru started to understand the way the sound of the chords, the voice and the lyrics worked. Dylan and Marley did not sound like Western singers, he tells me, they sounded like the Nagas. The defining feature of their songs, guru says, is their rawness, their emphasis on roots, and, because the songs are relatable to 'our songs', guru felt that he could sound like them even when he sang in his own language. Take, for example, he says, 'Redemption song' (1980) by Bob Marley.

> The lyrics and the sounds are very close together and it really reflects Naga village life – where we are also singing about oppression and yearning for freedom. Even though we were very rudimentary in our civilisation and although we don't have many facilities, we were living freely. But now the Indians and the Meitei community in Manipur – the majority – are exploiting us socially and economically. So 'Redemption song' reflects our situation. Emancipation is about freedom from mental slavery.

Marley was singing in a different place and time but his message cuts across. Guru uses Marley's song, 'Three little birds' (1980) (he sings: 'Don't worry about a thing, 'Cause every little thing gonna be all right. … Three little birds pitched by my doorstep … Sayin' "This is my message to you"'), to criticise the waywardness of the Christian Church. The song is about the trinity – the Father, the Son and the Holy Spirit. The message of the song, he says, is so unlike the kind of Christianity that Nagas are practising – shallow and inauthentic – in contrast to the deep spirituality evoked in this song.

The influence of Bob Marley on the musical landscape of the region comes from the music festivals, Roots and Roots on the Move, organised by activists like Keith Wallang and Anungla Zoe Longkumer since 2003.[17] Guru was also involved in these festivals and was in fact managed initially by Keith and Anungla through their company Springboard Surprises. The idea for Roots comes from Marley's lyric, which says – Anungla tells me – 'some are leaves, some are branches, but I and I are the roots'. What struck her about Marley and the Rastafarian movement was that they don't say 'we' for the collective, they normally say 'I and I'. And it was this sentiment – whether 'we' or 'I and I' – that led Keith and Anungla to organise a festival that was about reviving traditional identities in the region, amidst the suffering and ongoing militarisation and counter-insurgency brought about by the various nationalist movements claiming autonomy, self-determination and sovereignty (Baruah 1999; Longkumer 2020). This is how Anungla explained it to me:

> Our whole vision for the Roots festival was to fill this gap between our traditional thing and our contemporary thing that is going on in

the arts here in the Northeast. Even we grew up sort of displaced from our roots, so at least personally for me it was always this search in me for some sort of connection. The reason why we called it Roots … it's multi-layered, it's everything, us going back to the traditional thing, going back to nature, digging our roots in, so that we are unwavering in the winds of change.

Many of the themes around the revival of folk return to this idea of roots, both being rooted to land and tradition and looking back to a past associated with nostalgia and loss. Loss is a dominant feeling in my many interviews, but there is also a sense of hope for the future that artists like guru Mashangva (and the Roots festival) represent. While Marley was concerned with notions of social justice and roots, for guru the influence of Bob Dylan is paramount. Dylan's influence on the musical landscape in the last 50 years is immense, especially his poetry and protest songs connected with the civil rights and anti-nuclear movements, student revolts, the counter-cultural movement, and anti-war and Cold War propaganda. Like Dylan, guru Mashangva's musical influence lies in the resurgence of a folk tradition focusing on orality and a return to the pastoral, village, rural and personal roots through music (Shelton 2011; Sounes 2001).

The first Dylan album that he listened to was *Planet Waves* (1974). Matbam Rikhang, a friend who was a visual artist and worked in poster design in Bollywood (he was involved in the film *Bobby*, starring Rishi Kapoor), introduced guru to Dylan. When he first listened to Dylan, he was not very impressed by his vocal abilities. But when he listened to more of his music, the voice and the playing of the guitar sounded like his villagers playing; it was very simple. Guru could not understand the English lyrics so his friend Matbam translated them into Tangkhul. Guru then started to listen to other Dylan albums, in particular the way he strummed the acoustic guitar, which inspired his own way of playing. *Blowin' in the Wind* (1963), along with *Chimes of Freedom* (1964), had a significant impact on guru, especially Dylan's lyrical ability to relate to real-life events. Guru says, 'How many years have we been asking for sovereignty? How many times, and how many more years, do we have to wait to call us a man? Dylan's songs highlighted our yearning for freedom, peace, justice.' 'Blowin' in the wind' was the first Dylan song that he learnt to play, but with a guru Mashangva twist.

When I heard his guitar and vocal delivery, I really felt good. Some of the village elders, when they joked, their delivery sounded so much like Dylan's positivity in his songs. That feeling was present. Like when one listens to the stories, the humour, and the happiness – that was the feeling. Sometimes Dylan was just talking, sometimes singing. So this really touched my heart and I wanted to convey this kind of feeling and sing these kinds of songs. I don't know all of the meanings of his songs; sometimes I would translate one or two lines, or I would imagine that this must be this and that must be that.

Guru inherited from a friend a Dylan songbook that included most of his songs, and he has kept it to this day (Figure 1.5). From this songbook he would ask people to translate and help him understand songs related to peace, harmony, human rights and love. Two songs he particularly cherishes, he tells me, are 'Love minus zero' (1965) and 'Is your love in vain?' (1978). (He sings a little: 'Do you love me, or are you just extending good will?'). Much like Dylan, guru keeps the chord progressions simple; a three-chord structure is his preference.

Figure 1.5a Front cover of the Bob Dylan lyric book; courtesy of guru Rewben Mashangva and used with permission.

Figure 1.5b Back cover of the Bob Dylan lyric book; courtesy of guru Rewben Mashangva and used with permission.

For me, I have to follow the guitar chords that speak to me, and three chords is what I like and that allows me the freedom to combine the vocals, guitar chords, melody and lyrics. I play the A, E, D and G chords. I don't let minor and flat chords dominate, I use them primarily as a transition chord. These chords give structure to the songs. The guitar, and the lyrics, are simple, but when listening the music is very powerful.

Unlike major chords, minor chords, he says, don't bring happiness. The major chord structure, he notes, is also present in Naga folk traditional singing. That's why he could easily blend Dylan's songs with Tangkhul ones. He attempted this during the Naga Students' Federation (NSF) conference held in Ukhrul in 1992, which was a key moment in his career. Guru recalls that the NSF organisers were not keen on inviting him, fearing that his village style of music and his lack of English skills might put off the more urban and educated NSF members from all over the Naga regions. But they relented and gave him a chance to sing during the conference. Searching for inspiration, he opened his Dylan songbook and found the song 'Trust yourself' (1985). He then experimented with a traditional Tangkhul folk tune that was about Ayesho, who was a pretty girl coming to fetch water (he sings: 'Ayesho, Ayesho, senden ta-ra la-re'). When he combined this tune with the lyrics of 'Trust yourself', he was surprised to find that the metre matched perfectly. He sings: 'Trust yourself, trust yourself to do the things that only you know best ....' 'Trust yourself' was serendipitous. While it was clearly a Dylan song, the lyrics spoke to guru by giving him the courage to trust his instincts and to fashion his own path. The NSF audience was surprised by guru's fusion but pleased by guru's performance, accompanied by his friend Kelvin who played the harmonica and two back-up singers. He sang another Dylan song, 'Let me die in my footsteps' (1963), set to a folk tune. From then on, guru recalls, whenever he meets a member of the NSF audience they sing his version to him and not Dylan's.

Dylan was not the only artist guru emulated. His long-time friend and lyricist, Ngachonmi Chamroy, tells me that they would talk about Europe, South America and Africa and how songs influenced social and political movements. Using the lyrics of Bob Dylan, Bob Marley and Joan Baez, they would reflect on the situation in the Naga areas and similarly think about songs as the medium through which they could express some of the angst and frustration they were feeling. They felt that they could fuse their traditional songs with a 'dose of rock, jazz or blues and that these experiments were fine'. Ngachonmi said that Dylan's influence gave them a texture, a vast canvas, enough to accommodate the kind of music they wanted to experiment with.

The language of protest and resistance through music is visible in Northeast India. Two songs taken from the documentary *Sword of the Chosen One* come to my mind. The first is a song called 'Punshinba', by Kanglasha, a heavy metal band from Imphal, Manipur:

> Let us show our united strength,
> Let it shine the world over.
> Whom should we fear?
> Why should we depend on others for our freedom?
> With the united strength
> Only I, your mother, await.
>
> Don't make your eyes glow
> Looking, waiting, calling – wake up!
> The rainbow-coloured flag will flutter in the sky.[18]

This song is a reflection on the draconian Armed Forces Special Powers Act (AFSPA) and the hegemonic grip it has in Manipur, curtailing the freedom of its people. AFSPA has been imposed in many of the states in the region because of demands for autonomy and sovereignty, leading to armed insurgency, since Indian independence in 1947. AFSPA provides the Indian state with the power to stop and search any individual on mere suspicion of acting against the state, and has led to mass shootings and murders.[19] Members of Kanglasha lament the neglect shown by the Indian government towards the region, where human rights activists like Irom Sharmila had to go on continuous hunger strike for 16 years (2000–16) to advocate for the removal of AFSPA. Yet the status quo remains. In another example, this time against the institutional Church, Boomarang, a rock band from Aizawl, Mizoram, takes aim at the debilitating influence and the reach of the Christian-influenced Young Mizo Association (YMA), which acts as the local moral police. This song, 'King of pain', articulates their angst:

> There was once the kingdom of pain
> ruled by terror, many years he reigned.
> Truth was hidden by the lie he teaches,
> Justice was overruled by the power of riches,
> The knights were bribed with gold as their bride,
> The Church content with the laws he provide.
> …

When a new day is come, and a new sun is shone
My children will never taste your bitter shit no more …[20]

Guru and Christianity

Christianity has had a presence in the Naga areas from the mid-nineteenth century, when many converted. Indeed, over the years and in particular after Indian independence, the presence of Christianity and its widespread popularity gave rise to a sense of belonging, away from the dominant religions of India that held very little sway amongst the tribes of Northeast India (Downs 1992; Thomas 2016). With Christianity came a growing sense of pride and association with a 'universal' religion that superseded local traditions. However, along with the spread of Christianity came trepidation about the disappearance of traditional culture, a lament that is echoed quite widely in Christian circles, as well as by guru Mashangva and Ngachonmi Chamroy.

Spiritually, Ngachonmi says, Christians talk about Jerusalem from the Bible and sing from Western hymnals, but in doing this the Nagas have forgotten the Indigenous songs, rooted in this land. The American and British missionaries wanted local people to abandon their past without much accommodation and negotiation. Their zealotry was palpable in the early missionising period, and was adopted by local converts. The singing of traditional songs, the drinking of rice beer, the veneration of ancestors and animal sacrifices were discouraged. Thus, we see the advent of the 'dark ages' amongst the Nagas. Ngachonmi goes on to explain that the Nagas are aping Western culture, 'a Xerox copy of someone else rather than an original copy of ourselves'. But, after much discussion, guru and Ngachonmi realised that separating the two – traditional culture and Christianity – was not doing any good, so they started experimenting, initially mixing Dylan's lyrics with a traditional tune. Similarly, they experimented with the Christian hymn 'A shelter in the time of storm', fusing the lyrics with traditional tunes. When they do this, Ngachonmi and guru say, their worship and outlook bring them closer to God. The use of folk music to indigenise Christian practices and biblical themes is not uncommon in other parts of India (see Sherinian 2014).

But there is resistance to guru and Ngachonmi's approach amongst some Christians, who see it as propagating a kind of pseudo-Christianity, one that has been corrupted by the forces of tradition. And this idea of corruption, guru and Ngachonmi say, comes primarily from the ideology of 'Nagaland for Christ' – a geo-religious idea that promulgates Christian purity – propounded by various churches and groups like the National Socialist Council of Nagalim (NSCN), now fragmented into different factions (see Longkumer 2018b). For guru and Ngachonmi, there must be clear separation of Church and politics. There has been too much entanglement in the past, leading to immense confusion. Getting to the roots is of vital importance, and at times, the Church has been the barrier to this. In fact, they suggest, the two can coexist. 'Nagaland for Christ' is largely a slogan to make the Church, the Christian institutions and the wealth associated with the Church's power, the basis for maintaining the status quo. Rediscovering oneself through digging into one's roots is where the spiritual power lies, according to guru and Ngachonmi:

> So if we talk about Jerusalem and the Old Testament, we imagine a place far away, somewhere in Judaea, places we have never seen. We have only read about them in the Bible. So we also see Christianity as very abstract and some idea that has been transplanted from a faraway place like Jerusalem. So we are trying to bring Jesus closer to us, and make it more akin to us.

The kind of loss associated with the coming of Christianity and the forces of modernity have led to heavy hearts for many in the region. Stephen Angkang, a Tangkhul elder, bemoans this reality and warns of the dire consequences if these forces are left unchecked. He says that folk traditions are quickly disappearing because of the restrictions placed on them by Christian institutions. Newer and more attractive forms of art, music and technology are overtaking the oral culture, which transmits knowledge through the generations. Closely connected to this, he says, is that agricultural work has decreased, giving way to school education as a more desirable way of creating a future. With that, people are losing their work songs – (he chants) *he ho, he ho*. Do people, he asks, chant these while reading or writing?[21] Of course, this rhetorical question has a broader point, and that is the attraction of another culture over one's own. He notes that the Nagas are attracted to Hindi movie songs and Western music more than to their own traditional songs. Because the allurement of something novel and shiny because of mass media (social media, Bollywood, Hollywood) has often led to their acceptance, the assimilation of another culture can easily lead to the loss of one's own.[22] These are points that are helpfully discussed by Alobo, who runs a music school in Dimapur.

> I have a music school and I teach students from the baroque period, Mozart, etc., and I can do that because there are written documents

in the form of musical notations. We don't have any documentation in the form of musical notations, etc.; we have audio recordings now, but these documents are absent. So this is one of the scary things about our culture, and I have been working on this. Guru Rewben is promoting folk songs and culture through our music, but our generation will be the last to know, and the next generation might not remember.

Similarly, Stephen Angkang reminds us that Western music has tonic sol-fa (do-re-me-fa-so-la-ti-do) and staff notations. But Naga folk music lacks that. Appearing slightly exasperated on camera, he says, 'What symbol shall we give to record a particular sound or tune? I often propose to establish institutions where children can learn folk songs and musical instruments by paying them stipends. Otherwise these arts will disappear. A tribe or a nation or a community that has lost its own culture is finished! I often shout about this, but I don't know how many will hear my words.'[23] But others do not lay the blame squarely on Christianity (Kikon and McDuie-Ra 2021, 115–16). Alobo, for instance, emphasises that one of the positive aspects of Christianity has been the focus on singing. The hymns and the different musical traditions of the Church have always been a 'core value', which has allowed singing to evolve and continue, although in different forms.

Guru governmentality: the preservation and passing down of folk

In 2004, the North East Zone Cultural Centre (NEZCC), a regional institution that is part of the Indian Ministry of Culture, gave Rewben Mashangva the title 'guru'.[24] Here guru governmentality and guru logics (Copeman and Ikegame 2012b), the legitimation of authority by the state, release a kind of power. According to Michel Foucault, '"Government" did not refer only to political structures or to the management of states; rather, it designated the way in which the *conduct* of individuals or of groups might be directed: the government of children, of souls, of communities .... To govern, in this sense, is to *structure the possible field of action of others*' (1983, 221; emphasis added). This kind of rationale, which creates the condition for the exercise of power, is captured in the notion of a state-sanctioned 'guru', but also in the cultural capital that this term confers. Not only does he perform and travel to various festivals in India and abroad, but through this recognition he functions as a 'cultural ambassador' who highlights the folk traditions of India and exemplifies the Unity in Diversity that India is keen to project.

The NEZCC recognition is part of their Guru–Shishya Parampara scheme (teacher-to-student tradition). In an advert, the NEZCC calls for applications from candidates who have 'thorough knowledge for imparting training in any cultural field of the region, i.e. folk dance/songs, bamboo/cane/wood craft, folk theatre, woodcraft, mask making etc., emphasis is given on Dying & Vanishing art forms of the region'.[25] For one year, the guru will impart training to four shishyas (or students), with monthly stipends for all those involved. This is quite a large scheme; when he was an awardee, there were roughly 20 others from all over the Northeast, and it lasted for two years. Some gurus gain prominence through the scheme; others quietly fade away from public view. As part of it, and through the years, 15 shishyas have studied under him, particularly in teaching traditional folk music and the revival of Tangkhul culture. Guru was already pioneering the preservation of tradition through his music; the title was simply an elevation, in recognition of his efforts. His primary task, through this guruship, was to acknowledge traditional culture as 'good' and to tackle cultural amnesia. His desire is to make folk attractive. He jokes that playing the tingteila (fiddle) during the rainy days puts even the chickens to sleep. Because he wants to improvise and to make folk songs relevant, the songs need to evolve and be dynamic. 'Our folk is good,' he says, 'but it's too raw. That's why I am trying to make a fashionable thing out of the original so that all the grandeur is not lost.' For guru, then, some of the 'grandeur' of folk has been lost to modern music; in fusing the two, must there be an element of compromise? He would argue that 'folk' is not a moribund form, or a simple reinvention of the past. Everything modernises, in some way or another, or it dies. Naga music should modernise, rather than be pickled in aspic.

Initially Rewben was not keen on using the title guru, but gradually began to use it as a recognisable and honorific form of address. His initial questioning was based on the fact that people thought 'guru' was associated with Hinduism, as a term of reverence for someone with religious power: a miracle worker, renunciant or 'divine human'. People in the region failed to see, because of their Christianised culture, that 'guru' could also apply to music. Indeed, as Schippers (2007) argues in the context of north Indian classical music, the teacher–student relationship is central to the perpetuation of the oral tradition of music. Ironically, audiences in Myanmar, South Korea, China and Nepal recognised this fact, but people in his home town of Manipur questioned his allegiance. He sounds exasperated when remembering discussions in which 'guru' was viewed negatively as belonging to a Sanskritised Hindu cultural cosmos that had very little relevance for Christian hill tribes in Manipur. He would often engage in debate by asking critics to think about the various titles that people have – from Christian Reverend to the academic Dr or medical Doctor ('Dr' and Doctor' are colloquially distinguished thus in Northeast India) – which are unproblematic. Yet apprehension arises from the use of 'guru'. He continues by saying that one should not be afraid of embracing 'guru', partly because it is a 'universal language' that is instantly recognisable. This title is not only for the Tangkhuls or the Naga Nation, but it is for the whole world, he tells me.

One of his students, Freddie, remarked that when Rewben started using the term 'guru', he was very suspicious. Its strong association with the Hindu tradition and mainstream India made it difficult to accept. Once he learned the title was bestowed by a state-managed government scheme rather than a Hindu spiritual organisation, he came round. It was simply recognition of guru's work as a teacher, primarily in the secular mould as espoused by the scheme. However, in Tangkhul, Rewben is known as 'Awo', translated loosely as 'grandfather' but meaning someone who is also an elder and a keeper of knowledge and wisdom. 'Awo' also has a connotation of someone who blends tradition (his stage clothes, necklace, haircut) and modernity: 'someone who lives in the modern world, but trying to live in the times of our ancestors', as Freddie put it. When I asked if the title 'guru' was a state-driven agenda to promote the idea of 'Unity in Diversity', Alobo, the Dimapur musician, told me there is no political or national agenda. He believes that if the government awards the title 'guru' to someone within the region, one should accept and celebrate this recognition.

'Awo and guru is the same for us', says Augustine, the leader of the band Featherheads, which has been influenced by guru's approach to music. One title is local and the other is Indianised, but both mean a teacher or an elder who imparts knowledge so that others can learn and follow. This notion of passing down knowledge, or *parampara*, is something guru is keen to impart. Many come to see him play: rock musicians, church singers, and those interested in music. He tells them about the songs inspired by nature that humans engage in and how storytelling is in song. 'We don't have a book to share,' he says, 'but we must engage in the oral tradition of passing down knowledge, a *parampara*.' Even in his concerts, Alobo recalls, 'he shares folklore and folktales associated with the songs, so in this way, it is very enchanting.'

Our discussion of his guru status naturally revolves around the many identities that he manages and encompasses. He is a family man, a musician, an artist and creator of musical instruments, Christian, Tangkhul, Naga, Indian, teacher, traveller and performer. Yet, for him, these categories don't matter; they only box him in in unhelpful ways. Sometimes, certain identities emerge and are emphasised over others when he faces an audience. However, most important to guru is the fact that he, alongside his friend Ngachonmi and allies, is trying to create a movement, 'nothing less than a cultural revolution'. He is a cultural revivalist, a reviver of old practices and traditions, making them relevant to the present generation, emphasises Ngachonmi. Guru and his allies are battling the deep-seated anxiety, uncertainty and traumatic loss experienced as a result of British colonialism and Christian proselytisation, which drove Indigenous cultural practices underground. Material things were attacked: beads and necklaces were pounded with a wooden mortar and pestle and buried, as a sign of burying the past, on the encouragement of Christian zealots who saw these things as evil. To create a movement, guru has to encompass all walks of life.

His popularity has also meant that students from all over India want to study under him. But guru is unsure. His method of teaching is by *doing* – without his instruments, he says, he cannot lecture or talk to audiences for hours. If he started a school, the whole course would be over in two days, he tells me. Not used to question-and-answer sessions, nor to explaining the history of musical forms, guru is honest about his capacity and his way of teaching. For him, there has to be an element of self-discovery, or, as Tim Ingold explains in relation to his work with the Saami people in Finland, 'To know things you have to grow into them, and let them grow in you, so that they become a part of who you are' (2013, 1). Quoting Gregory Bateson's idea of 'deutero-learning', Ingold explains that this approach is not so much learning about the world as being taught by it (2013, 2). Perhaps this is what guru means when he talks about teaching by *doing*. Many from outside Imphal contact him with offers of money for tutelage, but he admits that this is a task he is uncomfortable to undertake. Instead, he says, he accommodates many events locally for free, and to fulfil his idea of taking pride in his work and his status he gives his time without conditions. 'I am now guru, this is a title that I cannot erase. I've used it for close to 20 years. India recognises this and the region recognised this in 2004 and for that I was very happy. I am now guru Rewben Mashangva.'

Parampara and the act of handing down knowledge

Central to his understanding of guruship is the act of handing down knowledge. Freddie, who is a Baptist pastor, a musician and an entrepreneur, remembers the first time he heard guru Mashangva, in 1995. It was an old videotape of guru's performance in Ukhrul during the 1992 NSF conference. 'Instantly', Freddie says, 'I fell in love with his music.' A few years later, when guru came to Shillong, the capital city of Meghalaya, he stayed with Freddie and his family and taught them a few of his songs. Freddie was playing covers of the British band Iron Maiden, and was massively influenced by the American glam rock of the 1980s and 1990s, only to see 'this guy come to the stage with his guitar, his haircut and playing traditional tunes, mixed with blues – this was all novel to us'. The band he formed, called Salt and Light Traveling Band, fuses traditional music with metal and reggae. Like guru, he wears the Raivat Kachon (Tangkhul body cloth), cuts his hair in the style of guru, and fuses various genres of music. But the band's lyrics are Christian gospel. Their idea, Freddie says, is to 'present the gospel to a secular stage'. Although guru claims to be one of the few people who sing traditional songs, Freddie reminds me that there are many Tangkhul Christian composers who combine traditional tunes with gospel lyrics; in fact, he notes, these songs are even purer than guru's, because there is no fusion of musical genres. So while guru may be the face of this musical movement, there are others working tirelessly in the background.

Augustine is another musician, from the band Featherheads, influenced by guru. They combine traditional Naga music with rock and metal. His is a story of travel and of the uprootedness that he experienced as a child. Because of his parents' jobs they moved around all over India, he says, like 'hippies and gypsies'. He had very little connection with his community in Ukhrul, which he now regrets. He trained as a DJ in Pune after listening to Linkin Park, an American rock band. He was particularly impressed by the DJ skills of Joe Hahn, whose scratching, turntables, sampling and programming were key to the sound of Linkin Park. It was while DJing that Augustine founded two bands – first Systemic Roots and then Featherheads – that were inspired by a variety of musical genres. They listened to bands like System of a Down and Bullet for My Valentine, and gravitated especially towards the Finnish symphonic metal band Nightwish. The latter's ability to combine traditional Finnish folk and the new metal genre gave Augustine the inspiration to carry on with Featherheads. When Augustine moved back to Ukhrul, he met up with guru. He had already heard of guru's early songs like 'Changkhom philava' and he began to adopt the Naga hairstyle, like guru, and his type of fusion music. He started playing with the traditional Naga clothes, again like guru. What drew him to guru was not only his music, but 'his way of becoming himself'. He is guru but also Awo, an elder who represented his vision of 'our love of ancestors'. Guru showed Augustine and the band how to bridge the time of their ancestors and the time of modernity. In sonic terms, what this highlights is the ability to recognise sound and place as sensed through their motion across space and time, remaining true to who they are as a people; perhaps guru's way of becoming himself is marked by these capacious temporal and spatial constellations.

Guru in many keys or the travelling, marketable guru

John and Jean Comaroff (2009) draw our attention to how the abstraction of capitalism becomes materialised and mediated in social formations, and how culture as a tradition-filled idiom is increasingly packaged as a commodity (see also Longkumer 2015). This process, however, is complex and multipronged, a cyclic loop that highlights the fundamental interconnection of culture, commodity and capitalism. '[T]he producers of culture', they write, 'are *also* its consumers, seeing and sensing and listening to themselves enact their identity – and, in the process, objectifying their own subjectivity, thus to (re)cognize its existence, to grasp it, to domesticate it, to act on and with it' (2009, 26; italics in original). Their provocative title, *Ethnicity, Inc.*, encapsulates some of the processes I too describe, especially as guru negotiates the complex terrain of culture in an age of mass publicity (Mazzarella 2003), where visuals and images that enter into circulation confound in their capacity to inspire, interrupt and exceed existing meanings in their exuberance. Folk culture needs the aptitude of individuals like guru, but at the same time it requires mass consumption and participation through the various media that I have been describing.

Guru knows that his persona enables a certain perception that can be expanded. He plays on the 'exotic' tribal card, so that he can be excused for his unpolished demeanour and lack of English. When he explains to people that he is from a small village in Manipur, near the Myanmar border, people automatically relate to the remoteness and agrarian life, and when he tells them that he learnt English by listening to the radio, or that he learnt conversational English (not reading or writing) on the roadside and attended school only up to class 5 (around 10 years of age), he creates a certain aura of a simple village boy, who has achieved so much from so little. The presentation of his identity – the traditional hairdo, the clothes and his demeanour – are carefully packaged so that the audience 'adores me', explains guru. There is also an element of charm, an almost childlike joy, in guru's voice that makes him him. His rawness, combined with the innocence he exudes, may not be the most appealing to an audience, Alobo argues. However, when he plays his music, the beauty and the roots of folk remains even as they are blended with blues or rock. 'When you listen to it,' Alobo continues, 'automatically there's a smile on your face.' In a recent interview about the Japanese pop band Shonen Knife, which focused on their singing in English, Daniel Robson remarks, 'The slight grammatical errors or strange pronunciations are part of Shonen Knife's charm, enhancing the innocence of their sound.' 'I don't want to sing perfectly in English', says Naoko, the lead singer. 'I prefer to sound original.'[26] In a way, guru encapsulates this sentiment too. He is confident and almost self-effacing when he sings and speaks in English; like Shonen Knife, he sounds original.

Guru is also a master at presenting himself to particular audiences, attracting attention. For instance, in places like Nagaland or Manipur, he tends to play his more blues- or rock-oriented songs, while in Mumbai or Bangalore he leans towards folk, as that is new to them, or 'even exotic', a kind of displaced orientalism. Isn't it odd, I suggest to guru, that it is the folk songs, where the lyrics are mostly (if not all) in Tangkhul, that are so popular with an audience that has no comprehension whatsoever? He sings in Tangkhul, he says, but adds a few lines in English so that they follow the story. For instance, in 'Changkhom philava', he will add in English 'princes of the mountain, princess of the mountain', so that the audience can get a sense of the plot. But language is no barrier for guru. His collaboration with the Raghu Dixit Project is a great example of this.[27] The song is called 'Basti ki masti' (house of fun), a catchy funky tune to which Raghu Dixit sings the Hindi and guru the Naga parts. So when they played it in front of a Hindi-speaking audience in Bihar, most knew the Naga lyric *'hopi pi, le ho le, hopi, hopi, le oh le'*, even though their knowledge of the Naga people is limited. The popularity of the song even spread to the office of the Rashtriya Swayamsevak Sangh (RSS), a Hindu-right group. When it was announced that guru would be awarded the Padma Shri in January 2021, the RSS invited him to their office in Imphal to honour his achievements. When the RSS asked him to play one of his songs, he replied to them in an allegorical way: 'I don't have anything to say, but I understand the language of fish, trees, natural things, so I will make the bamboo flute speak to you today.' He went on to play 'Basti ki masti', which the RSS cadres instantly recognised and clapped along to, some even moving to the rhythm of the song. Hindu *rashtra* (state) meets fusion music.

Other musicians also find his approach to music refreshing, says Ngachonmi. Bands like Agni, a popular rock band from Kerala, sought out guru after his performance in a concert in Bangalore and confessed that they had been studying his music. They said they were fed up, guru continues, with the heavy metal music they had been playing and wanted to mimic guru's philosophy of music or ecologies of creation. Mimesis, or to 'become and behave like someone else', is according to Walter Benjamin ([1933] 1976), an intrinsic human quality. This mimesis is triggered by a certain connection, allurement and social capital that guru's music and philosophy attain. In our age of planetary consumerism and mass media, then, guru's persona travels across national borders, providing what William Mazzarella, drawing from the philosopher Peter Sloterdijk (2011), calls a 'constitutive resonance' (Mazzarella 2017, 5).

Because of his fame, guru is frequently invited to cultural festivals around the country; he also represents India internationally. The celebration of folk by the Indian state suggests that it belongs to the 'nation', or, as George Revill says of English folk music, 'As mere temporary custodians of a common culture, "the folk" had no individual rights of ownership in what was clearly a heritage belonging to the nation as a whole' (2005, 700). That is why guru's music is celebrated by the Indian state through recognition, which also allows them to outsource his talents by performing a governmental function, perpetuating the 'idea of India'. In contrast, when he tours in China, South Korea or Myanmar, as part of the Government of India cultural troupe, people are often surprised when they see him, and question if he is indeed from India. When he was in China, people were astonished that he did not speak Mandarin. In South Korea, people thought he was Chinese, and in Myanmar they wanted him to speak Mandarin, suspecting that he was a kung fu master (primarily, he jokes, because of his long hair). His presence is an attempt to celebrate the Indian national imagination of Unity in Diversity, but this gets lost in translation when he is globetrotting. Shared cultural ideas increasingly become blurred.

Guru and the art of survival

Despite the success of guru's music and that of other artists in the Northeast, there is precarity in the art. What is folk music without the fused elements? This is a question that has always found a familiar answer. Guru reflects on the question of survival as an artist, always innovating, and constantly reflecting on new processes. He says: 'In order to go professional, you have to be creative and be able to refine the existing art. You should be able to please the listeners and viewers. Our art survives on their appreciation. If people don't buy our product, we are gone.'[28] This notion of sounding relevant is something that many artists speak about. Alobo explains how 'pure folk' (perhaps untainted by outside influence?) is not appealing. As artists, and particularly to be successful, they have to survive and think about entertaining an audience. Guru's music, he notes, is largely about presenting it in a new package that marries the best of both worlds. He says:

> So if it's like pure-pure folk, then, it's a very niche market. From an artist's point of view, I need to do something commercial if I need to be invited again. If I am full-on folk, my market is very limited. And I will be invited only in government events. But if I do fusion, both sides of the market will enjoy and I will gain an audience. Second, it is a smart way of selling your folk music. If there is someone coming from Assam singing his folk songs, I might not be interested. But if he puts a Metallica rift, and sings on top of that or if he has an EBM [electronic body music] beat with Assamese folk, then I'll be more interested in that. I think survival and marketing is one way of making an artist do that. For us artists, we have to blend a certain element of Western or popular music to be able to sell our trade and craft.

Alobo's point is that Naga folk music cannot compete with the dominant music based in the Hindi and English languages. State support is helpful for some artists, but this kind of association with the government provides very little patronage in the music industry that is now booming all over the world. Even simply singing in Hindi, Alobo notes, is beneficial in a market driven by familiarity, helping attract wealthy patrons who might invite them to play at private weddings or commercial, industry-related events. English may be a useful language to speak, but, at least in north India, without Hindi in their repertoire artists' prospects are limited.

Augustine from the Featherheads laments the way folk music is seen by the younger generation, as boring and without energy. He admits that listening to folk music requires patience, and realises that the only way to encourage the younger generation to appreciate folk is to move towards popular genres, hoping that 'someday the younger generation will come back to folk'. When probed as to why folk should be on a lower rung than popular music, Freddie asked me whether my line of questioning would be more helpful if it was the other way round: one should lay the emphasis on folk. He said: 'People will appreciate folk if I am able to fuse it with jazz, rock, blues and reggae.' There is bound to be some dilution when it comes to fusing and making music for the market, Freddie confesses. But Naga folk provides the originality in a market that is teeming with competition, talent and skill. If you remove the Naga folk elements, at least in the Northeast, all it is doing is copying the dominant music genres. Think of fusion as a 'new genre' that artists in the region are creating; don't think in terms of purity, originality, or even timeless pasts, Freddie tells me. His helpful intervention allows me to think about the hierarchy of musical genres that I have been discussing so far. Is Western music above folk, or is that the wrong way to look at this? Pierre Bourdieu offers us a prescient reminder of this dilemma when he says: 'the paradox of the imposition of legitimacy is that it makes it impossible ever to determine whether the dominant feature appears as distinguished or noble because it is dominant [...] or whether it is only because it is dominant that it appears as endowed with these qualities and [as] uniquely entitled to define them' (cited in Fellezs 2011, 20). Guru's music responds to these issues in nuanced and complex ways. While he is known widely as the 'King of Naga folk blues', and for creating a new genre of 'experimental indigenous rock',[29] he wants to be known for Hao music. Hao is not only the Indigenous name of the Tangkhul Nagas, it also relates to the pulsating rhythm of the daily grind of work – here voiced as 'hey-ho, hey-ho'.

Conclusion

This chapter is about the sonic guru. More importantly, it asks: what kind of guru is Mashangva? While the tradition of guruship is well established in India, in the Northeast it is still nascent. Guru Mashangva thus offers us a way to understand guruship, through his music and the way he fuses Tangkhul folk with modern sounds, particularly drawn from blues, and from the likes of Bob Dylan and Bob Marley. While guru is clear that he wants to establish a movement that is about preserving the tradition of singing in various Naga villages alongside the appreciation of the modern, popular music in the world, he is also the progenitor, a kind of bricoleur who is experimenting with the tools at his disposal. He is not shy of embracing fusion, nor is he reticent about newer influences. What he most clearly represents is what I have called the *ecologies of creation*, which are about fusion, place making and celebrating roots, but also about an open enquiry leading to growth. He has definitely come far, and the length and breadth of his travels gives weight to his immensely successful and diverse life as a guru, musician, teacher, national icon and international star. Indeed, guru Mashangva is an identity and association that is now inseparable from who he is. He is the light shining in a place that has experienced loss, and finding the *roots* to forge new *routes* establishes his guruship amongst gurus. Music is not only about the collective habitation, representation and performance of culture. For guru, it is about shining a light on a path for others to follow. To *be* as a way of living and taking pride in one's work, that's the true nature of a guru.

Acknowledgements

My thanks to Along Longkumer, who introduced me to Grace Jajo. Grace connected me with guru Rewben Mashangva and Ngachonmi Chamroy, who patiently answered all my questions and shared their ecologies of creation with me with kindness and generosity. My deepest gratitude. Tarun Bhartiya introduced me to Oinam Doren who generously shared his film, *Songs of Mashangva*, and gave me another insight into guru Rewben's music. Anungla Zoe Longkumer, Alobo Naga, Freddie Longleng, from Salt and Light Traveling Band, and Augustine Shimray, from Featherheads, shared their musical journeys with me. My thanks to them. Jacob Copeman, Bjørn Ola Tafjord and Lindsay Graham read versions of this chapter: my gratitude to them.

Notes

1. This opening scene is from the documentary *Songlines* (dir. Vasudha Joshi; https://psbt.org/films/songlines/, accessed 13 February 2023).
2. I use 'folk' here simply because guru and others use it. They use it as shorthand to encompass traditional village songs too, not in the sense that folk is representative of a static past, unchanging with the vicissitudes of life, but as a positive feature that imbues tradition. Folk songs are therefore slippery and multivalent; they not only represent the village-based traditions but are also rearranged and reinterpreted for an urban/government/popular audience. Folk music, as Stephan Fiol notes, is also positively valued as a token of 'plebeian identification, anti-colonial nationalism, and cultural regionalism' (2017, 72). Aspects of these are certainly present in what I will discuss below. In the wider Indian context, the tradition of 'folk' singing, versus the more 'classical' tradition, has been discussed at length by others who place emphasis on elite/non-elite distinctions which sometimes blur, especially when the popularity of one art form gains ascendancy. Usually, the influence of both traditions must be taken into account, and any divide between the two is blurry (see Fiol 2017; Manuel 2015).
3. He has released three studio albums: *Tantivy* (1999), *Creation* (2006) and *Our Story* (2012).
4. On 4 April 2023.

5 Somini Sengupta, 'Town in India rocks (no use to wonder why, babe)', *New York Times*, 23 June 2008. https://www.nytimes.com/2008/06/23/arts/music/23dylan.html.
6 https://www.youtube.com/watch?v=P39L_M5JYKk (accessed 13 February 2023).
7 'Guru Rewben Mashangva awarded Padma Shri', *Ukhrul Times*, 9 November 2021. https://ukhrultimes.com/guru-rewben-mashangva-awarded-padma-shri/ (accessed 1 May 2023).
8 I have come across only one piece of research on guru, by Dhiren Sadokpam (2018), which is a short study of guru and his music. For comparative examples of other musical forms in Northeast India see Borah 2018 and Rojio 2018. Another book, by Dolly Kikon and Duncan McDuie-Ra (2021) on the urban landscape of Dimapur in Nagaland, as a post-conflict place, explores what they call the 'Audible City'. Using music to navigate suffering, pain, loss and hope, they argue that music is intrinsic to the identity of Dimapur, creating 'audible experiences' of living in the city.
9 YouTube proliferates with various performances of guru. The video documentaries are available online, two of which are free. These are *Songlines* (see note 1) and *Sword of the Chosen One* (https://www.youtube.com/watch?v=XElsOGJ1SYU&t=1999s, accessed 13 February 2023); the other is *Songs of Mashangva* (https://www.docubay.com/songs-of-mashangva-2118). I am grateful to the director, Oinam Doren, for sharing the film with me.
10 In *Songs of Mashangva* he says that Burmese traders brought the strings from Myanmar.
11 *Songs of Mashangva*.
12 Shrinkhla Sahai, '"Social distancing fuels creativity"', *The Hindu*, 19 March 2020, https://www.thehindu.com/entertainment/art/social-distancing-fuels-creativity/article31109386.ece.
13 'Social distancing fuels creativity', *The Hindu*.
14 Taken from *Songs of Mashangva*.
15 *Songs of Mashangva*.
16 *Songs of Mashangva*.
17 The festival attracted anything from 3,000 in smaller venues to 10,000 and 20,000 people in larger locations. To get a glimpse of the festival Roots and the regional dynamics of music, politics, protest and insurgency in the Northeast, see the documentary *Roots of the Move*: https://vimeo.com/87651836?fbclid=IwAR1QBxlnHxRbfLoVko8x0-s4Q-6aLXnQtHHQfU3bv3Zunhbn65g09gMhPEI (accessed 13 February 2023).
18 The song is in the documentary *Sword of the Chosen One*.
19 The recent killing of innocent villagers by the Indian armed forces in Oting, Nagaland, is an example of the unprecedented use of force on mere suspicion (and in this case weak intelligence). See Rupa Chinai, 'Nagaland civilian killing: Oting revives bitter, painful memories for Nagas', *Outlook*, 28 December 2021. https://www.outlookindia.com/magazine/story/india-news-nagaland-civilian-killing-oting-revives-bitter-painful-memories-for-nagas/305296 (accessed 13 February 2023).
20 The song is in the documentary *Sword of the Chosen One*.
21 *Songs of Mashangva*.
22 *Songs of Mashangva*.
23 *Songs of Mashangva*
24 Alongside the Padma Shri and the NEZCC award, he has received numerous regional and state awards including the Manipur State Kala Akademi award for 'Tribal Folk Music' in 2004 and 2005.
25 https://ipr.nagaland.gov.in/nezcc-invites-applications-guru-shishya-parampara-scheme (accessed 5 April 2023).
26 Daniel Robson, '40 years of Japanese rockers Shonen Knife: "Nirvana looked wild – I was so scared!"', *The Guardian*, 3 December 2021. https://www.theguardian.com/music/2021/dec/03/40-years-of-japanese-rockers-shonen-knife-nirvana-looked-wild-i-was-so-scared (accessed 14 February 2023).
27 According to his website, Raghu Dixit is '[o]ften hailed as India's biggest cultural & musical export .... His music is strongly rooted in Indian traditions and culture and is presented with a very contemporary, global sound.' https://www.raghudixit.com/#intro (accessed 1 May 2023).
28 *Songs of Mashangva*.
29 Somini Sengupta, 'Town in India rocks (no use to wonder why, babe)', *New York Times*, 23 June 2008, quoting Kit Shangpliang of Summer Salt.

References

Alemchiba, M. 1968. *The Arts and Crafts of Nagaland*. Kohima: Naga Institute of Culture.

Altglas, Véronique. 2014. *From Yoga to Kabbalah: Religious exoticism and the logics of bricolage*. New York: Oxford University Press.

Aravamudan, Srinivas. 2005. *Guru English: South Asian religion in a cosmopolitan language*. Princeton, NJ: Princeton University Press.

Bakhtin, Mikhail. 1981. *The Dialogic Imagination: Four essays* (trans. Caryl Emerson and Michael Holquist). Austin: University of Texas Press.

Baruah, Sanjib. 1999. *India against Itself: Assam and the politics of nationality*. New Delhi: Oxford University Press.

Benjamin, Walter. [1933] 1978. 'On the mimetic faculty', in *Reflections: Essays, aphorisms, autobiographical writings* (ed. Peter Demetz, trans. Edmund Jephcott), 333–6. New York: Schocken Books.

Borah, Utpola. 2018. 'Music, body and sexuality in Bihu songs of Assam', in *Northeast India: A reader*, edited by Bhagat Oinam and Dhiren A. Sadokpam, 279–87. Abingdon: Routledge.

Chopy, G. Kanato. 2021. *Christianity and Politics in Tribal India: Baptist missionaries and Naga nationalism*. Albany, NY: SUNY Press.

Comaroff, John L. and Jean Comaroff. 2009. *Ethnicity, Inc*. Chicago, IL: University of Chicago Press.

Copeman, Jacob and Aya Ikegame. 2012a. 'The multifarious guru: An introduction', in *The Guru in South Asia: New interdisciplinary perspectives*, edited by Jacob Copeman and Aya Ikegame, 1–45. Abingdon: Routledge.

Copeman, Jacob and Aya Ikegame. 2012b. 'Guru logics', *HAU: Journal of Ethnographic Theory* 2 (1): 289–336. https://doi.org/10.14318/hau2.1.014.

Downs, Frederick S. 1992. *History of Christianity in India. Volume 5: North East India in the Nineteenth and Twentieth Centuries*. Bangalore: Church History Association of India.

Eastman, Ralph. 1988. 'Country blues performance and the oral tradition', *Black Music Research Journal* 8 (2): 161–76. https://doi.org/10.2307/779350.

Feld, Steven. 1996. 'Waterfalls of song: An acoustemology of place resounding in Bosavi, Papua New Guinea', in *Senses of Place*, edited by Steven Feld and Keith H. Basso, 91–135. Santa Fe, NM: School of American Research Press.

Fellezs, Kevin. 2011. *Birds of Fire: Jazz, rock, funk, and the creation of fusion*. Durham, NC: Duke University Press.

Fiol, Stefan. 2017. *Recasting Folk in the Himalayas: Indian music, media, and social mobility*. Urbana: University of Illinois Press.

Foucault, Michel. 1983. 'The subject and power', in Herbert L. Dreyfus and Paul Rabinow, *Michel Foucault: Beyond hermeneutics and structuralism*, 208–26. Chicago, IL: University of Chicago Press.

Gold, Daniel. 1987. *The Lord as Guru: Hindi sants in North Indian tradition*. New York: Oxford University Press.

Hirschkind, Charles. 2006. *The Ethical Soundscape: Cassette sermons and Islamic counterpublics*. New York: Columbia University Press.

Holt, Fabian. 2007. *Genre in Popular Music*. Chicago, IL: University of Chicago Press.

Ingold, Tim. 2013. *Making: Anthropology, archaeology, art and architecture*. Abingdon: Routledge.

Kikon, Dolly and Duncan McDuie-Ra. 2021. *Ceasefire City: Militarism, capitalism, and urbanism in Dimapur*. New Delhi: Oxford University Press.

Lévi-Strauss, Claude. 1966. *The Savage Mind*. London: Weidenfeld & Nicolson.

Longkumer, Arkotong. 2015. '"As our ancestors once lived": Representation, performance and constructing a national culture amongst the Nagas of India', *Himalaya: The Journal of the Association for Nepal and Himalayan Studies* 35 (1): 51–64.

Longkumer, Arkotong. 2018a. 'Spirits in a material world: Mediation and revitalization of woodcarvings in a Naga village', *Numen: International Review for the History of Religions* 65 (5–6): 467–98. https://doi.org/10.1163/15685276-12341509.

Longkumer, Arkotong. 2018b. 'Bible, guns and land: Sovereignty, indigeneity and nationalism amongst the Nagas of India', *Nations and Nationalism* 24 (4): 1097–1116. https://doi.org/10.1111/nana.12405.

Longkumer, Arkotong. 2019. '"Along Kingdom's Highway": The proliferation of Christianity, education, and print amongst the Nagas in Northeast India', *Contemporary South Asia* 27 (2): 160–78. https://doi.org/10.1080/09584935.2018.1471041.

Longkumer, Arkotong. 2020. *The Greater India Experiment: Hindutva and the northeast.* Stanford, CA: Stanford University Press.

Manuel, Peter. 2015. 'The intermediate sphere in North Indian music culture: Between and beyond "folk" and "classical"', *Ethnomusicology* 59 (1): 82–115. https://doi.org/10.5406/ethnomusicology.59.1.0082.

Mazzarella, William. 2003. *Shoveling Smoke: Advertising and globalization in contemporary India.* Durham, NC: Duke University Press.

Mazzarella, William. 2017. *The Mana of Mass Society.* Chicago, IL: University of Chicago Press.

Openshaw, Jeanne. 1998. '"Killing" the guru: Anti-hierarchical tendencies of "Bāuls" of Bengal', *Contributions to Indian Sociology* 32 (1): 1–19. https://doi.org/10.1177/006996679803200101.

Ranade, Ashok D. 1998. 'The guru-shishya parampara: A broader view', *Sangeet Natak* (129–130): 39–54.

Revill, George. 2005. 'Vernacular culture and the place of folk music', *Social & Cultural Geography* 6 (5): 693–706. https://doi.org/10.1080/14649360500258302.

Rogers, Matt. 2012. 'Contextualizing theories and practices of bricolage research', *Qualitative Report* 17: art. no. 7, 1–17. http://dx.doi.org/10.46743/2160-3715/2012.1704.

Rojio, Usham. 2018. 'Poetic discourse in the songs of Tapta', in *Northeast India: A reader,* edited by Bhagat Oinam and Dhiren A. Sadokpam, 298–308. Abingdon: Routledge.

Sadokpam, Dhiren A. 2018. 'Problematizing cultural appropriation: Tangkhul folk-blues and socio-political aspirations', in *Northeast India: A reader,* edited by Bhagat Oinam and Dhiren A. Sadokpam, 288–97. Abingdon: Routledge.

Schippers, Huib. 2007. 'The guru recontextualized? Perspectives on learning North Indian classical music in shifting environments for professional training', *Asian Music* 38 (1): 123–38. http://dx.doi.org/10.1353/amu.2007.0020.

Shelton, Robert. 2011. *No Direction Home: The life and music of Bob Dylan.* Milwaukee, WI: Backbeat Books.

Sherinian, Zoe C. 2014. *Tamil Folk Music as Dalit Liberation Theology.* Bloomington: Indiana University Press.

Sloterdijk, Peter. 2011. *Bubbles: Spheres Volume I: Microspherology.* Los Angeles, CA: Semiotexte.

Sounes, Howard. 2001. *Down the Highway: The life of Bob Dylan.* New York: Grove Press.

Srinivas, Tulasi. 2010. *Winged Faith: Rethinking globalization and religious pluralism through the Sathya Sai Movement.* New York: Columbia University Press.

Sterne, Jonathan. 2003. *The Audible Past: Cultural origins of sound reproduction.* Durham, NC: Duke University Press.

Thomas, John. 2016. *Evangelising the Nation: Religion and the formation of Naga political identity.* New Delhi: Routledge India.

Urban, Hugh B. 2016. *Zorba the Buddha: Sex, spirituality, and capitalism in the global Osho movement.* Oakland: University of California Press.

Werbner, Pnina. 2001. 'The limits of cultural hybridity: On ritual monsters, poetic licence and contested postcolonial purifications', *Journal of the Royal Anthropological Institute* 7 (1): 133–52. http://dx.doi.org/10.1111/1467-9655.00054.

2
'Non-human gurus': yoga dolls, online avatars and meaningful narratives

Patrick S. D. McCartney and Diego Lourenço

Introduction

The etymology of 'guru' appears to stretch back to the Proto-Indo-European root *gwere-*₁. 'Guru' has come to mean that someone can have a large presence through a sense of 'heaviness'. This signifies the *gravitas* of a charismatic authority figure such as a guru, who is considered an expert teacher capable of transmitting knowledge to disciples. Following on from this is the concept of preserving and perpetuating the transmission of knowledge through an intergenerational tradition (*paramparā*). However, as is the focus of this chapter, for this process to work a human guru might not always be required. Objects such as books have been regarded as gurus or forms of representation of a particular tradition's line. The best example of this is Sikhism's sacred book, the Guru Granth Sahib, which is legally considered to be a 'living guru' whose desecration carries lengthy prison terms (see Myrvold 2010). Likewise, contemporary yoga spread around the world initially through books and pamphlets even when such texts were not assigned to a known tradition or guru. The obvious function of the written word in prescribing and translating experience implies that guruship can occur so long as the act of reading can enact a sense of connection or discipleship in the reader. Indeed, that was the case in many countries, some which were at the centre of contemporary yoga developments, such as the UK (Newcombe 2019), and others at the periphery, such as Brazil (Lourenço 2021). Still, adding to the 'contemporary guru field' (Lucia 2022), we envision the guru principle to be preverbal and therefore more fundamental than what can be conveyed through language. Building on Copeman and Ikegame's (2012) notion of the uncontainability of the 'multifarious guru', we explore the mediatisation of the *guru-tattva* ('teacher's principle') through the categories of 'non-human' and 'non-anthropomorphic' gurus. The analysis focuses on children's 'fashion' and 'action' dolls and on toys related to the category of yoga dolls, which can be understood as 'non-human' gurus and thus potentially relate to yoga hybrids (see Newcombe 2012; Di Placido 2020; McCartney 2020, 2021a). The focus on such non-human gurus stresses the role of the guru principle in the intergenerational transmission of knowledge and behaviours from adults to children, which might mimic the dynamics of a *paramparā*.

Furthermore, the possible transmission of yoga through toys offers insight into the guru principle's operation beyond the level of language, or complex socio-spiritual configurations such as those associated with the global spread of the 'guru phenomenon' (Lucia 2020), which relied on more elaborate layers of meanings and cognition. At the most basic level of individual playful experiences, however, meaning can still be negotiated in a rather unbounded way, under greater levels of agency. The imaginative freedom of playing with yoga dolls in one's bedroom contrasts with the increasingly controlled yoga industry. We call this 'received consumption', which relates to the imposition of 'proper' understandings of what yoga means and competing biopolitical ideologies, from how to position the body in the space, and breathing and meditating in the 'right' way, to reformulating the essence of yoga through, for instance, a prosocial justice ethic (see Fleming et al. 2022).

Yoga dolls and toys act as potential gurus, providing children with access mainly to the perceived popular benefits of yoga for health and lifestyle. This completely bypasses the professional authority and orthodoxy of yoga teachers, styles and organisations and what might be regarded as legitimate and authentic in a yoga practice. Even the commercial element involved in the popularisation and acquisition of such items exists mainly in a context and mode estranged from the yoga industry and more traditional institutions. This being so, the toy industry is a reasonably novel domain within which yoga articulations are transmitted through gift-giving from adults to children. Therefore, we consider that the guru principle can be mediated through yoga dolls and playthings for children through explicit relational power differentials during transmission of social and cultural values. Thus, reciprocation from children would partly entail the assimilation of the context-bounded and culture-informed skills and knowledge that the guru might teach.

That is, partial transmission of yoga to children might ensue if and when children apprehend such knowledge.

Since children's play involves formulating ideal social roles and role models, we consider how such mediatisation occurs, potentially creating demand for the acquisition of yoga lifestyles, which are not necessarily spiritual but speak of a mode of living and being in the world that is, or is at least perceived to be, somewhat more refined than other, non-yogic lifestyles. Yogic lifestyles are often marketed as being perceptibly more sustainable. This moral enhancement is said to arise through the vague technique of raising one's consciousness, which is said to be linked to improving ecological, health and social issues. One way to perceive embodiment of yogic culture is as some sort of yoga *habitus*. Like any habitus, it entails parental transmission of recognisable social patterns to the child (Bourdieu 1984). Habitus is closely linked to the notion of *socioculture* (Rehbein 2020), which is used to understand how social structures and classes, which have long historical roots and specific habitus, operate as tradition lines transmitting privileged knowledge (and inequalities) from one generation to the next. This process of transmission includes defining the limits of what constitutes a particular broader identity within society with the accompanying social norms which should be understood not as mere conformity but as an understanding of what is perceived as morally right (Sayer 2011). Thus we consulted video and branding research that attempts to ground such identities historically, looking for the influence and significance of locally bound symbolism (Cayla and Arnould 2008). This search included looking for the existence or transmission of a yoga habitus, through yoga toys, which was mediated by the guru principle, that is, whether some form of moral training was present. Habitus are notably difficult to operationalise, and such operationalisation is a step ahead of what is introduced in this study, as it would require the research to be complemented by interviews with the children and parents as well as with parents and grandparents.

Our approach considers mostly the impact of commercial and political global brands upon distributed networks of consumers who, through shared consumption, become members of the 'global village' (McLuhan and Powers 1989). One of the aims has been to chart the narratives of both producers and consumers of yoga dolls through market segment and content analysis. We understand that such narratives play an important role in promoting yoga lifestyles to children and might relate to the guru principle.[1] The focus on narrative, as we propose, is not intended to emphasise storytelling as a pedagogical tool, or to expose or even reject the logic of grand narratives with a postmodern critique and its ontological relativism. Here, our understanding of narrative encompasses the reality of the world and its impact on the lives of individuals. Narrative is therefore a process of finding meaning or making sense of one's experience and context in a real world, even if the narrative itself may not be accurate and may change over time. From this perspective material causality is not a matter of perception; it is real and limits the scale of human experience, agency and interactions, regardless of the discourses it engenders (Bhaskar 2016). Importantly, narratives and meanings are not only individual constructs but also collective and social ones, which some industries have been more effective than others in exploring. That is the case with marketing practices such as branding, which are used by several commercial, political and religious organisations to create meaning and sell ideas through products and services.

The first section of this chapter introduces some of the major trajectories and narratives interconnecting yoga, gurus and dolls in Indian and global contexts. It highlights how they are infused with assumptions about desirable modes of living and social distinctions. The second section assesses the Indian government's aspirations for yoga and indigenous toys in light of its vision of India as the world's guru. The third section examines how, in the non-Indian context, yoga dolls are means of articulating idealised lifestyles and identities, as aspired to by the middle classes for their offspring. The section also explains why, at least among children, the mediation of the guru principle through yoga dolls and narratives occurs in a rather limited manner.

Histories, stories and narratives surrounding yoga, gurus and dolls

> The invention of toys in India took place during the Indus Valley Civilization, nearly 8000 years ago in history.
>
> (IMARC 2023)

> India has a rich legacy in toy-making. Historically Indian toys date back to 5000 years. The excavated toys and dolls found in Harappa and Mohenjo-Daro included small carts, dancing woman, etc.
>
> (Ministry of Tourism n.d.)

The ur-doll, as it were

The splicing of history, myth, nostalgia and aspiration plays an unremarked role in the mediation of the guru principle. For millennia, anthropomorphic dolls have been imbued with religious symbolism (*pratīkatva*, 'being an image or symbol'; *pratīka-darśana*, 'a symbolic conception'), as iconographic forms have been used for ceremonial and educational purposes (Wright 2021, 103). Children have used dolls in imaginative play scenarios to emulate the domestic surroundings within which they live, which complicates the relations between dolls that were religious accoutrements and those that were toys. However, material cultural remains demonstrate that some clear distinctions between religious symbols and toys existed. Nonetheless, in certain cases, there were overlapping forms and uses. Mishra and Roy (2017, 71) claimed that this '5000 years' of tradition is bound up in cloth dolls. This point, however, might not have much to do with yoga dolls and their antiquity, even though there are millennia-long continuities, all the way from ancient Mesopotamia to the contemporary south Indian incorporation of dolls within the Navarātri festival and their glocal commodification (Ilkama 2018; Parpola 2020).

Drawn from an area located across modern-day Punjab and Sindh and straddling parts of Pakistan and India, the archaeological record has revealed the perennial and universal nature of the figurine play that occurred during South Asia's earlier periods (see Renfrew et al. 2017). From several sites such as Harappa, Mohenjodaro, Chanhudaro and Kot Diji, Lothal and Kalibangan, numerous terracotta, stone and metal figurines have been excavated. The earliest terracotta representations have been dated to the pre-ceramic, Neolithic, Pre-Harappan Phase (3700–3300 BCE) and located at Mergarh in Balochistan, Pakistan (Hooda et al. 2018). So, too, during the initial Early Harappan Phase ('Ravi') of the Indus Valley Civilisation (IVC) at Harappa (3300–2600 BCE), and the maturing Kot Diji Phase (2800–2600 BCE), at the archaeological site of Kot Diji, several 'mother goddess' sculptures were discovered.

At these sites, clay toys of varying levels of complexity and style, including male and female dolls, carts and several animals, suggest children were engaged in mimetic play of daily domestic activities and household chores (Chase et al. 2014). Popular speculations about the IVC often inform narratives about yoga's past. Many essentialise it into a 'timeless and unchanging' past indexed by an uncritical '5,000 years old' date. By way of example, inconclusive information is overdetermined in interpretations of the 'Paśupati seal' (Proto-Śiva), which is consistently recycled as incontrovertible evidence of postural yoga's supposed pre-Vedic antiquity. John Marshall was the first to promote this idea (1931, 52–6), which reflects neo-Romantic sentiments about popular literature and academia. However, as Srinivasan (1984) explained, there is little evidence to support such claims. Parpola (2017, 2020) discussed how the symbolism inherent in this seal emerged in western Asia, in Uruk (ancient Sumeria, modern-day Iraq). It was central to the 'contest motif' that signalled royalty and an ancient Mesopotamian priestly class. This particular seal was probably worn to indicate social rank, while other seals were used to administer the state, identify property and enable migration, perhaps like travel documents.

Therefore, the Harappan seals are not some ancient card game for kids, and yoga's postural roots are not long enough to reach the IVC (Varma 2018). Similarly, the 'dancing girl' figurine makes an improbable first yoga doll.

Fashionable dolls, sustainable lifestyles

In the non-Indic context, the iconic Barbie doll emerged in 1959 (Spencer 2019), and fashion dolls emerged in Western Europe during the seventeenth and eighteenth centuries as a convenient and affordable way to distribute and promote novel fashion trends (Werlin 2019). Today, the gendered dichotomy separating 'action figures' for boys and 'fashion figures' for girls ultimately reduces both to 'toys' (Reece 2018). Still, anthropomorphic toys are an essential learning aid. Playing out imaginary real-world social activities and relations supports children's learning and the developmental process. Yoga and toys are similarly informed and validated through language. The biomedical discourse, for instance, accounts for about 90 per cent of academic literature on yoga published in the past 40 years (Lourenço 2019, 7). This layer of understanding of yoga praxis is not only an additional interpretation but a justification, a reasoning for doing it. It would appear that the subjectivity of playing with toys and the logic of the yoga practice both supposedly assume an objective public rationale encoded in the biomedical rhetoric. Just as playing with toys is promoted to benefit a child's psychological, physical and social development, across most wellness segments, including in India, yoga is encouraged mainly for health benefits. Thus, biomedical narratives are often used to promote yoga lifestyles and are linked to the general perception among yoga practitioners that such a lifestyle facilitates material personal transformation by encouraging steps towards lasting, positive change (Butera et al. 2021).

Furthermore, the proximity of yoga to the spiritual heritage of Indic, European and American cultures ensures that both discourses (biomedical and lifestyle) are infused with religious, esoteric and indigenous renderings. The promotion and consumption of yoga dolls benefit from appealing to both discourses. Desirable outcomes merge the dual biomedical discourse of promoting children's development, preparing them for a healthier youth and adulthood with possible (lifestyle) articulations about spirituality and tradition. A pertinent example is the way in which indigenous wellbeing is romanticised in tourism advertising (Phillips et al. 2021). Raj (2005, 140) explained one way in which a doll mediates the guru's presence. Some devotees of Mata Amritanandamayi, also known as Amma ('the mother'), or the 'hugging saint', carry dolls in her likeness. Available from Amma's website, the dolls are located under the Inspirations tab. For the devotees, Amma's most visible and symbolic good is her hug. This is her method of dispensing *darśana* ('exchange of vision'). The regular format for her large-scale public events includes people lining up, possibly for several hours, to receive a brief embrace. In lieu of an actual hug, many devotees have come to regard the dolls as literal containers of her divine energy and sacred presence. This leads the devotees to long for the – by proxy – 'tactile experience of an embrace' (Lucia 2014, 62). Mazzarella (2006, 496) suggested that Amma's perceived spiritual power partly results from the dolls being produced locally and from her discarded clothing. 'Closing the distance' between the devotee and the guru through an avatar-like doll possibly potentiates a dialectical effect of awe-inspiring authority and distanced obedience.

Each doll could be thought to act like a radio tower relaying information, transmitting and distributing the guru's attention, creating

Figure 2.1 'Barbie movimientos made to move opinion', by Maria Martinez Dukan. CC BY-NC-ND 2.0. https://www.flickr.com/photos/68421420@N03/31751584916.

a coherent ideological network of nodes (i.e., the dolls) through which the community's lifestyle is replicated. Through the distribution of the doll, the mediation of the guru's ambient gaze can be imagined as similar to a Wi-Fi signal or the panopticon vision of CCTV cameras, which unconsciously prime individuals towards prosocial and prescribed standards of behaviour. For example, an Amma doll staring across a devotee's bedroom would work, to some degree, to keep the devotee in check. In addition, the dolls appear to act as a buffer to reduce separation anxiety in individuals who long to be in the presence of their guru. It is, then, not surprising to know that some devotees quite literally consider that these 'dolls are Amma' (Lucia 2014, 64). However, even though the Amma doll is an interesting example of guru mediation, it does not neatly fit into the yoga doll category that is the focus of this chapter. It does provide a compelling template for considering the interpersonal and transhuman dynamics, while not forsaking the possibility that some devotees might 'do yoga' with the doll.

Results from experimental economic games demonstrate that the presence of 'witnesses', even if they are simply images of robots with large human-like eyes, encourages more altruistic behaviour and decision making when the allocation of scarce resources is involved (Bering 2006). The role of the ambient gaze in the transformative socialisation of the individual is further explained by a belief in watchful supernatural agents that militate against the psychological state of deindividuation, which causes people to follow group, instead of personal, norms. While deindividuation occurs during moments of ecstatic or devotional singing (*kīrtana*), in which an environment of collective identification can lead to the inculcation of a collectivised habitus, the subjective individual self remains. Regarding the cultivation of shared emotions, 'atmospheres' (affective properties) and 'moods' (affective states) work together to produce shared aesthetic experiences, which actively regulate behaviour by facilitating possibilities for expanding or retracting social connectedness (Trigg 2021).

In the case of the yoga dolls, one might speculate how the general concept of the guru's panopticon-like gaze, filtered through the facilitation of online yoga classes, might cultivate transitioning from an individuated state to one which is deindividuated. This transition is central to the perceived transformational power of the 'yogic lifestyle' and to the guru's power. Speculating, then, on the mediated role of the guru possibly embodied in the yogic identities of the animated versions of yoga dolls, we intend to develop a nuanced understanding of the dynamic role (and relationship) these yoga dolls (and their gazes) may have in transforming individuals. At the heart of this process is the perennial cultivation of affective desire, which is associated with German Romanticism and its move away from industrialisation and towards nature (Heelas 2008). This informs the emergence of the 'leisure class' and the environmentalist sentiment so ingrained in popular ideations of a yoga lifestyle.

However, since material wealth is not necessarily a predictor of emotional well-being (Kahneman and Deaton 2010), and time poverty negatively affects an individual's lifestyle during their lifespan regardless of their material resources, the effect of following a yoga lifestyle on practitioners' actual social capital is limited. This leads into Schlossberg's (2019) concept of 'inconspicuous consumption' and its inversion of Veblen's ([1899] 2009) idea; instead of displaying wealth and status via material or practical consumption, there is an impulse to consume things of an immaterial and esoteric nature. Thus, the symbolic capital generated through investing in oneself, responsibly and sustainably, in the ongoing march towards the accumulation of unbridled superpowers in a utopia-inspired *Übermenschlichkeit* ('superhumanity'), seems to be what informs the social distinction permeating the narratives about yoga lifestyles, products and services. Moreover, if narratives can remain ideologically coherent, while obscuring the reproduction of social inequalities, then the subject's perception of reality – as mediated through the (non-human) guru principle – requires the expansion of mythological boundaries into such places as yoga studios and retreats, and into other modes of identity and belonging. Meaning, then, is mediated in multiple ways and assumes its more personal and contextualised form according to multiple dimensions. The next two sections discuss how yoga dolls are infused with universal and particular meanings through macro narratives which attempt to appeal to individual and social identities.

Globally aspiring yoga gurus: the Indian government and an indigenous toy industry

In India's current consumer market, the relationship of caste to power has shifted. This is because of the tidal forces of modernisation that have compressed the central-peripheral distribution of 'purity' through the labour market's transformation of a traditional agrarian economy (Kothari and Das 2016). As the disarray of urbanisation has brought global brands into a glocal context, yoga's soft-power export has covered the globe, while mass-produced dolls spread to the remotest of Indian villages. Somewhere in the glocal meshing of yoga with dolls linger traditional and idealised notions of yoga and gurus. Still, it is challenging to find any

Indian-produced and -marketed yoga doll. One oblique example is the representations of gods, such as the toys and accompanying books produced by Modi Toys (2022), which target a Hindu consumer base. These plush dolls feature Hanumān, Kṛṣṇa, Dūrgā and Sarasvatī. Each has a button in the abdomen, which, once pressed, plays a deity-specific set of mantras. While not marketed explicitly as yoga dolls, they could be used in such a play scenario for such a purpose. They are, however, another way through which the mediation of the guru could occur. Though the toys are marketed for 0–2-year-olds, thereby expanding the definition of the mediation of the guru principle through non-human forms as the intergenerational transmission of knowledge, these plush toys of Hindu deities reciting mantras as part of didactic and informal pedagogy do mediate the guru principle, insofar as they are capable of informing behaviours and attitudes, and set the context for the establishment of a *paramparā*.

The Toy Association of India (2022) intends to facilitate trust and cooperation between India's 800 toy and game manufacturers in a domestic market valued at US$2 billion. This is approximately 1 per cent of the world market (IMARC 2022). India and China are expanding markets because of their population size and rising disposable incomes; however, India's toy industry struggles to meet domestic demand and expectations. Growth has been compromised by retailer preference for Chinese-made goods, which account for more than 90 per cent of the market. This scenario leads to local manufacturers being unable to meet consumer demand for locally made products (Dhar 2020). As a result, India's prime minister asserted that the time had come for the local industry to 'doll up' and increase production (Krishnakumar 2020). Parallel to this, the Self-reliant India campaign (Ātmanirbhar Bhārat) is a calculated approach aimed at helping India to rise in the global soft-power rankings by promoting 'Vocal for Local' products, in the hope that they will eventually transform into globally recognisable brands (McClory 2018; Dubey and Dubey 2020; Sharma and Gupta 2021; Atmanirbhar Bharat 2022). Perhaps, with Modi's stated intention to further India's global expansion through the international promotion of its '*swadeshi* toy industry', in the not-too-distant future various yoga-doll product lines might emerge (IANS 2020; IBEF n.d.).

To what degree might this new way forward limit or potentiate the promotion and mediation of the guru principle? For instance, at a global level, we consider 'What better way to increase awareness of kids to Yoga than to do so with YEGO?' (Coquelz 2020a, 2020b). This slogan was used by an individual who asked LEGO to create a YEGO line (yoga + LEGO). LEGO has an open system whereby individuals can petition the company, and LEGO might create the product if a minimum demand is reached. In this case, YEGO fell short of the required number of signatures and was not produced. Still, YEGO illustrates how more than goodwill and intentions are required to affect changes in consumer and producer demands and expectations. It also suggests that, although yoga enjoys mainstream levels of cultural interest and is in a mature, if not saturated, phase of its lifecycle, stretching the transformational lifestyle practice of yoga into the realm of children's toys seems a complicated option.

Furthermore, India's self-reliance, when combined with its new conservative vision, calls for a break from the past to move into a 'New India' (Banerjee 2020). While Modi considers this the only way forward, one might ponder how breaking with the past squares with promoting traditional handcrafts and cultures. In India, traditional toys compete with online gaming, particularly in the 15+ age groups. India is at a disadvantage in producing all things electronic. This is because of the high import duties on the equipment needed to expand the electronic toy market, which China and Taiwan already dominate. In the past, Modi has relied on a rhetorical device, referring to India as the 'viśva guru; world guru' (Singh 2014). Modi's political party, the Bharatiya Janata Party (BJP), or the Indian People's Party, contends that India's soft power does not operate at total capacity and that India can increase its 'magnetic power' by returning to the *viśva-guru* status it apparently once enjoyed (BJP 2014, 40). According to the BJP's manifestos, building a 'new and resurgent India' (p. 36) requires 'strengthening our cultural roots and preserving civilisational continuity' through the 'promotion of Sanskrit and Yoga' (BJP 2019, 36).

Globally, 'as the world celebrates 21st June as the International Yoga Day', the Indian government has sought to 'promote Yoga as a vital method to achieve physical wellness and spiritual rejuvenation across the globe and will continue to work towards training of Yoga practitioners' through 'rapid expansion of Yoga health hubs, Yoga tourism and research in Yoga' (BJP 2019, 36). The Indian state intends to position itself as the 'world guru' and leverage further nation-building expansionist aspirations across the US$4.5 trillion global wellness, leisure and cultural/spiritual tourism industry, in which intangible yoga-oriented, Sanskrit-inflected experiences are anticipated to draw many tourists because of 'Yoga tourism' being considered a force for potential transformation of the individual, communities and the world (Dillette et al. 2019). Although, at least in the north Indian state of Uttarakhand, which is home to the supposed 'yoga capital of the world', Rishikesh, the development rhetoric has materially transformed little (McCartney 2021b).

The BJP attempts to mediate the yoga guru through a non-human, anthropomorphically animated version of Modi, through the initiative

'Yoga with Modi' (BJP 2018; Yoga with Modi 2022). This avatar has some similarities to the online form Barbie and other dolls take. The viewers find Modi's avatar to be the sole participant in the room, and even though it is not Modi's voice giving the instructions, it looks as if Modi is the one teaching. In these instances, the claims of India be(com)ing the world guru are compressed into Modi's yoga guru avatar. However, while multiple 'yoga classes' are available in many languages (12 Indian and 12 non-Indian), the view ratios were relatively low. By comparison, as at April 2023, Modi's two official Twitter accounts have 87.5 and 52.7 million followers (Narendramodi 2022; PMOIndia 2022). But when we compared Modi's Twitter profiles with the official YouTube accounts, both 'Yoga with Modi' (64,300 subscribers) and 'Narendra Modi' (14.3 million subscribers), it is clear that while Modi is more popular through Twitter, his yoga YouTube channel has significantly fewer subscribers. This discloses a particular trend regarding the type of mediation of Modi's guru principle. These videos were uploaded in 2018, and the extent of their softer yogic power appears restrained, since 95 per cent of the total 1.7 million views came from within the Indic group of languages; even though geotagging of the views is not available, we assume that some come from the diaspora. Either way, this demonstrates a significant cultural and linguistic insularity. Notably, even though yoga teachers and studios have turned to the internet in order to provide yoga classes during these pandemic-constrained times of social distancing, no new videos have been uploaded on Yoga with Modi. If these videos were intended to broaden the International Day of Yoga's global reach, they appear to have fallen short of the mark.

The validation of guru yoga dolls requires further examination regarding their conceptualisation and production. Considering what specific lifestyles dolls such as Barbie represent, and whether this product can continue to diversify in an ever-changing environment (Pilu36 2022, 1), ethical issues arise concerning the translocation or imposition of the all-American Barbie into or on the clothes, tones and ethnicities of other cultures. According to Nemani, 'The way in which the current Barbie undergoes mere superficial ethnic modifications only furthers inaccurate and misguided cultural and gender-based stereotypes in young females' (2011, 36). Yet the Indian online retailer of children's toys, FirstCry, markets Indian Barbie dolls, in India, in the following way.

> Celebrate diversity with this unique fashion doll that encourages real-world storytelling and open-ended dreams. Dressed in a fashionable outfit designed to reflect the world girls see around

them, offering infinite ways to play out stories and express their style. This detailed, articulated doll is a perfect new addition to your child's doll collection.

(FirstCry 2022)

The alleged diversity of these uniquely costumed dolls, in saris, etc., presents a conservative representation of Indians through their being dressed in stereotypical costumes. While it is arguably ethnically sensible, there appears to be no Indian equivalent of the yoga doll or of, for example, Barbie's wellness/athleisure line. However, even though it is difficult to find examples of specifically Indian-made and *deśī*-('Indian'-) inspired yoga dolls, such items exist. They are sold through online vendors such as Amazon and Flipkart. While one is classified by its Indian retailer as a yoga doll (RV 2022), they differ from their global counterparts because they do not have articulated limbs and are advertised as 'Garden Yoga Dolls' (RV 2022). Flipkart, which is an Indian online retailer similar to Amazon, sells three brands of yoga dolls with articulated limbs. The first is from Barbie's Made to Move line (Barbie Doll 2022; Barbie Store 2022), while the other two are from the Indian brand Poksi (2022, 2023), even though information about this brand remains elusive. Both the Yoga Sparkle Girl Doll and the New Yoga Doll for Kids have purpose-built articulations; however, the newer doll can apparently 'perform all the aasanas' (Poksi 2023).

In contrast, the online retailer aptly named Desi Toys promotes its range of products as 'Classic timeless Indian toys and games, skill-enhancing and sustainable, 100% made in India', which are 'nostalgic' and 'iconic' (Desi Toys 2022). Desi Toys is a premier example of the type of Indian (*deśī*)-style material culture that Modi wants to use to become the world guru, though, even if they provide 'safe, durable and super fun iconic toys and games', which '[engage] and [enhance] essential life skills' (Desi Toys 2022), the types of toys amount to wooden spinning tops, miniature kitchen sets and chess boards. Importantly, neither yoga nor yoga dolls are mentioned.

Globally aspiring gurus from California: Mattel and AZ I AM

In 2019, the global toy market was valued at US$22.1 billion and was projected to grow at a compound annual growth rate (CAGR) of 1.4 per cent between 2020 and 2025 (Azoth Analytics 2020). North America

Figure 2.2 Hybrid 'yoga' doll: head is from Cy Girls XIXOX 'Bloody Rose' character and the body is a Soldier Story – large chest body. CC BY-NC-ND 2.0. https://www.flickr.com/photos/7972566@N02/1199388107.

Figure 2.3 'Made to move Barbie DHL84 (2015)', by shadow-doll. CC BY-NC-SA 2.0. https://www.flickr.com/photos/55615037@N02/25525812723.

headed the regional markets, as did the 9–15 years age category, which accounts for almost 50 per cent market share of the total global market across all segments and ages.

The following are some of the brands of yoga dolls available: Zita (Zita Element 2022); Yoga Kung Fu Monkey Dolls (Quaidenu 2022), Our Generation Lucy Grace Doll and Dress Along Dolly (Our Generation Store 2023); Black Girl Doll with Yoga Set (Nice2You 2022); Baby Stella (Manhattan Toys 2023), AZ I AM (AZ I AM 2022b) and the most popular of all, Barbie's Made to Move doll (see Figures 2.2 and 2.3), which, just like the other dolls, is ethnically diverse and comes with different skin tones, hair colours and styles. It is important to note that the inculturation into particular consumption modes extends into accessories and clothing. While a doll is only one unit, its wardrobe is incomplete because of the endless array of yoga-related athleisure wear outfits available to purchase.

In 2020, Mattel's Barbie brand generated gross sales of about US$1.35 billion, up from about US$1.16 billion in 2019, with over half of Mattel's revenues generated in the North American region (Statista 2022a, 2022b). In 2021, the Barbie brand was named the 2020 Top Global Toy Property of the Year and Europe's Top Gaining Toy Property by Category (NPD Group 2021). This demonstrates the mediatory power of Barbie. Richard Dickson, President and COO of Mattel, explained that

> Barbie is more than a doll, she is a pop culture icon. She has proven her staying power by remaining both timeless and timely, continuing to lead and reinvent the fashion doll category. Barbie has created new and compelling ways of engaging consumers through new product innovation, cultural relevance, digital dialog, and the celebration of female role models. In 2020 the brand also honored frontline healthcare workers and furthered its mission to inspire the limitless potential in every girl through the Barbie Dream Gap Project initiative.
>
> (Mattel 2023)

Mattel's (2021) initiative is an essential conduit for transmitting, translating and transforming the empowering message and the vessel, that is, the consumer, which welcomes it. As at April 2023, the Barbie brand has 456 items in its product line. These are intended for ages 2–7 years and fit within a dominant price bracket of up to US$25 (Mattel 2022a). Products are broken down by category, type, theme, age and price. The two most pertinent themes are *Self-Care* and *Made to Move*, in which there is considerable overlap (Mattel 2022b). There were approximately 20 dolls which specifically cite or obliquely reference yoga. This includes the two variations of the *Breathe with Me* dolls, and the *GRL PWR* (Girl Power) dolls. Figurines are available in White, Black and Asian ethnicities and come with different hair colours and costumes. Twenty 'yoga' dolls out of 456 is approximately 4.5 per cent. From this analysis, further insight is gained regarding the potency of and potential for these versions of Barbie dolls to promote yoga lifestyles (though it shows what a small part of Barbie's empire yoga is).

Mattel has a host of issues stemming from mismanagement, which can be divided into legal issues, international supply chain issues, and increased technology-based toys. Across the globe, similar trends occur, with traditional toys and games forced to compete with electronic games by digitising and adapting to remain relevant and viable (Mordor Intelligence 2022). These technological advances satisfy the increasing demand for high-tech toys, draining preference away from traditional toys. As a result, dolls are transitioning into roles and domains better suited to digitised times, including developing online personas within metaverses filled with avatars.

Mattel and others continue to build online worlds in which users can interact with their dolls' avatars, shop for clothes and other goods, design a virtual apartment, invite other children to play, and engage with a pretend 'Wellness line with Barbie' that is 'all about physical wellness and emotional well-being' (GeekSpin 2020). Barbie's animated avatar explained, replete with its own social media handle (@Barbie 2017), 'I love doing yoga. I try to practice it every single day. And it's called "yoga practice", cause it's not really about perfecting or mastering a move. It's about the practicing of it. It's the journey.' @Barbie (2017) continued to explain in its 'Yoga Challenge' vlog that some of its favourite yoga postures were 'Balancing table pose', 'Chair pose', 'King Dancer pose', 'Warrior 3', 'Tree pose', 'Palm Tree pose' and 'Savasana'. This instance of a Sanskrit term for a posture was rare. We speculate that it might have something to do with translating *śavāsana*, which relates to *śava* (corpse). We conjecture that this might be a bit too heavy for Barbie's consumer base. Furthermore, this cryptic pun, in the following statement, 'What's your favorite yoga pose? P.A.C.E. Om!', demonstrates some transfer of Indic lexicon not typically present in the yoga doll *identikit*. While the inclusion of the all-encompassing 'Om' (ॐ) is obvious, the acronym-inflected pun, P.A.C.E., appears to signal 'peace (*śānti*)'.

P.A.C.E. covertly promotes the London-based pedagogical system known as 'Play, Adventure and Community Enrichment' (PACE 2022). Nevertheless, the expansion into cyberspace also accompanied technological advances in the actual materials composing the toys. As yoga dolls require flexibility for yoga poses, some versions of Barbie come with 22 articulating joints, which are specifically intended to increase the flexibility of the previously inflexible Barbie. While Barbie has a more dynamic lifestyle in its digitised form, its morning routine includes meditation. Moreover, the Breathe with Me Barbie features five 30-second meditations, which are activated by pressing the moon-shaped necklace. The following scripts reveal the contents of the meditations. Each is punctuated by low-resolution temple bell chimes and wheezy breathing.

> Meditation 1: How are you feeling? Use your voice with me. Breathe. 'Aaaaah.' (Repeated five times.)
> Meditation 2: Let's take an imaginary bubble wand and blow an imaginary bubble. Breathe. 'Aaaah.'
> Meditation 3: Repeat after me, 'I am strong', 'I am loved', 'I am unique', 'I can be anything'.
> Meditation 4: Imagine your feelings are fluffy clouds. Now, let's breathe in and out like this. Breathe in and out. 'Aaaah.'
> Meditation 5: Take a deep breath in, like you are smelling a beautiful flower. Breathe out and in. 'Aaaah.'
>
> (Azusa Barbie 2020)

Mattel has also made attempts to combine explicit yoga-related skills and child play. Fisher-Price offers toddlers the Meditation Mouse, which obliquely references an Indic frame through the creation of a portmanteau using morphophonemic matching between nama(ste)+stay, as in 'to help your little one learn how to nama-stay relaxed' and the double sensorial appeal of sound through the guided meditation and touch from the cuddly experience.

> The Meditation Mouse from Fisher-Price® introduces your toddler to guided meditation through physical prompts and breathing exercises to help them unwind during the day and before bedtime. This soothing plush mouse is the go-to calming cuddle buddy to help your little one learn how to nama-stay relaxed. Choose from 3 calming modes, including a daytime relaxation session, a nighttime soothing sounds mode, and a 3-part bedtime wind-down exercise.
>
> (Mattel 2022c)

This blatant example of a mouse doll mediating the guru principle in a practical and emotionally meaningful fashion highlights the role of meaning and narratives in conceptualising the need for such a product. Meaning derives from resources available to people through their subjective experiences and personal, social, political, cultural and environmental contexts, which can be and are exploited by market forces. Thus, the popular perception of meditation as something beneficial and calming meets the context of contemporary busy parents of often over-stimulated children and assumes meanings such as 'soothing' or 'mindful toy' for the former and 'cuddle buddy' for the latter, facilitating the acceptance of the fluffy guru and its message by the family. Here, the purchasing act entails a commitment to what the guru envisions or represents and, to a certain extent, constitutes a symbolic conversion. Unlike human gurus, who are limited by their historical context, charisma and mortality, non-human gurus can capture ideas and ideals that, if not atemporal, are temporally meaningful, seamlessly moving between the material and the virtual and from one generation to the next, with the potential benefit of remaining culturally relevant through unlimited updates. This is even more the case in configurations which follow the logic of yoga-related offers in the spiritual and wellness markets.

As a meaning-making practice mainly taught by women to women, in the past decades contemporary yoga has incorporated developments intrinsically linked to womanhood and notions of femininity. Hybrids such as yoga for pregnancy, postnatal yoga, baby yoga, yoga for kids and teen yoga are all late but popular additions to the yoga portfolio that follow the cycle of motherhood and (gendered) nurturing roles. In this context, yoga dolls are not an unlikely fit. Indeed, they may have emerged in tune with these developments as a bridge between the values and lifestyles of mothers and their aspirations for their offspring. In this way, yoga dolls could be a prop used to teach yoga-related skills such as meditation, postures and breathing and individual and collective perceptions of the relevance of such practices as self-control, social responsibility, spiritual development and a naturalist lifestyle.

However, focusing on this well-intentioned development of yoga would obscure a crucial characteristic of its demographic; across the globe, yoga is overwhelmingly a middle- and upper-class phenomenon that fails to spread beyond its high socio-economic influences and their firmly gendered, racialised and educationally privileged divides. That is, the yogic habitus seems to be a desirable part of the Western and Westernised middle and upper classes' sociocultures. Although yoga dolls can reflect the meaningful interplay between yoga and motherhood encouraged by yoga practitioners, this interplay would not necessarily involve the production of new dolls. The nature of meaning-making practices is that they can easily be adapted to fit many contexts, which, arguably, any doll could. Consequently, the category of yoga doll as something the doll *is* rather than something that any doll *does* assumes such a form when broader ideological narratives (rather than personal and localised ones) are deployed. When yoga dolls are articulated in general terms by agents operating at the national or global levels of society, they tend to become instruments signalling a uniformity of meaning and identity.

In the context of mass-produced dolls, of which consumer culture determines the relevance and profitability, possibilities of meaning are diluted into mostly dominant-class ambitions that are currently centred on the environment, bodies and lifestyles, along with the unlikely – but not unexpected – combination of capitalist values such as individualism and meritocracy with liberal anxieties about diversity and inclusion. Barbie has many skin shades, hairstyles and fashionable items, but remains virtually young and healthy, fit and successful, independent and beautiful and, ultimately, never poor. A yoga Barbie is even better as it has every element of its life updated or justified by its commitment to mainstream optimistic assumptions of yoga lifestyles. As a result, it is not only better articulated, it is articulate. Its lithe body accompanies a mindful athleisure outfit; it is busy but meditates; it has a high socio-economic status but can give to charity and recycle; it is healthy because it cares for the environment through its lifestyle. Barbie's 'yogic' update is akin to adding another layer of privilege to the already privileged socio-economic context of those likely to pay for and play with it.

What is new in the process of yogification of dolls is that, unlike most yoga-related products, it is overwhelmingly an initiative from agents outside the yoga industry, whose engagement with yoga and perceived yogic values is notably minute. It is undoubtedly a market effort to ensure Barbie remains socially and culturally relevant. Thus, as a guru doll, it is hardly mediating any yoga learning besides recorded meditations, calls for breathing, and mobile limbs; instead, it seems to be mediating the reaffirmation of an identity marker and the transmission of updated class-based values and the habitus of a socioculture. This becomes explicit through the way yoga is informing its lifestyle, worldview and fashion, but keeps it unpretentiously marginal, orbiting its possibilities among other exciting activities in its middle-class menu, such as doing gymnastics and playing the guitar. Although Barbie's traditional 'biological' limitations have been addressed by competitors, whose freedom from nostalgia allows their dolls to be presented with more realistic bodies and ecologically sensitive materials, the considerably higher price tag of such dolls highlights how dolls potentiate more desirable lifestyles, and are often symbols of social distinction for a select consumer base which can afford and is already familiar with such values. That yoga dolls can express positive social change through yoga associations and yet reinforce the status quo is not surprising. For they are, above all, products in an economy constantly feeding on the wealth and profitable interests, ambitions and anxieties of its target – but never truly challenging them.

When yoga toys explicitly emerge within a context of familiarity with yoga culture, the potential for challenging the status quo as mediatised gurus appears to be more meaningful and thus relevant, but not necessarily freer. One ought to consider the irrepressible gravity of India's caste system and how yoga is mediated through it (see Argenal and Bajaj 2021).

One way yoga can reformulate things is through Yoga Joes, traditional plastic soldiers that, instead of carrying guns, are contorted into different yoga postures. They represent a concerted effort by individual agents to advance yoga beyond its usual demographics (Sinha 2018). Bringing yoga back into a hyper-masculine context linked to military activities (Pinch 2012) ironically re-articulates it as a practice befitting masculinity, in that conflict and uniformity are replaced by peaceniks and diversity of colourful yoga postures.

This initiative is an example of what yoga dolls can teach, how they can act as potential gurus and how they are always bound to their context and invented realities. The Yoga Joes are not challenging the perceived assumptions about masculinities and the perceptibly less flexible male body. They have no articulated parts, and their postures are rigid and reliant on physicality and strength. Besides, the notion of non-harming is at odds with the ideology represented by the military uniform. Rather than peace, yoga is already used to improve efficacy in attack and resilience in recovery from potentially traumatic military operations. It seems that if Yoga Joes could have the intended impact on male openness to yoga, that openness would still be negotiated in terms of conventional gendered norms and territories of masculinity. This reflection implies that the mediatisation of gurus through yoga dolls is largely limited by context and therefore unlikely to produce outcomes beyond familiarisation and perhaps identification with social and cultural elements already pervading children's experiences.

Mattel's new competitor and Barbie's next rival comes not from the toy industry but from yoga entrepreneurship. The AZ I AM yoga doll offers a range of ethnic identities and claims to be the world's first (AZ I AM 2022a). Despite its reference to Asianness, AZ I AM is based in Santa Monica, CA. Founded by a yoga teacher, the company provides activewear collections, 14 children's books with yoga and wellness themes and

'The World's First Yoga Doll and Soul Model collections'. A dominant narrative used by the company is the promotion of its branding in association with idealised forms of femininity and female spirituality, such as in 'Modern Goddess':

> Modern Goddess: (Noun)
>
> A self-sufficient human female who honors Nature, is confident in Spirit and powerfully aligned with Truth. Her actions exude Integrity. She does not sell her Sexuality for gain or profit; it is her Sacred Power. Her choices are Authentic and clear in respecting all Life. She flows in Synchronicity and radiates Consciousness. Never sacrifice the Divinity of who You are. Live True.
>
> (AZ IA M 2022a)

The brand's embellished language is characteristic of certain forms of contemporary yoga as practised in anglophone countries. Likewise, its dolls explicitly refer to classical yoga philosophical concepts familiar to yoga practitioners. As a boutique purveyor of yoga-inflected lifestyle accoutrements, AZ I AM includes in its suite of yoga dolls eight 'diverse' figures, each one apparently highlighting an aspect of the eight limbs of the Yogasūtras of Patañjali (c.350 CE), even though they adapted, and in places inverted, the original meanings found in the primary text.

> The AZ I AM® Girlz doll collection are teenage girls, beautiful from the inside out, making a positive difference in the world today. The dolls were single-handedly created by esteemed yoga instructor and founder of AZ I AM® Yoga, Alanna Zabel. The AZ I AM® brand is dedicated to teaching girls to love who they are, as they are. Using the basics of Yoga to teach positive self- and social- awareness, we have designed dolls, plush pets, clothing, accessories, bags, yoga products, jewelry, headwear, games, programs and books to make the wellness experience more colorful and fun for your Goddess in Progress®. ... Based on the ancient eight-limbed path and philosophy of Yoga, we have matched modern day play patterns of young girls today with the essence of the 8 Limbs of Yoga philosophy as taught by Patanjali. Our focused intention is to offer young girls a doll that is not solely focused on looking glamorous, but instead learning positive states of being and giving back to social causes while also inspiring girls to be active, kind, and love themselves AZ I AM®.
>
> (AZ I AM 2022b)

Insofar as popular narratives around Patañjalayoga are often crowded by misrepresentations (Jacobsen 2018; White 2014), AZ I AM promotes a typical rendition of yoga's perceived ethics as if they were intended or indeed could be used to 'teach young girls about empowerment, about confidence' (AZ I AM 2022b). AZ I AM yoga dolls 'mediate' these teachings, refashioning them into contemporary ideals for children based as much on the company's peculiar interpretation of yoga philosophy as on the popular stereotypical portrayal of other cultures. For instance, the doll associated with the second limb (*niyama*) is the Niyama Nature Girl, who lives in Manaus, Brazil. Thus, it is green and eco-sensitive, and loves exploring the Amazon forest and eating açai berries. It has a pet monkey and wants to be a doctor. The doll associated with the fourth limb (Pranayama) is the Prana Fashion Girl, who lives in Yunnan, China. It lives with its grandmother and loves designing and sewing clothes; it has a pet elephant and is organising its first fashion show.

In the well-intentioned attempt to appeal to diversity, the company has constructed simplistic representations of Brazil, China and other countries, unifying them under a yogic label that has hardly any meaning to their citizens. More problematic is the lack of insight into the social inequality underlying such representations. So that yoga and fitness aficionados can enjoy the benefits of a superfood and accessible fancy clothing in the Global North, Niyama's contemporaries will be left with the cheapest part of the fruit, while Prana's will be working long hours on low wages in clothing production (possibly leaving their children with the grandparents). Interestingly, Santa Monica's doll, Asana, is associated with the most prominent part of contemporary yoga, postures, and is the only yoga teacher among the dolls. It is not given any central aspiration, nor does it have any exotic pet or background; it has a dog and seems to have a normal life in California. Asana's only aspiration seems to be educating others in the world about yoga, 'unpretentiously'.

One glimpse into the rhetoric informing the lifestyle promoted by yoga dolls includes Barbie's recorded affirmations, such as 'I am strong, I am loved, I am unique, I can be anything'. In contrast, AZ I AM dolls are promoted with more directional phrases such as 'I am strong, I am active, I am team spirit, I am kind, I am giving back, I am beautiful, AZ I AM' (Zabel 2023). While Barbie appears to prefer a universalist or global yoga lifestyle more aligned with contemporary living and urbanity, the AZ I AM dolls promote a yoga lifestyle explicitly linked with a reimagined Yogasūtra tradition, a naturalist nostalgia and more rigid expectations concerning behaviour and identification with the brand. The formations of such narratives by the two companies are unconnected to each other and originated from different social phenomena. On the one hand, Barbie is an iconic doll adopting a yoga-related lifestyle to remain relevant to contemporary children. On the other, yoga is an iconic practice propelled into the children's universe and market to affirm its relevance. That Barbie's and yoga's largest market is the USA, and that the first doll claiming to espouse traditional yoga philosophy is not from India but from Santa Monica, is hardly a coincidence.

Furthermore, when yoga dolls and toys are, from the outset, conceptualised in conversation with yoga traditions by those engaged with yoga practice, as in the case of AZ I AM dolls, this must be understood against the backdrop of a much larger multibillion-dollar industry centred on yoga classes which are taught in usually attractive studios in more economically vibrant urban areas by vastly underpaid yoga teachers. The development of yoga props, clothing, art and toys is not necessarily a commitment to spreading the so-called yoga values or lifestyle and often represents an attempt by individual agents to make a living out of selling yoga courses, workshops, teacher training programmes, retreats and paraphernalia so that they themselves can live the so-called yoga lifestyle. The economic nature and sometimes ingenuity of such structures ensure a constant influx of new ideas, styles and products within the yoga industry following, rather than a yogic, a global capitalist logic with obvious demands from consumer culture. Besides, by adopting a narrative in which yoga dolls can improve society through promoting a yoga lifestyle, such individuals may portray themselves as agents of change, re-signifying and overselling their relationship with yoga, yoga teaching and society. The industry is replete with famous examples of yoga teachers who were committed not so much to spreading yoga as to their unique interpretations of it (Singleton and Goldberg 2014).

Conclusion

As instruments mediating experience in tender developmental phases of the human brain, dolls and toys can have a great impact on someone's life. The extent to which the influences from these objects can mediate the principle of the guru is debatable. If we consider this principle to be centred on the mere circulation of ideas, dolls are certainly used in that way by commercial and nationalist forces, particularly as a means of conceptualising ideals of social identity and promoting expected modes of behaviour and lifestyles. However, if we acknowledge that the guru principle is only fulfilled when the transmission of knowledge is assimilated at the recipient's end, we also must consider the role of human agency in this process. Although the impact of guru dolls on children is beyond the scope of this study, research based on how children play with yoga and dolls in stop-motion videos suggests that yoga is pervading their imagination, but not precisely as gurus or adults might intend.

The most common theme associated with dolls doing yoga in videos made by children is the perceived difficulty of postures and subsequent boredom. The most commonly shown posture is the downward dog. There is little inflection of idealised lifestyles, yoga philosophy or tacit support of Hindu supremacy in the videos produced by children. This could reflect what children hear about yoga from the adults around them, or represent their own frustrations with the play options. We tentatively suggest, based on our study, that as individual meaning is internalised and temporarily articulated by the children, it is more likely that yoga narratives are taking their own directions through child play. However, this requires further analysis through qualitative investigation. Further investigation could also assess the tension between capitalist forces aiming at transmitting a universal/globalist agenda through yoga dolls and socially dominant forces within political and religious spheres that use yoga dolls to establish localised spiritual identities, nationalism and idealised interpretations of yoga texts.

From responses and testimonials about yoga dolls, it is evident that those buying such items are already participants in yoga classes or subscribe to yoga's spiritual or wellness aspirations, which supports our understanding that the dolls are merely a prop to reinforce a lifestyle and (class) identity already familiar to the child (see Reeves 2019). That is, yoga dolls are one possible way by which aspects of class habitus can be transmitted from one generation to the next within the same socioculture. For instance, we found no evidence that children of parents who do not partake in yoga classes are given yoga dolls. Moreover, on the occasions on which they are given such dolls, there is no reason to suggest that the objects represent any meaningful yoga teaching. As the context and resources required for the emergence and transmission of a yoga habitus are not present, it is highly unlikely that a child who has not consistently been exposed to meditation by their role models in the family will benefit from the 'teachings' of a doll that gives instruction in meditation.

Therefore we suggest that, at least among children, the potential of yoga dolls to mediate the guru principle is substantially restricted in relation to the transmission of yoga teachings. It might only occur when a yoga habitus is already established in the children's environment. Nevertheless, we suggest that non-human, non-anthropomorphic mediatisation of the guru principle does exist in such dolls in situations involving non-specific rather than detailed yoga teachings, as they can be simply and vaguely articulated within broader universalistic narratives, such as those about a generic healthier lifestyle or flexible bodies. In these contexts, yoga dolls can be symbols of a lifestyle. They certainly communicate the commitment or the intention to transmit such messages to children. Finally, from the present study it is not possible to separate such non-human gurus from the narratives which give meaning to them. Although they may constitute different aspects of the same social phenomenon, we also speculate about the extent to which meaningful narratives alone, without a human and non-human material vortex to anchor meanings and experiences, could manifest the guru principle in the same way. This might open new avenues for research on ideologies.

Note

1   The collected data included promotional material and reviews from online vendors of yoga dolls, mostly from North America and India, given their relevance to the sales of such dolls. Importantly, for the purpose of studying children's engagement with yoga dolls, we only analysed data publicly available on children's social media and YouTube for their toy- and yoga-related content. Video transcripts were extracted either manually or via automation processes. The total quantity of metadata collected exceeded 20,000 discrete videos. After this list had been refined for relevance, approximately 50 individual videos were selected. Different software from Rieder (2015) was employed, such as the forced aligner, Gentle, which produces precise timing information for transcripts (Ochshorn and Hawkins 2022), which were then analysed using the concordance software AntConc (Anthony 2022).

References

Anthony, Laurence. 2022. 'AntConc.' http://www.laurenceanthony.net/software/antconc/ (accessed 8 May 2023).

Argenal, Amy and Monisha Bajaj. 2021. 'Reclaiming spaces, reshaping practices: Yoga for building community and nurturing families of color', in *Practicing Yoga as Resistance: Voices of color in search of freedom*, edited by Cara Hagan, 38–48. Abingdon & New York: Routledge.

Atmanirbhar Bharat. 2022. 'What is "vocal" about "local"?' https://web.archive.org/web/20220313162306/https://atmanirbharbharat.in/vocal-for-local/ (accessed 8 May 2023).

AZ I AM. 2022a. 'Goddess in Progress® – I AM Perfect AZ I AM®'. https://www.aziamkidz.com/ (accessed 8 May 2023).

AZ I AM. 2022b. '8 Limbs of Yoga'. https://www.aziamkidz.com/pages/8-limbs-of-yoga (accessed 8 May 2023).

Azoth Analytics. 2020. 'Global toy market: Analysis by product type, by age, by distribution channel, by region, by country (2020 edition): Market insights and outlook post Covid-19 pandemic (2020–2025)'. https://www.researchandmarkets.com/reports/5139335/global-toy-market-analysis-by-product-type-by?utm_source=CI&utm_medium=Press Release&utm_code=9k3sj9&utm_campaign=1436080+-+Global+Toy+Market+(2020+to+2025)+-+by+Product+Type%2c+Age%2c+Distribution+Channel%2c+Region%2c+%26+Country+&utm_exec=jamu273prd (accessed 8 May 2023).

Azusa Barbie. 2020. 'Meditate with Barbie'. YouTube. https://www.youtube.com/watch?v=dUi8cKk2bqY (accessed 15 February 2023).

Banerjee, Vikramjit. 2020. 'Tenets of new conservatism and the vision of Ātmanirbhar Bhārat'. Shyam Prashad Mukherjee Research Foundation, 8 September. https://www.spmrf.org/tenets-of-new-conservatism-and-the-vision-of-atmanirbhar-bharat/ (accessed 15 February 2023).

@Barbie. 2017. 'Barbie: Morning routine with meditation: Barbie vlogs: @Barbie'. YouTube. https://www.youtube.com/watch?v=DDTfDt8lCcY (accessed 15 February 2023).

Barbie Doll. 2022. 'Barbie Made to Move yoga doll'. https://www.flipkart.com/barbie-made-move-yoga-doll/p/itmf2a0d72f596fa?pid=DDHG5W8H4TXBSDQP&lid=LSTDDHG5W8H4TXBSDQPMZQOXN&marketplace=FLIPKART&q=yoga+doll&store=tng%2Fkks&srno=s_1_2&otracker=search&otracker1=search&fm=SEARCH&iid=d2dd9c5a-9ebe-4f53-ae51-3b96e9f7d053.DDHG5W8H4TXBSDQP.SEARCH&ppt=sp&ppn=sp&ssid=6nwjqtv07m1m8zk01642312288846&qH=c929f67d8070cd88 (accessed 15 February 2023).

Barbie Store. 2022. 'Barbie Made to Move doll (pink)'. https://www.amazon.in/Barbie-Made-Move-Doll-Pink/dp/B015EB27VY/ref=sr_1_1?crid=1XTTSEZYFFTDP&keywords=yoga+doll&qid=1641710263&s=toys&sprefix=yoga+doll%2Ctoys%2C372&sr=1-1 (accessed 15 February 2023).

Bering, Jesse M. 2006. 'The folk psychology of souls', *Behavioral and Brain Sciences* 29 (5): 453–98. https://doi.org/10.1017/s0140525x06009101.

Bhaskar, Roy. 2016. *Enlightened Common Sense: The philosophy of critical realism*. Abingdon: Routledge.

BJP. 2014. *Election Manifesto: 2014*. New Delhi: BJP.

BJP. 2018. 'Yoga with Modi (English)'. YouTube. https://www.youtube.com/watch?v=VWtHY710BL0 (accessed 15 February 2023).

BJP. 2019. 'Manifesto'. http://library.bjp.org/jspui/handle/123456789/2988 (accessed 15 February 2023).

Bourdieu, Pierre. 1984. *Distinction: A social critique of the judgement of taste*. Cambridge, MA: Harvard University Press.

Butera, Robert, Ilene S. Rosen and Jennifer Hilbert. 2021. *The Yoga Life: Applying comprehensive yoga therapy to all areas of your life*. Woodbury, MN: Llewellyn Publications.

Cayla, Julien and Eric J. Arnould. 2008. 'A cultural approach to branding in the global marketplace', *Journal of International Marketing* 16 (4): 86–112. https://www.doi.org/10.1509/jimk.16.4.86.

Chase, Brad, P. Ajithprasad, S. V. Rajesh, Ambika Patel and Bhanu Sharma. 2014. 'Materializing Harappan identities: Unity and diversity in the borderlands of the Indus Civilization', *Journal of Anthropological Archaeology* 35: 63–78. https://doi.org/10.1016/j.jaa.2014.04.005.

Copeman, Jacob and Aya Ikegame. 2012. 'The multifarious guru: An introduction', in *The Guru in South Asia: New interdisciplinary perspectives*, edited by Jacob Copeman and Aya Ikegame, 1–45. Abingdon: Routledge.

[Coquelz, Gregory]. 2020a. 'Yego'. Lego Ideas, 14 April. https://ideas.lego.com/projects/154cc77a-0764-4bc3-a17f-8ecc3916bd97 (accessed 15 February 2023).

Coquelz, Gregory. 2020b. 'Yego, a Lego Ideas project'. https://www.youtube.com/watch?v=0p4VyS2dEu8 (accessed 15 February 2023).

Desi Toys. 2022. 'Desi Toys'. https://www.desitoys.in/ (accessed 15 February 2023).

Dhar, Shobita. 2020. 'India's toy industry can't meet domestic demand, expectation', *Times of India*, 2 September. https://timesofindia.indiatimes.com/india/indias-toy-industry-cant-meet-domestic-demand-expectation/articleshow/77884539.cms (accessed 15 February 2023).

Dillette, Alana K., Alecia C. Douglas and Carey Andrzejewski. 2019. 'Yoga tourism: A catalyst for transformation?', *Annals of Leisure Research* 22 (1): 22–41. https://doi.org/10.1080/11745398.2018.1459195.

Di Placido, Matteo. 2020. 'Blending martial arts and yoga for health: From the last Samurai to the first Odaka Yoga Warrior', *Frontiers in Sociology* 5: art. no. 597845, 1–16. https://doi.org/10.3389/fsoc.2020.597845.

Dubey, Smita and Harish Kumar Dubey. 2020. 'Atmanirbhar Bharat Abhiyan: An analytical review', *UGC Care Group I Journal* 10 (7): 27–34. https://www.researchgate.net/publication/343139784_ATMANIRBHAR_BHARAT_ABHIYAN_AN_ANALYTICAL_REVIEW (accessed 28 March 2023).

FirstCry. 2022. 'Baby doll toy set & dollhouses for girls'. https://www.firstcry.com/barbie-dolls/5/91?scat=91@@@@@@@@~30@@1@0@20@@@@@@@@@&sort=Popularity?sort&q=as_BARBIE&asid=274 (accessed 15 February 2023).

Fleming, Crystal M., Veronica Y. Womack and Jeffrey Proulx (eds). 2022. *Beyond White Mindfulness: Critical perspectives on racism, well-being, and liberation.* Abingdon: Routledge.

GeekSpin. 2020. 'Breathe with me Barbie – these Barbie dolls help you meditate'. YouTube. https://www.youtube.com/watch?v=7YDuhM7s8bg (accessed 15 February 2023).

Heelas, Paul. 2008. *Spiritualities of Life: New Age Romanticism and consumptive capitalism.* Oxford: Blackwell.

Hooda, Rajesh, Rajpal and Kushal Parkash. 2018. 'Femininity in proto-historic South Asian art: An analytical study of Harappans', *Antrocom Online Journal of Anthropology* 14 (1): 139–47. http://www.antrocom.net/archives/2018/140118/Antrocom_14-1.pdf (accessed 4 May 2023).

IANS. 2020. 'PM chairs meeting to take "Swadeshi" toy industry global', *Siasat Daily*, 23 August. https://www.siasat.com/pm-chairs-meeting-to-take-swadeshi-toy-industry-global-1954883/ (accessed 15 February 2023).

IBEF. n.d. 'Indian toys'. Indian Brand Equity Foundation. https://www.ibef.org/indian-toys/ (accessed 5 July 2023).

Ilkama, Ina Marie Lunde. 2018. 'Dolls and demons: The materiality of Navarātri', in *Nine Nights of the Goddess: The Navarātri festival in South Asia*, edited by Caleb Simmons, Moumita Sen and Hillary Rodrigues, 157–78. Albany, NY: SUNY Press.

IMARC. 2022. 'Indian toys market: Industry trends, share, size, growth, opportunity and forecast 2023–2028'. IMARC, Noida, Uttar Pradesh. https://www.imarcgroup.com/indian-toys-market (accessed 8 May 2023).

Jacobsen, Knut A. 2018. *Yoga in Modern Hinduism: Hariharānanda Āraṇya and Sāṃkhyayoga.* Abingdon: Routledge.

Kahneman, Daniel and Angus Deaton. 2010. 'High income improves evaluation of life but not emotional well-being', *PNAS* 107 (38): 16489–93. https://doi.org/10.1073/pnas.1011492107.

Kothari, Ashish and Pallav Das. 2016. 'Power in India: Radical pathways', *CETRI: Southern Social Movements Newswire*, 1 February. https://www.cetri.be/Power-in-India-radical-pathways?lang=fr (accessed 15 February 2023).

Krishnakumar, Kritika. 2020. 'The Indian Toy Story: Rs.200 crore toy market is dominated 90% by China, time to doll-up for "local" production says PM Narendra Modi', *Indian Wire*, 31 August. https://www.theindianwire.com/business/the-indian-toy-story-rs-200-crore-toy-market-is-dominated-90-by-china-time-to-doll-up-for-local-production-says-pm-narendra-modi-287553/ (accessed 15 February 2023).

Lourenço, Diego. 2019. 'Has yoga teaching become a new type of yoga? An exploratory survey on yoga through UK yoga teachers'. MA dissertation, SOAS, University of London.

Lourenço, Diego. 2021. 'Le Brésil: Implantation du yoga dans une société multiculturelle', in *Yoga: L'encyclopédie*, edited by Ysé Tardan-Masquelier, 537–9. Paris: Albin Michel.

Lucia, Amanda J. 2014. *Reflections of Amma: Devotees in a global embrace.* Berkeley: University of California Press.

Lucia, Amanda. 2020. 'The global manifestation of the Hindu guru phenomenon', in *Routledge Handbook of South Asian Religions*, edited by Knut A. Jacobsen, 413–27. Abingdon: Routledge.

Lucia, Amanda. 2022. 'The contemporary guru field', *Religion Compass* 16 (2): art. no. e12427. https://doi.org/10.1111/rec3.12427.

Manhattan Toys. 2023. 'Wee Baby Stella 12" soft baby doll with yoga set'. Amazon. https://www.amazon.com/Manhattan-Toy-Baby-Stella-30-48cm/dp/B07NJKR7JD/ref=sr_1_2?keywords=manhattan+toys+baby+stella+yoga&sr=8-2 (accessed 5 May 2023).

Marshall, John (ed.). 1931. *Mohenjo-daro and the Indus Civilization: Being an official account of archaeological excavations at Mohenjo-daro carried out by the Government of India between the years 1922 and 1927*, vol. 1. London: Arthur Probsthain.

Mattel. 2021. 'Barbie named 2020 Top Global Toy Property of the year'. https://apnews.com/press-release/business-wire/lifestyle-business-north-america-recreation-and-leisure-consumer-products-and-services-f193b00e5ed645858341c4bf712cefaa (accessed 8 May 2023).

Mattel. 2022a. 'Barbie dolls'. https://www.mattel.com/collections/barbie-dolls#filter.vendor=Barbie (accessed 15 February 2023).

Mattel. 2022b. 'Barbie dolls [Self-care]'. https://www.mattel.com/collections/barbie-dolls#filter.ss_filter_tags_subtype=Self-Care (accessed 15 February 2023).

Mattel. 2022c. 'Fisher-Price Meditation 7.87" Mouse stuffed animal with soothing sounds'. https://www.mattel.com/products/meditation-mouse-toddler-plush-musical-toyfisher-price-grv08 (accessed 15 February 2023).

Mattel. 2023. 'What is the Dream Gap?' https://www.mattel.com/pages/barbie-dream-gap (accessed 5 July 2023).

Mazzarella, William. 2006. 'Internet X-ray: E-governance, transparency, and the politics of immediation in India', *Public Culture* 18 (3): 473–505. https://doi.org/10.1215/08992363-2006-016.

McCartney, Patrick. 2020. 'The X+Y+Zen of "Temple Yoga" in Japan: Heretically-sealed cultural hybridity', *Journal of Dharma Studies* 3: 45–58. https://doi.org/10.1007/s42240-020-00069-9.

McCartney, Patrick. 2021a. 'The not so united states of Yogaland: Post-nationalism, environmentalism, and applied + yoga's sustainable development', in *Nationalism: Past, present, and future*, edited by Thomas J. Keaney, 1–122. Hauppauge, NY: Nova Science.

McCartney, Patrick. 2021b. 'Where does India stand when it comes to Yoga tourism?' *The Wire*, 10 March. https://thewire.in/culture/india-yoga-tourism-uttarakhand (accessed 15 February 2023).

McClory, Jonathan. 2018. *The Soft Power 30: A global ranking of soft power 2018*. London: Portland Communications.

McLuhan, Marshall and Bruce R. Powers. 1989. *The Global Village: Transformations in world life and media in the 21st century*. Oxford: Oxford University Press.

Ministry of Tourism. n.d. 'Toy Story: Promotion of Indigenous toys of India'. https://eoivienna.gov.in/?pdf11699?000 (accessed 15 February 2023).

Mishra, Satyendra Kumar and Satyaki Roy. 2017. 'A story of languishing doll: Revival of cloth dolls of India', in *Research into Design for Communities. Volume 2: Proceedings of ICoRD 2017*, edited by Amaresh Chakrabarti and Debkumar Chakrabarti, 71–9. Singapore: Springer.

Modi Toys. 2022. 'Modi Toys'. http://www.moditoys.com (accessed 15 February 2023).

Mordor Intelligence. 2022. 'Traditional toys and games market: Growth, trends, COVID-19 impact, and forecasts (2023–2028)'. https://www.mordorintelligence.com/industry-reports/traditional-toys-and-games-market.

Myrvold, Kristina, ed. 2010. *The Death of Sacred Texts: Ritual disposal and renovation of texts in world religions*. Farnham: Ashgate.

Narendramodi. 2022. '@Narendramodi'. Twitter. https://twitter.com/narendramodi/media (accessed 15 February 2023).

NDP Group. 2021. 'The NPD Group presents its global and European Toy Industry Performance Awards for 2020'. https://www.npd.com/news/press-releases/2021/the-npd-group-presents-its-global-and-european-toy-industry-performance-awards-for-2020/ (accessed 15 February 2023).

Nemani, Priti. 2011. 'Globalization versus normative policy: A case study on the failure of the Barbie doll in the Indian market', *Asian Pacific Law and Policy Journal* 13 (1): 1–37. https://ssrn.com/abstract=1802793 (accessed 9 May 2023).

Newcombe, Suzanne. 2012. '"Global hybrids?" "Eastern traditions" of health and wellness in the West', in *The Gaze of the West and Framings of the East*, edited by Shanta Nair-Venugopal, 202–17. Basingstoke: Palgrave Macmillan.

Newcombe, Suzanne. 2019. *Yoga in Britain: Stretching spirituality and educating yogis*. Sheffield: Equinox.

Nice2you. 2022. 'Black Girl Doll with Fashion Clothes Set: Yoga Mat and Yoga Stretch Band'. https://www.amazon.com/Nice2you-American-African-Washable-Realistic/dp/B094XF89X8/ref=sr_1_13?crid=11H8UUK06Q8UP&keywords=yoga+dolls&qid=1641309147&sprefix=yoga+dolls%2Caps%2C252&sr=8-13 (accessed 24 January 2022).

Ochshorn, Robert M. and Max Hawkins. 2022. 'Gentle'. https://lowerquality.com/gentle/ (accessed 9 May 2023).

Our Generation Store. 2023. 'Lucy Grace: 18-inch yoga doll with mat'. https://ourgeneration.eu/products/lucy-grace-bd31184 (accessed 9 May 2023).

PACE. 2022. 'Play, adventure and community enrichment'. https://www.paceforall.com/ (accessed 15 February 2023).

Parpola, Asko. 2017. 'Indus seals and glyptic studies: An overview', in *Seals and Sealing in the Ancient World: Case studies from the Near East, Egypt, the Aegean, and South Asia*, edited by Marta Ameri, Sarah Kielt Costello, Gregg Jamison and Sarah Jarmer Scott, 127–43. New York: Cambridge University Press.

Parpola, Asko. 2020. 'Iconographic evidence of Mesopotamian influence on Harappan ideology and its survival in the royal rites of the Veda and Hinduism', in *In Context: The Reade Festschrift*, edited by Irving Hinkel and St John Simpson, 183–90. Oxford: Archaeopress Publishing.

Phillips, Tarryn, John Taylor, Edward Narain and Philippa Chandler. 2021. 'Selling authentic happiness: Indigenous wellbeing and romanticised inequality in tourism advertising', *Annals of Tourism Research* 87: art. no. 103115, 1–12. https://www.doi.org/10.1016/j.annals.2020.103115.

Pilu36. 2022. 'Dols [sic] of Mattel: Challenges on the global markets'. https://doi.org/https://www.termpaperwarehouse.com/essay-on/Dols-Of-Mattel-Challenges-On/202951.

Pinch, William R. 2012. *Warrior Ascetics and Indian Empires*. Cambridge: Cambridge University Press.

PMOIndia 2022. '@PMOIndia'. Twitter. https://twitter.com/PMOIndia.

Poksi. 2022. 'Poksi Yoga sparkle girl doll with long and gorgeous hairs'. https://www.flipkart.com/poksi-yoga-sparkle-girl-doll-long-gorgeous-hairs/p/itm6baa64e66aa8a?pid=DDHG8USUZW6GVHHG&lid=LSTDDHG8USUZW6GVHHG6KK4FA&marketplace=FLIPKART&q=yoga+dolls&store=tng&srno=s_1_3&otracker=search&otracker1=search&fm=organic&iid=b54f99e2-c917-4685-a060-e86e67f00254.DDHG8USUZW6GVHHG.SEARCH&ppt=None&ppn=None&ssid=k6vjxugaps0000001641710453246&qH=9d5626f169a49f21.

Poksi. 2023. 'New yoga doll for kids: Can perform all the aasanas |flexible legs and hand (Yellow)'. https://www.flipkart.com/poksi-new-yoga-doll-kids-can-perform-all-aasans-flexible-legs-hand/p/itm89892d6c120c1 (accessed 5 May 2023).

Quaidenu. 2022. 'Qaidenu Cute Monkey Man Doll, Kung Fu Monkey'. Amazon. https://www.amazon.com/live/video/089d930a6d6e4e638d43332b67fb623c (accessed 9 May 2023).

Raj, Selva J. 2005. 'Passage to America: Ammachi on American soil', in *Gurus in America*, edited by Thomas A. Forsthoefel and Cynthia Ann Humes, 123–46. Albany, NY: SUNY Press.

Reece, Steve. 2018. 'Action figure & fashion doll categories, trends and challenges'. Playing at Business: Toy and game business podcast, 6 September. https://playingatbusiness.libsyn.com/action-figure-fashion-doll-categories-trends-and-challenges.

Reeves, Aaron. 2019. 'How class identities shape highbrow consumption: A cross-national analysis of 30 European countries and regions', *Poetics* 76 (October): 1–43. https://doi.org/10.1016/j.poetic.2019.04.002.

Rehbein, Boike. 2020. 'Social inequality and sociocultures', *Methaodos Revista de Ciencias Sociales* 8 (1): 10–21. https://doi.org/10.17502/m.rcs.v8i1.331.

Renfrew, Colin, Iain Morley and Michael Boyd (eds). 2017. *Ritual, Play and Belief in Evolution and Early Human Societies*. Cambridge: Cambridge University Press.

Rieder, Bernhard. 2015. YouTube Data Tools (Version 1.22) [Software]. Available from https://tools.digitalmethods.net/netvizz/youtube/.

RV. 2022. 'RV's garden yoga dolls polyresin – (Set of 3)'. https://www.amazon.in/RVs-Garden-Yoga-Dolls-Polyresin/dp/B09KLRCP82/ref=sr_1_2?crid=1XTTSEZYFFTDP&keywords=yoga+doll&qid=1641710263&s=toys&sprefix=yoga+doll%2Ctoys%2C372&sr=1-2 (accessed 15 February 2023).

Sayer, Andrew. 2011. *Why Things Matter to People: Social science, values and ethical life*. Cambridge: Cambridge University Press.

Schlossberg, Tatiana. 2019. *Inconspicuous Consumption: The environmental impact you don't know you have*. New York: Balance.

Singh, Ramesh K. 2014. 'India can be Vishwa Guru', *The Pioneer*, 26 December. http://www.dailypioneer.com/todays-newspaper/india-can-be-vishwa-guru.html (accessed 15 February 2023).

Singleton, Mark and Ellen Goldberg (eds). 2014. *Gurus of Modern Yoga*. New York: Oxford University Press.

Sinha, Swati. 2018. 'When GI Joes practice yoga', *The Hindu*, 28 May. https://www.thehindu.com/sci-tech/health/when-gi-joes-practice-yoga/article24011213.ece (accessed 15 February 2023).

Sharma, Rajat and Sahil Gupta. 2021. 'Bharat towards Atmanirbharta: A Twitter based analysis', *Journal of Content, Community & Communication* 13 (7): 58–65. https://doi.org/10.31620/JCCC.06.21/07.

Spencer, Carol. 2019. *Dressing Barbie*. New York: Harper Design.

Srinivasan, Doris. 1984. 'Unhinging Śiva from the Indus Civilization', *Journal of the Royal Asiatic Society of Great Britain and Ireland* 116 (1): 77–89. https://doi.org/10.1017/S0035869X00166134.

Statista. 2022a. 'Gross sales of Mattel's Barbie brand worldwide from 2012 to 2021'. https://www.statista.com/statistics/370361/gross-sales-of-mattel-s-barbie-brand/ (accessed 15 February 2023).

Statista. 2022b. 'Revenue of Mattel worldwide from 2018 to 2021, by region'. https://www.statista.com/statistics/198722/international-revenue-of-mattel-by-region/ (accessed 15 February 2023).

Toy Association of India. 2022. 'About us'. https://tai-india.org/aboutus/ (accessed 15 February 2023).

Trigg, Dylan (ed.). 2021. *Atmospheres and Shared Emotions*. Abingdon: Routledge.

Varma, Supriya. 2018. 'Material culture and childhood in Harappan South Asia', in *The Oxford Handbook of the Archaeology of Childhood*, edited by Sally Crawford, Dawn Hadley and Gillian Shepherd, 179–96. Oxford: Oxford University Press.

Veblen, Thorstein. [1899] 2009. *The Theory of the Leisure Class* (ed. Martha Banta). Oxford: Oxford University Press.

Werlin, Katy. 2019. 'The fashion doll'. *The Fashion Historian* (blog). http://www.thefashionhistorian.com/2010/02/fashion-doll.html (accessed 15 February 2023).

White, David Gordon. 2014. *The Yoga Sutra of Patanjali: A biography*. Princeton, NJ: Princeton University Press.

Wright, J. Lenore. 2021. *Athena to Barbie: Bodies, archetypes, and women's search for self*. Minneapolis, MN: Fortress Press.

Yoga with Modi. 2022. 'Yoga with Modi'. YouTube. https://www.youtube.com/c/YogaWithModi/videos (accessed 5 July 2023).

Zabel, Alanna. 2022. 'Az I am Kidz'. https://www.aziamkidz.com/ (accessed 5 July 2023).

Zita Element. 2022. 'American 18 inch girl doll yoga Pilates clothes set'. https://www.amazon.com/ZITA-ELEMENT-American-Pilates-Included/dp/B08KRW8YMG (accessed May 2023).

3

Governing with a lockdown beard: the COVID-19 crisis as a laboratory for Narendra Modi's Hindutva

David Landau and Nina Rageth

Introduction

During the first two waves of the COVID-19 pandemic, the Indian prime minister Narendra Modi orchestrated a dramatic makeover of his image. Between approximately March 2020 and September 2021, he replaced his signature outfit – the sharp tailored Nehru jacket and kurta, designer glasses and luxury watches, and the carefully cropped beard and meticulous haircut – with a look that drew from the saintly idiom. In doing so, he effected an aesthetic transformation that had far-reaching significance for relations between the Indian state and Hinduism. Modi started appearing in public and in social media posts attired in the fashion of Hindu gurus, with increasingly long hair and a long, unkempt beard. By adopting this image, Modi ingeniously cultivated the symbolic language of gurus and used it during the crisis to articulate his political ambitions. This new look served perfectly to complement, strengthen and promote his agenda of elevating Hindu nationalism in Indian politics. Modi developed a visual grammar that communicated a congruous parallel between the length of his beard and his commitment to Hindutva ideologies. The longer the beard, the sharper the majoritarianism; the shorter the beard, the more emphasis on 'politics as usual'. This chapter focuses on Modi's performance of the Hindu guru as a way to understand the shifting contours of Indian politics, taking into consideration both the immense power that the figure of the Hindu guru holds in India and the central position that Modi himself occupies on the national stage.

In contemporary India, Hindu gurus are a ubiquitous phenomenon. Unlike other Hindu religious experts such as ritual specialists (*pujārī*) or temple priests (*purohit*), the guru is a teacher and counsellor. There are sectarian gurus, middle-class gurus, New Age gurus (Rudert 2010), local gurus, global gurus (Altglas 2007; Bauman 2012; Waghorne 2009, 2014, 2017), cosmopolitan gurus (Aravamudan 2006), high-profile gurus (Warrier 2005), vernacular gurus and anglophone gurus. There is a veritable guru market featuring competition, innovation and the possibility of choice (Lucia 2014b; Warrier 2003a). They show different organisational modes which are captured in terms such as 'devotional order' (Copeman 2009, 1), 'guru movements' (Spurr 2016), 'guru organizations' (Warrier 2003a, 2003b) or 'guru-centered associations' (Waghorne 2014, 187). One shared key feature of gurus is, as Copeman and Ikegame convincingly argue, their 'uncontainability' (2012a, 291). Jacob Copeman and Aya Ikegame describe gurus as 'domain crosser[s] par excellence' (2012a, 324). Gurus appear in a multitude of social arenas. They act as leaders of humanitarian projects (Copeman 2009; Lucia 2014a), experts in the medical domain (Rageth 2018), defenders of environmental concerns, promoters of well-being (Khalikova 2017; Goldberg and Singleton 2014) and finally, as we discuss in this chapter, they participate in politics.

One concern of this chapter is to uncover how Narendra Modi enacts the Hindu guru, closely examining the visual aesthetics but also considering the rhetorical possibilities of the guru figure. Writing about the broad phenomenon of gurus, Copeman and Ikegame convincingly argue that a primary strategy for showcasing guruship is mimesis of canonical markers of the guru. This makes performativity and theatricality aspects crucial for grasping the guru phenomenon (Copeman and Ikegame 2012b, 8). 'Dressing up', they state, 'enacts the very structure of performance and impersonation by which all guruship is assumed' (2012b, 8). In this vein, they argue that '"[g]uru culture" comprises a particularly dense complex of imitative registers' (Copeman and Ikegame 2012a, 297). These 'registers' are not to be confused with an invariable set of codes, or, in their words, 'the guru does not refer to a consistent body of knowledge and practice' (2012a, 324). Rather, guruship comprises certain logics, 'the guru logics' (Copeman and Ikegame 2012a), which aspiring gurus are to reproduce. Following this argument, we discuss Modi's novel appearance as a form of performance. By imitating the figure of the Hindu guru, Modi benefits from the power that the figure of the Hindu guru has garnered in the last century.

Scholars have observed and examined the figure and political phenomenon of Modi from a variety of angles, which has yielded a large body of research. Christophe Jaffrelot (2021b) recently published a voluminous monograph which scrupulously documents and analyses Modi's capture of power. A number of scholars have focused on Modi's use of social media and other technologies such as the holographic speeches (Baishya 2015; Menon 2014; Rai 2019; Rao 2018). Research has been done on the relationship between Modi's popularisation of yoga, as in his inauguration of the International Yoga Day, Hindutva politics, and global spirituality (Jain 2020). Sanjay Srivastava (2015) applies a gender perspective to examine Modi's masculinity, which he intersects with forms of new consumerist aspirations. And, to mention one more perspective, others focused on the situation of minorities, especially the Muslim minority since Modi's election (Waikar 2018; Wright 2015). Although research has offered a range of insights and perspectives into Modi's character, this scholarship has so far not given focused attention to his enactment of the Hindu guru. Analysing the figure of the Hindu guru and Modi's employment of its many symbolic layers serves to untangle Modi's agenda of ideology and populism. Although there are aspects of Modi's much-discussed 'strongman' politics and the performance of the Hindu guru that overlap, there are notable differences, particularly regarding the guru's capacity to forge a new kind of Hindutva politics that departs from India's original democratic framework. Moreover, the Modi-as-guru figure resonates differently with the public from Modi-as-strongman, and the guru holds the potential to reach an even wider audience. We hold that there is no parallel figure in India which is as widely understood and recognised as the Hindu god-man. In other words, the guru figure resonates throughout and across different areas and communities in India, which turns it into a particularly powerful figure.

In this chapter, we place Modi's changing outward appearance – including his beard – in the wider context of his Hindutva project to restructure Hindu and Indian identity. An examination of Modi's Hindutva reveals it as promoting a homogenised version of Hinduism, which is fuelled by a need to dominate Indian culture. We understand his embodiment of the figure of the guru, or the guru prime minister, as merging two aspects of his Hindutva, namely the original revivalist credo of Hindu nationalism, and a strongman style of politics championed by Modi himself. Exponents of neo-Hinduism such as Vivekananda, Gandhi or Aurobindo, to name a few highly prominent figures, all displayed religious and political aspirations and acted as religious and political representatives. Modi's experiment with blending religious and political symbols is different in that it is an attempt at gaining more power than is contained in any singular frame of reference, political or religious. Modi reached the position of prime minister thanks to his successful political career and now he is expanding his aura to include the figure of the guru. Other figures, such as Vivekananda and Aurobindo, used the capital they accumulated through their religious activities to influence the sphere of politics. Gandhi is harder to categorise, as it seems his political and spiritual activities developed in tandem and were complementary. Modi's combination of prime minister and figure of religious authority is brand new and holds the potential for far-reaching changes in Indian politics.

The COVID-19 crisis has been an opportunity to speed up processes that were already taking place: erosion of democratic principles, strengthening of the Modi cult, and detachment from challenging realities such as the economic crisis and tensions with China. Modi has used these crises to test, refine and calibrate different combinations of religious and political symbols, potentially setting Indian politics on a new course. In this chapter, we focus on the context of Modi's transformation, then discuss the figure of the guru that he draws upon. We move on to discussing the dynamics of gurus and politics in India before suggesting some possible motivations for Modi's dramatic shift, and its possible implications.

Modi's shape shifting

Adopting the imagery of the Hindu guru

During the COVID-19 pandemic, India's prime minister Narendra Modi dramatically changed his appearance. Before the pandemic, Modi's self-presentation emphasised traditional values alongside advocacy of economic progress and state development, while occasionally flirting with Hindu symbols. In the first year or so after the outbreak of the virus, Modi presented himself as a white-bearded guru, dressing in the style of Indian holy men and growing a long and at times ragged beard. It is impossible to pinpoint the exact beginning of Modi's makeover, but it occurred at some point during the first national lockdown, which started at the end of March 2020. Indeed, the first commentaries on Modi's new look called it a 'lockdown look' or 'lockdown beard' (Sikander 2020). And though we too believe that the adoption of a new look was tightly connected to the lockdown, or more precisely to the humanitarian crisis unfolding in India because of the pandemic, we argue that this transformation was not the result of the rupture in normality. Rather, Modi used the extraordinary situation as a testing ground for a new kind of politics.

Modi's aesthetic transformation did not come unexpectedly. It followed the trajectory of his image management: a strategy of continuous shape shifting producing a number of public identities that sometimes replace one another, sometimes coexist, and sometimes contradict and sometimes complement each other (on Modi's image making see Baishya 2015; Pal 2015; Rai 2019; R. Sen 2016; Srivastava 2015).[1] Modi's guru look was immaculate. Part of its power was the minute attention to detail with which Modi (and presumably his team) styled his public persona. This attention to detail ensured that every viewer with a sense of guru ascetics would immediately recognise Modi's new persona. One of the early dramatic guru enactments took place on 5 April in 2020, on the ninth day of India's first lockdown. Modi was shown on major Indian TV channels such as *India Today* lighting a *diyā*, an oil lamp, in silence, engaging in darshan, gazing at a devotional object, and performing a nine-minute act of solidarity with and for the nation (*India Today* 2020). This spectacle framed Modi as a spiritually devout man, in humble clothing, a lone seeker with nobody but his mother at his side. This moment roughly marks the beginning of Modi's employment of guru aesthetics. Moreover, it was a rare occasion on which Modi not only appeared as a guru but also acted like one. Most of his public appearances during the pandemic were in the guru garb but his actions were of a political nature. Moreover, as we discuss below, Modi expressed his shift predominantly through visual aesthetics, and he did not invest in the adaptation of his linguistic register. It seems that in a media-saturated society the visual image is Modi's most powerful tool to promulgate his image makeover.

Modi started to experiment with the guru motif at the beginning of the pandemic by drawing on the canonical marker of the guru's long beard. As mentioned above, following Copeman and Ikegame (2012a, 2012b), performativity and mimesis are crucial aspects of modern guru-hood. The visibly growing beard, coupled with a traditional Hindu wardrobe, served as a clear message of a new turn in his public persona. He appeared with loose-fitting clothes, choosing a new cut and traditional-looking fabrics. This sartorial flair was reminiscent of both modern gurus in the trajectory of Vivekananda and pre-colonial courtly dress (Houghteling 2017). The clothes were often in earthy colours and expressed comfort and opulence. On specific occasions he even presented himself wearing saffron, a colour that signals renunciation, or initiation into a monastic order, especially into a Shaivite sect (*sampradāya*); moreover, it is the representative colour of the Hindu right (Jha 2014). It became rare for him to be photographed without a shawl or a scarf. A good example of his sage-like appearance is a photo circulated on his social media accounts and in different newspapers that depicts him addressing the Indo-Japan Samwad Conference via video in December

2020. He is shown in a garden with a statue of the Buddha behind him wearing a perfectly ironed simple white shirt and a colourful shawl placed very neatly over his left shoulder (Mukhopadhyay 2021). The placing of the shawl is unmistakably evoking religious garb in which only one shoulder is covered.

Along with his new clothing style, Modi played with the guru's haircut and beard. Throughout the different stages of growth and trimming, his hairstyle and beard were of great public interest and evoked different interpretations. This is not surprising, hairstyle and type of beard being recognisable indicators of religious life and religious authority in the Indian context. Modi's shoulder-long groomed hair and at times ragged beard were part of his new sannyasi-esque appearance, clearly employing the style of famous Hindu gurus such as Mahesh Yogi, Sri Sri Ravi Sankar, Sadhguru and Baba Ramdev, and contrasting with the monk-like style of Yogi Adityanath with his shaven head. 'Well maintained long hair and beard' is suggestive of a person 'who is in the world, but not of the world, someone who leads a celibate and simple life, but is not extreme in asceticism and not circumscribed by the minutiae of a specific monastic order' (Jacobs 2015, 132–3). Modi was experimenting with his image by testing both 'worldliness' and asceticism, positioning himself 'in the world, but not of the world' by letting his beard grow ragged at times (especially during the March–April 2021 West Bengal elections), and at times appearing with a flowing but well-groomed beard.

Some commenters claimed he was so busy dealing with the pandemic that he did not have time for a haircut, while others speculated that he had undertaken a vow not to cut his hair until the construction of the Ram Mandir temple in Ayodhya was completed (Babu 2020). However, Modi was ridiculed for trying to associate himself with historical figures. For example, in April 2021, during the election campaign in West Bengal, when his beard was at its most unruly stage, his look was compared with that of the Bengali poet Rabindranath Tagore. His main opponent in West Bengal, Mamta Banerjee, ridiculed Modi's beard and look: 'The Indian economy has gone for a toss. There is no industrial growth. There is no growth except for the beard of Narendra Modiji. At times he dresses like Rabindranath Tagore and at times like Mahatma Gandhi' (*The Economic Times* 2021).[2]

While Modi is clearly experimenting with the image of the Hindu guru, linking this image to specific historical figures, as Mamta Banerjee does, simplifies the issue.[3] The image of the Hindu guru is so variegated that rooting its origin in one specific figure is impossible. It is more instructive to employ Deleuze and Guattari's image of a rhizome in order to think of gurus as forming assemblages out of shared symbols (Deleuze and Guattari 2003). When Modi appears as a guru, he evokes a multitude of references. He is both a humble spiritual seeker and a wise teacher, both a sage from Hinduism's golden past and a modern worldly guru. A rhizome has no origin, no chain of events and no direction of development. Rather, the roots intertwine and feed into each other, making a genealogy impossible. There are certainly distinct figures that left potent imprints on that image and shaped its form-taking, an exemplary case being Gandhi. Gandhi established key characteristics such as asceticism, self-discipline and selfless service, which invites a reading of Modi's new appearance as an imitation of Gandhi (see for example Jaffrelot 2021b, 463). However, though similarities between Modi and Gandhi abound, there are also remarkable differences, and it does not seem helpful to brush them aside.[4] Rather than reading Modi's new mode of self-representation as a copy of one distinct guru persona, we suggest reading Modi's appearance as the mimicking of 'guru logics' (Copeman and Ikegame 2012a), which brings together the influences of different guru personas, establishing a solid framework for guruship within which Modi acts.

From virile ruler to ascetic guru

Modi's guru-esque appearance is particularly striking when contrasted with the pre-guru image of Modi as the decisive leader. Modi's 'persona as the savior of the country' (Kaul 2017, 531) consisted of an ingenious mixture of the business-friendly entrepreneur, the clever developer and the solid traditionalist. Market-led development and liberalisation, prosperity and progression for India: such were the key promises that Modi made during the election campaign and in the aftermath of the 2014 general elections, echoing economic ideals of the post-1990s. The hashtag #acchedin (good days [are coming]) encapsulates the dominant electoral rhetoric and gives a sense of Modi's performance as the harbinger of a historical period marked by India's resurrection after years of Congress rule (Kaur 2015; Menon 2014; Rai 2019). He cultivated a larger-than-life image manifested in different ways, such as the suit emblazoned with his name which he donned for meeting Barack Obama in 2015.[5] He promotes grand projects, such as the construction and inauguration of the statue of Sardar Patel, the world's largest, and his multibillion-dollar project to redevelop Lutyens's central vista in New Delhi. Modi was hardly ever seen wearing the common dress of Indian male politicians, that is, 'khadi or at least the colour white' (Chakrabarty 2001, 29). Instead, he was known for sporting a well-crafted look with the sharp kurta and Nehru jacket and the closely cropped beard.

Moreover, an integral part of the branding, suggestive of professionalism and efficacy, of economic aspirations and national pride, was the performance of hyper-masculinity. Modi cast an image of the broad-chested ruler, of a solid and potent body governing the nation. In Nigam's words, Modi 'was projected as one who is [a] stereotypically, alpha, muscular, macho, powerful, strong, megalomaniacal, metaphoric superman who could instill fear in his enemies' (Nigam 2018, unpaginated). Modi's '56-inch chest' became a stable reference in the election campaign to denote his virility and manhood (see Kinnvall 2019; Srivastava 2015).

However, alongside the larger-than-life persona that Modi projected, he also famously played with symbols of the Hindu saint. After his election, he was eager to foster the image of the celibate, kinless, abstinent and devout ascetic. This image is drawn in the official biographical story of Modi, which recounts how he renounced conventional ties by leaving his family and wife at the young age of 18, roaming through India and travelling to the Ramakrishna Mission in Belur Math, driven by a yearning to become a mendicant (*parivrājak*) (Marino 2014, 25–9). Moreover, Modi chooses to stage public acts which present him to the world as a person with particularly strong spiritual dispositions. Towards the end of the Lok Sabha election in May 2019, Modi chose to spend 15 hours meditating in a cave at the Kedarnath shrine. Photographs of Modi sitting cross-legged, eyes closed and covered with an orange shawl went viral (Elsa 2019). Modi's supporters are even known as devotees, as bhakts. This shows that the image of the ascetic guru was always part of the larger 'Modi myth' (Kaul 2017). However, it is a recent and notable phenomenon that the guru appearance is overriding other aspects of the previously multifarious Modi. While previously, as Kaul convincingly argues, Modi integrated the imaginaries of the 'ascetic, paternal, and decisive ruler' (Kaul 2017, 533), we witnessed for a moment a subtle but clear shift towards the exclusive enactment of the ascetic guru.

Hindu gurus in Indian politics

At this point, a cursory examination of the figure of the Hindu guru in Indian politics is required to grasp and contextualise Modi's self-styling. As stated, the guru is a multifaceted, plural and flexible figure that evades all efforts at generalisation. Examining previous intersections between the guru figure and politics helps us to understand how Modi is acting within a familiar set-up and at the same time introducing a novel mode of the guru politician.

It is publicly acknowledged that many contemporary Hindu gurus often act in conjunction with the agenda of the current BJP government.

The affinity and consonance between Hindu gurus and BJP politicians have become particularly evident through saffron-clad gurus such as Baba Ramdev, a promoter of Hindutva ideologies (Chakraborty 2006, 2007; Jaffrelot 2011; Kanungo 2019; Khalikova 2017; Longkumer 2018; Sarbacker 2014). Baba Ramdev is an overt supporter of Modi and has ingeniously promoted loyalty to the nation above all. His vision of it is that it is a proud and self-sufficient nation, more precisely, a *Hindu* nation.[6] The phenomenon of Hindutva-sympathetic gurus is not limited to north India, but extends into the south of India, far beyond the BJP's Hindi belt. Jaggi Vasudev, better known as Sadhguru, whose headquarters are in Tamil Nadu, publicly displays his closeness to Narendra Modi and, reciprocally, Modi pays tribute to the southern yogi (Choudhury 2019). This alliance is made palpable when Jaggi Vasudev praises Modi for his Swachh Bharat Mission (Clean India Mission) (Republic Bharat 2018),[7] or when he speaks out in favour of the Citizenship Amendment Act (Chandra 2020), and in 2017 Modi travelled to the ashram's headquarters to unveil the so-called Adiyogi statue, a significant icon for Sadhguru's Isha foundation.[8] Obviously, not all current Hindu gurus are open supporters of BJP politics. However, many Hindu gurus further the growth of Hindu nationalism by spreading and commodifying the notion of the supremacy of Hindu spirituality and the image of Hinduism as a way of life rooted in the Indian nation-state.

The intersection of Hindu gurus and the political economy of Hindu nationalism has a long and complex history.[9] 'The volatile mixture of politics and religion' (Aravamudan 2006, 221) goes back to luminaries such as Vivekananda and the Ramakrishna Mission, Aurobindo, Tagore and Gandhi. These men shared a strong agenda of reforming Hinduism, invoking social transformations, and ultimately bringing about political change. Their ideology fused religious and national reformation to the extent that they would often become indistinguishable. These early reformers were Indian nationalists, and their main objective was the betterment of the nation (Chakraborty 2007, 1175; Jaffrelot 2012, 80). Their nationalist zeal was directed first and foremost towards resistance against British colonialism, and it did not carry the fascist overtones of the later Hindu nationalism. Nevertheless, their work to reform Hinduism and revitalise Hindu identity, and the centrality of ideas related to spirituality in their version of Indian nationalism, co-constituted the ground for the later emergence of Hindu nationalism (Beckerlegge 2000, 2006; Chakraborty 2007, 1174–80; Gold 1991; Katju 2003; McKean 1996; Van der Veer 2001, 47). It is striking to see that in recent years the BJP government has shown a renewed interest in such figures. It promotes and celebrates them as early proponents of a Hindu nationalist ideology, even though many of these Hindu reformists clearly spoke out against a communalist ideology for which they are now instrumentalised. Perhaps the defining feature of RSS-style Hindu nationalism is its anti-minority discourse. Therefore, it is important to differentiate between early proponents of a Hindu nationalism that emphasised a pan-Indian identity and envisaged Hindus, alongside Muslims and other minorities, freed from colonialism, but was not based on enmity to the 'Other'. In particular, these early proponents of Hindu nationalism did not think of India as an exclusively Hindu nation. Under Modi's leadership there has been a campaign to rewrite the history of Hindu reform movements and to place different forms of Hindu nationalism that competed with the RSS during the decades leading up to independence under the umbrella of the RSS ideology. Hence, though it would be misleading to frame all Hindu reformers as early exponents of the current Hindu nationalist agenda, it is important to acknowledge the long-standing alliance between spirituality discourses and Hindu nationalism. Particularly relevant in this regard is the close association of early Hindu gurus and the RSS, the fountainhead of Hindu nationalism (founded in 1925 by K. B. Hedgewar) and the VHP (Vishva Hindu Parishad), a Hindu coalition fundamental to the development of militant Hindu nationalism (founded in 1964 by M. S. Golwalkar). Not only have some Hindu gurus been in favour of the ideologies of the Hindu right, but Hindu nationalist bodies have actively cultivated the figure of the Hindu guru as representative of the very type of Hinduism which they promoted.[10]

Returning to the present, it seems safe to say that the position of Hindu gurus in the political landscape is undergoing a shift. Though Hindu gurus have been a crucial voice in the ecosystem of authority since the independence movement, and have fostered a complicated alliance with Hindu nationalism, it is only recently that they have publicly exhibited their alliance with elected politicians, and, even more so, that they have themselves acted as political agitators. In the 2010s, during the anti-corruption campaign, Ramdev faced heavy criticism for his involvement in politics, 'for illegitimately mixing yogic spirituality with politics' (Copeman and Ikegame 2012a, 318). While until Modi came onto the national stage the guru–politician relationship was one of reciprocal support and mutual promotion, gurus have now started to be directly involved in political affairs. Since the ascendance of the Hindu right in Indian politics, and particularly since Modi's election in 2014, politicians such as Yogi Adityanath (CM of Uttar Pradesh from 2018), Uma Bharati (MP from 2014 to 2019) and Sakshi Maharaj (MP from 2014) have overtly displayed their religious affiliations.[11] In other words, a shift appears to be taking place which is erasing the division between politics and gurus, and we increasingly see figures who are both gurus and politicians. What we are witnessing is the merging of a Hindu guru and a politician in one and the same person.

Modi's orchestration of the Hindu guru marks the pinnacle of this development. When the Indian Prime Minister appears today as a Hindu guru, he is uniting both positions: he is king and king's guru, raja and raj guru. By blurring the boundary between the ruler and the spiritual adviser, he is circumventing an established division. He is creating a new and all-powerful position which has not gone unnoticed in Indian society and which has evoked – at least in some sections of the political landscape – disapproval and objection. Though power dynamics between religious and political leaders have certainly shaped Indian history, we still hold that what we are witnessing here is a new constellation. The emergence of a space in which religious and political power merge and overlap under Modi occurs within the context of conditions vastly different from the religion–politics interplay in previous periods. In the globalised age of the nation-state and digital technology, the consequences of the current confluence of religion and politics are potentially much greater.

Just looks?

Modi's transformation is most obvious in the visual aesthetics he employs. But what about his rhetoric? Is his makeover limited to the visual aspect of appearance, or has he also invested in the adaptation of his linguistic register? In order to examine the depth of Modi's makeover, we investigated his use of language. Specifically, we analysed the rhetoric in his monthly radio show *Mann Ki Baat* ('words from the heart') between spring 2020 and summer 2021, and compared it with the pre-pandemic content. We examined some of his political speeches, such as his addresses on Independence Day in August 2020 and 2021, and studied some of his many public appearances during the West Bengal election campaign in 2021. Also, we studied his Twitter and Facebook feeds, as well as the content of the Narendra Modi app.

An examination of Modi's utterances during the pandemic revealed no clear findings. Modi is a prolific social media user across different platforms and regularly gives speeches in different settings throughout India, one of his 'masterstroke[s] in the use of media' (Sharma and Dubey 2021, 535) being his very own radio programme *Mann Ki Baat*.[12] The sheer quantity of Modi's words serves to keep him at the centre of the nation's attention, but it can also serve to obscure changes, subtle or otherwise. Our analysis did not expose discernible changes in his rhetorical strategies towards a more overtly guru-like tone. Because of the pandemic the tone and subject matter shifted, but there is no clear increase in religious references that could have been interpreted as a break from his previous utterances, such as quotes from religious texts, mention of mythological stories, claims of an unmediated connection to God, declarations of magical powers, emphasising a guru lineage, etc. In other words, there were religious references scattered throughout his speeches, but the number seems to be the same as in pre-pandemic times. We tread carefully here, since there is obviously space for an in-depth discourse analysis, but that is not the focus of this chapter. Further research would need to focus on Modi's rhetoric, including an analysis of the use of anecdotes, repetition, subject matter and other markers of guru discourses, rather than politicians' speech.

It seems that Modi's recasting as a Hindu guru is engineered mainly by focusing on the visual. Perhaps for a figure of Modi's stature the image and self-presentation might be more important than the texts and speeches themselves. The significance of the visual can be explained in terms of the media-saturated society in which current politics take place. With 340 million in the year 2020, India has the largest number of monthly Facebook users (Singh and Deep 2020, 2978). As at April 2023, Modi himself has 48 million followers on his Facebook page and almost 88 million Twitter followers, and he is the most followed sitting world leader on Instagram (Monteiro 2020, 96). With his millions of followers thirsty for visual feeds from their PM, Modi understood how to use, as Sardesai pointed out, 'his wardrobe as a power statement and for deft image-building' (Sardesai 2019, 65). These digital media favour the visual rather than the textual, which gives extra weight to Modi's wardrobe, hairstyle and beard, and demeanour.

It is indisputable that appearance carries a semiotic function and that it serves as a means of communication (Owyong 2009, 192). Historically, clothing matters have been particularly sensitive and powerful issues in India. The most prominent example is of Gandhi's khadi, which was turned into a powerful political symbol, a sign of anti-imperial struggle and of nationalist fervour, and which was used as an enormous exercise in mass mobilisation (see Chakrabarty 2001; Ramagundam 2018; Tarlo 1996). Tarlo argues that by 'adopting the loincloth he was able to communicate all his most important messages through the medium of dress' (1996, 62). What do Modi's clothes represent? While his previous style signalled a blend of tradition, modernity and efficiency, with his 'Modi kurta' and tailored Indian suits, we inquire into the messages carried in his guru attire.

What is at stake in Modi's politics of guru performance? What kinds of ends does he want to achieve? And what consequences might his politics of guru performance have in the short and long runs?

Towards new modes of Hindutva politics

Credibility in moments of crisis

From sifting through images of Modi and comparing them with newspaper reports from and about India, it is clear that Modi's beard reached its unruliest stages as the second wave of the pandemic in India was starting to peak at the end of May 2021. After weathering the first wave in a way that surprised many commentators, Modi boasted about India's dealing with the crisis, including during his speech at the online World Economic Forum in January 2021: 'In a country which is home to 18% of the world population, that country has saved humanity from a big disaster by containing corona effectively' (PM India 2021). Just a few months later, India was in the grip of a deadly second wave which spun out of control, with large numbers of people dying. Despite clear indications that a second wave was imminent, Modi and his government promoted two events which brought millions of people together, the April 2021 Kumbh Mela in Haridwar and the March–April elections in West Bengal. Both events were politically important for Modi, but they were disastrous for the containment of the pandemic.[13] The management of the pandemic in India was a severe failure that resulted in the collapse of the system; this led the political activist Arundhati Roy to speak of 'a crime against humanity' (A. Roy 2021). Alongside the COVID-19 crisis, the Modi government was dealing with at least two other large-scale crises which occupied the news cycle, namely the farmers' protests against the new Farm Bills, and military stand-offs on the border with China. The farmers' protests were a challenge, since it was harder to apply the BJP playbook of accusing its opponent of being anti-nationalists. The crisis on the border held the potential for humiliation, as China clearly had the upper hand. Media reports on these different crises, and particularly on the catastrophic development of the pandemic in India, abound. In the following we discuss a number of parallel and intertwined interpretations of Modi's guru image, and suggest some of our own. As it is too early to state things with confidence, what follows should be read as an attempt to chart different potential motivations for Modi's experimentation with the 'guru logic'.

At the height of this turmoil, against the backdrop of the above challenges, Modi was losing support. His approval rating fell from 66 per cent to 24 per cent (*The Wire* 2021), and hashtags such as #ModiMustResign or #ModiHaiToFailureHai were trending. During this unprecedented challenge to his authority, Modi chose to stage the image of a Hindu guru. The confluence of these different events invites the obvious question: Was Modi's guru image a way of transcending his failures in managing the different crises? Though it is possible to imagine a scenario in which Modi could have recovered his popularity without taking any action, it does not seem far-fetched to link his guru appearance to negative polls. Modi's transformation can be read as a way of circumventing responsibility for the disastrous management of the crises. As a guru he locates himself as the spiritual leader of the nation offering moral rather than material support. As a guru, he is not expected to take practical actions and solve problems, his duty is to soothe and to provide an assuring presence. Jaffrelot (2021b, 464) highlights the connection between guruhood and the dodging of political responsibility, stating: 'Charisma is above accountability, and Modi has grasped these dynamics.' As is well known, charisma is one of Max Weber's central sociological terms related to the legitimisation of authority. According to Weber, personalised charisma means 'a certain quality of an individual personality by virtue of which he [*sic*] is considered extraordinary and treated as endowed with supernatural, superhuman, or at least specifically exceptional powers or qualities' (1968, 241). More precisely, charisma does not mark a personal quality, but a successful claim to a quality, or, in Weber's words, 'recognition on the part of those subject to authority' (1968, 242).

Why is Modi's claim of guru-hood accepted and reinforced? Why is he endowed with charismatic authority when he enacts the Hindu guru? We hold that these dynamics are linked to the powerful presence of the image of the modern guru in post-colonial India. As discussed above, alongside the consolidation of India as a nation, gurus became nationally recognised figures, with high levels of credibility. By enacting the guru figure, Modi is exploiting the power of that image. As we argued above, what we are witnessing here is not a completely unexpected and abrupt transformation. The image of the ascetic guru has always been one thread in the larger 'Modi myth' (Kaul 2017). However, it has now, for a moment, superseded other aspects of the multifarious image that Modi promotes. Britta Ohm writes that the challenges of the pandemic 'magnified dominant characteristics of people as much as of leaderships around the world' (Ohm 2021, 502). While we agree with the gist of that statement, we also want to bring attention to Modi's agency in that process. Modi's image of the guru is not a mere reaction to challenges. Rather, it is a conscious utilisation of them. The pandemic created a rupture in normal politics and Modi used the situation as a laboratory to explore a new kind of politics. We assume that this was partly a strategy to evade responsibility in a moment of severe crises. However, it also seems likely that Modi is following an even larger goal by enacting the god-man. Modi's guru appearance is closely intertwined with his determination to realise his political agenda of creating a Hindu state and of attaining unprecedented dominance in Indian politics and history.

Hindutva at a crossroads

Seeing the Indian Prime Minister appear as a guru is particularly striking in the context of the strict division between electoral politics and the RSS that existed until very recently. The Sangh Parivar (family of the co-religionists), a term in use since the 1950s to refer to the expansive network of affiliated Hindutva organisations, is known for its order and its rigid division of labour (see Jaffrelot 2021b, 17). At the core of the network sits the RSS (Rashtriya Swayamsevak Sangh). It was founded in 1925 by K. B. Hedgewar as a Hindu revivalist movement with paramilitary overtones and a stringent anti-minority, anti-Muslim discourse. It focused on training young men to promote and defend Hindu values. In the decades following the founding of the organisation, its members branched out and established many sister organisations with separate constitutions and structures in order to reach and influence as many Hindus as possible and to counter other ideologies, such as communism. These organisations range from workers' and farmers' unions, India's largest student union (Akhil Bharatiya Vidyarthi Parishad) to the VHP, a coalition of Hindu organisations whose aim is to 'protect the Hindu Dharma' (VHP 2022). All of these unions became dominant players in their respective fields, with their own programmes, schemes and target groups (see Jaffrelot 2005, 10). Initially, the ideology of the RSS was to influence society from below through education and mobilisation, which still holds true today.[14] However, after being banned, following Gandhi's murder by a former RSS member, the leaders decided that they needed political power as well in order to promote their cause. Therefore, from the 1950s onwards, the RSS established political parties, starting with the BJS (Bharatiya Jana Sangh, established in 1951), the BJP (Bharatiya Janata Party, established in 1980) being its latest avatar. There has always been a dynamic division between the RSS and the BJP, whose fluctuations were dominated by political calculations. The idea was that the BJP was to focus on gaining political power even at the cost of diluting Hindutva ideology, while the RSS was tasked with protecting this very ideology. After a period in which the BJP had to obscure its association with the RSS in order to appease its various coalition partners, following the BJP's electoral successes in 2014 and especially 2019, the relationship between the two organisations was more publicly acknowledged (on the relationship between the RSS and BJP, *see* Jaffrelot 2012, 88–94; Kanungo 2006). Modi embodied the arrival of RSS ideology, with its Hindu supremacist fervour and aggressive anti-minority propaganda, in the mainstream of Indian politics. Modi's guru performance can be interpreted as marking a transition in the established order. When Modi, in his position as prime minister and leader of the BJP, orchestrates the Hindu guru, he is establishing a new configuration of the Sangh. As mentioned above, a dominant strategy of the Hindutva movement was to split into different groups in order to reach as diverse an audience as possible. Today, Hindutva is the dominant political force in India and no longer needs to water down its stated ideology. It seems likely that, at this stage, the movement is rethinking its strategy and experimenting with new possibilities. Modi's enactment of the Hindu guru could be read as marking a crossroads in the tactics of the Sangh. The figure of the Hindu guru as prime minister weaves together the distinct domains of the BJP and the RSS and creates new possibilities for extending and wielding power.

Following this line of thought, one could go a step further. What we see is not just the reorganisation of the Sangh Parivar, but an expression of Modi's larger political goal. Modi follows the conspicuous agenda of creating some version of a Hindu ethnocracy.[15] In Modi's ethnocracy the old structure of the Sangh Parivar is no longer needed. The 'old order' is only good for 'the old India', that is, a democratic India. Through his political actions, he is consolidating a Hindu public sphere and facilitating the marginalisation of minorities. India, which used to be a role model for democracy in the Global South, has transitioned first into a '*de facto* ethnic democracy' since Modi's election to power in 2014, and lately, with a number of drastic changes and amendments in the law and constitution, into a '*de jure* ethnic democracy' (Jaffrelot 2021b, 128–30).

As discussed above, the figure of the Hindu guru helps Modi to promote this political goal. To deliver his message and to win people's (that is, Hindus') support for his cause, Modi has to speak a language that is understood nationwide. There is no parallel figure in India which is as widely understood and recognised as that of the Hindu god-man. In other words, for the Hindu collective identity the figure of the guru elicits the most identification. People from disparate regions and classes understand the language of the Hindu guru, a language of which the grammar has come to centre on a Hindu supremacist ideology, a zeal to revive ancient Hindu traditions and return to an untarnished past, and a determination to heal the wounds of Muslim influence and colonialism. By orchestrating the Hindu guru, Modi is effectively tapping into this semiotic register. When the Prime Minister appears as a Hindu guru, he does not appear as a representative of Indian citizens but as a representative of Hindus only. The guru garb marks him as a leader of Hindus, implicitly unifying them against all non-Hindus. To put it bluntly, Modi's guru look fosters his agenda of establishing a Hindu ethnocracy, without naming it explicitly. Modi's self-fashioning as the Hindu guru is a conscious aesthetic effort of immense significance for the contours of democracy or ethnocracy in India. Modi's makeover during the pandemic needs to be linked with his ambitions to radically alter Indian democracy.

Conclusion

Modi's aesthetic transformation has the potential to be of immense significance. In spring 2020, at a moment when the Prime Minister was faced with an array of severe crises, he took on the image of the Hindu guru. His guru makeover was achieved by blending a marked change in his sartorial style and the length and cut of his beard and hair. One and a half years later, Modi suspended the carefully crafted guru look. In September 2021, when Modi set out on his first trip abroad since the pandemic, he presented himself to the nation and the world with a trimmed beard and cut hair. He still looked different from the pre-COVID Modi, as his beard was noticeably longer. However, at this point he shed the guru image and presented himself as a man who is prepared for worldly affairs (Sharma 2021). It is too early to understand what this latest makeover indicates. Did the period of Modi's guru-hood come to an end, or did he just put the experiment on hold? Will Modi now create a middle ground in which he presents himself as a guru and as an international power broker, depending on his audience?

Having closely examined Modi's performance of the Hindu guru, we have shown how he played with a well-established and powerful imagery of the Hindu guru. Through adopting the guru logic, he introduced a novel mode of the guru politician. In our discussion of Modi's striking shape shifting, we put particular emphasis on the intersection of Hindu gurus and the political economy of Hindutva, a pivotal issue in the history of the Indian nation-state. We have examined possible motivations for the image makeover and considered the short- and long-term consequences that Modi's guru-esque appearance might have for himself, but also for the future of India and particularly of Indian democracy. We have interpreted Modi's makeover as a way of circumventing responsibility for the disastrous management of the pandemic and failures with regard to other severe crises. Furthermore, we have shown how Modi's display of Hindu guru-hood is shaking up or even undermining the established division of labour in the Sangh Parivar. This has led us to suggest that Modi's transformation should be read as a deliberate way of espousing and advancing his agenda of building the foundation for an ethnocratic Hindu nation-state.

There is another element that needs to be taken into consideration when unpacking Modi's display of guru aesthetic, and that we have, so far, left out. Modi's actions can also be read as an expression of 'Moditva' (Kanungo and Farooqui 2008). That is, it is unclear whether Modi's experiments with the symbols of guru-hood have to do with a vision of Hindutva or with an attempt to gain as much personal power as possible. Perhaps rather than reorganising the Sangh Parivar, Modi is destabilising it in order to create a new order which is about Modi himself. Perhaps Modi's embodiment of the guru is not only about Hindutva ideology. Rather, he is doing this because the figure of the guru promises absolute power to himself. This is in line with contemporary strongman leaders such as Trump, Bolsonaro, Duterte and others whose emphasis is often more on spectacle than on promoting a specific coherent ideology. Being the centre of attention becomes the ideology, much as commodification of the self is a marker of our neoliberal age. An example of Modi's taking centre stage and deliberately sidelining the RSS hierarchy occurred in August 2020, when he did not invite prominent Hindutva leaders, who had been instrumental in the Ramjanmabhoomi movement, to the laying of the cornerstone for the new Ram temple in Ayodhya. Traditionally the RSS and the Sangh promoted loyalty to the cause and the organisation, and were suspicious of charismatic individuals. This is where Modi seems to be breaking free. Through his guru enactment he is building the foundation for this new type of political structure, namely, strongman leadership. Modi's Hindutva, or Moditva if you like, includes leader worship, majoritarianism, muscular Hinduism and grandiose building projects. Finally, and perhaps most importantly, Modi's style of leadership has created an atmosphere of fear among those who dare oppose him.

Modi's performance as the Hindu guru testifies to his ability to use a crisis as an opportunity to experiment and further his agenda. While part of his sharp change in appearance was 'just' an immediate response to the multiple challenges he faced, we argue that his experiment has gone further and that he has skilfully used the extraordinary situation as a laboratory for future plans. Modi's experimentation with the figure of the Hindu guru has revealed that his future political path might include a mixture of religious symbolism that would be novel for an Indian prime minister, and that poses a real threat to religious minorities. Moreover, Modi's taking on the figure of the guru might signal a further shift towards weakening the secular framework of the state and government. The atmosphere in India today for minorities and dissenters is quite grim. Modi remains silent when Hindu leaders call for genocide of Muslims, but posts numerous comments about other issues on his social media feeds. Modi's guru look allows him to implicitly support more extreme strains of Hindutva while giving him space for plausible denial should things get out of hand. He signals Hindutva but can very rarely be directly quoted on it. This is sufficient for his followers and allows him to continue to participate on the world stage without being directly held responsible for the atmosphere of fear that pervades India under his rule.

Notes

1 An incident that compellingly illustrates Modi's ability to stage image makeovers took place in the run-up to the parliamentary elections in 2014 and his early period in office. Modi used a range of communication strategies to rebrand his image as a totalitarian leader, which haunted him from his decade as Chief Minister of Gujarat and, moreover, his image as a CM who instigated and endorsed a pogrom against the Muslim minority in 2002.

2 Quotation translated from the Bengali original by *The Economic Times*.

3 Similarly, Nandy identifies Aurobindo as 'India's first modern guru' (Nandy 2010, 97), a bold statement that he does not elaborate or explain.

4 For a comparison between Gandhi and Modi see Basu 2020; for a comparison between Gandhi and current Hindu gurus in Gujarat see Mehta 2017.

5 When Modi had received Barack Obama as an official state guest at the Republic Day celebrations in 2015, he was wearing a suit with small golden letters spelling out his name repeatedly in the pinstripes. It was a highly controversial moment. Modi's move to wear a monogrammed suit at a US president's visit was interpreted by many as a narcissistic step too far and an expression of Modi's megalomaniac character.

6 In 2016, Baba Ramdev received a lot of media attention (#TalibaniRamdev), after publicly stating that people who refuse to say the Hindu patriotic slogan 'Bharat Mata Ki Jai' (Hail to Mother India) should be beheaded (*The Indian Express* 2016).

7 The official goal of the Swachh Bharat Mission is to end open defecation and to implement a country-wide solid waste management (Swachh Bharat Mission 2021).

8 Another example of a god-man based in south India who is committed to Hindu nationalist politics is Sri Sri Ravi Shankar, who spearheads the Art of Living Foundation (on the Art of Living Foundation see Jacobs 2015; Tøllefsen 2011).

9 The relationship between political and religious leaders in India, and particularly the role of religious experts in politics, is a subject often discussed among scholars of the history of religion on the Indian subcontinent (see for example Appadurai 1981; Dirks 1987; Dumont 1980; Gold 1987; Sears 2014).

10 On the promotion of Hindu gurus by the VHP and the Hindu gurus as the main supporters of the organisation, see Jaffrelot (2001). For a short description of the development of the

Sangh–guru alliance, see Kanungo (2019, 121–2). Lucia also provides a summary of the conjunction of Hindu gurus and Hindu nationalism (2020, 420–3). For a discussion of the relationship between Hindu gurus and political authorities, with a focus on the RSS as the Raj guru of the ruling party, see Jaffrelot (2012).

11 Another example is Baba Ramdev, who founded the Bharat Swabhiman Trust with decidedly political goals (Gupta and Copeman 2019).

12 For an analysis of Modi's use of his addresses to the nation through *Mann Ki Baat*, see Jaffrelot 2021b, 113–15; Sharma and Dubey 2021.

13 The Kumbh Mela was a symbol of resurgent Hinduism and an occasion for consolidating the image of Modi as promoting Hindu tradition in the face of modern scientific interference. The elections in West Bengal were crucial for the BJP's plan of increasing their power, and the polls showed that they had a chance to win in West Bengal for the first time in history. In the end, the BJP lost the election and the Trinamool Congress stayed in power.

14 In this regard, Anderson and Longkumer describe the Hindutva organisations as 'committed to root-and-branch societal transformation – in the form of a so-called "Hindu Renaissance" – and to this end have made inroads into education, development, the environment, industry, culture, and almost every other aspect of public life' (Anderson and Longkumer 2018, 372).

15 The term ethnocracy was popularised by the Israeli sociologist Oren Yiftachel. Yiftachel uses the term to describe 'a specific expression of nationalism that exists in contested territories where a dominant ethnos gains political control and uses the state apparatus to ethnicize the territory and society in question' (Yiftachel 2000, 730). For work that applies the concept to the Indian context, see especially Adeney 2021; Jaffrelot 2021a; I. Roy 2021; S. Sen 2015.

References

Adeney, Katharine. 2021. 'How can we model ethnic democracy? An application to contemporary India', *Nations and Nationalism* 27 (2): 393–411. https://doi.org/10.1111/nana.12654.

Altglas, Veronique. 2007. 'The global diffusion and Westernization of neo-Hindu movements: Siddha Yoga and Sivananda Centres', *Religions of South Asia* 1 (2): 217–37. https://doi.org/10.1558/rosa.v1i2.217.

Anderson, Edward and Arkotong Longkumer. 2018. '"Neo-Hindutva": Evolving forms, spaces, and expressions of Hindu nationalism', *Contemporary South Asia* 26 (4): 371–7. https://doi.org/10.1080/09584935.2018.1548576.

Appadurai, Arjun. 1981. *Worship and Conflict under Colonial Rule: A South Indian case*. Cambridge: Cambridge University Press.

Aravamudan, Srinivas. 2006. *Guru English: South Asian religion in a cosmopolitan language*. Princeton, NJ: Princeton University Press.

Babu, Venkatesha. 2020. 'Pejwara seer has a theory about PM Modi's growing beard, hair', *Hindustan Times*, 28 December. https://www.hindustantimes.com/india-news/pejwara-seer-reveals-secret-behind-pm-modi-s-growing-beard-hair/story-Va6qyDvuFEyR0Jjm4FcOAI.html (accessed 17 February 2023).

Baishya, Anirban K. 2015. 'Selfies| #NaMo: The political work of the selfie in the 2014 Indian general elections', *International Journal of Communication* 9 (May): 1686–1700.

Basu, Amrita. 2020. 'From Gandhi to Modi: Enlisting the Rudolphs to understand charismatic leadership', in *Interpreting Politics: Situated knowledge, India, and the Rudolph legacy*, edited by John Echeverri-Gent and Kamal Sadiq, 239–65. New Delhi: Oxford University Press.

Bauman, Chad. 2012. 'Sathya Sai Baba: At home abroad in Midwestern America', in *Public Hinduisms*, edited by John Zavos, Pralay Kanungo, Deepa S. Reddy, Maya Warrier and Raymond Brady Williams, 141–59. New Delhi: Sage.

Beckerlegge, Gwilym. 2000. *The Ramakrishna Mission: The making of a modern Hindu movement*. New Delhi: Oxford University Press.

Beckerlegge, Gwilym. 2006. *Swami Vivekananda's Legacy of Service: A study of the Ramakrishna Math and Mission*. New Delhi: Oxford University Press.

Chakrabarty, Dipesh. 2001. 'Clothing the political man: A reading of the use of khadi/white in Indian public life', *Postcolonial Studies* 4 (1): 27–38. https://doi.org/10.1080/13688790120046852.

Chakraborty, Chandrima. 2006. 'Ramdev and somatic nationalism: Embodying the nation, desiring the global', *Economic and Political Weekly* 41 (5): 387–90. http://dx.doi.org/10.2307/4417755.

Chakraborty, Chandrima. 2007. 'The Hindu ascetic as fitness instructor: Reviving faith in yoga', *International Journal of the History of Sport* 24 (9): 1172–86. https://doi.org/10.1080/09523360701448307.

Chandra, Rajshree. 2020. 'An (un)enlightened Sadhguru in King Modi's court', *The Wire*, 1 January. https://thewire.in/politics/an-unenlightened-sadhguru-in-king-modis-court (accessed 17 February 2023).

Choudhury, Angshuman. 2019. 'Why Hindutva nationalists need a Sadhguru', *The Wire*, 9 March. https://thewire.in/politics/why-hindutva-nationalists-need-a-sadhguru (accessed 17 February 2023).

Copeman, Jacob. 2009. *Veins of Devotion: Blood donation and religious experience in north India*. New Brunswick, NJ: Rutgers University Press.

Copeman, Jacob and Aya Ikegame. 2012a. 'Guru logics', *HAU: Journal of Ethnographic Theory* 2 (1): 289–336. https://doi.org/10.14318/hau2.1.014.

Copeman, Jacob and Aya Ikegame. 2012b. 'The multifarious guru: An introduction', in *The Guru in South Asia: New interdisciplinary perspectives*, edited by Jacob Copeman and Aya Ikegame, 1–45. Abingdon: Routledge.

Deleuze, Gilles and Félix Guattari. 2003. *A Thousand Plateaus: Capitalism and schizophrenia*. London: Continuum.

Dirks, Nicholas B. 1987. *The Hollow Crown: Ethnohistory of an Indian kingdom*. Cambridge: Cambridge University Press.

Dumont, Louis. 1980. *Homo Hierarchicus: The caste system and its implications* (trans. Mark Sainsbury, Louis Dumont and Basia Gulati), rev. English edn. Chicago, IL: University of Chicago Press.

Economic Times, The. 2021. 'PM's growing beard inversely proportional to the state of country's economy: Mamata Banerjee', *Economic Times*, 26 March. https://economictimes.indiatimes.com/news/elections/assembly-elections/west-bengal/pms-growing-beard-inversely-proportional-to-the-state-of-countrys-economy-mamata-banerjee/articleshow/81710632.cms?from=mdr (accessed 17 February 2023).

Elsa, Evangelina. 2019. 'India PM Modi meditates in a cave, pictures go viral', *Gulf News*, 18 May. https://gulfnews.com/world/asia/india/indian-pm-modi-meditates-in-a-cave-pictures-go-viral-1.64028532.

Gold, Daniel. 1987. *The Lord as Guru: Hindi sants in North Indian tradition*. New York: Oxford University Press.

Gold, Daniel. 1991. 'Organized Hinduisms: From Vedic truth to Hindu nation', in *Fundamentalisms Observed*, edited by Martin E. Marty and R. Scott Appleby, 531–93. Chicago, IL: University of Chicago Press.

Goldberg, Ellen and Mark Singleton. 2014. 'Introduction', in *Gurus of Modern Yoga*, edited by Mark Singleton and Ellen Goldberg, 1–14. Oxford: Oxford University Press.

Gupta, Bhuvi and Jacob Copeman. 2019. 'Awakening Hindu nationalism through yoga: Swami Ramdev and the Bharat Swabhiman movement', *Contemporary South Asia* 27 (3): 313–29. https://doi.org/10.1080/09584935.2019.1587386.

Houghteling, Sylvia. 2017. 'The emperor's humbler clothes: Textures of courtly dress in seventeenth-century South Asia', *Ars Orientalis* 47: 91–116. https://doi.org/10.3998/ars.13441566.0047.005.

India Today. 2020. 'PM Modi lighting diya at his residence in Delhi', 5 April. Video posted on YouTube. https://www.youtube.com/watch?v=nbLQcF2hObA&t=6s (accessed 17 February 2023).

Indian Express, The. 2016. 'Guru Ramdev: If no law, would have cut the heads of those who don't say Bharat Mata ki jai', 3 April. Video posted on YouTube https://www.youtube.com/watch?v=0G4Wr1Xwijk (accessed 17 February 2023).

Jacobs, Stephen. 2015. *The Art of Living Foundation: Spirituality and wellbeing in the global context*. Farnham: Ashgate.

Jaffrelot, Christophe. 2001. 'The Vishva Hindu Parishad: A nationalist but mimetic attempt at federating the Hindu sects', in *Charisma and Canon: Essays on the religious history of the Indian subcontinent*, edited by Vasudha Dalmia, Angelika Malinar and Martin Christof, 388–411. New Delhi: Oxford University Press.

Jaffrelot, Christophe. 2005. 'Introduction', in *The Sangh Parivar: A reader*, edited by Christophe Jaffrelot, 1–22. New Delhi: Oxford University Press.

Jaffrelot, Christophe. 2011. *Religion, Caste, and Politics in India*. New York: Columbia University Press.

Jaffrelot, Christophe. 2012. 'The political guru: The guru as éminence grise', in *The Guru in South Asia: New interdisciplinary perspectives*, edited by Jacob Copeman and Aya Ikegame, 80–96. Abingdon: Routledge.

Jaffrelot, Christophe. 2021a. 'From Hindu Rashtra to Hindu Raj? A *de facto* or a *de jure* ethnic democracy?', in *Routledge Handbook of Autocratization in South Asia*, edited by Sten Widmalm, 127–38. Abingdon: Routledge.

Jaffrelot, Christophe. 2021b. *Modi's India: Hindu nationalism and the rise of ethnic democracy* (trans. Cynthia Schoch). Princeton, NJ: Princeton University Press.

Jain, Andrea R. 2020. *Peace Love Yoga: The politics of global spirituality*. New York: Oxford University Press.

Jha, Sadan. 2014. 'Challenges in the history of colours: The case of saffron', *Indian Economic & Social History Review* 51 (2): 199–229. https://doi.org/10.1177/0019464614525723.

Kanungo, Pralaya. 2006. 'Myth of the monolith: The RSS wrestles to discipline its political progeny', *Social Scientist* 34 (11/12): 51–69.

Kanungo, Pralay. 2019. 'Gurus and the Hindu nationalist politics: The Baba Ramdev–BJP partnership in the 2014 elections', in *The Algebra of Warfare-Welfare: A long view of India's 2014 election*, edited by Irfan Ahmad and Pralay Kanungo, 119–42. New Delhi: Oxford University Press.

Kanungo, Pralay and Adnan Farooqui. 2008. 'Tracking Moditva: An analysis of the 2007 Gujarat elections campaign', *Contemporary Perspectives* 2 (2): 222–45. https://doi.org/10.1177/223080750800200202.

Katju, Manjari. 2003. *Vishva Hindu Parishad and Indian Politics*. New Delhi: Orient Longman.

Kaul, Nitasha. 2017. 'Rise of the political right in India: Hindutva-Development mix, Modi myth, and dualities', *Journal of Labor and Society* 20 (4): 523–48. https://doi.org/10.1111/wusa.12318.

Kaur, Ravinder. 2015. 'Good times, brought to you by Brand Modi', *Television & New Media* 16 (4): 323–30. https://doi.org/10.1177/1527476415575492.

Khalikova, Venera R. 2017. 'The Ayurveda of Baba Ramdev: Biomoral consumerism, national duty and the biopolitics of "homegrown" medicine in India', *South Asia: Journal of South Asian Studies* 40 (1): 105–22. https://doi.org/10.1080/00856401.2017.1266987.

Kinnvall, Catarina. 2019. 'Populism, ontological insecurity and Hindutva: Modi and the masculinization of Indian politics', *Cambridge Review of International Affairs* 32 (3): 283–302. https://doi.org/10.1080/09557571.2019.1588851.

Longkumer, Arkotong. 2018. '"Nagas can't sit lotus style": Baba Ramdev, Patanjali, and Neo-Hindutva', *Contemporary South Asia* 26 (4): 400–20. https://doi.org/10.1080/09584935.2018.1545008.

Lucia, Amanda. 2014a. '"Give me *sevā* overtime": Selfless service and humanitarianism in Mata Amritanandamayi's transnational guru movement', *History of Religions* 54 (2): 188–207. https://doi.org/10.1086/677812.

Lucia, Amanda. 2014b. 'Innovative gurus: Tradition and change in contemporary Hinduism', *International Journal of Hindu Studies* 18 (2): 221–63. https://doi.org/10.1007/s11407-014-9159-5.

Lucia, Amanda. 2020. 'The global manifestation of the Hindu guru phenomenon', in *Routledge Handbook of South Asian Religions*, edited by Knut A. Jacobsen, 413–27. Abingdon: Routledge.

Marino, Andy. 2014. *Narendra Modi: A political biography*. Noida, Uttar Pradesh: HarperCollins Publishers India.

McKean, Lise. 1996. *Divine Enterprise: Gurus and the Hindu nationalist movement*. Chicago, IL: University of Chicago Press.

Mehta, Mona G. 2017. 'From Gandhi to gurus: The rise of the "guru-sphere"', *South Asia: Journal of South Asian Studies* 40 (3): 500–16. https://doi.org/10.1080/00856401.2017.1302047.

Menon, Ramesh. 2014. *Modi Demystified: The making of a prime minister*. Noida: HarperCollins India.

Monteiro, Stephen. 2020. '"Welcome to selfiestan": Identity and the networked gaze in Indian mobile media', *Media, Culture & Society* 42 (1): 93–108. https://doi.org/10.1177/0163443719846610.

Mukhopadhyay, Nilanjan. 2021. 'With "sage" makeover, Brand Modi reinvents itself again', *Deccan Herald*, 5 January. https://www.deccanherald.com/opinion/with-sage-makeover-brand-modi-reinvents-itself-again-934577.html (accessed 17 February 2023).

Nandy, Ashis. 2010. *The Intimate Enemy: Loss and recovery of self under colonialism*, 2nd edn. New Delhi: Oxford University Press.

Nigam, Shalu. 2018. 'The cult of 56-inches and toxic masculinity.' SSRN Scholarly Paper ID 3201493. Social Science Research Network. https://doi.org/10.2139/ssrn.3201493.

Ohm, Britta. 2021. 'Defying responsibility: Modes of silence, religious symbolism, and biopolitics in the COVID-19 pandemic', in *The Routledge Handbook of Religion, Medicine, and Health*, edited by Dorothea Lüddeckens, Philipp Hetmanczyk, Pamela E. Klassen and Justin B. Stein, 502–8. Abingdon and New York: Routledge.

Owyong, Yuet See Monica. 2009. 'Clothing semiotics and the social construction of power relations', *Social Semiotics* 19 (2): 191–211. https://doi.org/10.1080/10350330902816434.

Pal, Joyojeet. 2015. 'Banalities turned viral: Narendra Modi and the political tweet', *Television & New Media* 16 (4): 378–87. https://doi.org/10.1177/1527476415573956.

PM India. 2021. 'PM's address at the World Economic Forum's Davos Dialogue', PM India, 28 January. https://www.pmindia.gov.in/en/news_updates/pms-address-at-the-world-economic-forums-davos-dialogue/ (accessed 17 February 2023).

Rageth, Nina. 2018. 'A reciprocal relationship: Siddha medicine in the context of a Hindu guru organization', *Asian Medicine* 13 (1–2): 222–46. https://doi.org/10.1163/15734218-12341414.

Rai, Swapnil. 2019. '"May the force be with you": Narendra Modi and the celebritization of Indian politics', *Communication, Culture and Critique* 12 (3): 323–39. https://doi.org/10.1093/ccc/tcz013.

Ramagundam, Rahul. 2018. *Gandhi's Khadi: A history of contention and conciliation*. Hyderabad: Orient Blackswan.

Rao, Shakuntala. 2018. 'Making of selfie nationalism: Narendra Modi, the paradigm shift to social media governance, and crisis of democracy', *Journal of Communication Inquiry* 42 (2): 166–83. https://doi.org/10.1177/0196859917754053.

Republic Bharat. 2018. 'Sadhguru Jaggi Vasudev joins PM Narendra Modi's "Swacchata Hi Seva" drive', 15 September. Video posted on YouTube. https://www.youtube.com/watch?v=wFRpjev6PDo (accessed 17 February 2023).

Roy, Arundhati. 2021. '"We are witnessing a crime against humanity": Arundhati Roy on India's Covid catastrophe', *The Guardian*, 28 April. https://www.theguardian.com/news/2021/apr/28/crime-against-humanity-arundhati-roy-india-covid-catastrophe (accessed 17 February 2023).

Roy, Indrajit. 2021. 'India: From the world's largest democracy to an ethnocracy', *India Forum*, 17 August. https://www.theindiaforum.in/article/india-world-s-largest-democracy-ethnocracy (accessed 17 February 2023).

Rudert, Angela. 2010. 'Research on contemporary Indian gurus: What's new about New Age gurus?', *Religion Compass* 4 (10): 629–42. https://doi.org/10.1111/j.1749-8171.2010.00245.x.

Sarbacker, Stuart Ray. 2014. 'Swami Ramdev: Modern yoga revolutionary', in *Gurus of Modern Yoga*, edited by Mark Singleton and Ellen Goldberg, 351–71. Oxford: Oxford University Press.

Sardesai, Rajdeep. 2019. *2019: How Modi won India*. Noida: HarperCollins.

Sears, Tamara I. 2014. *Worldly Gurus and Spiritual Kings: Architecture and asceticism in medieval India*. New Haven, CT: Yale University Press.

Sen, Ronojoy. 2016. 'Narendra Modi's makeover and the politics of symbolism', *Journal of Asian Public Policy* 9 (2): 98–111. https://doi.org/10.1080/17516234.2016.1165248.

Sen, Satadru. 2015. 'Ethnocracy, Israel and India', *History and Sociology of South Asia* 9 (2): 107–25. https://doi.org/10.1177/2230807515572211.

Sharma, Daneshwar and Akash D. Dubey. 2021. 'The political leader's motivating language use and his perceived effectiveness: The case of Narendra Modi's Mann Ki Baat', *Asian Politics & Policy* 13 (4): 534–53. https://doi.org/10.1111/aspp.12613.

Sharma, Unnati. 2021. 'Modi sheds his "ascetic" look, lands in US with trimmed beard & hair, "ready for business"', *The Print*, 23 September. https://theprint.in/india/modi-sheds-his-ascetic-look-lands-in-us-with-trimmed-beard-hair-ready-for-business/738865/ (accessed 17 February 2023).

Sikander, Zainab. 2020. 'Modi's lockdown beard is here to stay: It has much to achieve, politically', *The Print*, 26 October. https://theprint.in/opinion/modis-lockdown-beard-is-here-to-stay-it-has-much-to-achieve-politically/529735/ (accessed 17 February 2023).

Singh, Paramveer and Aman Deep. 2020. 'Growth of Facebook as a tool of electioneering: Reasons and facts', *Journal of Critical Reviews* 7 (19): 2977–85. http://dx.doi.org/10.31838/jcr.07.19.362.

Spurr, Michael James. 2016. 'Modern Hindu guru movements', in *Hinduism in India: Modern and contemporary movements*, edited by Will Sweetman and Aditya Malik, 141–75. Los Angeles: Sage.

Srivastava, Sanjay. 2015. 'Modi-masculinity: Media, manhood, and "traditions" in a time of consumerism', *Television & New Media* 16 (4): 331–8. https://doi.org/10.1177/1527476415575498.

Swachh Bharat Mission. 2021. 'Vision and objectives', Swachh Bharat Mission, 12 August. https://swachhbharatmission.gov.in/SBMCMS/about-us.htm (accessed 17 February 2023).

Tarlo, Emma. 1996. *Clothing Matters: Dress and identity in India*. London: Hurst.

Tøllefsen, Inga Bårdsen. 2011. 'Art of living: Religious entrepreneurship and legitimation strategies', *International Journal for the Study of New Religions* 2 (2): 255–79. http://dx.doi.org/10.1558/ijsnr.v2i2.255.

Van der Veer, Peter. 2001. *Imperial Encounters: Religion and modernity in India and Britain*. Princeton, NJ: Princeton University Press.

VHP. 2022. 'VHP at a glance: Introduction.' Vishva Hindu Parishad Official Website, 25 April. https://vhp.org/introduction/ (accessed 17 February 2023).

Waghorne, Joanne Punzo. 2009. 'Global gurus and the third stream of American religiosity: Between Hindu nationalism and liberal pluralism', in *Political Hinduism: The religious imagination in public spheres*, edited by Vinay Lal, 122–49. New Delhi: Oxford University Press.

Waghorne, Joanne Punzo. 2014. 'From diaspora to (global) civil society: Global gurus and the processes of de-ritualization and de-ethnization in Singapore', in *Hindu Ritual at the Margins: Innovations, transformations, reconsiderations*, edited by Linda Penkower and Tracy Pintchman, 186–207. Columbia: University of South Carolina Press.

Waghorne, Joanne Punzo. 2017. 'Alone together: Global gurus, cosmopolitan space, and community', in *Place/No-Place in Urban Asian Religiosity*, edited by Joanne Punzo Waghorne, 71–90. Singapore: Springer.

Waikar, Prashant. 2018. 'Reading Islamophobia in Hindutva: An analysis of Narendra Modi's political discourse', *Islamophobia Studies Journal* 4 (2): 161–80. https://doi.org/10.13169/islastudj.4.2.0161.

Warrier, Maya. 2003a. 'Guru choice and spiritual seeking in contemporary India', *International Journal of Hindu Studies* 7 (1): 31–54. http://dx.doi.org/10.1007/s11407-003-0002-7.

Warrier, Maya. 2003b. 'Processes of secularization in contemporary India: Guru faith in the Mata Amritanandamayi Mission', *Modern Asian Studies* 37 (1): 213–53. https://doi.org/10.1017/S0026749X03001070.

Warrier, Maya. 2005. *Hindu Selves in a Modern World: Guru faith in the Mata Amritanandamayi Mission*. Abingdon: RoutledgeCurzon.

Weber, Max. 1968. *Economy and Society: An outline of interpretive sociology*, vol. 1. New York: Bedminster Press.

Wire, The. 2021. 'Support for Modi as "best choice for PM" falls from 66% to 24% in a year, India Today poll finds', *The Wire*, 16 August. https://thewire.in/government/narendra-modi-prime-minister-adityanath-india-today-poll (accessed 17 February 2023).

Wright, Theodore. 2015. 'Modi and the Muslims: The dilemma for the Muslim minority in the 2014 Indian national elections', *Journal of South Asian and Middle Eastern Studies* 38 (2): 65–72. https://doi.org/10.1353/jsa.2015.0002.

Yiftachel, Oren. 2000. '"Ethnocracy" and its discontents: Minorities, protests, and the Israeli polity', *Critical Inquiry* 26 (4): 725–56. https://doi.org/10.1086/448989.

4
'Immortal Gurus of *Bhārata*': the social biography of a contemporary image

Raphaël Voix

Over the last 20 years or so in India, it has not been unusual to come across a particular type of religious image that appears to borrow from the theological inclusiveness of caste Hinduism while referring to sectarian saintly figures. In these images the gurus placed side by side represent different sectarian affiliations, although all belong to religious communities originating on the South Asian continent. They look like 'class photographs' of ascetics. The images, more prevalent in north India and very likely originating in Bengal, are most often found in places of worship dedicated to a saint, even though they are not themselves objects of worship and no ritual seems to be associated with them. What then is their function? What exactly do they represent? What is the logic behind the choice of characters represented?

In order to answer these questions, I shall start with a study of the corpus of the images and give a broad outline of the shared characteristics that establish this corpus as a particular 'type'. Next, I shall set up a social biography (Appadurai 1986) of one of these images, analysing its genesis and the variations it presents. According to the logic I will identify, I will, in my final section, consider the relationship with the other that these figures give rise to. I shall endeavour especially to explain the paradox whereby these sectarian figures, generally worshipped in an exclusive manner, are gathered together here to bring about a modality peculiar to Hindu pluralism, which I shall call 'egalitarian pluralism'. The aim in this study will be, on the one hand, to give an account of a singular relationship to otherness in which the habitual theological and regional boundaries are dispensed with in favour of a religious identity common to the whole Indian subcontinent and, on the other, to accentuate the limits of this 'inclusivism'; through a process of working in the dark, the figure of the religious other will become visible, that figure which cannot be integrated into the 'Immortal Gurus of *Bhārata*'.

A type of modern *deśika* image

The images that are the subject of this chapter belong to a Hindu iconographic tradition of which the sole object is the representation of human beings. Daniel Smith has suggested qualifying this tradition as '*deśika*'. Derived from the Sanskrit term *deśa*, 'country, place, region or province', this neologism refers to a 'local', that is, an individual born in a specific place with which he is familiar. Figuratively, the term *deśika* connotes the idea of a 'guide, an extraordinary inhabitant', and may refer to a '*guru* or spiritual teacher' (Smith 1978, 61 n. 1). Smith constructs this term to contrast with '*devata*' ('deity'), with which he associates the entire assembly of Hindu representations of gods and goddesses as well as deified elements of non-human origin (animals and others) that are objects of worship (p. 40). The former differs from the latter in that a personage is 'never represented with several body parts' (p. 40). The *devata* images and *deśika* images, in contrast, have a human physical appearance (two arms, a head, a pair of legs, etc.) which is simply the 'visual reminder of the terrestrial origin, human nature and worldly virtues that the figure represented is meant to immortalise' (p. 61). A wide variety of Hindu images thus belong to this *deśika* category, and especially all represent-ations of religious personages, often known and sometimes forgotten, whether of distant epochs or recent – that is, contemporary – times, who benefit from regional or pan-Indian celebrity and may be depicted in such varied ways as holy father (*bābā*), holy mother (*āmmā*), saint (*sant*), swami (*svāmi*), hero (*virā*), yogi (*yogīn*), and, too, as devotee (*bhakta*), seer-sage (*ṛṣī*), ascetic (*tapasas*), bard (*kavyavacakas*) (p. 61 nn. 1, 2).

The *deśika* images analysed in this chapter display a homogeneity that leads us to say that they constitute a particular 'type', distinguished by common characteristics in terms of composition, historical origin and usage.

A characteristic composition

All the 10 or so images collected, of which three are shown here (Figures 4.1–4.3), are in A4 size and landscape format, with a general title,

Figure 4.1 *The sons of ambrosia.* The forty-two monks of India. Front row (12 portraits): Buddha, Śaṅkarācārya, Nanāk, Dhanajayadas, Pranavananda, Bhaskarananda, Caitanya, Nigamananda, Vivekananda, Jalaram, Gambirnath, Balananda Maharaj. Second row (12 portraits): Mahāvīra, Padmapādācārya, Haridāsa, Shirdi Sai Baba, Nityānanda, Kabīr, Tulsīdās, Rāmānuja, Goraknāth, Totapuri, Devraha Baba, Santadas Kathiya Baba. Third row (12 portraits): Madhusūdana Sarasvatī, Visuddhananda Paramahamsa, Bijoykrishna Gosvami, Aurobindo Ghose, Vishuddhananda Sarasvati, Ramana Maharshi, Rāmprasād Sen, Bamakhepa, Lahiri Mahasaya, Ram Thakur, Jagadbandhu, Bholananda giri. Fourth row (6 portraits): Mahavatar Babaji, Ramdas Kathiya Baba, Trailanga Svami, Bholanath, Lokenath Brahmachari, Ramakrishna.

Figure 4.2 *The great incarnations of eternal India.* Fifty immortal gurus of Bharat.

'IMMORTAL GURUS OF *BHĀRATA*': SOCIAL BIOGRAPHY OF AN IMAGE   151

Figure 4.3 *Saints of India.*

and comprise several rows of juxtaposed portraits followed by a box containing a subtitle, below which we can read the names of the personages represented.[1] These images differ in whether they are in black and white or colour, in background (plain or not) and in the number and nature of the portraits, but they are all composed of a central iconographic area surrounded by graphic segments. These last comprise a title and a subtitle that, although they differ from one image to another, in their language as well as in the terms they use, include two elements: the 'type' of personages represented and the 'territory' with which they are associated.[2]

The 'type' of personage
The images display different qualifiers to designate the personages represented. In Indian languages, whether Sanskrit or one of the vernacular languages (Hindi, Bengali, Tamil), three different expressions are used: 'Sons of ambrosia' (*amṛtasya putrāḥ*), which is a fairly rare Sanskrit formulation designating beings established in a state of bliss and immortality,[3] and two more common expressions, *ṛṣi*, which designates 'an inspired poet or sage …; a saint or sanctified sage in general, an ascetic, anchorite' (Monier-Williams 1899, 226, 227), and *mahā muni*, 'a [great] saint, sage, seer, ascetic, monk, devotee, hermit' (Monier-Williams 1899, 823). These three expressions share a Vedic origin, a point of the

utmost importance, as we will see. It is noteworthy that none of the more current terms, such as 'descent' (*avatāra*), 'great soul' (*mahātma*), devotee (*bhakta*), holy father (*bābā*), ascetic (*sādhu*), holy mother (*āmmā*), 'yogi' (*yogī*), saint (*sant*), 'hero' (*virā*), 'ascetic' (*tapasas*), 'bard' (*kavyavacakas*) or even 'renunciant' (*saṃnyāsī*), is used. This is no doubt because all these terms refer either to a specific theology or to a specific societal state, which is exactly what the image is intended to do away with.[4] With their titles carrying few theological and social connotations, the images analysed in this chapter are able to encompass ascetics of different obediences, another very important point. In the English-language versions of this image, the words 'monks', 'saints' and 'incarnations', which have no exact equivalents in Indian languages, are used indiscriminately.[5] The last term frequently used is 'guru', a Sanskrit term meaning 'heavy' and commonly used in all Indian languages from pre-modern times. In the texts, it often refers to a 'spiritual teacher' with whom the disciples have a particularly 'personal' and 'emotional' relationship (Hara 1979, 94); nowadays the term 'possesses the "semiotic limitlessness" characteristic of the floating signifier' and gurus become 'multifarious' agents of South Asian social life (Copeman and Ikegame 2012, 38). Beyond differences in terms, let us remember that the personages represented in the various images are all 'ascetics'. By this I mean people, mostly celibate, though sometimes married, who adhere to a religious way of life out of deliberate choice.[6]

The 'territory'

The second element present in the text of these images concerns the territory these gurus are associated with. Two words are indifferently employed to designate it: '*bhārata*' (equally *bhāratavarṣa*) and 'India'. The first is ancient and of Sanskrit origin. It refers in the Purāṇas to an idea of spatial and social insularity (Clémentin-Ojha 2014, 2). It thus designates territory within the Indian subcontinent where the ideal Brahmanical social system, based on the recognition of the Veda as supreme authority, prevailed. '*Bhārata*', however, never corresponded to a politically oriented entity before the nineteenth century, when its meaning incorporated geographical and political concepts imported by British colonisation, from which came the 'indigenous name given to a nascent nation' (Clémentin-Ojha 2014, 3).

The second term, 'India', just as ancient but of Graeco-Latin origin (Greek *Indikê*, Latin *India*), has been employed to designate a great variety of territories in southern Asia before coming, under colonisation, to designate what was 'mapped and organised by the British' (Clémentin-Ojha 2014, 3). There is thus a long historical and cultural process that has seen the meaning of these two terms evolve to be considered as quasi-synonyms, as witnessed by the fact that, after independence, when Indian legislators were drafting the constitution of the nascent nation, they employed these terms interchangeably, at least in legal and political contexts. Besides being a sign of the contemporality of the images, the undifferentiated use of the terms here seems to refer rather to a philosophical and religious level. These gurus have, in fact, a single trait in common, that of having exercised their charisma in South Asia but over a territory that extends beyond present regional and national borders. A number of the gurus depicted in the image are notably of East Bengal origin, a region today estranged from the Indian nation-state.

A modern group of portraits

In South Asia, representations by material images of gods, of a religious leader or of a perfect soul go back to the second century BCE, a period when Vedic circles would have accommodated the use of this type of religious image (Colas 2010: 529). It seems that a number of representations of personages found in temples serve as souvenirs for the devotees.[7] Not all these representations constitute 'portraits', however, in the strict sense of the term. Referring to the classical definition of a 'portrait' – according to which 'portraits are art works, intentionally made of living or once living people by artists, in a variety of media, and for an audience' (Brilliant 1991, 8) – Lefebvre adds three criteria to distinguish a simple 'image' from a portrait. First is the 'intention': a portrait results from a deliberate choice to represent a person whose historical existence is attested; second is the 'perception': the person whose portrait is drawn must be identifiable by the observer; if not, it is nothing but an 'image'; and third is the 'function': a portrait is distinguished by the specific use made of it (Lefebvre 2011, 18; 2018, 34). Because it represents different individuals who have existed and are identifiable, the *deśika* image analysed in this chapter may be called a 'group of portraits'.

Such a group of portraits is unprecedented in the history of Hinduism.[8] Though the earliest groups of portraits of Hindu gurus appear in the medieval era in Vaisnava devotional milieux, they represent, exclusively, members of a single sect.[9] When the groups of portraits of Hindu gurus of different sectarian obediences appear, they are of male saints participating in the same soteriological movement. This is notably the case with the Sants, those medieval poets of different theological inclinations who nevertheless share the same critique of doctrinal distinctions and preach a religion of divine love.[10] By bringing together individuals from the same region of the world in a photograph with the legend 'East-Asian group', the image created seemed to associate territorial belonging with religious unity, a feature which is at the heart of the image that is the subject of this chapter.

The advent of photography in India in the middle of the nineteenth century could only confirm this trend: the earliest photographs of the group of ascetics show members of the same sectarian tradition exclusively.[11] In 1893, however, one case in particular stands out. During the World's Parliament of Religions, which took place on the fringe of the World's Columbian Exposition in Chicago with a view to setting up a global interreligious dialogue, several photographs of groups of religious leaders were taken. Aside from the well-known image of the closing ceremony in which all the members present are sitting side by side (Barrows 1893, frontispiece; Seager 1995, 93), another image gained a wide circulation in India. Entitled 'East Indian group', it shows five of the Indian leaders present at Chicago standing side by side (Houghton 1893, 534), including representatives of Hinduism, Buddhism and Jainism.[12]

All the same, according to our survey, the earliest group of portraits of Indian holy men referring to different epochs and obediences dates from the first quarter of the twentieth century.[13] Entitled 'A group of thirty religious men of India' and sub-titled 'Paradise' (*nandanakānana*), the image conforms to the same kind of composition as the type of *deśika* images analysed here (Figure 4.4). There is an iconographic area where several personages are placed side by side and two explanatory graphic areas. The central figure, wearing a blue loincloth and standing with his arms raised towards the sky, is Caitanya, which leads us to suppose that the image is of Vaisnava inspiration. We will return to this image in the Conclusion.[14]

An image with diverse functions

These images bringing together portraits of saints are usually framed under glass or, more rarely, rolled up. Unlike the other types of *deśika* images they are not known to be available as greetings cards, key rings, etc., nor as articles such as hologram cards, in which the portrait of a saint is superposed on a divine representation. These are on sale on stalls around the places where the saint is venerated and are available in digital format on the internet (via websites or social networks). They may also be edited into online videos, in which a progressive zoom on the image and then on each portrait is accompanied by devotional music.[15] Unlike other images of male Hindu saints, this type of image is not an object of veneration within a particular cult. They may be hung on the wall of a

Figure 4.4 *A group of thirty religious men of India*. Front row: Bijoykrishna Gosvami, Nanāk, Buddha, Śaṅkara, Ramakrishna, Vivekananda. Second row: Jagadbandhu, illegible, Lokenath Bramachari, Trailanga Svami, Bhaskarananda, Hariguru Swami, illegible, illegible. Third row: Rammohan Roy, Debendranath Tagore, Keshubchandra Sen, Dayananda Sarasvati, illegible, Nityānanda, Keśava Bhāratī, Caitanya, Rāmānuja, Sivanarayan, Vallabha, illegible, Brahmananda, Kabīr, Haridāsa.

house or kept in a temple but do not, for all that, have a purely aesthetic or decorative function. In India, as elsewhere, a portrait is not distinguished from the model from whom it is derived. Without becoming objects of worship, the portraits act as a 'substitute' for or 'souvenir' of the model they represent and will even be 'impregnated with his presence' (Lefèvre 2018: 43–6).[16] This is how these images operate as a reminder to the observer of a particular presence.

Cultural biography of the 'Immortal Gurus of *Bhārata*'

The characteristics of this type of *deśika* image having been outlined in broad strokes we turn to a series of images that we will call the 'Immortal Gurus of *Bhārata*', who all originate from the same 'source image' (Figure 4.1); I shall attempt to outline a cultural biography for them.[17] Initiated by Appadurai (1986), this method consists in following the tracks of an object as it goes through the different stages of its existence and different regimes of value. We shall look first at the initial manufacture of the source image and then at its circulation and the transformations it undergoes. In so doing we shall attempt to see what these different logics of production of the image have to teach us about the relationship with the other in sectarian Hinduism.

From the assemblage of heterogeneous portraits to the creation of a monolithic image

The detailed observation of the source image and its different declensions allows, in default of knowing the exact origin, identification of the principles of its making. To compose the harmonious image we have in front of us, the original author of the image had to choose the portraits of the ascetics before assembling and retouching them.

A heterogeneous selection of gurus

The construction of this image (Figure 4.1) starts with the selection of 42 portraits. The choice conforms to two criteria: the portraits are exclusively of male and deceased personages. They are divided into two kinds, however: paintings or drawings of gurus who lived before the nineteenth century, and photographs of gurus born after 1800.

There are 13 of the first kind, including the founders of religions[18] that grew up in South Asia from the same soil as Hinduism, including the Buddha,[19] founder of Buddhism, and Jina Mahāvīra, founder of Jainism. Present too is Guru Nanak (1469–1539), founder of Sikhism, a tradition that has become independent of Hinduism. The rest of the gurus are generally considered to be 'Hindus'. We find several founders of sectarian traditions (*sampradāya*), including Śaṅkara (788–820), the principal founding teacher (*ācārya*) of the school of Advaita Vedānta, to which the *Daśanāmī sampradāya* order claims allegiance. His presence is a reminder that he is an essential reference for a number of modern Hindu gurus. Padmapādācārya too is there, disciple of Śaṅkara and author of the treatise *Pañcapādikā* (1992), with which is associated the foundation of Dvārakā Pīṭha (in Gujarat), the headquarters in the west of India of Śaṅkara's monastic tradition. Next come several founders of Vaiṣṇava sectarian traditions: Rāmānujā (1050–1139), founder of the sect of Śrīvaiṣṇava (Śrī Sampradāya) and the school of Viśiṣṭādvaita (qualified non-dualism), a theist interpretation of Vedānta; Caitanya (1486–1533), founder of the Bengal Vaiṣṇava (*gauḍīya vaiṣṇava*); his close disciple Nityānanda (sixteenth century); and finally Haridāsa (*c*.1480–1575), founder of the eponymous sect Haridāsī Sampradāya. The only Śaiva represented among these medieval gurus is Gorakhnāth, (twelfth-century) guru of the sect of Nāth yogis. Besides these founders we find some personages celebrated in north Indian Hinduism: Kabīr (1440–1518) the mystic-poet of Benares, who preaches a religion of love for a supreme, unique deity and is a prominent representative the stream of the *sant*; Madhusūdana Sarasvatī (1540–1640), propagator of Advaita, and his friend Tulsīdās (1543–1623), a prolific poet and the author of the *Rāmcaritmānas* (1574).

The second type of portrait, elaborated from retouched photographic images, contains 31 modern gurus.[20] Of these more than two thirds are of Bengali origin. Some, such as Vivekananda (1883–1903) and his guru Ramakrishna (1836–86), have international reputations,[21] while others are known only in north and east India but are part of defined sectarian lineages;[22] finally there are those who are outside any sectarian framework and whose popularity is only regional, in this case Bengali.[23] We also note the presence of north Indian ascetics who were initiated into Hindu sects but subsequently lived and acted independently of those sects.[24] On the other hand, surprisingly, no modern superior of a monastic headquarters in the Shankarian tradition is shown, even though some enjoy great renown.[25] Finally, the presence of several little-known members of the Ramakrishna Mission contrasts with figures who are more celebrated but belong to reform movements originating in other parts of Bengal.[26] These features, taken together, lead me to believe that we are dealing with an image that originated in modern Bengali Hindu circles, a point to which we shall return.

Realistic portraits

The image thus combines painted or drawn portraits of ascetics who lived before the advent of photography with photographs (black-and-white or sepia) of ascetics taken during their lifetimes. All the same, the demarcation line between these two types of portrait is fluid and hard to discern at first glance. Techniques as diverse as cropping, composite printing, scratching and photomontage have always been central to the practice of photography. In South Asia, this manipulation was primarily done through 'painted photographs' (Gutman 1982; Pinney 1997; Dewan 2012), to the extent of their being considered as an 'autonomous genre' forming a 'legitimate expression of popular culture' (Allana and Kumar 2008). Just a few years after their introduction into the British Raj, and following the decline of the princely states with their patronage, most photographic studios employed artists who specialised in the production of Mughal miniature paintings to decorate photographs. By deepening some hues, by adding a subtle touch of colour, by adding jewellery, textiles and embroidery to a portrait or associating it with a luxurious and opulent frame, these artists were able to transform reality. Photographs of families, sovereigns or ascetics were transformed into dreamlike and surreal images by being coloured with oil paint, watercolours or gouache, which created a unique visual culture.[27]

In the same way, to make the source image, the artist-photographer retouches each portrait by hand. His work seems to be guided by two aims. The first is that every portrait should be photorealistic even if its origin is in painting. Through technical work in the course of which exposure, contrasts and clouds are modified and colours smoothed, the artist-photographer is trying not so much to decorate a photograph as to produce the 'embellished reality' (Dewan 2012) which has made these images painted in India famous, as to render each portrait hyperrealistic. It is this that gives the viewer the illusion of the reality of the image in its grouping. The second axis guiding the work of the artist-photographer is to take each portrait out of the socio-religious context of its origin. The work of retouching usually consists of adding objects to embellish the photograph, while here the aim is to remove parts of the real so as to minimise marks of sectarian affiliation. A *deśika* portrait is generally enriched with 'clues' to the sectarian framework of the figure and to his wider socio-historical context. Gestures with the hands (*hasta-mūdras*), postures, attitudes and ornamentation (accessories, landscape, illustration of miracles, etc.) place the ascetic in a visual context and by so doing give meaning to the image. As in the case of images of deities, these clues mean that *deśika* images may be recognised in the Hindu communities to which they refer (Smith 1978, 61). Here the artist seems to adopt a reverse approach: having extracted the portrait from its socio-cultural environment, he accentuates the very recognisable manifestations of its religious identity. He thus separates the portrait from the accompanying background and may suppress an ornament, a necklace, a staff or a sectarian insignia. In other words, the artist-photographer removes from each portrait the spatio-temporal and theological markers that make it too recognisably unique, making sure at the same time that the subject of the portrait is identifiable, or it would no longer be a portrait. In so doing he manages to erase the plurality of identities. He has thus created what might be called a 'mono-iconic' image, which is certainly his mission: to give a monolithic appearance to a composite image.

A harmonious overall appearance

The final step in the making of this image consists in placing the portraits side by side and giving the totality a harmonious appearance. First of all, to give this impression, each portrait is represented independently of the sectarian lineage, if any, to which the subject belongs. Most of them are shown without their ascendants, companions or disciples, unlike the more classical iconographies of the sectarian milieu. When several personages of the same lineage are represented, they are separated from one another. Furthermore, all the figures are in the same seated posture, whatever their usual iconography may be. Caitanya (1486–1533), a Bengali mystic known for the intensity of his devotion to Krishna, is shown seated even though he is classically represented standing on the sole of one foot with the other bare foot forward and both arms raised, countenance absorbed in divine intoxication (Smith 1978, 54). Finally, the overall harmony of the 'Immortal Gurus of *Bhārata*' is reinforced by the choice of a plain black background (Figures 4.1, 4.6, 4.8) or a coloured one (with some exceptions that we shall analyse), and the fact that the difference in shades between the portraits is accentuated makes the singularity of the 'Immortal Gurus of *Bhārata*' more striking.

To illustrate even better the 'Immortal Gurus of *Bhārata*', let us look at Figure 4.5. Although it also consists of a grouping of male and female saints, it is different in every way from the analysis above. First of all, it brings together divine figures of different natures, some historical, others mythological, which does not correspond at all to a group of portraits in the strict sense of the term. Then, it keeps each figure in its iconographic universe of origin: along with a collection of sectarian insignia, in

Figure 4.5 Potpourri of divine figures.

company with his co-religionists, or in the posture the community expects to see him in, not necessarily seated. Moreover, there is no work of fusion or smoothing of colour, which gives the image the appearance of a kaleidoscope of divine figures. Finally, these different images are arranged chronologically, each row corresponding to a different historical period. From the first image, which shows a Vedic sacrifice (*yājña*), to the last, which is a graphic representation of the sound Om, considered as the primordial seed containing the totality of the Vedic revelation, all the images together are grouped by epoch.[28]

Circulation, reproduction and variations

The monolithic appearance of the source image would lead us to suppose that its assemblage would be beyond question. In reality, the image has, since its elaboration, had a life of its own. By a process of repeated aggregation, each community, temple or devotee has been able to transform it to adapt it to its own socio-religious context. The techniques of hand colouring (paint application, retouching or colouring) that comprised the source image have disappeared from modern studios in India, to be replaced by digital techniques. The source image has thus been the object of various reappropriations, reminding us that 'no visual image is self-sufficient, bounded, insulated; instead, it is open, porous, permeable, and ever available for appropriation', resulting in the emergence of an interocular or intervisual work of art (Ramaswamy 2003, xvi).

Variant 1

It is common for the artist-photographer to take the opportunity to introduce his own guru into the image. Figure 4.6 is the exact replica of the source image (Figure 4.1) except that the author has added to the back row the portrait of Sri Sri Nitaichaitanya Paramhansadev (Figure 4.7), a Vaisnava guru whose reputation is limited to the district of Birbhum in West Bengal. The author of this image has renamed it 'The forty-three monks of India' and has distributed it through his own social networks. One would not recognise the source image, since there is no clue that would point to this being a variant. Thus, contrary to the idea that the development of modern media (films, radio, scholarly textbooks, journals, reviews and paperbacks) would cause the disappearance of local religiosity in favour of more regional or pan-Indian forms, we see that the reappearance of this image may contribute to the establishment of local charisma.

Figure 4.6 *The forty-three monks of India.* Front row (12 portraits): Buddha, Śaṅkarācārya, Nanāk, Dhanajayadas, Pranavananda, Bhaskarananda, Caitanya, Nigamananda, Vivekananda, Jalaram, Gambirnath, Balananda Maharaj. Second row (12 portraits): Mahāvīra, Padmapādācārya, Haridāsa, Shirdi Sai Baba, Nityānanda, Kabīr, Tulsīdās, Rāmānuja, Goraknāth, Totapuri, Devraha Baba, Santadas Kathiya Baba. Third row (12 portraits): Madhusūdana Sarasvatī, Visuddhananda Paramahamsa, Bijoykrishna Gosvami, Aurobindo Ghose, Vishuddhananda Sarasvati, Ramana Maharshi, Rāmprasād Sen, Bamakhepa, Lahiri Mahasaya, Ram Thakur, Jagadbandhu, Bholananda giri. Fourth row (seven portraits): Sri Sri NitaiChaitanya Paramhansadev, Mahavatar Babaji, Ramdas Kathiya Baba, Trailanga Svami, Bholanath, Lokenath Brahmachari, Ramakrishna.

Figure 4.7   Portrait of Sri Sri Nitaichaitanya Paramhansadev.

Variant 2

In contrast, other variants are distinguished by the fact that the author has not concealed the cutting and pasting work. We see this in Figure 4.8, which has been elaborated in Kerala. The author has added nine portraits of gurus to the source image, pasting them at the ends of each row but without trying to unify the colour, so that their brighter portraits stand out from the others. Among these additions are a large number of gurus of Kerala: Narayana Guru (1856?–1928), a saintly figure celebrated in Kerala as much among Muslims and Christians as among Hindus who has many local masters associated with him, such as Chattampi Swamikal (1853–1924), Shubhananda Swami (1882–1950) and Nataraja Guru (1895–1973); Bhagawan Nityananda (1888–1961) of the siddha yoga; and Ramdas Ramdas (1884–1963), disciple of Ramana Maharsi. Adding

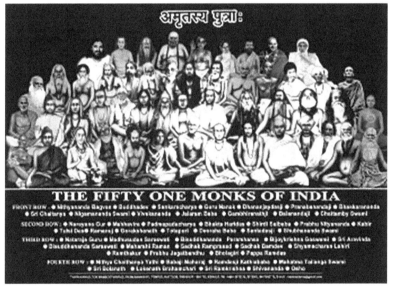

Figure 4.8 *The fifty-one monks of India.* Front row (14 portraits): Bhagawan Nityananda, Buddha, Śaṅkarācārya, Nanāk, Dhanajayadas, Pranavananda, Bhaskarananda, Caitanya, Nigamananda, Vivekananda, Jalaram, Gambirnath, Balananda Maharaj, Chattampi Swamikal. Second row (14 portraits): Narayana Guru, Mahāvīra, Padmapādācārya, Haridāsa, Shirdi Sai Baba, Nityānanda, Kabīr, Tulsīdās, Rāmānuja, Goraknāth, Totapuri, Devraha Baba, Santadas Kathiya Baba, Shubhananda Swami. Third row (14 portraits): Nataraja guru, Madhusūdana Sarasvatī, Visuddhananda Paramahamsa, Bijoykrishna Gosvami, Aurobindo Ghose, Vishuddhananda Sarasvati, Ramana Maharshi, Rāmprasād Sen, Bamakhepa, Lahiri Mahasaya, Ram Thakur, Jagadbandhu, Bholananda giri, Ramdas. Fourth row (nine portraits): Mahavatar Babaji, Ramdas Kathiya Baba, Trailanga Svami, Bholanath, Lokenath Brahmachari, Ramakrishna, Sivananda, Osho-Rajneesh.

Figure 4.9 *The forty-two monks of India* (photo Raphaël Voix). Front row (12 portraits): Buddha, Śaṅkarācārya, Nanāk, Dhanajayadas, Pranavananda, Bhaskarananda, Caitanya, Nigamananda, Vivekananda, Jalaram, Gambirnath, Balananda Maharaj. Second row (12 portraits): Mahāvīra, Padmapādācārya, Haridāsa, Shirdi Sai Baba, Nityānanda, Kabīr, Tulsīdās, Rāmānuja, Goraknāth, Totapuri, Devraha Baba, Santadas Kathiya Baba. Third row (12 portraits): Madhusūdana Sarasvatī, Visuddhananda Paramahamsa, Bijoykrishna Gosvami, Aurobindo Ghose, Vishuddhananda Sarasvati, Ramana Maharshi, Rāmprasād Sen, Bamakhepa, Lahiri Mahasaya, Ram Thakur, Jagadbandhu, Bholananda giri. Fourth row (6 portraits): Mahavatar Babaji, Ramdas Kathiya Baba, Trailanga Svami, Bholanath, Lokenath Brahmachari, Ramakrishna.

specifically local figures assists in the regional reinscription of the image. Also added are several figures celebrated abroad: Sivananda (1887–1963), founder of the Divine Life Society, and Rajneesh, later known as Osho (1931–90), founder of the Rajneesh movement.

Variant 3

Another way of transforming the source image is to insert specifically Hindu symbols. It is this type of reappropriation that we see on the cover illustration (Figure 4.9) of the English translation of the Bengali work *Jñānaganja*, whose author Gopinath Kaviraj (1887–1976) was a celebrated Bengali pandit and mystic, intimate with several gurus of his time.[29] To the left is a representation of the saint Caitanya (1486–1533) standing with his arms raised towards the sky according to his classic iconography; at the centre a stylised Shiva lingam bears the three strokes (*tripuṇḍra*) of the sectarian Saiva mark, encompassed by a cobra and with a luminous halo above him; to the right is the modern effigy of the god Vishnu, haloed by a glittering circle and with some of his typical attributes – the conch (*sankha*), the mace (*gadā*), the lotus (*padma*), the bow (*dhanu*) and the disc (*cakra*) – and, enclosed in a stylised graphic representation in Devanagari letters, Om, the sacred syllable (*praṇava*) which is for the Hindus the 'primordial seed' representing the essence of the Vedic revelation (*śruti*).[30] The image in its entirety is placed above a mountainous landscape that evokes the Himalaya, a Saiva icon.

In adding these various symbols to the source image, the image's author fits it into an explicitly Hindu cultural and mythological framework. Not only does the presence of divine images (*mūrti*), which are objects of worship in temples, break with the use of human portraits alone, but the representation of mountains in the background places this image squarely in the wider mythological framework, in line with the subject matter of the work for which the image is the front cover. In fact, *jñānaganja*, the title of the book, is a Sanskrit technical term certainly used in the Tantric context (*tāntrika*) to designate those realms where the circles of perfect beings (*siddha*) live in their bodies of light. It refers to a tantric cosmology according to which ascetics who in their lifetime have acquired extraordinary powers gain access after their physical death (*samādhi*) to that same place of eternal rest (Kaviraj 2014, 94). That space called *jñānaganja* is of an 'imaginal' nature. By this expression, taken from Henri Corbin, André Padoux refers to a type of reality in Indian studies that is 'imaginary' in that it appeals to the imagination of the yogi who visualises it, but which is no less 'true', since the yogi is able actually to experience it (Padoux 2013, 10). However, according to Kaviraj, *jñānaganja* refers, too, to a real area situated in the Himalaya, beyond Mount Kailash on the border of Tibet (p. 80). The image then takes on quite another dimension, symbolising the assembly of perfect beings and thereby referring to an assumed mythological corpus.

Variant 4

The fourth variant of the image (Figure 4.10) is entitled 'The family of ambrosia' (*amṛtasya pārivāraḥ*), with the subtitle 'The group of sixty great seer sages of Bhārata' (*bhāratvarṣera ṣāṭjana mahā muni ṛṣigaṇa*). It takes up the selection of Figure 4.1 by extending it to comprise 60 exclusively male personages. With 18 figures added, placed either at the ends of the rows existing in the source image, or on a new, higher, row, the process of aggregation to the work multiplies the bodies of the yogis and confers an even more powerful force on the image. While no personage has been subtracted, several have been displaced. For example, the first row brings together the same dozen portraits as the source image

Figure 4.10 *The family of ambrosia*. The group of sixty great spirits of Bhāratavarṣa. First row (12 portraits): Buddha, Śaṅkarācārya, Nanāk, Dhanajayadas, Pranavananda, Bhaskarananda, Caitanya, Nigamananda, Brahmananda, Jalaram, Gambirnath, Balananda Maharaj. Second row (13 portraits): Sitaram Omkarnath, Mahāvīra, Padmapādācārya, Haridāsa, Shirdi Sai Baba, Nityānanda, Kabīr, Tulsīdās, Rāmānuja, Goraknāth, Totapuri, Devraha Baba, Santadas Kathiya Baba. Third row (13 portraits): Mohananda Brahmachari, Madhusūdana Sarasvatī, Visuddhananda Paramahamsa, Bijoykrishna Gosvami, Aurobindo Ghose, Vishudananda Sarasvatī, Ramana Maharshi, Rāmprasād Sen, Bamakhepa, Lahiri Mahasaya, Ram Thakur, Jagadbandhu, Bholananda Giri. Fourth row (14 portraits): Dayananda Sarasvati, Samartha Rāmdās, Bhaba Pagla, Anukulchandra, Mahavatar Babaji, Ramdas Kathiya Baba, Trailanga Svami, A.C. Bhaktivedanta, Lokenath Brahmachari, Harichand Thakur, ?????, Hariharananda Aranya, Paramananda, Yogananda. Fifth row (8 portraits): Durgaprassana, Jñāndev, Vivekananda, Ramakrishna, Abhedananda, Satyananda, Swarupananda, Prajnananda.

with the exception of Vivekanana, whose head is replaced with that of Brahmananda, his close disciple and spiritual companion. This feature is of particular interest as it recalls the bricolage nature of this collage logic. To maintain the harmony of the original image, instead of removing Vivekananda in order to replace him with Brahmananda, the author is content to replace the face of the former (Figure 4.11) with that of the latter (Figure 4.12), creating thereby a hybrid ascetic (Figure 4.13), the head of Brahmananda on the body of Vivekananda.[31]

Through the use of a well-known photograph – taken in Jaipur in 1886 and used as the cover of his *Complete Works* (Vivekananda 2019) – which shows him in his distinctive monastic habit, the reinsertion of Vivekananda at the summit (fifth row of Figure 4.10) gives the image a new meaning. Now dominated by the central and disproportionate

Figure 4.11 Vivekananda, Calcutta.

Figure 4.12 Brahmananda, Calcutta.

portrait of Ramakrishna, who is seen flanked by two of his turbaned disciples (Vivekananda to the left and Abhedananda to the right), the image would seem to be dominated by the Ramakrishna Mission.

Variant 5

The last variant is entitled 'The extraordinary (*ālokita*) children (*santān*) of ambrosia (*amṛta*)' (Figure 4.14). The image is framed and displayed in

Figure 4.13 False brahmananda.

a temple in south Kolkata.[32] Aside from its Bengali origin, its being in colour, and the very large number of saints it depicts, it is remarkable in that it includes several female ascetics or mystics (*sādhikā*), some not of South Asian origin. There are nine of these women, all placed in the top row. There we find Mīrābāī (sixteenth century), a saint celebrated for her songs, and two holy women associated with Ramakrishna: Bhairavi Brahmani (nineteenth century), who is said to have given Ramakrishna tantric initiation, and Sarada Devi (1853–1920), his young wife. As well as Anandamayi Ma (1896–1982), the holy woman of Bengal, there are two mystics associated with Sri Aurobindo: Mirra Alfassa (1910–73), his spiritual companion, and Indira Devi, disciple of Dilip Kumar Roy – himself a disciple of Sri Aurobindo – with whom she founded the temple of Hare Krishna at Pune.

This feminisation of the image most likely originates from the personal inclination of B. K. Shital, its author, whose initials suggest that he may have been a member of the Brahma Kumaris World Spiritual University.[33] Founded in 1937 at Sindh, BKWS is a Vaisnava sect known, since women have always held a central position in it, for its 'indigenous feminism' (Babb 1984), in contrast to the prevailing view of female asceticism in India.[34] The image thus incorporates the founder, a diamond dealer called Lekhraj K. Kripalani (1871–1969) (first from the left in row 5), as well as the first two administrative superiors of the sect, Jagadamba Sarasvati (1920–65), venerated as the Mother Superior, and Prakashmani (1922–2007), venerated as the Sister Superior. It should be noted that two

Figure 4.14 *The extraordinary children of ambrosia*. Front row (12 portraits): Buddha, Śaṅkarācārya, Nanāk, Dhanajayadas, Pranavananda, Bhaskarananda, Caitanya, Nigamananda, Vivekananda, Jalaram, Gambirnath, Balananda Maharaj. Second row (12 portraits): Mahāvīra, Padmapādācārya, Haridāsa, Shirdi Sai Baba, Nityānanda, Kabīr, Tulsīdās, Rāmānuja, Goraknāth, Totapuri, Devraha Baba, Santadas Kathiya Baba. Third row (13 portraits): Madhusūdana Sarasvatī, Visuddhananda Paramahamsa, Bijoykrishna Gosvami, Aurobindo Ghose, Vishudananda Sarasvati, Ramana Maharshi, Rāmprasād Sen, Bamakhepa, Lahiri Mahasaya, Ram Thakur, Jagadbandhu, Bholananda Giri, Bhaktisiddhanta Sarasvati. Fourth row (13 portraits): Janakinath Brahmachari, Bamakhepa, Sanskar puri, Mahavatar Babaji, Ramdas Kathiya Baba, Trailanga Svami, Bholanath, Lokenath Brahmachari, Ramakrishna. Abhedananda, Swarupananda, Durgaprasana, Ram Chandra Lalaji. Fifth row (13 portraits): Mahanambrata Brahmachari, Nagmahasay, Manamohan Datta, Surathnath Brahmachari, A. C. Bhaktivedanta, Jyotirsvarananda, Brojananda Sarasvati, Benimadhav Brahmachari, Brahmananda Bharati, Anandamurti, Bhaba Pagla, Harichand Thakur, Sitaram Omkarnath. Sixth row (13 portraits): Dada Lekhraj, Lalan Fakir, Anukulchandra, Bhairavi Brahmani, Sarada Devi, Mīrābāī, Anandamayi Ma, Mirra Alfassa, Jagadamba Sarasvati, Indira Devi, Prakashmani, Devi Ma, Balak Bramachari.

of these nine women are not Indian, even though they lived for a long time in India: the French Mirra Alfassa, a spiritual companion of Sri Aurobindo, who lived in Pondicherry from 1920,[35] and, still more surprising, the Australian Devi Ma (top row, second figure from the right), disciple of Swami Shankarananda, in the lineage of the Siddha-yoga of Muktananda.[36] We note too that several personages who appear in the image had been subjects of controversy.[37] In addition to the assembly processes we have just analysed, we have been interested in analysing the logics that run through this aggregation. It is necessary now to examine the semantics of this image, that is, its ability to transmit different messages.

An imaginary pluralistic Hindu community

In showing a single unified community in a precise territory, this collection of images is part of a 'process of religious unification'. In the history of the Indian subcontinent, this type of process has taken different forms (ritual, philosophical, institutional, iconographic, etc.) and in some cases has benefited from political support.[38] Let us then analyse the singularity of the process at work in the 'Immortal Gurus of *Bhārata*'.

By bringing onto the scene an assembly of gurus of diverse historical, regional and sectarian origin, this image would seem to wipe out religious otherness on a number of levels. In associating the ascetics who follow the teachings of Shiva or the Goddess (*śakti*) with the devotees of Vishnu, including beside them personalities who are outside all traditional transmission lineages (*parampara*), the image not only does away with Hindu sectarian borders but goes beyond institutional logic. In so doing it is reminiscent of certain 'hagiographic collectives' (Keune 2007, 169), like, for example, the well-known *Bhaktamāla* ('garland of devotees').[39] In this text, which he composed at the beginning of the seventeenth century, Nābhādās shows a community of devotees outside the strict framework of the Rāmānandī tradition of which he is a member (Hare 2011a, 2011b). The text thus brings together biographies of mythological characters, born in 'puranic' times, and those of recent historical personages belonging to different castes and sects. Nevertheless, whether men or women, Śaiva or Vaiṣṇava, rich or poor, Brahman or Śūdra, all the personages included share the same religious sensibility, that of loving devotion (*bhakti*) to the supreme deity, the deity the text intends to eulogise by enriching the praises with the qualities of each of these 'exemplary devotees'. By encompassing characters with very different religious sensibilities, the image that is the subject of this chapter goes beyond that attitude. Not only does the image group together Hindu ascetics of different obediences, it also attaches portraits of the Buddha, Mahāvīra and Nanāk, and systematically includes the religions born in the Indian subcontinent; this is without doubt its most remarkable feature.

How, then, are the dynamics at work in aggregation in this process to be qualified? Paul Hacker (1913–79) calls the ideal of empirical and doctrinal tolerance, often attributed, during the modern epoch, to Hinduism, 'inclusivism'. By this term he means the fundamental tendency of Hindu traditions to assimilate or appropriate elements that were initially foreign (Halbfass 1988, 403–546), a tendency at work in both the domain of ritual practice (worship, prayer, pilgrimage, etc.) and that of religious writings (theological treatises, doxography or mythological tales). The heuristic force of this term comes from the fact that it allows for the qualification of different processes, like, for example, integrating a facultative ritual practice into an obligation or integrating into a new religion elements of an older one. This concept is, however, axiologically biased. In using it, Hacker, who was a Christian apologetic, blindly denounces the approach he perceived at work in Hinduism that consisted in integrating all foreign ideas into its own conception and subordinating them (Halbfass 1988, 406; Nicholson 2010, 185–90). If, in fact, we find in numerous ancient Hindu doctrinaire expositions the notion that the author's system is integrating the imperfect doctrines of other systems, that idea comes from a hierarchical and non-egalitarian logic: the doctrine of the author is presented as intrinsically superior. Other authors have elaborated a similar critique. Thus, for Parekh,[40] the religious pluralism that Hindus have prided themselves on since the nineteenth century is not in reality egalitarian. If different sects and ways of life co-exist within Hinduism, not everybody benefits from the same status: some people are considered superior, others inferior, so much so that Hindu pluralism is 'structured in a hierarchical manner' (Parekh 2003), even if that hierarchy cannot be absolute.

Although it does not challenge the analysis, the image studied in this article seems to suggest another form of Hindu pluralism that I would qualify as 'egalitarian'. No saint seems to have been put in a superior position in relation to any other. This is further testified to by the fact that they are all presented in the same way under the epithet of 'saint or monk' while each of them is certainly considered by his disciples to be a 'god'.[41] We have seen that this image is the fruit of an artisanal process in the course of which the author has sought, by a meticulous work of retouching – a sort of ancient Photoshop – to obscure the difference between historical portraits taken from photographs and painted portraits in order to give the whole image not only a realistic appearance but also a harmonious one. Through the erasing of sectarian markers and the disarticulation of a line, all these saints are rendered equivalent. Kabīr, the iconoclastic medieval master, is found beside Śankarācārya, the ancient Brahman theologian, and Bama Ksepa, the contemporaneous 'fool of God' whose ashram is a cremation ground and whose aura is exclusively local.

By placing these gurus from different periods, obediences, doctrines and regions side by side, this image participates in the construction of an 'imaginary community' which goes beyond all historical, sociological and theological distinction, its unity coming from the territory of origin of its members. Far from reflecting a reality, this image suggests and brings into being a 'possibility', that may be constantly reinvented and enlarged through modern Photoshop techniques.

The egalitarian character of the image is confirmed by various comments made on it by devotees that I have been able to collect. A devotee of Lokenath Bahmachari, Mr Saha, has constructed a personal temple, open to the neighbourhood, on the façade of which he has hung the portraits of different saints in large format. 'If people see a portrait of their saint here, they will be content', he says.[42] A similar reason seems to have prompted the members of the Sri Sri Lokenath Mandir to hang the 'Immortal Gurus of *Bhārata*' in the Lokenath community temple (*mandira*) that they founded in 2014. Though it benefits from a dedicated officiant and a solid structure, it is distinguished from Hindu temples by the public nature of its cult image. Usually such an image is situated at the heart of the temple, sheltered from the view of the outside world. Here, on the contrary, the cult image is visible from the street so that passers-by may benefit from the sanctified vision (*darśana*) of Lokenath without even entering the temple. This is, in fact, a characteristic feature of the quotidian religiosity offered by these street shrines (Larios and Voix 2018). It is in the end the same dynamic that prompts a devotee to post the 'Immortal Gurus of *Bhārata*' on social media with the following commentary: 'I pay homage to all the world's great men without distinction of race, religion or caste. They are all dear to us for their important and outstanding contributions. They have proposed different names for human well-being according to the needs of each age' (Facebook post of a follower of Lokenath Brahmachari, August 2014). By positing the pre-eminence of territoriality over any other form of religious identity this iconic egalitarian plurality does away with the otherness of theologies and of religious practices that favour one pan-Indian religious identity which is without a name, the term 'Hindu' being absent from the images.

The emergence of such a visual contestation of communitarian differences is explained by the period, the culture and the socio-religious milieu of which the image is the product. By disregarding all mythical figures and representing only those beings whose existence is historically attested, the image participates in that 'religion of humanity' (*mānava dharma, mānuṣer dharma* or *mānuṣya dharma*) and the humanist discourse associated with it.[43] Not only does the appearance of this

'Hindu humanism' constitute the most important 'development of the religious world of modern India' (Hatcher 1994, 158) but it is inseparable from another transformation of Hindu representations, that is, the elevation of gurus to the level of exemplary religious figures of modern India. This process, qualified as 'sadhuization' (Singer 1970, cited in Bharati 1970, 277), or 'ascetisation' (Dobe 2015), constitutes, however, a return to communal representation. In the first half of the nineteenth century, under the influence of orientalist ideas and Protestant values, the initial Hindu reform movements had vigorously attacked ritualism and asceticism. Instead of domestic priests (*purohita*) and ascetics (*sannyāsin*), who, in the eyes of its members, embodied corrupted Hinduism, the Brahmo samaj elevated the 'householder' engaged in action in the role of 'scholar, humanist or moralist' to the level of exemplary religious figures (Dobe 2015, 86). It was only at the end of the nineteenth century that the figure of the holy man fashioned from that of the mythic Vedic seer-sage (*ṛsi*) became not only a praiseworthy character of religious modernity but also 'the "media form par excellence" [an expression borrowed from Hirschkind 2006, 3] of the so-called Hindu Renaissance' (Dobe 2015, 77). Dating back to the beginning of the nineteenth century, the image I evoked at the beginning of this chapter (Figure 4.4) seems thus to have been at a halfway point in this reversal, since it counts among the religious men it glorifies ascetics, certainly, but also householders – Rammohan Roy (1772–1833), Debendranath Tagore (1817–1905) and Keshubchandra Sen (1838–84) – who will disappear from later images.

In addition to its modernity, the relationship with the other that the 'Immortal Gurus of *Bhārata*' emphasises seems characteristic of a somewhat unorthodox socio-religious milieu. The prominence of portraits of gurus, sometimes without any religious instruction and outside any sectarian tradition, as well as certain errors of attribution of names, leads us to think that this image has its origin in circles relatively lacking in knowledge on the religious level. Unlike other processes of religious unification at work on the Indian subcontinent, this kind of imaging is not part of an intellectual construction that aims, for example, to promote the acceptance of theological diversity. Yet it is precisely there that its potential inclusivism is to be found: by being associated with only a minimal text, this image avoids the question of the 'religious norm' (Hatcher 1994) and, that accomplished, can absorb diversity and religious otherness into itself just as these have been internalised into Indian territory. Furthermore, far from its being an obstacle, the fact that the image has no institutional legitimacy and that its author is unknown adds to the semiological power of the image. Through the use of digital craft technology, it may also be the object of numerous individual reappropriations to adapt it to different theological and devotional contexts. Despite its relatively recent origin, the image has come to form a sort of common heritage with which a significant number of Indians can identify. Moreover, if the image seems to blur distinctions of caste and sect, it is no less rooted in a specific region: the preponderance of ascetics of Bengali origin and the scant presence of ascetics of south Indian origin, as we have seen, shows that its source is in Bengali regional territory. Bengal has a singular regional religious culture: having remained for a long time on the fringes of Brahmanism, it has seen local religious traditions Hinduised belatedly and gradually (Chakrabarti 2001).[44]

If the image embodies a form of 'egalitarian pluralism' which allows for the integration of an assembly of people otherwise considered to come from different traditions, it does so within certain limits that indicate to us which figures of religious 'otherness' fall outside this potential integration. First, although the image crosses sectarian, religious and lineage boundaries, it does not include male saints who spoke in religious idioms that did not originate on the Indian subcontinent. Even though Christianity and Islam, because of their long presence on the subcontinent, are marked with the social forms of Hindu religious life, the absence of gurus associated with these religions is glaring. Even more remarkable is that, from the second half of the nineteenth century, and especially in the writings of Keshub Chandra Sen (1838–84), numbers of Hindu masters considered Christ a 'great yogi' and established his worship within their organisations, and that for a long time in India a large number of Muslim saints have been worshipped locally by Hindus in the culture of the dargah.[45] The only saints of Muslim origin portrayed in the image show an ambivalent religious belonging. So we see Kabīr, who belonged to a caste of weavers (julāhā) recently converted to Islam; his teachings are very much influenced by Sufiism but he is never presented as a Muslim (Vaudeville 1959). As for Sai Baba, he is also a composite figure belonging as much to Islam as to Hinduism (McLain 2011).

Does this mean that the image may be seen in the same light as the 'exclusivist reductionism' that Parekh denounced? Parekh (2003) meant by this expression that Hindu pluralism would be the base of a new hierarchy, at the summit of which would be Hinduism: it is because Hinduism had discovered, recognised and respected the truth according to which all religions were partial and limited because of the infinite nature of ultimate reality, that it would be superior to other religions, particularly to those which, like Islam or Christianity, claim universal truth. Ultimately, if this image is popular in India today and is the object of diverse reappropriations, this is precisely because of its semiotic virtuosity, that is, its capacity to signal complex social messages – on the one hand egalitarian pluralism and on the other exclusivist reductionism – and so to illustrate the ambivalence towards relations with the other in contemporary Hinduism.

Notes

1 Unless otherwise stated, all the images presented here were collected by myself between 2002 and 2020 in West Bengal, either from private houses or from temples. Some of them also circulate on the internet in forums or on particular sites.

2 Often, but not systematically, the 'number' of characters is added (as here in Figures 4.1 and 4.2). Among the 10 or so images collected, the number of gurus represented varies from 40 to 80 (50, 51, 54, 60, 75, etc.) without any symbolic criterion seeming to govern this choice. The only practical considerations are that there should be a sufficient number of figures for the observer to get an impression of collectivity, and that each portrait should remain identifiable as an individual, since if it were not it would no longer be a group of 'portraits'.

3 In the Veda, ambrosia is associated with *soma*, an intoxicating drink with ecstatic properties that 'stimulates speech, provokes a kind of ecstasy, and confers all bliss' (Renou and Filliozat 1947, 327). It is also associated with 'immortality'. With the exception of certain collections of 'divine lives', such as that of ten monks of the Ramakrishna Mission (N. Bhattacharya 1959) or that of twenty Assamese (Deka 1996), it should be noted that this expression 'Sons of ambrosia' is not frequently used in Hinduism.

4 Used in Hindu mythological narratives later than the Veda, the term *avatāra* ('descent') designates the divine being who descends to earth to combat disorder (adharma). While in a strict sense it refers to a type of theatrical appearance in the context of a crisis of royal power (Biardeau 1976, 176; Couture 2001, 323), its meaning was later expanded to equate a set of indigenous deities with the Brahmanical pantheon and its social and ritual order (Coleman 2013). In the early twentieth century, it even came to refer not only to mythical figures, but also to local ascetics or mystics, sometimes with unorthodox behaviours like Ramakrishna (1836–86) or more recently Sathya Sai Baba (1926–2011). One can assume that, if the term is not used, that is precisely because it refers to a particular 'process of deification' (Voix 2019a) to which many sects do not adhere, that of a 'divine descent' more related to the various manifestations of the god Vishnu.

5 Monasticism as a 'social state, organised with a view to a religious life, in an autonomous and specific way, apart from the clergy proper' (Boureau 2010, 749; my translation) originally relates to Christianity exclusively. However, certain Buddhist or Hindu ascetics are called 'monks' (Boureau 2010). The term 'saint' has no strict equivalent in the vernacular languages of northern India. The two main Bengali biographies of Caitanya, for example, refer to him as a 'descent' (*avatāra*) and not as a 'saint' (F. Bhattacharya 2001, 185). For all that, in Indian studies, the word 'saint' has been employed for a wide variety of 'mediating figures', such as the '*devarṣi*' (Tiefenauer 2018, 243). As André Couture reminds us, the use of Christian terminology to refer to Hindu ascetics is misleading, because, for Hindus, these women and men have already realised their own divinity in their present bodies and are in their lifetime treated as deities (Couture 2001). As for the term 'incarnation', its closest Hindu concept is *avatāra*. For a comparison of the Hindu concept of *avatāra* and the Christian doctrine of the incarnation of Jesus see especially Brockington (1992), and for more extensive bibliographical indications see Coleman (2013).

6 For a sociological distinction between 'ascetic' and 'renouncer', see in particular Clémentin-Ojha 2006, 536–7.

7 Representations of 'vanished' religious figures, whether they have attained 'extinction' (*nirvāṇa*) Buddhist or 'liberation' (*mokṣa*) Hindu, constitute a 'paradox since they cannot act as intermediaries with divine forces' (Colas 2010, 531).

8 However, images close to the type that is the subject of this chapter can be found in the Muslim traditions of South Asia. From the early twentieth century, bazaar painters, illustrators and

collagists have produced a wide variety of Muslim pious images, including 'depictions of the calligraphic verses of the Qur'an, views of the holy sites of Mecca and Medina, the Prophet Muhammad's heavenly mount Buraq, members of the Holy Family (*ahl al-bait*), Shi'a Imams and martyrs of Karbala, Islamic heroes, as well as figurative narrative scenes with Quranic themes' (Frembgen 2010, 239). Displayed in private spaces (homes, offices) or public spaces (shops, restaurants, barber shops, shrines, etc.), they serve as a medium of piety in everyday religiosity. Among the most popular is a type of print called 'Assembly of Saints' (*mehfil-e-auliyā*) or 'Royal Court of Saints' (*darbar-e-auliyā*), which has the particularity of grouping on the same image many – up to 60 – Sufi saints (*awliyā'*) from different territories (of Arabia) and lineages of masters. This type of image has many features in common with the image that we analyse here. First, it brings together saints from different periods and geographical origins. To account for the imaginary and the atemporal character of the meeting between these saints who lived in different times Frembgen proposes to call them a 'timeless conclave' (Frembgen 2006, 31, 34). In fact, these images are the pure product of 'the imagination and faith of the devout' and have no institutional source. They appear as vernacular productions far from Islamic orthodoxy, which forbids this type of figurative representation. Secondly, they are made using the same technique of handicraft production consisting of collage, and each portrait has a number referring to an index of the saints present. Important distinctive features are also to be noted. First, unlike in our image, all the saints are not represented equally: they are grouped around 'Abdul Qadir Jilani, thus marking the spiritual pre-eminence of the latter; some are even represented twice, which emphasises their authority. Secondly, a set of Islamic iconographic references in addition to the portraits of saints have been inserted: representations of holy places (the specific shrine of a saint, Mecca, Medina); symbolic motifs (the rose, the pigeon, the candle, the oil lamp and the crown) and calligraphic elements, referring either to pan-Islamic themes (Qur'anic verses, standard Islamic formulas, such as 'bismillah' and 'kalima' or invocations of Allah, Muhammad and Ali) or to the specific verses and devotional formulas of a saint. In short, all these elements contribute to the reinforcement of the Islamic character of the image. Finally, thanks to the importance of bright colours, there emerges from this image an 'exuberance and gaiety' that seem characteristic of the visual aesthetics of popular Muslim religious art, but which is absent from our image. For an analysis of these engravings see Frembgen 2006 as well as the site 'Visual Pilgrim: Mapping popular visuality and devotional media at Sufi shrines and other Islamic institutions in South Asia': https://www.asia-europe.uni-heidelberg.de/en/research/heidelberg-research-architecture-new/digital-output/visual-pilgrim.html (accessed 13 May 2023).

9   One thinks in particular of the lithographs of Tamil saint-poets (*ālvārs*), who were members of the *śrīvaiṣṇava* sect or teachers (*gosvāmīs*) of Bengali Vishnuism (*gaudīavaiṣṇava*).

10 See for example the image of Ravidas, Kabir and two other saints at http://www.tasveergharindia.net/AdvanceSearch.html?conentType=0&searchterms=saint&lst_Subject=0#lg=1&slide=8 (accessed 17 February 2023). Note that some of Sant's images display Indian sufis alongside them; see for example Schomer and McLeod 1987.

11 The earliest known photo of Hindu monks side by side is dated 30 January 1887 (see Beckerlegge 2008, 8, illustration 4). It shows Vivekananda with his 'brothers in guru' (*gurubhaī*), with whom he lived in a house in Baranagar (Calcutta), following the death of their master, Ramakrishna, in August 1886. Vivekananda, third from the left, stands surrounded by seven co-religionists; in the front row four others are seated. Although he was the leader of this small group, Vivekananda's appearance, apart from his turban, which would become one of his distinguishing marks some years later, was very similar to that of his co-religionists. He has a full beard, long hair and an ochre-coloured (*geruā*) shawl draped over his shoulder, revealing different parts of his body, all signs of renunciation of the world. A few days before this photo was taken, the various protagonists performed their own funeral rites (*śrāddha*) marking the entry into renunciation (*saṃnyāsa*) (Dhar 1975, 216–18, cited in Killingley 2010). Coming from the British-educated Bengali bourgeoisie, they adopted a monastic life as well as the regular practice of spiritual exercises, and thus formed the first 'monastery' (*maṭha*) of the movement associated with the figure of Ramakrishna, a decade before the foundation, in 1897, of the Ramakrishna Mission. The photo reflects this spirit of communal renunciation: it shows a group identity in which no individual particularly stands out. Vivekananda thus appears as a 'renunciant man, a member of a simple monastery' (Beckerlegge 2004, 50) surrounded by other gurus, of whom he seems to be the equal. This is in stark contrast to later pictures of him. The British Library collection shows no chromolithographs prior to this image: such an

arrangement of portraits of gurus seems to be non-existent in the great Calcutta photo studios of the nineteenth century (Chore Bhagan Art Studio or Calcutta Art Studio), as well as in the work of Ravi Varma. https://research.britishmuseum.org/research/collection_online/ collection_object_details.aspx?objectId=3275857&partId=1&people=141601&p eoA=141601-2-61&page=1. On the other hand, there are some photographs of members of the same sect. See for example Gutman 1982, 102.

12 Among the five are Nagārika Dharmapāla (1864–1933), a Buddhist monk from Ceylon, Swami Vivekananda (1863–1904), a Hindu monk and disciple of Ramakrishna, and Virchand Gandhi (1864–1901), a layman representing Jainism.

13 This image cannot be dated accurately. The fact that it was found hanging in the room of Mahendranath Gupta (1854–1932), author of the most important biography of Ramakrishna (the *Sri Sri Ramakrishna Kathamrita*) after his death, suggests that it was known to be in existence in 1932, and, as it only includes people who were already dead (including Vivekananda, who died in 1902), it probably dates back to the first quarter of the twentieth century.

14 Another, more recent, example of this type of group portraiture is the 1947 mural by the Bengali artist Benod Behari Mukherjee. Painted on the wall of the Hindi pavilion of Vishva-Bharati University (Shantiniketan, West Bengal), it depicts an assembly of medieval and contemporary saints facing the Ganges. Representing a nation of united saint-poets, this fresco was intended as a response to the 1946 Noakhali riots between Muslims and Hindus.

15 Present on online video platforms such as YouTube. See for example 'The forty-three monks of India', https://www.youtube.com/watch?v=c_PfY1uX_Qs and 'The fifty-four monks of India'. https://www.youtube.com/watch?v=R9CnPE1lVtA. Another video, entitled 'Great saints of India', https://www.youtube.com/watch?v=2P7XGQBk75g, shows separate images of saints, always set to devotional music (all accessed 18 February 2023).

16 Although portraits are very common in India, there is no term other than 'image' to refer to them. For a definition of these different expressions and their etymological details, see Lefèvre 2018, 42.

17 My choice is Figure 4.1 because there are many variants.

18 By 'founders of religions' I mean persons whom particular socio-religious communities hold as such, although in many cases this process is retroactive (Hatcher 2006, 51).

19 The representation of the Buddha has long been the subject of controversy The oldest iconographic sources of Buddhism are, moreover, aniconic: they do not represent the master, but his absence (Colas 2010, 531).

20 For a detailed list of these gurus see Voix 2021, 95–8.

21 Indeed, we do not find gurus originating in Bengal who were successful elsewhere, especially within a non-Indian community as is the case with Yogananda (1893–1952), who lived for many years in the USA (Foxen 2017), and Ananda Acharya (1881–1945), the first Bengali missionary in the Nordic countries (Jacobsen 2020).

22 Among them are several Kāṭhiya Bābās, ascetics who wear a wooden belt to affirm their absolute celibacy and belong to a branch of the Nimbārka Sampradāya, whose founder, Nimbārka (twelfth–thirteenth century), is, we remember, absent from the picture. Also absent are Bholananda Giri (d. 1929), Bijoykrishna Gosvami (1841–99) and Balananda Maharaj (d. 1937).

23 This is the case with Lokenath Brahmachari (d. 1890), Bamakhepa (1837–1911), Devraha Baba (d. 1990), Jagadbandhu (18711921) and Ram Thakur (1860–1949).

24 As renunciants who acted independently of their lineage, we find Bhaskarananda (1833–99) and Trailanga Svami (d. 1887), two renunciants (*saṃnyāsī*) of high birth who were initiated into the Paramahaṃsas and Sārasvatī lineages respectively. Although they were thus affiliated with an *akhāṛā* of the Dasanāmī Sampradāya, both were based in Benares and lived there independently of their *akhāṛā*. Note that they were also related to many of the ascetics shown in the image.

25 One thinks in particular of Svāmī Karpātrī (1907–82), a monk of the Dasanāmī Sampradāya order, of which he was the superior, and famous for both his theological works and his political commitment: he founded the conservative party Assembly of the Kingdom of Rāma (Rāma-rājya-pariṣad) with the objective of establishing the 'reign of dharma' (*dharmarājya*); it was, however, opposed to the theses of the Hindu ultra-nationalist organisations. One also thinks of Svāmī Svarūpānanda, the superior of Dvārakā pīṭha (Gujarat) and Jyotiṣ pīṭha (Uttarkhand), and of Shantananda Saraswati.

26 One finds several monks associated with the Ramakrishna Mission, such as Brahmananda (1863–1922), its first president, and Abhedananda (1866–1939), the founder of the Ramakrishna Vedanta Math (Kolkata, 1923). One thinks in particular of Gujarati Hinduism, such as the Swaminarayan sect, or even of one of its most popular contemporary expressions, Bochasanwasi Akshar Purushottam Swaminarayan Sanstha (BAPS) and its founder, Pramukh Swami.

27 See on portraits in the history of photography in India, the famous collection of Anil Relia available online as well as the various books *The Indian Portraits* (I–XI) which are issued from it: http://www.theindianportrait.com.

28 A lineage is thus traced from the Buddha to some contemporary saints, passing through the figure of Vyāsa transmitting the Mahābhārata, the medieval saints of bhakti, and representatives of medieval devotion. Note in particular some of the absent portraits of the 'Immortal Gurus of *Bhārata*': in addition to the mythological figures (Vishnu, etc.), there are several saints from south India (but also Sister Nivedita, the European disciple of Vivekananda).

29 With the title of 'Venerable Preceptor' (*Mahāmahopādhyāya*), Gopinath Kaviraj was principal of the prestigious Government Sanskrit College in Benares from 1924 to 1937. He took initiation from Swami Vishudhananda (1853–1937), a thaumaturgist tantric from Benares, before becoming a devotee of Anandamayi Ma (1896–1982). The translator, Gautam Chatterjee, is a Bengali resident of Benares. Born in 1963 into a family associated with the prestigious social reformer Iswarchandra Vidyasagar (1820–91), he received a mantra from Gopinath Kaviraj a few days before the latter's death and thus declared himself his disciple (Kaviraj 2014, 6).

30 The origin of this iconography of Vishnu is unknown; it seems to be inspired either by the 'calendar art' of the lithographic press or even (without representing the famous style of Raja Ravi Varma) by the Indian mythological films of the 1950s.

31 The confusion of bodies and faces is not new. In his famous mural *The Indian Medieval Saints* on the walls of the library of the Hindi Department (Hindi Bhavan) of Vishabharati University in Shantiniketan (West Bengal), the avant-garde Bengali artist Binode Bihari Mukherjee (1904–80) had painted Ramananda's face from Ramakrishna's (Sheikh 1983, 16, cited in Sinha 2007, 70 n. 13).

32 This temple, dedicated to the worship of Lokenath Brahmachari, is located in the Santoshpur district (15, Kali Kumar Majumdar Road) in Kolkata. The image was acquired in Baradi (Bangladesh) by one of the founding members of the temple during the annual commemoration of the death of Lokenath Brahmachari: dated 2 June 2011, this image even seems to have been created precisely for the occasion.

33 Although the headquarters of the sect has been located since 1951 in Mount Abu (Rajasthan), BKWS is present all over the world through 'Raja Yoga' centres, and is thus also present in Bangladesh.

34 While, throughout history, exceptional women have become gurus and have been considered 'Mothers' (*mātājī*), the Brahmanical tradition envisages female asceticism only in the context of married life, ascetic celibacy being reserved for men. Indeed, classical texts allow renunciation only for male members of the three highest varṇas, i.e., the twice-born (*dvija*), who have access to the Veda and are qualified to offer sacrifices, and Hindu monastic orders have opened female branches only in the last century (Clémentin-Ojha 2013).

35 She refused Indian naturalisation because she would have had to give up her French citizenship.

36 Indeed, Devi Ma has always lived in Australia, where she led the Australian Yoga Teachers Association (2002–7) and took the renunciation in 2009, that is to say only two years before the making of this image.

37 Anandamurti was convicted of murder (Voix 2008b), Devi Ma was accused of hiding the sexual abuse perpetrated by her guru Swami Shankarananda in Australia, and Balak Brahmachari's disciples are accused of deception (Voix 2019).

38 The research group Les figures de l'unification religieuse dans le monde indien, directed by V. Bouillier and C. Clémentin-Ojha (2012–14), had highlighted several processes of unification. In addition to distinguishing between indigenous processes and external processes (etc.), such as those elaborated by certain Indianists with a view to thinking of Hinduism as a unified whole, the team had distinguished, in particular: the work of synthesising doctrinal positions, such as that instigated in Rajasthan by Jaisingh II (1688–1743) in order to unite the different Vaiṣṇava groups of his kingdom, or, more recently, the work carried out by the philosopher and politician S. Radhakrishnan; pilgrimage practices, such as the Kumbha Melā, which bring rival sects

together in the same place at a specific ritual time; and ritual practices, such as the adoption by all Hindus of tantric ritual practices, i.e., those based on a revelation other than the Veda.

39 Note the work of the collective hagiography *Bhārater Sādhaka* (Roy 1949–54), many of whose characters are identical to the characters of the 'Holy Family of Bhārata'.

40 This point has been identified by various authors who have described Hinduism as an 'orthopraxy' as opposed to an 'orthodoxy'. For Parekh (2003), Hindu 'tolerance' is based on four 'beliefs' or 'principles': first, the 'primacy of conduct over doctrine', which makes theological disputes futile; second, a 'dharmic view of morality' according to which each individual must follow an ethic appropriate to his or her idiosyncrasy, with the consequence that there can be no question of imposing one's own behaviour on others; third, 'individual uniqueness', according to which each person is fully responsible for his or her own salvation, so that there can be no religion imposed on all; fourth, 'religious pluralism', the belief that, being of an infinite nature, the ultimate reality cannot be grasped in its totality by the human soul, which obliges the coexistence of a plurality of ways to grasp it. If many of these assertions deserve comment, let us stop at his conception of Hindu pluralism.

41 To Anandamayi Ma's followers, who reject her categorisation as 'holy,' she is 'god'; see Hallstrom 1999, ix.

42 Interview with Mr Saha, Kolkata, 15 November 2017.

43 Note indeed the absence of Vālmīki, mythical author of the Mahābhārata, who is nonetheless often depicted as a holy man, as in the Bhārat Mātā to Mother India (McKean 1996).

44 Note further that in the vernacular forms of Islam present in East Bengal, there are lists of Muslim saints that may have inspired the present image. For example, in Chittagong, Bangladesh, the phrase 'land of the twelve saints' (*bāro āuliyāra deśa*) refers to 12 medieval Muslim saints held responsible for the Islamisation of the region. According to one legend, the name Chittagong, which litrally means the 'village of the lamp' (*caṭṭagrām*), is said to have originated from the belief that the 12 saints lit a lamp on their arrival to scare away evil spirits (jinn) and fairies (pari), and without them the city would have 'perished long ago' (Harder 2011, 11, 13). The number 12 does not refer to a definite list of saints but fluctuates according to the interlocutors. The village Baro Auliya, a few kilometres north of Sitakunda, has a mausoleum dedicated to the 12 saints (*bāro āuliyā*) (Harder 2011, 11, n19).

45 On the Hindu sanctification of Christ see, for example, Yogananda's discussion of Christ (Foxen 2017, 151); on the integration of his cult within the Yogoda Society (Yogananda [1946] 1975 II) or the Ramakrishna Mission; and the integration of Christ within the Amar Chitra Katha series (Hawley 1995,107). On dargah culture in India, see, for example, Bigelow 2010 and Bellamy 2011.

References

Allana, Rahaab and Pramod Kumar K. G. (eds). 2008. *Painted Photographs: Coloured portraiture in India*. Ahmedabad: Mapin.

Appadurai, Arjun. 1986. *The Social Life of Things: Commodities in cultural perspective*. Cambridge: Cambridge University Press.

Babb, Lawrence A. 1984. 'Indigenous feminism in a modern Hindu sect', *Signs* 9 (3): 399–416.

Barrows, John Henry. 1893. *The World's Parliament of Religions: An illustrated and popular story of the World's First Parliament of Religions, held in Chicago in connection with the Columbian Exposition of 1893*. Chicago: Parliament Publishing Company.

Beckerlegge, Gwilym. 2004. 'Iconographic representations of renunciation and activism in the Ramakrishna math and mission and the Rashtriya Swayamsevak Sangh', *Journal of Contemporary Religion* 19 (1): 47–66. https://doi.org/10.1080/1353790032000165113.

Beckerlegge, Gwilym. 2008. 'Svāmī Vivekānanda's iconic presence and conventions of nineteenth-century photographic portraiture', *International Journal of Hindu Studies* 12 (1): 1–40. https://doi.org/10.1007/s11407-008-9056-x.

Bellamy, Carla. 2011. *The Powerful Ephemeral: Everyday healing in an ambiguously Islamic place*. Berkeley and Los Angeles: University of California Press.

Bharati, Agehananda. 1970. 'The Hindu Renaissance and its apologetic patterns', *Journal of Asian Studies* 29 (2): 267–87. https://doi.org/10.2307/2942625.

Bhattacharya, France. 2001. 'La construction de la figure de l'homme-dieu selon les deux principales hagiographies bengali de Śrī Kṛṣṇa Caitanya', in *Constructions hagiographiques dans le monde indien: Entre mythe et histoire*, edited by Françoise Mallison, 183–203. Paris: Librairie Honoré Champion.

Bhattacharya, Nandalal. 1959. *Amṛtasya putrāḥ*. Kolkata: Lipika.

Biardeau, Madeleine. 1976. 'Études de mythologie hindoue (IV): Bhakti et avatāra', *Bulletin de l'Ecole française d'Extrême-Orient* 63: 111–263. https://doi.org/10.3406/befeo.1976.3888.

Bigelow, Anna. 2010. *Sharing the Sacred: Practicing pluralism in Muslim North India*. New York: Oxford University Press.

Bouillier, Véronique. 2010. 'Y a-t-il des monastères dans l'hindouisme? Quelques exemples shivaïtes', in *Moines et moniales de par le monde: La vie monastique au miroir de la parenté*, edited by Adeline Herrou and Gisèle Krauskopff, 25–35. Paris: L'Harmattan.

Boureau, Alain. 2019. 'Monachisme', in *Dictionnaire des faits religieux*, edited by Régine Azria and Danièle Hervieu-Léger, 819–23. Paris: Presses Universitaires de France.

Brilliant, Richard. 1991. *Portraiture*. London: Reaktion Books.

Brockington, John. 1992. *Hinduism and Christianity*. Basingstoke: Macmillan.

Chakrabarti, Kunal. 2001. *Religious Process: The Purânas and the making of a regional tradition*. New Delhi: Oxford University Press.

Clémentin-Ojha, Catherine. 2006. 'Replacing the abbot: Rituals of monastic ordination and investiture in modern Hinduism', *Asiatische Studien/Etudes Asiatiques* 60 (3): 535–73.

Clémentin-Ojha, Catherine. 2013. 'Female ascetics', in *Brill's Encyclopedia of Hinduism*, edited by Knut A. Jacobsen, Helene Basu, Angelika Malinar and Vasudha Narayanan, vol. 3, 60–7. Leiden: Brill.

Clémentin-Ojha, Catherine. 2014. '"India, that is Bharat ...": One country, two names', *South Asia Multidisciplinary Academic Journal* 10: 1–21. https://doi.org/10.4000/samaj.3717.

Colas, Gérard. 2010. 'Iconography and images (murtī): Ancient concepts', in *Brill's Encyclopedia of Hinduism*, edited by Knut A. Jacobsen, Helene Basu, Angelika Malinar and Vasudha Narayanan, vol. 2, 529–36. Leiden: Brill.

Coleman, Tracy. 2013. 'Avatāra', in *Oxford Bibliographies Online*. https://doi.org/10.1093/OBO/9780195399318-0009.

Copeman, Jacob and Aya Ikegame. 2012. 'The multifarious guru: An introduction', in *The Guru in South Asia: New interdisciplinary perspectives*, edited by Jacob Copeman and Aya Ikegame, 1–45. Abingdon: Routledge.

Couture, André. 2001. 'From Viṣṇu's deeds to Viṣṇu's play, or Observations on the word *avatāra* as a designation for the manifestations of Viṣṇu', *Journal of Indian Philosophy* 29: 313–26.

Deka, Kanakacandra. 1996. *Amṛtasya Putrāḥ* (Divine lives). Guwahati: Champavati prakashan.

Dewan, Deepali. 2012. *Embellished Reality: Indian painted photographs: Towards a transcultural history of photography*. Toronto: Royal Ontario Museum Press.

Dhar, Sailendra Nath. 1975. *A Comprehensive Biography of Swami Vivekananda*, vol. 1. Madras: Vivekananda Prakashan Kendra.

Dobe, Timothy S. 2015. *Hindu Christian Faqir: Modern monks, global Christianity, and Indian sainthood*. New York: Oxford University Press.

Foxen, Anya. P. 2017. *Biography of a Yogi: Paramahansa Yogananda and the origins of modern yoga*. New York: Oxford University Press.

Frembgen, Jürgen Wasim. 2006. *The Friends of God: Sufi saints in Islam: Popular poster art from Pakistan*. Karachi: Oxford University Press.

Frembgen, Jürgen Wasim. 2010. 'Icons of love and devotion: Sufi posters from Pakistan depicting Lal Shahbaz Qalandar', in *Religiöse Blicke – Blicke auf das Religiöse: Visualität und Religion*, edited by Bärbel Beinhauer-Köhler, Daria Pezzoli-Olgiati and Joachim Valentin, 227–42. Zurich: TVZ.

Gutman, Judith Mara. 1982. *Through Indian Eyes: 19th and early 20th century photography from India*. New York: Oxford University Press.

Halbfass, Wilhelm. 1988. *India and Europe: An essay in understanding*. Albany, NY: SUNY Press.

Hallstrom, Lisa Lassel. 1999. *Mother of Bliss: Ānandamayī Mā (1896–1982)*. New York: Oxford University Press.

Hara, Minoru, 1979. 'Hindu concepts of teacher, Sanskrit *guru* and *acaryā*', in *Sanskrit and Indian Studies: Essays in honour of Daniel H. H. Ingalls*, edited by Masatoshi Nagatomi, Bimal Krishna Matilal, Judith M. Masson and Edward C. Dimock, 93–118. Dordrecht: D. Reidel Publishing Company.

Harder, Hans. 2011. *Sufism and Saint Veneration in Contemporary Bangladesh: The Maijbhandaris of Chittagong*. Abingdon: Routledge.

Hare, James P. 2011a. 'Garland of devotees: Nābhādās' *Bhaktamāl* and modern Hinduism.' PhD dissertation, Columbia University.

Hare, James P. 2011b. 'Contested communities and the re-imagination of Nābhādās' *Bhaktamāl*', in *Time, History and the Religious Imaginary in South Asia*, edited by Anne Murphy, 150–66. Abingdon: Routledge.

Hatcher, Brian A. 1994. '"The cosmos is one family" (*vasudhaiva kutumbakam*): Problematic mantra of Hindu humanism', *Contributions to Indian Sociology* 28 (1): 149–62. https://doi.org/10.1177/006996694028001006.

Hatcher, Brian. 2006. 'Remembering Rammohan: An essay on the (re-)emergence of modern Hinduism', *History of Religions* 46 (1): 50–80.

Hawley, John Stratton. 1995. 'The saints subdued: Domestic virtue and national integration in *Amar Chitra Katha*', in *Media and the Transformation of Religion in South Asia*, edited by Lawrence A. Babb and Susan S. Wadley, 107–36. Philadelphia: University of Pennsylvania Press.

Hirschkind, Charles. 2006. *The Ethical Soundscape: Cassette sermons and Islamic counterpublics*. New York: Columbia University Press.

Houghton, Walter Raleigh. 1893. *Neely's History of the Parliament of Religions and Religious Congresses at the World's Columbian Exposition*. Chicago, IL: Frank Tennyson Neely.

Jacobsen, Knut. A. 2020. 'Hindu traditions in Norway', in *Handbook of Hinduism in Europe*, edited by Knut A. Jacobsen and Ferdinando Sardella, vol. 2, 1241–64. Leiden: Brill.

Kaviraj, Gopinath. 2014. *Jñānaganja: A space for timeless divinity* (trans. Gautam Chatterjee). Varanasi: Indian Mind.

Keune, Jon. 2007. 'Gathering the bhaktas in Marāṭhi: The *Bhaktavijay* of Mahipati', *Journal of Vaishnava Studies* 15 (2): 169–87.

Killingley, Dermot H. 2010. 'Vivekananda', in *Brill's Encyclopedia of Hinduism*, edited by Knut A. Jacobsen, Helena Basu, Angelika Malinar and Vasu Narayanan. Leiden: Brill.

Larios, Borayin and Raphaël Voix. 2018. 'Wayside shrines in India: An everyday defiant religiosity', *South Asia Multidisciplinary Academic Journal* 18. https://doi.org/10.4000/samaj.4546.

Lefèvre, Vincent. 2011. *Portraiture in Early India: Between transience and eternity*. Leiden: Brill.

Lefèvre, Vincent. 2018. 'Portrait or image? Some literary and terminological perspectives on portraiture in early India', in *Portraiture in South Asia since the Mughals: Art, representation and history*, edited by Crispin Branfoot, 34–49. London: I. B. Tauris.

McKean, Lise. 1996. 'Bhārat Mātā and her militant matriots', in *Devī: Goddesses of India*, edited by John Stratton Hawley and Donna Marie Wulff, 250–80. Berkeley: University of California Press.

McLain, Karline. 2011 'Be united, be virtuous: Composite culture and the growth of Shirdi Sai Baba devotion', *Nova Religio* 15: 20–49. https://doi.org/10.1525/nr.2011.15.2.20.

Monier-Williams, Monier. 1899. *A Sanskrit-English Dictionary: Etymologically and philologically arranged with special reference to cognate Indo-European languages*. Oxford: Clarendon Press.

Nicholson, Andrew J. 2010. *Unifying Hinduism: Philosophy and identity in Indian intellectual history*. New York: Columbia University Press.

Padoux, André. 2013. *The Heart of the Yoginī: The Yoginīhṛdaya, a Sanskrit tantric treatise*. New York: Oxford University Press.

Padmapādācārya. 1992. *Śrī Padmapādācārya's Pañcapādikā with the Commentaries Vivaraṇa by Śrī Prakāśātmanmuni, Tattvadīpana by Śrī Akhaṇḍānanda Muni, and Ṛjvuvivaraṇa by Śrī Viṣṇubhaṭṭopādhyāya* (ed. S. Subrahmanya Sastri). Varanasi: Mahesh Research Institute.

Parekh, Bhikhu. 2003. 'Some reflections on the Hindu theory of tolerance', *India Seminar* 521 http://www.india-seminar.com/2003/521/521%20bhikhu%20parekh.htm (accessed 20 February 2023).

Pinney, Christopher. 1997. *Camera Indica: Social life of Indian photographs*. Chicago, IL: University of Chicago Press.

Ramaswamy, Sumathi. 2003. *Beyond Appearances? Visual practices and ideologies in modern India*. New Delhi: Sage.

Ray, S. N. 1949–54. *Bhārater Sādhak*, 12 vols. Kolkata: Karuna Prakashanee.

Renou, Louis and Jean Filliozat. 1947. *L'Inde classique: Manuel des études indiennes*. Paris: Payot.

Schomer, Karine and W. H. McLeod, eds. 1987. *The Sants: Studies in a devotional tradition of India*. Delhi: Motilal Barnarsidass.

Seager, Richard Hughes. 1995. *The World's Parliament of Religions: The East/West Encounter, Chicago, 1893*. Bloomington: Indiana University Press.

Sheikh, Gulam Mohammad. 1983. 'Viewer's view: Looking at pictures', *Journal of Arts & Ideas* 1983 (3): 5–20.

Singer, Philip. 1970. *Sadhus and Charisma*. Bombay and New York: Asia Publishing House.

Sinha, Ajay. 2007. 'Against allegory: Binode Bihari Mukherjee's *Medieval Saints* at Shantiniketan', in *Picturing the Nation: Iconographies of modern India*, edited by Richard H. Davis, 66–91. New Delhi: Orient Longman.

Smith, H. Daniel. 1978. 'Hindu "deśika"-figures: Some notes on a minor iconographic tradition', *Religion* 8 (1): 40–67. https://doi.org/10.1016/0048-721X(78)90031-3.

Stchoupak, Nadine, Luigia Nitti and Louis Renou. 1959. *Dictionnaire Sanskrit-Français*. Paris: Adrien Maisonneuve.

Tiefenauer, Marc. 2018. *Les Enfers indiens: Histoire multiple d'un lieu commun*. Leiden: Brill.

Vaudeville, Charlotte. 1959. *Au cabaret de l'amour: Paroles de Kabîr*. Paris: Librairie Gallimard.

Vivekananda. 2019. *The Complete Works of Swami Vivekananda*, vol. 6. New York: Discovery Publisher.

Voix, Raphaël. 2008. 'Denied violence, glorified fighting: Spiritual discipline and controversy in Ananda Marga', *Nova Religio* 12 (1): 3–25. https://doi.org/10.1525/nr.2008.12.1.3.

Voix, Raphaël. 2019a. 'Déification', in *Dictionnaire des faits religieux*, edited by Régine Azria and Danièle Hervieu-Léger, 241–6. Paris: Presses Universitaires de France.

Voix, Raphaël. 2019b. 'Dans l'attente du vrai leader: Apocalypse et régénérescence en Inde hindoue', *Terrain, Anthropologie et Sciences Humaines* 71. https://doi.org/10.4000/terrain.18374.

Voix, Raphaël. 2021. 'La 'Sainte-Famille de Bhārata': Inclusivisme et pluralisme égalitaire dans l'hindouisme sectaire', *Puruṣārtha* 38: 69–110.

Yogananda, Paramahamsa. [1946] 1958. *Autobiography of a Yogi*. Bombay: Jaico Publishing House.

5
Languages of longing: Indian gurus, Western disciples, and practices of letter writing

Somak Biswas

This chapter will look at the role of letters as a medium for constituting discipleship. I examine three Indian guru figures – the Hindu monk Swami Vivekananda (1863–1902), the poet Rabindranath Tagore (1861–1941), the nationalist leader Mahatma Gandhi (1869–1948) – and their relationships with close Western disciples. Located firmly in a time of high British imperialism, this chapter charts the important work letters did in moulding sympathetic Western men and women into intimate disciples serving a range of Indian causes.

The cast of Western disciples gathered around these guru figures came from a variety of backgrounds. C. F. Andrews and William Pearson were Christian missionaries (Anglican and Baptist respectively), Margaret Noble, Sara Bull and Josephine MacLeod were involved in various heterodox initiatives (linked to Hindu eclecticism), Madeleine Slade was the daughter of a British Admiral. Many of them, such as Sister Nivedita (Margaret Noble), C. F. Andrews and Mira Behn (Madeleine Slade), came to occupy major roles in Indian cultural and political nationalism. Ashram experiments, especially Shantiniketan and Sabarmati (Belur Math less so, given its male monastic character), became aspirational communities that inspired their Indophilia, defined broadly as romanticised engagements around Hindu forms of India. Western followers' profound spiritual disquiet was rooted in the mechanisation of life produced by the onset of industrial modernity and violence in the West; gurus and ashrams constituted part of a larger 'seeking'. All of them were attracted to forms of immanent spirituality that inhered in the figures of Vivekananda, Gandhi and Tagore.

Context

Several interlinked developments undergird the emergence of the modern letter in colonial India. The rapid proliferation of postal networks scaled time and distance, emerging as key to imperial governance (Gupta 2016, 219). The introduction of the Indian penny post in 1854 saw an explosion of postal communication that continued over the next century. The diffusion of India's postal system had a remarkable uptake in urban and rural areas (Frost 2016, 1058), across new literary publics as well as non-literate populations.

In Victorian Britain, letter-writing manuals offered instruction in the art of letter writing, considered necessary education for building the character of young men and women in their public conduct. Private letters were understood to reveal the 'authentic character of an individual even if their public conduct could not' (Poskett 2019, 118). The private letter was a site to produce and perform a true individual moral self. It was to this epistolary tradition that Western disciples like Andrews, Pearson, Noble and Slade belonged.

Indian correspondents, on the other hand, came from a different, if not unrelated, tradition. The rationalisation of postal communication, while it introduced new forms of letter writing, transformed pre-colonial forms as well. The emergence of the private letter changed conventions and meanings around letter-writing practices for the Indian elite educated in the English language. Colonial literary modernity paved the way for a more individualised process of articulation, giving birth to a new critical individual subjectivity that took itself very seriously (Orsini 2006, 235). Older epistolary forms were not effaced, but the advent of a modern selfhood helped chart a self-individualisation that greatly affected the nature of authors and audiences emerging around the form.

An influential class of English-educated (but bilingual)[1] Indian elite pioneered ideas and institutions that refracted notions of citizenship and civil rights dominant in metropolitan discourse. The lateral networks forged between members of this class and sympathetic white Western figures (British/European, American) formed part of a complex interlocution. Letters played a key role in them. Western disciples formed a precipitating point in the interlocution of these rights and discourses, vocally arguing for the extension of metropolitan rights and privileges to the empire. Their active presence in non-/anti-colonial Indian projects became a morally legitimising force.

Indophile letters bring to the fore that rare intimacy between iconic Indian figures hailing from a critical class of Western-educated elite and their white disciples. They form a minor, if influential, trend in a time of high imperial consolidation, of Western men and women who willingly became the disciples of Indian figures and stood against the imperial politics of their own nation and racial privilege. Tagore and Vivekananda of course made concessions in distinguishing Western culture from Western imperialism, but this distinction was generally under strain. Western disciples consciously sought to identify with romanticised ideas of India, broadly upper-caste Hindu (but not strictly orthodox) in derivation. Indophile performances routinely transgressed and reified regimes around race, class, caste and gender, a few of which will be illustrated in this chapter.

Epistolary communities

The community of letters formed out of this cast of Indian and Indophile characters was expansive.[2] Anxious for physical and emotional proximity to their mentors, followers found that letters compensated for both. Enthralled by their mentors' personalities, disciples wanted a larger stake in their lives and works. The letters passing through this small but influential community can be broadly categorised into primary and secondary epistolary networks. Primary epistolary networks constituted the entire corpus of letters exchanged directly between disciples and their Indian gurus. In these, disciples poured out their hearts to mentors and sought instruction. As emotional practice, letters between mentors and their disciples record the gradual shifts and shifting sensibilities facilitated by letter writing. This is not to suggest that these relationships were forever beholden to the greatness of the guru, or that the spell never broke. They came under frequent strain; primary epistolary networks provide a rich narrative of this densely constituted interiority.

Undergirding these major epistolary networks were various ancillary connections that refer to lateral correspondence exchanged between followers and their close confidant(e)s, and between various Indian mentors and members of their wider circles. These include Noble's correspondence with other Western disciples of Vivekananda (Sara Bull and Josephine MacLeod) and the diaries and accounts of Gandhi's associates (Mahadev Desai and Pyarelal) that shed light on primary networks. Also in this category are letters exchanged between Gandhi and Tagore, Andrews and Pearson, and members of their wider circles, such as the Swiss-French littérateur Romain Rolland, Tagore's British associate Leonard Elmhirst (who worked on his Sriniketan community enterprise), the moderate Congress politician Gopal Krishna Gokhale, the Arya Samaj leader Munshi Ram and the Wesleyan missionary Edward J. Thompson. Secondary epistolary networks consist of these parallel epistolary connections. They illuminate and complicate the dynamics of the relationships forged between gurus and disciples. They elaborate on how desire, love and jealousy were interwoven in the making of these discipleships and the tensions that cohered in the epistolary practice of these intimacies. Together, they constitute the broader epistolary community referred to throughout the chapter. Romain Rolland has provided the most consistent record of these intersecting networks (Rolland 1960). A European pacifist literary figure with a deep interest in Indian culture and philosophy, he had personally met and been in touch with Vivekananda, Gandhi, Tagore, and all of their Western disciples. He had even 'gifted' Slade to Gandhi. Each of them confided in Rolland their doubts, hopes and fears about others. Rolland's diary unifies these different sets of disciples within a shared tradition of Western Indophilia. Culled from personal exchanges with them, his diary entries offer valuable comparative insight on the cumulative convergences at work.

Letters regularly helped contain effusions of love (particularly between men) within a relatively non-threatening framework.[3] Epistolary expressions of desire for a closer presence continually underlined the impossibility of any further physical fulfilment. Letters sustained a language of perpetual deferral, while also making possible quiet upheavals. The following sections analyse several aspects of these relationships through their letters.

Letters to the guru

Charles Freer Andrews joined the Cambridge Brotherhood Mission in Delhi (St Stephen's College) in 1904 as an Anglican missionary. Known for his reformist and unorthodox views, Andrews courted frequent controversy within missionary and Anglo-Indian circles in India, as well as in England. His missionary dialectics strongly advocated an Indianisation of Christ and Christianity. He had been influential in the selection of S. K. Rudra as the first Indian Christian to head St Stephen's College. Between 1905 and 1910, years that saw the proliferation of the Swadeshi movement in Bengal, along with the rise of extremist politics and revolutionary terrorism, Andrews emerged as a distinctive liberal Christian voice.

William Winstanley Pearson was a Baptist missionary teaching at the London Missionary College in Calcutta. He sought to quit the mission in

1911, dissatisfied with the stifling theological atmosphere in the college, and wished to continue in India as an independent worker. Andrews's eclecticism (his position against conversion, belief in a fulfilment theology) had by then already spread in Indian missionary circles. Pearson was attracted to Andrews's reformist streak, and the latter introduced Pearson to Tagore in London (Tinker 1998, 45–6). The two men had a shared experience of a Cambridge education and missionary service in India.

By the 1910s, Tagore had already left behind his interest and association with the Swadeshi movement in Bengal. Increasingly disillusioned and, later, critical of the exclusionary Hindu cultural nationalism that had come to dominate the movement, he had moved towards pantheism and a language of universal humanism. In 1912, his *Gitanjali* poems – translated into English from their Bengali originals – created a stir in London literary circles. Their mysticism and lofty spiritual language had moved poets like W. B. Yeats, and paved the path for his Nobel Prize, within a year, in 1913.

Andrews and Pearson had first met Tagore at a reading session in London and were greatly moved by his poetry and personality. Within weeks of their first meeting in London, Andrews wrote to Tagore:

> My thoughts are with you so constantly and I seem at times to pass whole days with you altogether, remembering you in my prayers and thinking of you …, and also longing to be with you. … I want you to tell me anything you would wish me to do to help you.
>
> (Andrews to Tagore, 18 March 1913)[4]

Tagore became part of this projection, in his daily prayer and longing, thought and habit. Pearson, on the other hand, was ready to give up his missionary vocation after their London encounter. He wanted to join Tagore's educational ashram at Shantiniketan:

> You told me in London that you wanted to capture me for Shantiniketan and now I am able to write and tell you that I am a willing captive and that it is only a question of time now for the captive to enter the place where the bonds of affection have been woven.
>
> (Pearson to Tagore, 17 December 1912)[5]

Both Andrews and Pearson were in the process of imagining a putative intimacy with Tagore, already the vaunted *gurudev* (the guru as god). Tagore warmly reciprocated both Pearson's and Andrews's overtures, in lofty terms. Pearson's letter 'stirred [Tagore's] heart to its depths' (Tagore to Pearson,

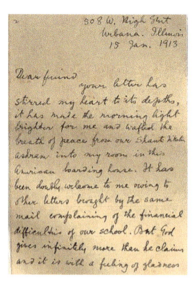

Figure 5.1 Tagore's letter to Pearson, 15 January 1913. Courtesy: Rabindra Bhavana, Visva Bharati.

15 January 1913; see Figure 5.1).[6] Acknowledging Andrews's affection, Tagore wrote: '[H]ow your love has made my life richer and I count it as one of the gains of my life that will abide. Have faith in my love when I am silent' (Tagore to Andrews, 13 May 1915).[7] Andrews and Pearson visited Tagore's ashram in his absence to help with ashram activities and constantly wrote letters that affirmed their loyalty (see Figure 5.2).

Like Andrews and Pearson, Noble and Slade wished to be part of their mentors' lives and works. Letters became the medium through which to express their desires. Never having met Gandhi in person, Slade came to know of him first through Romain Rolland, in 1924.[8] She had wanted to join Sabarmati ashram immediately but Gandhi advised caution, suggesting a preparatory interval of one year before taking a final decision. After a year, Slade reiterated her request:

Most Dear Master,

… The first impulse has never faded, but on the contrary my desire to serve you has grown ever more and more fervent. … My being is filled with a great joy … of giving all I have to you and to your people and the anguish of being able to give so little. I pine for the day when I shall come to India. …

Dear Master, may I come?

(Slade to Gandhi, 29 May 1925)[9]

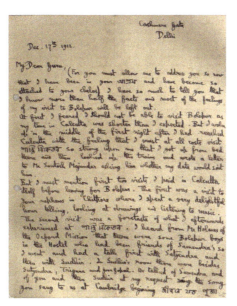

Figure 5.2 Pearson asking to refer to Tagore as guru, 17 December 1912. Courtesy: Rabindra Bhavana, Visva Bharati.

She gave up 'the drinking of all wines, beers or spirits' and 'meat of any kind', and began to spin and read Hindi (Slade to Gandhi, 29 May 1925). In a similar vein, Noble's guru Swami Vivekananda had initially advised against her coming to India. Noble was already active in the London Vedanta Society that Vivekananda had established with the help of British disciples. Vivekananda acknowledged that she had 'the making ... of a world mover' but felt she 'could do more work for us in England than by coming here' (Vivekananda to Noble, 23 July 1897). A cautious Vivekananda confided to Sara Ole Bull, a wealthy American patron-disciple, who also knew Noble:

> I do not think any European or American will be of any service here just now, and it will be hard for any Westerner to bear the climate. Mrs. Annie Besant with her exceptional powers works only among the Theosophists and thus she submits to all the indignities of isolation which a Mlechchha [outcaste] is made to undergo here. Even Goodwin smarts now and then and has to be called to order. He is doing good work as he is a man and can mix with the people. Women have no place in men's society here, and she can do good

only among her own sex in India. The English friends that came over to India have not been of any help as yet and do not know whether they will be of any in the future. With all these, if anybody wants to try she is welcome.

(Vivekananda to Bull, 19 August 1897)

In 1898, Josiah Goodwin, a British monastic disciple of Vivekananda, had passed away from severe exhaustion and physical illness while working in India.[10] Goodwin's death precisely exemplified Vivekananda's anxieties. It was only after other disciples interceded on Noble's behalf regarding her single-minded determination to visit India that he conceded (Vivekananda to Noble, 29 July 1897). Both Gandhi and Vivekananda warned of the lack of general European comforts, and of everyday deterrents that ranged from casteism, racism and poverty to language and climate barriers. Aspiring disciples regarded these ordeals as a testament to the purity of their resolve.

Self-abnegation and suffering formed a common arc for disciples to prove their worthiness. Exalted references such as Master, *Bapu* (Father) and *Gurudev* served to underscore a relationship of subservience and worshipful reverence. Nivedita exemplified this yearning:

[T]oday I want to do things only because they are my Father's [Vivekananda's] will. ... One longs to serve for serving's sake, for ever and ever, dear Master – not for our miserable little life!

(Noble to Vivekananda, 13 January 1900)

Declarations of subservience placed them on a par with the Indian disciples gathered around these figures, who were already familiar with the idiom of *gurubhakti* (devotion to the guru). Yet, even as it rendered them in equal relation to their fellow Indian disciples, their extraordinariness was well understood. Their letters, often suffused with (spiritual) invocations of complete surrender, continued to perform physical and symbolic inversions of everyday hierarchy.

Love in letters

The expectation of reciprocity was fundamental to the act of letter writing (Poustie 2010, 12). Or at least the promise of it led disciples to continue writing. Given the very itinerant lives of gurus, letters remained the preferred mode of communication. Letter writing re-enacted the affective ties of their relationship. Vivekananda comforted Noble:

> Every word you write I value, and every letter is welcome a hundred times. Write whenever ... and whatever you like, knowing that nothing will be misinterpreted, nothing unappreciated.
> (Vivekananda to Nivedita, 20 June 1897)

For Noble, writing to her guru was an eagerly anticipated exercise. She would playfully assert the joy of that act: 'All day I have been promising myself the joy of writing to you. Haven't I been a bad daughter? To my poor old father, too!' (Noble to Vivekananda, 15 December 1899).

This assertion, seemingly light and playful, of a filial relationship between Vivekananda and Nivedita, however, was also part of a continual attempt to frame that relationship in desexualised terms.[11] Josephine MacLeod, a fellow woman-disciple, felt that Nivedita had the 'lover's adoration' for the swami.[12] Her letters became a medium for both expressing and controlling those feelings. By thinking and writing so, she could couch her 'unruly' love in appropriately filial terms. Heterosexual discipleships between Gandhi, Vivekananda and their women disciples were always subjugated into the frame of a father–daughter relationship, to tame potential slippages.

Feelings of love and affection were framed through different kinds of operative limits. Gandhi was the least inhibited in declaring and naming this love, to both his male and female disciples. Gandhi cherished writing 'love letters' to his Western followers, who included the likes of his South African Jewish colleagues Henry Polak and Hermann Kallenbach (the latter a body-builder), and later Andrews and Slade. Gandhi referred to Kallenbach's letters as 'charming love notes' and each had, on at least one recorded occasion, pledged in uninhibited terms a deep love for the other, while Kallenbach regarded Gandhi's wife Kasturba as his 'mother' (Gandhi to Kallenbach, 30 August 1909). Gandhi did not shy away from acknowledging the homoerotics in his relationship with Kallenbach.[13] In a letter written from London, Gandhi reminisced:

> Your portrait (the only one) stands on my mantelpiece in the bedroom. The mantelpiece is opposite to the bed. ... The pen I use ... in each letter it traces makes me think of you. If, therefore, I wanted to dismiss you from my thoughts, I could not do it. ... The point ... is to show to you and me how completely you have taken possession of my body. This is slavery with a vengeance.
> (Gandhi to Kallenbach, 24 September 1909)

Material artefacts – portrait, bed, pen – came together to stage a 'possession' of Gandhi's body. Absence evoked romantic longing. And love-letters helped correspondents to imagine a co-presence. That Gandhi destroyed many of Kallenbach's early letters to preserve their confidentiality limits us from speculating too much on the nature of this possession. In this, he seemed to have acted on Kallenbach's insistence on their not being read by anybody else.[14] Gandhi censured his powerful love but did not forbid or dissuade him: 'Everyone considers that your love for me is excessive' (Gandhi to Kallenbach, 10 September 1909). Homoeroticism figured frequently under the benign sign of mentor–disciple relationship, which illustrates how male intimacy was constantly recoded in letters.

Kallenbach's 'excessive love' soon manifested itself in resentment towards C. F. Andrews. In 1914, Andrews's emergence as a trusted associate of Gandhi in South Africa provoked Kallenbach's jealousy. Gandhi reassured him repeatedly: 'Though I love and almost adore Andrews so, I would not exchange you for him' (Gandhi to Kallenbach, 27 February 1914). Evidently, the reassurance was not enough, for within two months we find sterner replies to Kallenbach: 'you seem to have been hasty in judging Andrews. I fancy that I know him better' (Gandhi to Kallenbach, 7 April 1914). Gandhi chided Kallenbach for being 'petty' (Gandhi to Kallenbach, 12 April 1914). Interestingly, it was to Andrews that Gandhi turned for help in getting Kallenbach to India in 1915 after his return from South Africa, with the outbreak of the war (Kallenbach was German, and in later life became Zionist).[15] From Shantiniketan, where Gandhi's Phoenix School boys were temporarily lodged, he remembered Kallenbach while working on sanitary reform with Andrews and Pearson:

> Extraordinary changes have been made in the Santiniketan school, Andrews and Pearson rose to the occasion and Pearson and I, whilst we were working away at sanitation reform, thought of you – how you would have thrown yourself into the work.
> (Gandhi to Kallenbach, 13 March 1915)

We do not know whether such letters soothed Kallenbach's jealousy, but he did correctly identify Andrews as a major contender for Gandhi's affections.

On their first encounter, Andrews had stooped to touch Gandhi's feet in a racially polarised South Africa. He was shunned by the white press and population. But this act had gained him the immediate affection of both Gandhi and the Indian community. Though his stay was brief, he played an important role in the brokering of the Gandhi–Smuts Agreement in the same year. Andrews's regard for Gandhi found clear expression in his letters to Tagore, his other (already) great love:

> The English in Natal are far worse than the English in Calcutta. What is exercising them … is the fact that I [as an Englishman] took the dust of Mr. Gandhi's feet – the feet of an Asiatic – on landing. I am afraid I shall never be forgiven.
> (Andrews to Tagore, 6 January 1914)

Andrews hoped that his transgressive acts in Natal would make him worthy of Tagore's love:

> I long – Oh! How deeply I cannot tell you to take this love itself and lay it at the feet of Gurudev. I am longing and hoping that by and through this experience I shall not be made less unworthy of his love.
> (Andrews to Gandhi, 5 April 1914)

The need to 'love' became an existential, almost desperate, need for Andrews. The act of taking Gandhi's dust and the desire to lay himself at Tagore's feet suggested his readiness to transgress the strict racial codes of British colonial life.

Andrews constantly compared his feelings for Gandhi with those he had for Tagore and found the former fell short: 'I could not love him immediately, instinctively, as I loved you when I saw you in England' (Andrews to Tagore, 14 January 1914). Unlike with Tagore and at Shantiniketan, he felt he had to: 'cut channels, for love to run freely … and to get past the barriers of mere kindness and friendliness which falls short of true love' (Andrews to Tagore, 14 January 1914). Compared to the rustic, unfettered freedom of Shantiniketan, Phoenix and Tolstoy Farm were highly regulated spaces, purpose-built for carrying out political struggles. Andrews's proprietary tendency to compare affections, with Tagore as the gold standard, often betrayed his insecurities. In his letters, he would confide his love for Gandhi to Tagore, that for Tagore to Gandhi, and for both Gandhi and Tagore to Gokhale, creating a thick affective trail. Aboard a ship bound for India from Cape Town, he yearned for 'Mohan' (Gandhi):

> I have been thinking so much about you on this voyage – more even, I think, than on my voyage from the Cape. It is the coming closer to India that brings me even closer to you. … [H]ow sane and true you

were, Mohan, when we were in Pretoria and I was questioning myself of going to the [passive resistance] march with you if it were to begin once more ....

(Andrews to Gandhi, 13 April [1914?])

Reciprocating this embrace, Gandhi's 'love letter' playfully noted:

If you cannot have a nurse like me, who should make love to you but at the same time enforce strict obedience to doctor's orders, you need a wife who should see that you had your food properly served, you never went out without an abdominal bandage .... But marriage is probably too late. And not being able to nurse you I can only fret.

(Gandhi to Andrews, 6 August 1918)

'Love letters' such as these virtually reconstituted co-presence. An intensely intimate letter, it painted a vivid image of domestic affection. The attention to material details of care – food, bandages – and the invocation of specific roles such as nurse and wife enabled this intense co-presencing. The references to 'love-making' and wifely care by a strictly celibate Gandhi made possible a language of homoerotic intimacy. Like a doting wife, he portrayed Andrews as the suffering husband, evoking a vision of conjugal domesticity.

Andrews's desire to love and be loved by prominent men such as Munshi Ram (later Swami Shraddhanand), Tagore and Gandhi helped him realise his 'feminine' self. As he confided to his colleague and friend at St Stephen's College, S. K. Rudra, he was 'too much of a woman by nature ... and cannot help' expressing his love and concern (Andrews to Rudra, 4 May 1915). Seeing his sentimentality as a 'feminine' attribute greatly complicated the nature of his male intimacies. Perhaps anticipating its potently risqué sexuality, he qualified this 'feminine' self as essentially maternal:

[I]t is because of this unchanging motherly influence that the 'mother' in me has grown so strong. My life seems only able to blossom into flower when I can pour out my affection upon others as my mother did upon me.

(Andrews to Tagore, 27 January 1914)[16]

Homoeroticism had to be carefully contained within desexualised maternal terms. To love India was construed as essentially an effect of this strong maternal urge. Andrews felt powerfully attracted to different kinds of masculinity embodied by these 'great' men. To be able to come into their close confidence was a dual affirmation of his 'womanliness' and their manliness. It evinced his 'feminine' ability to 'love' and 'long' for their presence while also sublimating it under an abstracted Indophilia.

Epistolary projections form part of a longer invocation of homoerotic intimacy practised through letters. Gandhi's 'love letters' to Western followers became a major site to stage this language. Letters provided the form and space to express languages of longing without their having to be actualised in practice. Potent attractions of disciples to their mentors could be contained, their sexualities could be sublimated within non-threatening idioms of affection. Epistolary spaces manifested and indeed celebrated these intimate transgressions less readily achievable in more formal spaces. It 'queered' languages of intimacy within standard idioms of discipleship, a point rarely recognised within mainstream scholarship.[17]

When the discipleship was heterosexual, like that of Gandhi and Mira, 'love letters' both expressed and contained mutual love. Justifying his habit, he wrote to Mira:

> Though you absolve me from having to write to you I cannot deny myself the joy of writing to you every Monday. Writing love letters is a recreation, not a task one would seek an excuse to shirk.
>
> (Gandhi to Mira, 4 April 1927)

'Love letters' induced Mira to continually project her 'love'. Like Nivedita, Mira had the 'lover's adoration' for Gandhi, as Rolland observed in his journal (Prabuddhaprana 1990, 217). To cultivate physical distance, Mira was sent to different ashrams to hone her Hindustani and, more importantly, to stem her over-attachment to Gandhi. Love letters became a mode of instruction in Gandhian syncretism:

> I have all your love letters. The one about the repugnance against Mussalmans is disturbing. It is the fear of conversion that has caused this repugnance.
>
> (Gandhi to Mira, 27 December 1926)

Though letter writing is a relational practice and based on reciprocity, the desire to please Gandhi had led Mira to forfeit even that expectation. At times, Mira did not even seek his acknowledgement of her 'love letters', satisfied in the knowledge that they would be read by him, despite his busy schedule. She wrote voluminously, sometimes, as Gandhi complained, not 'shorter than ten pages' (Gandhi to Rukminidevi and Benarsilal Bajaj, 8 January 1933). For Mira, to be replied to was a rare privilege in itself, even if it was a two-liner. Gandhi's replies – often short and curt – were hardly effusive. They followed up on her training in the ashram and other practicalities, such as learning Hindi:

> You should give me your day's doings, and describe the prayers, the studies and the meals. Tell me what you are eating. How are your bowels acting? What is the quantity of milk you are taking? … Are there mosquitoes there? Do you take your walks regularly? Do you write any Hindi?
>
> (Gandhi to Mira, 11 December 1926)

Gandhi's ashram letters generally served a didactic function. They reflected his constant pursuit of ideal dietary regimes and minimalist lifestyles.

Anxieties of longing

Disciples sought an amplified sense of their guru's self in letters, and generally found it. Through letters, they felt the guru's touch and presence. Distance imparted meaning to the epistolary embodiments, compensating for physical absences. Andrews wrote to Tagore:

> It was such an intense pleasure to see your dear handwriting again. I had been looking for it mail after mail hoping against hope … and my heart overflowed when it came at last with its opening word of 'friend'. I wish I could tell you what that means to me, but it must be told in other ways than letters!
>
> (Andrews to Tagore, 8 May 1913)[18]

The 'mail' – embedded in a larger history of imperial networks and postal modernity – reordered epistolary meanings of intimacy through space and time. The wait for the letter created the momentum for its realisation. Postal and epistolary modernity came to manifest new languages of emotion around the private letter, shaping its correspondents' expectations and intentions. The handwriting and signature came together to reconstitute this cultural-material embodiment. Even as Andrews fretted to Tagore, 'I could never tell you in words how I love you' (Andrews to Tagore, 2 October 1913), letters came closest to embodying this love.

Disciples' love for gurus could not remain impervious to the anti-colonial ethos of their projects. While Tagore did not participate in mainstream political endeavours as Gandhi did, he nevertheless remained a critic of empire. Epistolary texts bore testimony to confessions of complicity and failure. An anguished Andrews confessed to Tagore about his failings:

> I have failed many times. The greatest failure was last year when to my surprise the missionary societies, one and all, asked me to write a book for their younger people to study. I accepted the task …. I was ashamed of the book …, especially when I met you and stayed with you. But the sense of shame has increased since I came back to India and visited the ashram. … [B]ut I will *never* write a book on those lines again! I want to realise a truer self … and I am going to make a great claim upon your friendship and ask you to help me to do so.
>
> (Andrews to Tagore, 8 March 1913; emphasis mine)

Andrews's book – *The Renaissance in India: Its missionary aspect* (1912) – credited missionary Christianity in India with being responsible for its new social, cultural and political awakening. In letter after letter to Tagore, he expressed torment over his deeds and sought penitence. Tagore's letters gave him new life:

> [S]trangely enough, though things are still so uncertain, since your letter came my mind has been wonderfully relieved. The assurance of your love and the call to your side have changed the aspect of affairs, and I am happy.
>
> (Andrews to Tagore, 15 May 1913)

Andrews could not wait to be 'freed from all … claims, as soon as possible, of Government and Mission and Anglo India with its social calls and conventions'. Meeting Tagore had only made the 'longing stronger', along with a 'liberalising of [his] own Christian thoughts' (Andrews to Tagore, 8 May 1913). Pearson underwent a similar experience. Despite his Baptist missionary affiliation, he was impatient to offer his services for Tagore's ashram 'with the humility and reverence of a worshipper', 'trying to give up thinking of the poverty and failures of [his] own life and try to fix a steadfast gaze on the ideal for which the as[h]ram stands' (Pearson to Tagore, 6 May 1913). Pearson wanted to work quietly on his Bengali and leave his Baptist missionary obligations before immersing himself in Shantiniketan. Pearson's love for Tagore elicited in Andrews a similar feeling:

> It has been very beautiful on this voyage to watch Willie's love for you, and it has given me a deep joy which I cannot express in words. …To speak of you, as we do together, has been his great and widest comfort.
>
> (Andrews to Tagore, 5 October 1915)

He wished to follow in Pearson's footsteps: to learn Bengali and Sanskrit, travel widely and live in India with eminent Indians, engaging with Indian philosophy and thought. He wanted to try, from a 'completely independent standpoint (not as a paid agent)', to express Christian thought in the East: 'I have been proud and conceited in the past and underrated Hinduism; I would be so no longer' (Andrews to Tagore, 28 July 1913). Letters reflect this inter-referentiality of shared affections, for Tagore, India and Hinduism. Love for Tagore spilled into new investments (see Figure 5.3), linking them in a relationship of transitivity:

> [T]here has come, I know not how, through my love for you, a new confidence and a new assurance. I have entered into the heritage of India herself and been made one with her spiritual experiences and felt its depth and power. ... But the fountain of my own heart was still partly sealed and only since I have learnt to love you has it burst its bonds and overflowed. It is this which has made the last year of my life richer in love for all who love India than it had ever been before. It has taught me to love ... all the dear friends I have made at the ashram.
> (Andrews to Tagore, 13 December 1913)

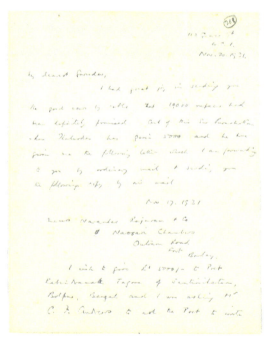

Figure 5.3 C. F. Andrews fundraising for Shantiniketan, 20 November 1931. Courtesy: Rabindra Bhavana, Visva Bharati.

Andrews's 'love talk' for Tagore and Shantiniketan was, however, interpreted as a sign of his 'going native' by missionary colleagues and English newspapers. He wrote to Gandhi of his intense state of turmoil:

> That attack on me in the English newspapers for my 'Hindu' proclivities … The missionaries are probably saying … that I am going to become a 'Hindu' and if I go to Bolpur and resign the Delhi Mission this will be universally believed.
>
> (Andrews to Gandhi, 13 April [1914?])

His coming closer to Tagore signified a moving away from missionary ties:

> I could not be true to my love for you, if I did not seek to share them [his difficulties] with you and I trust your love enough to be sure that you will welcome the burden …. [I]t was my very meeting with you, which has made me realize more clearly my own position and become dissatisfied with it. I could not share your life, without feeling the confinement of the narrow walls of my own. … If I remain a missionary, in a somewhat narrow Missionary Society, I am in a sort of bondage.
>
> (Andrews to Tagore, 28 July 1913)

Tagore and Shantiniketan continued to figure in almost every letter from and between Andrews and Pearson, reminding them of the parochiality of mission life and the promise of freedom that ashram life offered. Visions of being with Tagore heightened the longing to unlearn, if not always disown, their cultural inheritances.

Work became worship and gurus became near-divine characters. Mira, bouncing between ashrams all over India, remained 'immersed in [her] Bapu'. Her letters to Gandhi show the painful negotiation of a new cultural self – living a simplified Indian ashram life – and her fear of failure:

> Bapu dearest, another long and precious letter from you has just arrived! I could not, even if I tried, be anything else but what I am before you, and that is why, however I am ashamed of my weakness, I have to lay bear [sic] before my Bapu – Yes – you are indeed father and *mother* and what is more than all, you are Bapu, *my Bapu* – in whom I live, and in whom I have that utter confidence that only boundless love can inspire – and it is Bapu alone who can make me what I should be. The strength and love of my Bapu are ever with me now … Nothing that bears the slightest shade of *untruth* can stand before you.
>
> (Mira to Gandhi, 15 May 1927, emphasis in original)

Gandhi's consequent replies to Mira are almost clinical in their brevity and directness. He referred to his disciplining of Mira's passionate desire to be close to Gandhi as a necessary 'operation':

> I sent you away too quickly after a serious operation. But the sending you away was part of the operation. … Jamnalalji says I should have kept you with me. Well, you are going to belie their fears and … keep quite well and cheerful.
>
> (Gandhi to Mira, 2 October 1927)

Almost like a mandate, Gandhi's instructions to Mira brought more sorrow than solace. The attempt to excise personal attachment almost broke Mira. Love letters bore testimony to the continued cycle of distress and relief that characterised their relationship.

Becoming idealised objects

The bodies of white women and their deployments in specific projects became sites of gendered spectacle. Both Noble and Slade adopted vows of Hindu celibate asceticism or *brahmacharya,* becoming Nivedita and Mira respectively. Vivekananda had anticipated for Noble the role of delivering manhood to Indian men:

> What was wanted was not a man but a woman; a real lioness, to work for the Indians, women especially.
>
> India cannot yet produce great women, she must borrow them from other nations. Your education, sincerity, purity, immense love, determination and above all, the Celtic blood make you just the woman wanted.
>
> (Vivekananda to Nivedita, 29 July 1897)

In letter after letter, Vivekananda continued to spell out what the Indian nation needed Nivedita to embody: purity, education and a Celtic racial valour mobilised to deliver manhood. He continued to warn her of people who stood in the way of such a project:

> [A]s long as you go on mixing with that [Tagore] family, I must go on sounding my gong. Remember that that family has poured a flood of erotic venom over Bengal …. [M]y mission is simply to bring MANHOOD to this people.
>
> (Nivedita to MacLeod, 12 March 1899)[19]

Nivedita in due course became a central figure in a Hindu cultural nationalism that hinged on a politics of deficit masculinity, dominant in colonial Bengal and India in the early twentieth century. Creating a desexualised but forceful language of discipleship was crucial for Vivekananda.

Gandhi, attuned to a different vision of Hinduism and masculinity from Vivekananda's, exercised different expectations on Mira. Mira adopted celibacy and took her vows in Gandhi's presence in 1927. Her letters were frequently circulated by Gandhi as objects of education for ashram inmates. Gandhi told Mira:

> [Y]ou should perhaps know that I send most of your letters to the Ashram for being read to the members. They are so beautiful. Those that contain criticism of the attitude of the Kanya Gurukul I did not send. I destroyed them. ... I do not want you to restrain yourself because other eyes may see the letter.
>
> (Gandhi to Mira, 24 January 1927)

The practice of circulating letters gave them a performative role. Selectively destroying critical letters betrayed Gandhi's concern to curate a prescriptive ideal self for consumption by his ashram community. This simultaneous gesture of approval, through circulation of her appreciative letters, and control, by destroying more critical letters, formed part of a larger disciplining exercise.

Mira's coming closer to a syncretic and 'essential' Hinduism reflected her desire to identify with an aspirational collective:

> Every day of my life I become more and more deeply in love with the Hindu nature – I don't know how to express it Bapu – I just feel as if it were the highest development of humanity which we have in this world, with its inborn gentleness, forgiveness and tolerance – its simpleness and natural feeling for God. ... I get the feeling that to pass into the Hindu nature is the natural, perhaps *the* road to salvation. ... [A]s long as one remains to any extent outside it, one feels oneself to be to that extent a barbarian. ... I now realise that barbarism in myself and sooner or later I will overcome it. ... If I cannot all together overcome it in this life, then I ask nothing better than to be born a Hindu in the next birth – and this the Blessed Way will at last become open to me.
>
> (Mira to Gandhi, 29 January 1929)

The strong desire to be Hindu produced the experience of being so. Mira was far less prominent than Nivedita in Indian nationalist discourse, but both became extraordinary examples of an Indianness they were not born into. In women such as Noble and Slade, therefore, we see a nationalist appropriation already at work that ranged from swadeshi to social work. By voluntarily choosing to side with anti-colonial politics and its Indian proponents, these disciples reworked a racialised symmetry of power both personally and politically. Indian nationalist politics, both political and cultural, generally remained sensitive to the strategic use of these figures. Their racial difference made Western discipleships extraordinary, and therefore useful. The bind this claim created on white women disciples led to further disciplining of their bodies and desires.

Archipelago of affect

The anthropologist Monique Scheer has argued that emotions are not merely cognitively rooted but also consistently material, embodied and embedded in practice (Scheer 2012, 194–6). Since historians can only access the expression of an emotional experience, not the experience itself, languages of expression assume primacy in understanding emotions as practice. Letters and letter writing were a distinctive mode of such emotional practice. The act of writing made physical acts around them more real. Conversely, physical acts informed by epistolary dialectics reinforced their convictions. Letters made possible a dense archipelago of affect.

Epistolary narratives of discipleship are replete with ruptures. Mentors resisted, not infrequently, the continuous proprietary appropriations of their disciples. Vivekananda and Gandhi continued to sermonise on the dangers of 'personal love'. The problem of the 'personal' lingered in relationships with women disciples. Letters also became a way to insert personal distance. Vivekananda clarified to Nivedita that despite 'persons giving [him] almost the whole of their love', he 'must not give any one the whole of [his] in return, for that day the work would be ruined. … A leader must be impersonal.' Similarly, Mira's continuous desire for physical proximity to Gandhi irked him. He chided her sharply:

> Why hanker after my company! Why touch or kiss the feet that must one day be dead cold? There is nothing in the body. … Experience and effort will unravel it before you, never my association in the manner you wish. … Why so helplessly rely on me? Why do everything to please me? Why not independently of me and even in spite of me? … Break the idol to pieces if you can and will.
>
> (Gandhi to Mira, 24 June 1929)

Gandhi pushed back against Mira's constant 'clinging'. Invocations of impersonality and the idea of a greater (implicitly spiritual) cause served to stem the dangers of excessive personal adoration. But the desires of the guru remained a perpetual driving force for disciples' sacrifices, particularly around the incipient nation. The conjoining of *gurubhakti* (devotion to the guru) and *deshbhakti* (devotion to the country) has long been an integral part of the nationalist project in India, since at least the late nineteenth century, and with important consequences for many forms of *bhakti*.[20]

Gandhi was always fearful of sexual transgression, and his own lifelong experiments with celibacy bore witness to that anxiety. Thwarted by her own mentor, she could only 'remain immersed in [her] Bapu' from afar. Letters allowed an acceptable mode of expressing love and longing. Vivekananda struggled with the incessant rumour-mongering about his chastity, usually perpetrated by detractors.[21] Creating a desexualised and sacralised language of discipleship was required, given the prominence of celibacy, or *brahmacharya*, in Gandhi and Vivekananda's projects, both personally and publicly.

With male disciples, disenchantments played out differently. There was no imminent fear of sexual transgression that loomed large, unlike with women disciples, and this might explain their relative lack of censure. Tagore and Gandhi agreed to 'share' Andrews between themselves. Gandhi wrote to Tagore:

> Much as I should like to keep Mr. Andrews with me a little longer, I feel sure that he must leave for Calcutta tonight. ... And you must have him while you need him. ... I would ask you ... to lend me ... Andrews now and then. His guidance at times is most precious to me.
>
> (Gandhi to Tagore, 30 April [1918])

Secondary epistolary exchanges such as these reveal what Indian mentors thought about their Indophile mentees and each other. They brought to the fore doubts, differences and dismissals. Tagore, for instance, did not hesitate to criticise Gandhi's practices to Andrews, anticipating much of their later differences in opinion:

> Only a moral tyrant like Gandhi can think that he has the dreadful power to make his ideas prevail through the means of slavery. It is absurd to think that you must create slaves to make your ideas free. I would much rather see my ideas perish than to leave them in

charge of slaves to be nourished. There are men who make idols of their ideas and sacrifice humanity before their altars.

(Tagore to Andrews, 7 July 1915)

Tagore continued to air his differences with Gandhi both privately and publicly; Andrews remained a trusted aide in the communication between these two figures. Even as disciples sought to stake a claim in Tagore, he resisted their zealous overtures in his ashram and his literary endeavours. He played truant whenever his disciples' desire for physical proximity became overwhelming, and continued to dispense transcendent wisdom from a suitable epistolary distance. Andrews recognised the strain his tendency to act as custodian put on his relationship with Tagore. He rationalised:

[O]ne with a strong personality tends to weaken the characters of those who are closely associated with him, whenever they remain too long at his side and become dependent on him. ... This danger I have experienced personally. ... I was too eager to be continually present with the Poet, ... whom I deeply loved, and it became an oppression to him because he saw with his fine instinct that it was weakening my individual character. Therefore, in the gentlest manner possible, he warned me from this.

(Andrews to Rothenstein, 3 August 1916, cited in Tinker 1979, 129)

The 'oppression' such declarations of love conferred on Tagore was not minor. Edward J. Thompson, a Wesleyan missionary, poet and admirer of Tagore, was scathing about Andrews as 'beneath contempt as regards judgement and intellect generally', and for fanning Tagore's vanity.[22] He did not hesitate to convey this opinion to Tagore's British associates, including the poet Robert Bridges and the artist William Rothenstein. Thompson's offers to translate Tagore had often been thwarted by Tagore himself, who had 'every hope that Andrews will be willing to help me in this work' (Tagore to Thompson, 15 February 1914).[23] Yet this closeness and help occasionally brought its own allegations. Always uncertain of the literary merit of his English translations, Tagore felt annoyed that his close association with Andrews had led people to suspect that he owed his literary success to Andrews, 'which is so false that [he] can afford to laugh at it' (Tagore to Rothenstein, 4 April 1915, cited in Lago 1972). Nevertheless, all this suggests Andrews's inordinate influence with the poet that led Thompson to blame him for 'annex[ing] Tagore as a private possession', a feeling shared by another British follower, the agricultural educationist Leonard Elmhirst.

Tagore frequently appealed to the lofty language of freedom to distance himself. Letters became vectors to intimate such distance. Yet disciples too occasionally rebelled at the continuous demands made on their person. Pearson, often travelling with Tagore on his international voyages and having to act as his secretary, chafed at this imposition. This came as a discovery to Tagore, who immediately sought to free him from such binds of duty:

> You must have freedom, not only for your sake but for mine. That I had been forcing you to a life from which you had been struggling to be free is a discovery which is the most difficult of all the burdens that I am bearing at present. ... You know I love you, and therefore any service you offer to me which is irksome to you is doing injustice to me.
>
> (Tagore to Pearson, 23 December 1920)

Yet Tagore's habit of using English secretaries remained, especially on his Western tours; they were usually his close followers. Declarations of love went both ways to act as reason for control and freedom. Disciples generally opened themselves up to their mentors in order to grow closer to them. Intimacies intensified when mentors returned this gesture. Tagore confided in Andrews about the extreme agony of his inadequacy to serve the ashram, his family, zamindari and country (Pal 1997, 10). He was 'struggling ... through the wilderness[,] ... [t]he toll of suffering ... to be paid in full' (Tagore to Andrews, 21 May 1914). Andrews, who was undergoing a similar turmoil owing to a crisis of faith in his missionary vocation, was deeply touched that Tagore had confided in him and sought to share his pain and crisis with him (Andrews to Tagore, 23 May 1914). Hitherto, it had mostly been Andrews pouring out his heart and mind to a lofty 'Gurudev', from whom he sought guidance and inspiration. Tagore's inner sufferings somehow made him more human, for which Andrews could 'love [him] all the more' (Andrews to Tagore, 25 May 1914).

Dreams became part of such projections, in which disciples could enter the subconscious of their gurus. Pearson dreamt a vision of a battle-worn Tagore:

> Your face was deathly pale, full of profoundest sorrow. I did not know the reason but it seemed to me quite natural. ...[Y]ou were wounded in your right arm. ... It was an intense suffering for me, I suppose it was your pain which was transferred to my heart. Then I woke up.
>
> (Tagore to Pearson, 11 October 1915)

Pearson's ability to empathise with Tagore's (supposed) pain in his dream-reality reflected his love for him. Tagore evoked feelings of (once again) 'maternal' affection in Pearson: 'Watching Gurudev's face, his white haired and bearded face my maternal affections would spill over – I felt like hugging him close to my chest like a little child.'[24]

Conclusion

Letter writing brought disciples closer to the world of their mentors. They testify to trying (and often failing) to be part of the guru's spiritual, emotional and cultural world. The fracturing of Western cultural selves, and, along with it, belief in an innate sense of cultural and racial superiority, were part of this emotional upheaval.

The act of letter writing reflected the continuous grappling of Western disciples with a new set of idioms and individuals, all of which were distinctively Indian. Informed and mediated by the politics of race, nation, class and gender, the letter became a point of convergence between individuals located in various positions of power. They became agentic in intermeshing big discourses in their everyday contexts and power relationships. Letters, like ashramic spaces, became active sites for renegotiating a relationship of identity with Indian gurus. Even a simple act of narrating or describing real-life colonial experiences became an integral aspect of this self-articulation.

Epistolary texts abound in a language of loss, the will to intimacy constantly riven by disciples' doubts of self-worth. The tendency to

Figure 5.4 Envelope (in Tagore's hand) addressed to Andrews, then residing with Gandhi at Sabarmati, 1918. Courtesy: Rabindra Bhavana, Visva Bharati.

overcompensate is writ large in much epistolary articulation, but this is particularly telling in the initial phase of discipleship. In time, these intimacies were transformed, serving as nodes for transnational discourses that drew a wider audience in India and abroad.

Notes

1   I use 'bilingual' in the sense of English and one vernacular language; there were vibrant traditions of non-English bilingualism in the subcontinent, disrupted by the growing importance of English.

2   Gandhi's and Tagore's, as also their disciples', epistolary accounts are more complete than Vivekananda's. This is largely due to censorship practised by the Ramakrishna Mission over the archival traces of the legacies of its founder and his disciples' (both Indian and Western).

3   Jacob Copeman and Aya Ikegame (2012) show how central the trope around the uncontainability of gurus is. To contain what is uncontainable is an old rhetoric in Hindu religious metaphor, though this claim, often made by and for gurus, is used to mark power and authority in the wider social world.

4   Original letters from C. F. Andrews to Rabindranath Tagore, Visva Bharati, Shantinikentan, Rabindra Bhavan Archives. Henceforth MSS/CFA/RBVB/F/4-11, MSS/CFA/RBVB/F/4-11.

5   Folder 287(ii), Letters from William W. Pearson to Rabindranath Tagore, Rabindra Bhavan, Visva Bharati. Henceforth MSS/WP/RBVB/F/287 (ii).

6   Folder 287(i), Letters from Tagore to Pearson. Henceforth MSS/RT/RBVB/F/287(i).

7   File no. 1, Original Letters from Rabindranath Tagore to C. F. Andrews, CFA PAPERS, File: 1-26, 28 (ii), CD No: RBVB-018. Henceforth MSS/RT/RBVB/F/1-26, 28 (ii)

8   Through the publication of Rolland's book (Rolland 1924).

9   Suhrud and Weber 2014, 11–12. All letters between Gandhi and Mira/Madeleine Slade are taken from this volume unless otherwise stated.

10   Goodwin is an underexplored figure in the Ramakrishna–Vivekananda tradition. Enlisted as a stenographer by Vivekananda's wealthy patrons in America, he went on to become one of his staunchest followers. In India, though, he could not fit in with Vivekananda's Indian disciples. The only proper reference to his life is Pravrajika Vrajaprana (1994).

11   See Leslie A. Fiedler's (1972) comparable insight on interracial relationships: as long as there is no mingling of blood, love doesn't become a threatening enough force to reckon with in interracial relationships (p. 148).

12   Rolland writes of this in his journal (Rolland 1960), cited in Prabuddhaprana 1990, p. 217.

13   For instance, the Agreement signed by Gandhi and Kallenbach on 29 July 1911, on the eve of Kallenbach's visit to his family in Europe, for 'more love, and yet more love ... such ... as the world had never seen' is particularly insightful (Gandhi 1958, vol. 96).

14   Gandhi to Kallenbach, 30 July 1909: 'I know that you do not want them to be read by anybody else' (Gandhi 1958, vol. 96, p. 21).

15   Kallenbach's German nationality was a problem in his entering British India on the eve of the First World War. Gandhi consulted Andrews before writing to the Viceroy, Hardinge, to see what steps could be taken. Gandhi to Kallenbach, 17 February 1915 (Gandhi 1958, vol. 96, p. 202).

16   Fraser–Tagore Collection, press clippings 91–200, University of Edinburgh.

17   As for instance Uma Dasgupta's (2018) framing of the relationship between Tagore, Gandhi and Andrews as lofty 'friendships of largeness and freedom', formed in the shadow of colonial rule and India's freedom struggle.

18   MSS/CFA/RBVB/F/4-11. All letters from Andrews to Tagore are from this series.

19   All letters by Sister Nivedita are taken from *Letters of Sister Nivedita*, vols 1 and 2 (Nivedita 1960).

20   Jacob Copeman (2008) offers a comparative insight into the powerful role of the guru in influencing disciples' sacrifices around donating blood for the Indian armed forces in post-colonial India, and how this has been embraced by some sects influenced by reformist Hinduism.

21 See a letter from his Brother Disciples to Vivekananda, March 1894 (*Vivekananda* 2011), about rumours spread by the Brahmo preacher Protap Mazoomdar of him 'committing every sin under the sun in America – especially "unchastity" of the most degraded type!!!' (Burke 1984, 90).

22 Edward P. Thompson (1993, 33) received an uneven response from Tagore throughout his engagement with the poet.

23 Edward J. Thompson papers, general correspondence, Tagore; Oxford Bodleian Libraries MS. Eng. c. 5318, fols 1–40.

24 Urmila Devi, 'Winstanley Pearson', Pearson Smriti, Calcutta, 1923, Folder 287 (viii), Rabindra Bhavan.

References

Primary sources

C. F. Andrews, Pearson and Tagore papers, Rabindra Bhavana, Shantiniketan.
Fraser–Tagore collection, University of Edinburgh.
E. J. Thompson papers, Bodleian Library, University of Oxford.

Secondary sources

Burke, Marie Louise. 1984. *Swami Vivekananda in the West: New discoveries*, 3rd edn, vol. 2. Calcutta: Advaita Ashrama.

Copeman, Jacob. 2008. 'Violence, non-violence, and blood donation in India', *Journal of the Royal Anthropological Institute* 14 (2): 278–96. https://doi.org/10.1111/j.1467-9655.2008.00501.x.

Copeman, Jacob and Aya Ikegame. 2012. 'The multifarious guru: An introduction', in *The Guru in South Asia: New interdisciplinary perspectives*, edited by Jacob Copeman and Aya Ikegame, 1–45. Abingdon: Routledge.

Dasgupta, Uma (ed.). 2018. *Friendships of 'Largeness and Freedom': Andrews, Tagore, and Gandhi: An epistolary account, 1912–1940*. New Delhi: Oxford University Press.

Fiedler, Leslie A. 1972. 'Come back to the raft ag'in, Huck honey', in *An End to Innocence: Essays on culture and politics*, 2nd edn. New York: Madison.

Frost, Mark R. 2016. 'Pandora's post box: Empire and information in India, 1854–1914', *English Historical Review* 131 (552): 1043–73. https://doi.org/10.1093/ehr/cew270.

Gandhi, Mahatma. 1958. *Complete Works of Mahatma Gandhi*, vols 14, 52 and 96. https://www.gandhiashramsevagram.org/gandhi-literature/collected-works-of-mahatma-gandhi-volume-1-to-98.php (accessed 21 February 2023).

Gupta, Devyani. 2016. 'Stamping empire: Postal standardization in nineteenth-century India', in *Global Scientific Practice in an Age of Revolutions, 1750–1850*, edited by Patrick Manning and Daniel Rood, 216–34. Pittsburgh, PA: University of Pittsburgh Press.

Lago, Mary. 1972. *Imperfect Encounter: Letters of William Rothenstein and Rabindranath Tagore, 1911–1941*. Cambridge, MA: Harvard University Press.

Nivedita, Sister. 1960. *Letters of Sister Nivedita* (ed. Sankari Prasad Basu), vols 1 and 2. Calcutta: Nababharat.

Orsini, Francesca. 2006. 'Love letters', in *Love in South Asia: A cultural history*, edited by Francesca Orsini, 228–58. Cambridge: Cambridge University Press.

Pal, Prashanta. 1997. *Rabijibani*, vol. 7. Calcutta: Ananda.

Poskett, James. 2019. *Materials of the Mind: Phrenology, race, and the global history of science, 1815–1920*. Chicago, IL: University of Chicago Press.

Poustie, Sarah. 2010. 'Re-theorising letters and "letterness".' Olive Schreiner Letters Project, Working Papers on Letters, Letterness & Epistolary Networks no. 1, University of Edinburgh.

Prabuddhaprana, Pravrajika. 1990. *Tantine: The life of Josephine MacLeod, friend of Swami Vivekananda*. Calcutta: Sri Sarada Math.

Rolland, Romain.1924. *Mahatma Gandhi: The man who became one with the universal being* (trans. Caroline D. Groth). London: Swarthmore Press.

Rolland, Romain. 1960. *Inde: Journal (1915–1943)*. Paris: Albin Michel.

Scheer, Monique. 2012. 'Are emotions a kind of practice (and is that what makes them have a history)? A Bourdieuian approach to understanding emotion', *History and Theory* 51 (2): 193–220. https://doi.org/10.1111/j.1468-2303.2012.00621.x.

Suhrud, Tridip and Thomas Weber. 2014. *Beloved Bapu: The Gandhi–Mirabehn correspondence*. New Delhi: Orient Blackswan.

Thompson, Edward P. 1993. *'Alien Homage': Edward Thompson and Rabindranath Tagore*. Delhi: Oxford University Press.

Tinker, Hugh. 1998. *The Ordeal of Love: C. F. Andrews and India*. Delhi: Oxford University Press.

Vivekananda, Swami. 2011. *Letters of Swami Vivekananda*. Calcutta: Advaita Ashrama.

Vrajaprana, Pravrajika. 1994. *'My Faithful Goodwin'*. Calcutta: Advaita Ashrama.

6
Śabda-guru: conflicts of guruship, mediational phenomenology and *Śabda*-philosophy in Sikhism

Arvind-Pal Singh Mandair

Introduction

Sikhism is often referred to as a 'Guru' tradition par excellence, and not surprisingly, because it had 10 living, or personal, Gurus as well as an authoritative scripture called the Guru Granth Sahib. Moreover, the term 'Guru' is quite possibly the most prevalent in the Sikh conceptual lexicon, giving rise to such terms as *gurmat* (the logic or philosophy of the Guru), *gurprsād* (by the Guru's grace), *gurbāṇī* (the utterance of the Guru), *gurdarśan* (the Guru's vision), to name but a few. One might therefore conclude that Sikhism is just like any other of the many Indian guru traditions. Doesn't the prevalence of personal gurus within the wider Sikh Panth (community), in the form of Baba-sects, *dera*-Babas, Sants[1] and related sectarian figures, attest to the long-held view, reflected by the scholar of Sikhism W. Owen Cole, that it is to 'that Indian religious tradition that we must turn in our attempt to understand the major distinct concept of Sikhism, that of guruship' (Cole 1982, 1)? Indeed, as Cole states, although 'India has seen the emergence of many guru cults in its long history' and although '[m]any have disappeared soon after the death of the preceptor', so that the 'guru becomes lost to memory save for a samadhi, a tomb or memorial shrine', evidently this is not the case for Sikhism, which 'may be regarded as a gurucult which has persisted and in doing so made a distinctive contribution to the concept of guru in the Indian religious tradition' (Cole 1982, 2).

Although Cole was not incorrect to emphasise the 'distinctive contribution to the concept of guru', his categorisation of Sikhism as a 'gurucult', albeit one with greater longevity than others, is certainly an oversimplification, as is the suggestion that its notion of guruship can be unproblematically fixed into 'Indian religious tradition'. If we carefully probe the meaning and implications of the concepts of Guru and guruship in Sikh literature and its early history, what emerges is both surprising and, in some ways, almost un-Indian. The term 'Guru', especially when linked to the term *śabda* (for example in *śabda-guru*, the Guru as Word or Word as Guru), refers less to a person than to an incorporeal concept that radically undermines all vestiges of personhood. As I argue in this chapter, *śabda-guru* is not only one of the conceptual building blocks of any Sikh philosophy, but is also rooted in an evolving phenomenology which starts out (during their lifetimes) with the Gurus communicating authority according to the Indic tradition of oral mediation; from here, mediation of authority transitions from a living person, to a sacred text in conjunction with a living person; from here it transitions further to a sacred text in conjunction with a community *minus* a living personal Guru; it culminates in a situation today where the figure of Guru is dispersed between sacred text, community and digital forms of media (digital text, sound, in multiple languages) and available on laptop, tablet and smartphone (Mandair 2019). At all times during its evolution, the form of mediation is itself accompanied and underpinned by a philosophical concept, the notion of incorporeal Word (*anhad śabda*). It is the Word's incorporeal nature that pushes the relation between Guru and Sikh towards a state of absolute depersonalised, formless non-mediation (or immediacy), characteristic of pure consciousness. Needless to say, this movement from mediation to immediacy has potentially important ramifications for the way in which political authority and sovereignty are conceived within and outside the Sikh community. By depersonalising the tendency to vest authority in living gurus, the concept of *śabda-guru* complicates the notion of spiritual-political authority in ways that not only place it at odds with an 'Indian religious tradition' that privileges personalised guruship, but also present a challenge to mainstream Khalsa Sikhism. For even as the latter enshrines *śabda-guru* as its central doctrine, its tendency to iconise and idolise this doctrine in the form of religious ritual (especially after the nineteenth century), rather than to examine it philosophically for its salvific potential, inadvertently causes a fault line within popular Sikhism's understanding of authority that has been exploited on the one hand by 'gurucults' such as the *dera*-Babas and on the other hand by political organisations vying for votes.

In this chapter, I shed some light on the mediational phenomenology in relation to the societal, philosophical and political-theological implications of this equation of *śabda* with *guru*. How does this concept sit with the community's collective memory and practice, which retain an emotional link to a personal Guru? In what way does the tension between the mediational and the philosophical aspects of *śabda-guru* create one of the fault lines between mainstream Sikhism (Khalsa tradition) and the popular tradition of paying reverence to the so-called 'Baba' sects such as the Radhaswamis, the Nirankaris, and contemporary Sant-based groups? Can the concept of *śabda-guru* transform notions of sovereignty especially in the diaspora, as loyalty comes to be invested in a geographically non-locatable, non-historical principle?

Contesting narratives of guruship

Students and many scholars encountering Sikhism for the first time are often struck by the ubiquity of the term 'guru' both as a figure and as a concept, in the phenomenology of Sikh ritual process, its way of life, its literature as well as its philosophical teachings. This is hardly surprising, given that historically there was a continuous succession of 10 living Gurus, starting with the founder Nanak and ending with the tenth Guru, Gobind Singh, who ended the formal line of personal or living guruship, known as *gurgaddhi*, shortly before his death in 1708. Instead of nominating a living (*dehdhari*) guru as his successor he nominated the Sikh scripture (Adi Granth) as the eternal guide of the Sikhs in conjunction with a minimal community of five Sikhs initiated into the order of the Khalsa (a spiritual-political order established by Guru Gobind Singh in 1699).

As historians have long noted, the nomination of a successor was often a contested issue, with rival claimants to the *gurgaddhi* either being marginalised, setting up their own sectarian bases or, in certain cases, colluding with powerful state forces to help undermine the authority of the chosen leader of the Sikhs (McLeod 1997; Grewal 2009). Not surprisingly, refusal to compromise on the part of overlooked claimants at times led to schisms within the early Sikh community. This became something of a pattern especially after the fifth Guru, Arjan, was selected in place of his elder brother Prithi Chand, as the historian W. H. McLeod has noted:

> As a result Arjan had to face the disappointed and determined enmity of his eldest brother, Prithi Chand, and quarrels over the succession became a feature of the remainder of the Guru period. At least three of these disappointed contenders formed panths of their own, claiming to be the legitimate descendants from Nanak.
>
> (McLeod 1997, 29)

For years his opposition proved a great difficulty for Guru Arjan, particularly after Arjan's son was born, when Prithi Chand seems to have attempted something serious in the hope of undermining the child's claims to succession. There is sound evidence for this particular episode, which indicates that Prithi Chand was contemplating serious injury to (possibly assassination of) Arjan's only child, the future Guru Hargobind. As proof we have the testimony of both Guru Arjan and Bhai Gurdas. Prithi Chand, having failed in his attempt, set himself up as a rival Guru. To followers of the legitimate line, they were the Minas or 'scoundrels' (McLeod 1997, 30).

Having learned from this episode and anticipating future schisms and hostilities from external forces such as the Mughal sultanate, which was undergoing its own wars of succession, Guru Arjan took steps to consolidate and diversify the nature of authority within the community, which till then centred on the figure of the living Guru. Arguably the most important step was the compilation of a scripture (Adi Granth) containing the compositions of the preceding Gurus. Hymns contributed to the Adi Granth by six of the Sikh Gurus (Nanak, Angad, Amardas, Ramdas, Arjan and Tegh Bahadur) not only carried the authorising stamp of the name 'Nanak' (each Guru signed in the name of 'Nanak'), but respective Sikh Gurus could be distinguished by the code word *mohalla* (lit. 'house' or 'neighbourhood'), abbreviated to 'M' within the text of the Adi Granth. These Gurus therefore signed off as M1, M2, M3, M4, M5, M9 (Shackle and Mandair 2005, xviii). The key point here is that the designation 'M' referred not only to the *bodily identity* of each Guru but to the house or neighbourhood, which can also be seen as a metaphorical reference to the nature of a *sovereign consciousness* that was shared by each individual Guru in order to be recognised as the legitimate occupant of the *gurgaddhi*. Thus, to be officially nominated as 'Guru' by the incumbent master, the initiate had to manifest evidence of being possessed by this consciousness, which could only be verified by the master through specific tests, the importance of which was that they showed the new Guru's ability to channel the revelation of *gurbani*.[2]

A second step implemented by Guru Arjan was to install formally the Adi Granth in the newly constructed Harimandir, which thenceforward became the central pilgrimage site for the Sikh community. During the installation Arjan publicly prostrated himself before the Adi Granth and placed the scripture on a podium higher than his own sitting position, in effect treating it as if it were his Guru. The message to his followers (and to his detractors within and outside the community) was unambiguous: spiritual authority lay not only with the person of the living Guru, but, from now on, with the Adi Granth, not only with the corporeal text but, even more importantly, with the incorporeal teaching contained within its verses. This practice was continued by the later Gurus (Hargobind, Har Rai, Harkrishen and Tegh Bahadur) until the last days of Guru Gobind Singh, who formally ended the line of living Gurus by transferring guruship jointly onto the text, which was renamed the Guru Granth Sahib, and the community, with the proviso that it was to be led by the Khalsa. To quote McLeod again:

> Before he died, realizing his end was near, the Guru summoned his Sikhs and declared that the line of personal Gurus was now at an end. Thereafter they should regard the functions of the Guru as vested in the Granth (which became the Guru Granth) and the Panth (the Guru Panth). In this way the Guru will remain ever-present and ever-accessible to his Sikhs. … The line of personal Gurus was at an end and the Guru would thereafter be present in the Granth and the Panth.
>
> (McLeod 1997, 58–9)

This brief foray into early Sikh tradition shows us that the figure of the Guru, and with it the concept of guruship, were intimately tied to issues of sovereignty and authority. Indeed the question of sovereignty is central to the various scenes of nomination that resulted in the investiture of a living personal Guru from the late fifteenth century to 1708, or the investiture of the scriptural text as Guru parallel to the living Guru (1603), or the investiture of the Adi Granth as Guru in 1708, and of course the designation of Khalsa's right to lead the community. What is often forgotten (at times by Sikh traditionalists themselves) is that the primary reason for creating the Khalsa was not so much to create an external identity where one did not exist, or to formalise a new spiritual-political order, the primary *raison d'être* of Khalsa was (and remains) to conserve the teaching of the house of Guru Nanak, whose foundational principle is the sovereign consciousness passed from one living Guru to another and enshrined within the text as a philosophico-spiritual principle of liberation: *śabda-guru* – the idea that Guru is Word. As a doctrine, *śabda-guru* incorporates two seemingly contradictory functions. On the one hand, it mediates between (1) Guru Nanak and the materiality of the Adi Granth, (2) the body of the text and the visual and sonic presence of the living Guru, and (3) the sonic resonances of the text as it is read, recited, memorised and sung, communally and individually. On the other hand, and in paradoxical fashion, its philosophical concept *mediates immediacy*, in the sense that it provides access to a liberating epistemology which annihilates all manner of duality: Guru versus Sikh, self versus other, subject versus object, materiality versus ideality. In other words, it pushes physical mediation (embodiment, textuality, sonic resonance) towards an absolute immediacy signified by the term *anhad sabda* (incorporeal word, soundless sound, unpulsed vibration). It is this paradoxical principle that grounds Sikh epistemology, and informs its ontological ethics and therefore the potential for it to be shared with the wider world. It is this principle more than any other aspect that has prevented Sikhism becoming just another Indian sect or guru cult. At the same time, however, it marks a central point of divergence between those who prefer a living preceptor, whose voice and physical presence mediate authority, to mainstream Khalsa Sikhism, which adheres to the *śabda-guru* principle as it has manifested either in various forms, or formlessly as a spiritual-philosophical principle.

This broad divergence between Khalsa Sikhism's *śabda*-centrism and the preference of non-Khalsa sects and *dehdhari* gurus can also be seen as a fault line within the broader Sikh community. Although this fault line has been exacerbated by local and national politics (see below), the nature of its disjuncture has also been somewhat misunderstood by an influential strand of scholarship which has significantly underplayed the politico-theological, philosophical and mystical nuances of *śabda-guru* as a doctrine. Until relatively recently, the dominant strand of scholarship in modern Sikh studies exhibited a tendency (1) to highlight the more visible aspects of guruship, notably the master's *living* presence, personal charisma and holiness, and (2) to stress that the Guru and his teaching are 'essentially religious', resulting in a praxical ideal of detachment and non-engagement in worldly and political affairs. This is especially the case with the work of W. H. McLeod and scholars who followed his lead in the decades between the late 1960s and 2010 (McLeod 1968, 1975; Cole 1978, 1982; Nesbitt 2005; Fenech 2008; Jakobsh 2012). Based on a largely positivist form of historiography,[3] McLeod's work suggested that there was a qualitative and progressive deviation or fall from the pristine religiosity of Nanak (to which he attributes the closest proximity to the divine source) and that of the later Gurus who became involved in political affairs (Mandair 2009). From this perspective, events such as the creation of the Khalsa are represented as epitomising the divergence from 'explicitly religious' and peaceful origins associated with the Nanak Panth, towards the kind of political involvement in violence, social justice and affairs of the state characteristic of Khalsa Sikhism (Mandair 2022a).

From here on, the false assumption concerning the 'fundamental change in the dominant philosophy of Panth' (McLeod 1984, 11) from the peaceful message of the early Nanak Panth to the violent message of the later Sikh Gurus, culminating in the Khalsa Panth, becomes centralised in discourses of Sikh studies, South Asian studies and the history of religions. Furthermore, once this narrative was normalised within academic discourses, it was but a short step to portraying the Khalsa as a suspect entity prone to anti-state activity and spreading anarchic violence. This negative stereotype about Khalsa Sikhs was deployed by the Indian state via its think tanks, which fed the Indian and global media from the late 1970s onwards. As I have argued at length elsewhere, at best this thesis says more about the political ideology and governance mechanisms of modern liberal states than it does about early Sikh history (Mandair 2009, 2015, 2022a). At worst it reflects an imperialising tendency inherent within the modern state (British and Indian) that deprives indigenous traditions of the right to define and participate in their own sense of sovereign consciousness.

While the dominant Sikh political system, represented by the Akali Dal and its ecclesiastical arm the Shiromani Gurdwara Parbhandhak Committee (SGPC), has tried to minimise tensions between Khalsa and non-Khalsa formations in the broader Sikh community, at various times throughout the twentieth century the fault line erupted into violent confrontations between Khalsa and non-Khalsa denominations. In most cases the tensions can be attributed to perceived external challenges to the centrality of the Guru Granth Sahib as the source of spiritual-political authority, and therefore also to the Khalsa Panth. Since the 1970s, whenever such confrontations occurred, the mainly state-controlled India media have tended to categorise Khalsa-centrism as a conservative religious orthodoxy unwilling to entertain plurality within the Sikh political-spiritual system (Ballard 1984; Kapur 1986; R. D. Mann 2016).[4]

While this is neither entirely untrue nor entirely different from other disputes concerning guru traditions, in which contestations over authority are common and widespread, nevertheless the overly negative stereotyping of Khalsa as a regressive, anti-pluralistic entity overlooks a factor of crucial importance, one that is specific to the Sikh context. It has to do with the fact that the 'Guru' is not just a corporeal entity (the Granth or scripture), but, perhaps more importantly, also an axial philosophical, and therefore incorporeal, *concept* in Sikhi or *gurmat*. This can be seen in the lexicon of the Guru Granth Sahib and related literature, which gives rise to terms such as *gurmat* (logic or teaching of the guru), *gurprasad* or *gurdwara* or *gurbani*, all of which are intimately woven into Sikh life-practices. If we probe the meaning of 'Guru' in this literature, and specifically its linkage to the term *śabda* (Word/language of the guru), what emerges is an impersonal concept of *śabda-guru* which, in addition to being a pivotal concept in the Sikh lexicon, radically undermines all vestiges of personhood and personal sovereignty. In other words *śabda-guru* might be regarded as an onto-epistemological concept that paradoxically sustains what might be considered a 'radical orthopraxy' (Khalsa-centrism) by shifting the tradition away from vesting authority in a person, towards consciousness in general.

In the following section I would like to explore some political-theological implications of equating *śabda* with *guru* as *śabda-guru*. However, to further emphasise the need for understanding this concept, it may be helpful to highlight some recent examples of flashpoints that have exacerbated existing fault lines between mainstream (Khalsa-centric) Sikhism and sectarian groups that pay reverence to personal gurus often referred to as 'Babas' or 'Sant-Babas'. I ask how some of the sectarian Baba movements play on the community's collective mnemopraxis and visual imagination, which continue to retain an emotional link to the living presence of charismatic preceptors vis-à-vis the 10 historical Sikh Gurus. Conversely, to what extent does the mainstream Khalsa Panth's often thorny relationship with *dera*-Babas and related guru cults mirror a long-standing ideological struggle and fundamental difference between Sikh and Vedic doctrine? And to what extent is the latter struggle reflected in the current political tensions between the Sikhs and contemporary Hindu nationalism? This will allow us to contextualise more carefully the philosophical concept of *śabda*-as-guru within contemporary Sikh culture. I conclude by asking whether (and if so how) the concept of *śabda-guru* can transform notions of sovereignty, especially in the diaspora, as loyalty comes to be invested in a geographically non-locatable, non-historical principle.

Fault lines, personal gurus and sectarian violence

Although it should not be regarded as a rule of thumb, the fault line between Khalsa-centrism and anti-Khalsa-centrism is a helpful indicator of broader tendencies within Sikhism towards or away from personal gurus. This is particularly evident in the way the intellectual, social and political movements to modernise Sikhism instigated by the Singh Sabha reformists in the late nineteenth century culminated in the establishment of the Sikh code of conduct, the *Sikh Rahit Maryada* (SRM), in 1950–4, under the auspices of the SGPC (McLeod 1989). The SRM affirms the definition of a Sikh as a 'person who professes the Sikh religion, believes and follows the teachings of the Sri Guru Granth Sahib and the ten Gurus' (McLeod 1984, 79; see also McLeod 2003).

The key point about this definition is that it re-establishes the centrality or axiomatic status of the nature of guruship, and therefore authority in the global Sikh community, as vested not only in the corpus of the scripture as a canonical scriptural text, the 'Book' as many modern-day Sikhs call it, but even more importantly in the instructional logic or teaching (lit. *gurmat*) contained within the texts. The emphasis on *gurmat* was crucial to the Singh Sabha's entire scholarly effort over a period of 70 years (from the 1880s to the 1950s) to re-establish the nature and location of authority. I shall return to this point in more detail in the next section of this chapter, as it harbours a fault line *within* a fault line – what might be called an interiorising fault line that is often missed in modern Western Sikh studies and to some extent even by traditionalist Khalsa-centric Sikh scholars. In this section, I would like to probe some of the social implications and manifestations of the Khalsa–anti-Khalsa fault line.

The main societal implication arises from the fact that, within the global Sikh community, there are a number of groups which did not accept that, just before his death, Guru Gobind Singh uttered the injunction '*guru manio granth, pargat guran ki deh*' (consider this Granth/ text to be the embodiment of the Guru), which effectively ended the line of living, personal Gurus.[5] This refusal can be seen in their continuation of lines of human gurus. Exemplary of this kind of reluctance to accept the Adi Granth as Guru, or acceptance of Khalsa-centrism, are groups such as the Namdharis, the Nirankaris, the Radhasoamis, and other organisations loosely categorised as Sant-groups or *dera*-Babas. Presented below are a few characteristics of each of these groups, after which I focus on the Nirankaris and *dera*-Babas which have come into violent conflict over the question of personal guruship.

Namdharis

The Namdharis (ones who wear the divine Name on the fabric of the body-mind) observe the Khalsa form, a central feature of their praxis being constant remembrance of *nam* (divine Name(s)),[6] hence the meaning of Namdhari as one who wears the *nam* on their body and mind. Where they differ from orthodox Khalsa practice is in their belief in a continuation of the line of living gurus. According to Namdhari belief, Guru Gobind Singh was wounded after receiving a dagger blow from a Pathan assassin in 1708, but did not pass away as is generally accepted by the wider Sikh community. Rather, he spent his last days as a recluse, calling himself Ajapal Singh, and before his death he selected Balak Singh as his successor (Takhar 2005). The Namdhari doctrine of religious authority is similar to the Muslim Shia teaching about the Hidden Imam. Accordingly, the Adi Granth is positioned alongside the current living guru and successors of Balak Singh. In addition, for Namdharis the central position in their *dharamsala* (as opposed to Sikh gurdwaras, a term that was instated by the SGPC in 1925) is occupied by a picture or the actual personage of the regnant *satguru*, at the time of writing Jagjit Singh. Unlike in mainstream Khalsa practice, Namdhari marriages and birth ceremonies are based on the performance of *havan* or the traditional fire ceremony, following the ancient Vedic style (*yajna*).

Nirankaris

Unlike the Namdharis, the Nirankaris do not emphasise the Khalsa form and external symbols, instead promoting the 'interiorized nature of Guru Nanak's teaching' (Takhar 2014, 353; see also Cole 1982). The Nirankari sect was founded by Baba Dyal, a non-Khalsa or *sahaj-dhari* Sikh (1783–1855) and contemporary of Maharaja Ranjit Singh. Baba Dyal Singh encouraged his followers to focus on the formless (*nirankar*) nature of the divine, a move that was motivated in part by the fact that during the reign of Maharaja Ranjit Singh, Brahmanical rituals and idol worship had regained a foothold amongst the Sikh masses. Refocusing attention on *nirankar* brought Sikhs closer to the message of the Guru Granth Sahib, and as a result the Nirankari sect is considered a precursor of the Singh Sabha's wide-ranging reforms aimed at re-establishing the Guru Granth Sahib at the heart of Sikh praxis. Despite these early efforts to centralise the GGS, the Nirankaris' non-insistence on Khalsa external symbolism has led to this sect being labelled Nanak Panthis. After partition in 1947 the Nirankaris re-established their headquarters in Chandigarh and remained relatively marginal until 1978, when their leader brought them into violent conflict with Khalsa-centric Sikh groups (see below).

Sants

This brings me to the charismatic persons belonging to the so-called Sant tradition (Schomer and McLeod 1987), who individually and through their followers exerted significant influence in the global Sikh community.

The term Sant is derived from the Sanskrit *satya* (being-truth) and normally refers to a charismatic spiritual master, literally one who knows the truth of being and non-being. The word Sant appears often in Sikh scripture, where it is synonymous with terms such as *gursikh*, *gurmukh*, *sadh*, *sadhu* and *bhagat* (Nesbitt 2014, 360). Thus the term Sant both pre- and post-dates the line of 10 Sikh Gurus beginning with Nanak and ending with Gobind Singh. According to one scholar the Sant movement can be regarded as a 'nonconformist counter tradition [largely associated with Kabir, Ravidas and Namdev and Nanak] that transcended established religious categories and challenged many of the beliefs and practices of orthodox *bhakti* (Schomer 1987, 8). The relationship between mainstream Sikhism and the Sant movement is a contested one. As Eleanor Nesbitt explains,

> Not only the Gurus but also unsuccessful aspirants to the *gaddi* ('throne' of Guruship) drew followers during the sixteenth and seventeenth centuries. Despite the ending of the line of personal Gurus in 1708, the ancient master/disciple tradition survived, though the master could never be called a guru .... Many Sikhs attached themselves to preceptors who had acquired reputations as teachers or exemplars and who eventually acquired the title of *sant*.
> (Nesbitt 2014, 361).

However, if a particular person, in acquiring the title 'Sant', is seen by the mainstream Sikh community to accord to himself (or to be accorded by his followers) the title of 'Guru', this often becomes a contentious issue, at times leading to violence because of its overt or implicit challenge to the narrative that Guru Gobind Singh closed the line of human gurus in 1708 and accorded sovereignty jointly to the Guru Granth Sahib and the Khalsa community. In the Punjab heartlands some Sants have tended to establish residential centres called *deras* (lit. dwelling place of a Sant), which serve as locations where Sants impart instruction in Sikh beliefs and spiritual practices (Takhar 2005; Nesbitt 2014).

Throughout the twentieth century, individual Sants have been involved in different kinds of political movements in ways that have taken their influence well beyond their *deras*. The politics of Sants falls roughly in line with the Khalsa/non-Khalsa fault line noted earlier. For example, at the height of British rule, Sant Attar Singh Mastuana-wale (1866–1927) 'played an important grassroots role in furthering the Tat-Khalsa reforms and later on supported the Akali movement's anticolonial struggle to remove *mahants* or corrupt custodians of Sikh historical shrines' (Nesbitt 2014, 362). In the 1960s Sant Fateh Singh fasted to death in the political struggle to establish a Punjabi-speaking state. More recent examples include Sant Harchand Singh Longowal (1932–85), who led the Akali Dal in the early 1980s and organised non-violent campaigns or *morchas* against the ruling Congress Party. Longowal was assassinated in 1985 after signing a peace accord with India's prime minister Rajiv Gandhi. Even more 'spectacular' in his political involvement against the Indian state was Sant Jarnail Singh Bhindranwale, who became head of a leading Sikh missionary centre (Damdami Taksaal), and was killed in the Indian Army's attack on the Golden Temple complex in Operation Blue Star (June 1984). For many Sikhs, Bhindranwale was an exemplary modern *shahid* or martyr for a noble cause (Grewal 2009, 305).

The above-mentioned Sants were fully embedded within, and promoted a key tenet of, Khalsa-centric doctrine, namely that a Sant or any charismatic figure in a leadership role cannot regard him- or herself as either on a par with the Guru Granth Sahib or above the will of the Sikh community, especially the Khalsa community. There are, however, other Sant groups who have encouraged styles of veneration and reverence, ranging from deference towards a psycho-spiritual and charismatic personality, to veritable personality cults around authoritarian 'Babas' who became fully embroiled in often violent sectarian clashes with Khalsa Sikhs. Examples of the latter include violent clashes between orthodox Khalsa groups and the Sant Nirankari Baba, Gurbachan Singh (1978), the attack in Vienna on Sant Niranjan Dass and Sant Rammanand of Dera Sachkhand Ballan (2009), and several clashes with devotees of the Dera Sacha Sauda Baba, Gurmeet Ram Rahim Singh (2007).

Babas and violence

Arguably the bloodiest clash triggered by the contentious issue of personal guruship and the challenge it posed to mainstream Khalsa Sikhism took place on 13 April 1978 in the city of Amritsar in Punjab. According to the news media at the time members of two orthodox Sikh groups, the Akhand Kirtani Jatha and the Damdami Taksaal, were protesting against a planned convention and parade organised by the Sant Nirankari Mission (SNM). The Sant Nirankaris had split off from the main Nirankari sect in the early twentieth century. Whereas the latter upheld the spiritual temporal authority of the Guru Granth Sahib, the splintered Sant Nirankaris believed in a personal living guru.

In 1963 the fourth leader of the sect, Baba Gurbachan Singh, began proclaiming himself a god-man and incarnation of Guru Nanak, at the same time encouraging his followers to call him *bajjan-wala* (Master of the Hawk), which in Sikh lore is an unambiguous reference to Guru Gobind Singh. By the 1970s the Sant Nirankari Baba Gurbachan Singh had started to project his status as being above the Guru Granth Sahib, and had introduced innovations that challenged the standard Tat Khalsa rites of initiation. In the lead-up to the Baisakhi day celebrations of 13 April 1978, the Sant Nirankari Baba had held a series of parades in other cities in Punjab on an open-top bus, with himself seated next to and slightly above a copy of the Guru Granth (Grewal 2009, 310). When a group of unarmed civilians belonging to the Akhand Kirtani Jatha (AKJ) and Damdami Taksaal (DT) tried to prevent the parade taking place in Amritsar, the Baba's security guards pulled out sub-machine guns and shot many of the protesters, killing 13 of them. Most of the dead, including the leader of the group Fauja Singh, belonged to either the AKJ or the DT. This incident is widely regarded as the spark that led to the events of Operation Blue Star and the militant insurgencies of the 1980s (Mahmood 1996, 78). Scholars are now generally in agreement that the rise of Baba Gurbachan Singh and the entire Sant Nirankari episode had been politically engineered by the ruling Congress Party and the Jan Sangh (a precursor of the BJP) to destabilise the Akali Dal and the Sikh political system (G. Singh and Shani 2022).

The unusually rapid growth of the Sant Nirankari sect, the odd composition of the sect's followers, who included gazetted police officers and deputy commissioners with powers to allot land and attract large numbers from poor sectors of Punjabi society, and of course the arming of this group with the latest sub-machine guns, suggested that the Sant Nirankari Baba was part of a broader political engineering project that could undermine mainstream Sikh power in Punjab (Mahmood 1996, 79; Grewal 2009). In the context of this chapter, however, the key take-away from this episode is the ease with which agent provocateurs were able to manipulate the fault line between personal and scriptural Guru.

Almost three decades later, history seemed to repeat itself when Indian news media were reporting clashes between Khalsa Sikhs and the followers of a new *dera*-Baba, Gurmeet Ram Rahim Singh, who had become the third leader of the Dera Sacha Sauda. Widely described as a religious sect, this *dera* achieved notoriety through its overt involvement in state and local politics, openly encouraging its people to vote for political parties favoured by the *dera*-Baba himself (Copeman 2009). In the 2007 Punjab state elections, the Dera Sacha Sauda supported the Congress Party, helping it to exert influence in the Malwa region previously controlled by the Akali Dal. In the run-up to the elections Gurmeet Ram Rahim Singh openly courted controversy when he appeared in newspaper adverts impersonating iconic religious figures, such as Guru Gobind Singh and Lord Vishnu.

Sikh critics of the Dera noted that the tactics deployed by the Baba were very similar to those used by the Sant Nirankari chief in 1978. Khalsa Sikhs alleged that he was not only actively undermining Sikh faith in the Guru Granth Sahib, but also trying to destabilise the Sikh political system by manipulating the contentious issue of personal guruship. In May 2007 these allegations spilled over into violent clashes between followers of the Dera Sacha Sauda and the Akali Dal, and news media made overt comparisons between the violence of the 1970s instigated by the Congress–Sant Nirankari partnership (Copeman 2009, 122–3). At the behest of the Akali Dal, the Akal Takht *jathedar* issued a proclamation demanding closure of all *deras* in Punjab and encouraged its own followers to organise protests and strikes (*bandhs*). As a result of this intensive political pressure Gurmeet Ram Rahim Singh issued a formal apology, but it was deemed insufficient and rejected by the Akal Takht. Marches and boycotts against the Dera continued for several weeks amidst escalating violence (Copeman 2009, 121).

The Dera Sacha Sauda's involvement in state politics did not end with the violent altercations of 2007. In the run-up to the 2012 state elections, the Punjab Congress leader, Capt. Amarinder Singh, and his family visited the *dera*-Baba and requested his support to oust the Akali Dal, led by Parkash Singh Badal (Gopal 2017). Two years later, in 2014, and again in 2015, BJP leaders in the Haryana and Bihar state elections approached Gurmeet Ram Rahim for support, and as a result the Dera Sacha Sauda encouraged its followers to vote for the BJP in both states (Sharma 2016). In August 2017, however, prompted by allegations of sexual assault and other misdemeanours, a long-standing criminal investigation by the CBI caught up with the *dera*-Baba and he was indicted on charges of sexual assault against two female devotees (Dera Sadhvis). Following the court's verdict the Baba's followers rioted throughout northern India, which led to the deaths of dozens of people in Punjab and Haryana.[7]

A rather different example of the long-standing tensions between mainstream Sikhism and *dera*-Babas is that of the Dera Sachkhand Ballan. In 2009 militant Sikhs attacked important representatives of this *dera* at a *satsang* in Vienna. One of the *dera* leaders hurt in the attack was Sant Niranjan Dass. His deputy Sant Rammanand was killed. News of the attack led to widespread rioting in Punjab by followers of the Dera. What made this incident different from other confrontations is that the Dera Sachkhand Ballan 'highlights the troubling dynamic of caste amidst an increasingly diverse diaspora' (Nesbitt 2014, 367). Although Dalits comprise at least 30 per cent of the population of Punjab, and despite *chamar* icons such as Bhagat Ravidas being included in the Sikh scripture, the *chamar* community itself has continued to be marginalised by dominant caste groups in the Sikh Panth, especially Jats and Khatris. This has led Dalit Sikhs to distance themselves from mainstream Sikhism by self-identifying as Ravidasia. The violence in Vienna in 2009 is one of the most dramatic manifestations of this tendency; it led to the formalisation of a new religious movement called Ravidas Dharam on 29 January 2010 by the Dera Sachkhand Ballan, with its own scripture (*Amrit Bani* of Guru Ravidas).

Although it is rarely discussed in the scholarly literature, the formation of a separate scripture, and the elevation of the figure of Ravidas from 'Bhagat' (in the Adi Granth) to 'Guru' in response to its caste-based marginalisation by mainstream Khalsa Sikhs, is highly ironic for the simple reason that Tat Khalsa Sikhism distinguished itself from other forms of Sikhism by its strong anti-caste emphasis. This was especially the case in the late nineteenth and early twentieth centuries when reformist Tat Khalsa Sikhs managed to marginalise the so-called 'Sanatan Sikh' groups which were led by Khatri Sikhs such as Baba Khem Singh Bedi, who claimed to be a descendant of Guru Nanak and refused to accept caste-mixing (Oberoi 1994). But caste is only one way to understand the fault line, and, as shown by the above example of the Ravidas Dharam, it is not an entirely reliable indicator. A better way to probe (with a view to resolving) the nature of the fault line that defines the wars over guruship is to bring into view the almost complete marginalisation and misunderstanding of the implications of the *śabda-guru* as the philosophical principle that constitutes the vitality of guruship as a principle of polity. It is to this much misunderstood yet axiomatic principle that I would like to turn.

'Guru' as an epistemic principle: *śabda-guru*

Before I turn this discussion towards the philosophical concept of *śabda-guru*, let me start by reiterating, and elaborating on, a point that was signalled at the outset of this chapter. During the lifetime of the Sikh Gurus, the Guru–Sikh relationship remained largely within the Indic tradition of oral mediation. The ontological question 'what is a guru?' did not arise (Mandair 2009, 263). A living Guru's spoken word and personality were taken as marks of authority. This continued during the lifetimes of the first nine Gurus (from Nanak to Tegh Bahadur), but when the last living Guru declared that guruship would pass to the Adi Granth and to the community, led by the Khalsa Panth, the doctrine of dual sovereignty, *Guru Granth* (Guru-as-text) and *Guru Panth* (Guru-as-Khalsa), emerged as central. Arguably, the primary role of the Khalsa was to safeguard the spiritual sovereignty of the Guru Granth and specifically its role as repository of the ultimate or true Guru, the *satguru*.

As the historian J. S. Grewal has argued, especially in the eighteenth century the doctrine of dual authority provided 'a sense of solidarity and unity of action' (Grewal 1996, 46) and consolidated the belief that the Guru was ever-present amongst the Sikhs, both as text (Granth) and as community (Panth). This in turn aided the evolution of a related institution, known as *Gurumata*, which played a crucial role in fostering expressions of political and spiritual sovereignty for the Sikh Panth.[8]

Throughout much of the eighteenth century, although the power of the Mughal empire was steadily declining, Khalsa forces nevertheless remained preoccupied with survival and warfare. As a result, the management of Sikh historical shrines and centres of learning (*taksaals*) passed into the custodianship of Udasi and Nirmala sects. This trend continued in the early decades of the nineteenth century under the Sikh ruler Maharaja Ranjit Singh, who not only patronised Udasi and Nirmala ashrams, but also abolished the institution of *Gurumata*. An important consequence of this was a pronounced diffusion of Vedic and Puranic concepts into existing Sikh interpretive frameworks. Udasi and Nirmala scholars generally subscribed to a worldview determined by the Brahmanical *sanātana dharma*, an axiomatic principle of Hindu orthodoxy governed by the theological paradigm of 'Eternal Sanskrit' (Deshpande 1993) and the centrality of the Veda. At the core of the eternal Sanskrit paradigm are several interlinked assumptions. The first is that the essence of language (*śabda*) is voice (*vāk*), and *vāk* indicates the living presence of a person capable of sounding *vāk* here and now. Secondly, because *vāk* is eternal and immutable, it is intrinsically sacred. Thirdly, there is a prohibition against *vāk* being written, because the written signifier represented the death of the living presence or person.[9] Taken together, these aspects of the doctrine of eternal Sanskrit translated into a cultural preference within the *sanātan dharma* worldview for personal (*dehdhāri*) gurus whose living presence was a conduit for *vāk* and *śabda*.

As I have argued in greater detail elsewhere, it is precisely this principle that is resisted by mainstream Khalsa mnemopraxis and the Sikh philosophical conception of *śabda-guru*. This mnemopraxis is broadly encompassed by the term *gurmat* (teaching, logic or philosophy of the Guru). While the most obvious example of such resistance to *sanatana dharma* is in Guru Gobind Singh's performative closure of the line of living Gurus and prostration before the Adi Granth, formally conferring the title of Guru, it was by no means a new event. For example, as noted earlier, the fifth Guru, Arjan, who compiled the Adi Granth in 1603, had already elevated the scriptural text above his own personal status, by formally installing it in the Harimandar Sahib, thus giving it the central place in the development of Sikh rituals and ceremonial practices (P. Singh 2003).

However, it is important to note that the depersonalisation of guruship does not begin with Arjan, but with the first Guru, Nanak himself. Although Nanak formally initiated the succession of personal Gurus by passing the *gurgaddhi* to his chosen successor Angad, it is important to note *what* exactly he had passed on and why. Thus, while scholars are generally agreed that Nanak passed on a *pothi* or corpus of manuscripts containing his own authorised poetic compositions (G. S. Mann 1999; P. Singh 2003), what is underplayed in this scholarship is the incorporeal teaching or philosophy (*gurmat*) at the heart of these writings. For at the core of this teaching is an answer to the question: What is a guru? Or what is a guru for? – an answer that is expressed in terms of the philosophical concept of *śabda-guru* as the preferred vehicle for effecting spiritual liberation or self-transformation. It is because soteriology is intimately tied to the concept of *śabda-guru*, and because *śabda-guru* is a cornerstone of Nanak's own experience and his teaching, that this principle becomes a measure of the kind of sovereign consciousness that the last living Guru (Gobind Singh) bequeathed to the Khalsa, which in turn enshrined this consciousness into its praxical memory and endeavoured to protect and defend it, often at the cost of individual life itself. It became literally a matter of living and dying (Mandair 2022b, 64–6). With this in mind, let me return briefly to look more closely at *śabda-guru* as a philosophical concept.

Satguru as *Śabda*: depersonalising the function of Guru

One thing that cuts across all guru traditions and guru sects is the term *satguru* (or *sadhguru*), which refers to the ultimate, true or real Guru, the one who claims authority to teach and instruct others on the basis of personal experience. In the Indian wisdom traditions, and those Sikh sects which defer to the authority of these traditions (for example Radhasoamis, Sant-Nirankaris and many *dera*-Babas), the authoritative source of the teaching, instruction, technique or path leading to enlightenment is usually provided by a living person acting as a preceptor.

By contrast, mainstream Sikhism, beginning with Nanak's distinctive deployment of the term *satguru*, indicates that the kind of spiritual transformation articulated in texts such as the Guru Granth Sahib should not be reliant on a living human preceptor. It is more efficacious to try and attain it directly through one's own effort, for the simple reason that the desired experience is singular in nature. It is not only unique to each person but the state of consciousness it enjoins students to achieve is marked by immediacy, a lack of quantifiable distance, a state that can only be realised within the interiority of one's consciousness. Of course, as any perceptive student of Indian thought knows, this emphasis on immediacy and interior consciousness was first discovered and recorded in the early Upanishads, after which it was endlessly analysed and debated in the philosophical schools. If that is the case, how does Sikhism differ? The short answer lies in how the principle of immediacy and/or access to interior consciousness as a vehicle of liberation is socially implemented and institutionalised. Whereas orthodox Hinduism restricted access mainly to the Brahmin caste (the theology of Eternal Sanskrit and the *varna-ashram-dharma* being essential tools for this task), Guru Nanak enshrined it at the centre of his teaching, on every page of the Adi Granth, in every form of mnemopraxis, and eventually, through the agency of his successor Gurus, within the form of the community known as Khalsa. With Brahminism the point was to conserve authority and conserve a social in-group by policing consciousness, whereas for Khalsa Sikhism the whole point is to devolve authority, to give the means of liberation back to the people. In terms of mediational phenomenology, Brahminical Hinduism shifts the function of *mediation* back to the personal figure of the Brahmin as the conservator of Veda and Eternal Sanskrit, and of the *varna* system: in this way Brahminism is a highly effective system for preserving the sovereignty of the self. In contradistinction, the *śabda-guru* principle in conjunction with the Khalsa as a social formation works (in theory at least) to 'annihilate' ego (liberating the self from itself) and to prevent the accumulation of personal sovereignty as the basis for mediating authority.

This rejection of personal sovereignty is explained by Nanak himself in one of his compositions known as *Siddh Gosht* (Dialogue with the Siddhas). The dialogue itself involves a discussion about the ultimate source of Nanak's authority as a spiritual master in his own right. As Nanak explains, the source of his authority is the *satguru* (true Guru) but when asked who his *satguru* is, Nanak suggests that it derives from a non-human source which resides in the interior of one's consciousness. Although *satguru* is rather conveniently translated as 'God', more precisely it refers to an absolutely interior wellspring, a living force inherent within all life that remains hidden from us because of the kind of psychic orientation attained through acculturation to conventional societal norms. In stanzas 43 and 44 of the *Siddh Gosht,* the debate between Nanak and the Siddhas reaches a climax as the Siddhas directly confront Nanak about the source of his knowledge and therefore about the source of his authority as a spiritual master.

Siddhas (43)
What is the origin [of your power]?
What system of knowledge commands respect today?
Who is your guru? Whose disciple are you?
Which knowledge leads to detachment?
Let Nanak speak and explain to us
Which Word [or teaching] can liberate us?

Nanak replies (44):
Breath is the origin [of my practice and power].
The Guru's logic is the knowledge in this age.
Word is Guru: Consciousness attuned to it is the disciple.
Through the Incorporeal Word, detachment can be attained.
Only through the Word (*śabda*) can the state of Oneness be described,
Embodying Oneness/detachment, the gurmukh quenches the fire of ego.

What stands out in these stanzas is the directness and specificity of Nanak's reply regarding what a *satguru* is. For Nanak, and for each of the Gurus in the lineage up to the tenth Nanak, Gobind Singh, *satguru* is *śabda* (expression/word/desire/concept), which is also referred to as *anhad śabda* (unpulsed/incorporeal Word), a pure or egoless speech and thought that resonates with the underlying sonic-mnemic theme of creation (*nam*), and in resonating unlocks and reveals the creative potentials inherent within human consciousness (see Mandair 2022b). From this perspective it is not incorrect to say that *śabda* is the non-human, anthropomorphic agent of revelation, and revelation in Nanak's philosophy (which cannot be equated with the Abrahamic sense of the speaking-hearing of God's Voice) is tied to the epistemic function of *śabda* as the non-anthropomorphic agent of spiritual self-realisation.

A more productive way of thinking about this is to regard *satguru* as the force immanent within conscious life that enables a transformation of the psyche from its everyday, contracted or egocentric state of consciousness (*manmukh* in Nanak's lexicon) to an expanded state of consciousness which, paradoxically, is achieved only by ego loss. The clearest indication of this transformed state is registered through various modes of expression (language/thought/desire) comprising our aesthetic sensibility.

The agent of this transformation is *śabda*, almost strictly *anhad śabda* (unpulsed or incorporeal word/vibration). The qualifier *anhad*, which literally means unbeaten or unpulsed, unstruck, is crucially important not only for understanding what *śabda* is (its ontology) but also how it functions in the conversion/transforming process, and therefore how and why it replaces the personal touch of human mediation. Throughout his compositions Nanak emphasises that *śabda* is only attained by 'dying to the word' or 'dying to the self', meaning that an individual must sacrifice herself to the word. The references to sacrifice and dying are in fact indicators of a performative mnemopraxis called *nam simaran* that Sikhs are supposed to inculcate into their lives. *Nam simaran* literally means to remember *nam*, to bring *nam* to mind in each and every moment. But to do so requires a performative – real and symbolic – death of the self at the very moment in which the self is generated. If one can achieve the balance (*sahaj*) of living and dying and weave it into the very fabric of the self, this new 'self' that emerges can no longer see itself as an objectifiable entity representable as manifold forms (*sargun*). It is 'now' neither form nor formless (*nirgun*), neither self nor non-self, but only *pure relation to all that exists*. The most evident marker of this *self-as-pure-relation* is the change in its mode of expression. It expresses itself only in the form of poiesis, melody, rhythm, which are all modes that reflect its central characteristic, which is neither thing-ness nor no-thingness, but only vibration (*nad* or *śabda*), or more accurately *anhad śabda* (spontaneous or effortless vibration, or unpulsed, unstruck, uncaused word-sound). All of these references to vibration or resonance are metaphorical ways of describing the nature of self as pure relation. That is to say, the self as a force of connection or relation to the world, a fundamental opening of the self to its outside, its other, so that the duality of self (what is near) and world (the far) is merged in the vibration that is *nam*.

Implications of *śabda* philosophy

In light of the above, what might be some socio-political implications of understanding *satguru-as-śabda*, or to consider *śabda* as *anhad śabda* (pure resonance)? The first and most obvious is the depersonalisation of the concept of Guru, which in turn functions to displace the need for human mediation in the spiritual quest for perfection of the psyche. As a principle it indicates both the immediacy of the spiritual experience and that this experience is open to anyone. Because the emphasis of Nanak's teaching seems to be on im/mediation rather than mediation, a human agent is unnecessary. Accordingly the sovereign experience through which this resonant force is released (or 'revealed') itself becomes the touchstone of all authority in a way that has implications for social and political practice. Although the philosophical conception of *śabda* might seem somewhat esoteric and beyond the pale of media journalism, which has always found it more expedient to present spectacles of violence associated with misleading clichés of violent Khalsa Sikhism versus pacifist Sikhism of the Sants and Babas, it is worth noting that the concept of *śabda-guru* is routinely discussed within exegetical discourses of mainstream Khalsa Sikhism by itinerant preachers, *kirtanias* and *katha vachiks*. From this perspective alone it ought to be regarded as a notion that encourages tendencies towards 'democratising' spirituality by never allowing it to accumulate in a person. Conversely, from the perspective that emerges from the teachings of the Sikh Gurus, the practice of certain *dera*-Babas and Sant groups, of concentrating authority in a person, might be regarded as an 'anti-democratic' preference for silent and pliable *sangats*, thereby hiding highly exploitable proto-fascist tendencies under the veil of unquestioning 'devotion' to a charismatic master. As the rise and mediatisation of guru cults and militant *sadhus* throughout north India have shown us, the veneer of 'devotion' has been cleverly exploited by major political formations such as the BJP, with party leaders themselves performing the role of *sadhu/guru*-in-chief. The concept of *śabda-guru*, as practised by the Sikh Gurus and enshrined into the socio-political *raison d'être* of the Khalsa, was designed to circumvent any tendency towards any such fascism (in the psycho-political sense) that might arise. The reasons for Khalsa Sikhism not being able to entirely live up to the promise of this concept could be laid, in part, at the door of the political system that was adopted after the British relinquished control of Sikh shrines to the Akalis (Sikh Gurdwaras Act of 1925), after which Khalsa Sikhism redefined its role as the body politic of Sikhism. For over a century the Akali leadership was able to leverage a new self-definition of Sikhism as a 'religion'. The problem with the category of religion, however, is that it was invented in the modern era and served a very specific function on behalf of the liberal state. Basically religion was a legal category of governance in keeping with the liberal statecraft of the British, and deployed with clinical efficiency by the imperial British and post-independence Indian states. On the other hand (and this is a direct consequence of the legal religionisation of the Khalsa following the Sikh Gurdwaras Act 1925) the blame lies in a lack of introspection and application of the *śabda-guru* concept to the Khalsa itself. In other words, for the Khalsa to rule (and stay true to its invocation of '*Raj Karega Khalsa*') it needs to surrender spiritually to the *śabda-guru* principle.

Notes

1 'Sants' (upper-case 'S') are historical figures, such as Namdev and Ravidas. Without the capital 'sant' can apply to contemporary figures who assume this title.

2 As I have noted elsewhere (Mandair 2022b, 63), it would not be incorrect to suggest that *śabda* is the non-human agent of revelation. I use the word 'revelation' with some caution here, for I want to underscore that it does not necessarily correspond to the Abrahamic notion of revelation as the literal speaking of God's Word to man either directly or through the agency of supernatural beings such as angels. Revelation in Guru Nanak's philosophy is intrinsically tied to the role of *śabda* as the non-anthropomorphic agent of spiritual self-realisation.

3 See for example McLeod (1994).

4 Throughout the 1980s there was a noticeable trend for many Western and Indian scholars to present the very idea of the Khalsa in a particularly negative light. Their articles and books contributed to feeding Western and state-sanctioned Indian media with an orientalist stereotype of a 'pacifist Nanak Panth' in contrast to a more violence-prone Khalsa Panth. Amongst the many examples of this trend is the work of Roger Ballard and Rajiv Kapur. The recent work by Richard D. Mann (2016) published in the journal *Sikh Formations* challenges these earlier trends by exposing the role of Indian and Western media in 'framing' Khalsa Sikhism as essentially violent.

5 For a discussion of the sources that authenticate this statement see Harbans Singh 1983, 107–9.

6 Often translated theologically as 'divine Name', *nam* can be more usefully considered to be a creative impulse, a term expressing the central attribute of a paradoxical divine that is existent and non-existent at the same time.

7 Srinivasa Prasad, 'Gurmeet Ram Rahim convicted: Godman become powerful as "cautious" media shies away from reporting their crimes', *Firstpost*, 26 August 2017: https://www.firstpost.com/india/gurmeet-ram-rahim-convicted-of-rape-godmen-become-powerful-as-cautious-media-shies-away-from-reporting-their-crimes-3977103.html; Ankit Tyagi, 'Ram Rahim sentencing: Dera-run newspaper gives rape convict clean chit, slams media for negative reporting', *India Today*, 30 August 2017: https://www.indiatoday.in/india/story/dera-sacha-sauda-gurmeet-ram-rahim-singh-sach-kahu-rape-1034554-2017-08-30; Tushar Dhara, 'How the international media covered the Ram Rahim Singh riots', *News18*, 26 August 2017: https://www.news18.com/news/india/how-the-international-media-covered-the-ram-rahim-singh-riots-1502083.html; 'Gurmeet Ram Rahim Singh convictin: Media target', *The India Express*, 26 August 2017: https://indianexpress.com/article/india/gurmeet-ram-rahim-singh-conviction-media-targeted-4813927/ (all accessed 21 February 2023).

8 The word *mata* in Punjabi means a decision agreed by common assent in democratically convened meetings. Hence the *gurumata* was seen as a morally binding resolution and as a medium of expression for political sovereignty.

9 As I have noted elsewhere (Mandair 2009) it is fairly well known that the predominance of orality in Indian tradition was not the result of Indians' inability to write but a conscious decision sustained over a long period of time to restrict the mediation of knowledge to orality, thereby suppressing written sources. The ultimate purpose was to preserve the ritual purity of Aryas vis-à-vis *dharma* and sociolinguistic identity. This prohibition goes back to the early Upanishads, which stipulated that a Brahmin should not recite or orally transmit the Veda after he has eaten meat, seen a dead body or blood, or engaged in writing. In short, words that were written were considered signifiers of death.

References

Cole, W. Owen. 1978. *The Sikhs: Their beliefs and practices*. London: Routledge & Kegan Paul.

Cole, W. Owen. 1982. *The Guru in Sikhism*. London: Darton, Longman and Todd.

Copeman, Jacob. 2009. *Veins of Devotion: Blood donation and religious experience in north India*. New Brunswick, NJ: Rutgers University Press.

Deshpande, Madhav M. 1993. *Sanskrit and Prakrit: Sociolinguistic issues*. Delhi: Motilal Banarsidass.

Fenech, Louis. 2008. *The Darbar of the Sikh Gurus: The court of God in the world of men*. New Delhi: Oxford University Press.

Gopal, Navjeevan. 2012. 'Amid depleting clout, dera chief's kin loses', *The Indian Express*, 7 March.

Grewal, J. S. 1996. *Sikh Ideology, Polity, and Social Order*. Delhi: Manohar.

Grewal, J. S. 2009. *The Sikhs: Ideology, institutions, and identity*. New Delhi: Oxford University Press.

Jakobsch, Doris. 2012. *Sikhism*. Honolulu: University of Hawai'i Press.

Kapur, Rajiv A. 1986. *Sikh Separatism: The politics of faith*. London: Allen & Unwin.

Mahmood, Cynthia Keppley. 1996. *Fighting for Faith and Nation: Dialogues with Sikh militants*. Philadelphia: University of Pennsylvania Press.

Mandair, Arvind-Pal S. 2009. *Religion and the Specter of the West: Sikhism, India, postcoloniality, and the politics of translation*. New York: Columbia University Press.

Mandair, Arvind-Pal. 2015. 'Sikhs, sovereignty and modern government', in *Religion as a Category of Government and Sovereignty*, edited by Trevor Stack, Naomi R. Goldenberg and Timothy Fitzgerald, 115–42. Leiden: Brill.

Mandair, Arvind-Pal S. 2019. 'Im/materialities: Translation technologies and the disenchantment of diasporic life-worlds', *Religion* 49 (3): 413–38. https://doi.org/10.1080/0048721X.2019.1635331.

Mandair, Arvind-Pal S. 2022a. *Violence and the Sikhs*. Cambridge: Cambridge University Press.

Mandair, Arvind-Pal S. 2022b. *Sikh Philosophy: Exploring gurmat concepts in a decolonizing world*. London: Bloomsbury Academic.

Mann, Gurinder Singh. 1999. *The Making of Sikh Scripture*. New York: Oxford University Press.

Mann, Richard D. 2016. 'Media framing and the myth of religious violence: The othering of Sikhs in *The Times of India*', *Sikh Formations* 12 (2–3): 120–41. https://doi.org/10.1080/174487 27.2017.1315521.

McLeod, W. H. 1968. *Gurū Nānak and the Sikh Religion*. Oxford: Clarendon Press.

McLeod, W. H. 1975. *The Evolution of the Sikh Community: Five essays*. Oxford: Clarendon Press.

McLeod, W. H. 1984. *Textual Sources for the Study of Sikhism*. Manchester: Manchester University Press.

McLeod, W. H. 1989. *Who Is a Sikh? The problem of Sikh identity*. Oxford: Clarendon Press.

McLeod, W. H. 1994. 'Cries of outrage: History versus tradition in the study of the Sikh community', *South Asia Research* 14 (2): 121–34. https://doi.org/10.1177/026272809401400201.

McLeod, W. H. 1997. *Sikhism*. London: Penguin.

McLeod, W. H. 2003. *Sikhs of the Khalsa: A history of the Khalsa Rahit*. New Delhi: Oxford University Press.

Nesbitt, Eleanor. 2005. *Sikhism: A very short introduction*. Oxford: Oxford University Press.

Nesbitt, Eleanor. 2014. 'Sikh *sants* and their establishments in India and abroad', in *The Oxford Handbook of Sikh Studies*, edited by Pashaura Singh and Louis E. Fenech, 360–71. Oxford: Oxford University Press.

Oberoi, Harjot. 1994. *The Construction of Religious Boundaries: Culture, identity and diversity in the Sikh tradition*. New Delhi: Oxford University Press.

Schomer, Karine. 1987. 'The Sant tradition in perspective', in *The Sants: Studies in a devotional tradition of India*, edited by Karine Schomer and W. H. McLeod, 1–17. Delhi: Motilal Banarsidass.

Shackle, Christopher and Arvind-Pal S. Mandair (eds and trans.). 2005. *Teachings of the Sikh Gurus: Selections from the Sikh scriptures*. Abingdon: Routledge.

Sharma, Nidhi. 2016. 'Dera chiefs play gurus to tallest of politicians', *The Economic Times*, 2 December. https://economictimes.indiatimes.com/news/politics-and-nation/dera-chiefs-play-gurus-to-tallest-of-politicians/articleshow/55736977.cms?from=mdr (accessed 22 February 2023).

Singh, Gurharpal and Giorgio Shani. 2022. *Sikh Nationalism: From a dominant minority to an ethno-religious diaspora*. Cambridge: Cambridge University Press.

Singh, Harbans. 1983. *The Heritage of the Sikhs*. New Delhi: Manohar.

Singh, Pashaura. 2003. *The Guru Granth Sahib: Canon, meaning and authority*. New Delhi: Oxford University Press.

Takhar, Opinderjit Kaur. 2005. *Sikh Identity: An exploration of groups among Sikhs*. Aldershot: Ashgate.

Takhar, Opinderjit Kaur. 2014. 'Sikh sects', in *The Oxford Handbook of Sikh Studies*, edited by Pashaura Singh and Louis Fenech, 350–9. Oxford: Oxford University Press.

7
Hacking God: Ganesh Yourself, an incarnation experiment in human divine circuitry

Emmanuel Grimaud

Bappa 1.0 was launched in Mumbai during the Ganapati festival in 2014 and advertised, with a hint of exaggeration, as 'the first ever robot of a god'. It was in fact conceived by the artist Zaven Paré and myself for an 'incarnation experiment' named Ganesh Yourself.[1] With its uncanny resemblance to the god Ganesh, the interface allowed anyone to put themselves in God's shoes and experience this impossible perspective framed as a conversation with another. Operated by a controller (or 'embodier') tasked with doing 'God's voice', with a webcam displaying their face in the robot by internal back projection, the tele-operated machine presented an opportunity for a rather more interactive dialogue than usual encounters with silent idols. To our considerable surprise, Bappa was quickly adopted, without major issues but not in the way we expected. Hindu priests incorporated it into their rituals as a prop for broadcasting mantras. Astrologers used it for their consultations, seeing in such an interface the potential for a different type of dialogue with clients. Political activists, from environmentalists to gays and feminists, harnessed the machine to spread reformist messages, recognising that an interface that looked like a god was a good way to get oneself heard. What if the Ganesh Yourself incarnation game was a shortcut to becoming a guru, amplifying one's own aura and making disciples? It was a risk, but the following account will show that it was not so simple. What if all gurus' performances were actually incarnation experiments unaware of their possibilities of circuitry? Originally conceived as a small experiment in divine (media) performance, Ganesh Yourself was bound to fail.

Figure 7.1 *Ganesh Yourself*, film, 2016, credit E. Grimaud.

A divine posture is not easy to achieve or maintain: it is neither a self declared-act nor something you can easily delegate to a machine; it involves other qualities. But, through failure, the incarnation game became much more than a provocative exercise in design or a burlesque experience in divine stuttering, a veritable experiment in deconstruction of guruship, effects of divinity, authority and conviction: to what extent can we speak on behalf of God without being considered an imposter? How far can a machine serve as an effective 'god trap'[2] and an invisible being genuinely enter a machine? Can God be rebooted, reset or even 'hacked'? What advantages could such an act of re-mediation entail? Rather like the dismantling of a motor in a garage, Ganesh Yourself might help us to explore the fragility of incarnation experiments in general and to understand better the hidden possibilities of *human divine circuitry*, a critical zone of experimentation where gurus have always found innovative ways to position themselves.

The interactive game of Ganesh Yourself

The science fiction writer Philip K. Dick made an interesting observation: 'God is the only theological entity that can be found everywhere, from the gutter to the stars.' In *The Exegesis*, his journal of over 1,000 pages, Dick takes wry pleasure in speculating on God's forms, imagining a world just like our own, in which 'every man will carry a bit of God inside him, like a walkie-talkie' (Dick 2011, 167). And what if God were some kind of 'great artificial intelligence system', highly active, constantly slipping up but always getting back on its feet? Or a 'form of plasmatic electricity saturated with information, alive and intelligent', sending us encrypted signals via a multitude of information channels? Attentive to the new faces this entity might adopt in a world overflowing with technologies of every kind, Dick raises a profoundly speculative but current question that few anthropologists have dared tackle with people:[3] what forms might God take in a continuously evolving world?

The Ganesh Yourself experiment was a speculative exercise to open up new possibilities of incarnation, but before the interface was actually tested and operated by people, it would have been hazardous to make any prediction about its possible use. Anyone could volunteer to embody Ganesh. Some of them did it because they were convinced they had the natural authority to do so. Others claimed they had a special proximity with the god, a special talent, a message to convey. And many did it out of curiosity, to test their own ability to address an audience, suddenly projected into a 'guru' position, feeling empowered by their Ganesh appearance. And very early in the process, as soon as they are caught inside the machine, the volunteer realises they are engaged in a risky incarnation exercise, in which any visitor could approach to challenge their legitimacy as a 'voice of God' or as his mouthpiece. They have to recall whatever Sanskrit and mantras they know, and all the formulas they have heard, including punchlines from gurus or other authorities. If the formulas fail – and they do most of the time – the volunteer has no other choice than to find their own voice.

Most experiments in psychology have hypotheses to test. We didn't; we just had a contraption to propose. What if, no sooner incarnated in this overly human form, God was cast out, returning to his spectral existence in the depths of the unseen? The Ganesh Yourself experiment involved not only anthropology and theology, but also robotics, and, more broadly, the ecology of non-humans, populated with uncooperative, unstable, elusive entities. The issue of the right instrument to give voice to a recalcitrant being elicits very varied answers, depending on the context of the enquiry. Designing an acceptable divine interface or a new kind of religious media in India presents its own set of challenges. There is no need to recall the profusion of ethnographic enquiries carried out throughout the subcontinent, pointing out the myriad flexible forms of Hindu deities, sometimes fixed, sometimes mobile, deliberately considered as *entity clusters* (avatars, etc.), offering the chance for far more rewarding incarnation games than would be possible in other religious worlds. Yet pinpointing the threshold of what can be embodied in such a context, or indeed the line beyond which a device would be rejected as useless, bad or downright blasphemous, is not always straightforward. These limits are precisely what Ganesh Yourself made it possible to test, provoke or stimulate, like an energy point in acupuncture. If God only comes forth under certain conditions, there is no reason *a priori* that he should not implant himself in a machine, so long as the requirements of convocation (or invocation) for the entity to manifest have been satisfied. Among embodiers and interlocutors alike, there were many who started out expressing their scepticism, though this did not discourage them from putting the system to the test, gauging the controller's ability to embody the voice of God, which gave us a concrete opportunity to capture live the conditions for potential divine effects to

Figure 7.2   *Ganesh Yourself*, film, 2016, credit E. Grimaud.

occur under. Like two voices blending polyphonically to create a third, phenomena of emergence adhere to a simple formula: $1 + 1 = 3$. By extension, *does one human plus one machine suffice to bring forth a god*? There is nothing to prevent us theorising in this regard; in practice, however, it is less clear if divinity is better obtained through addition than through subtraction.

Interaction 1: 'Who's there?'

When it comes to God's voice and his mission, everyone has their own ideas. Adopting a divine posture from the outset, rather than earning it patiently, was the chosen strategy of Karan, our first embodier. We had recruited this 26-year-old business graduate from Gwalior through a classified ad. On the surface, there was nothing remarkable about this rather shy, softly spoken individual, but when he closed his eyes and settled into a meditative state there was no doubt in his mind that he was Ganesh, which is why we had chosen him. 'Ganesh is in me!' he would say. And every time he prepared to embody Ganesh, he would do a few breathing exercises to get into the mindset, repeating the syllable *Oṃ* or the expression *Oṃ namaḥ śivāya* over and over. His guttural sounds and peculiar breathing drew people in, who would pause, some longer than others, in front of the robot, intrigued.

Unbeknown to us, Karan had a plan. He was determined not to end up in the sea, the fate usually reserved for Ganesh idols at the end of the ritual festivities. During his first interaction with some children, this was the first thing he told them, almost as if trying to convince himself: 'Unlike all other idols, I will not be submerged. Why not? Because I am an electronic Ganesh.' No one had mentioned anything of the sort to him beforehand. Karan had identified himself with the machine, incorporated it into his being. 'I came to earth with a mission. My goal concerns you all. You must heighten your devotion towards the god Ganesh. I will travel all around the city to this end. I am Ganesh, son of Gauri. And you may ask me questions.'

When he was asked, 'Where do you come from?', Karan had an answer ready: 'I am the son of our great god Shankara. My father has many names. I came down from Mount Kailash to be with you. I was configured in an eye-opening rite [*prāṇa pratiṣṭha*]. What is the total number of gods and goddesses? Thirty-three thousand and I am one among them!' And when the child asked, 'Where's your mount gone? What have you done with your rat?', he improvised a curious response: 'As you can see, I have lost my mount. I am trying to find it. I meditate every day, after which I speak with people. I am looking for the rat that serves as my mount during my meditation. It is here somewhere. Do you know what meditation involves?' Receiving a negative response, Karan felt obliged to explain: 'Meditation is about connecting to your inner self and seeing another world. Anyone can meditate. Because that is how you can become very strong, you should all meditate. Now, repeat after me: *Oṃ namaḥ śivāya …*'

We were in a fishing village along the Bay, a quintessential shanty town. Just a few metres away, people were relieving themselves on the beach. Meditation was a middle-class pursuit, of minor interest to fishermen. But Karan was there to convert them, to educate them about his religion of the great Brahmanical gods, a form of religiosity nowadays built on two pillars: ritual and meditation.

Thanks to Karan, we understood Ganesh Yourself would not just be a game. The danger lay in succumbing to a form of robotically assisted evangelism, or in every interaction becoming mired in a mythological Q&A, in which the god served as a teacher of good conduct, or even in stirring up class conflict through divine intervention. Karan was unconcerned with any of these risks, leaping headfirst into every trap set for him. And he could say and do as he pleased. Seeking confrontation was risky. He might rise brilliantly to the occasion, or he might fail his self-set test, and in so doing risk the entire credibility of the device. Whatever the outcome, it was his decision to proceed in this way. Incarnation would be his own ordeal.

One of the most delicate interactions he had was with a fisherman's wife who asked perfectly reasonable questions. Just as Karan felt he had his own mission, so did she. 'Devījī [a respectful form of address to a woman], approach me. Do you have a question?' Karan asked as she stepped timidly forward. 'Yes,' she said, gesturing towards him. 'I want to know who we're dealing with here. What is this thing?' 'I am the electronic Ganesh,' replied Karan. 'I come from Mount Kailash. I am Ganesh, son of Parvati. Ask me your question.' The woman frowned aggressively. 'We've never seen anything like this before!' But Karan felt imbued with a special legitimacy. 'I have come to earth in this form for the first time. My purpose is to heighten devotion towards me, through this medium, this Ganesh …'

The woman remained sceptical: 'We didn't know that was your purpose. Why the need?' 'I sensed that I needed to come to see you, to speak to you,' said Karan. 'All the idols of Ganesh that you have seen until now could not speak. But I have the gift of speech. I have come to talk with you and find solutions to your problems. You can find me through devotion and meditation [*sādhana*]. If you see me in this form, it will heighten your faith and devotion.' His interlocutor was unconvinced and continued voicing her doubts: 'The Ganesh we see in his traditional form is quite enough for us. We don't know what's true or not, if you're a real god or an imposter. We've never seen you in human form.' To which Karan replied: 'On this earth, man must achieve everything by his own good deeds. He alone must judge what is true and what is not.'

Karan, and through him all the gods, were now really put to the test. 'If there is truth in devotion, why can't this truth be grasped?' she asked. Karan replied that God was the only truth; she could find him through devotion and so receive anything she desired. 'But that's never happened to me!' she exclaimed. 'I practise devotion, I perform all the rituals, but the more I do, the more injustice I encounter!' Karan had nothing to offer but a promise: 'This injustice will end. Your devotion must be sincere. Worship Ganesh. Worship me.' The woman asked if all her desires would truly be granted and if her situation could really change from one day to the next like that. 'Everything that you can think of will be granted,' vowed Karan. 'That's never happened before!' she rejoined.

Her frustration and anger were palpable. At this point, she raised her voice: 'If people pray sincerely for their wishes to be met, why then do they still have problems?' Karan answered that her wishes would certainly be met, that the problems she encountered were the result of her actions, good and bad. Here, she interjected angrily: 'Our wishes are granted, but we're still going through hard times, we don't see any way out. Even when our patience is rewarded, hostile forces return to mock us!'

After a moment's reflection, Karan, ever calm, seemed to have found a solution: 'Life is made of ups and downs. If your enemies mock you, you must ignore them. You must focus on positive actions. Your goal on earth must be devotion. Worship God, Shiva, Ganesh … You must worship them all. Then your wishes will come true.' Despite her rancour, the woman continued to address Karan respectfully, though not without a hint of irony: 'That's it then! Everything you say must come true. Everyone prays to God. If someone's wish is granted, wonderful, heaven on earth!' Karan kept up his promotion of a magical god granting and dispensing wishes, one deemed untenable by his interlocutor: 'You must worship me all the time,' he said. 'You do not need to go to the temple. You can worship me at home. You can ask me what you want, as long as it is done with conviction. You must think about your goal at all times, morning and night. And you must think about how you can achieve it, everything that it takes. If you picture it, you will get it, wealth, recognition, fame or something else. You can have anything in this world, depending on your attitude.' But the woman refused to let herself be hypnotised: 'That would be great if it was true!' she told him. Karan kept trying: 'I will grant your wishes. Close your eyes and picture your desire, but do not say it aloud in front of everyone, say it in your head.' She closed her eyes a few seconds, but opened them again before long.

Interestingly, she then switched abruptly to a theological plane: 'Is there any truth in the notion that God exists in our minds?' she asked. Faced with such unsated metaphysical thirst, Karan could have seized the opportunity to change tactics and perhaps construct a new god born out of genuine collaboration. To do so would have required the same question to be asked in return then and there; Karan would have had to confess to being as unenlightened as his interlocutor. But he was too wedded to his original design, using the machine to plunge his listeners into an altered state of consciousness that permitted the acceptance of all paradoxes. 'God exists in this world,' he told her. 'Brahmaji, father of the universe, created man and woman. In life, good and bad are part of this world. Your goal must be devotion.'

Karan reeled off his prepared statements without realising his interlocutor wanted to engage him in a far deeper exercise, namely a radical re-evaluation of his own being: 'Why can't we see God? The god we worship so ardently, why doesn't he show himself? Why doesn't he appear before us?' Whereas before she had been directing her recriminations partly at God himself and partly at his professed embodier, by now she had accepted the latter's ambiguity so long as he could help her illuminate the former's mystery. But Karan was providing answers as a machine, as succinctly as possible, inevitably leading us back to the old covenant binding humans and gods by *promise*: 'The fact that we cannot see God', he said, 'does not mean that he does not exist. He does exist. He listens to your desires. Ask your question.'

Evidently, he could not conceive of his mission any other way. But she did not see it like that.

'Why did you come in this strange form?' she asked again.

Admittedly, Karan was in a tricky position. Unacceptable as a god, forever being relegated to go-between status, he had to prove himself as a liminal vessel. In its remotely operated form, this new variant of God, a unique combination of close-up voice and remote image, unleashed any repressed grievances. This was no doubt its main selling point: a complete factory reset on God. Karan had to come up with something new. Even the invisibility and silence in which the gods had up to now deliberately been enshrouded, an entire ritual technocracy complicitly orchestrating their presence-absence, was no longer a given.

'I am the electronic Ganesh,' said Karan. 'I was created by scientists and an appropriate ritual was performed for which I descended from Mount Kailash. I came to talk with you all. Ask your question, Deviji.'

'But I've never seen Mount Kailash!' she cried. 'We're human beings. We only know earth!' Karan insisted: 'Without worshipping me, nobody will receive anything.' The glaring paradox of the situation was that now it was he imploring her, not the other way around. When he urged her to think hard about her desire, she countered, 'I'm going to ask you to grant it, then I'll check if it comes true or not!'

Sensing he was getting nowhere, Karan tried a new approach: 'Deviji, tell me what your problems are.' This only unleashed a new wave of anger: 'Are our problems hidden? If you are God, surely you know our wishes and our desires?' Karan played his most gentle hand: 'I know, but I need to hear it from your lips. And if possible ...' She interrupted again. 'Do I really need to say it aloud? If you want to grant our wishes, you should be aware of our desires. You should know the needs of every human that worships you!' At Karan's continued insistence, she finally expressed her deepest wish, for her children to be educated and succeed, since 'that's every parent's dream'. And Karan offered a surprising response: 'Your wish shall be granted, your children will be educated and accomplish what they want to do. For this to happen, you must be organised, you must plan their education. You must ask them regularly what their plans are for the future and help them when they encounter difficulties.' Against all expectations, Karan too had engaged in a subversive logic. His eagerness to establish a magical relationship with his interlocutor had been a means to undermine her from within before introducing a little pragmatism. 'Won't you give me your blessing now I've expressed my desire with sincere devotion?' she replied. So he uttered two *Oṃ namaḥ śivāya*. She did likewise and the interaction came to a close with all the respect due a deity.

Karan was hardly the first god in the history of religion to speak in such redundancies. Like some old conversational computer program endowed with a very limited number of potential responses, he continued repeating the same messages until the interlocutor was worn down. Karan could have belonged to the first generation of robotic gods, those that employ a limited number of statements, seeking to lull their interlocutors into an altered state of consciousness, halfway between hypnosis and meditation, to then restore their confidence.

His discourse was even more mechanical than his mask suggested. But he was undoubtedly one of the few gods to state clearly his intention to draw more devotion and not simply resolve people's issues, a sort of narcissistic god, hungry for love, fuelled by the veneration he receives, without ever making good his promises. Before him was someone speaking on behalf of a group, all those who, like her, performed rituals without deriving any benefit truly attributable to the deity. How had Karan come to defend this minimal cycle of devotional reward when his interlocutor was offering proof of his lack of reciprocity and his trying to find a way out? How had he become the champion of magical thinking? Was he not risking being unmasked? To think of God is to think 'miracle', yet for miracles to occur, he said, there was no need for magic formulas, so long as you made your request with 'sincerity' and reflected on the best course of action.

Karan was willing to try anything for his interlocutor to internalise him, to embody him just as he had embodied Ganesh. But through her reflexive outburst, the woman was resisting. It had only taken God to be granted the power of speech – or rather a bare minimum of interactivity, for God's word has always existed – for all the cracks in the usual devotional relationship to appear. The interlocutor would not be pushed around. She cast doubt on his form, his mission, and – through Karan – she called into question the entire devotional apparatus as a system of quantifiable acquisition, a balance of gains and losses, right down to the presumption of divine omniscience and the intimate communion of thoughts that underpinned it.

She soon realised that addressing a machine god was not quite the same as addressing a god in the temple. She could afford to be more demanding and, once the power balance had been calibrated, throw down a final gauntlet: if her wish did come true, she would continue to worship the temple gods without a second thought. For his part, Karan knew he was not going to be held to account, and so he could promise something without anyone coming back to reproach him for not making good. And in response to his interlocutor's perfectly reasonable concern for her children's future, Karan played his part. Here, as before, he used his position to disseminate positive thinking techniques. One could hardly blame him. He had sought to be a successful embodiment, and for him this meant offering hope by any means. And although his interlocutor was not desperate, it had not taken much to unearth those doubts buried deep. At first, she had had no particular question to ask him; the question had been him.

Regarding his capacity to arouse doubt, the embodier had had to learn on the go. These doubts were usually expressed with a certain level of respect. The more Karan interacted, the more he learned, gradually fine-tuning his prepared statements. 'I reside in the idol. I go everywhere my idols are placed. But this time, I am appearing through an electronic medium. I can speak to you through the interface. I can resolve your problems,' he would say. A well-known manufacturer of idols approached the machine. 'I have no doubts about Ganesh,' he said. 'My only doubt is about you. Ganesh is so important to us, we couldn't possibly desecrate him. We respect Ganesh the way he is. We might be less careful when it comes to goddesses, but we're very cautious about moving a Ganesh idol. There could be problems if we do. That's why we keep it fixed in place. So yes, we do have questions. Everyone here is curious about your electronic form. Is this new form truly Ganesh's idol? You may be a scientific marvel, but you're creating a lot of uncertainty.'

Karan had not suspected he might arouse so much suspicion. By mimicking meditation, he had unwittingly kept God in almost the same state of motionlessness in which manufacturers of idols deliberately fixed him. The absence of movement had averted any question-and-answer games. To justify his ability to move and speak, the embodier had limited options. Either he banked on a perfect symbiosis between God and himself, or he stressed that he was only a representation, an actor wearing a mask, but this was equally unacceptable. In this way, Bappa gradually came to individuate itself, from one embodier to the next, initially taking the fusion between God and the embodier for granted, when in fact it remained to be seen. It became apparent before long that the embodier's presumed fusion was unviable. They had to learn to be God before proclaiming themselves as such. Karan discovered this the hard way, just as he was starting to improve his conversational feedback. 'I am the same

Figure 7.3 *Ganesh Yourself*, film, 2016, credit E. Grimaud.

Ganesh. I have two ears. I have a trunk. You can touch it and feel it. I can hear and feel your presence in my trunk. You can touch my trunk. I travel from one place to the other on my rat mount. Do not be shy. I came here for you. I came from far away, from Mount Kailash, just for my followers. If you do not come to me, I will disappear forever.'

Interaction 2: 'I will teach you how to incarnate God!'

Karan had played along with the incarnation until the moment someone tried to disprove him. This was a bus driver by the name of Nitin Parwar, who also ran a *mandal*, one of the neighbourhood organisations that collected funds for the Festival of Ganesh, produced a local idol for those interested and arranged the relevant rituals. The same organisation had erected a scaffold in the middle of a small square to accommodate a three-metre-tall idol where visitors could come to worship. Nitin was also well known locally for his charity work with various associations. He had agreed that we could set up our robot nearby, along with a few chairs to allow anyone to take part in the incarnation and spectate. To set an example, he was the first to open a dialogue with Bappa, surrounded by a crowd of local schoolchildren, all sitting quietly.

'As you know, Mumbai has major traffic issues. The city's become very crowded. What would you suggest to solve this problem?' asked Nitin Pawar. 'This is a human problem. The solution lies within you,' said Karan apathetically.

'We're trying solutions,' Nitin went on, 'but I want to know yours. There are many accidents. Young people don't follow the rules. They're obsessed with speed. What advice would you give them?'

'I would advise the young people to slow down,' stammered Karan.

Nitin was surprised to hear such a banal response: 'That's a bit of an empty answer …. And what about the potholes in the roads? The council doesn't do anything, even when you write to them. What would be your message to these corrupt officials?'

Karan fell silent. After a long pause, he muttered, 'No.'

'No, what?' asked Nitin.

'I'm thinking about the problem,' the embodier replied.

'Oh, you're thinking …. As you are Knowledge incarnate, I thought you might already have the answer. Is my question so difficult even Ganapati Bappa has to think about it?'

Karan seemed a little unnerved. 'No, my son. I am simply thinking about something.'

With every pause, Nitin doubled down. 'Right, so even God has to think when it comes to corruption? Bappa, everyone's waiting. You always seem so caught up in your thoughts!'

'You should avoid such things as much as possible,' Karan countered.

'What should we avoid?' asked Nitin.

'We should neither take nor offer bribes,' stated Karan.

'But that's just the way it is now! Even to get a school placement, you have to bribe someone. How can we solve this problem?' Nitin pressed.

This time, Karan answered immediately: 'This problem is something you created. The solution lies in you.' As before, it seemed Karan knew just the magic words to provoke his interlocutor.

'You're not offering any constructive solutions,' exclaimed Nitin. 'You're shirking all responsibility. You say these are human problems. But God created the human mind. Man wasn't born with a computer instead of a mind. And that same mind is to blame for all these problems. So how can we cleanse the human brain? [Silence.] Bappa … are you thinking again?'

Nitin's outbursts were drawing consistent laughter from the audience. But I wondered if Nitin was as conscious of the device as we were. How could he disregard the machine like this, willingly ignore the subtle mechanism of remote presence, to focus only on the man before him? Any technology is designed to fade into the background. In all remote communications, we eventually forget the intolerable energy costs, the cables criss-crossing our oceans, the data centres, and the monstrous distances travelled around the globe by our signals. Nitin seemed to be giving the same impression of ignorance. But as we will see, this was all a strategic ruse, and he had never actually forgotten about the device. He simply wanted to play the game and get straight to the point: a face-to-face showdown between him and God. Or rather between *us* and God, since he had managed to get the crowd onside, acting as their self-appointed representative. Whereas, before, the apparatus had been the target of all the questions, serving as a barrier to communication, it had now become peripheral. No one was paying any attention to how the word was conveyed, though everyone was seemingly taking the god seriously, offering up their most weird and wonderful problems. The embodier found himself trapped once more, but in a precisely symmetrical fashion, not because people doubted his divinity, but because they were trying to show that this was *all* the god was.

After more reflection, Karan resumed.

'You should not offer bribes.'

'Without bribes,' Nitin went on, 'you can't even get someone cremated. To gather the ashes after the last rites, you have to pay. In my experience, at least. That's not a human problem. You blame humans. So what has to be done to cleanse their brains? These people ought to be publicly shot or executed.'

Karan could feel a trap had been laid for him, and his pauses were growing longer and longer. 'No,' he said. 'You must work together to find a solution.' Nitin was acting as if he had accepted him as a god the better to put him to the test, but Karan was failing to improvise back convincingly.

'What's your solution?' asked Nitin. 'That's what I want to know. You are Knowledge incarnate!'

'Do not offer nor take bribes,' Karan repeated.

'I'll say it again,' Nitin insisted, 'that bribes have become tradition now. Corruption is rampant. The average person encounters corruption from the day they're born to the day they die. Even after a birth, nurses, doctors, everyone needs a bribe. We even have to bribe someone for a death certificate. I understand all these problems are man-made. But you must have thought of a punishment for these people. How can they be punished? In my opinion, these people should be killed in the street.'

Karan did not seem to approve of this solution. 'No, certainly not,' he replied confidently, but Nitin was unmoved.

'So, what's the answer? Bappa, what are you thinking about? Are my questions too vague?'

Karan was more silent than ever, lost in his thoughts, and Nitin was growing increasingly impatient.

'You can keep thinking,' he fired, 'but everyone's looking at you. Everyone wants to know why Bappa thinks so much! Bappa is the god of Knowledge! Everyone expects immediate answers from Bappa. Does Bappa need to do his homework?'

At this point, all Karan wanted to do was escape, melt away, resume his fixed form, retreat into a deep meditation, the only viable state for the god he wanted to be. And then he had the bright idea of beating his retreat by falling back on the only formula he could think of: '*Oṃ namaḥ śivāya … Oṃ namaḥ śivāya … Oṃ namaḥ śivāya ….*'

But Nitin was not remotely impressed: 'Chanting *Oṃ namaḥ śivāya* is not the answer to my question. Anyone can chant *Oṃ namaḥ śivāya* to escape their responsibilities. *Oṃ namaḥ śivāya* is not an answer, sir!' he exclaimed.

'I was chanting mantras as I thought …,' Karan excused himself.

'Chanting mantras? Bappa is thinking and everyone's watching Bappa. Everyone wants to know. Your facial expressions have changed. Bappa is annoyed now. Perhaps Bappa hasn't done his homework?' Nitin cast a glance around the crowd, whose laughter was becoming increasingly derisive.

Ganesh's silence spoke volumes. No doubt someone more experienced could have done better, but his mute retreat just as he had been expected to publicly demonstrate his wisdom is telling. It had only taken granting a god the power of speech and having a human assume the right to speak in his name to unlock a variable that had been hidden until then. *Better for gods to stay quiet to stay gods.* Karan took his time, but he pulled himself together. 'Very well. Tell me the situations where you have had to bribe someone.' Nitin rattled off a quick list: 'In hospitals. It's not funny. Listen, this is my personal experience. When my father was in hospital, I had to pay to take his body to be cremated. And I'm not the only one. There are other people here who've had similar incidents. But no one has the courage to speak out.'

For a moment, Karan transformed into an empathetic questioner, a stance that would not last long. 'Have you ever reported this to the police?' he asked.

'Yes, we've reported it,' said Nitin. 'But no one ever does anything about it. They tell us corruption is just a fact of life. They tell us they can't do anything about it. Eighty per cent of the police is corrupt and demand bribes. Everyone sitting here has experienced these things for themselves. There are many children here who had to offer 150,000 INR as a "donation" to get into a school. They queue all day for a chance to get in and they're forced to make a donation.'

At this point, Karan turned representative for the status quo, and they began arguing at cross purposes.

'The money you give to gain entry to a school is to receive quality services. The more money you give, the better the service you get,' Karan declared robotically.

'So what's a poor person to do then? Where does a poor man's child go to school?' cried Nitin. To which Karan replied, 'They should go to state schools.'

Nitin was not convinced. 'We have to offer bribes in state schools too!' he stressed.

'Aren't entrance exams open to all?' remarked Karan.

'The costs aren't covered. The money gets charged towards other things, in the name of welfare, but it's all corruption!' Nitin spat with contempt.

Karan told him this was not so, but Nitin was convinced otherwise, saddened that God could be so wilfully ignorant of the situation.

'If you want access to higher education,' Karan said, 'you have to take entrance exams. And those who pass are accepted.'

It was clear to Nitin that Karan was completely detached from reality, referring to another time, when admissions had been truly meritocratic. 'Bappa, we're not going to end corruption,' he said. 'Right now, Mumbai is the most corrupt place of all, including the police and politicians. So I don't think you have an answer to this problem.'

Karan would have liked to roll out his pre-prepared script, a mash-up of mythology and science fiction, the same one he had carefully honed, but the poor man was being confronted with issues of corruption and school access rights, bogged down in very concrete matters of local politics. These were surely the only questions worth asking, in Nitin's mind, to gauge what this god pretender was truly an incarnation of. And Karan was doing little more than stoking his interlocutor's resentment further.

'These problems were created by you,' he said.

'You're just repeating yourself. You aren't offering solutions,' replied Nitin.

'But you have the solution!' Karan fired back.

'Yes, I have the solution. I'm going to shoot them, with your blessing! It's the only answer I have. Every corrupt person needs to be locked up and killed!' Nitin declared furiously.

'This problem must be exorcised permanently from our homes,' Karan continued. 'When you have a child at home, you corrupt them with sweets. Is bribing children with sweets not a form of corruption? Rewarding a child for passing their exams, is that not the same as a bribe?' On this point, Nitin agreed. Offering a child sweets could be likened to corruption or bribery in certain circumstances.

'The practice of corruption thus began with you,' concluded Karan. Nitin's irritation had now peaked. 'You're a broken record, shirking all responsibility. You keep saying you haven't done anything .... As you are the Source of all Knowledge, we just want to know. We ask you to please instil some good manners in these corrupt individuals. Some parents sell their jewellery to pay for their children's donations, or remortgage their houses. If this situation is man-made, then all humans should be exterminated. Why does Ganesh hold an axe [parśu]? Could you tell me, since you've assumed Ganapati's form?'

We were helpless bystanders at this unusually violent debate. Nitin was not alone in having used his interaction with Bappa to vent his problems and turn the apparatus into a trial. Was there any other way to play politics? With Karan struggling, we surmised it might be time to change embodier, that it was not enough to have Ganesh within to have the answer for everything. In the end, however, Nitin took the initiative, to stop the experiment devolving into chaos, fluctuating according to the quality of the participants. All the digressions and failures would not undo the process. Quite the contrary: the more the embodier failed to grasp the transcendentals, the more Nitin felt emboldened to take the god by the hand and *teach him how to be a god*. The best way to avoid falling back into old habits, the cycle of promise and demand, was to consider this god to be on a learning curve and to teach him his role.

'Ganapati Bappa is armed with an axe to ward off harmful impulses,' said Nitin. 'If Ganesh can't come to this earth to punish these corrupt individuals, we ask him to transfer us his powers so we can take appropriate measures against them.'

But Karan was not prepared to go that far. 'The power to change things is within you,' he said.

'Not at all,' answered Nitin. 'We have to bribe people, even to vote. Today, eighty per cent of politicians live off bribes and false promises.'

'But were you not the one to elect them?' asked Karan.

'There you go blaming others again,' fired back Karan. 'Please, don't pass the buck. Be constructive! If humans are responsible for everything, then what does God do?' Karan's answer was clear-cut, final: 'God does nothing.'

'God does nothing?' Nitin repeated. 'God did create the universe,' Karan clarified.

'And all he asks of humans', Nitin added sarcastically, 'is to live as they see fit? God created the universe and gave humans the freedom to live as they please? I don't think so! Birth and death are in God's hands; so are intelligence and the ability to think. If none of that is in God's hands, then humans should have the right to punish corrupt individuals themselves. And if God chooses me to carry out this task, the only punishment I can give is death!'

By a curious feat of dispossession, Nitin no longer felt entitled to act of his own accord, as if God had rescinded all free will and the divine firewall had to be lifted before one could take back control. Nitin was desperately seeking the support of some *vague force* targeting world affairs as a whole, not focused on any particular object, but with the power to involve itself in all earthly matters. It was precisely this indeterminate energy that Nitin was trying to redirect, draw out, renew the covenant with. But there was more to it than this (lest we overlook the crux of the dialogue).

There was something in crisis here, something twisted, gnarled, even rotten, in the contract between Nitin and his god, something he was deliberately challenging, with a certain contrarian irony, by recalling to mind the purity of a divine power balance. To solve this crisis, his tactic was to set the embodier an unsolvable moral question, a trial by contortion, from which Ganesh, friend of the people, moral and responsible deity, had to emerge twisted, disfigured, perhaps even monstrous.

This being so, the meat of their misunderstanding was not so much the existence of God as a technical issue, one of 'circuitousness', to borrow a term from Alfred Gell.[4] Karan had become the wretched guinea pig in a boundary-pushing experiment designed to test how far a follower could entrap a god and reverse the transfer of power. How to get through this contortion? How to bend God, to twist him to the point of disfigurement? How to twist morality? One understands the dilemma facing the embodier, who would have preferred to hang back in the shadows. Ultimately, Karan retreated further, ever more powerless, resolved to invoke other figures.

'The good and bad deeds of corrupt individuals are accounted for by Chitragupta [god who records the actions of human beings],' said Karan, as robotically as before.

'Then make me Chitragupta, let me be Chitragupta! Or make me *Yamaduta* [a messenger of Yama, god of death],' implored Nitin.

'They will all be punished by Chitragupta,' said Karan.

'But Chitragupta can't come down to earth!' exclaimed Nitin.

'Chitragupta records all the actions of corrupt individuals,' said Karan, explaining the old scratched mythological record.

Nitin refused to back down: 'We know Chitragupta records all actions, but who's ever actually seen him? When we're alive, no one sees him come down, and he doesn't show up after you die either. So how can we possibly know what punishment Chitragupta will inflict on the corrupt?'

Karan could take some comfort in the fact that he and Nitin were at least now speaking in the same terms. It was fun to see Nitin toying so smartly with the machine. He never questioned whether God could take human form or not, and he took advantage, with a certain irony, of this convenient medium to push its limits, as if the incarnation game were the perfect opportunity for a makeover, to straighten out those frayed divine circuits, subvert the dusty old personifications, put mythological images to the test of reality. How to regain that higher level? To reconnect with that for which the gods are named, but which has been lost by assimilating them to people? Karan had no other solution than to be his own mythological film and drag Nitin into it with him. Nitin, meanwhile, had no alternative but to undermine this film from within by any means.

'Everyone will reap the consequences of their actions when the time comes,' warned Karan. 'We are in the *Kaliyuga*. We are no longer in the age of *Satyayuga*, when I could act by a little magic and appear on command.'

Did Karan know at this point which direction the dialogue would take? It was not only corrupt people and politicians that Nitin resented, but gurus who claimed to 'perform magic and miracles' too:

'Who are these people then?' he said. 'Why do people admire them so much? They're just magicians, they're not real ascetics, they don't have any special powers. They do magic tricks! They do magic tricks to seduce people. They take advantage of your innocence. They drive luxury cars, and you all line up to see them.'

And Karan added fuel to the fire. 'And all thanks to your support, the people. Why do you support them?' he asked.

'While we're getting rid of the corrupt, we also have to fight the babas and disindoctrinate the idiots that let them take advantage of them!' raged Nitin. 'And will you be the one to rid us of them?' said Karan.

'If you give me the chance, I'll grab a hockey stick and knock each and every one of them out. I'll kill them all!'

Silence.

Nitin calmed himself a little, before taking the hand of a young girl to his right.

'This little girl wants to ask you a question now,' he said.

Karan and Nitin had wrestled to the point of exhaustion. They needed a break. In the face of such an unprecedented challenge, the divine word had never been so hard fought for. Let us consider what is at work in the moments when the embodier gets stuck. He fails to appease his interlocutor. Perhaps it is in those moments when a rattled, hesitant, confused Karan pauses, when nothing seems to be happening, that the void is felt as a pure driving force. This is only one interpretation at this stage, to which we will come back in more detail later. Unbeknown to the embodier, the interaction with Nitin would not have had the same texture, the same dynamic, without his pauses for breath, his slip-ups, his stammers. And this was undoubtedly one way to bring a god to life, through the void, that Karan unwittingly demonstrates.

Since embodying the void or absence was deeply uncomfortable, Karan had tried several times to calm Nitin by chanting mantras, but was caught mid-flight. Everyone was watching him, avidly awaiting his response. And Nitin was looking for a fight, for catharsis. Until that point, Karan had done his best to embody the detached god, uninvolved in worldly affairs, powerless to offer his followers more than a little comfort or confidence. To him, God was but some kind of small machine to be rescued from the coming submersion. All grievances were automatically perceived as an attack. Nitin had forced this god out of his comfort zone, but, curiously, it was the inner workings of the circuit linking him to the deity that were revealed.

With all seemingly mired in profound crisis (power, action, responsibility, confidence, legitimacy), with magic no longer effective, and because his version of God had retreated, no longer willing to be so easily manipulated, there was nothing left for Nitin but to embrace his own will to act, in its forms simultaneously creative and destructive. There would be no one to make him Chitragupta, the great scorekeeper of human actions, or to instate him as Yamadut, messenger of death.

Having exhausted all avenues for agreement, Karan and Nitin reversed roles. It was Nitin's turn to embody. But first, Nitin did all he could to teach Karan how to be a 'good god'. Beckoning over a little disabled girl, he encouraged her to ask Bappa when she would walk again. Her mother asked Bappa to do everything in his power to help her walk again by the following year. Karan responded: 'Of course. You must pray to Ganesh as much as possible. And in the end, he will grant your wish.'

But Nitin was not satisfied. 'Bappa, it's not enough to simply say "of course". It has to happen. There has to be a definitive result. There are many innocent children who can't walk. There are many children who go hungry.'

Karan replied that Ganapati Bappa always helped those faithful to him. But Nitin had clearly resolved to apprise Bappa of all the world's current ills and the possible ways to address them.

'Rather than making offerings in temples and mosques,' suggested Nitin, 'it would be better to simply feed a hungry person.'

The learning contract had been laid bare. Karan listened, taking on board the solutions proffered by his instructor.

'My goal', he said, 'is to inform you of all these things. This is why I came down from Mount Kailash and I am talking with you all.' But Nitin was unsatisfied. Each time Karan reverted to his blissful divine posture, Nitin did everything to steer him back to a state of unease.

'You may have come down from Mont Kailash,' he stated, 'but we've lived our whole lives here on Pali Pathar. We may as well just send all our problems up to Mount Kailash! When we do finally make it to Mount Kailash [which also means the heavenly abode after death], it's not like we'll be able to come back here, right? As long as there's life in us, we'll fight to do something.'

And every time Karan retreated to his old adages ('Anything can happen if you will it'; 'Think hard and your wishes will be granted'), Nitin introduced a new angle, each as unsettling to the god as the last.

'Bappa, I get the impression my questions are confusing you,' he said.

'No, I'm thinking about something,' answered Karan.

'Okay, you keep thinking,' replied Nitin. 'There are people gathered here. We'd like to use this medium, this form you've taken right now, to spread positive messages, useful messages to people through this good form of yours.'

'Naturally, that is my intention,' said Karan. 'That is why I came to this earth.'

A man stepped forward to ask his question: 'Which mistakes should be tolerated and which should not? Which misdeeds committed by humans should be pardoned and which should be punished?' To which Karan replied: 'If you make a mistake, you must compensate for it with a good deed. Sometimes, we run over a snake while driving. In that case, it is enough to offer up a copper image of a snake to the god Shiva.'

Despite having been ready to cede his place to others, Nitin became angrier than ever here.

'That's just blind faith! If I kill someone by mistake, I can't just offer up a copper image of a man to God by way of repentance! If I accidentally kill someone on the road, I can't just make an offering in a temple to erase my misdeed. I have to go to prison. Sir, I work as a bus driver in the public transport system. An accident may be an act of fate, but if I or anyone else from my company is implicated, I'll have committed a punishable crime. I can't simply go to a temple and make an offering. I'll end up behind bars for sure!' To which Karan replied: 'If you deliberately steered your vehicle into the person, you will be sent to prison; but otherwise, you are innocent.'

Nitin Pawar had done all he could to steer God's message, to help Karan say all he could. But in vain. Karan then addressed the children, telling them to repeat *Oṃ namaḥ śivāya*, before asking who among them practised meditation.

'What's meditation?' asked one.

'Meditation is something that you can do at any moment,' said Karan, 'whether you are lying down on the ground or sitting up. All you need to do is close your eyes and turn your palms to the sky. And you take control of your mind. Whenever you meditate, take care not to let your thoughts overwhelm you. You can improve your power of concentration through meditation.'

Whereupon Nitin flew off the handle once more.

'Bappa, these days, kids are all hooked on their phones,' he cried out. 'They go to bed and all they think about is texting. That's their meditation! Kids today don't know how to chant mantras. There's not a single child today that knows a full mantra. But tell them to send a text and they'll do it straight away. Kids see the image of Ganesh on their phones and simply say "Ganapati Bappa", but none of them feel any true devotion to him, and no one wants to chant mantras. Facebook is their only mantra! We have a proverb in Marathi that says: man spends his life in pursuit of pleasure, and only remembers God when the time comes for him to die.'

Karan responded that venerating God only as one neared death was not a good thing, that it was good to do so as young as possible. As for mobile phones, he offered nothing better than his usual refrain: 'You have the solution to this problem. It all depends on you.'

In the face of a god refusing to engage with his version of society, Nitin had initially sought his approval to take justice into his own hands. In the face of such a man in search of 'empowerment', Karan had acted more like a robot than a god. He was of course human, but he often behaved like an actual robot, with which dialogue may be possible, but a dead-end dialogue in which he would latch onto one word, or fail to understand the whole sentence, or twist its meaning. In the course of an argument, he would suddenly give the impression of knowing better or differently, and the fight would resume, as if his lack of understanding was only ever a ploy to steer the interaction in a new direction and always keep it moving.

In the face of a god seemingly still so out of reach, albeit growing increasingly coherent, strengthening his respondence (the term I use to denote the embodier's capacity to answer the questions asked of him) little by little, Nitin remained a model of patience, even stubbornness. Karan would repeat what he was told, creating some semblance of accord, before veering off into some new disagreement. Nitin's efforts to persuade him were never completely fruitless, but the Ganesh before him seemed to exhibit a moral resistance to being used. Nitin had done everything to make him into an idealised god, one in touch with the people's problems, an interface to spread the good word, a pragmatic message, full of practical answers to questions relating to the common good. A modern god, of this world, manifested through the sum of all good thoughts and deeds.

The more Karan mastered his role, the more the dialogue evolved from a mere call for devotion, but whenever social matters arose, the response was always the same: in his view, people had to accept their responsibilities, and stop blaming God and depending on him for everything and anything; hence his consistent sidestepping, absolving God, condemning the 'magic' of rituals while simultaneously promoting a form of mentalist magic ('you need only think very hard to get what you want'), passing the buck to his interlocutor, who found himself accused of everything. For his part, Nitin was eager to close this vicious circle, for God to be no longer the one of whom we ask everything, more than he can give. He recognised that one did not accumulate 'karmic' merit simply by leaving a coconut on an altar, though he could not envisage any other kind of covenant.

How then to move past this relationship of giving and reciprocating, an eternal balancing act between request and (dis)satisfaction, unless the entity in question were simply a crystallisation, a materialisation of people's positive intentions, providing an 'image' of the path to follow? But why bother with all the ritual apparatus in that case? If God is just an ornament, a decorative accessory, rather than a crucial anchor point for our actions, responsible at least for their 'results', then we should either let him go, or else profoundly reassess our relationship with this *reclusive, invisible*, often *indifferent* entity that Karan personified so well.

'Bappa, if we do have to do everything ourselves, then why should we keep you?' Nitin had raised the stakes.

'It is for you to take all necessary measures to obtain results,' the god returned.

'Understood,' said Nitin. 'Actions are the remit of humans. But are their consequences not a matter for God? Who makes the consequences of actions apparent?'

Karan replied that God made them apparent only in the actions of humans, while the Constitution of India anticipated different types of punishment for almost any wrongdoing. An aggrieved Nitin fought back.

'Can you tell us how many people respect the principles of the Constitution these days? How many people truly follow it? The courts are the only place it's followed!'

When Karan continued to insist that humans alone were responsible for this situation, Nitin accused him one last time of ignoring his responsibility.

'You keep saying we're responsible for everything that goes wrong. If that's the case, then we're the worst criminals of all! And we don't deserve the presence of the god Ganesh in our homes. We're not worthy of worshipping him.'

Karan closed the exchange with these words.

'If you are a criminal, you will be punished. You can diminish your misdeeds by worshipping Ganesh. [*To the children*] Children, please ask me any questions. Come closer. You may touch my truck. I am listening. Come forward. *Oṃ namaḥ śivāya, Oṃ namaḥ śivāya …*'

Nitin had been backed into a corner by an indifferent god. He had to repent for being 'the worst criminal of all' and his only recourse was to worship Ganesh and hope the consequences of his misdeeds would be diminished! With Karan, the divine word was manifesting in its starkest form, like a meme or a 'psychic module' of self-control, combining self-regulation and responsibility for one's own confidence (through meditation): 'If you think that ... then you need only worship me ...' Without thinking, almost inadvertently, Karan had covered a number of different possible postures, from detached or irresponsible god to occasional cultural dope; often empathetic, he had nonetheless taken the side of the state against the weak, and this god of the state, wavering between impartiality and indifference, had ended up as an accusing god reiterating parasitic demands for mindless devotion.

This last display of narcissism had roused something in Nitin that no one could have foreseen. It was his turn to become Ganesh now. Karan had done everything on his side to bring it to this point, awakening a desire in his interlocutor to fabricate his own god or else become one. It seemed disagreement had won the day. But as a result of their bout, and because they understood that something here needed rethinking, even sublimating, beyond their irreconcilable stances, Karan and Nitin had both given Ganesh good reason to decant himself into a further form. Nitin went to find Karan in the little booth set up for the occasion, grabbed the helmet from him, and started to address the children.

'I am your Bappa. I live among you always. My name is Nitin Pawar. I am the Bappa of your area. My goal is to touch your hearts and minds to free you from any negative tendencies. Envy is a dangerous thing. Jealousy can ruin lives. If you try to overtake me on the road, even at the risk of causing an accident, that is greed. Traffic and congestion are caused by greed. If someone earns more than me, I will do anything to get rich or steal. The source of corruption is greed. Mastering your desires is the ultimate solution. If I am poor, I must be content with what I have. If I am less smart, I must study harder. If my motorbike has a 125-horsepower engine, I do not need a more powerful one. Do not stop dreaming, however. Your success must not be at another's cost. Greed has undermined the veneration of God. It perverts worship and devotion. It is at the root of all our ills. Greed is our new God.'

We might have expected something different from Nitin, something more revolutionary. Instead, he was inviting resignation, moderation, self-control: the same interchangeable values that Karan had made his trademark. But the tone of Nitin's words was more significant than their content. Self-assured and full of confidence, he had replaced an embodier found wanting, as if to say: 'I will teach you how to incarnate God!'

Dynamics of the interaction: from scepticism to the possibility of bliss

The constraints of this chapter do not allow for further case studies. I refer those wishing to explore the full range of interactions to the *Ganesh Yourself* film (2016) and to the book (Grimaud 2021). These respond to a similar dynamic. In the face of a human trying to embody God, the expected reaction might be: 'Who do they think they are, pretending to be a god?' And yet this question never really arises as such, as if people found it more interesting to play along with this ambiguous contraption, while still reserving their doubts. For the interest of such a device lies in its very ontological uncertainty (individual, machine, god); and in the inability to ever resolve the ideas expressed or poured forth through it. It is clear that those who come forward to consult the god are able to differentiate between (1) the embodier sitting behind the robot with all their subjectivity, (2) the possibility that the god could be embodied in the interface so long as the embodier speaks well, and (3) the god Ganesh as a *potential*, *spectral* and *fluctuating* entity that cannot be reduced to his incarnations. All three scenarios are compatible in the best of cases, or completely dissociable in the worst, to the point of creating rifts or even conflict. The test of incarnation becomes even harder when questions relate to politically sensitive social issues (corruption, etc.), or when the person tries to catch the god out, asking him to support his violent urges and legitimise his vigilantism. The conversation takes a surprising final twist: the man takes the embodier by the hand and tells him, in almost schoolteacher tones, what it means to be a god and how to keep the job. 'Since you do not know how to be God, I will show you!' After realising that this version of Ganesh has no constructive solutions to offer, the man seems to be left with no other choice than to persuade him to approve his course of action. But why, after so many unanswered questions and unmet demands, go to such lengths for the blessing of someone unable to convincingly embody the divine word? Is it because an inability to respond is not sufficient reason to disqualify a god? Or because there is still a chance the god can be felt in the interface, even when the embodier no longer knows what to say?

One thing is certain: the more the embodier struggles to present a god acceptable to his interlocutor, the more the god continues to live on elsewhere, in a *spectral* state. It is clear that the participants in the proposed incarnation game have been motivated by mere metaphysical curiosity, or by a desire to settle their differences with God, or both. Here, we diverge from a basic Turing test, which would simply consist in determining the status of the vague entity in question (in Turing's case, human or machine, man or woman). Compared to an ordinary Turing test (more on this later), God's ever-present shadow looms over the machine, unlocking yet another possibility: is this a human pretending to be God? A god taking human form? A deified machine operated by a human? A god possessing a machine through a human? A human possessed by a god through a machine? A tricky question to be sure, but it is this complexity that results in such a lengthy dialogue. The interlocutor *suspects* this 'animated god' in both senses of the word: he may be suspicious of the device's claim to embody God; or else suspect that God may well be in there. In any case, the interlocutor's question is less 'Who are you?' or 'Are you real or not?', and more 'What connections are possible through you but not through other idols?' This sidestepping implies an engagement with a discursive flow, a recognition that there is less to gain from first establishing the status of the entity than from embracing a healthy dose of *ontological vagueness* in order to reap the fruits of the dialogue.

A few parameters of interaction

There is not enough space here to discuss all the interactions and sometimes heated debates the residents of Mumbai engaged in via the interface. Nonetheless, we can confidently state that the impetus behind each conversation with Bappa was a desire to test his capacities, in a technical sense. What concrete and innovative possibilities can a machine–human interface offer to human divine circuitology? People would normally sit down next to the robot to gauge its worth as an instrument of manifestation and dialogue. Human divine engineering might have its own ways of creating circuits, cables and transmission that many engineers ignore but that many gurus consciously or unconsciously play with. In any case, innovation in the field of human divine circuitry or mediation (Lucia 2014) requires reliability tests. And for most of the people we met, the only way was to have an interaction to test out the experience for themselves. So let us examine more closely the parameters of interaction established in this way.

Doubt

Doubt is a key factor in any interaction with Bappa, varying in intensity and taking many forms: 'I should warn you, I don't believe in your thing at all'; 'I believe in God, but I don't believe he can be here …'; 'Why have you taken this form?'; 'We've never seen you like this, explain this form you've taken!'; 'I don't believe in all that, but since you're here, here's a question for you, Ganesh ...' There is something of Coleridge's 'poetic faith'[5] at work here, if defined as something other than the *consensual suspension of disbelief* to which it is often reduced. In many cases, there is *consensual (or not) affirmation of scepticism*, even a willingness to deconstruct one's own faith – though only to see it transformed, for it cannot bear to go unanswered. Once doubt has been expressed, the interaction must then be overcome or sublimated.

Respondence

As mentioned above, this is the embodier's capacity to answer the questions asked of him. When it became clear the god was not necessarily going to tell them their future, many people left, some losing no time in insulting him: 'Stupid b—!'; 'A god should submit to any test!' But for the most part, respect prevailed. People were polite and started to interact as they would with a god, playing along, though not without expressing some doubt or reticence. The participant could then ask questions, to test him or catch him out, or simply because they believed the embodier would be able to help them make decisions or solve philosophical problems. Many people complained to the robot: 'We constantly pray for you and to you, what do you do for us?'; 'What's your answer to the overpopulation problem?' The unspoken pact with the gods was thus called into question, as in the previous interaction above, and the embodier was inevitably drawn back into the difficulty of embodying the divine word. The interlocutor was quick to point out the excessive confidence exhibited by ordinary followers, and to chasten the god over his ineffective handling of current affairs. Others sought answers to metaphysical questions ('Are we right to believe in reincarnation?'; 'Is yoga of action better than yoga of knowledge for attaining liberation?', etc.) without much concern as to the kind of consultant they were engaged with (avatar? astrologer? sage?). Respondence is as variable as doubt. The constant demand was reflected in answers marked by hesitation, stammering, delays or silences, varying in degree from one interaction to another or depending on the problem posed. A cycle of respondence was quickly established from the moment the participant decided to sit down and ask questions. It did not matter to them if this was Ganesh, a charlatan, a hybrid or some ill-defined composite; what mattered was the answers it could give, which could only be evaluated through dialogue.

Personhood

Compared to a Ganesh idol, with its idealised traits conforming to a certain standard of beauty, Bappa only has the face of a singular human. This excess of *personhood* must also be resolved, accepted or overcome. Some people tried to erase themselves behind the god figure, others argued that they were a singular individual, and their expressed point of view was very much theirs, yet ought to be acceptable as that of a god. Each embodier had to overcome this difficulty, either by hiding behind the point of view of a universal god, or by declaring themselves a singular deity. Some embodiers envisioned and presented themselves as a new, entirely separate form: 'I am an electronic Ganesh, ask me your question'; 'I am this or that Ganesh'; 'I personally believe that Action is better than Knowledge'; 'I am a trans Ganesh'; 'I am a gay activist Ganesh'; 'I am an environmentalist Ganesh', etc. The experiment showed that nothing precluded such statements. On the contrary, the interface proved an effective way to generate a Ganesh of many voices and many faces. In this regard, the problem faced by participants was less whether the person they were dealing with *was* Ganesh, but rather *which* Ganesh it was.

Disembodiment

For the embodier, Bappa provided the opportunity to be someone else. Not everybody experienced the interaction the same way; but when the dialogue went deeper, touching on themes the embodier would never have thought of, several told us: 'It didn't feel like me talking, but someone else through me.' Another confided: 'It was like my inner voice, that person I talk to in private, who was suddenly front and centre, on the outside, and I thought to myself: is that person really me?' Notably, this same shift could occur on the interlocutor's side. Since this was their first time addressing a god in public, outside the intimate conditions of prayer or a temple visit, they could be persuaded to bring up delicate or deeper issues they would never have considered, such as the nature of belief, or the very function of the gods. By *disembodiment*, I mean that the voice in question can be ascribed to another entity outside itself and taken as the instrument of a voice distinct from the embodier's subjectivity.

Concretion

In most cases, the person consulting the god could tolerate the fact they were dealing with a tentative voice, an incarnation in progress rather than a perfectly stabilised entity. In the dialogue, a *concretion* (in the chemical sense of the term) occurs between several bodies – individual, machine and god converging and consolidating as one, more successfully in some cases than in others – and this process determines a set of possibilities for dialogue. The test could last a while, depending on the appetite for interaction and Ganesh's ability to hold the questioner's attention or provide acceptable responses. The embodier always emerged from the interaction exhausted; yet, to our great surprise, any hesitation, stammering or silences as they sought to conform in one way or another to a standard of the divine word were rarely perceived as a digression or as breaking character. Whenever an answer seemed to align with their conception of God's voice, the questioner was left with the feeling of having spoken to Ganesh, or that there was certainly something of God in this interface. In the worst cases, they rejected the incarnation interface because of its flawed human aspect; in the best, they left thinking: 'For the first time, I had the chance to speak to a human, a machine and a god all at once!'

Beyond Turing

A successful agglutination (along the lines of '… and … and …') necessarily occurs at the expense of the clarity of the component parts, but to grasp the implications of this evolved form of ontological ambiguation, we must refer again to the famous Turing test. In his renowned article of 1950, Turing proposes a paradigm shift to designers of 'intelligent' machines. Instead of 'Can machines think?', Turing prefers to ask under which conditions a machine can make us believe it is thinking, the only question he considers worth asking. And so he suggests the following game: Person X is in a room exchanging notes with a machine located in another room alongside Person Y. The machine's task is to make Person X believe it is a woman; Person Y's task is to muddy the waters; and Person X's task is to guess with whom he or she is interacting. Turing's experiment was designed to produce as much ambiguity as possible in order to deceive the questioner, testing a machine's capacity to fool us in terms of not only machine-ness, but gender too. Drawing on the well-known 'imitation game', the machine's bluffing abilities can be evaluated. In other words, for Turing, machines only seem to possess intentionality if they deceive us as to their true machine nature, and because they stimulate to varying extents the generosity of our attributive faculties.

Ganesh offers a different approach to this problem, inevitably for an entity trying to pass as something other than what it is. With Turing, the ontological confusion is sought, envisaged in binary terms of an '... or ...' to be overcome (human or machine, man or woman), a dilemma that cannot go unresolved, but tilts in favour of the deceiving element (the machine) when the experiment is successful. While a relationship based on ontological *confusion* is never particularly healthy, can there be one based on a positive conception of *ambiguation*? Imagine that a machine sends us a message saying: 'I am a human being'. How would we react? According to attribution psychology, we can take this signal at face value, accept it, and engage with this machine as we would with a human. But since it is, ultimately, a machine, it will struggle to conceal its machine traits for very long. It is therefore likely that something more complex is afoot and that these signals are creating a misunderstanding, a conflict of 'ontological' categories (between human and machine) or a contradiction between two 'inferential systems', as we say in the cognitive sciences: the one that leads you to identify a human and interact with them as you normally would with a human; and the one that tells you it is an object, determining a different type of behaviour. The situation can be complexified further: imagine you have a very strong desire to view this machine as human, but the machine periodically slips up, indicating that it is just an object. Either you ignore this, or you find a way or a compromise to manage this paradoxical information, these mixed *signals*.

Now imagine that a human sitting behind a machine sends us a message saying: 'I am a god'. We can take this signal at face value, accept it, and engage with this human behind their machine as we would with a god. But since it is, ultimately, a human behind a machine, there is the possibility of addressing three distinct entities: seeing a human and interacting with them as we would with another human, seeing a god and interacting with it as with a god, and seeing a machine and interacting with it as with an object. At first glance, the question seems simple if we subscribe to theories of causal attribution: we must know which kind of entity we are dealing with in order to interact appropriately with it, but it is only by interacting with it that we can truly grasp what it is before us. Thus, any interaction with such unsteady entities, which could at any point emit contradictory signals, requires a moment of convergence in which each participants identifies and wins over the other, followed by a phase of coming to terms with the nature of the given entity.

Yet reality, as we have seen with Ganesh, transpires quite differently. True, there is still the choice here between three terms – god, machine and human (the controller) – brought together in a single interface (an avatar), though without ever being totally equivalent. But in practice, there is no choice; we are confronted with a *borderline presence* that can never be completely formalised into a maxim along the lines of '… or this … or that'. It adheres to a spectral principle of variable intensity, whereby the entity oscillates (upgrades or downgrades) between several possibilities. In this case, Ganesh oscillates between the material, the organic and the etheric.

The fact that the 'spectre' in our scenario comprises three thresholds or levels (god, human, machine) may complicate things somewhat in relation to the Turing test's two (human or machine). But for any interaction with Bappa to be of equal value to both questioner and questionee, it must go beyond Turing-style guessing games ('are you real or not') to test the actual elasticity of the entity. And this spectral range can only be experienced through interaction, it cannot be predetermined. A person wants to be a god; a god seeks itself in a person; a machine allows itself to be possessed, serving as a conduit between the other two. And even if they try to hide behind one or other of these entities ('I am a machine'; 'I am a god'; 'I myself am Person X'), the embodier must answer the questions asked of them and manage this complex ventriloquist arrangement as best they can. It is what is exchanged in such a context that prevails, the device's ability to provide an acceptable echo, some answers, an affective intimacy. The ambiguity of the being before us ('Is it an avatar?', 'How can we integrate this medium into the panoply of Ganesh's existing forms?') is ultimately of less importance than the pertinence of the answers conveyed by this vague entity.

Would such an interface of divine deconstruction have produced similar results if tested outside the context of Hindu polytheism? Evidently not. In a monotheistic context, something else would have had to be conceived, a quantum machine for example, capable of providing answers, an abstract entity with which a dialogue could be established. Nonetheless, it is in polytheistic worlds, so often erroneously reduced to a catalogue of ready-made, inherited forms, that the most elaborate experiments to test the effects of divinity must be devised. Barbara Cassin offers an apt remark in regard to paganism in Homer's time: anyone appearing before us could at any moment be a god, but this presupposes having proof of it, testing it (Cassin 2006).

What happens when the machine gets involved? Does this strengthen the authority of the word, or, inversely, generate more scepticism? In our digital age of remote communication technologies, the question 'Who is there?', 'Who speaks?' or 'Whose voice is it?' is essential, but, as we have seen with Ganesh Yourself, there can be no simple answer to this question.[6] It must be seen in context how the vagueness surrounding the given entity is, in different cases, either amplified or else resolved through dialogue.

In any event, it is worth considering which direction robotics and artificial intelligence would have taken or would take if we changed the experimental framework entirely, and if the Turing test were not binary (based on competition between human and machine) and did not strive for 'ontological confusion'[7] but rather a form of ambiguation conducive to generating *poetic faith* in potential entities. Would our relationship with machines be the same? This is where the Ganesh experiment is interesting, in that the same reasoning can be applied to God: once the potential to act on the world has been externalised in this form, it seems more difficult to re-internalise it, unless we are given the tools or the medium through which to accomplish this repatriation. In approaching Bappa, the first thought is not 'Another god to worship!' or 'Another guru in the making!', but rather 'How can I benefit from this strange circuitry?' In other words, although we do not expect miracles, we cultivate an air of attentiveness towards this vessel through which a little divinity may be expressed, irrespective of the medium in question.

Conclusion

Bappa has something of an *anti-machine*, enough of a machine to represent the mechanical species, but not sophisticated enough to make further claims without being operated by a complicit human. There is no better way to tangle delicately strung wires and analogue cables; it has its own unique way of belonging to another age or putting up resistance, in its *fragility*. Ganesh's trunk hangs by a single thread from its sensor, the counterweight requiring regular readjustment to avoid tangling the trunk's wire. At peak fragility, the mechanics and programming are kept to a bare minimum. Ganesh Yourself was a strange media experiment, an attempt at divine (re-)engineering, provoking questions more than solving problems.[8] It could have been a good tool for locating unknown gurus, revealing their auras to those who would otherwise ignore them. Their rhetorical abilities could have been reinforced. It could have been a subliminal test for potential new gods and gurus in the making. But in fact, because it could lead to both – *guruisation*, or its opposite, *guru-retrogradation* – and finally leave all actors of the game with a crisis of (divine) representation to overcome, I think its main lessons lie elsewhere. Revealing the fragility of incarnation, the limits of claims and mythic scenarios, it directly points out the unconscious ingredients necessary for a presence or a word to be felt as 'divine'. Bappa is an *anti-god* as well. What distinguishes it from a classical idol is obvious: turning the mirror back onto the worshipper, Bappa is a mere impulse of deification in search of itself, crystallised into an object. Who could have thought such a contraption would be good for much else than to make a god stutter, or that the resulting experience would be both political and metaphysical?

While offering everyone the chance to plumb their inner depths for the necessary resources to compose the divine word, this little deconstructive machine is also killing two birds with one stone: it fractures the being by revealing their machinelike side, their little routines and thought reflexes; and everything needed in terms of delegation, the unconscious and the miraculous to construct a viable voice. There is not enough room here to examine all the moments when the embodier, looking to escape a somewhat aggressive interaction, transforms into a *mantra-*dispensing machine, justifying their indifference or lack of empathy by the notion that God could well be nothing more than a machine or a program, the very first algorithm ever created. No matter the embodier's chosen tactic, the interaction becomes the plane of consistency where the god falls from his pedestal and man loses his ability to make sense of it. A successful interaction with Bappa invariably leads to a form of *tabula rasa* as to what lies behind the 'god' label, and a reassessment of how far one may legitimately speak in his name. Ganesh Yourself is ultimately a positive reset device with all the risks this entails for those who participate. Once the deconstruction of different possibilities of divine postures has occurred,

Figure 7.4   *Ganesh Yourself*, film, 2016, credit E. Grimaud.

the embodier has no choice but to commit themselves to the process of reconstitution, whether another voice emerges from the rubble of deconstructed gods – a bespoke Ganesh of their own making – or another tradition emerges through his intermediary, one without precedent in the pantheon of existing gods.

Notes

1 The experiment was made into a film. See E. Grimaud, *Ganesh Yourself*, film, Arte/Rouge International, 70′, 2016.
2 Trap, as a notion, has been the subject of extensive glosses in anthropology. Long before Gell (1996), Otis Mason proposed the following definition: 'A trap is an invention for the purpose of inducing animals to commit incarceration, self-arrest, or suicide' (Mason 1900, 657). After him, Leroi-Gourhan (1945) saw in the *lure* 'an instrument of seduction combined with one of death'. A very sensitive use of these classical definitions is proposed by Nick Seaver (2018), who looks at digital algorithms as traps.
3 'Anthropology is philosophy with the people in' (Ingold 1992, 696).
4 'What distinguishes "technique" from non-technique is a certain degree of circuitousness in the achievement of any given objective' (Gell 1988, 6).
5 '[A] semblance of truth sufficient to procure for these shadows of imagination that willing suspension of disbelief for the moment, which constitutes poetic faith' (Coleridge [1817] 2004, chap. 14).
6 The way in which humans are led to perceive personhood in things or in other beings is simultaneously a question of psychology, an ethical and political debate, and a historical problem. The possibilities of fusion and confusion between object, presence and person (and especially god) are, depending on context and era, widely exploited or channelled. On this point, see Grimaud, Taylor, et al. 2016.
7 A link between the Turing test and the prophecies mentioned earlier appears self-evident. Turing certainly seems happy to fuel them: 'At some stage therefore we should have to expect the machines to take control, in the way that is mentioned in Samuel Butler's *Erewhon*', his article 'Intelligent machinery, a heretical theory' ([1951] 1996) concludes.
8 'Experimental systems are vehicles for materializing questions' (Rheinberger 1997, 28).

References

Cassin, Barbara. 2006. 'dieux, Dieu', *Critique* 704–5: 7–18.
Coleridge, Samuel Taylor. [1817] 2004. *Biographia Literaria or Biographical sketches of my literary life and opinions*. https://www.gutenberg.org/files/6081/6081-h/6081-h.htm#link2HCH0014 (accessed 1 March 2023).
Dick, Philip K. 2011. *The Exegesis of Philip K. Dick* (ed. Pamela Jackson and Jonathan Lethem). Boston, MA: Houghton Mifflin Harcourt.
Gell, Alfred. 1988. 'Technology and magic', *Anthropology Today* 4 (2): 6–9. https://doi.org/10.2307/3033230.
Gell, Alfred. 1996. 'Vogel's net: Traps as artworks and artworks as traps', *Journal of Material Culture* 1 (1): 15–38. https://doi.org/10.1177/135918359600100102.
Grimaud, Emmanuel. 2021. *Dieu Point Zéro: Une anthropologie expérimentale*. Paris: Presses Universitaires de France.
Grimaud, Emmanuel, Anne-Christine Taylor, Denis Vidal and Thierry Dufrêne. 2016. 'Qui est là? Présences-limites et effets de personne', in *Persona: Étrangement humain* (exhibition catalogue), 11–19. Paris: Musée du quai Branly, Actes sud.
Ingold, Tim. 1992. 'Editorial', *Man* ns 27 (4): 693–6. http://www.jstor.org/stable/2804169.
Leroi-Gourhan, André. 1945. *Milieu et techniques: Evolution et techniques*. Paris: Albin Michel.

Lucia, Amanda. 2014. 'Innovative gurus: Tradition and change in contemporary Hinduism', *International Journal of Hindu Studies* 18 (2): 221–63. https://doi.org/10.1007/s11407-014-9159-5.

Mason, Otis T. 1900. 'Traps of the Amerinds: A study in psychology and invention', *American Anthropologist* ns 2 (4): 657–75. https://doi.org/10.1525/aa.1900.2.4.02a00050.

Rheinberger, Hans-Jörg. 1997. *Toward a History of Epistemic Things: Synthesizing proteins in the test tube*. Stanford, CA: Stanford University Press.

Seaver, Nick. 2018. 'Captivating algorithms: Recommender systems as traps', *Journal of Material Culture* 24 (4): 421–36. https://doi.org/10.1177/1359183518820366.

Turing, Alan. 1950. 'Computing machinery and intelligence', *Mind* 59 (236): 433–60. https://doi.org/10.1093/mind/LIX.236.433.

Turing, Alan. [1951] 1996. 'Intelligent machinery, a heretical theory', *Philosophia Mathematica* 4 (3): 256–60.

8
Flooding the Web: absence-presence and the media strategies of Nithyananda's digital empire

Amanda Lucia

In 2013, just before a busy pedestrian bridge at the Kumbh Mela[1] in Prayagraj, India, a sari-clad *videśī* (foreign[er]) *brahmacāriṇī* (renunciate aspirant) invited me into her guru Swami Nithyananda's camp. The camp exterior was the towering façade of the famed Meenakshi temple of Madurai, made from thin decoratively painted plywood suspended on bamboo scaffolding. Inside at the centre was a golden *siṇhāsan* (altar throne), upon which a richly adorned golden figure of Shiva was seated with his trident, *ḍamaru* (drum), diamond earrings and silk turban, replete with a bejewelled golden Parvati perched delicately on his lap. To the right was a life-sized wax statue of the guru, Swami Nithyananda. He was similarly turbaned and wore a *rudrakṣa mālā* (prayer necklace), bracelets and armbands, and diamond bling; all three wore rich, high-quality flower *mālās* (garlands). The life-sized wax figurine of Nithyananda sat in lotus position, cross-legged on a bed of ochre brocaded silk with his right hand raised in the *abhayamudrā* ('fear not' hand gesture).

Several days earlier, in a secret ceremony, the Mahanirvani Akhara (a sect of Daśnami *saṃnyāsis*, Shaivite world-renouncing ascetics) had appointed Swami Nithyananda as a Māhāmaṇḍaleśwar, a high-ranking title of religious leadership. That year, by chance I had befriended several *sādhus* (ascetics) of the sect, and from them I learned that several of them were honoured that Nithyananda had been given such a prestigious title in their *akhāṛa* (ascetic sect), and one showed me pictures of him on his mobile phone, proud of his proximity to the famed guru. But soon controversy began to erupt. The president of the Akhil Bharatiya Akhara Parishad (ABAP, the apex body of the 13 Akhāṛas) decried that 'he

[Nithyananda] had acquired the rank with the use of money'. Another spokesperson of the Parishad suggested that it was because '[Nithyananda's] image had taken a beating after the sex scandal and he wanted to get himself elevated to the rank of a mahamandelshwar so that he could join the top seers [ṛṣīs, rishis: sages] of the country' (*Voice of India* 2013). In the midst of the controversy, Nithyananda did not attend the *śahi snān*, the most auspicious bathing day, with his new Akhāṛa; only the life-sized wax figurine was present, a signifier of the absconded and notorious guru.

In fact, one of the most fascinating aspects of Nithyananda's persona as guru in recent years has been that he is physically absent, all the while being notoriously present in the media and in popular discourse. The guru – like his life-sized wax figure – is a poignant signifier of the ambivalences and play of 'present absence' and 'absent presence' of post-Derridean media theory (McQuire 2017). This chapter explores the affective registers of absence and presence that are generated in the multi-platform media representations disseminated in Nithyananda's name. I argue that the guru's assemblage of media representations creates a presence that replaces, alleviates, and even erases, his conspicuous absence. Furthermore, I show how, in this case, scandal and strategies of media proliferation – what I name as the strategy of 'flooding' – are correlated, and interdependent. That is to say that as Nithyananda became mired in scandal, his visage and exploits increasingly occupied headlines in popular media. In response, he began to use his own social media presence and media platforms to defend himself by mobilising counter-narratives. The result is that the more the guru has been persecuted and pursued – and the more he absconded – the less physically present he can be, and, as a result, the more his media representations effectively replace any semblance of the 'real' guru's presence.

Confronting the impact of scandal, Nithyananda has deployed defensive counter-narratives by flooding the field with media represent-ations, obscuring and suppressing other, more critical narratives. This media strategy that I am calling flooding is, in fact, a common legal strategy, used in the context of 'predatory discovery', which Nithyananda's advocates deploy in legal contexts as well.[2] In analysing how this strategy enables a Derridean 'play' of representation, I consider how this type of hyper-mediated guru enacts what Jean Baudrillard (1994) famously called the 'simulacra' of modernity. Overarchingly, this chapter questions if guru embodiment holds the same import as it once did, in a hyperreal world in which only the spectre of embodiment appears to be necessary, and virtual interaction with the guru convincingly generates the affective experience of guru devotion for millions of followers.

Corresponding to the increase in criminal charges levied against him, Nithyananda has become progressively more absent. During his trial for rape, he attended court for the first session on 5 June 2018, but then he was absent from all subsequent sessions. From that moment and continuing into the following year, he was also absent from his Bidadi Ashram (Yadav 2019). In 2019, he had also failed to appear in more than 50 hearings on charges of kidnapping, according to Gujarat Police (Express Web Desk 2020). Most remarkably, despite the fact that his passport expired on 30 September 2018, Nithyananda is reported to have absconded from India, clandestinely and illegally fleeing the country. His devotees claim that he has travelled to an island off the coast of Ecuador, and has established a new nation called Kailash, which is an asylum for persecuted Hindus – like himself. But, in response, the Ecuadorian government has denied ever having given him asylum (Basu 2019). Astoundingly, even today, the notorious guru has effectively vanished, evading both the Indian police and Interpol for the past several years.

But in this period of physical absence the guru is also surprisingly present. On the one hand, his story and his image are ubiquitously present, topping the headlines of Indian media publications so routinely as to become identifiable tabloid fodder. The secular media seems to have a ravenous appetite for Nithyananda-related speculation, rumour and gossip. His exploits are quickly turned into sensationalist accounts that decry his debauchery and gall. In response, probably in an attempt to counterbalance such critiques, Nithyananda and his followers have also been producing large quantities of media content, which they disseminate on social media, on Google's video-sharing platform YouTube, and on Nithyananda Foundation-related websites and online publications. The guru's presence is conveyed through multiple media representations, and his physical absence is itself erased by this constructed, if receding, speculative and sometimes falsified presence. That is to say that so many different agents are making media content in Nithyananda's name and with photographs and recorded videos of him that they generate an *assemblage* (Deleuze and Guattari 1987, 84) of presence, even when the guru is notably absent.

Furthermore, Nithyananda's media representations seem to be using additional strategies to confuse and disrupt any suspicion of the guru's absence. Online messaging from the guru and his ashram is regular and constant; from Facebook alone, Nithyananda's 'live darshan' notifications occur multiple times each day. This creates an affective feeling of the guru's presence despite his absence, creating a constancy and persistence which I signal through performative interruptions in the narration of this chapter, as in: 'LIVE DARSHAN | WEBINAR | UNRAVEL MYSTERIES OF PARALLEL UNIVERSE | 16 JAN 2022', 'PARASHAKTI AKASHIC READING | 17 JAN 2022'.

Production value in such 'live darshan' sessions is relatively high, with rapidly shifting visual imagery and booming symphonic orchestration, which creates an affective feeling of a movie trailer. These online *satsaṅgs* (devotional gatherings) occur regularly, during which teams of the guru's *brahmacarī/iṇīs* (celibate renouncers) lecture and provide spiritual exegesis on Hindu concepts, often framing their teachings as *akashic readings*, an intuitive reading of the 'cosmic memory bank'.[3] These videos are spliced with pre-recorded, often archival footage of Nithyananda giving spiritual discourses. Even these archival videos of the guru are themselves spliced with several camera angles and slightly different settings and costumes, which reveal that they are composites drawn from multiple recordings taken at different times. To confuse matters even further, many of the different *brahmacārīs* who perform pujas (ritual devotions) and give discourses in these videos physically resemble Nithyananda in age, attire and comportment. While I cannot speculate on the intention behind this effective doubling, their similarity of appearance also contributes to a sort of abstract signification of the guru's presence, when in fact he is absent.

Stop. Interruption. My phone buzzes. There's a notification: 'KAILASA'S SPH JGM Nithyananda Paramashivam is live now'. The elusive Nithyananda is 'live' giving a satsaṅg *on Facebook. I stop typing, click in, and there he is: turbaned and adorned with* rudrakṣa mālās *(prayer necklaces), a ruby-red dhoti (traditional cloth wrap), tiger-print cummerbund – all symbols of Lord Shiva – and a fixed broad smile. Seated barefoot in the lotus position on a golden throne, he gently rocks back and forth as he speaks with percussive English diction. His presence signifies opulence and wealth. He is bejewelled with multi-stranded golden chains, diamond tikka* māng *(traditional forehead jewellery) and golden rings on every finger. His golden throne is surrounded by gold and brass lions, goddess figures, fans, pillars,* ḍamaru *(Shiva's drum), and urns, all made of gold (probably brass polished to look like gold). His throne is adorned with bundles of peacock feathers, a symbol of Lord Krishna.*

Today, he speaks of 'manifesting abundance', which he articulates as the 'economic policies of Paramashiva'. He tells his virtual audience that they must 'manifest' physical and mental health through cultivating the 'science of conscious sovereignty'. He invites his listeners to 'manifest this conscious sovereignty-centric ecosystem' either with him in Kailaasa or by learning it now from him and then activating it in their home communities. He claims that he will teach how to 'manifest supermind, which manifests all powers – extreme joy, ecstasy, bliss, completion – powers'. He instructs them to 'declare you are Paramashiva, the ultimate conscious being', right here and now. 'Even if you are experiencing self-doubt, self-denial, self-hatred', 'all of this, too, is part of the Paramashivatva', or the essence of Paramashiva.

But then, the image morphs in such a way that Nithyananda's image shifts a few inches, and Nithyananda abruptly stops speaking. His virtual figure is still, static, completely frozen in his seated lotus posture on his golden throne; his broad smile still stretches mechanically across his face. The ticker tape scrolling across the bottom reads 'we will be right back ... stay tuned!' After a few moments of silence, a traditionally high-pitched female Indian vocalist begins to sing a bhajan *(devotional song) offered in praise of the guru: 'Ooh Nithyananda, Ooh Nithyananda ...'. After several moments, the guru returns, and with a brief explanation of how extraordinarily complex the 'science of conscious sovereignty' is, he promises to explain more in future satsangs. He concludes with Sanskrit prayers that grant the darshan the ethos of tradition and authenticity, and as he closes, he says, 'With this, I bless you all ...' He then raises his hands into a* 'namaste' *prayer position and rolls his eyes into the back of his head so that only the whites are showing. The camera zooms in and focuses on the unseeing whites of his eyes, pulsating there for some time. Then red velvet curtains – or the CGI likeness thereof – close in front of him. Darshan is complete. A chorus of male voices sings Sanskrit prayers to the guru, accompanied by the traditional drone of the tambura. The ticker tape continues to roll across the bottom of the screen with the invitation: 'Apply now for a free passport:* https://joinkailaasa.org/freepassport *be an ekailsian today and enjoy the enlightenment ecosystem:* https://joinkailaasa.org' *(Facebook 2022a).*

As the guru disappears behind the red velvet curtain, I have a somatic feeling of having seen and experienced the guru, of having had darshan. I also note a feeling of interruption, an incomplete suspension that fosters a desire for resolution. I can imagine this emotion transforming into a feeling of devotional longing among the faithful. Perhaps that is the intent. Presence. Absence. Interruption. Desire. Attachment. Devotion.

Becoming Nithyananda

Born in 1978 under the name Arunachalam Rajasekaran in Tiruvannamalai, Tamil Nadu, the swami began his life as the guru Nithyananda in 2002, and established his ashram the following year. According to the Nithyananda Dhyanapeetam trust account, within five years, by 2007, the movement had spread to 33 different countries, and had been endorsed by the then President of India, A. P. J. Abdul Kalam. Nithyananda also found success in the United States, cultivating significant donations from wealthy Indian-Americans and establishing ashrams in multiple cities. That same year, he was invited to serve as the chairman of the Hindu University of America by Braham Aggarwal, the university's founder, a devoted disciple, and an occasional companion of some of the most world-renowned global gurus (including Baba Ramdev, Sadhvi Ritambhara and Swami Mukundananda) (YouTube 2021). Nithyananda, who was by then referred to as 'His Divine Holiness', greatly expanded his 'mission' to 'reinterpret traditional Vedic wisdom in the light of modern living'. His discourses and methods used approachable language to distil Vedic, yogic and bhakti (devotional) aspects of traditional Hindu religiosity. But he also blended this inherited tradition with easily implementable daily skills and tactics that he promised would augment material success and psychological wellness. Put simply, he promised that his strategies would increase happiness and invite material prosperity; following his teachings would 'help you enjoy your life more' (YouTube 2010).

In the first decade of the twenty-first century, Swami Nithyananda published a flurry of books, effectively inundating the guru market with his ideas and persona. Most notably, his 999-page manifesto, entitled *Living Enlightenment*, with the biblically inflected subtitle 'the *Gospel of Paramahamsa Nithyananda*', provided readers with a spiritual treatise that guided readers toward 'superconsciousness' through instructions based in 'everyday life solutions'. In accessible and practical language, the book – and the Nithyananda Mission more generally – claim to help 'people discover the simple secrets of conflict-free, productive and blissful living'.[4] Published by the Life Bliss Foundation, it has sections with soothing therapeutic titles like 'flow in love', 'there is nothing to worry', 'excel without stress', 'face your fears and be free', 'pain is a great teacher', 'desire is a dynamic energy', 'guilt is the original sin', 'you can unclutch from the mind maze', and 'global peace begins from you'. After listing the 'top 10 reasons to get enlightened' in 10 pithy slogans promising emotional fulfilment, worldly success, ultimate knowledge and God-like existence, the book focuses on practical spiritual advice and meditation techniques. It also includes a compact disc containing Nithyananda's teachings, and directs readers to 'the largest spiritual library in the world' available at www.YouTube.com/LifeBlissFoundation. The publication was, in fact, symbiotically fuelled by his online media engine, and together his print publications and online messaging created a media blitz that catalysed his global influence.

Nithyananda's empire expanded enormously and is now represented by his trust, Nithyananda Dhyanapeetam, which has temples, *gurukulas* (religious schools) and ashrams in multiple countries, with Indian headquarters in Bidadi, near Bengaluru, and an international headquarters in Montclair, California (a suburb of Los Angeles). His latest venture has been the rapid establishment of NGOs around the world that aim to create a global fundraising network. In 2020, there were 10 different NGOs established in his name in the United States alone (Kumar 2020). All of this fundraising infrastructure operates in service of Nithyananda's new nation: Kailasa, 'the Revival of the Ancient Enlightened Hindu Civilizational Nation', which he established to prevent a 'Hindu Holocaust' (Srikailasa n.d.a). As will be discussed, Nithyananda designs ambiguity around Kailash intentionally, referring to it as simultaneously a mental state of consciousness, a nation with a geographical location with a central bank and a distinct currency (*News 18* 2020), and an e-nation replete with e-passports and e-citizenship, a complete 'digital enlightenment ecosystem' (Srikailasa n.d.a.; see also Srikailasa n.d.b). In Nithyananda's language, it is all of these, with the promise: 'If you cannot come to KAILASA, KAILASA can come to you! KAILASA coming to you is E-KAILASA' (Srikailasa n.d.b).

The message

One of the primary reasons Nithyananda became globally famous was the miraculous 'mystical powers' that he has claimed he can cultivate in others through 'superconsciousness breakthrough'. He made news headlines in 2018, when he announced that his technique would enable animals (monkeys, lions, tigers, bulls and cows) to grow vocal cords and speak in Sanskrit and Tamil.[5] He has also taught his technique of 'superconsciousness breakthrough' to children (*bālasants*, child Hindu monks) in his *gurukul* (religious school).[6] According to ashram publications, these *balasants* give *akashic* readings daily in the Nithyananda Gurukul and online, offering their services to humanity free of cost.[7] YouTube videos also circulate in which the children of Nithyananda's *gurukul* demonstrate their powers by allowing themselves to be blindfolded and then reading books, writing messages and drawing pictures. The most famous of these is Ma Nithya Yogamaathananda (Ma Yogamata), who has become one of the primary exemplars and defenders of the practice (YouTube 2017). When a 2015 video of her demonstrating her 'superpower' went viral (now with more than 10 million views), she was only nine years old (YouTube 2015). The video begins with an elegant sari-clad Indian woman introducing

Ma Yogamata to an older upper-class Indian crowd seated in chairs at the Los Angeles ashram, while white camerapersons record the event for online dissemination. The child then demonstrates her 'superpower' by reading text and replicating patterns supplied by the audience, all the while blindfolded.

The video then transitions to a different environment, in which Ma Yogamata appears with her mother, both in traditional Indian Hindu dress conveying wealth, tradition and devotion. The interviewer is Frank Elaridi of Modern Nirvana, an organisation self-described as dedicated to catalysing spiritual transformation and human potential.[8] Elaridi presents himself as an outsider who was contacted by the Nithyananda temple about Ma Yogamata's abilities, but says, 'I had to see it for myself' (YouTube 2015). The rest of the video shows Elaridi working with Ma Yogamata closely, blindfolding her and giving her tests to demonstrate her 'superpower' of akashic reading. It closes with contact information to learn more about 'Third Eye Awakening process or Inner Awakening Program', with an email address and a Los Angeles phone number for Nithyananda University.[9] The explanation given for her and the other *gurukul* children's paranormal abilities is their training with Nithyananda. According to Nithyananda, anyone can learn the skill of *akashic* reading through his 21-day course in 'third eye awakening', which costs US$10,000. Nithyananda articulates the reasoning behind the practice of *akashic* reading as follows:

> Akashic Reading is a record created in space. Whatever has happened in time, is there as a file. When a being realizes he is beyond time and space he will be able to decode those Akashic recordings, spell it out in the language you understand, in the frequency you can receive for your betterment, to improve the life, and reach your ultimate goal and the ultimate goal of humanity – enlightenment.
>
> It is not prediction, it is reading from the records. There is no such thing as past, present and future. Beyond space, creation and destruction happen simultaneously. In dimension of time, starts the past, present and future. But in Akashic Records, there is no past, present and future, that is why what you call as happened, happening, yet to happen are clearly already recorded.[10]

Nithyananda and his supporters have held numerous public demonstrations of children performing *akashic* readings. When Ma Swarupapriyananda (now Sarah Landry) left the ashram in September 2019, she made a YouTube video (YouTube 2019a) that included allegations of child abuse relating to the practice, stating that children at the *gurukul* knew the practice was fake and were beaten severely when they failed to produce clairvoyant skills. Indian media outlets swiftly deployed Landry's video footage to denounce the guru, who was already accused of fraud, kidnapping and rape, among other charges (*Republic TV Investigation* 2019, no longer available). Since then, other allegations of criminal activity in Nithyananda's organisation, including child abuse related to Nithyananda's demand that ashram children perform *akashic* readings, have been made even more visible. Multiple allegations, including those of Sarah Landry and ashram children, are collated in the documentary film series *My Daughter Joined a Cult* (Saraiya 2022). But Nithyananda continues to tout *akashic* reading as a straightforward, simple and solution-oriented tactic, mostly geared towards providing solutions to problems of modern living, as in 'Solutions for physical, mental and emotional problems', 'Solution for chronic ailments', 'Solution for depression', 'Solution for addiction', and 'Solution for fear of death' (Nithyananda 2008, 224–7).

In addition to claiming to provide solutions to the discontent of modern living, Nithyananda's teachings promise to guide aspirants not only to spiritual enlightenment, but also to material wealth. Far from demanding that aspirants either renounce or denounce the material world, Nithyananda's teachings affirm worldly material success. He encourages his devotees to envision and manifest material prosperity, and his teachings resemble a Hindu formulation of prosperity gospel. Prosperity gospel, or the gospel of 'health and wealth', is a Protestant Christian concept, which has gained a strong foothold in many Evangelical churches (Bowler 2013) and in Black churches (Walton 2014), and it has even transferred into religious fields like New Age religion through New Thought metaphysics, as in the practice of 'manifesting abundance' (Lucia 2020, 137–43). In the Christian context, prosperity gospel practices are justified through multiple biblical passages that promise material rewards for believers (see James 4:2 and Jeremiah 20:11), and particularly for those who give money to the church (see Malachi 3:10). Many of these biblical verses are controversial, with detractors claiming that they are extracted from their ancient cultural context and misunderstood, and adherents defending them as a covenant with God promising financial gain for good works.

Despite his self-identification as the Supreme Pontiff of Hinduism, Nithyananda's 'Gospel' (2008) has considerable Christian overtones. His message implements prosperity gospel maxims, excerpted from their Christian context and reformulated with Hindu New Age ideals, that spiritual seekers can transform reality by shifting their consciousnesses. He articulates this principle by deploying the New Thought metaphysical ideal that 'thoughts manifest into reality' and also the human potential movement's assertion of the 'power of positive thinking' to support his claim that mental fluctuations can change reality. He then intertwines these philosophical foundations to mobilise prosperity gospel promises, claiming that if his followers only recalibrate their minds, that they can 'manifest' material benefit.

Stop. Interruption. My phone buzzes. There's a notification: 'KAILASA's Courtyard Manifesting Powers' is live now. The elusive Nithyananda is 'live' giving a satsang *on Facebook. I stop typing, click in and there he is sitting on the golden dais smiling broadly at me. I am introduced to the 'Kailash Courtyard Manifesting Power DAILY ROUTINE JNANAPADA', which begins with the* māhāvākya *(grand, profound saying):* 'Om Nithyānanda Paramaśivo ham'. *The* māhāvākya *mantra is repeated in a rhythmic, hypnotic, droning chant with a driving percussive accompaniment, and I am encouraged by a young Indian* brahmacāriṇī *in ochre robes and* rudrakṣa mālās *to chant along. The session promises that through meditation on the* māhāvākya *participants will gain the ability to manifest flakes of gold in the palm of their hand. The* brahmacāriṇī *leading the meditation shows a power point slide show replete with X-rays providing evidence that dedicated meditators have produced precious foreign objects in their throats while chanting the* māhāvākya. *Attendees are told to focus steadily on this practice of chanting the* māhāvākya *in order to manifest wealth and abundance in their lives (Facebook 2022b). In the days that follow, multiple devotees post photographic evidence of the efficacy of this manifestation practice to this Facebook account's home page. Although this is advertised as a 'Facebook live' satsang with the guru, the imprint on the video footage of Nithyananda reads 'Nithyananda University 2018'.*

Many of Nithyananda's discourses and meditations focus on helping his followers to access material rewards and to materialise wealth. In the 'viral video' previously discussed, when Ma Yogamata demonstrates her 'super-power' of *akashic* reading, she names material gain as its primary benefit. She says:

Elaridi:	There is no difference between a wish and a will. What does that mean?
Ma Yogamata:	I mean like, if for example, I want a toy. I want a toy and I wished for it, and then it just happens, like …
Elaridi:	You just get it?
Ma Yogamata:	Yeah, I just get it.
Elaridi:	Because you wanted it.
Ma Yogamata:	I just wish, oh, I want a Lego and it just happens!
	(YouTube 2015)

Nithyananda's prosperity gospel provides evidence of the strengthening importance of an Indian New Age religiosity, which is responding to the pressures of neoliberal capitalism and the desires and aspirations of India's growing middle classes (T. Srinivas 2018). His teachings and meditation techniques are presented as a set of easily implementable tactics that will help his followers to set boundaries, to recalibrate their relation to their minds and emotions, to cure their ailments and unhappiness and to set themselves free from stress, worry and pain. He guides his followers through pithy slogans, short exercises and moderate commitments, all the while applauding their efforts with highly encouraging language and feel-good messages. His rhetoric is affirming and supportive, emblematic of the practice of 'love bombing' (Hassan 1988, 14), and includes pledges that aspirants will receive Nithyananda's full support and guidance if they apply his teachings.

In so doing he operates in a field of Indian New Age gurus who are marketing their messages and practices as avenues to building business success, financial wealth and personal happiness (Karapanagiotis 2021; Lucia 2022; Moodie 2020). New Age aspirational rhetoric, encouraging platitudes and easily implemented practices are surrounded by exaggerated Hindu affective signifiers, such as richly traditional Hindu yet ascetic costuming, gilded thrones, references to Vedic knowledge and ritualised Sanskrit recitations. Nithyananda, positioned as 'Paramaśiva' and as 'the Supreme Pontiff of Hinduism' (SPH), authenticates this unique hybridisation between an Indian New Age religion and a hyperbolic Vedic Hinduism. Such rhetoric, combined with conventional signifiers of Hinduism, provides ample evidence of an Indian New Age that is prolific and independent of its expressions in the West (Rudert 2017, 29; S. Srinivas 2008, 338).

Flooding as media strategy

There is perhaps no better contemporary guru to think through the relationship between gurus and media than Swami Nithyananda. Nithyananda's followers boast that he has the largest internet presence of any living guru, and he is unique in his methods of media engagement and message proliferation. During his rise to global fame, Nithyananda has directed his followers to build his social influence by creating and disseminating his presence on media platforms. In his ashrams, children and adults alike are instructed to make videos and posts advocating for and defending their guru; these materials are then disseminated on platforms like YouTube, Facebook, Twitter, Instagram, TikTok and WhatsApp. Marion Braun, an ex-Nithyananda devotee who ran his programmes in Germany and Australia, reported that every day they 'had to share [Nithyananda's] messages' on social media. 'They took it very seriously, we all had to do three videos a day talking about him and our lives at the ashram' (Oelbaum 2020). These videos are usually posted multiple times on different online platforms; devotees have uploaded tens of thousands of videos with Nithyananda content and in praise of Nithyananda, all of which exist independently of the official ashram-sponsored channels.[11]

The official Nithyananda channel (KAILASA's SPH Nithyananda) on YouTube has 314,000 subscribers, but there are dozens of others that are constantly producing new Nithyananda content. For example, among just the 'featured channels' that scroll across the top of the screen there are additional channels, such as 'Guaranteed Solutions From' (5,820 subscribers), 'KAILASA's Nithyananda Yoga (12,000 subscribers), KAILASA'S Nithyananda Sangha (33,600 subscribers), 108Nithyananda Videos (4,390 subscribers), KAILASA's The Avatar Clicks (83,300 subscribers), KAILASA'a Nithyananda Top (13,800 subscribers), Nithyananda Truth (1,920 subscribers), KAILASA'a Nithyananda Sarvajna (3,540 subscribers) and several others. Each of these featured sub-channels opens to a separate screen filled with dozens upon dozens of individual webinars, many with more than 300,000 views. Some ardent devotees, like Sri Nithya Dridhananda (Blissful Athlete) and his partner Prasiddha (Kundalini Yogini), are self-proclaimed 'influencers' with large followings on their own YouTube channels (37,000 and 56,200 respectively). Sri Nithya Dridhananda (Blissful Athlete) pays homage to his guru Nithyananda throughout his videos and is often accompanied by a fabricated image of Nithyananda, whether a life-sized cardboard cut-out or a superimposed CGI image.[12]

In addition to his sizeable YouTube presence, Nithyananda focuses particularly on disseminating his messages on Facebook, probably in recognition that Facebook is the most popular social networking site in his home region of Tamil Nadu. In a 2013 sample study, media scholar Shriram Vekatraman found that of all the social media sites, Facebook was the most commonly used (84 per cent), followed by WhatsApp (62 per cent), both only distantly followed by Twitter (34 per cent) (Venkatraman 2017, 36). Venkatraman's research revealed that Facebook users in southern India are largely younger people, in particular literate, employed men (less so women and the elderly), and most had access to the social media platform through prepaid internet connections on their personal smartphones (p. 37). Social networking through social media, particularly Facebook, is very popular and increasingly important in the middle and business classes of south Indian society; in 2014 mobile phone penetration was close to 70 per cent among its sizeable populations of skilled IT workers, in 2014, in contrast to the 21 per cent national average (p. 32). Tellingly, Venkatraman notes that many users create 'fake' and 'multiple' Facebook profiles in order to conceal their identities, to create curated identities for different populations. This practice results in 'the fracturing of their personalities through multiple profiles [as] an authentic and necessary way of maintaining their identity' (Venkatraman 2017, 45).

In southern India and around the world, followers of the guru are notified on their mobile phones several times per day when Nithyananda is 'Live' on Facebook. Nithyananda devotees replicate this 'Facebook Live' strategy on other social media platforms, comprising one node of the strategy of flooding the Web. This strategy is complemented by a complex network of websites and YouTube channels/videos that produce Nithyananda-supportive content. In addition, Nithyananda has curated a robust online archive of his spiritual teachings, named Nithyanandapedia (https://nithyanandapedia.org), which is designed for easy consumption in the bustle of fast-paced modern living. Kailasa's Nithyanandapedia defines itself as 'The Core of the Supreme Pontiff of Hinduism, Jagatguru Mahannidhanam, His Divine Holiness Bhagavan Sri Nithyananda Paramashivam (HDH) teachings'.[13] It claims to include 1.3 million+ photos, 176,920+ Wiki pages, 1,126+ books, 6,770+ audios, 5,949+ courses and 624+ articles, with links to search for Nithyananda materials in both Tamil and Telugu. Nithyanandapedia.org also has a page listing 'Kailasas around the world'. Nithyananda is widely celebrated among his devotees as the guru with the most teachings on the internet, and Nithyanandapedia, in particular, attempts to impress with its sheer volume of materials. Any given search opens to a litany of Hindu parables, collected materials and videos (with accompanying transcripts) of the guru speaking on any topic of inquiry.[14]

With this arsenal, Nithyananda floods the Web by creating a massive amount of scaffolded and interlaced media content that effectively enables even those with a casual interest to become quickly inundated, consumed and even lost in the 'rabbit hole' of Nithyananda-supportive content. Nithyananda's flooding strategy has close parallels with other online movements in which casual users who inadvertently stumble upon content are easily inundated and surrounded with what appear to be separate, but are in fact networked and commonly sourced information channels that together reinforce a singular message. Movements that use similar strategies, for example white nationalist extremism, Islamic extremism, and QAnon, have proved to be successful in radicalising casual users, who began their internet inquiries with only moderate feelings of social discontent.[15]

Other powerful figures have deployed a similar strategic method, and aspects are visible in the actions of both the Church of Scientology and the former United States President Donald Trump. In the first example, when faced with detractors, the Church of Scientology inundated its opponents with information, bombarding them with hundreds of lawsuits and effectively burying its enemies in data and bureaucracy.[16] In so doing, it activated a common legal strategy, known as an abuse of the process of discovery or 'predatory discovery'. In their article detailing abuses of the discovery process, William Hopwood, Carl Pacini and George Young write that the term 'predatory discovery' originates from *Marrese v. Amer. Academy of Orthopedic Surgeons*, 726 F. 2d 1150, 1162 (7th Cir. 1984), and refers to when discovery is 'sought not to gather evidence that will help the party seeking discovery to prevail on the merits of his case but to coerce his opposition to settle regardless of the merits' (2014, 57). They list multiple strategies of predatory discovery, each of which results in obstruction in some form. The closest to the Nithyananda's media strategy of flooding is what they call the 'document dump' (pp. 66–7), whereby 'a responding party provides thousands and thousands of pages of poorly organized documents to the requesting party' and 'Sometimes the responding party will bury relevant documents within huge stacks of irrelevant documents the other party never requested'.

The former US President Donald Trump and the multiple political organisations advocating for his political platform used similar tactics to overwhelm and discredit critics. His producers also flooded the media with narratives that distracted from and effectively buried his critics' voices. He also waged a war against media corporations, and maligned them as corrupt and 'fake news' media. This strategy was aimed at deflecting criticism by sowing distrust in both media representation and, more fundamentally, in facts. In Susannah Crockford's words, Donald Trump's term 'fake news' 'has since been used in a similar way to how "conspiracy theory" itself is used, as a way of undermining and dismissing dissent, often by those in power, not those outside of it. … [This] fractured nature of authority … has serious implications for a consensus agreement on what is valid knowledge, what is "true", even what constitutes "reality"' (Crockford 2021, 173). Such distrust of the nature of truth itself has become a lasting legacy of Trump's political moment, and one that continues to impact

American opinions on science, climate change (Ward 2018) and COVID-19 (Owen 2020).

Combining these two strategies, Nithyananda produced a 742-page report, entitled *Hindu Holocaust, The Untold Story: 10 years of organized, systematic persecution on his Divine Holiness Paramahamsa Nithyananda*. In it the authors use the term 'fake' 146 times, the most common usages being 'fake rape allegations', 'fake [legal] case', 'fake police complaint', 'fake obscene videos', 'fake video', 'fake witness', 'fake trial', 'fake interview', 'fake media coverage' and 'fake news'. The lengthy treatise details Nithyananda's 'persecution' by the 'state-police-media-mafia', and attributes his scapegoating to 'media crimes against humanity' (Nithyananda n.d., 675), because of his minority religious identity (Adi Shaivite) (p. 300), his ethnic identity (p. 675) and his gender identity (multi-gender) (p. 459).

Deployed together, these tactics complement each other: allegations of 'fake news' destabilise any singular notion of the truth, while the flooding with information overwhelms and fosters doubt. Researchers at the Observatory on Social Media have shown how 'information overload' (and the associated fact of 'limited attention span') can explain how 'fake news' goes viral. In a clinical trial that analysed the circulation of memes on social media, researchers found that, as the quantity of memes went up, the quality of those that propagated fell (see Qiu et al. 2017, cited in Menczer and Hills 2020). In short, the strategy of flooding audiences with media creates an information overload, which enables 'fake news' to spread more vigorously.

For Nithyananda, the media strategy of flooding buries critique in a deluge of laudatory propaganda created and disseminated by his devotees. This is particularly true when social media and search algorithms are considered, because, when Nithyananda and his devotees produce enough material to occupy the majority of the sites in a given internet search, they effectively suppress critical articles by pushing them to the bottom of the first page of 'hits', to the second page, or even further, forcing them to recede into the digital ether. Additionally, Nithyananda and his media-savvy devotees seem to activate strategies that are specifically designed to confuse search engines and their algorithms. For example, if one searches for 'Nithyananda finances' to access the guru's income or net worth, one is instead bombarded with sites announcing the new Reserve Bank of Kailash and Kailashian dollars, the new currency Nithyananda launched for Kailash. While Nithyananda's motives for establishing a central bank and a currency for his new nation are unclear, it is a convenient side effect that his announcement of a Kailash currency buries articles related to his organisational finances and net worth. This is particularly useful because one of the highest estimates for Nithyananda's net worth places him second only to the notorious Asaram Bapu (at the time of writing in prison in Jodhpur, Rajasthan), with a net worth of US$1.5 billion (Rs 10,000 crore) (Rajit 2017), though, of course, significantly more modest estimates also circulate.

Flooding the real in representation

This practice of multiplying representations in order to obfuscate the real draws to mind postmodern theorists such as Jacques Derrida and Jean Baudrillard, who challenged the semiotic relation of signifier and signified, and the correlation of image (representation) and meaning (signification). In recent decades, the proliferation of media representations and their powerful psychological and affective impacts has destabilised Walter Benjamin's famed assertion that there is a presence or 'aura' located in the original, which is either diminished or vacated from the copy.[17] Instead, powerful images circulate and proliferate on the internet in countless refractions, reproductions and augmentations, to the extent that the original itself is split, inverted, repurposed, obfuscated, and even erased (think, for example, of internet memes). In contrast, both Jacques Derrida and Jean Baudrillard offer increasingly valuable insights on representation that are applicable in the era of the internet, whether in helping us to think through the splitting of the original in its representation or in the implosion of meaning enacted through its representation. If readers will abide a brief detour into both of these philosophers' thoughts on representation, it will enable a clearer analytical pathway, which will help us to understand the functionality of the multiple representations of Nithyananda, and what I have called the tactic of flooding in digital media platforms.

In short, Derrida took the broadest view, with his argument on writing, which built on Saussurean semiotics to question the relationality between idea and its representation, and, more precisely, between meaning, language and writing. As is well known, Derrida argued that meaning-making was not, in fact, readily visible in a one-to-one relation of sign and signified, but rather enacted a play of signifiers and a process of endless deferral – or *différance* – of meaning signification. He used this insight to question the logocentric view, which, in his argument, asserts a false presence at the centre of meaning-making. Instead, Derrida wrote:

Representation mingles with what it represents, to the point where one speaks as one writes, one thinks as if the represented were nothing more than the shadow or reflection of the representer. A dangerous promiscuity and a nefarious complicity between the reflection and the reflected which lets itself be seduced narcissistically. In this play of representation, the point of origin becomes ungraspable. There are things like reflecting pools, and images, an infinite reference from one to the other, but no longer a source, a spring. There is no longer a simple origin. For what is reflected is split in itself and not only as an addition to itself of its image.

(Derrida 1997, 36)

In *On Grammatology*, Derrida applied this deconstructionist analysis to all forms of representation, even its simplest phenomenological forms, and thus made a marked contribution to the fields of semiotics and linguistics.

But Derrida's intervention has occupied an important position in media studies as well, as a field consumed by analyses of representation of that which is presumed real, but often, in fact, is not. As a genre, media – at least the fictional narrative – invoke the willing suspension of disbelief, and demand audience consent to imagine the representation as the real, if only for the duration of the film. Media scholars Sarah Gretter, Aman Yadav and Benjamin Gleason show how the internet, in particular, 'blurs boundaries between reality and fiction, rendering the distinction between factual and fictional information more difficult'. This blurring of fact and fiction facilitates propaganda, and many studies show that audiences are unable to distinguish between 'facts and opinion, entertainment and outright disinformation' (2017, 7). Studies have also shown how social media sites have become anonymous and decentralised radicalising spaces, whether the radicalisation is political, social or religious, by using 'narrative transportation', meaning the shifting of a singular narrative across multiple media platforms (p. 9).

Devotees' intentional, proliferating and exponential reproduction of Nithyananda's image and message results in what postmodern theorist Jean Baudrillard calls the 'implosion of meaning', that which he regards as a definitive feature of modernity or the 'era of simulation'. In his famed treatise on modernity, *Simulacra and Simulation*, Baudrillard argues that 'there are no more media in the literal sense of the word ... – that is, of a mediating power between one reality and another, between one state of the real and another. Neither in content, nor in form' (Baudrillard 1994, 82). He writes of this implosion of meaning as the negation of the traditional sense of the real, but also of the positive creation of modernity as the *hyperreal*, defined as 'the disappearance of objects in their very representation' (p. 45). Of the hyperreal, he writes:

> Therein objects shine in a sort of hyperresemblance ... that makes it so that fundamentally they no longer resemble anything, except the empty figure of resemblance, the empty form of representation.
> (Baudrillard 1994, 45)

In naming the multiplicity and fluidity of refracted representations – as seen in media, but also in history-making and daily living in modernity, Baudrillard argues that

> the confusion of the medium and the message ... is the first great formula of this new era. There is no longer a medium in the literal sense: it is now intangible, diffused, and diffracted in the real, and one can no longer even say that the medium is altered by it.
> (Baudrillard 1994, 30)

Baudrillard's positing of the hyperreal also disrupts the conventional semiotic equivalence of the relation of sign to signifier as a meaning-making referent. Instead of any presumed constancy and singularity of meaning, there is an 'implosion of meaning' which refracts through space–time, emplacing representation in a funhouse of mirrors. The result is that in this proliferation, splitting and implosion of meaning-making representations, truth, facts, reality and historical events become interrupted, confused and intentionally obfuscated. Coupled with the distrust of authority and individualistic neoliberalism that inform New Age thinking (Crockford 2021; Jain 2020; Lucia 2020), spiritual circles that consume Nithyananda's teachings are particularly vulnerable to such a tactic. Nithyananda's media strategy relies on devotees to disrupt the rhetorical and ideological power of the singular meaning-making projects and truth claims of his critics. Devotees do this by flooding the media with representations of Nithyananda, his message and his accolades (healings, miracles, coronations and spiritual powers), thus splitting and imploding any singularity of the guru's presence, or guilt.

Absence-presence and scandal

Although Nithyananda has most certainly built his absence-presence and his social capital through the media, at times the media has also provided platforms for his most forceful detractors. After he was filmed in 'compromising positions' with Tamil film actress Ranjitha, the Tamil television station *Sun News* broadcast the video, beginning on 2 March 2010 and continued to air the footage with sensationalist tabloid-style coverage of the guru. In response, both Nithyananda and Ranjitha claimed that their images had been tampered with ('morphed') in the footage, and Atmaprabhananda, manager of Nithyananda's Dhyanapeeta Charitable Trust, argued that *Sun TV* had demanded money to stop running the video footage (PTI 2011). In 2012, Nithyananda reinforced these claims by mobilising his American devotees to solicit the opinions of four independent US-based media experts, each of whom analysed the video footage and concluded that the content was 'fake' and 'morphed' (*The Hindu* 2012). In yet another act of absence-presence – guru disappearance – Nithyananda's California-based non-profit organisations Life Bliss Foundation and Nithyananda Dhyanapeetam Temple & Cultural Center filed a US\$290 million RICO[18] complaint against Sun TV Network, Nakkheeran Publications (a Tamil magazine that ran many sensationalist anti-Nithyananda articles) and 13 others in federal court; charges included extortion, criminal intimidation and assault. Nithyananda, the then 35-year-old guru, was not even a party to the lawsuit (Reynolds 2013).

Instead, Nithyananda took to virtual spaces to issue his own call to arms. He wrote on his website in 2014:

> We will take the route of Social Media to educate the world about the Guru Bashing going on this country. … I request all my disciples, devotees, followers, you will all be warriors protecting Santana Hindu Dharma in Social Media- FB [Facebook], Twitter, Internet. Exposing this [*sic*] conspirators against Hinduism because in this country, Hindu gurus are judged before investigation.[19]

Facing a scandal that was quickly circulating globally, Nithyananda employed his devotional armies to activate social media as a populist arsenal that could create the appearance of controversy and multiple possible realities, despite the presence of clear video footage. The responsive assault began with a full denial: devotees argued that the video was 'fake' and the news reports surrounding it were 'fake news'. Nithyananda's defenders also activated the Orientalist trope of the 'scientific West' versus the 'superstitious East', by deploying the scientific credibility of technical experts in the United States to prove that the video was 'morphed', while deriding Indian media critics as gullible anti-guru forces.

After the story broke, in 2010 and 2013, there was a split in the Los Angeles ashram, as one-time supporters of the guru who had contributed financially to his vision of creating a Vedic University in Los Angeles filed lawsuits against the Nithyananda Foundation, claiming that they had been defrauded.[20] In the 2013 lawsuit, the plaintiffs argued that Nithayananda had 'personally admitted' that the 'videotape accurately depicted SWAMI with a woman engaging in a sex act in his private quarters at his Indian ashram', that he 'had in fact had sex with more than one woman', and that 'the NDAs [non-disclosure agreements] existed going back to 2005', but had been intentionally concealed.[21]

The non-disclosure agreement referred to above has been widely circulated on the internet as one of the most damning pieces of evidence that refute Nithyananda's claims to be celibate. It reads:

A3. Volunteer understands that the Program may involve the learning and practice of ancient tantric secrets associated with male and female ecstasy … Volunteer understands that these activities could be physically and mentally challenging, and may involve nudity, access to visual images, graphic visual depictions, and descriptions of nudity and sexual activity, close physical proximity and intimacy, verbal and written descriptions and audio sounds of a sexually oriented, and erotic nature, etc. By reading and signing this addendum, Volunteer irrevocably acknowledges that he/she is voluntarily giving his unconditional acceptance of such activities and discharges the Leader and the Foundation, and anyone else not specifically mentioned here but directly or indirectly involved in the organization, management, or conduct of any such programs from any liability, direct or indirect, arising from such activities.[22]

The Superior Court of the State of California, San Bernardino County, found the defendant, Nithyananda Foundation, guilty of fraud and racketeering, and awarded US$1.565 million to Popatlal Savla, who had filed his lawsuit in 2010, seeking damages to recuperate his donation of US$1.7 million to Nithyananda.[23] In 2015, the second lawsuit was settled out of court for US$1 million, again to recuperate the cost of previous donations; the award was divided among multiple plaintiffs. Thus, court evidence asserts that both plaintiffs were successful in their lawsuits against the Nithyananda Foundation and related entities. But Nithyananda's media engine effectively used the strategy of flooding to create a counter-narrative; multiple Nithyananda-related websites actively publicised that all charges were dismissed. For example, one reads: 'On January 10, 2013, a U.S. Federal Court dismissed, with prejudice, the entire case of *Popatlal K. Savla v. Nithyananda Foundation, et al*. All claims have been dismissed and the matter has been resolved.' The page also displays an image of an official court document from the United States District Court Central District of California dismissing the case.[24] Thus, even a casual internet search opens into a pre-existing battleground for the truth, in which Nithyananda's devotees and critics are staging an ongoing war. The conflict, the arsenal and even the legal case are created in and through digital media. In fact, *Shinde v. Nithyananda Foundation* was one of the first legal cases on record in which 'the court ruled that "service through a Facebook account was permissible on a defendant located in India, a signatory to the Hague Convention" and comported with due process' (Nussbaum 2018).

Simultaneously, while Nithyananda's devotees flooded the Web to deflect criticism, they also began to create new possible worlds. They mounted a global campaign that 'flipped the script' to recode Nithyananda and his followers not as criminals or frauds, but rather as persecuted and innocent victims of Hinduphobia. This view echoes the recent strategies of Hindu nationalists who dominate Indian politics and society but claim to be persecuted minorities.[25] In defence of this position, on 18 September 2018, Nithyananda submitted a 'Special Report to the United Nations Office of the High Commissioner for Human Rights', in which he argued that he was being persecuted by violent Hindu majoritarian militants because of his minority 'Adi Shaivite' religion (Nithyananda 2018). In 2019, Nithyananda presented the aforementioned 742-page report, *Hindu Holocaust, The Untold Story*, to the United Nations. The guru appealed to the United Nations for refugee status because of religious, ethnic and gendered persecution in India, including 'mob lynching' and 'assassination' attempts (Karthikeyan 2019). In November 2019, Nithyananda fled India and claimed to have established a private island, Kailash, which he explains 'offers a safe haven to all the world's practicing, aspiring or persecuted Hindus, irrespective of race, gender, sect, caste, or creed, where they can peacefully live and express their spirituality, arts, and culture free from denigration, interference and violence' (Srikailasa n.d.d). This archetypal combination of a powerful charismatic figure, a theology that destabilises reality, allegations of financial and sexual impropriety, a narrative of active persecution, the retreat to an isolated island, and the adoption of defensive pre-emptive counter-attack position, would – and should – make any scholar of minority religions nervous (Dawson 2006).

Conclusion

The media has played a significant role in creating and destroying Nithyananda as a powerful global guru, and the guru has used the media to wage a digital war on his critics. As Jacob Copeman and Aya Ikegame have written, 'The guru [Nithyananda] was betrayed by the very same technologies that had hitherto enabled the global circulation of his image and teachings, proliferating his influence and "presence"' (Copeman and Ikegame 2012, 20). It is thus through media analysis that we can build a useful reformulation of the import of the guru's presence and the impacts of mass mediation under late capitalism and globalisation. For in Nithyananda's case the guru has all but disappeared – in one last magical, global vanishing act – and all that is left is speculation, his spectre and the propagation of his virtual presence by so many of his advocates and detractors.

In this chapter, I have argued that the strategy of media flooding is correlated to guru scandal, because it effectively disrupts the monopoly of his critics' truth claims by proliferating multiple layers of counter-narratives. These counter-narratives split and implode representations of fact and presence, effectively raising the possibility of doubt, and destabilising critical truth claims. The tactic of media flooding enacted by Nithyananda's devotees uses the strategy of narrative transportation across online platforms, to effectively blur boundaries between real and fiction. Their assemblage of representations of the guru and his ideas 'stands in' for the physical presence of the guru and disrupt the appositional relationship of absence and presence, representation and the real. Instead, like Derrida's reflecting pools, the proliferation of media representations creates infinite references that not only eclipse but split the original. And in that splitting they form a signifying aspect of modernity, what Baudrillard calls the hyperreal: the disappearance of objects into the multiplicities of their representation. Quite practically, multiple media representations also obscure the truth of Nithyananda's physical location, as he is depicted simultaneously in multiple 'live' videos, which are, in fact, spliced with his presence from pre-recorded archived materials. This splitting, implosion and proliferation of the guru creates a figure who is simultaneously hyper-present in the media and physically absent in the world. This guru miracle – or media mirage – enables Nithyananda to maintain his robust empire of followers, while effectively evading legal authorities.

Notes

1. The Kumbh Mela is a quadrennial Hindu ritual bathing festival that drew 120 million pilgrims that year.
2. In a 2022 podcast interview, Sarah Landry, once a high-ranking devotee in Nithyananda's community, reported that Nithyananda intentionally adopted strategies, practices and institutional structures from Scientology (Bernstein 2022). What I am calling 'flooding' provides support for this claim because Scientologists implemented a similar practice in analogue form during the Wollersheim case (Bernstein 2022, 183), and they continue to use it as a digital combat strategy; see Urban 2011, 178–200.
3. Wouter Hanegraaff argues that the practice of clairvoyantly intuiting from the Akashic record is in fact a method that was put into practice by the theosophists in the nineteenth century. He suggests that the notion of Akashic records or the 'universal cosmic "memory bank"' is dependent on authors such Agrippa or Paracelsus rather than 'Oriental' sources (1998, 454).
4. Amazon.com 2021.
5. The video in which Nithyananda promises these animal superpowers went viral on Twitter and in popular media; see Radha-Udayakumar 2018.
6. *Kailasa's Hinduism Now!* 2017.
7. Yoga Shaktis n.d.
8. *Modern Nirvana* n.d.
9. Nithyananda University 2022.
10. Yoga Shaktis n.d.
11. See, as one of thousands of possible examples, Facebook 2022c, an hour-long lecture on the *Śri Guru Gītā* by Ma Durga, uploaded and disseminated on the Nithyananda-related page 'Kailasa Singapore-Aadheenam'.
12. See YouTube 2022, and for an example of the implementation of the life-sized cardboard cut-out of Nithyananda see YouTube 2019b.
13. https://nithyanandapedia.org (accessed 18 May 2023).
14. See for example Nithyanandapedia 2022.
15. On social media and extremism, see Conway et al. 2019 and Williams et al. 2021, and on QAnon 'rabbit holes' see Wong 2020.
16. In its feud with the Cult Awareness Network (CAN), the Church of Scientology 'bombarded CAN with more than fifty lawsuits and launched an aggressive plan to undermine and discredit the network' (Urban 2011, 149). The Church of Scientology used a similar strategy in its battle against the Internal Revenue Service (IRS), launching 'hundreds or even thousands of lawsuits' in an attempt to 'overwhelm' it (Urban 2011, 171).
17. Benjamin 2019, originally published in 1935.
18. RICO is the Racketeer Influenced and Corrupt Organizations (RICO) Act of 1970.
19. Nithyananda 2014. Also cited in Oelbaum 2020.
20. *Popatlal K. Savla v. Nithyananda Foundation et al.* (2010) [Superior Court of the State of California, San Bernadino County, CIVRS 1008116], 8.
21. *Dr Manohar Shinde et al. v. Nithyananda Foundation et al.* (2013) [US District Court for the Central District of California, 5:2013cv00363], 52.
22. *Dr Manohar Shinde et al. v. Nithyananda Foundation et al.* (2013), Exhibit A, p. 9 of 10, 84.
23. *Popatlal K. Savla v. Nithyananda Foundation et al.* (2012) [Superior Court of the State of California, San Bernadino County, Verdict form: 5:11-cv-01304-SVW-SP].
24. E-Narada 2013. See also www.nithyanandatruth.org and http://prweb.com, accessed 12 February 2022.
25. Srikailasa n.d.c, 'Persecution of Hinduism'. For a broader explanation of Hindutva claims of persecution, see Appadurai 2006.

References

Amazon.com. 2021.'*Living Enlightenment*: About the author.' https://www.amazon.com/Living-Enlightenment-Nithyananda/dp/1606070487 (accessed 2 March 2023).

Appadurai, Arjun. 2006. *Fear of Small Numbers: An essay on the geography of anger*. Durham, NC: Duke University Press.

Basu, Nayanima. 2019. 'Ecuador claims didn't help Nithyananda, but it has been a favourite of fugitives for long', *The Print*, 6 December. https://theprint.in/world/ecuador-claims-didnt-help-nithyananda-but-it-has-been-a-favourite-of-fugitives-for-long/331377/ (accessed 2 March 2023).

Baudrillard, Jean. 1994. *Simulacra and Simulation* (trans. Sheila Faria Glaser). Ann Arbor: University of Michigan Press.

Benjamin, Walter. 2019. 'The work of art in the age of mechanical reproduction', in *Illuminations: Essays and reflections* (ed. Hannah Arendt, trans. Harry Zohn), 166–95. Boston, MA: Mariner Books.

Bernstein, Rachel (host). 2022. 'The tyrant behind the mask 'w/Sarah Landry'. *Indoctri Nation* podcast, 14 December. https://soundcloud.com/indoctrinationshow/the-tyrant-behind-the-mask-wsarah-landry.

Bowler, Kate. 2013. *Blessed: A history of the American prosperity gospel*. New York: Oxford University Press.

Conway, Maura, Ryan Scrivens and Logan Macnair. 2019. 'Right-wing extremists' persistent online presence: History and contemporary trends.' International Centre for Counter-terrorism Policy Brief, 1–24. https://doi.org/10.19165/2019.3.12.

Copeman, Jacob and Aya Ikegame. 2012. 'The multifarious guru: An introduction', in *The Guru in South Asia: New interdisciplinary perspectives*, edited by Jacob Copeman and Aya Ikegame, 1–45. Abingdon: Routledge.

Crockford, Susannah. 2021. *Ripples of the Universe: Spirituality in Sedona, Arizona*. Chicago, IL: University of Chicago Press.

Dawson, Lorne L. 2006. 'Psychopathologies and the attribution of charisma: A critical introduction to the psychology of charisma and the explanation of violence in new religious movements', *Nova Religio* 10 (2) (November): 3–28. https://doi.org/10.1525/nr.2006.10.2.3.

Deleuze, Gilles and Félix Guattari. 1987. *A Thousand Plateaus: Capitalism and schizophrenia* (trans. Brian Massumi). Minneapolis: University of Minnesota Press.

Derrida, Jacques. 1997. *Of Grammatology* (trans. Gayatri Chakravorty Spivak). Baltimore, MD: Johns Hopkins University Press.

E-Narada. 2013. 'Nithyananda Ashram won a case in United States District Court', 15 January. https://enarada.com/nithyananda-ashram-have-won-a-case-in-united-states-district-court (accessed 2 March 2023).

Express Web Desk. 2020. 'Fugitive godman Nithyananda announces visa, flights to his "country" Kailasa from Australia', *Indian Express*, 19 December. https://indianexpress.com/article/india/nithyananda-kailasa-visa-flight-7109833/ (accessed 2 March 2023).

Facebook. 2022a. 'Parashakti Akasihc [*sic*] Reading', KAILASA's SPH JGM Nithyananda Paramashivam.' Live video. https://www.facebook.com/search/top?q=kailasa%27s%20sph%20jgm%20nithyananda%20paramashivam (accessed 8 January 2022).

Facebook. 2022b. 'Materialisation.' Live video. KAILASA's Courtyard Manifesting Powers. https://m.facebook.com/story.php?story_fbid=4996821550382607&id=2426025547462 233&m_entstream_source=timeline (accessed 8 February 2022). Duplicated at YouTube 2022, 'Power to Manifest Gold Flecks | POWER MANIFESTATION THROUGH THIRD EYE'. https://youtu.be/auvIP-lH7Bw, 8 February 2022.

Facebook. 2022c. 'Shri Guru Gita #21: The Song of the Absolute, as revealed by Paramashiva to Devi Parvati.' Live video. Kailasa Singapore Aadheenam, 9 February. https://www.facebook.com/SingaporeNithyanandaSangha/videos/4945076598878550 (accessed 2 March 2023).

Gretter, Sarah, Aman Yadav and Benjamin W. Gleason. 2017. 'Walking the line between reality and fiction in online spaces: Understanding the effects of narrative transportation', *Journal of Media Literacy Education* 9 (1): 1–21. https://doi.org/10.23860/JMLE-2017-9-1-2.

Hanegraaff, Wouter. J. 1998. *New Age Religion and Western Culture: Esotericism in the mirror of secular thought*. Albany, NY: SUNY Press.

Hassan, Steven. 1988. *Combatting Cult Mind Control*. Rochester, VT: Park Street Press.

Hindu, The. 2012. 'Nithyananda cites U.S. experts to claim videotape is fake', 16 March. https://www.thehindu.com/news/national/tamil-nadu/nithyananda-cites-us-experts-to-claim-videotape-is-fake/article2999685.ece (accessed 6 November 2021).

Hopwood, William, Carl Pacini and George Young. 2014. 'Fighting discovery abuse in litigation', *Journal of Forensic & Investigative Accounting* 6 (2) (July–December): 52–80.

Jain, Andrea R. 2020. *Peace, Love, Yoga: The politics of global spirituality.* New York: Oxford University Press.

Kailasa's Hinduism Now! 2017. 'Nithyananda Gurukul: Mindblowing mystic school in southern India.' https://hinduismnow.org/blog/2017/01/16/nithyananda-gurukul-mindblowing-mystic-school-southern-india (accessed 2 March 2023).

Karapanagiotis, Nicole. 2021. *Branding Bhakti: Krishna consciousness and the makeover of a movement.* Bloomington: Indiana University Press.

Karthikeyan, Suchitra. 2019. 'ACCESSED: Nithyananda's slanderous 742-page anti-India report to United Nations', *RepublicWorld.Com*, 13 December. https://www.republicworld.com/india-news/general-news/accessed-nithyanandas-slanderous-742-page-anti-india-report.html (accessed 2 March 2023).

Kumar, Ankit. 2020. 'Exclusive: Behind Nithyananda's Kailaasa empire, a hidden maze of companies and NGOs', *India Today*, 22 August. https://www.indiatoday.in/india/story/exclusive-behind-nithyananda-kailaasa-empire-hidden-maze-of-companies-and-ngos-1713691-2020-08-21 (accessed 2 March 2023).

Lucia, Amanda. 2020. *White Utopias: The religious exoticism of transformational festivals.* Oakland: University of California Press.

Lucia, Amanda. 2022. 'The contemporary guru field', *Religion Compass* 16 (2): art. no. e12427, 1–15. https://doi.org/10.1111/rec3.12427.

McQuire, Scott. 2017. 'Media theory 2017', *Media Theory*, 1 (1) (October): 34–42. http://journalcontent.mediatheoryjournal.org/index.php/mt/article/view/15 (accessed 22 March 2023).

Menczer, Filippo and Thomas Hills. 2020. 'The attention economy', *Scientific American* 323 (6): 54–61.

Modern Nirvana. n.d. 'Who we are.' https://www.modernnirvana.com/who-we-are (accessed 2 March 2023).

Moodie, Deonnie. 2020. 'Corporate Hinduism: An argument for attention to sites of authority in a nascent field of research', *Religion Compass* 15 (2): art. no. e12387, 1–9. https://doi.org/10.1111/rec3.12387.

News 18. 2020. 'Rape-accused Nithyananda unveils currency of "Reserve Bank of Kailasa" on Ganesh Chaturthi', *News 18*, 22 August. https://www.news18.com/news/india/rape-accused-nithyananda-unveils-currency-of-reserve-bank-of-kailasa-on-ganesh-chaturthi-2810619.html (accessed 6 February 2022).

Nithyananda. n.d. *Hindu Holocaust, the Untold Story: 10 years of organized, systematic persecution on his Divine Holiness Paramahamsa Nithyananda.* Available on Scribd. Uploaded by ankit (13 December 2019). https://www.scribd.com/document/439639383/Persecution-of-His-Divine-Holiness-Paramahamsa-Nithyananda-Grand-Narrative-The-Hindu-Holocaust#from_embed (accessed 2 March 2023).

Nithyananda. 2008. *Living Enlightenment (Gospel of Paramahamsa Nithyananda).* Montclair, CA: Life Bliss Foundation.

Nithyananda. 2014. 'Nithyananda Diary 2nd March 2014.' https://www.nithyananda.org/photo-gallery/nithyananda-diary-2nd-march-2014-anti-spiritual-elements-suicide-day-padukapuja-nithya#gsc.tab=0 (accessed 10 February 2022).

Nithyananda. 2018. 'Special Report to the United Nations Office of the High Commissioner for Human Rights: Persecution of Adi Shaivite Minority Tradition in India.' 18 September. Available on Scribd. Uploaded by ankit. https://www.scribd.com/document/439639234/UN-Special-Report-on-ASMT-Persecution (accessed 3 March 2023).

Nithyananda University. 2022. https://nithyanandahinduuniversity.org (accessed 3 March 2023).

Nithyanandapedia. 2022. 'Akashic readings on death.' https://nithyanandapedia.org/wiki/Akashic_Readings_on_Death (accessed 3 March 2023).

Nussbaum, Rob. 2018. 'International service of process through social media', *Trending Law Blog*, 1 March. https://trendinglawblog.com/category/service-of-process (accessed 3 March 2023).

Oelbaum, Jed. 2020. 'She built a shady guru's YouTube army. Now she's his fiercest critic – but who will believe her?' *Gizmodo*, 17 June. https://gizmodo.com/she-built-a-shady-guru-s-youtube-army-now-she-s-his-fi-1843283794 (accessed 3 March 2023).

Owen, Laura Hazard. 2020. 'Older people and Republicans are most likely to share Covid-19 stories from fake news sites on Twitter', *NiemanLab*, 26 October. https://www.niemanlab.org/2020/10/older-people-and-republicans-are-most-likely-to-share-covid-19-stories-from-fake-news-sites-on-twitter (accessed 3 March 2023).

PTI. 2011. 'Nithyananda files criminal complaint against Sun TV COO Hansraj Saxena', *The Economic Times*, 13 July. https://economictimes.indiatimes.com/news/politics-and-nation/nithyananda-files-criminal-complaint-against-sun-tv-coo-hansraj-saxena/articleshow/9211757.cms (accessed 3 March 2023).

Qiu, Xiaoyan, Diego F. M. Oliveira, Alireza Sahami Shirazi, Alessandro Flammini and Filippo Menczer. 2017. 'Limited individual attention and online virality of low-quality information', *Nature Human Behaviour* 1 (7): art. no. 0132. https://doi.org/10.1038/s41562-017-0132.

Radha-Udayakumar, Ganesh. 2018. 'Swami Nithyananda: I can make cows speak in Tamil and Sanskrit', *India Today*, 19 September. https://www.indiatoday.in/india/story/swami-nithyananda-says-can-make-cows-speak-tamil-1343545-2018-09-19 (accessed 3 March 2023).

Rajit, Khaidem. 2017. 'India's top-notch 5 richest saint and guru', *KHBuzz*, 1 October. https://www.khbuzz.com/2017/10/01/indias-top-notch-5-richest-saint-guru/ (accessed 3 March 2023).

Republic TV Investigation. 2019. 'Former disciple Sarah Landry exposes the atrocities children faced at Nithyananda's ashram', 21 November. https://youtu.be/bviQh4twgIQ (accessed 30 January 2022).

Reynolds, Matt. 2013. 'Big trouble at the ashram', *Courthouse News Service*, 6 March. https://www.courthousenews.com/big-trouble-at-the-ashram/ (accessed 3 March 2023).

Rudert, Angela. 2017. *Shakti's New Voice: Guru devotion in a woman-led spiritual movement*. Lanham, MD: Lexington Books.

Saraiya, Naman (dir.). 2022. *My Daughter Joined a Cult*. Available on Discovery Plus and Amazon.com.

Srikailasa. n.d.a. 'Kailasa'. https://gov.shrikailasa.org (accessed 3 March 2023).

Srikailasa. n.d.b. 'E-Kailasa'. https://gov.shrikailasa.org/ekailasa (accessed 3 March 2023).

Srikailasa. n.d.c. 'Persecution of Hinduism'. https://gov.shrikailasa.org/persecution (accessed 18 May 2023).

Srikailasa. n.d.d. 'Vision & mission'. https://kailaasa.org/about/vision-mission/ (accessed 18 May 2023).

Srinivas, Smriti. 2008. *In the Presence of Sai Baba: Body, city, and memory in a global religious movement*. Leiden: Brill.

Srinivas, Tulasi. 2018. *The Cow in the Elevator: An anthropology of wonder*. Durham, NC: Duke University Press.

Urban, Hugh B. 2011. *The Church of Scientology: A history of a new religion*. Princeton, NJ: Princeton University Press.

Venkatraman, Shriram. 2017. *Social Media in South India*. London: UCL Press.

Voice of India. 2013. '"Mahamandaleshwar" Nithyananda skips Kumbh bath, will be stripped of bought title – Deccan Herald', 17 February. https://bharatabharati.in/2013/02/17/mahamandaleshwar-nithyananda-skips-kumbh-bath-will-be-stripped-of-bought-title-deccan-herald (accessed 3 March 2023).

Walton, Jonathan L. 2014. 'Prosperity gospel and African American theology', in *The Oxford Handbook of African American Theology*, edited by Anthony B. Pinn and Katie G. Cannon, 453–67. New York: Oxford University Press. https://doi.org/10.1093/oxfordhb/9780199755653.013.0032.

Ward, Bob. 2018. 'President Trump's fake news about climate change'. Grantham Research Institute on Climate Change and the Environment, London School of Economics and Political Science. 30 January. https://www.lse.ac.uk/granthaminstitute/news/president-trump-fake-news-climate-change (accessed 3 March 2023).

Williams, Heather J., Alexandra T. Evans, Jamie Ryan, Erik E. Mueller and Bryce Downing. 2021. 'Understanding the virtual extremist ecosystem', in *The Online Extremist System: Its evolution and a framework for separating extreme from mainstream*, 4–13. Santa Monica, CA: RAND Corporation.

Wong, Julia Carrie. 2020. 'Down the rabbit hole: How QAnon conspiracies thrive on Facebook', *The Guardian*, 11 February. https://www.theguardian.com/technology/2020/jun/25/qanon-facebook-conspiracy-theories-algorithm (accessed 3 March 2023).

Yadav, Umesh R. 2019. 'Nithyananda has skipped trials, not seen in ashram', *Deccan Herald*, 23 November. https://www.deccanherald.com/state/top-karnataka-stories/nithyananda-has-skipped-trials-not-seen-in-ashram-778993.html (accessed 7 January 2022).

Yoga Shaktis. n.d. 'Akashic readings and the spiritual power to go beyond time'. https://yogashaktis.innerawakening.org/akashic-readings-spiritual-power-go-beyond-time/ (accessed 4 April 2023).

YouTube. 2010. 'Inner Awakening – a 21 day transformational meditation workshop with Nithyananda', 21 January. https://youtu.be/XDq64gzwbYI (accessed 3 March 2023).

YouTube. 2015.'Girl demonstrates cool superpower (third eye)', 30 July. https://youtu.be/ZtLkzg8bFgA (accessed 3 March 2023).

YouTube. 2017. 'I'm the girl who demonstrates a cool superpower, third eye! Now learn how …', 28 June. https://youtu.be/n9VKilkYoTom (accessed 3 March 2023).

YouTube. 2019a. Sarah Stephanie Landry, 'Brainwashed by Nithyananda; Now I'm speaking out about his DANGEROUS CULT!', 16 September. https://youtu.be/XsnxFh1orY4 accessed 3 March 2023)..

YouTube. 2019b. Kailasa's Blissful Athlete, 'How to overcome laziness + be disciplined | LIVE Q&A!', 13 July. https://youtu.be/-ieIhJWBkoY (accessed 3 March 2023).

YouTube. 2021. 'Celebrating the life of Braham Aggarwal', 24 January. https://youtu.be/ppAnbKOzqLQ (accessed 3 March 2023).

YouTube. 2022. 'Kailasa's Blissful Athlete, "About"'. https://www.youtube.com/c/Blissful Athlete/about (accessed 3 March 2023).

9
When God dies: multi-mediation, the elsewhere and crypto-futurity in a global guru movement

Tulasi Srinivas

The end is the beginning

It was not the end that Shri Sathya Sai Baba, global guru and spiritual leader of several million followers, had envisaged for himself. He had repeatedly prophesied that he would 'leave his body' at the ripe old age of 96 and remain healthy until then (Babb 1986). But on 24 April 2011, Easter Sunday morning, the BBC reported, at the top of the news hour, that Sathya Sai Baba had died at 7.40 a.m. in the super-specialty hospital named after him in his home town of Puttaparthi, in rural south India, at the age of 84. The news flashed through his network of followers spread across the globe,[1] carried as banner headlines by his own media empire of Sai Television and Sai Radio, and through to other Indian and global news organisations.

This was the beginning of a media crush in Puttaparthi, as national and international television crews and newspaper reporters rushed to this small provincial town in south India to cover the story of the guru's illness and death. As journalist Adnan Adibi of Reuters noted, mourners were allowed to 'pay their last respects' to a 'man revered as a living god', following which the funeral and interment took place at the Sai ashram.[2]

As hundreds of thousands of mourners made their way to the ashram, Sai Baba's body was placed in an air-conditioned crystal coffin, ordered at great expense by the Sai Trust from the nearby city of Bangalore, to cool the guru's body in the searing heat of the south Indian plains. Indian television stations broadcast (in real time) footage of the endless queues of mourners, filing in to view Sai Baba as he lay in state, with a military guard surrounding the coffin. A rolling chyron at the foot of the television screen reminded viewers that local officials had extended the viewing time of Sai Baba's body by two days to accommodate the endless influx of devotees. Some news reports estimated the number of mourners who overran this small town to be over a million people.

Following two days of state mourning, the body of Sai Baba was handed over to a phalanx of orange-robed priests and white-uniformed Sai officials for Hindu religious funeral services that were broadcast live through the day. Television coverage focused on the plural nature of Sai devotion, showing powerful images of Tibetan monks, Muslim clerics, top politicians including the President of India, military officers, business tycoons and Bollywood stars who sat with family and Sai Trust members to commemorate the charismatic guru.

As Sai Baba's body was sprinkled with water from the sacred river Ganges, and hymns and mantras to speed the soul on its way were chanted, the body was lowered into a deep crypt under the Sai Kulwant darshan hall. The mourners threw perfumed ash into the crypt before it was sealed tight, as a 21-gun salute boomed over the town.

In the following pages I interrogate the events around Sai Baba's death, funeral and entombment as an example of a 'didactic death' (Copeman and Reddy 2012), whereby 'much is to be learned' from one individual's act of dying.[3] Sai Baba's illness, death, funeral and subsequent burial in a crypt created a new instructional idiom of godly dying that requires different epistemological and ontological framing if we are to understand the timeless and mediated relationship between the living and the dead.

Having conducted substantial ethnographic research on the Sathya Sai Baba Movement over nine years in six countries while Sai Baba was still alive (Srinivas 2010), here I rethink tropes of Hindu sacred personhood (Gold 1987) in terms of the 'afterlife' of a guru figure (McLain 2016) and the endurance of a religious movement (Lambek 2013).[4]

Building upon the idea that death is an instructional act, in which 'a kind of moral drama' unfolds (Copeman and Reddy 2012), I argue that Sathya Sai Baba's death was *a multi-mediated event,* by which I mean not only that it was relayed on different platforms to his devotees across the world, but also that it mediated different temporal, geographical and affective worlds (Copeman and Reddy 2012). Sai Baba's death was itself a medium between different temporalities, of human life and immediate concerns, and the eternal life of the guru; the funeral was a venue for *mediatisation,* by which I mean its expansion through various media channels including television, photographs, the internet, newspapers and other media broadcasts, and for *disintermediation*, by which I mean a reduction in the intermediaries required to gain access to the guru (Copeman and Ikegame 2012a; Copeman and Quack 2015, 51–2).

Sai Baba's death and encryption, by which I mean literally the putting of his body into a crypt as well as putting text into a cipher, has the power of many meanings as well as the volatile movement of internal complexity, and that they build, in sometimes surprising ways, on the earlier foundations of our understandings of death in India, with its inherited modes of classifying the world and its typical understandings of human identity and religious experience.

As Sai Baba's body was lowered into the crypt, three different yet interdigitised religious processes unfolded: first, the encrypting of Sai Baba's body converted what I have termed his 'nomadic charisma' (Srinivas 2010) into the geographical sacredness of the samadhi or mausoleum (Bayly 1989);[5] second, this encryption gestures towards a cosmological Elsewhere which allows Sai devotees to continue to venerate the guru through haptic logics (Lucia 2018) regardless of his embodied state;[6] and third, the crypt and mausoleum rendered Sai Baba eternally present (Taneja 2012), creating a crypto-futurity which allows it to endure, by which I mean a future that relies on the hidden to propel it forward. I suggest that the ontological primacy of the Elsewhere is also inextricably connected not just to the past, as Anand Taneja argued in his brilliant study of Muslim saints' dargahs (tombs) in Delhi (2012), but also to the future, to the extended life of the Sai movement in a post-Sai Baba era.

In Sai Baba's case, his death and encryption foreshadow this crypto-futurity, in which a future life for the movement is based on this secreting of the body and the affects it exudes into space.[7] I draw on Yael Navaro-Yashin's concept of 'affective space' (2012, 173) that conceives of bodies and things through the energies they 'exude to their environment'. The devotees' veneration of Sai Baba at and through his samadhi, I argue, hinges upon the magical character of his body which 'gives presence' (Böhme 1993, 119) to its material surroundings, which devotees travel to Puttaparthi to see and to touch, which they feel and dream about, a reality that is hidden, yet everyday.

Indeed, Sai's encryption, which evolves over time into a samadhi,[8] offers a space for Sai Baba to remain both alive and not-alive, hidden and yet present for eternity, and emergent in a future time (Ssorin-Chaikov 2006). It represents what Amira Mittermaier terms the 'imaginal Elsewhere', a cosmological time–space bridge between the material and the spiritual that allows Sai Baba to remain ever alive and agentive, yet removed from his body (Mittermaier 2011, 4), thereby giving devotees an eternal space, and a different medium, for connection to the supposed divinity of Sai Baba.

Fever archives: a god's death in an age of global media

On 28 March 2010, Sathya Sai Baba was admitted to the eponymous hospital in Puttaparthi with 'breathing difficulties'. The *Times of India* noted: 'Doctors said he was suffering from pneumonia and water has entered his lungs.' They also stated that J. Ratnakar, a member of Sai Baba's family, who was also a member of the influential Sai Trust, reassured devotees that Sai Baba was being treated and was 'recovering'.[9] But the news magazine *India Today*,[10] known as 'India's *Time* magazine', reported a week after Sai Baba was admitted to the hospital that he was on a ventilator and kidney dialysis support after enduring the installation of a pacemaker. By the evening of the same day the news of Sai Baba's illness had travelled via the grapevine and concerned devotees started to gather in a small group near the entrance to the hospital. Every day this anxious group of devotees grew, and soon a large crowd was gathered near the gates of the hospital.

NDTV, a popular television satellite channel, covered Sai Baba's worsening health and the lingering crowd of devotees. Their narration stated, 'Hundreds of concerned devotees have been thronging the gates of the hospital ever since [Sai Baba's admssion], forcing the administration to enforce prohibitory orders to keep the crowds at bay.'[11] Reportage, both television and newsprint, initially focused on the mood of the crowd of devotees gathered at the gates. They reported that the state administration sent police troops to control the crowds for fear of widespread civil unrest as the news circled the globe via various media channels.

But then rumours began to circulate among devotees in Puttaparthi and around the world, via the internet and social media, that he was lying in the hospital and not being cared for properly. Devotees were anxious. Conspiracy theories broke out that Sai Baba had died several weeks earlier and the fact was being hidden from the public while Sai officials battled over the matter of the succession and inheritance of his US$9-billion spiritual empire. A few concerned devotees broke into the hospital trying to locate Sai Baba, and even entered a ward before they were caught and returned to the crowd at the gates.

Newspapers and TV stations worldwide carried coverage of Sai Baba's illness. Shailaja Bajpai, a journalist with the *Indian Express* group of newspapers, stated that coverage of the medical bulletins every day was seen as 'breaking news'.[12] She added, 'The TV reporters were left standing outside the hospital or the Sathya Sai Baba Trust premises, trying to play the interpreters of maladies or biographers of his ailments.' But the crowd outside the hospital grew restive. Riot police were despatched.[13] They pitched a large tent outside the hospital and kept a round-the-clock guard.

To combat the rumours circulating among devotees, the medical director of the hospital, Dr N. Safaya, took to giving daily bulletins about Sai Baba's health, which the press reported. NDTV stated that a minister of the Andhra Pradesh government and a devotee, Gita Reddy, had visited Sai Baba. 'I have seen Baba myself and I have seen that there is a lot of improvement. He responds if you tell him something, he is blinking, but because of the ventilator, he can't speak. He gives signs that he does understand', Reddy said in an interview to the press.[14]

Between 8 and 20 April Dr N. Safaya's bulletins grew increasingly obscure and terse, with the use of more medical jargon seemingly indicating Sai Baba's worsening health. On 21 April Safaya's bulletin described Sai Baba as 'very critical', and, accordingly, stories about Sathya Sai Baba's health being 'critical' figured in the national news channels and Web portals of newspapers. But despite the grave reports, alternative news stories focused on the expectation of the devotees that the god-man would recover, since he had predicted that he would live until he was 96 years old.

On 24 April 2011, the tone of the morning news on television grew dire, signalling that Sai Baba had died, though that word was never used. NDTV 24x7 reported (in a 3:44-minute segment in the morning news) that the usual health bulletin had not been issued that morning, and 'something' had happened the previous day, though there still was no 'official confirmation'. Security had been enhanced in Puttaparthi, and the roads leading to the hospital where Sai Baba was admitted had been blocked by police.

Later the same day, the hospital announced his death.

The *Times of India* marked the occasion by printing a photo of the police beating Sai devotees with batons at the entrance to the hospital as they stormed the gates, desperate for a glimpse of their god.[15]

An enigmatic god

NDTV 24x7 broadcast a total of 17 stories on Sai Baba on the day of his death, setting the stage for the post-Sai era (Mohammad 2010). Apart from tributes and condolences from various well-known names in politics, cinema, sports and religion, the stories highlighted his philanthropy as a guru and god-man. NDTV also broadcast two special obituaries in the evening, a 16-minute story on 'The early years of Sathya Sai Baba', and a 21-minute story titled 'The man who touched all'. Yet despite all their attempts to trace and illuminate his miraculous life, Sai Baba, like many other gurus and god-men, remained an enigma.

Sathya Sai Baba, born a peasant boy named Sathyanarayana Raju in 1926 in the village of Puttaparthi in rural south India, rose to prominence when he declared his divinity at the age of 14: '"I am Sai, I belong to Apasthamba Suthra [a Brahma Sutra], I am of the Bharadwaja Gothra [lineal descent from the Hindu sage Bharadwaja]; I am Sai Baba; I have come to ward off all your troubles; and to keep your houses clean and pure"' (Kasturi 1962, 39); thus he claimed affiliation with the revered Sufi fakir (holy man) Shirdi Sai Baba, who died in 1918.[16] With that pronouncement he created an enduring subcontinental, syncretic religious tradition classified by some scholars as 'neo-Hindu' (Palmer 2005).

Sai Baba is believed to be *Bhagawan* (God) by his devotees, and is referred to by this name or simply as Swami (the Lord). He is thought by some to be a charismatic guru (teacher) and by others to be a seer, a saint, a fakir (Muslim holy man), or, as many believe, an avatar (incarnation) of the Hindu god Shiva (Srinivas 2010, 55–70).

In 1950 he built the Sai ashram at Puttaparthi, which heralded the start of the transformation of the village into a Sai Baba wonderland spread over some 10 square miles (26 square kilometres), a vast complex of dormitories, libraries, hotels, resorts, university buildings, museums, hospitals, an airport and shops, all thronging with devotees. Sai Baba's huge global popularity may be explained by his non-dogmatic, non-doctrinal approach to religion and his claim that the only religion he believed in was 'love'. Devotees came from around the world to meet him, claiming that Sai Baba had visited them in a dream or had serendipitously summoned them to Puttaparthi.

The central act of devotion during Sai Baba's life was darshan (viewing or witnessing God), in which most devotees attempted to touch and speak with him, to petition him and, often, to be healed. In addition, his mystical ability to manifest *vibhuti* (holy ash), food, jewellery and watches out of thin air was often cited as further proof of his divinity, akin to the 'miracles' ascribed to past prophets (Morgan 2010). For decades, various scientists, rationalists and magicians had attempted to debunk the guru and his 'doubtful illusions', which they claimed were 'mere magic' (Srinivas 2017). In the mid-1970s, the Indian magician P. C. Sorcar duplicated one of Sathya Sai Baba's signature miracles: conjuring things out of thin air, from sacred ash to Swiss watches. '"His magical tricks never impressed me. They were not of high quality," Sorcar told *TIME* [magazine].'[17] But devotees claimed that the form of Sai Baba that they saw during darshan veiled his 'true' and eternal divinity (Srinivas 2010, 210). Ideally, devotees wished for a 'private darshan' where they could interact closely with him face to face and one to one to resolve their difficulties and get his blessings.

The Sai movement grew nationally and then internationally during his lifetime. Estimates of the total number of Sai Baba devotees around the world vary between 10 and a self-reported 50 million, though in 2002 the news magazine *India Today* estimated their strength at 20 million in 137 countries and their net worth at approximately US$6 billion.[18] Unlike other transnational, charismatic, civil religious movements emerging out of India, the Sai following is not confined to the Indian diaspora (Babb 1986) but has expanded to include the cosmopolitan and professional middle classes of many different countries and cultures. He was what Weiss aptly calls 'a prophet of the jet-set more than … a guru of peasants' (2005, 7).

In the 1970s Sathya Sai Baba began to take on the role of philanthropist, transforming the small ashram in his home town of Puttaparthi into a multimillion-dollar complex for the public good. His charitable trust ran schools, hospitals, colleges, stadia and a planetarium, and created a piped drinking-water project serving more than 750 villages in the surrounding areas. These humanitarian projects attracted donations from around the world, most notably a US$108 million gift from Isaac Tigrett, the founder of Hard Rock Cafe. The huge sums of money added another veil of power and mystery to Sai Baba and his movement.

A damning rumour that swirled around Sai Baba in the early 1970s, and grew into a whisper campaign, was accusations of sexual harassment and assault of young male devotees. Though the ideal-typical guru is an asexual being, Sai Baba was repeatedly accused of paedophilia and sexual harassment (Srinivas 2010). But the accusations were always dismissed out of hand by the tightly controlled Sai Baba organisation.

The rumours came to a head in 1993 with the gruesome killing of four young men who had broken into his secure quarters, supposedly with the intent of doing him harm; they were shot dead by the police. By the early 1990s, several former devotees in Europe and Australia had archived the various allegations, and then they sought to have Sai Baba investigated. In the early 2000s a young man named Alaya Rahm, a former devotee, lodged a sexual harassment case against the Sai Baba Organization in Orange County, California. Rahm claimed Sai Baba had assaulted him, but the case was negotiated in an out-of-court settlement. Finally, in 2004, the BBC produced a film titled 'The Secret Swami' that contained input from former devotees, which detailed several allegations against him, causing scandal at the ashram. The accusations built to a crescendo. And yet, as Norris Palmer writes, the guru's 'divinity is maintained ... by the very fact that he transgresses our ideas of what is or should be holy. ... [T]he greater the transgression, the more certain his divinity' (Palmer 2005, 118).

By the time Sai Baba was admitted to hospital in 2011, the accusations had dissipated into the ether. Sai Baba's reputation as a living god on earth remained intact.

A televised funeral for a living god

On 27 April 2011, all the national news channels – both English and Hindi – and many of the regional ones as well, particularly those from the south, broadcast live the funeral of Sathya Sai Baba. Satellite news channels, including Star News, Aaj Tak, India TV, NDTV India, NDTV 24x7, DD News, IBN7, CNN-IBN, News 24, ETV Jharkhand, Total TV, India News, Live India, Times Now and Headlines Today, carried live footage of the event.

The daily news was relegated to the scrolling chyron at the bottom of the television screen, as the funeral was broadcast not just in the country but across the globe, particularly to those 160-odd countries where Sathya Sai Centres exist, transforming the broadcast into nothing less than what Dayan and Katz (1992, quoted in Das 2015, 84) would call a 'historic media event'; these are broadcast events that have become world rituals with the potential to transform societies even as they transfix viewers around the globe.

The reporter's narration drew the audience's attention repeatedly to the body of Sathya Sai Baba lying inside the glass coffin. Intermediate shots of devotees singing devotional songs in the Kulwant Darshan hall, now a funeral stage, were the background to the reporters' narration, which focused on the growth of the Sai movement and centres since the 1950s.

The underlying theme of the broadcast was of the high-profile death of a 'god on earth', as the NDTV reporter Maya Sharma stated. Reporters repeatedly mentioned the hagiography of Sathya Sai Baba as a reincarnation of the nineteenth-century saint Sai Baba of Shirdi, and the former's declaration that he would soon be reborn in the Mandya district of neighbouring Karnataka. Maya Sharna said: "'This belief is held by many devotees we spoke to here. Sathya Sai Baba will be back. [...] While there were tears, sorrow among people, some spoke of faith being renewed'" (quoted in Das 2015, 97).

Though Shailaja Bajpai spoke of the muted nature of the television coverage, both NDTV and the BBC showed crowds of devotees rocked by waves of grief, wailing, crying, sobbing and looking dazed while waiting to see their 'Swami' in the flower-adorned crystal coffin. As the Associated Press reported, 'Women selling marigold garlands broke down in tears outside the ashram, while devotees began flocking to the temple complex where the guru's body will lie through Tuesday' (Quraishi 2011). Shailaja Bajpai of NDTV said that such instances of devotees mourning their loss were the 'most moving moments' and that 'when the Hindi news channels found devotees who spoke of their devotion and what Sathya Sai Baba meant to them, these were seen as authentic and powerful' (Das 2015).

The spectacular nature of the funeral as media event was unignorable. Besides focusing upon the pomp and splendour of the event – the flowers, banners, marching bands, the phalanx of priests and crowds of mourners – the coverage zoomed in on elite politicians and celebrities on the stage. Bajpai noted that sports star Sachin Tendulkar, a world-renowned cricketer, was 'stalked' by cameras. Tendulkar's weeping, with his wife Anjali solicitously watching him and offering him a handkerchief, transfixed news channels, especially national Hindi news channels, and these images were played on a loop over and over again, making the funeral seem immediate and personal.

Devotees all over the world watched the television footage mesmerised. I watched with a group of devotees in Boston, MA. The devotees wore white (the Hindu colour of mourning) and stood with hands folded in front of their televisions or computers as Sai Baba's body in the crystal coffin was driven into the hall and arranged on the dais. The coffin, draped in the Indian tricolour flag, and surrounded by a military guard of honour, was greeted with veneration. Devotees whom I interviewed years later commented that they remembered the gigantic photographic banner of Sai Baba, with hands raised in blessing on the right side of the coffin, as being 'so lifelike' and 'beautiful!'

Devotees said they 'felt close' to Sai Baba and his embodied power and 'were glad to be at Puttaparthi'. In San Diego, Shiksha, a young woman devotee, stayed up all night to watch the funeral. She had been glued to Indian television and her computer for a month, watching all the available streaming footage of Sai Baba's hospitalisation. She said meditatively:

> Every time we saw some news story around Swami, we were better prepared for the eventuality. Imagine if suddenly we had to hear the news! With this coverage I could actually see Bhagawan's (god's) face up close. It was like he was sleeping.

Shiksha said watching the funeral helped her family and friends, all of whom were devotees of Sai Baba, to come to terms with Sai Baba's mortal end.

Another devotee, Sai Ram, who watched the footage with his family in Delhi, bowed in veneration to the images of Sai Baba on screen. He told me, 'It was like we were there! We heard the news and my wife said, let us go to Puttaparthi, but where to get tickets for a train or plane? All sold out! We couldn't go, but thanks to all the coverage it was like we all were there to see Swami (the lord).' His wife added, 'They did all the last rites. My mother-in-law said they did it all perfectly. When they prayed, we also prayed at home. We kept our photo of Baba nearby and garlanded it and all.' The wall-to-wall television coverage of the funeral transported anxious devotees to Puttaparthi and allowed them a front-row seat at the moral drama of Sai Baba's death (see Das 2015, 99 for a description of how one family watched the funeral).

But the funeral also rendered time out of joint. The mediatisation of the funeral events made them immediate and immediately present for globally dispersed devotees. William Mazzarella speaks of 'a politics of immediation' in which mediation is 'the ambiguous foundation of all social life' and its practices 'are formalized as mechanisms, externalized as technologies, and naturalized as social orders' (Mazzarella 2006, 476). Here the funeral as media event was the beginning of an encryption process opening a pattern of materialising in an archive that was once living action.

'The visuals and narration around the state honours, such as the 21-gun salute, the draping of the body in the national flag by the police personnel, and the presence of national political leaders, cutting across party lines, were all symbols and imageries that transformed the event into a national mourning' (Das 2015, 96). Greg, a devotee from Boston, said, 'It's good that the government is recognising Bhagawan's importance to the world.'

Sai devotees, watching the footage of Sai Baba's death and documentaries of his life nearly constantly for a week, were drawn into these mediated politics of death where time was twisted into a media loop.

Bhashyam, a middle-aged Sai devotee, the director of a small widget-making company in Mumbai, and his wife Krithika, watched the funeral together. They prayed to Baba and cried at their loss. They touched the television in veneration when the coverage showed Sai Baba's body, particularly his feet, performing *pada namaskaram* (the veneration of the feet). They bowed down with hands folded as the cannons boomed and the priests chanted. Bhashyam said:

> I watched the television for all the days they showed Bhagawan. Fully! So nice he looked. As though he was just sleeping. Every day I watched! The whole week. I have a small television in the office so there also I watched. I told my boys at work also and they used to come on lunch break and all and watch. For three days I did not even look at the account books!

Krithika concurred, saying, 'We spent all the time simply watching!' Like Bhashyam and Krithika, Sai devotees spent the entire week in front of the television watching Sai Baba's body and the activities in the ashram. As a result they felt they had been to the funeral, and spoke about it with expert knowledge: who the celebrities attending were, where the military stood, how the crystal coffin arrived at the Hall, how the ritual of the funeral was performed, the flowers, the banners, and so on.

Ten years later Bhashyam told me that he took the trouble that day to record the funeral coverage onto a VCR, which he hangs on to despite changes in technology that do not allow him to play the videotape any more. He showed it to me as a relic of an earlier era, saying, 'Now everything is always available on the internet! How many times Krithika and I watched this tape. But now we have signed up for the live feed to the samadhi and so when we pray in the morning we just watch the live feed!'

But during that month in 2011 Sai Baba's illness, funeral and encryption broke into devotees' everyday routines for several weeks through the broadcast on television with wall-to-wall coverage. This was a Derridean 'time out of joint' (1994).

In *Specters of Marx*, Derrida, in the name of what he terms 'hauntology', establishes a series of concerns around the spectral that are foundational to our inquiry here: a respect for the *revenant* that complicates a metaphysics of presence through a spectral figure that is neither present nor absent, dead nor alive, but nonetheless powerful; and the temporality of the hauntology is the *contretemps* of a 'time out of joint'. The television coverage of the funeral allowed this endless looping of time, of a time out of joint, an intermingling of past and present, of death and life.

The encryption of Sai Baba

Just before the final rites were to start and the lid of the crystal coffin was to be removed to place Sai Baba's body in the crypt, the NDTV reporter Maya Sharma emphasised the sense of overwhelming loss that devotees felt:

> We have *lakhs* of devotees in Puttaparthi. A very sorrow[ful] moment .... But not just sorrow, but also peace. [...] Many devotees, we talked to, telling us that Sathya Sai Baba will be with them always. In fact, Sathya Sai Baba himself said that he will be reincarnated in Mandya District of Karnataka within a few years['] time. And that is a belief that many of his followers have faith in. While they bury his mortal body today, they say he will be back. Sathya Sai Baba, himself at the age of 14, declared that he was the reincarnation of Shirdi Sai Baba, and he would once again come back as Prema Sai in Mandya district of Karnataka.
> (Maya Sharma, NDTV, quoted in Das 2015, 97)

Though Sai Baba was Hindu, his body was not cremated, as was usual for Hindus, but buried, in keeping with both his birth caste status as Kuruba (shepherd caste) and his special status as spiritual leader and god-man. The burial was a private event, restricted to a handful of family members and an inner circle of Sai trust officials. After the public funeral, maroon velvet curtains dropped from the ceiling to hide the entire dais. Some people were ushered off the dais, as the curtain was drawn.

The crowd chanted the mantra known as the Sai Gayathri 108 times: *Om Saieshwaraya Vidmahe, Sathya Devaya Dheemahi, Thanna Sarvah Prachodayath* (We know Sri Sathya Sai as Supreme Divinity Incarnate, We meditate on this God of Truth, May Almighty God lead us to Liberation).[19] As the powerful mantra was chanted, Sai Baba's body was lowered into the crypt behind the curtain. Television footage deprived of the immediate image of the lowering of the body cut to real-time footage of drums rolling, cannons firing, flags flying and crowds sobbing. The public face of the media event was focused on loss, and it lingered on the crypt as a space of the last view of that loss.

But Sai television went 'behind the curtain' as it were, giving devotees a look at the private funeral. It showed the encryption of Sai Baba's body in pitiless detail. The body was moved out of the crystal coffin and lowered on a simple bier into a deep pit, 7 feet by 12. As the priests chanted mantras, Sai Baba's family members and Sai officials on the dais lifted handfuls of sacred ash from an enormous silver bowl and threw them into the crypt. The outlines of Sai Baba's body began to blur and then his face disappeared as he was buried in the scented ash. As Derrida notes, 'No crypt presents itself. The grounds [lieux] are so disposed as to disguise and to hide: something, always a body in some way. But also to disguise the act of hiding and to hide the disguise: the crypt hides as it holds' (1986, xiv).

The encryption of Sai Baba's physical body into the space of the marble crypt in Puttaparthi suggests a different spectral outcome from the Derridean wandering ghost (Gordon 2008), separating his presence, marked as eternal, from his body. Alexei Yurchak (2015) argues, in his thoughtful study of Lenin's death, funeral and mummification, that the Russian Politburo separated the physical decomposing body of Lenin from his larger persona as an embodiment of the Russian state. Indeed, as Yurchak notes, this 'doubling' of the royal body allowed its conservation as an artefact of the state.[20] Preserving Lenin's body thus became the project of the cultivation of devotion to the Soviet state. In Sai Baba's case, the separation of physical body from charismatic godhood allowed the powerful Sai presence that had agency similar to that of the living Sai Baba to be conceived of as lingering in the crypt. Preservation of the crypt became akin to the cultivation of Sai devotion in the absent presence of Sai Baba.

Andrew McDowell (2019), in his ground-breaking study of tuberculosis in Rajasthan, India, argues that ghosts, the spectres of the people that are lost, are lost themselves, and seek their kith and kin in order to haunt them. Though McDowell is ostensibly thinking about voice and authorship, importantly for our purposes, he argues that the spectral in India is *not* Other as Derrida presupposes, but kin in the village, self and yet not self, bound by familial and geographical ties. So in the supposed achronology of ghostly life that Derrida highlights, the 'spectres of a place and time out of joint', historical or suprahistorical, are actually rooted in the rhythms and sociality of local village life, as the ghost returns to that which was familiar in life to a chronology of the present through the past (Bashir 2014). Though McDowell's essay is focused on retrieving the voice of the ghost pivoting towards new intergenerational ethical claims, he returns repeatedly to the spatiality of the spectral, creating a new ontology, of and for the ghost, that refocuses on locality and its intersections with time, the visible and the hidden, rather than on the flattened horizons of the temporal alone (McDowell 2019, 514). And, indeed, focusing on space rather than time, I argue, transfers our attention from loss and history to possible elsewheres and potential futures.

The mausoleum as Elsewhere

A year after the funeral and encryption, Bhashyam and Krithika stood in the Sai Kulwant Hall 10 feet away from the marble samadhi of Sai Baba in front of the dais that bore the chiselled motto and logo of the Sai movement, 'Love all Serve all'. The pristine white marble mausoleum, covered in bright red roses, offered them 'peace', they said. They stood at its foot, touched the marble briefly and touched their foreheads in namaskaram, as they did to the living Sai Baba's feet.[21]

Krithika quoted the Sathya Sai webpage almost verbatim in educating me about the space of the hall. Gesturing to the marble sarcophagus, she said, 'This is called the Mahasamadhi. This place means not only the conscious departure from the physical body of a realised soul but also the shrine where the body is buried.' She added, 'Bhagawan Sri Sathya Sai "took" Mahasamadhi on 24 April 2011', by which she meant that was the day he died. Among devotees, Sai Baba is believed to have chosen the date and time of his death voluntarily, as is exemplary for great gurus and saints.

Several groups of devotees sat in the hall. Some stood at its far end. Others sat in meditation in the hall some distance from the samadhi. Two women in the corner were crying silently, wiping tears from their eyes with handkerchiefs. An elderly man in another section of the hall was reading from a prayer book and coughing loudly. Some devotees seemed to pass through the hall, standing at the base of the stage staring towards the white marble – a simple low-slung box-like oblong samadhi – closing their eyes, saying a prayer, and continuing on their way.

Krithika stared at the marble samadhi, which had garlands of flowers wreathed around it and stiff flower arrangements of gladioli and roses in baskets all around it. To the left was Sai Baba's empty throne and behind the samadhi was a life-sized photograph of Sai Baba, his hands raised in blessing in a gold frame. The photograph was built into a solid chiselled silver and gold panel that imitated ancient Hindu temple frescoes and that rose to the ceiling. The photograph was garlanded, and there were spray-like fresh flower arrangements of roses and gladioli in front of it, similar to flower arrangements I had seen in churches in Bangalore.

As I have argued before, images of the guru, however large or small, have an opaque status between sacred relic and consumer good (Srinivas 2012). Such images reflect Michael Taussig's (1993, 134–5) accounts of the 'fetish-power of appearance' and objects that 'exceed … symbolic signification'. For devotees, the aura of sacred images like the one of Sai Baba behind the samadhi releases their presence into the space, animating it. These images mark the threshold of reality, a porous experience that floats between dreams to the waking world.

The samadhi played to Sai Baba's syncretic Hindu–Muslim faith, drawing from his supposed incarnation of Shiva and Shirdi Sai Baba. While the marble sarcophagus was simple, like a Muslim fakir's dargah, the wall behind him, with its excessive silver and gold decoration of sculpted guardians of the gate, the *yali mukha* (dragon guardians), and eternally lit lamps, was rife with Hindu iconography of deities and demigods, similar to the sculptures on Hindu temples.

The samadhi offers devotees like Bhashyam a place to go to and worship Sai Baba even though he is gone. The mausoleum is a place-based understanding of Sai Baba's charisma, where the elision from his person to the place occurs. But during the funeral this nomadic charisma was captured, and interred into the crypt and mausoleum. Yet at the same time this charisma was transmitted globally via the media, simultaneously contained in the place of the crypt and in Puttaparthi, and transmissible, or uncontained, via live video feeds and on television.

With regard to gurus and saints in particular, the physical bodies of religious leaders are often thought to be so powerful that they continue to emit power and charisma even after the body's death (Lucia 2018, 965). In Orianne Aymard's powerful description of what she terms the 'post-mortem cult' of the guru, she describes pilgrimages to the samadhis of gurus, and refers to the mausoleum as a 'central point' where the presence of the saint is believed to be the strongest, a liminal 'point of junction between the earth and the heavens' (Aymard 2014, 90).

The encryption of Sai Baba's body in the mausoleum marks the space of the samadhi as a space of 'spiritual corporeity' in absentia (Carrette 2000, 139) and transfers the power of the guru into that space. In death as in life, the corporeal body of the guru, filled with so much sacred power that it overflows, transfers this sacred power to anything it has come into contact with: in life, the magical objects materialised for devotees, the clothes Sai Baba wore, his apartments and objects, and in death the space that houses his body. As Lucia points out with regard to the guru Ma Amritanandamayi and her bracelets, this transference of power is linked to temporality (2018, 965). Ma Amritanandamayi's bracelets are sold to devotees at prices based on how long she has worn them or how close they have been to her body. Hence a bracelet worn once is less valuable than one worn every day, as the longer it stays on the powerful body of the guru the more likely it is to have absorbed the shakti (power) of the guru.

Similarly, being close to the guru's body, what the Sai movement now calls 'the Divine physical frame' (to indicate its separation from the essential non-material divinity of Sai Baba), increases the potential for the devotee to feel and absorb the shakti of the guru. As Lucia notes, the concentration of the guru's shakti becomes more intense in direct proximity to the guru's physical body. 'In essence, the closer one gets to the guru's physical body, the more powerful the transmission of *śakti*' (Lucia 2018, 966). 'Such a presumption relies on princip[le]s of contagious magic, the belief that things that have once been conjoined remain connected even after having been severed from each other' (Lucia 2018, 964). Devotees have miraculous stories of being healed by the guru's touch, his or her grace passing through the guru's body and into the devotee's. So devotees clamour for a glimpse of the guru, or to touch him or her, and they purchase or 'even steal items that the guru has used or worn', in the hope that the power of the guru will be vested in them.

For devotees like Bhashyam and Kritika, this imaginal world of the guru's power in the samadhi is ontologically real, with the imagination a privileged locus of experience, transformation, and relation to the divine. For Aymard, as for Bhashyam, the body of the guru[22] within the mausoleum gives it power and bridges the living and the dead, creating a cosmological Elsewhere where the guru and his power reside in eternity. At the same time, the guru's death signifies his or her embodied dissolution but also their permeation into all aspects of existence. One can only access the guru after their death through the imaginal Elsewhere, either at the samadhi space or through one's dreams of them.

Perfumed crypts and elegiac dreams

Krithika said she and Bhashyam had both dreamed that Sai Baba has asked them to come and pay him a visit in Puttaparthi. He showed them his samadhi and told them to visit him. As soon as they awoke she and her brother called one another to relay their identical dream and recognised it as Sai Baba's call. They made plans to travel to Puttaparthi from their homes in Mumbai. 'If we couldn't get flight, we said, we'll take train. If we can't get train, we'll hire car. If not car, we'll come by walk. Bhagawan has invited us. We had to come!' Krithika and Bhashyam understood the dream of Sai Baba's mausoleum as a veridical and visionary experience that conveyed an invitation to the Elsewhere.

As testaments to the reality of the imagination, Corbin underlines both 'dreaming' that opens onto the imaginal and visionary dreams as bearers of other-worldly knowledge (Corbin and Horine 1976, 10–12). Corbin's viewpoint is integral to understanding saintly veridical dreams and their idea of an imaginal Elsewhere (Mittermaier 2012). In the case of Sai Baba's samadhi, the earthly world and the realm of the transcendent interlink, allowing the mourners to locate the 'spiritual' as embedded in the 'corporeal' of Sai Baba's magical body eternally at rest. Sai Baba's earthly body holds the imaginary 'remnants' of the Elsewhere (Navaro-Yashin 2012, 15) sedimented in the samadhi. The samadhi becomes a pivot point linking this world with the imaginal Elsewhere.

Standing in front of the samadhi, Krithika fell into a trance. She suddenly seemed to wake and commented that the samadhi gave off a perfume like that of roses and jasmine, just as in her dream.[23] This was unsurprising, since the samadhi was enveloped in scented garlands, but Kritika claimed it was not the flowers but the perfume of Sai Baba's body within that played through her dream and lingered in her home afterwards.[24] To Krithika and Bhashyam, the presence of the scent indicated a nocturnal visit from Sai Baba, his presence lingering through the scent, which drew them to the samadhi. Devotees like Krithika and Bhashyam believe that Sai Baba is present at the samadhi, just not visible to them. He has agency to act in the world, to do saintly work, to bless his devotees and protect them. They believe that Sai's presence in the crypt is no Othered Derridean ghost, but kin, linked by affinal and geographical bonds to them. Devotees travel to the mausoleum and petition the Sai presence to do saintly work on their behalf in the world. Therefore I argue that this encrypted figure is no Freudian site of silenced trauma, but is an anti-Freudian actor in its agency and power to act in the world. The perfume is the subtle manifestation of Sai Baba's invisible agentive presence among the living.

After they heard Krithika many devotees seated in the hall commented on the perfume from the mausoleum. One of the elderly women who had been sitting in a corner came up to the samadhi to bow and pray, and she breathed in deeply. She and Krithika got talking about the perfume, and its lingering scent that followed them. She described it as 'heavenly'. Another simply gestured at the samadhi and said by way of explanation, 'His presence'. Sarah Chavosian traces the presence of fragrances emanating from the tombs of Iranian martyrs (2020). The presence of the perfume around the tombs elevates it from a vaguely experienced fragrance to a distinct olfactory sensation, indicative of both the exceptional body within the tomb, and the connection to the imaginal Elsewhere that the tomb represents. The elderly lady agreed and said in veneration, 'Whereas ordinary people's bodies give off a stench when they are decayed [*badhbhoo*], the body of a guru gives off this extraordinary scent of flowers.' Then she added, to give emphasis to his presence, 'Many times I used to have private darshan and touch his feet. This fragrance is like the hem of his robe.' Others nodded in agreement.

For devotees on that day it seemed that being able to smell the perfume was a sign of attunement to Sai Baba's subtle presence, and, as Chavosian notes, the presence of the perfume and the ability to smell it 'dilated the site into an Elsewhere', a place where Sai Baba remained alive (2020, 153). The acknowledgement of the fragrance charged Krithika's dream with a sense of reality, finding the dream in the waking world, and thus causing an increased intimacy with the deceased body of Sai Baba.

Mourners who approach the white marble sarcophagus touch it reverently, and touch their foreheads afterwards, indicating the divinity of Sai Baba that imbues the marble with sacred powers of healing. The haptic logics of touch are key in Hindu worship and in memorialisation as well. Touching the samadhi reverentially venerates that which is within, hidden yet held. The haptic logics surrounding the guru, as Lucia argues, presuppose that the guru's charismatic energy is a potent 'transferable force' magically able to move to the devotee through touch. And so devotees clamour to be physically close to the guru, in what I have elsewhere termed a 'proxemic desire' (Srinivas 2010, 167).

As Amanda Lucia states, 'the guru's physical form is the epicenter of his or her [power or] *śakti*, and the guru's *śakti* is believed to radiate outward from his or her physical form', and 'The believed moral perfection and spiritual exceptionalism of the guru is exhibited and transmitted through contact with his or her physical form' (Lucia 2018, 964). But even after death, as Orianne Aymard demonstrates in her study of the 'post-mortem cult' of guru Ma Amritananadamayi, the samadhi and the relics of the guru become what Stanley Tambiah envisions as an 'anthropomorphic extension' of the shakti of the saint, an intimacy with Sai Baba not possible in his life (Aymard 2014, 98).

Sakshim, a young man I met at the mausoleum in 2012, who had sunk down next to it with his hands on the cool marble, spoke to this intimacy. 'When I come to the Mahasamadhi I feel Bhagawan is alive, only

I cannot see him; but he is here not only in our hearts, but he is here, just sleeping. I feel I can touch him, see him, be blessed by him.' Krithika added, 'He *is* here. Only we cannot see him because we are blinded by the *maya* [illusion] of existence.' The devotees agreed that they felt that Sai Baba was present but veiled and that he could act in the world, blessing them and removing obstacles in their lives. In other words, the mourners perceived what they thought of as the intermediary power of the samadhi as a connecting force between the living-yet-dead guru and living supplicants. The samadhi is the material trace of 'a medium of absence' (Meyer 2015, 165) in which, paradoxically, the presence of Sai Baba is felt and maintained by devotees.

In his article 'Dream kitsch', Walter Benjamin ([1927] 2004) refers to the mundane aspect of dream-reality to indicate the interpenetration of the dreaming and waking worlds. 'Dream-realities', according to Benjamin, stand against the ahistorical Freudian unconscious harking back to a historically specific phenomenon like the elderly woman's prior visit to Sai Baba when she knelt at his feet. The dream and waking worlds are interpolated through the subtle perfume, allowing the ordinary to acquire greater significance and the Elsewhere to be present in the here and now.

Krithika's recognition of the perfume enabled a blurring of boundaries between dream and reality, between alive and dead, between presence and absence, for all the devotees, expanding the idea of the samadhi as a conduit to the Elsewhere, allowing devotees to feel the presence of Sai Baba as intimately alive and present. Though subtle, it productively unsettles ideations of space and time, dream and reality, history and future.

Crypto-futurities: samadhi as theatres of the living dead

This interment of the magical body and the samadhi as Elsewhere are not limited to Sathya Sai Baba. In fact it is a well-established Sufi Muslim tradition in the subcontinent that the Sathya Sai movement has incorporated (Taneja 2012). Sufi dargahs or tomb shrines like samadhis are often seen as sites of healing. As Taneja notes about the dargahs of Sufi pirs (saints) in the ruins of Delhi, believers visit the sites to petition the jinns who live there to solve problems or for healing of illness. These sites are experienced not as locations of the historical past but as sites of *hazrat*, the presence of the pir (2012, 558). Visiting them is seen as a moment out of time. Taneja argues that this is a different way of knowing the dead, not just through remembering but also through dreams, visions and imagining.

In studying the dargahs of Sufi saints as sites of healing and moral warfare, Carla Bellamy too develops a wonderful exposition of dargah culture and its association with dreaming, fragrance and healing through a particular venue known as Husain Tekri, or 'Husain Hill' (Bellamy 2011). Tracing the healing that takes place at the dargah, she argues that the dargah functions as a court of appeal in which chronically ill people who are harassed by malevolent spirits or jinns petition the dead saint to intervene on their behalf and battle the jinns. She, like Taneja, argues that the dargah gains its power of healing and judgement through a conjured context, as it were, where the hazrat or presence of the saint, known through subtle traces such as their arrival in dreams or a distinctive scent, offers the solution. The dargah mediates the saints' response from the Elsewhere, offering a radical continuity between life and death in opposition to the 'rupture' that occurs in Christianity when one is born again and the old self is seen as dead (Engelke 2004).

Often, as Taneja and Bellamy suggest, gurus' or fakirs' tombs are part of a pilgrimage circuit for anxious and unwell devotees. The most illustrious example is the samadhi of the Muslim saint Shirdi Sai Baba, whom Sai Baba claimed as a spiritual ancestor. In their study of the town of Shirdi itself and its relationship to the dargah of Shirdi Sai Baba, Shinde and Pinkney (2013) trace how the city emerged as a religious tourism destination at the epicentre of the global Shirdi Sai Baba movement.

Shirdi, the town, has an estimated annual influx of eight million short-term visitors to Shirdi Sai Baba's mausoleum, which is popularly referred to as Sai 'mandir' or temple. Religious tourists far outnumber locals. A city has sprung up to cater to them; shops, restaurants, bus stands, hostels and rental accommodations, hospitals and pharmacies, and parks and recreational spaces, all surround the mandir. They do brisk business all year round, supported by the pilgrims from all over India and the world. As Shinde and Pinkney note, it is clear that the city of Shirdi owes its growth to the pilgrims who visit the mausoleum of Shirdi Sai Baba. One could say that the atmosphere of the city of Shirdi is shaped by the 'affective exudations' (Navaro-Yashin 2012, 174) of the mausoleum.

But neither the popularity of mausoleums as pilgrimage sites nor the crossover between Hindu and Muslim saints is anything new in the subcontinent. Susan Bayly's ambitious historical study of the landscape of Hindu, Christian and Muslim tombs from eighteenth- to twentieth-century Tamil Nadu, and the pilgrimage circuits around them, develops the idea of the mausoleum as the seat of the saint in eternity.[25] In a telling illustration Bayly recounts the story of Yusuf Khan, a soldier of fortune who fought for the British in south India in the 1750s, and was later beheaded by the local Nawab. His magical tomb had become such a popular pilgrimage site by the 1820s that dargahs across Tamil Nadu said to contain parts of his dismembered body proliferated, and kunmi or narrative ballads about him and his magical tomb were sung among Hindu martial castes such as the Kallars. Bayly demonstrates that Islamic modes of disposal and deification influenced the landscape of Hindu shrines and extended the pantheon of Hindu saints, a pattern that extends into the contemporary landscape of south India.

For in Puttaparthi too, in and around Sai Baba's ashram there are several shops, hotels, restaurants and other commercial establishments that catered to devotees and pilgrims who came to get darshan of Sai Baba during his lifetime. Soon after Sai Baba's funeral, the city wore a forlorn look, and traders who dealt in images and photos of Sai Baba reported a drop in their sales, with few pilgrims arriving. Since the building of the Samadhi, though, the number of pilgrims visiting the ashram has increased, and the sales in the area around the main street have got brisker.

The success of Shirdi is what Puttaparthi hopes to emulate, to have hundreds of thousands of devotees worship at the mausoleum and for it to develop as a site of devotee healing and petitioning for justice. Devotees believe that through such a presence in his samadhi, Sai Baba, like Shirdi Baba, will capacitate a new future for the movement, one that is yet to be eventuated.

Conclusion: decrypting the future

This chapter attempts an impossibility, to recoup the irrecoverable by focusing on those remnants that are left behind. Joseph Smith and William Kerrigan (1988, viii) suggest that such phenomena need to be studied with an 'eye toward the contingent, the haphazard, the chance event or lapse'. The phrase an 'eye toward the contingent' reminds us that the contingency of death is always present in life, and it threatens, particularly in the case of a spiritual leader like Sathya Sai Baba, to engulf life itself.

We have detailed the layered media presences at Sai Baba's death: place as mediator (of the guru's presence in a particular space), the Samadhi as mediator (of the guru's presence in and across time frames), conventional media around the funeral such as television and newspapers (that make the guru's presence virtual).

In the case of Sai Baba, a silent and radical inscriptive opening onto ethics is made via the dead yet living presence of the guru. The guru's presence is not a Derridean ghost; despite being dead, he is not an Other on the subhuman or human level but he is transcendent, an encrypted divine self. The notion of the encrypted guru-self runs counter to the Freudian notion of the ghost as Other. The transcendent guru-self sees the living as kin. For devotees, then, the samadhi is a technology of connection to the space of this living dead kin. The encrypting of Sai Baba's body into a samadhi, a sepulchre, ensures that the body that is dead is also alive in the Elsewhere, and the mausoleum acts as a medium to that which is dead that goes on living and influencing actions. And because it is kin it can be petitioned to heal and provide.

But the idea of a Derridean hauntology itself makes ethical claims upon the world which we cannot and should not ignore. Derrida writes, 'If I am getting ready to speak about ghosts, inheritance, and generations, generations of ghosts, which is to say about certain others who are not present, nor presently living, either to us, in us, or outside us, it is in the name of justice' (1994, xix). This ethical claim on life attained through death in the corner of the world that is Puttaparthi rests, as we have seen, on a mechanism of encryption and decryption.

This doubled process of encrypting and decrypting is a refusal of death as termination, and the refusal of the trauma of its final partitioning. It is a recognition of saint work as opposed to ghost work, not found in the crypt but founded upon and structured by it. It makes the work of the living yet dead saint, their healing work, central to their immortality and the endurance of the movement. And in these dark times, healing is a hopeful pivot towards life and possible futures.

Notes

1 Burke 2011.
2 Abibi 2011.
3 Though Copeman and Reddy (2012) speak of didactic death as the instructional idiom of a 'big man' dying in India, in order to trace the pedagogical value of such a death, I use the idea of an instructional death more broadly, to explore death as an act in the life of the guru.
4 As Copeman notes, Sai Baba's presence in the crypt forms an interesting parallel with the Sacha Sauda guru's presence in prison, namely that gurus, even when they disappear from the public eye, never really leave (pers. comm.).
5 Susan Bayly's ground-breaking work on the burial of saints in their tombs and mausoleums, and on pilgrimage, forms the basis on which this chapter stands.
6 Here I am thinking of Yurchak's exciting work (2015) on Lenin's body.
7 Ssorin-Chaikov's breath-taking article (2006) on the exhibition of Stalin's birthday gifts in 1949 and how it gestures towards differential temporalities – 'heterochrony' – argues that the circles of reciprocity implicit in gift giving cancel time. Playing on the word 'present', he suggests that 'time gaps' in gift giving allow understandings of the future to emerge by enabling a 'leap forward'.
8 Samadhi (tomb, mausoleum) translates literally as 'seat of eternal rest'.

9 'Sri Satya Sai Baba hospitalised', *Times of India*, 29 March 2011. https://timesofindia. indiatimes.com/city/hyderabad/sri-satya-sai-baba-hospitalised/articleshow/7812494.cms (accessed 4 March 2023).

10 [Headlines Today Bureau], 'Tension rises over Sathya Sai Baba's health', *India Today*, 11 April 2011. https://www.indiatoday.in/india/south/story/tension-rises-over-sathya-sai-babas-health-131656-2011-04-05 (accessed 4 March 2023).

11 NDTV correspondent, 'Sai Baba's condition stable, say doctors', NDTV, 6 April 2011. https://www.ndtv.com/india-news/sai-babas-condition-stable-say-doctors-452317 (accessed 4 March 2023).

12 Shailaja Bajpal, 'A funeral, a wedding, a spectacle', *Indian Express*, 6 May 2011. https://indianexpress.com/article/news-archive/web/a-funeral-a-wedding-a-spectacle-2/ (accessed 4 March 2023).

13 This is reminiscent of Partha Chatterjee's description of 'crowd trouble' at the death of Balak Brahmachari, leader of the Santan Dal, a religious sect with a large following in southern Bengal. Chatterjee describes Brahmachari's controversial death, which was in some aspects similar to Sai Baba's as it occurred in a large hospital after a severe illness. Also similarly, Brahmachari's devotees were brought into a certain political relationship of opposition to the state because they refused to accept his death (2006, 38). Santan Dal activists argued that on a prior occasion Balak Brahmachari had voluntarily 'gone into samadhi for twenty-two days during which, from all outward appearances, he was dead' (p. 42), but he awoke thereafter. So the devotees took his body to their ashram and placed it on ice to keep vigil for Balak Brahmachari's reawakening. After two weeks, the municipal authorities demanded the body and protesters let off firecrackers outside the ashram, but the devotees persisted. A month after his official death, residents of the neighbourhood started complaining of an unholy stench. The state despatched a police detachment of several thousand to the ashram to take possession of the body of Balak Brahmachari. They were attacked with home-made weapons and Molotov cocktails by Santan Dal activists as the guru's brother performed the last rites and cremated the body of Balak Brahmachari. For several months after, Santan Dal activists attacked the government in the newspapers and in public talks, claiming that it overreached its powers and questioning its secular bona fides. The extension of the secular state into religious matters in a civil society coalesces in this potent example.

14 NDTV correspondent, 'Sai Baba's condition stable, say doctors', as above.

15 TimesContent, 'Devotee', 24 April 2011. https://timescontent.com/syndication-photos/reprint/news/222964/devotee-follower-prasanthi-nilayam.html (accessed 4 March 2023).

16 Shirdi Sai Baba was originally from Shirdi, a town in Maharashtra state, and at the time of his death had a large following among the Indian middle classes.

17 Jyoti Thottam, 'Sathya Sai Baba: The man who was God is dead', *Time*, 26 April 2011. http://content.time.com/time/magazine/article/0,9171,2068080,00.html (accessed 4 March 2023).

18 Antonio Rigopoulos (1993, 377) reported that there were close to 10 million devotees. Today, there are 1,200 Sai Baba Centres for promoting the religion in 137 different countries. Another source puts the number at over 6,500 Sai Baba Centres. During the 1970s, the pace of the movement grew. In addition, Sai Baba's group formed a Sai foundation in California and they also publish a Sathya Sai newsletter there.

19 For devotees, the Sai Gayathri mantra is akin to a Veda mantra, a rune of intense magical and secret power, and the belief is that the full power or siddhi of this secret mantra is realised when it is chanted 108 times.

20 Among the fascinating aspects Yurchak details of the mummification of Lenin's body and its preparation for public viewing for nine decades is the problem of deteriorating skin surfaces and hair. His interviews with the officials in charge of the body, about their needling the skin's surface to replace lost fats and their inserting fake eyelashes underneath the dead Lenin's eyelids, make gruesome reading (2015, 139).

21 This is before Covid. When Covid protocols were in place, touching of the samadhi and distribution of sacred food were not allowed. Only masked devotees were allowed to stand briefly before the samadhi before they were briskly ushered away.

22 Shahzad Bashir, in his brilliant (2013) work on Sufi saints of the fourteenth and fifteenth centuries in Iran, argues that the mystic's body was the primary shuttle between interior

(batin) and exterior (zahir) reality, and that the corporeality of the saint was deeply linked to the cosmos.

23 Mittermaier in her study of Egyptian divine dreamers speaks of 'visitational dreams' prior to pilgrimage and the occasions on which dreams are incited during pilgrimage (2008, 58–62).

24 When I mentioned the perfume at the samadhi to another devotee, she said simply, 'his presence', indicating Sai Baba's fragrant absent-presence.

25 Bayly's study overall seeks to seeks to undermine the conception of religious traditions as hermetically sealed systems of orthodoxy founded in textual canons, arguing instead for the affinity of religious practices across traditions, similar patterns of deification of saints, and social concerns and strategies shared between a variety of Hindu, Muslim and Christian groups.

References

Abibi, Adnan. 2011. 'Sai Baba buried in state funeral, thousands grieve.' Reuters. https://www. reuters.com/article/idINIndia-56592720110427 (accessed 3 March 2023).

Aymard, Orianne. 2014. *When a Goddess Dies: Worshipping Mā Ānandamayī after her death*. New York: Oxford University Press.

Babb, Lawrence A. 1986. *Redemptive Encounters: Three modern styles in the Hindu tradition*. Berkeley: University of California Press.

Babb, Lawrence A. and Susan Wadley (eds). 1995. *Media and the Transformation of Religion in South Asia*. Philadelphia: University of Pennsylvania Press.

Bashir, Shahzad. 2013. *Sufi Bodies: Religion and society in medieval Islam*. New York: Columbia University Press.

Bashir, Shahzad. 2014. 'On Islamic time: Rethinking chronology in the historiography of Muslim societies', *History and Theory* 53 (4): 519–44. https://doi.org/10.1111/hith.10729.

Bayly, Susan. 1989. *Saints, Goddesses and Kings: Muslims and Christians in South Indian society, 1700–1900*. Cambridge: Cambridge University Press.

Benjamin, Walter. [1927] 2004. 'Dream kitsch: Gloss on surrealism', in *Walter Benjamin: Selected writings. Volume 2, Part 1: 1927–1930* (ed. Michael W. Jennings, Howard Eiland and Gary Smith, trans. Rodney Livingstone and others), 3–16. Cambridge, MA: Belknap Press of Harvard University Press.

Böhme, Gernot. 1993. 'Atmosphere as the fundamental concept of a new aesthetics', *Thesis Eleven* 36 (1): 113–26. https://doi.org/10.1177/072551369303600107.

Burke, Jason. 2011. 'Sai Baba, spiritual guru to millions, dies at 85', *The Guardian*, 24 April. https://www.theguardian.com/world/2011/apr/24/sri-sathya-sai-baba-dies (accessed 3 March 2023)

Carrette, Jeremy R. 2000. *Foucault and Religion: Spiritual corporeality and political spirituality*. London: Routledge.

Chatterjee, Partha. 2006. *The Politics of the Governed: Reflections on popular politics in most of the world*. New York: Columbia University Press.

Chavosian, Sarah. 2020. 'Dream-realities: Rematerializing martyrs and missing soldiers of the Iran-Iraq war', *Religion and Society*, 11 (1): 148–62. https://doi.org/10.3167/arrs.2020.110111.

Copeman, Jacob and Aya Ikegame. 2012a. 'Guru logics', *HAU: Journal of Ethnographic Theory* 2 (1): 289–336. https://doi.org/10.14318/hau2.1.014.

Copeman, Jacob and Aya Ikegame. 2012b. *The Guru in South Asia: New interdisciplinary perspectives*. Abingdon: Routledge.

Copeman, Jacob and Johannes Quack. 2015. 'Godless people and dead bodies: Materiality and the morality of atheist materialism', *Social Analysis* 59 (2): 40–61. https://doi.org/10.3167/sa.2015.590203.

Copeman, Jacob and Deepa S. Reddy. 2012. 'The didactic death: Publicity, instruction and body donation', *HAU: Journal of Ethnographic Theory* 2 (2): 59–83. https://doi.org/10.14318/hau2.2.005.

Corbin, Henry. 1976. *Mundus Imaginalis: or, The imaginary and the imaginal* (trans. Ruth Horine). Ipswich: Golgonooza Press.

Csordas, Thomas J. 2004. 'Asymptote of the ineffable: Embodiment, alterity, and the theory of religion', *Current Anthropology* 45 (2): 163–85. https://doi.org/10.1086/381046.

Das, Manoj Kumar. 2015. 'Televising religion: A study of Sathya Sai Baba's funeral broadcast in Gangtok, India', *Anthropological Notebooks* 21 (3): 83–104.

Derrida, Jacques. 1986. 'Foreword: *Fors*. The Anglish words of Nicolas Abraham and Maria Torok' (trans. Barbara Johnson), in *The Wolf Man's Magic Word: A cryptonymy*, xi–xlviii. Minneapolis: University of Minnesota Press.

Derrida, Jacques. 1994. *Specters of Marx: The state of the debt, the work of mourning and the New International* (trans. Peggy Kamuf). New York: Routledge.

Engelke, Matthew. 2004. 'Discontinuity and the discourse of conversion', *Journal of Religion in Africa* 34 (1–2): 82–109. https://doi.org/10.1163/157006604323056732.

Freud, Sigmund. [1919] 1976. 'The "uncanny"' (trans. James Strachey), *New Literary History* 7 (3): 619–45. https://doi.org/10.2307/468561.

Gold, Daniel. 1987. *The Lord as Guru: Hindu sants in the North Indian tradition*. New York: Oxford University Press.

Gordon, Avery F. 2008. *Ghostly Matters: Haunting and the sociological imagination*, 2nd University of Minnesota Press edn. Minneapolis: University of Minnesota Press.

Kasturi, Narayan. 1962. *Sathyam Sivam Sundaram: The life of Bhagavan Sri Sathya Sai Baba*, vol. 1. Prasanthi Nilayam: Sri Sathya Sai Books and Publications; repr. Tustin, CA: Sathya Sai Book Center of America, 1969. http://vahini.org/sss/sss.html (accessed 5 March 2023).

Lambek, Michael. 2013. 'What is "religion" for anthropology? And what has anthropology brought to "religion"?', in *A Companion to the Anthropology of Religion*, edited by Janice Boddy and Michael Lambek, 1–32. Chichester: Wiley-Blackwell.

Lucia, Amanda. 2018. 'Guru sex: Charisma, proxemic desire, and the haptic logics of the guru–disciple relationship', *Journal of the American Academy of Religion* 86 (4): 953–88. https://doi.org/10.1093/jaarel/lfy025.

Mazzarella, William. 2006. 'Internet X-ray: E-governance, transparency, and the politics of immediation in India', *Public Culture* 18 (3): 473–505. https://doi.org/10.1215/08992363-2006-016.

McDowell, Andrew J. 2019. 'Chunnilal's hauntology: Rajasthan's ghosts, time going badly, and anthropological voice', *Ethos* 47 (4): 501–18. ('Special thematic collection: Hauntology in psychological anthropology', edited by Byron J. Good and Sadeq Rahimi.) https://doi.org/10.1111/etho.12261.

McLain, Karline. 2016. *The Afterlife of Sai Baba: Competing visions of a global saint*. Seattle: University of Washington Press.

Meyer, Brigit. 2015. 'How pictures matter: Religious objects and the imagination in Ghana', in *Objects and Imagination: Perspectives on materialization and meaning*, edited by Øivind Fuglerud and Leon Wainwright, 160–84. New York: Berghahn Books.

Mittermaier, Amira. 2008. '(Re)imagining space: Dreams and saint shrines in Egypt', in *Dimensions of Locality: Muslim saints, their place and space*, edited by Georg Stauth and Samuli Schielke, 47–66. Bielefeld: transcript Verlag.

Mittermaier, Amira. 2011. *Dreams that Matter: Egyptian landscapes of the imagination*. Berkeley: University of California Press.

Mohammad, Afsar, 2010. 'Telling stories: Hindu–Muslim worship in South India', *Journal of Hindu Studies* 3 (2): 157–88. https://doi.org/10.1093/jhs/hiq014.

Morgan, David (ed). 2010. *Religion and Material Culture: The matter of belief*. Abingdon: Routledge.

Navaro-Yashin, Yael. 2012. *The Make-Believe Space: Affective geography in a postwar polity*. Durham, NC: Duke University Press.

Palmer, Norris W. 2005. 'Baba's world: A global guru and his movement', in *Gurus in America*, edited by Thomas A. Forsthoefel and Cynthia Ann Humes, 97–122. Albany, NY: SUNY Press.

Quraishi, Mustafa. 2011. 'Hindu guru Sathya Sai Baba dies', *Times Union*, 25 April.

Rigopoulos, Antonio. 1993. *The Life and Teachings of Sai Baba of Shirdi*. Albany, NY: SUNY Press.

Shinde, Kiran A. 2008.'Religious tourism: Exploring a new form of sacred journey in North India', in *Asian Tourism: Growth and change*, edited by Janet Cochrane, 245–57. Oxford: Elsevier.

Shinde, Kiran A. and Andrea Marion Pinkney. 2013. 'Shirdi in transition: Guru devotion, urbanisation and regional pluralism in India', *South Asia: Journal of South Asian Studies* 36 (4): 554–70. https://doi.org/10.1080/00856401.2012.726605.

Smith, Joseph and William Kerrigan. 1988. *Taking Chances: Derrida, psychoanalysis and literature*. Baltimore, MD: Johns Hopkins University Press.

Srinivas, Tulasi. 2010. *Winged Faith: Rethinking globalization and religious pluralism through the Sathya Sai movement*. New York: Columbia University Press.

Srinivas, Tulasi. 2012. 'Relics of faith: Fleshly desires, ascetic disciplines and devotional affect in the transnational Sathya Sai movement', in *The Routledge Handbook of Body Studies*, edited by Bryan Turner, 185–205. Abingdon: Routledge.

Srinivas, Tulasi. 2017. 'Doubtful illusions: Magic, wonder and the politics of virtue in the Sathya Sai Movement', *Journal of Asian and African Studies* 52 (4): 381–411. https://doi.org/10.1177/0021909615595987.

Ssorkin-Chaikov. 2006. 'On heterochrony: Birthday gifts to Stalin, 1949', *Journal of the Royal Anthropological Institute* NS 12 (2): 355–75. http://dx.doi.org/10.1111/j.1467-9655.2006.00295.x.

Taneja, Anand Vivek. 2012. 'Saintly visions: Other histories and history's others in the medieval ruins of Delhi', *Indian Economic and Social History Review* 49 (4): 557–90. https://doi.org/10.1177/0019464612463843.

Taussig, Michael. 1993. *Mimesis and Alterity: A particular history of the senses*. London: Routledge.

Taylor, Lawrence. 2012. 'Epilogue: Pilgrimage, moral geography and contemporary religion in the West', in *Gender, Nation and Religion in European Pilgrimage*, edited by Willy Jansen and Catrien Notermans, 209–20. London: Routledge.

Weiss, Richard. 2005. 'The global guru: Sai Baba and the miracle of the modern', *New Zealand Journal of Asian Studies* 7 (2): 5–19.

Yurchak, Alexei. 2015. 'Bodies of Lenin: The hidden science of communist sovereignty', *Representations* 129 (1): 116–57. https://doi.org/10.1525/rep.2015.129.1.116.

10
Envisioning silence: Ramana Maharshi and the rise of Advaitic photography

Yagna Nag Chowdhuri

Many stories of meetings with and accidentally encountering the guru or master are found in the memoirs written by seekers. Gurus emerge from glimpses of meeting in dreams and in moments of recognition, while the seekers are looking into the guru's eyes or at a photograph. Gurus and masters appear through the power of their voice, vision or action. In this chapter, I analyse the making and remaking of such a figure, namely Ramana Maharshi, within a complex matrix of recognition and encounter through texts and media. I read his thought and practice through the concept of the 'figure', to highlight the processes by which he came into being and is continually remade. I argue that he drew upon older philosophies of self-transformation and refashioned these through media technologies, such as photography, thus giving rise to new discourses and practices that were further shaped by transnational encounters between gurus and disciples. Out of these discourses, practices and encounters, Ramana Maharshi emerged as a 'figure'.[1] I propose that theorising the figure is a broad mode of analysis, which enables the study of different relationalities, discourses, media and practices, and of the circulation of ideas. Hence, I contend that this mode of analysis can be applied to unpack varied gurus and their worlds. I further assert that the theory of the figure emerges from a matrix of relationalities, and therefore does not have a singular place of origin.

Theory of the figure

In developing this theory, I build on Jacob Copeman and Aya Ikegame's understanding of gurus as 'multifarious' and 'uncontainable' agents with a capacity to 'harvest' in situations in order to carry themselves forward. They argue that

> gurus have crossed domains and become apt for given situations, drawing in and re-composing diverse aspects of Indian social life in the process: from sexuality to new media; from slavery to imagination and transgression; from Brahmanical orthodoxy to the arts of government; from milieus of modernizing reformist fervour to those of convention and continuity. Needless to say, while intervening in and mediating these phenomena in various ways, the guru is not reducible to any of them.
>
> (Copeman and Ikegame 2012, 3)

This sense of spilling over into diverse phenomena and producing multiple effects emphasises the idea of uncontainability and multiple relationalities that are inherent in the idea of the guru. Building on such characterisations, I argue that the guru needs to be understood as a *figure* produced within an assemblage that takes into account the multiplicity of relations, effects and materials. I choose the term 'figure' in order to highlight the discourses, practices and circulations that contribute to the making of the guru. I am drawing here on several connotations of the term 'figure'. The French literary theorist Gérard Genette describes it as more than a literal expression, always with a surplus of meaning, which pertains to not only an 'object, a fact, a thought, but also their affective value'. The figure is understood to mean multiple things from individuals to objects and affects (Genette 1984). Literary scholar Erich Auerbach locates the origin of the 'figure' in *figura*, its Latin root – related to the Latin *fingere* and to 'effigy'– meaning 'plastic form' (1984, 11). This connotation highlights the term's connection with fluidity and the moulding of a form. This suggests the making of something in resemblance as well as its renewing and remaking (ibid). In relation to this iteration of the figure, James Clifford connects the practice of ethnographic writing with *'fingere'*. He says that ethnographic writings are fictional in the sense of 'something made or fashioned' (1986, 6). He adds: 'it is important to preserve the meaning not merely of making, but also of making up, of inventing things not actually real. (*Fingere*, in some of its uses, implied a degree of falsehood.)' (1986, 6). This innovative way of viewing the relationship between ethnographic writing and the 'figure' is the methodological starting point of this chapter, in which we see how the (guru) figure comes into being through the stories told by interlocutors and the narratives that I as an ethnographer construct.

These various connotations of the term 'figure' evoke multiplicity of form, fluidity, and remaking. The idea of assemblage builds on precisely these multiplicities. That is, the figure is constituted by, and emerges out of, an assemblage. The figure is thus constituted by a multiplicity of traditions, spaces and communities, rather than having a single point of origin. It is within such a matrix that the figure comes into being.

According to Deleuze (who coined the most popular usage of the term in critical theory), an assemblage

> is a multiplicity which is made up of many heterogeneous terms and which establishes liaisons, relations between them, across ages, sexes and reigns – different natures. Thus, the assemblage's only unity is that of co-functioning: it is a symbiosis, a 'sympathy'. It is never filiations which are important, but alliances, alloys; these are not successions, lines of descent, but contagions, epidemics, the wind.
>
> (Deleuze and Parnet 2007, 69)

In other words, figures are assemblages constituted not just by the relationality between individuals (followers, readers, practitioners or commune members) but also by material and symbolic artefacts. The artefacts that make up the figure include media objects (photographs, books, videos, speeches and meditations), practices of self-transformation and devotion, and the spaces of ashrams and schools, as well as the modes of circulation of these objects and practices.

Such an understanding of the figure as assemblage defies a historically linear mapping, giving rise to a dynamic and non-linear perspective, according to which time is simultaneous, moving between the past and the present. This non-linearity is a result not just of the deep investment in questions of preservation (by seekers and communities) of the past in order to maintain the future, but also of the endless potentiality or possibilities inherent in such assemblages. Media is recycled into new forms, meditation practices change and give rise to newer forms, and an oral discourse may transform into a self-help book and later a film. Amit Rai, a media theorist, argues for the 'media assemblage' approach to explain the 'stochastic' and 'non-linear' experiences of Bollywood in the contemporary world (2009, 8). His theorisation of the media assemblage approach helps our understanding of the experience of Bollywood viewing across different platforms, from cinema screens to mobile phones, which shape bodies of viewers and media consumption practices. Such an approach provides insights into the multiplicity of experiences and media forms across time and space. Rai, referring to Lalitha Gopalan's *Cinema of Interruptions*, says, 'There are moments in her study of action genres in Indian cinema where the thought of what I am calling media assemblages (contagious and continuous multiplicities, or ecologies of matter, media, and sensation) proliferates beyond the dialectic of interruption and continuity – that is, moments where a certain complicity is marked and made strange by its becoming something else' (2009, 8).

In this chapter, I delve into one such figure, Ramana Maharshi. In particular I examine the means through which texts and practices associated with him have found renewed life through processes of remembrance and preservation. While, through these processes, Ramana Maharshi has found many afterlives, practices and texts have also proliferated in their own ways, constituting him as the figure, and often possessing unpredictable trajectories of their own. The capacity to be affected and to affect is recognised as having an infinite set of potentials. The practices of meditation, silence and reading of texts not only change with the creation of different digital and virtual platforms or archives, but also produce a certain kind of seeker or practitioner, who in turn renews the life of the figure. I am thus led to examine the communities of seekers. Indeed, it is stories like those told by seekers who were once drawn to the face of Ramana on the cover of a book in a time and place far removed from the figures and then found themselves spending their lives in communities as followers, which demonstrate the element of unpredictability as inherent within this model of contagion.

Who was Ramana Maharshi or Bhagvan?

Ramana Maharshi was born in 1879 in Tiruchuli, India. In 1896, he suddenly felt he was going to die, and was gripped by a sudden fear of death. He described this experience thus: 'the shock made me at once introspective or "introverted". I said to myself mentally: "Now death has come. What does it mean? What is it that is dying? This body dies ... But with the death of this body, am 'I' dead? Is the body 'I'? ... All this was not a mere intellectual process. It flashed before me vividly as living truth"' (Kamath 1936, 1–2).

Soon after this experience, Ramana left his home in search of the Arunachala mountains. On reaching Tiruvannamalai, where the mountains are located, he resided in various temples before finally settling in the mountain caves. By then, many people in the surrounding areas had come to hear of him and would visit him. As is described in a popular biography, 'about this time, the Swami began to attract the attention of also a few educated people; and the notes they left give us a glimpse of his life and his teachings at the time' (Kamath 1936, 12). These visitors included Kavyakanta, a well-known scholar and poet of that time, Ramasami Aiyar, the Public Works Department overseer of Tiruvannamalai, *sadhus* in the surrounding areas, and F. H. Humphreys, a police superintendent of the area. Ramana would engage in dialogue and answer questions, and remain silent for long periods. He started to walk daily to a spot near the base of the hill, which later became the site of the current ashram. This is the place where visitors, devotees and seekers from all over the world started to come. The ashram has remained small; a few houses for accommodation in and around its campus have been built by devotees over the years.

Upon moving to the ashram, Ramana remarked, 'Not of my own accord I moved … Something placed me here and I obeyed … it is the will of others' (Kamath 1936, 14). The 'will of others' found a more concrete form in the devotees and visitors who played a role in making Ramana known and spreading his message. As visitors from all over the world, and animals,[2] found their way to the ashram, it became a unique and vibrant space. It slowly developed into a transnational community consisting of devotees who also engaged with photography. Devotees, such as Paul Brunton, Arthur Osborne and David Godman, played a central role in writing about him, and photographers, such as Henri Cartier-Bresson (who famously published a series of photographs documenting the last days of Gandhi, Ramana and Aurobindo), made his images available to the world.

An interest in documentation and historical preservation was ingrained in the minds of followers and devotees from the time of the conception of the ashram space. Today, visitors can see walls studded with photographs celebrating the life of the ashram. There are photographs of its construction over decades and of its daily life and activities, and images of devotees with Ramana. This self-conscious preservation is central to the process of being known to the world and of creating the transnational identity of the ashram.

Ramana can also be described as a kind of 'modern advaitin' (Lucas 2011) in light of his universalisation of the simple question, 'Who am I?' His message was unique in many ways, since it did not rely on any scriptural understanding or the presence of a teacher. While the ideas of Advaita had been popularised, both in India and in the West, much earlier, Ramana's version of Advaita differed in terms of both content and how it was popularised. Vedanta's scriptural base lies in the classical Upanishads, which contain much internal diversity and can be interpreted in many ways.

Ramana's modern Advaita,[3] like Vivekananda's, did not stick to any strict scriptural interpretations of it and was offered to the world at large. Ramana's message, however, relied on personal experience alone and was more focused, setting seekers to ask themselves the fundamental question: 'Who am I?' In contrast to Vivekananda's efforts to globalise himself and his message, Ramana made no attempts either to travel around the world (or even around India) or to establish any ashrams. The small ashram in Tiruvannamalai was the initiative of his devotees. The appeal of Ramana lies in the non-scriptural form of philosophy he espoused and his non-missionary zeal. His resistance to the formation of a lineage may also have allowed multiple lineages to emerge: since Ramana's dictum of self-inquiry remained 'simple' and straightforward, disposing of the need of a teacher or institution, it could easily be adopted by a range of other seekers, philosophers or teachers.[4]

In the next few sections of this chapter, I will interrogate the making of Ramana through different media. How did his mode of self-inquiry surface in the practice of photography? I will demonstrate that photography, in particular, gives us many clues to unpacking Ramana's philosophy and the creation of Ramana as a figure. As will be shown, seekers and devotees from all over the world were attracted to Ramana's presence through his photographs, his practice of self-inquiry – notably the dictum 'Who am I?', and his approach to embracing the 'other'.

Coalmine worker:	Larry, you sound like a very religious man who doesn't believe in God.
Larry:	I am not sure I believe in anything.
Coalmine worker:	Have you ever thought of going to the east, India for instance?
Larry:	No.
Coalmine worker:	I went there. I met a strange man, a man I never thought to meet in this world – a Saint. People go from all parts of India to see him to ask for his advice on their troubles, to listen to his teachings and they go away strengthened in soul and in peace. But it's not his teaching that matters, it's the man himself.

(Goulding 1946)

Figure 10.1 Still from *The Razor's Edge*, 1946.

This scene from the film *The Razor's Edge* (1946),[5] which was based on a popular novel by W. Somerset Maugham, presents a glimpse of Larry's journey in search of meaning. In Figure 10.1, we see him admiring the Arunachala mountain. (As I will discuss later in the chapter, the Arunachala mountain was considered by Ramana to be his guru. Devotees and seekers were always advised to walk up it on their visits to the ashram.) Larry, the protagonist of the film, faces a very particular kind of dilemma: a desire, a longing and restlessness to find his true self. Larry leaves his fiancée in America, against her wishes, to spend time in Paris 'to clear his head'. He works in a coal mine in order to 'work below', and finally heads to India. He has returned from the First World War traumatised by the death of a fellow soldier, which will not leave his mind. He finally declares that he wants to 'loaf' around the world and ends up at the Ramana ashram. Ramana advises him to climb the Arunachala mountain and spend time in the cave there. Having walked around the mountain, he finds himself transformed forever. Even though he has no desire to return to America, on the insistence of Ramana he agrees to go back.

In the novel, Maugham introduces Advaita philosophy through an interaction between Larry and Ramana, who is disguised as a fictional character named Sri Ganesha. The title of the novel and the film is taken from a verse from the Katha Upanishad. The novel was published in 1944 and based on the post-war period of exploration by the kind of 'seekers' who form the central cast in this chapter. The popular novel gives us a glimpse into how Ramana captured the imagination of these 'seekers'. Ramana has continued to be imagined as a saint or teacher who provided simple methods of self-enquiry and contemplation.

Below, I demonstrate that Ramana as a *figure* is produced within a matrix of photography, Advaitic thought and the writing of biographies. In other words, he is constituted by an assemblage consisting of multiple relationalities between individuals (followers and seekers), media objects (photographs and books) and practices of self-transformation. I particularly highlight the *discourses of self-transformation* which emerge out of this assemblage, such as the method of self-enquiry, the incorporation of the 'other' and the practices of photography. I argue that a new practice of Advaitic photography is born out of these discourses, which further defines the relationship between Ramana (figure) and the medium of photography (media). These practices and discourses take shape within the space of *transnational encounters*, which are located at the Ramana ashram and are facilitated through his philosophical discourses on the 'other'.

Journeys with the Ramana photo

Encounters with the portrait

While doing fieldwork, I unexpectedly encountered the Ramana photograph during conversations with a close friend. I met the friend, Vijaya, for an early-morning coffee in Delhi, for the first time in almost two years. She started to narrate her experience of a recent meditation retreat. I knew Vijaya had been practising Zen Buddhist meditation for several years. Many times she had tried to lure me into it too, but for one reason or another I had never been able to join her. As we talked, my research and travels came up. 'Tiruvannamalai! Oh, I love that place and the mountains. Many of our retreats happen there!' I was excited to hear that she had been there many times. I asked if she had heard of Ramana Maharshi. She exclaimed, 'Of course! When I was there the last time, I was smitten by his photograph. I was drawn to his eyes and face. His kindness emanates from the photo. I bought the photo and have placed it on my desk at home. I look at it every day.' Later she sent me the photo of Ramana over WhatsApp.

Figure 10.2 'Welling Bust' (1946). Taken by G. G. Welling. Source: Ramana Ashram bookstore.

This was not the first time I had heard of the magnetism of this particular Ramana photo. On my first visit to the Ramana ashram in Tiruvannamalai, I had encountered, on the wall of my room, the same photo that my friend had sent. The room was quite austere and the only form of decoration was this famous photo, known as the 'Welling Bust' (Figure 10.2).

I found myself pondering over many questions. Was Ramana posing? Who took the photo? Did others also feel drawn to it in the same way? The 'Welling Bust', as I discovered later in the archives, was taken by the photographer G. G. Welling on a short visit to the ashram in 1946. He had taken the photo with a handmade wooden box camera, according to the ashram archivist. An ashram newsletter relates: 'When he was readying to take Bhagavan's photo, Bhagavan asked if there was sufficient light. "Bhagavan, you are the light!", Mr Welling said' (Ramanasramam 2013). Later, the photographer presented Bhagavan with a photo album containing the portraits of Bhagavan, Chinnaswami and Alamelu, as well as the images of the Big Temple and the Hill' (Ramanasramam 2013). The Welling Bust is one of the most popular photos of Ramana today, often sold at the ashram gift shop. It can also be found on stamps issued by the Indian government in 1971.

One feels instantly drawn to this portrait of Ramana; the slight tilt of the face, a faint smile and the eyes convey an endless sense of kindness and grace. The photograph draws all attention to the face of Ramana. Welling had taken a couple of other portraits of Ramana, and the choice of the portrait as a form is perhaps not surprising. The religious studies scholar Gwilym Beckerlegge (2008) has investigated the use of photography by devotees to create the iconic status of Swami Vivekananda. He argues that the 'conventions of portraiture … were becoming increasingly familiar as photographic studios spread in different regions of the world'. Further, Beckerlegge argues that, 'the face was the window on the inner person … It should not display any vulgar emotion, but instead calmness, dignity, and self-control' (p. 3). Following Beckerlegge's lead, I argue that the photographic genre of the portrait made it possible for seekers to access Ramana directly. The 'bust', in particular, allows one to pay attention to the face alone. The fact that the photograph has no background or foreground strips away context. In their absence, does this form of photograph have any historical context? By removing context, it seems as though the photographer portrays Ramana as a timeless figure. Especially in the Welling Busts, Ramana acquires a divine status: eternal and timeless. This, as we will see, does not necessarily hold true for the numerous other photos of Ramana, where the context is an important historical marker. As Beckerlegge has contended, the role and significance of these photographs needs to be understood within the framework of the idea of the 'iconic', rather than that of the *murti* (idol), which signifies divinity and worship (p. 34). This iconography has been produced through common and identifiable norms of portraiture, which could easily be transferred across geographical boundaries.

Another photo of this kind is the popular 'Mani Bust' (Figure 10.3), taken in the 1930s. Ramana looks younger and his eyes shine, though he also appears somewhat sceptical, with a slight squint in his eyes. This photo was taken by P. R. S. Mani, who went on to work in the early film industry in Madras. While Mani took other photos of Ramana, those in the Mani Bust series are the most popular. Such portrait photos generate a form of intimacy in which the onlooker is drawn to the image of Ramana and able to form a unique and *individual* connection. In the moment of looking, only Ramana and the onlooker exist and somehow they forge a union.

Roland Barthes, in his famous work *Camera Lucida* (1980), describes the portrait photograph as a 'closed field of forces'. He explains that there are 'four image-repertoires' that intersect, oppose and distort each other: 'In front of the lens, I am at the same time: the one I think I am, the one I want others to think I am, the one the photographer thinks

Figure 10.3 'Mani Bust' (1930s). Taken by P. R. S. Mani. Source: Ramana Ashram bookstore.

I am, and the one he makes use of to exhibit his art' (Barthes 1980, 13). Thus the portrait photograph is constituted by the opposing and simultaneous forces of the four image-repertoires producing it as an object for circulation (a universal and portable image), an object of self-making and transformation and an object of intimacy and devotion.

Further, he suggests that, in the act of posing, one starts to imitate oneself when one is neither subject nor object, but rather 'a subject who feels he is becoming an object' and hence experiences a 'micro-version of death' and becomes a 'specter' (p. 14). In portrait photography, a transformation from subject to object takes place, or, as Barthes puts it, a transformation into a 'museum object' (p. 13). In the earliest photographic portraits, around the 1840s, the subject would simulate being an object in that they had to pose for a long time under bright sunlight without moving. In the case of the Ramana portraits (the Welling and Mani Busts), he patiently posed for the photographer. Perhaps it came easily to him to stay still and wait as the photographer adjusted the light.

This stillness prefigures the mortality of the photographed subject. Barthes explains the experience of micro-death, or becoming an object: 'Ultimately, what I am seeking in the photograph taken of me … is Death. Death is the *eidos* of that Photograph' (p. 15). If death is the essence of a photograph, was Ramana experiencing self-death through the photographs taken of him? And by extension, can this form of photography be seen as a form of self-denial, rather than as an attachment to or reproduction of the self? I suggest that each act of posing by Ramana can be understood as a rejection of the self. For Ramana, being photographed made possible further experimentation with self-denial; it allowed him to take further his method of self-enquiry. In this unselfing, Ramana conveyed the message and power of stillness to allow one to enter into a state of contemplation and transformation simply by asking the question 'Who am I?'

Photography can also be viewed as a meditation on the possible lives of an individual after their passing. Building on Barthes's insights, the literary theorist Eduardo Cadava (1997, 11) argues that 'Photography is a mode of bereavement. It speaks to us of mortification.' Photography as a form is inextricably linked to death and it is also a way of remembrance after death. As the ashram authorities, devotees and photographers took photos of Ramana, they also anticipated his death. Ramana himself may have been aware of the photograph as a mode of bereavement. Cadava writes:

> [T]he lesson of the photograph for history … is that every attempt to bring the other to the light of day, to keep the other alive, silently presumes that it is mortal, that it is always already touched (or retouched) by death. The survival of the photographed is therefore never only the survival of its life, but also of its death. It forms part of the 'history of how a person *lives on*, and precisely how this afterlife, with its own history, is embedded in life'.
>
> (1997, 11–13)

Following this, I suggest that devotees and photographers were already mourning the death of Ramana while he was alive. The abundance of photographs may indicate precisely the fear of losing him and the desire to preserve their intimacy with him.

Photographs and devotees

Followers of Ramana relate to his photographs in numerous ways. Intimacies created through his photographs can take the shape of devotion, healing, inspiration and meditation. Susan Visvanathan, in her moving account of illness and recovery through her devotion to Ramana, writes of the photographs at the ashram. She says:

> My room has a black and white picture of Ramana looking extremely skeptical. It's interesting how photographs convey so much of the presence of the Maharshi, the sense of here and now so integral to

his philosophy. If there is any deification at the asramam [ashram], it is the sense of the photographs functioning as the living image. Devotees plead with Ramana's pictures – understand us, remember us, give us light, salvation, freedom from fear – and the curious miracle of Ramana's presence is that there are visible signs of his hearing prayers.

(Visvanathan 2010, 115)

For Visvanathan, the photographs are objects of devotion, which embody Ramana's presence in the everyday life of the ashram. This enduring quality of Ramana, the sense of here and now conveyed through the photographs, structures the space of the ashram. All the halls and buildings of the ashram display photographs. There are photos of the different phases of ashram construction, of devotees who lived in it, of Ramana, of the sacred Arunachala mountains surrounding the ashram, and of devotees with their families. The entire space of the ashram feels like a museum, memorialising the life and community formed around Ramana. The dining hall, in particular, has several large photos of Ramana from different phases of his life, with some of his important devotees. As the visitors and devotees eat in silence, their eyes fall only on these images. The silence created while they are eating, surrounded by the large silent photographs, engenders a meditative mode. Surrounded by these images, one also feels part of a much larger community and one's connection with Ramana is further strengthened.

Devotees recall how when they first saw Ramana's photos they were captured or drawn to them in a moment of *recognition.* Devotees often said during interviews that they were able to identify him as their guru at this moment and felt an uncontrollable desire and feeling of being swept up by the image. This is when the charisma of Ramana takes hold. This moment of recognition is central to the narrative of devotion to him and the creation of his community. The moment constitutes both the devotee/seeker and Ramana as guru/teacher, and is thus both an autobiographical and a biographical moment. As the literary theorist Paul de Man (1979, 921) says, 'The autobiographical moment happens as an alignment between the two subjects involved in the process of reading in which they determine each other by mutual reflective substitution.' Similar to the process of reading, this moment of looking at a photograph is also a moment of mutual constitution. The figure of Ramana is constituted by all the attachments and intimacies associated with devotion to a guru, teacher or philosopher. The anthropologists Shaila Bhatti and Christopher Pinney term such a heightened moment of looking at an image 'intermingling' (2011, 227). Underlying this looking is a kind of 'corpothetics', a combination of 'the sensory, corporeal and aesthetic'. In this practice there is a mutuality of seeing and being seen (de Man 1979, 921). All the senses come together in this mutual constitution of Ramana and the devotee. This subject formation, then, marks the beginning of a journey of self-transformation stimulated by the image. Further, I suggest there is an *excess* to this act of looking – an uncontrollable, unmistakable recognition of being drawn to Ramana as *the* guru; an experience similar to that of falling in love. This was often the way in which many of the devotees described the process to me. Many had seen Ramana's photos in another part of the world, on book covers or posters, and had decided to make the long journey to the ashram, just to learn more about him or be in his presence. Such is the force of the Ramana photographs.

The photographs also play a role in constructing the community of followers and the figure of Ramana himself. While there has been a clear attempt by the ashram authorities to preserve, archive and display the photographs in a somewhat organised fashion, photographs are still found scattered around the ashram in various nooks and corners. They exist in abundance and in excess. For instance, many photographs in the archives do not carry captions, and everywhere in the ashram scattered photos can be found without an intent to display. In the ashram bookstore they are sold in many forms, such as calendar art, posters and postcards. These photographs circulate in abundance within the ashram and outside, having their own lives and afterlives. Anyone is welcome to take photos, buy photos, and visit the archive and donate photos that they may have taken in the past. As they circulate, they form new communities and attachments, thus renewing the life of the ashram and the figure of Ramana. In other words, the photographs not only act as a medium of devotion, remembrance and intimacy for many generations of followers: they also reach new communities and seekers.

These photos include depictions of Ramana going on his daily walk to his beloved Arunachala, eating a meal, being with his favourite animals, walking in the ashram premises and reading a book or a newspaper (Figure 10.4). These can be considered candid photographs, which serve the purpose of creating an image of Ramana as leading a regular life of austerity and simplicity. He is always dressed in a *langoti,* clothing often associated with holy men, and was never photographed in a studio space. As these images circulated, they perhaps created a resemblance to, and referred to, the imagined images of holy men, *sadhus*, and other figures of austerity. By displaying Ramana in what may be called his 'natural habitat', the photographs created a language or vocabulary for thinking about him as a spiritual figure, namely, an

Figure 10.4 Ramana reading (date and photographer unknown). Source: Ramana Ashram.

enlightened man living in a small town in India. These photos play an important role for devotees in enabling a continuing attachment to the *body* of Ramana. In these photos, he is seen in different poses, sometimes with an air of childlike enthusiasm, and at other times appearing calm and relaxed, surrounded by devotees. Ramana's almost naked body often forms a stark contrast with those around him. Looking at these photos, devotees observe the body of Ramana. They notice how he walks, tilts his head when he sits, and sits on the floor while eating a meal, and how his body always looks relaxed. According to many devotees, his relaxed demeanour reflects his *sahaja*[6] and enlightened nature. A devotee in the ashram once remarked, 'Do you notice how Ramana always sits in such a relaxed manner? He is never trying to sit in any yogic posture.' His calm state of being, especially when conducting mundane daily activities such as walking, eating, reading or sitting, is reflected in photos that denote his *sahaja* state at all times. These photos also demonstrate an intimacy between the photographer and Ramana and the former's desire to capture the many mundane moments of his daily life. These photos give insight into his personal life and make him a relatable figure, creating new forms of intimacy.

The ashram houses a photo archive that devotees can access. I met the ashram photo archivist on the first day of my visit. When I asked what drew him to the ashram, he had a familiar story to tell. He had seen a Ramana photo in England in the puja (prayer) room of a British female devotee in the 1970s. He was instantly deeply moved by it, and many years later he found his way to the ashram to finally settle there. He took over the role of archivist, as he is a photographer himself, and has an interest in the preservation of the photographs. His approach to the archive has been to collect and preserve as many photographs as possible. Many devotees have donated their photograph collections to the archive in recent years. The archive has emerged as an experiential space that devotees actively participate in creating. One of the major objectives of the archive is to provide specific photos to devotees on request. They are often viewed as one might view family photo albums. Many devotees stop by at the ashram photo archive to look at their favourite photos or search for a particular one. Many can recount stories connected to them: about the setting or the person in the photo, whether a devotee or Ramana himself. His photos are considered to be the most important in the collection. While some visitors to the archive come out of curiosity or as part of their day visit to the ashram, others come actively in search of specific photographs that are precious to them, for instance ones that document the visit of a family member to the ashram many years before.

Towards an Advaitic photography

In this subsection, I build on my previous analysis to read a photograph from the ashram archive as I seek to theorise death, the body and silence in relation to the figure of Ramana and his philosophy. These are crucial to his method of self-enquiry. I will argue that photographs taken of Ramana have resulted in the creation of a unique form of photographic practice, namely Advaitic photography.

Figure 10.5 is a photograph from a series by the French photographer Henri Cartier-Bresson.[7] The image is captioned 'Last Day' in the ashram archives and was the first image to strike me as I was looking over some of the more well-known photos of Ramana. The last days of his life were extensively documented by Cartier-Bresson. This particular photograph was taken when Ramana was at an advanced stage of illness in 1950. One may ask why he agreed to be photographed at such a time. Was he aware of his impending death? Ramana looks straight at the camera with a solemn expression and a sense of certainty. I found this photograph

340   GURUS AND MEDIA

Figure 10.5 '"Last day" of Ramana' (1950). Taken by Henri Cartier-Bresson. Source: Ramana Ashram Archive.

significant for another reason: the appearance in the background of images of two important national figures, Gandhi and Nehru. By placing these three figures (Ramana, Gandhi and Nehru) in the same frame, what might Cartier-Bresson have wanted to suggest? While there is no way of knowing the answers to these questions for certain, I use this photograph to advance some interpretations.

Cartier-Bresson had been with Gandhi in his last days, and had photographed him at that time, and had then photographed his funeral procession. The coincidence of Cartier-Bresson being with both Ramana and Gandhi in their last days is hard to ignore, as the imagery of Ramana and Gandhi bears many similarities. Both dressed in the garb of an 'ascetic' or 'renunciant', and made a claim to austerity. However, they had different approaches towards politics and the world. The story in the ashram is that Gandhi would often send his political workers to stay there when they felt tired of politics. One of the major distinctions between Ramana and Gandhi, as discussed by followers, has been that the latter was a man of *karma* (man of politics/the world), and the former was a *jnani* (self-realised person), who practised the path of silence and Advaita.

Returning to the photograph, we see that the calendar on the wall has a picture of a map of India (it is unclear whether it is pre-partition or not), with a rising Nehru in the background. Ramana's relationship to India as a nation and the idea of space comes across clearly in his talks with devotees. He believed that the category of space was irrelevant, because for him where one lived was not as important as how one lived. In this photograph we see Nehru, the first prime minister and visionary leader of the new India, who actively engaged with politics, Gandhi, representing the enduring voice of freedom, and Ramana representing the inner life and the importance of self-transformation. By bringing these three figures together in the same frame, Cartier-Bresson, in fact, represents an emerging Indian nation. The past, present and future – Gandhi, Ramana and Nehru – are all represented in the photograph. This places Ramana within the political canon of the nation.

This photograph was taken in Ramana's room, 10 days before his death on 4 April 1950. His arm had been operated on many times, and the bandage can be seen in the photograph. The photograph documents his long period of illness and his approaching death. We may ask, what was Ramana's relationship to death? Many devotee accounts spoke of the lack of pain he experienced, even after multiple surgeries. He was certain that the pain was only of the 'body' and the body should be allowed to take its own course. After the third operation on the malignant tumour in his arm, the cancer continued to spread through the bloodstream. The designated official photographer of the ashram, T. N. Krishnaswami, who spent a lot of time with Ramana, wrote in his account:

> It was sad indeed to look at the suffering of his body but the mystery was his attitude to it. He described all the pain and suffering as though the body belonged to someone else. The question arose whether he suffered or not. How could he describe the pain and suffering so accurately and locate it in the body and yet remain unaffected by it? He always said, 'There is pain' and not 'I have pain'.
> (Krishnaswami 1967, 36)

In another account, Ramana's doctor wrote, 'Disease and pain left no impression on his mind. If he allowed himself to be treated for the ailment, it was more because his devotees wanted it than because he desired relief' (Rao 2015, 138).

In a rather brilliant exposition, Ramana spoke himself of the relationship between the science of photography, and pain and the body; indeed, Ramana often employed photography in order to explain philosophical principles:

> 'When taking a picture the silver salts are coated over a film in the dark and when the film is exposed in the camera, you get an impression caused by light outside. If the film is exposed to light

before you put it in the camera there can be no impression on it. So is it with our *jiva*. When it is still in darkness, impression can be made on it by the little light that leaks in. But when the light of knowledge has already flooded it, there is no impression of external objects to be obtained.'

(Rao 2015, 140, quoting Ramana)

This quote suggests both Ramana's active participation in the discourse of photography and the articulation of Advaita. It also demonstrates that he found similarities between the technical apparatus of photography and his own philosophical foundations. In creating a parallel between his body and the exposed film, he suggests that if one has already been exposed to the light of knowledge, then no amount of external influence (pain) can cause any harm.

T. N. Krishnaswami accidentally fell into the role of the ashram's official photographer after he became the first visitor to take a photo of Ramana. He said that, at first, he felt that he had *captured* Ramana in his metal camera, but later he realised that it was Ramana who had captured him in his heart. This relationship of intimacy and devotion started with him taking photographs of Ramana. He was drawn to the body of Ramana. He said:

'Sometimes, I used to wonder if it was not ridiculous of me to pay so much attention to photographing his form when Bhagavan's teaching was "I am not the body". Was I not chasing the shadow and trying to perpetuate it? Somehow, so long as I was seeing him with my eyes, the teaching did not assume any importance to me. His person was seen by me and I felt drawn and attracted to him. It gave me immense pleasure to take photographs of him. He was more important to me than his teaching. Every little movement, every one of his acts and gestures, was highly valued by me and they always carried some divine fragrance. Simply to watch him, no matter what he was doing, was highly gratifying.'

(Ganesan 2013, 370, quoting Krishnaswami)

Here the act of taking photographs can be understood as a performance of devotion. This is manifested in the form of an intimacy with the body of Ramana, his gestures and body movements. For Krishnaswami, devotion to Ramana's body exceeds even the value of his teachings. This strong desire to be close to Ramana's presence is at the heart of the practice of his photography, but this desire creates dilemmas, as it seems to conflict with Ramana's teachings. However, as discussed earlier, photography in the case of Ramana can also be understood as a form of self-denial.

In another account Krishnaswami explains:

> Not once did Bhagavan tell me, directly or indirectly, ... to stop taking photos. On the other hand, he unhesitatingly stood or sat in whatever pose I asked him for. No one will believe if I tell now that I used to ask him, "Turn your face this side, look up, look sideways, keep the arms down or keep the arms like this", and that he acceded to my requests instantly. ... If anyone had been there and seen Bhagavan obeying me, they would have mistaken Bhagavan to be obsessed with being photographed. The real truth is that he, as my guru, was fulfilling my desires, my insatiable longing to photograph him and that was all.
>
> (Ganesan 2013, 370, quoting Krishnaswami)

Ramana thus actively participated in the process of being photographed, which no longer makes him solely a distant object of reverence. It also signals a sense of surrender to the will of the devotee or photographer. As Krishnaswami asks Ramana to pose, and to enact and re-enact himself, he not only imagines Ramana as guru but also enacts his own devotion. As a guru, Ramana reciprocates the affection and intimacy of the devotee, thus making the distance between the photographer and the object of photography (Ramana) disappear. I argue that this is how the practice of Advaitic photography emerges.

Zahid Chaudhary (2012), in his provocative work on photography in nineteenth-century India, analyses the 'phenomenological scene of photographic practice itself' and the way it transformed the 'perceptual apparatus' (p. 25). According to him, the camera provided the ability to extend the photographer's sense perception and become an extension of the body, eye or senses of the photographer him-/herself. In this interpretation, the camera is both a 'sense organ' and an instrument. Krishnaswami's use of the camera becomes a way of enabling his *own senses* to connect, to come into contact with Ramana. The camera allows a heightened sensory experience, which his vision alone could not have made possible.

The photograph thus acted as the ultimate Advaitic object, eliminating the distance between the body of Ramana and the photographer. Advaita refers to non-duality and an interpretation of reality that is constituted not by parts, but by a whole. In this photographic practice, the photographer is erased and the camera exists as an extension of the 'eye'

Figure 10.6 Photographer T. N. Krishnaswami with Ramana (date and photographer unknown). Source: Ramana Ashram Archive.

or the 'I' (without the Self). In other words, the distances between the camera, photographer and the figure (Ramana) are all obliterated, which forms a union. In the moment of encounter between the photographer and Ramana they meet through the camera, which acts as a medium of transformation. That is, the space of the encounter is one of transformation and union. The practice of Advaitic photography born in this encounter provides us with a way to understand the relationship between the figure (Ramana), the devotee (the photographer) and the medium (photography).

In another photograph, Krishnaswami is seen bowing to Ramana. In this unique photograph, we see the photographer in the same frame as Ramana, with the Arunachala mountain in the background (Figure 10.6). (One can see the foothills of the mountains, a familiar sight for devotees who visit the ashram often.) This photograph provides an excellent example of the practice of Advaitic photography. Ramana is Krishnaswami's object of devotion and the mountain is Ramana's object of devotion. When the three come together in the same frame, there seems to be a seamless union between them all.

Conclusion

In this chapter, I have examined how the figure of Ramana is produced within the sites of photography, the Advaitic tradition, practices of self-transformation, and encounters within the ashram. I have argued that the *figure* of Ramana is produced through *discourses of self-transformation*, such as Advaitic photography, and the practice of self-enquiry ('Who am I?'). These discourses take shape within the context of *transnational encounters* and the ashram space. While some devotees and seekers from different parts of the world come to the ashram for retreats, others have made it their home. Ramana's emphasis on inclusivity and non-duality, embracing the Other, continues to attract seekers from all over the world.

I began the chapter with a discussion of the simplicity of Ramana's method of self-enquiry, its popularity amongst devotees and also, later, neo-advaitin teachers. I also demonstrated that interpretation and commentaries have been an integral part of the formulation of this method. To highlight the role of mediation and interpretation in the making of Ramana as a figure, I then explored the role of photography. Ramana's Advaita was unique in several ways. First, a simple method of self-enquiry, which could be practised by anyone, irrespective of their subject position, was central to this articulation. Devotees had the freedom to choose both their method of practice and the circumstances under which they practised. Second, practices of silence and solitude facilitate these processes of self-transformation.

Taking as examples his most popular photographs, namely the Mani and Welling Busts, I demonstrated how portrait photography facilitates intimate moments of *recognition* between Ramana and devotees. I argued that the portrait photograph is composed as an object of circulation (a universal, portable image), of self-making and transformation, and of intimacy and devotion. I explored why Ramana chose to be photographed, speculating that the act of posing itself forms a pre-emptive enactment of death and performance of self-denial. That is to say, this mode of photography made experimentation with self-denial possible. These photographs also played a crucial role in forming a community of seekers. Found in abundance both within the ashram spaces and outside, they play a significant role in reaching new seekers and thereby renewing the life of the figure. Finally, I have argued that *Advaitic photography* emerges in this milieu. In this photographic practice, the distances between the camera, the photographer and the figure (Ramana) are all obliterated, thus forming a union. The practice of Advaitic photography provides a way of understanding the relationship between the figure (Ramana) and the devotee (photographer).

Notes

1   Jacob Copeman and Aya Ikegame have provided provocative conceptual tools that open up new possibilities for theorising the guru. They highlight the 'uncontainability' of the guru phenomenon, arguing that '[g]uru-ship is a suggestible form: as a principle-cum-model it affords movement between domains; the extension and transformation of modes of power; scaling up/down; the expansion/containment of persons' (Copeman and Ikegame 2012, 37). Further, they suggest that the guru is a 'prolific producer of "domaining effects"; effects that occur when the logic of an idea associated with one domain is transferred to another, often with interesting or unanticipated results' (p. 2), or even that the guru is a 'floating signifier'. Such conceptualisations of the guru are quite compelling, as they take the *making* of one seriously and highlight their discursive production. Here, by introducing the term 'figure', I further offer a way of understanding the guru in this discursive mode.

2   Ramana Maharshi was known to have unique abilities to connect with animals and often developed compassionate relationships with them. Several animals visited him at the ashram and spent time there. Some famous animals were Lakshmi (a cow), Jackie (a dog), and peacocks, deer, snakes and monkeys.

3   Here is a brief gloss of the term Advaita Vedanta: 'Advaita Vedānta is the non-dualistic system of Vedānta expounded primarily by Śamkara (*ca.* 788–820). … Śamkara's system is best labeled "non-dualistic" rather than "monistic" to distinguish it from any position that views reality as a single order of *objective* being. Advaita Vedānta is concerned to show the ultimate non-reality of all distinctions – that Reality is not constituted by parts, that in essence it is not-different from the Self' (Deutsch 1969, 3).

4   Forsthoefel, who has written on Ramana's contribution to Advaita philosophy, suggests that he succeeded in deeply internalising the truth of non-dualism, which renders all external phenomenal differences meaningless, giving rise to an 'egalitarian universalism'. He says: 'Ramana, by neatly weaving together his metaphysic and internal epistemology, profoundly relativizes traditional renunciant culture … he liberates Advaita from its local context; his internalism facilitates the universalism implicit in Advaita metaphysics' (Forsthoefel 2002, 124). Forsthoefel also notes that there must be personal experience in order to achieve liberation, a claim based on Ramana's own understanding. Ramana repeatedly warns his devotees not to get lost in bookish knowledge and that the Self could never be found in books: 'Ramana's life and teaching thus represents a particularly modern form of spirituality whose appeal in part lies in the promise of an immediate experience of the divine, uninflected by cultural forms, and available to all, regardless of culture or society' (Forsthoefel 2001, 32).

5   Somerset Maugham opens the novel on which the film is based with this quotation: 'The sharp edge of a razor is difficult to pass over; thus the wise say the path to Salvation is hard.' Katha-Upanishad[, 3.14] (Maugham 1944).

6   *Sahaja* is a state of silent awareness, which is continuous and does not change under any circumstances.

7   Henri Cartier-Bresson, a renowned French photographer, travelled across India and took a number of 'candid' photographs of Indian life. A unique and powerful record, they document a newly emerging Indian nation. Taken between the years 1947 and 1950, they include glimpses of the last days of Gandhi's life, images of rural life and scenes from the city of Bombay.

References

Auerbach, Erich. 1984. *Scenes from the Drama of European Literature*. Minneapolis: University of Minnesota Press.

Barthes, Ronald. 1980. *Camera Lucida: Reflections on photography* (trans. Richard Howard). New York: Hill and Wang.

Beckerlegge, Gwilym. 2008. 'Svāmī Vivekānanda's iconic presence and conventions of nineteenth-century photographic portraiture', *International Journal of Hindu Studies* 12 (1): 1–40. https://doi.org/10.1007/s11407-008-9056-x.

Bhatti, Shaila and Christopher Pinney, 2011. 'Optic-clash: Modes of visuality in India', in *A Companion to the Anthropology of India*, edited by Isabelle Clark-Decès, 225–40. Malden, MA: Wiley-Blackwell.

Cadava, Eduardo. 1997. *Words on Light: Theses on the photography of history.* Princeton, NJ: Princeton University of Press.

Chaudhary, Zahid R. 2012. *Afterimage of Empire: Photography in nineteenth-century India.* Minnesota: University of Minnesota Press.

Clifford, James. 1986. 'Introduction: Partial truths', in *Writing Culture: The poetics and politics of ethnography*, edited by James Clifford and George E. Marcus, 1–26. Berkeley: University of California Press.

Copeman, Jacob and Aya Ikegame. 2012. 'The multifarious guru: An introduction', in *The Guru in South Asia: New interdisciplinary perspectives*, edited by Jacob Copeman and Aya Ikegame, 1–45. Abingdon: Routledge.

Deleuze, Gilles and Claire Parnet. 2007. *Dialogues II* (trans. Hugh Tomlinson and Barbara Habberjam). New York: Columbia University Press.

de Man, Paul. 1979. 'Autobiography as de-facement', *MLN* 94 (5): 919–30. https://doi.org/10.2307/2906560.

Deutsch, Eliot. 1969. *Advaita Vedanta: A philosophical reconstruction.* Honolulu: University of Hawai'i Press.

Forsthoefel, Thomas A. 2001. 'The sage of pure experience: The appeal of Ramana Maharsi in the West', *Journal of Hindu-Christian Studies* 14: art. no. 10. http://dx.doi.org/10.7825/2164-6279.1253.

Forsthoefel, Thomas A. 2002. *Knowing beyond Knowledge: Epistemologies of religious experience in classical and modern Advaita.* Burlington, VT: Ashgate.

Ganesan, V. 2013. *Ramana Periya Puranam: Inner journey of 75 old devotees.* Tiruvannamalai: Ramana Asramam.

Genette, Gérard. 1984. *Figures of Literary Discourse* (trans. Alan Sheridan). New York: Columbia University Press.

Goulding, Edmund (dir.). 1946. *The Razor's Edge.* 20th Century Fox.

Kamath, M. Subbaraya. 1936. *Sri Maharshi: A short life sketch.* Tiruvannamalai: Sri Ramanasramam.

Krishnaswami, T. N. 1967. 'By an eye-witness', in *Ramana Pictorial Souvenir,* edited by Arthur Osborne, 36–7. Tiruvannamalai: Ramanasramam.

Lucas, Phillip Charles. 2011. 'When a movement is not a movement: Ramana Maharshi and Neo-Advaita in North America', *Nova Religio: The Journal of Alternative and Emergent Religions*, 15 (2): 93–114. https://doi.org/10.1525/nr.2011.15.2.93.

Maugham, W. Somerset. 1944. *The Razor's Edge.* Garden City, NY: Doubleday, Doran.

Rai, Amit. 2009. *Untimely Bollywood: Globalization and India's new media assemblage.* Durham, NC: Duke University Press.

Ramanasramam. 2013. 'In profile: Mr. G. G. Welling', *Saranagati* 7 (6): 5.

Rao, Shankar. 2015. 'Treatment to Sri Bhagavan: An account', in *The Silent Power,* edited by V. S. Ramanan, 135–41. Tiruvannamalai: Sri Ramanasramam.

Visvanathan, Susan. 2010. *The Children of Nature: The life and legacy of Ramana Maharshi.* New Delhi: Roli Books.

11

'Christ the guru': artistic representations of Jesus Christ in south India and their mediated notions of guru-ness

E. Dawson Varughese

It was in a hotel lobby in Munnar, Kerala, south India in late 2016 that I spotted the image of Christ as guru; he seemed to be watching over me, a framed image, hanging high above the reception desk. Positioned alone and located centrally in a panel of wooden wall cladding, the radiant and luminous white of his robes emanated from the otherwise dark surface surrounding him. This moment of 'seeing' was powerful for me, not having experienced such an intimate moment with a visual rendition of Christ portrayed as a guru in such a 'secular' space before. I experienced the guru-ness through his seated, cross-legged posture and his lightly closed eyes, and in his symbolic hand gesture (*mudra*). The owner of the Munnar hotel is a friend and so I was able to find out about the image, which I came to learn is entitled *Christ the Guru*. Eventually, I purchased an A1-sized print of it through the Christian Musicological Society of India based in Kochi, Kerala,[1] where this particular image has been adopted – practically, if not formally.[2] The appellation of *Christ the Guru* for this piece came from Dr Palackal, the founding member of the society.[3] The circulation of images of Jesus Christ is common in south India – on paper, as framed prints and in other ways – and Visvanathan, in her book *The Christians of Kerala* (2010), talks of the importance of visual representation of Christ in Keralite homes when she writes:

> A Christian house can be recognized by the 'holy' pictures on the walls. … Pictures of Mary with the infant Christ are also frequently

displayed, as also those of the saints Gevarghese and Thomas. Geverghese [*sic*] (St George) is shown in combat with a dragon, referred to as *pambu* or snake by the Christians, while Thomas is often represented as standing with his feet placed on Malabar, on a globe in the centre of a starlit universe.

(Visvanathan 2010, 75)

Christ the Guru – the image I saw hanging in the Munnar hotel – is an oil painting by M. P. Manoj which he completed in 1993 as a commission for a Fr Mathias in Bangalore. Fr Mathias commissioned 'an Indian-style Christ'[4] and M. P. Manoj's original oil painting currently hangs in Christu Jayanthi Kindergarten in Kakkanad, Ernakulum, Kerala. In this chapter, I place M. P. Manoj's *Christ the Guru* (Figure 11.2) in dialogue with two other visual portrayals of Christ as 'guru', namely a 2003, concrete-moulded tableau in St Anthony's Friary Church, Bengaluru by artist Fr Saji Mathew (Figures 11.3, 11.4), and the 'source' artwork for both M.P. Manoj's and Mathew's works (Figure 11.1), a mosaic installation from 1974, mounted on the façade of the Dharmaram College in Bengaluru. In order to examine the visual representation of Jesus Christ as guru in a comparative manner, I examine two additional paintings which are not associated by artist or style with the 'Christ the Guru' works noted above. I focus on two paintings from the 1980s by the renowned Bengaluru-based Christian artist Jyoti Sahi, which have known various titles (in English, German and other languages) over the years, and so I reference them here as *Missio I* (Figure 11.5) and *Missio II* (Figure 11.6). Both pieces were created by Sahi in 1986 for Missio Germany (which is part of the International Catholic Mission Society),[5] and they formed part of a series of 16 paintings on 'The Sermon on the Mount' (referencing the Gospel of Matthew). With its main offices in Aachen and Munich in Germany, Missio Germany describes itself as providing 'both financial and non-material support for the mission of local Churches in Africa, Asia, and Oceania' (www.missio.com). In my analysis below, I discuss Missio Germany in connection with its magazine publication *Weltweit* ('Worldwide'), in which some of Sahi's works appeared.

By virtue of being visual artworks, these portrayals of 'Christ', or, as I will argue in the case of three of the pieces, 'Jesus', engage with the apophatic, reminding us that no matter how many words or how careful the choice of words, none can suitably or properly describe the holy mystery that is the divine. Voss Roberts, a scholar of comparative theologies, acknowledges the apophatic – how God is ultimately 'unknowable' – in both Hindu and Christian thought when she writes:

The apophatic strand of theology, including its experiential dimensions, has provided fertile ground for theologies of Hindu–Christian encounter. If – as both traditions affirm – the ultimate reality is beyond human grasp, and if all of our words ultimately fail, then there is a place of silence, beyond doctrines, where the traditions meet.

(2021, 347)

In my discussion of these five visual representations and visual expressions of Jesus Christ, I recognise here that such portrayals are far more entrenched in Catholic and Orthodox Christian traditions than they are in Protestant traditions such as Methodism or some Baptist denominations, a difference that is often foregrounded even in the display of Christianity's iconic 'cross': a crucifix (representing the crucified Jesus) for Catholic and Orthodox, and a (simple) cross, without the crucified Christ figure, for Methodist and Baptist denominations. All five artworks examined here stem from a Syro-Malabar Catholic tradition, namely 'St Anthony's Shrine' at St Anthony's Friary Church, Bengaluru; Dharmaram College, Bengaluru (a major seminary of the Carmelites of Mary Immaculate congregation) and including Jyoti Sahi as a Catholic Christian artist based in Silvepura village, in north Bengaluru. Additionally, *Christ the Guru* by M. P. Manoj circulates in Orthodox Christian traditions within south India in particular (see http://christianmusicologicalsocietyofindia.com/), and Manoj's original painting is on display at a CMI (Carmelites of Mary Immaculate – the Apostolic Church of St Thomas) school in Kerala, south India. Whilst researching the five images discussed here, I happened to be reading *Names of the Women* by Jeet Thayil (2021), an author of Indian fiction in English whose works have received great acclaim during the post-millennial years. Born into a Syrian Christian family in Kerala in 1959, in *Names of the Women* Thayil radically reimagines the lives of the women who met and spent time with Jesus. In the opening pages Thayil writes of Jesus's relationship with his mother, and a particular passage from the novel returned to my mind on several occasions as I developed my ideas around Jesus as 'Son of God' and Jesus as 'Christ'. It reads:

Imma, I said to her, Gabriel was his name, don't you remember? She said, I remember only what he said, that my son would die on the cross, the terrible words that made me forget every other thing. Then she told me to live the days of my life fully. To learn the ways of men. To seek in my spirit first, then in my mind and at last in my body. To give myself to the answer.

(Thayil, 2021, 2)

The trope of the (Indian) 'guru'

As Copeman and Ikegame's volume *The Guru in South Asia* neatly outlines, the guru has always been 'a social form of peculiar suggestibility' (2012, 2) and a 'prolific producer of "domaining effects"; effects that occur when the logic of an idea associated with one domain is transferred to another, often with interesting or unanticipated results' (2012, 2). For my interests here, I refer to scholarship on 'guru-ness' in relation to Jesus/Christ that has been produced from a Christian-oriented perspective, in order to examine this body of research against the five Christian-oriented artworks ('Christian-oriented' by virtue of the artist or the nature of the commission).

Significantly, in the late sixteenth and early seventeenth centuries, the Jesuit missionary Roberto de Nobili separated out the Christian and Hindu ideas of incarnation by distinguishing 'the Christian doctrine of Incarnation as *mānusa avatāra*, "human descent", from the Hindu concept of *avatāras* as *deva avatāra*, "divine descent", on the basis that according to the Christian view God assumes human nature, which is body and soul together as one reality' (Brockington 1992, 41). In other words, God assumes human nature or is human and divine simultaneously in the Christian tradition, whereas in Hinduism the Divine may reside within the human being itself (*antaryami*), be omnipresent as Brahma, or may exist as individual deities within a spiritual world. In this vein of exploring the various facets of Hindu–Christian traditions, de Nobili adopted the term 'guru' for 'Christ'; Brockington documents this, explaining that de Nobili especially used *sadguru*, 'true teacher', partly because of 'its intrinsic appropriateness' (1992, 41). Furthermore, Richard Lannoy acknowledges that 'The *guru–shishya* [teacher–disciple] relationship incarnates a specific form of psychological bond; with the disintegration of traditional social roles and institutions it tends to be diffused or imprinted on relationships in no way connected with, let alone confined to, the religious domain with which it was originally associated' (1974, 348). Here Lannoy reminds us of the extensive ideas and semantics associated with the notion of the guru and of the importance of various agents, institutions and organisations which play a central role in how the notion of guru is refracted through societies, within India and beyond. We might consider the psychological bond that Lannoy calls attention to as an integral part of a relationship 'imprinted' by power, redolent of a 'knower' and a 'seeker of knowledge', clearly applicable to the religious domain, and also beyond it. With this in mind, we might read the notion of the guru in significantly fluid terms, and, as this edited volume deftly identifies, the notion of 'guru' within, and indeed outside, India is undeniably a multifaceted figure. I suggest that the term 'guru' is rendered thus through *specific* cultural interpretations as much as through *transcultural*, *globalised* ideas of the same. As I demonstrate by my choice of five artworks, a major feature of the 'visual' guru trope is a male figure, seated in *padmasana* – also known as the 'lotus posture' – whereby the legs are crossed with the feet laid in the hip crease with the soles of the feet turned uppermost, in meditative mode, usually positioned under a banyan or peepal tree and often displaying hand gestures (*mudra*) that are associated with 'teaching'. These aspects, when taken together, are emblematic of a yogi in meditation as well as referencing Lord Buddha in meditation, specifically when visualised under a fig tree (known as the 'bodhi' tree in popular parlance because of this cultural association). If we reflect on this demonstration of 'teacher-ness' as part of the guru figure, then, I suggest, the artworks examined here rely on certain visual 'clues' to reveal an almost intrinsic sense of the guru as teacher, and the motif of the seated, meditative male figure is one of them. The theologian and sociologist Jan Schouten emphasises the relational dynamics between a guru and their student(s):

> [A] guru is more than a teacher in the usual sense of the word. He not only passes on knowledge but embodies that knowledge himself as well. Doctrine and life are linked very closely. He does not present any theses for academic discussion. He does not stand alongside his students in order to seek out the truth with them. On the contrary, he teaches with absolute authority. He has appropriated the mystic insight about which he speaks. And the way in which he travels the pathway of life is in complete agreement with his message. That is why his followers can entrust themselves to him without any hesitation. Thus, in Hinduism, the relationship between a guru and his students is of a particularly intense nature.
>
> (2008, 269)

Similarly, Lannoy writes: 'The realized man becomes a sacred authority who radiates a beneficent numen; he is worshipped as an embodiment of Truth, the man who has resolved the contradictions of life. Whether he teaches or not is immaterial, for his charisma itself is a sermon' (1974, 347). If, then, the notion of guru is bound by ideas of 'power' and a seeking-offering of knowledge, what Lannoy refers to here as 'Truth' is an extension of what might be considered the 'knowledge' that is being sought by the pupil. Following Lannoy's idea of guru-ness, I argue that it is the idea of 'the realized man' worthy of being 'worshipped' because he has attained a freedom from life's 'contradictions' that we see visualised in the images analysed in this chapter, and that this is realised through a variety of artistic means, including colour palette, style and composition.

The scholar Enrico Beltramini describes the work of the eminent south Indian theologian Michael Amaladoss (b. 1936) as being 'characteristic of a certain period in the development of Indian theology, a period marked by the independence of the country, the rise of an Indian liberal state, and the ambition of a new generation of Indian theologians to articulate a true Indian Indian theology' (Beltramini 2021, 1). For Amaladoss, the motif of guru-as-teacher is paramount, as he states in his important text *The Asian Jesus*:

> Used in a spiritual context, it ['guru'] refers to those who have walked along the way and have experienced, or at least have had a glimpse of, the goal one is looking for. Therefore they are capable of guiding disciples (*sishyas*) in their own search. They can instruct them, solve their doubts and difficulties. They can authenticate their experiences. It is traditional in India that gurus do not go out looking for disciples. On the contrary, it is the disciples who seek a guru, someone competent to guide them along their spiritual path because of the guru's prior experience of having walked successfully along that path.
>
> (2006, 69)

Moreover, Amaladoss describes Jesus as a 'guru of an apostolic social movement' when he writes:

> The foreseen goal is double. Every person reaches personal fulfillment. But this is part of the fulfillment of all. We can recall here the Buddhist bodhisattva ideal in which the bodhisattva – a person who has attained liberation or fulfillment –postpones its completion in order to help others attain final liberation so that at the end everyone is fulfilled together. As a guru, Jesus is not merely guiding people toward personal fulfillment. He is launching and animating a global project that works for the fulfillment of all humans and of the whole universe. The project of Jesus is therefore both personal and social/cosmic.
>
> (2006, 75)

Central to this 'global project' is the recognition and practice of prayer. Amaladoss writes of the apostles:

They do[, however,] ask him to teach them to pray, and Jesus teaches them the Our Father (Lk 11:1–4). Made up of praise and petition, it has become a model prayer. It can also be seen as a summary of the mission on which Jesus is sending them.

(2006, 82)

In the case of Jesus Christ as guru, we might recognise the multitudes that followed him as his 'disciples', whilst we learn in the Gospel of Luke (6:12) about the 'apostles'. The Gospel explains that Jesus walked up a mountain to pray. It is reported that he prayed to God all night, and in the morning he returned to those who had accompanied him, choosing 12 of them to be his apostles. The 12 apostles were *chosen* by Jesus whereas those *who chose* to follow him (in multitudes) might be considered disciples of a guru, all embarked on their own search for spiritual guidance and support. These combined definitions of 'guru' from Lannoy and Amaladoss allow us to identify seven tropes of guru-ness; I find these particularly productive when analysing the artistic depictions of 'Jesus/Christ as guru' in this chapter. These seven tropes describe the guru as: (1) a sacred authority who radiates beneficent numen, (2) a guide (who can initiate and lead), (3) one who 'becomes' (a sense of 'formation'), (4) one whom others seek out for discipleship, (5) one who works for the fulfilment of all peoples, (6) one who fosters 'community building', and (7) one who recognises and practises the importance of faith and prayer. I attempt to trace these tropes through my analyses of the five pieces of artwork in order to understand how these visual portrayals of Jesus Christ embody and communicate a sense of 'guru-ness'.

Analysis of the artwork

Of twentieth-century south Indian artists, the names Jyoti Sahi (b. 1948), Angela Trindade (1909–80), Angelo da Fonseca (1902–67), Vinayak Masoji (1897–1977), Solomon Raj (1921–2019) and, sometimes, Francis Newton Souza (1924–2002) are generally associated with a body of Christian-themed artwork by Christian artists in south India. These artists have collectively contributed to and curated an immense oeuvre, and this body of work has been complemented by north Indian Christians' works, as well as by non-Christian Indians' artworks. Of the south Indian artists listed above, the motif of the guru can be traced across a number of their paintings and artworks; examples of this are: Angela Trindade's *Christ and the Woman of Samaria*, in which we see Christ positioned under a banyan tree, in saffron robes, a halo of light emanating from his head, a serene and pensive look upon his face; Vinayak Masoji's *The Last Supper*, of Jesus Christ surrounded by his disciples; and Solomom Raj's batik *Padmasana*, in which Jesus Christ is seen sitting within a lotus flower, afloat on water with his head in heaven, as the Lord of the universe, his hands in *mudra* and wearing a saffron-coloured robe. In my examination of five artworks, I notice how the trope of the seated, cross-legged image of Jesus Christ is central to building a sense of guru-ness. So is the use of *mudra*. In terms of their provenance, all these five visual representations of Jesus/Christ as guru analysed here share a territory – the city of Bengaluru[6] and the hinterland of Kerala – through the artists Fr Joy Elamkunnapuzha, Fr Saji Mathew and M. P. Manoj.

The most recently created artwork I examine is *St Anthony's Shrine*, a painted, concrete-moulded tableau installed in 2003 at St Anthony's Friary Church in Bengaluru. It was designed and created by the Keralite artist and Franciscan priest Fr Saji Mathew. At the other end of the timeline, the well-known, large mosaic on the façade of the Dharmaram College, which is also in Bengaluru, was created by Keralite artist V. Balan in 1974. The image of Jesus sitting cross-legged was originally sketched by the Keralite Fr Joy Elamkunnapuzha, and it was from this drawing that V. Balan created the mosaic façade. Another interpretation of this image was created in the early 1990s when a Keralite artist, M. P. Manoj was commissioned by a Fr Mathias to paint 'an Indian-style Christ', inspired by the Dharmaram mosaic of 1974. M. P. Manoj painted this piece in oils and the image has come to be associated with the Christian Musicological Society of India and its founding member, Dr Palackal, who entitled it 'Christ the Guru'; it is the image used on the Society's home page, and the site offers prints of the painting for sale.[7]

My overall interest here is in notions of 'guru-ness', but in order to help me to focus the analyses of the artworks, I take as a starting point the linguistic specifics of the appellations 'Christ' and 'Jesus', the former denoting an appellation of 'deity' (with the same meaning as 'Messiah') and the latter being the 'human name' given to the Son of God. I suggest that two of the three visual portrayals of 'Christ the Guru' examined here help us to ruminate on this semantic distinction. On the one hand, M. P. Manoj's oil painting, entitled *Christ the Guru*, from 1993 is inspired by the large 1970s mosaic, and both these images of 'Christ as Guru' represent, I suggest, a deified, revered Christ. On the other hand, the 2003 concrete tableau *St Anthony's Shrine*, by Fr Saji Mathew, represents something more of Jesus in his 'human nature', that is, Jesus as 'the Son of God'. In the analysis below, Fr Saji Mathew acknowledges that his design was inspired by having seen Jesus as guru 'here and there over time'[8] but makes no direct reference to V. Balan's or M. P. Manoj's works. Furthermore, I recognise that Jyoti Sahi's two paintings, which he prepared for Missio Germany in 1985–6, have tended to be referred to as representations of 'Jesus' and not of 'Christ'. This appellation of 'Jesus' is in line with most of Sahi's work in which the Son of God is pictured (see for example Lott and Sahi 2008; Amaladass and Löwner 2012, 268–76; Jyoti Art Ashram 2007) rather than a deified Christ figure. In my discussion of the *Missio* paintings below, I suggest that Sahi's interest in and commitment to folk art (especially that of Karnataka and the Konkan coast), Dalit identities and experiences of marginal (broken) existence resonate with the 'Jesus' figure ('Son of God') more than with the deified appellation of 'Christ'. Beldio writes of Sahi's interest in expressing and representing marginal existence, suggesting: 'Sahi seeks a union of justice and beauty in his work, a way to create culture and a way of life that can discover the risen Christ within the brokenness of the Earth and those who are marginalized like the Christian *dalits* of his community near Bangalore' (2021, 276, emphasis in the original).

Christ the Guru

I begin by looking at the two interrelated 'Christ the Guru' images (Figures 11.1 and 11.2). The mosaic from 1974 (Figure 11.1) can still be seen on the façade of Dharmaram College in Bengaluru. Figure 11.2 shows the oil painting from 1993 by M. P. Manoj that I came across in the hotel lobby in Munnar. In examining both pieces, which are separated by 20 years, I note that M. P. Manoj has created a painting that is particularly faithful to the 1974 mosaic created by V. Balan and designed by Fr Joy Elamkunnapuzha in terms of both composition and subject. Although V. Balan died in 2002, Fr Joy Elamkunnapuzha is still in service, currently working in north India.[9] Fr Joy's design of the mosaic clearly looks to display a meditative Jesus Christ, as we see him in *padmasana*, his eyes lightly closed, a serene expression on his face and his hands in the *jnanamudra*, a symbolic hand gesture in which the index finger and the thumb lightly touch and the remaining fingers stretch upwards. This *mudra*, usually held at chest height, signifies knowledge, teaching and 'the Wheel of Law' (specifically the circle made with the forefinger and the thumb). This visual semiotic might be read as one which demonstrates Amaladoss's notion of guru 'as a guide' (trope 2), and Lannoy and Amaladoss's one who 'becomes' (trope 3), since he has experienced what his followers are going through (in Amaladoss's

Figure 11.1 Façade of Dharmaram College, Bengaluru; mosaic by V. Balan (1974), design by Fr J. Elamkunnapuzha.

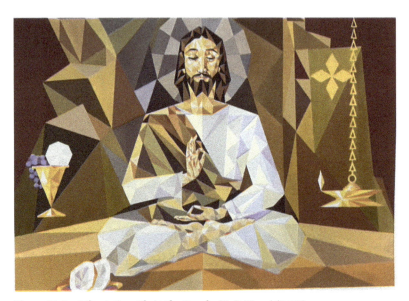

Figure 11.2 Oil painting: *Christ the Guru* by M. P. Manoj (1993).

words, 'the guru's prior experience of having walked successfully along that path' (2006, 69)).

The visual artist V. Balan was a Hindu Keralite from a Pillai family who studied at Cochin School of Art before becoming a freelance artist, residing mostly in south India (Chennai, formerly Madras; Bengaluru, formerly Bangalore), although his work took him all around the country. The ceramic materials that V. Balan used in creating the 1974 mosaic (Figure 11.1) were integral to the form and thus the final appearance of the artwork; here we experience 'Christ the Guru' denoted by straight lines and angular corners according to the nature of the small ceramic tiles that he used to build up the image. In M. P. Manoj's oil painting rendition (Figure 11.2), *Christ the Guru*, the process and creation of the image were not bound to such a geometry, given the materials M. P. Manoj chose to work with: brush, oil paints and canvas. It is curious, therefore, that M. P. Manoj decided to recast *his* portrayal of an 'Indian-style Christ' (commissioned by Fr Mathias), using lines and angles as 'triangles' specifically, to paint his 1993 piece. This decision meant that the two artworks, different in material, era of production and location (the mosaic is chiefly a static artwork, although images of it can be found online; the oil painting circulates widely as both a physical print and an electronic image), are placed in dialogue: an intertextuality that works productively to sustain a body of art in south India that celebrates Jesus Christ as a 'guru' figure. Moreover, the intertextuality foregrounds a sense of the reverence and respect that Manoj has for the original Balan mosaic; the junior artist holds the artist-elder in high regard and celebrates the earlier work of the master. In short, I suggest, a type of guru–pupil relationship exists between the two artists.

M. P. Manoj takes forward the geometrical form of the image created by V. Balan as well as the contrasting hues of light and dark that V. Balan achieves through his choice of ceramic tiles. However, M. P. Manoj develops this colour contrast by choosing warmer colours of oranges, browns and ochre, whilst rendering Christ's robes in an iridescent white. The use of the triangular form alongside the complementary colours gives significant depth to M. P. Manoj's painting, and this style is not unlike some of Jehangir Sabavala's (1922–2011) works, especially those of his later years (the first decade of the twenty-first century), such as *The Monks* (2006), *Mohalla* (2007) and *Yatra* (2001), all oil on canvas. Through this use of the triangular form, we see in M. P. Manoj's *Christ the Guru* that the image of Christ in the middle of the painting looks as if he is levitating, given the combination of colour palette and careful use of geometric design. This image might be interpreted as representing Lannoy's notion of guru as 'a sacred authority who radiates a beneficent numen' (1974, 347) (trope 1). Although the European art movement of Cubism, as well as the fact that M. P. Manoj was trained in European Fine Arts in Kerala, might easily be invoked here, we notice that *only* triangles are used, and that unlike in some Cubist artworks, in which a subject is broken up to be reassembled in an abstract manner, M. P. Manoj is careful in his placing and use of scalene, obtuse and acute triangles to recreate a familiar and representational image of Christ. The use of complementary yet contrasting colours means that, as we gaze at the image, the three points of the (various types of) triangles become emphasised, potentially leading 'the observer to concentrate[,] which leads to silent absorption' (Amaladoss 2021, 426).

Unlike Balan's rendition (Figure 11.1), in which triangular shapes organically appear out of the arrangement of small, mosaic tiles, M. P. Manoj works directly and concisely with the triangular form. Even the familiar visual tropes of 'Christ' appear as a triangle, the crucifixion marks on his hands and feet as well as the hair and beard detail. Moreover, the chalice, wafer, split coconut and *thookuvilaku*,[10] including its flame, are all crafted through careful use of colour and the triangular form. I suggest that through this dominant motif of the repeated triangle, the form takes on a new role, signifying and referencing *outside* of the image. M. P. Manoj aimed to employ the triangle shape in order to signify the Trinity within Christian traditions, representing a sense of 'God in three'.[11] Furthermore, I read these repeated triangular forms as an echo, inviting a *japa*-like rhythm (a meditative repetition of a mantra or a divine name) to the image as we see over, and over, and over, the presence of the triangular form (trope 7). More interculturally, we might read the motif of the triangle as one which connects with Hindu traditions such as the role of the triangle in geometric temple design, the geometric base of *rangoli* design, the yogic *trikonasana*, and of Shiv/Shakti. And so, rather than reading the triangular form as representing the Trinity (as 'three'), we might read it as an embodiment of an Indian Christian spirituality as being *advaita* (non-dualistic). Amaladoss (2021) suggests that, in contrast to the Western view of reality as dualistic, 'the Indian religious tradition affirms that God and the human are neither one nor two, but not-two' (2021, 425). Amaladoss goes on to connect this notion to moments in the Bible that speak of what Western readers would most likely recognise as the 'Trinity'; specifically, he quotes the Gospel of John, 'The Father and I are one' (John 10:30) and 'As you, Father, are in me and I am in you, may they also be in us' (John 17:21).

As noted above, I suggest that the guru-ness we recognise in M. P. Manoj's oil painting (Figure 11.2) is manifest through Christ's seated, cross-legged posture, *padmasana* (lotus flower pose), his lightly closed eyes,

Figure 11.3 *St Anthony's Shrine*, a painted, concrete-moulded tableau installed in 2003 at St Anthony's Friary Church, Bengaluru by the Keralite artist, Fr Saji Mathew.

serene facial expression and, importantly, the *jnanamudra* (the symbolic hand gesture held at chest height). Significantly, all of these aspects feature in the original 1974 mosaic designed by Fr Joy Elamkunnapuzha and made by V. Balan for Dharmaram (see Figure 11.1). I wish to extend this artistic lineage of 'making' to connect it with a more recent artwork, Fr Saji's 2003 installation (Figure 11.3), a painted, concrete-moulded tableau entitled *St Anthony's Shrine* (which is around two miles from Dharmaram College, along the Hosur Road), an artwork that I suggest also invokes the notion of guru. St Anthony's Shrine was set up in 2003, to provide a quiet place for reflection and prayer.[12] Until then, devotees had gathered at the Blessed Sacrament[13] chapel at the St Anthony's Friary Church complex, where a collection of statues of saints was kept in glass display cases. Because of the number of visitors and the lighting of oil lamps and candles, it was decided that a bigger area was needed, for worshippers to enter safely and to provide adequate space for all who come to worship. As Figure 11.3 shows, the statues in the glass boxes were transferred into this new space, which was named St Anthony's Shrine when it was inaugurated in 2003. The tableau of the meditative Jesus, sitting underneath the banyan tree, is far larger than the glass-boxed statues and occupies most of the wall to which it is affixed. Fr Saji Mathew designed the installation in this manner to enable Jesus to 'embrace all' and be 'the central focus' in this meditative space (tropes 6 and 7).[14] Influenced by other visualisations of Christ/Jesus as guru that Fr Saji Mathew reports 'having seen here and there over time',[15] he worked with a Keralite 'maker' from Kochi to construct the concrete tableau. The 'maker' is known to Fr Saji Mathew simply as 'Mr George' and was, apparently, a student of the late V. Balan, the chief craftsperson behind the Dharmaram mosaic, which I discussed above.

In his personal blog, Fr Saji Mathew describes 'St Anthony's Shrine' as a place for healing and quiet. He writes:

> Here in the shrine, this large sized relief work of serene image of Jesus has a cathartic effect on people who arrive here with various difficulties and challenges of everyday life. This central image of Jesus gives direction to, scattered, and at times misdirected, personal Christian devotions to saints and other pieties.[16]

Here, we might read the image of Jesus as guru in terms of Amaladoss's assertion that 'He [Jesus] is launching and animating a global project that works for the fulfillment of all humans and of the whole universe' (2006, 75) (trope 5). St Anthony's Friary complex is located in central Bengaluru, a city that has undergone immense change in urban infrastructure as well as in socio-cultural lifestyles over the last 25 years. The sociologist Smitha Radhakrishnan writes:

> Bangalore [Bengaluru] is the beating heart of India's IT industry, the most visible city in a short but growing list of Indian IT cities that includes Mumbai, Hyderabad, Chennai, Pune, and Gurgaon. ... In Bangalore, more than practically any other Indian city, the positive effects of the IT industry seem pervasive, whether in the crowded mall or the mushrooming tech parks, in the innumerable engineering colleges or the new high-end international airport.
>
> (2011, 26)

I suggest that the installation of *St Anthony's Shrine* might be read as a creative and spiritual intervention into such changed lifestyles and pace of living, and I am reminded of Lannoy, writing in 1974, when he said:

> At least as long as India continues to be in transition from a sacred to a secular society, the guru-figure will remain the model for the Indian charismatic leader, not because India is more or less religious than the supposedly advanced cultures, but because the guru-figure answers a cluster of psychological needs.
>
> (1974, 348)

Figure 11.4 'In *padmasana* posture': *St Anthony's Shrine*, a painted, concrete-moulded tableau installed in 2003 at St Anthony's Friary Church, Bengaluru by the Keralite artist, Fr Saji Mathew (detail).

Fr Saji Mathew entitles the blog piece I quote above 'Jesus the guru in Buddhist meditative posture', and he writes of the importance of 'the modern, inclusive inter-religious Indian Christian Psyche [sic]'.[17] The title of his blog (and thus the artwork) makes direct reference to Buddhism whilst manifestly being anchored in Christian tradition in terms of its physical location in the church in Bengaluru and its Christian (Fr) artist. We might understand this combination of religious traditions as a mindful, *personal* expression of the 'modern, inclusive, inter-religious Indian Christian Psyche' that Fr Saji Mathew both writes of and shares himself. Unlike the earlier pieces of 'Christ the Guru' (V. Balan; M. P. Manoj), where we experienced a deified rendition of Christ, I suggest that Fr Saji Mathew's installation, through the symbolism of quietude and meditation, through the simple 'woodcut-style' depiction of the natural world (the banyan) enhanced by the shades of brown on the installation itself, foregrounds 'Jesus' over a glorified 'Christ'. Here (Figure 11.4), 'Jesus' is represented as guru through the recognisable *padmasana* posture, and the *abhaya* 'fearless' *mudra* communicating a sense of divine protection and safety (the *abhaya mudra* uses an upright, raised, flat hand at chest height with the palm facing away from the body) (tropes 1, 2 and 4). On the presence of *mudras* in Christian Byzantine art, Rajaram Sharma writes, 'The gestures of Reassurance, Benedicto Latina, Benedicto Graeca and miscellaneous other gestures in Byzantine Art and religious practices form interesting parallels with the *mudras*' (2021, 38).

The guru-ness in Figure 11.3 is further exemplified by the figure being seated specifically under a banyan tree, with the tree's long tendril-like roots searching for the ground below it (emblematic of trope 3). The banyan (*Ficus benghalensis*) tree, ubiquitous across India and the wider region of South Asia, is strongly associated with Lord Buddha as it is believed that he attained enlightenment whilst meditating underneath such a tree. Within Hinduism, as well, the banyan is a revered tree, known as *Kalpavriksha*, representing longevity and the divine creator, Lord Brahma. The tableau at St Anthony's Shrine clearly identifies the tree as a banyan, the roots hanging down from the branches, the wide trunk within which Jesus Christ is seated and its broad canopy sheltering the Lord and all who seek shelter within and under it (trope 1). Schouten reminds us that 'Shri Ramakrishna attempted to fathom the meaning of Christ through meditation. He saw in him the mystic who through methodical practice was able to realize the divine in his life. For him, the guru Jesus had become a yoga master' (2008, 259). This idea of Jesus as a 'yoga master' connects somewhat with Lannoy's reference to 'a quasi-divine figure and without economic function' (1974, 347) and as one who 'must submit to a dedication that largely cuts him off from normal satisfactions. ... [H]e is supposed, first of all, to be a competent therapist, and second, capable of supplying correct answers to the riddles of life because he has transcended the law of opposites' (1974, 349) (thus tropes 2, 3 and 4 mentioned above).

In order to consider these attributes of 'Jesus' and guru-ness further, we turn to two paintings by Jyoti Sahi from the 'Sermon on the Mount' series of artworks, made for Missio Germany in the mid-1980s.

Missio I and *Missio II*

Whilst I have referred to the three images discussed above as 'Christ the Guru' because of their intertextuality in relation to V. Balan and the Dharmaram mosaic, the Jyoti Sahi images I examine here have hitherto escaped such a distinct 'naming'. What I call *Missio I* and *Missio II* are two of Jyoti Sahi's images from his 1986 'Sermon on the Mount' series (16 paintings in total), which has circulated transnationally and thus by way of several languages and socio-cultural interpretations. A long-time friend and colleague of Jyoti Sahi, the Rev. Dr Eric Lott,

Figure 11.5 *Missio I*, 1986, by Jyoti Sahi ('Missio': International Catholic Mission Society, Germany).

chose to entitle *Missio I* 'Teacher on the Plain' in his book (co-created with Jyoti Sahi) *Faces of Vision* (2008). He described the painting in these words:

> Jesus is here surrounded by flame-like figures, leaping in ecstasy. They are also the fire-like blossoms that fall from a flame of the forest tree. So brilliant at the time of the pre-monsoon showers, one of these is prominent in Jyoti's garden. For several weeks of the year, the brilliant colours of this flame tree are what Jyoti looks at each day, often too forming a brilliant carpet underfoot.
>
> (Lott and Sahi 2008, 23)

The Rev. Dr Eric Lott's description reveals his friendship with Jyoti Sahi through his significantly personal interpretation of the image in terms of the 'fire-like' blossoms of the flame tree in Jyoti Sahi's garden. The year after the creation of the 16 paintings for Missio in Germany, Missio's magazine publication *Weltweit* ('Worldwide') showcased them in a special feature issue. From this special issue of *Weltweit*, the text in German which accompanies the painting (*Missio I*) reads:

> 'Flammende Blütenpracht': Wie kleine Flammen springen nach dem Monsunregen die Blüten der Regenlilie auf. Dieses Schauspiel hat mich als Kind immer erinnert an die feurigen Zungen des Pfingstfestes. Später fand ich bei einem alten Kirchenvater eine Beschreibung der Verklärung Christi, wo es heißt: Nicht nur die Gestalt Christi habe geleuchtet wie die Sonne, sondern dieser Glanz habe übergegriffen auf den ganzen Berg und jede Blume auf ihm sei verwandelt worden in eine Flamme, so dass die Jünger den Anblick nicht ertragen konnten.
>
> (J. Übelmesser, *Weltweit* 1986, 14)

> 'Flaming Blossoms': the rain lily's blossoms which always follow the monsoon rains are just like little flames of fire. When I was a child, this spectacle always reminded me of the flaming tongues of Pentecost. Later on in life, I found a description of the Transfiguration of Christ by an early Church Father which said: the figure of Christ not only lit up like the sun, but for those disciples present unable to behold the splendour, his radiance spread out over the entire mountain, whereby every flower was transformed into a flame.
>
> Translation by the author.

The German text above was penned by Fr Joe Übelmesser, and through personal communication with Jyoti Sahi I learnt that Fr Joe had commissioned a series of paintings on the subject of the Sermon on the Mount. These paintings were in memory of Fr Joe Übelmesser's friend, Fr Matthew Lederle, who had died suddenly in Goa in 1986.

Thanks to a careful, and thorough, archival practice on Jyoti Sahi's part, he was able to retrieve some of the letters he wrote to Fr Joe Übelmesser in the mid- to late 1980s. During my own correspondence with Jyoti Sahi (via email and online video conversations), I was struck by how central the exchange of letters and thus ideas with the German Missio Fathers had been to Sahi's creative work during this time. Jyoti Sahi had spent time at the seminary in Pune with both Fr Joe Übelmesser and Fr Matthew Lederle, and a series of talks he gave there was published by Routledge & Kegan Paul, entitled *The Child and the Serpent: Reflections on popular Indian symbols* (1980). In one of our email exchanges Sahi told me:

> The typed copy of the letter I sent to Fr. Joe is quite long, in which I set out the underlying ideas behind my work on the 'Dharma of Jesus' as articulated in what he presented as 'The Beatitudes'. Here I talk about

the 'lilies of the field … and how Solomon in all his glory was not arrayed like one of these. To see the lilies in this way, requires a new vision.' … I do not find in this paper mention of the rain lilies, but it is certainly true that for me, especially in my childhood, the way the rain lilies burst into a sudden splash of colour after the rains, was something very impressive. I must have mentioned this to Fr. Joe. I go on to say: 'Both in Matthew and Luke, the transfiguration of Jesus has a central place. One father of the Desert said that at the time of the transfiguration of Jesus, even the flowers on the hill of Thabor were transfigured. Jesus the teacher is transfigured before the eyes of his disciples, reminding us of Moses who also was transfigured when he returned with the tables of the Law, so that people found it difficult to look at the glory [of] his face.'[18]

The insight that Jyoti Sahi's archived letters provides allows us to appreciate the kind of friendship – indeed, a Christian kinship – that these men shared during these years, and the archived letters further document the profoundly intercultural and negotiated ideas of Jesus as a 'teacher' and a 'guru' that were often at the centre of their discussions.

Whereas the three images discussed above have circulated predominantly within India, *Missio I* and *Missio II* have intentionally travelled across cultures and languages. I suggest that this is chiefly due to the friendship Jyoti Sahi and the Missio German Fathers shared. Here, in *Missio I* (Figure 11.5), Jesus is seated cross-legged in *padmasana* whilst those around him seem to be in movement or dance, as indicated by the way the limbs, in particular, are depicted. The guru figure we understand to be Jesus is draped in a robe, seated and with his arms raised. Although the gesture of his right hand is somewhat indistinct, we can see the left hand is raised and we might interpret this as being an *abhaya* or 'fearless' *mudra*, to communicate a sense of divine protection and safety (we see this also in Figure 11.3: *St Anthony's Shrine* in Bengaluru) (tropes 1 and 2). This *mudra* is emboldened by the depiction of those surrounding Jesus as flames, their bodies drawn using heavily curved lines, lines that imitate the licking and flickering of a flame. Moreover, the figures' heads stretch upwards and their bodies flow into one another just as the flames of a fire do. Jyoti Sahi paints these figures in shades of red, ochre and orange which seem to spread outwards, covering the ground around them. I suggest that this depiction of the guru Jesus's followers foregrounds Amaladoss's notion of the guru as one who is 'capable of guiding disciples (*sishyas*) in their own search. They [the guru] can instruct them, solve their doubts and difficulties. They can authenticate their experiences' (2006, 69) (tropes 2, 3 and 4).

We might assume that the tree under which Jesus is seated is a banyan tree, given the guru trope as one which often combines a seated sage and a broad banyan canopy (see above for a discussion of *Kalpavriksha*). In *Missio I* (Figure 11.5) the tree itself is made up of human forms, their limbs curving and bending as if they were the trunk and branches of the great tree. This section of the composition is coloured in hues of dark blue, grey and black, and frames the bodies dancing like flames around Jesus. The melding of form, human and arboreal, allows the figure of the seated guru to be seen as though he shared the flame-like profile, and this creates the sense that he is simultaneously *with* and *apart* from those who surround him (trope 6). This foregrounding of the guru motif but with a simultaneous anchoring of the guru in and of 'the people' communicates the idea of Jesus as more than a 'Teacher'; rather, as Eric Lott writes, 'the Guru somehow shares the life of God, within himself and with his disciples. In such a context no one can speak of Jesus as "only as a teacher"; such a Teacher, even with his Word, and imparting his Way, mediates the inner life of God' (Lott and Sahi 2008, 26).

In *Missio II* (Figure 11.6), we see Jesus once again seated underneath a tree but here he is also seated on an anthill, and the text from a special issue of the *Weltweit* magazine reads:

'Die vom Ameisenhaufen': Als der indische Dichter Valmiki das Ramayana-Epos schrieb, war er einmal so sehr in Meditation versunken – sagt die Legende, – dass er nicht bemerkte, wie unter ihm ein Ameisenhaufen aufwuchs. Von dieser Begebenheit leitet sich der Name des Dichters ab: Valmiki – der vom Ameisenhaufen. Und ebenso nennt man heute in Indien die Unterdrückten und Armen: Valmikis – die vom Ameisenhaufen.

(J. Übelmesser, *Weltweit* 1986, 6)

'People of the anthill': Legend has it that when he was composing the Ramayana epic, the Indian poet Valmiki was at one point so deep in meditation that he did not realise an anthill was taking shape beneath him. It is from this incident that the poet got the name 'Valmiki – the one from the anthill'. To this day, in India, the oppressed and poor are called 'Valmikis' – the people of the anthill.

Translation by the author.

As in *Missio I*, in *Missio II* the figure of Jesus is seated, cross-legged and in a recognisable visual semiotic of 'teaching/imparting wisdom'; he is

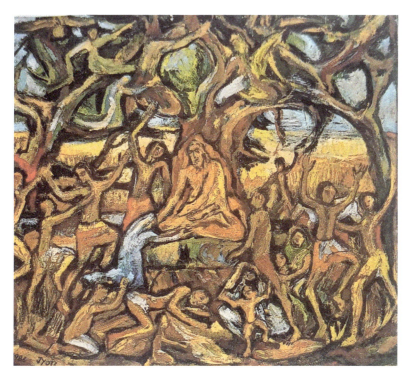

Figure 11.6 *Missio II*, 1986, by Jyoti Sahi ('Missio': International Catholic Mission Society, Germany).

central to the composition and people are gathered around him (tropes 1, 2 and 6). We notice in particular, through the luminescent hues of the clothes, the figure that has fallen at Jesus's feet (is it a woman?), the figure's head to Jesus's knee, the arms outstretched towards his feet. This depiction of falling at Jesus's feet further foregrounds the interpretation of Jesus as a benevolent figure, one it is possible to reach out to and touch (tropes 1 and 5), and, as Lannoy writes, 'The more active ideal of the spiritual "teacher" is associated with the Indian concept of compassion, or *karuṇā*' (1974, 348). We might also read this act as touching an elder's feet out of respect, seen in many Hindu traditions. This central aspect of both the composition of the image and the message of 'Jesus' (*karuṇā*) works productively with the overarching theme of Jesus's connection with the people of the earth, interpreted here as the *anawim*: the poorest, those who are outcasts and those who are persecuted. Through this connection with the oppressed, *Missio II* depicts Jesus as being literally part of the earth (he is *part of* the anthill), and I suggest that we might read this as emblematic of guru-ness (tropes 5 and 6). If we read the image as Jesus being 'one' with the earth – he is sitting atop the anthill, his body in direct contact with the clay and soil – then we might consider this to be an act that accentuates that 'the way to God is not through faithful observance of ritual and law but through fidelity to the fundamental demands of a love that reaches out preferentially to the poor and the oppressed' (Amaladoss 2006, 72). Other works of Jyoti Sahi created around this time – the late 1980s – explored a similar theme, and an image which prefaces chapter 6 in *The Child and the Serpent* (1990) shows a figure not unlike 'Jesus', as a yogi, lost in meditation, contained within an anthill. Sahi writes of this picture: 'The yogi lost in meditation. His body assumes the still, cone-like form of a mountain. (There are even stories of yogis who get lost inside an ant hill as the termites build their clay castle around the yogi without him noticing.)' (Sahi 1990, 68). Such 'Indian' cultural symbolism of the yogi and the anthill is visually manifest in Sahi's *Missio II* painting (Figure 11.6), making connections outside the frame to specifically Hindu, rather than Christian, traditions. The reading of Jesus the guru/yogi-like figure invokes what Amaladoss asserts is 'in-culturation', a term which

> is patterned on the term 'incarnation', which refers to the Word of God taking on human flesh to become human in Jesus (John 1:14). Christians believe that the Word becomes human in Jesus in order to divinize them as children of God. This divinization of humans also involves the transformation of their cultures and ways of life.
>
> (2021, 417)

I suggest that across *Missio I* and *Missio II*, Jyoti Sahi employs the visual semiotic of the guru figure to foreground the semiotic of 'Jesus' ('the Son of God') over a more deified, 'Christ' semiotic (tropes 4, 5 and 6). Jyoti Sahi realises this through the combination of composition, style of painting and the colour palettes he employs, which communicate a sense of a *guru* who is connected with the people of the earth, who listens and who also guides and transforms them (tropes 2, 4 and 7).

Conclusion

In the presentation and examination of five visual artworks in which Jesus/Christ is portrayed as guru, this chapter has attempted to trace a series of seven guru tropes (compiled from the work of Amaladoss, Lannoy and Schouten) across these artworks. Overall, the figure of 'the

Jesus (Christ) guru' is represented through a seated, male figure, in a meditative and/or teaching state. I have argued that it is through composition, style, artistic medium and colour palette that the tropes of guru examined here are communicated. Furthermore, I have outlined how these are employed to foreground a deified image of Christ or a more grounded, Son of God representation of Jesus. A Hindu reception of these representations of Jesus Christ has not been a focus of this chapter but it is productive to consider Lott's words:

> For many more Hindus, though, Jesus was seen as Guru. And the Guru may begin as 'teacher', but one whose personal charisma and spiritual potency – in the case of Jesus especially seen in his self-giving acts of healing and eventual dying – draw us nearer to God and even mediate the very character and being of God. The Guru then becomes far more than 'just a teacher'.
>
> (2008, 25–6)

I suggest that this quote demonstrates the transcultural and trans-spiritual qualities of the notion of guru when it moves beyond a simple understanding of 'guru = teacher'. Notably, Lott describes the guru as one who 'mediates the inner life of God' and therefore might be thought of as a being through which we reach God. Moreover, here Lott's sense of guru even suggests a being who is *of* God and is therefore knowable and yet 'unknowable' in the same moment. The beginning of this chapter referenced the apophatic through Voss Roberts's work; I argue that the visual representation of Jesus/Christ, over the verbal or textual representation of the same, extends and deepens our insight into 'no matter how many words or how careful the choice of words, none can suitably or properly describe the holy mystery that is the divine' (Voss Roberts 2021, 347).

The analysis of the guru-Jesus images in relation to the apophatic and 'seeing' foregrounds the capacity of the non-verbal/non-textual by highlighting 'the alternative cognitive structures of the visual' (Hirsch 2004, 1211). Through the trope of the guru, the gazer is invited into a moment of 'seeing' that transcends the spoken or written word and opens up a more intimate space for 'knowing' and 'feeling'. I argue that the channelling of the nature/character/message of Jesus Christ through the visual trope of the guru reveals facets of guru-ness that encode ideas of what it is to recognise oneself as both Christian and Indian. The analysis of the images has attempted to identify such facets and examine how they find expression through the visual medium. As Fr Saji Mathew's 2003 *St Anthony's Shrine* installation shows us, there is much scope for post-millennial expressions of guru-ness, and in this particular case we might recognise the effectiveness of such an installation in its 'attempt to tap various sources of power to overcome challenging situations in life' (Ponniah 2021, 223). India and ideas of 'Indianness' (see Dawson Varughese 2021, 2018a, 2018b) continue to evolve in the post-millennial period. Policy changes, such as the Citizenship (Amendment) Act (CAA, 2019) – whereby 'religion' has been used overtly to grant citizenship under Indian law – mean that it is more important than ever that we understand that 'citizenship concerns more than rights to participate in politics'. Indeed, citizenship 'concerns the moral and performative dimensions of membership that define the meanings and practices of belonging to a society' (Holston and Appadurai 1996, 200).

Notes

1 This organisation is committed to building up a 'digital library of Christian music, arts and literature of India', and features research work in Syriac chants and Aramaic and Christian art. http://christianmusicologicalsocietyofindia.com/ (accessed 8 March 2023).
2 Dr Joseph Palackal, pers. comm., August 2020.
3 M. P. Manoj, pers. comm., December 2021.
4 M. P. Manoj, pers. comm., December 2021.
5 See www.missio.com (accessed 8 March 2023).
6 Bengaluru, the capital of Karnataka state, is about 160 miles (260 km) north-east of its border with (northern) Kerala and has various transport connections for interstate travel.
7 http://christianmusicologicalsocietyofindia.com/.
8 Fr Saji Mathew, pers. comm., November 2021.
9 Dr Joseph Palackal, pers. comm., September 2021.
10 The thookuvilaku (a hanging lamp) hangs to the right of Christ as you look at the image, further situating the image regionally and culturally within South Asia.
11 M. P. Manoj, pers. comm., December 2021.
12 Fr Saji Mathew, pers. comm., November 2021.
13 http://friaryparish.com/40_hours_adoration.html (accessed December 2021).
14 Fr Saji Mathew, pers. comm. November 2021.
15 Fr Saji Mathew, pers. comm. November 2021.
16 See 'Jesus the guru in Buddhist meditative posture'. https://www.photographartdesign. com/2012/10/relief-work-jesus-at-st-anthonys.html (accessed 8 March 2023).
17 See 'Jesus the guru in Buddhist meditative posture'.
18 Jyoti Sahi, pers. comm., November 2021.

References

Amaladass, Anand and Gudrun Löwner. 2012. *Christian Themes in Indian Art: From the Mogul times till today.* [New Delhi]: Manohar.
Amaladoss, Michael. 2006. *The Asian Jesus.* Maryknoll, NY: Orbis Books.
Amaladoss, Michael. 2021. 'Inculturation', in *The Routledge Handbook of Hindu–Christian Relations*, edited by Chad M. Bauman and Michelle Voss Roberts, 417–29. Abingdon: Routledge.
Beldio, Patrick M. 2021. 'Aesthetics, art, and visual culture in Hindu–Christian relations', in *The Routledge Handbook of Hindu–Christian Relations*, edited by Chad M. Bauman and Michelle Voss Roberts, 268–79. Abingdon: Routledge.

Beltramini, Enrico. 2021. 'The "wisdom writer": Michael Amaladoss and his thought', *Religions* 12 (6): art. no. 396, 1–13. https://doi.org/10.3390/rel12060396.

Brockington, John. 1992. *Hinduism and Christianity*. Basingstoke: Macmillan.

Copeman, J. and A. Ikegame. 2012. 'The multifarious guru: An introduction', in *The Guru in South Asia*, edited by Jacob Copeman and Aya Ikegame, 1–45. Abingdon: Routledge.

Dawson Varughese, E. 2018a. *Visuality and Identity in Post-millennial Indian Graphic Narratives*. New York: Palgrave Macmillan.

Dawson Varughese, E. 2018b. '(Social) memory, movements and messaging on Tulsi Pipe Road: "Seeing" public wall art in Mumbai', *South Asia: Journal of South Asian Studies* 41 (1): 173–93. https://doi.org/10.1080/00856401.2018.1385671.

Dawson Varughese, E. 2021. 'Public wall art on Tulsi Pipe Road, Mumbai: The Indian post-millennial contemporary, sexual violence and "femaleness"', *Postcolonial Interventions* 6 (2): 14–44. https://postcolonialinterventions.com/archive/ (accessed 9 March 2023). https://doi.org/10.5281/zenodo.5106479.

Hirsch, Marianne. 2004. 'Editor's column: Collateral damage', *PMLA* 119 (5): 1209–15. https://doi.org/10.1632/003081204X17798.

Holston, James and Arjun Appadurai. 1996. 'Cities and citizenship', *Public Culture* 8 (2): 187–204. https://doi.org/10.1215/08992363-8-2-187.

Jyoti Art Ashram. 2007. https://jyotiartashram.blogspot.com/.

Lannoy, Richard. 1974. *The Speaking Tree: A study of Indian culture and society*. London: Oxford University Press.

Lott, Eric and Jyoti Sahi. 2008. *Faces of Vision: Images of life and faith*. Leicester: Christians Aware.

Ponniah, James. 2021. 'Popular religious traditions and shared religious spaces', in *The Routledge Handbook of Hindu–Christian Relations*, edited by Chad M. Bauman and Michelle Voss Roberts, 219–29. Abingdon: Routledge.

Radhakrishnan, Smitha. 2011. *Appropriately Indian: Gender and culture in a new transnational class*. Durham, NC: Duke University Press.

Sahi, Jyoti. 1990. *The Child and the Serpent: Reflections on popular Indian symbols*. London: Arkana.

Schouten, Jan Peter. 2008. *Jesus as Guru: The image of Christ among Hindus and Christians in India* (trans. Henry and Lucy Jansen). Amsterdam and New York: Rodopi.

Sharma, Rajaram. 2021. 'Buddhist art of India and Orthodox Christian art of the Byzantine Empire', in *Ratna Dipa: New dimensions of Indian art history and theory: Essays in honour of Prof. Ratan Parimoo*, edited by Gauri Parimoo Krishnan and Raghavendra Rao H. Kulkarni, 37–47. New Delhi: Agam Kala Prakashan.

Thayil, Jeet. 2021. *Names of the Women*. London: Jonathan Cape.

Visvanathan, Susan. 2010. *The Christians of Kerala: History, belief and ritual among the Yakoba*. New Delhi: Oxford University Press.

Voss Roberts, M. 2021. 'A theology of Hindu–Christian relations', in *The Routledge Handbook of Hindu–Christian Relations*, edited by Chad M. Bauman and Michelle Voss Roberts, 345–54. Abingdon: Routledge.

12
The total guru: film star guruship in the time of Hindutva
Jacob Copeman and Koonal Duggal

On 25 January 2017, at the Dera Sacha Sauda (DSS) headquarters in Sirsa, Haryana, the guru made his grand entrance before an audience of tens of thousands of devotees. It was an unusual sight, even in a devotional context where the unusual had become usual, to see him arrive on the stage astride an army tank, wearing black goggles and attire, gold embellishments and jewellery. As he sat atop the tank and saluted his devotee audience, flashes of colourful spotlights added to the dramatic effect. The guru was received with dancing, cheering and thunderous applause. Many in the crowd recorded the moment on their mobile phone cameras. High-volume synthesisers and drumbeats from the live orchestra provided the soundtrack as the guru descended from the tank and walked towards his cheering devotees, saluting and waving at them. If the scene was reminiscent of the dramatic entry of a hero in Bollywood films, it also recalled the grand entries of pop stars such as Michael Jackson in their live concerts. These are more than analogies, for by then the DSS guru had himself become a pop and film star, as well as having begun to perform a number of other roles not normally associated with spiritual guruship. Significantly, it was not only his roles that were changing. As his guruship unfolded over time, the roles of bhakt (devotee), spectator and fan became progressively folded together. If the movement's emphasis on the content of its teachings and practices appeared to decrease over this time, its 'exorbitant magnitude'[1] and focus on devotional spectacle centred on the guru starkly intensified. The DSS had developed into what we call a 'devotion of attractions'. If such techniques for the production of awe and surprise as the grand entrance of the guru had been integrated from Bollywood films and live rock and pop concerts, these were roles that he had also already begun to perform. Indeed, given that the DSS was already a devotion of attractions, it wasn't a complete surprise – indeed it seemed fitting – when rumours of the first instalment of his *MSG: Messenger of God* feature-film franchise, in which the guru would play himself, surfaced in 2015. In 2017, however, the DSS guru was sentenced to 20 years in prison for the rape of two female ascetics living in his *dera*.[2] Later, in 2019, he was convicted of the murder of an investigative journalist and sentenced to life imprisonment.[3] While these crimes are not our primary concern in this chapter, we do explore the sovereign conditions that enabled them and allowed him to evade imprisonment for many years, and his imprisonment casts a shadow over all present discussion of the movement.

Before his imprisonment, we began to see an increasing use of terms belonging to modern urban lingo – rock star, bling, dude, etc. – that defined him in ways that emphasised his 'being at home' in India's post-liberalisation era and that sought to attract millennials. When asked in an interview about his rock star persona and penchant for wearing fashionable blingy attire, the DSS guru explained that it formed part of an attempt to make his teachings and welfare measures attractive to young people who, drawn to the DSS, would then refrain from taking drugs.[4] If this suggests that the guru's adventurous masculine acts are necessary to keep the devotional economy in circulation, it is also, appropriately enough, a typical Bollywood trope, with acts of self-indulgence and ostentation coming to be sanctioned and recognised as virtuous if they can be shown to be socially concerned and public-spirited rather than narrowly self-interested (Vanita 2002, 155). Tales abound of sophisticated middle-class audiences walking out of the badly produced DSS films. The DSS guru is considered by them to be gaudy and crass (one critic pointing to a 'cringing parade of crazy costumes'). But for adherents the films' quality lies elsewhere. As one of the guru's aides told us in 2021, 'The main motive of the films is their message irrespective of their quality. To sugar-coat the bitter medicine for cure against drugs, bad habits and all evils.' While we suggest that is not the only motive, 'sugar-coating' is indeed a common trope employed by gurus for 'reeling in' devotees for deeper purposes. The 'tacky' miraculous production of *vibhuti* (sacred ash) by south Indian guru Sathya Sai Baba was famously explicated by him in such terms: 'I give you what you want so that you may want what I want to give you' (T. Srinivas 2012, 270).

There exist established genres of devotional and mythological film (Vasudevan 2005; Hughes 2005). Some of these films – for example *Sant Tukaram*, which narrates the story of the eponymous saint (Fattelal and Damle 1936) – famously contributed to the growth in popularity of the figures or the devotional practices they depicted.

Jai Santoshi Maa (1975), in particular, was notable for performatively creating the devotional phenomena it described (Das 1981): it led to new rituals of fasting among female adherents. In a double movement, such films at once produce existing devotees as film spectators and seek to convert non-devotee spectators into future devotees. Moreover, early devotional films stirred secular opposition because of their portrayal of miracles (Vasudevan 2005), something that also followed the release of the first film in the MSG franchise, *MSG: The Messenger of God* (2015). Early devotional films such as *Sant Tukaram* and *Jai Santoshi Maa*, clearly, are notable forebears of the *MSG* franchise. But there are significant differences. The *MSG* series of films innovatively combined the mythological and feature-film genres of Indian cinema. Full of mythological tropes, their stylisation also conforms to that of India's popular cinema, with music, dance and stylised violence and exaggeration. Indeed, they enact the kind of melodrama that is fairly typical of *masala* movies, featuring drama, action and dance sequences, and with an array of borrowings from and parodies of mainstream Bollywood. These are visible in scenes such as one which resembles Amitabh Bachchan's iconic slow-motion running sequence in *Agneepath* (1990) and the deliriously incongruous adoption of mannerisms made famous by the film star Shah Rukh Khan. The opening of the first *MSG* film borrows, too, from the well-known *Mein Samay Hoon* sequence featured in B. R. Chopra's *Mahabharata* TV serial.

Throughout, the guru performs an abundance of special-effect-produced miracles. Yet the DSS has its roots in *sant* social reform traditions that criticise 'showing off' and exorbitance. Performed in order to generate an aura of the miraculous that could attract new followers and so contribute to the movement's expansion, cinematic special effects allowed the guru to enact ostentatiously the miracles he otherwise railed against in his regular *satsang*[5] addresses. The state Censor Board attempted to ban the film on account of these miracles: it deemed that the guru, given that he was playing a version of himself, was not sufficiently dissociable from the acts he performed. Indeed, that, arguably, was exactly the point, from the DSS's point of view. The Board, however, was overruled by the BJP-led government, for whom the DSS guru had instructed his followers to vote, highlighting once again the entanglement of gurus in electoral politics.[6]

The *MSG* franchise – five films in total – was, then, as genuinely innovative as it was extraordinarily derivative. In this chapter we examine the relationship of these films to the state and also why a guru who already performed live *satsang* events across various televisual and digital platforms additionally sought to enter the cinematic medium. Production and consumption of the films were collapsed together, with audiences (specifically devotees and government and state authorities) being also active participants in their composition, as we shall see. Through this blending, the films sought of course to reach a further intended audience: non-devotees who might be persuaded by them to become followers. The guru's interfacing of 'the theological and the technological' (De Vries 2001, 46) in the production of special-effect miracles is particularly significant here. Could these be dispassionately dismissed as mere VFX wizardry or might they dupe credulous viewers? In its consideration of *MSG 1* the Censor Board evidently inclined towards the latter view. We shall see how, for the DSS, it was important to maintain a productive ambiguity on this question. Further, if the mobilising sway of the guru suggests domination and even an extractive approach towards devotees (see Introduction), the guru's exaggerated spectacles equally form welcome opportunities for devotees, frequently from disadvantaged backgrounds, 'to participate in omnipotence' and 'enjoy themselves in him' (Mazzarella 2022). Since these spectacles entirely depend on such participation, the relationship between leader and followers genuinely constitutes a kind of 'mutually amplifying feedback loop' (Mazzarella 2022).

Outlining what we call a model of total guruship, we see how DSS filmmaking is employed to facilitate and extend what was already a bhakti of expansion and exorbitance. That the films might function to some extent as a repository of the guru's id is suggested by their remarkable concentration of miraculous feats and his attempt to occupy every subject position both in terms of production – lead actor, script writer, sound editor, VFX creative director and more, amounting to at least 30 categories – and narrative: his turning of enemies into images of himself and the incorporation of devotees, deities, legendary heroes and earlier gurus into his ever-enlarging persona. The figure of the total guru is suggested by the multiplication of roles and repeat references by devotees to his versatility and his being 'all-in-one'. 'For the narcissist', as Christopher Lasch (1991, 19) put it, 'the world is a mirror'. The guru constructs the world as his mirror through tried and tested techniques such as mimetic suggestion, but also more innovative, cinematically dependent ones such as special-effect-assisted metamorphoses.[7] His 'grandiose self' (Lash 1991, 19) reflects back at him not only from the attention and admiration of others but through a double movement in which he projects his own self onto those others while also seeking to incorporate them. But to reiterate the point, so far as the underprivileged devotee is concerned such incorporation is frequently desired; the devotee finds in 'the superhuman scale of the leader's gestures' certain compensations for their own conditions (Mazzarella 2022).

The films also show signs of a carefully constructed defence against what was then the growing possibility of the guru's imprisonment.

Coterminous with their production were key developments in local and national electoral politics, especially the elevation of Narendra Modi from chief minister of Gujarat to the office of prime minister. The guru, as mentioned, supported Modi's Bharatiya Janata Party (BJP) at election time. The films collectively have a double relationship to Modi and his politics.

(1) They seek to copy Modi and repackage his politics to the extent that they become 'messengers of Modi' as much as of God. This recalls Alfred Gell's (1997) account of how gifts of praise amount to an Indic model of attempting to control entities 'superior' to the praise-giver, drawing them into a relationship of interdependence: exaltation effects neutralisation. This makes sense in light of the court cases the guru then faced. Both the films, then, and his support of Modi at election time form part of the same quid pro quo strategy, for he, likewise, was going to need Modi's support.[8] However, the guru not only endorsed Modi's approach and agenda; he sought to replicate it, mirroring both his politics and his tactics in seeking to extend his reach to become a national guru rather than a merely provincial one, just as Modi had successfully made the move from regional to national political leader.

(2) At the same time, the films carried – at least initially – a sense of threat. If the first tactic was the carrot, this was the stick. With its million-plus devotee extras, the guru's first film demonstrated the guru's power and might while containing narrative forewarnings about the possible unrest and civil strife that would result were the guru to be imprisoned on the charges he then faced.

The films contained, then, both obsequiousness and coded threats towards government and state authorities as differing but complementary means of building up the defences of the guru and his 'little fiefdom' (S. K. Singh 2017).

The guru's first feature film, *MSG: The Messenger of God*, was released in India in 2015. As well as starring as a version of himself, the guru is also credited with writing and co-directing it. Four more films quickly followed before the guru's imprisonment. With the guru having already experimented extensively with pop music and visual media forms (e.g. fashion photography),[9] the films sought to translate the guru's charismatic and performative appeal from printed to moving image, from small to big/cinematic screen, and from saint/baba/guru to cinematic icon. It is well known that certain film stars, particularly in south India, are worshipped, often in the cinema hall itself (S. V. Srinivas 1996). Here we find the reversal of this, namely one who is already worshipped turning into a film star. Indeed, his transformation from 'Saint' into 'Star', whose daredevil stunts drew comparisons with Tamil cinema icon Rajnikanth, inverts standard narratives about fan bhakti (devotion) in which film stars typically become semi-mythological figures and fans turn bhakt (devotee). Moreover, *MSG* embodied a shift from depiction of gurus in film to the guru as a film star playing (a version of) himself.[10] Perhaps it was for this reason that devotees did not respond in the same way to the film as Rajnikanth's devotees do to his:

> At the 9.15 am screening of the sequel to *MSG: Messenger of God* in midtown Mumbai, [the guru's] followers ensured that there were few seats to spare. But unlike Rajnikanth's devotees, they did not throw flowers at the screen when their hero appeared. Nor did they cheer when the credits revealed that Singh was *MSG 2: The Messenger*'s writer, editor, music composer, lyricist, production designer, choreographer, director and producer. Instead, the audience received *MSG 2* in reverential silence, as though at a prayer meeting or a video-streaming of a sermon.
>
> (Ramnath 2015)

While the guru's project connects to a broader global context in which 'religion and entertainment are increasingly difficult to distinguish from each other' (Hughes and Meyer 2005, 150) – a convergence witnessed for instance in the case of the pop star, film actor and Catholic priest Marcelo Rossi (Abreu 2005) – it also of course has its own local and national significance.[11] The opening half of the chapter concentrates on the first *MSG* film, *MSG: Messenger of God*, in particular the prominence within it of special effect miracles as well as its combative attitude towards the state authorities threatening to imprison the guru. The second half focuses on the later *MSG* films, which embody the guru's particular instantiation of the wider 'Hindutva turn' (Mohammad-Arif and Naudet 2020), a turn away, in his case, from confrontation with the state towards active collaboration with Modi's de facto majoritarian Hindu rashtra (Jaffrelot 2021, 6). Threaded through the sections is a concern with the guru's dream of totality.

Dreams of totality

Like other devotional movements with their origins in the north Indian *sant* heritage – 'the creed of the saints, a tradition associated with such figures as Kabir and Nanak' (Babb 1986, 17) – the DSS, founded in 1948, is an avowedly social reformist spiritual organisation, which aims – according to its official website – to 'save people from the complex ties, malpractices and superficial rituals that had been afflicting religion'.[12] Its teachings do not markedly differ from other devotional orders that have their origin in the north Indian *sant* heritage. Common to most of these orders are: guru-bhakti – devotion to a living spiritual master; devotee constituencies made up of both Hindus and Sikhs; an emphasis on the recitation of sacred words; a conception of transcendence as being open to all regardless of caste or gender; a social reformist agenda; and a set of teachings inherited from a family of non-sectarian *sants*, or saints, which began to emerge in the medieval period. Distinctions between Hindus and non-Hindus, and indeed distinctions of caste and other internal differentiations of community, tend to be downplayed, at least rhetorically, in favour of shared devotional attachment to a spiritual master. Many Dalits have been drawn to the DSS from Sikhism partly for this reason, with many gurdwaras in Punjab and its environs continuing to fail to live up to the religion's message of social equality (S. Singh 2019). The provision of numerous welfare services by the DSS is another key factor. In tension with the high-profile adventures of its guru, official DSS teachings propound a strong anti-'show-off' message: 'Dera Sacha Sauda does not believe in any kind of false practices, false pretensions, misguidance or any kind of show off which has nothing to do with spiritualism and those ritual practices which take you away from your real goal.'[13] The movement's professed aversion to ritual and 'show off' (*tamasha*) situates it in a reformist tradition that has been determined to undermine 'superstitious ritual'. All this is fairly standard for this devotional milieu. As we have pointed out elsewhere, however, what does set it apart – quite dramatically – from comparable *sant* orders are innovations introduced since the accession to the guruship of Gurmeet Ram Rahim Singh Ji Insan in 1990.[14] The DSS has in recent years come to possess a very particular relationship with excess. Its leaders and devotees alike understand the movement to be on a very special mission, its guru a figure of the stature of Krishna or Jesus. It seeks massive expansion. 'The day will come soon when every child in this world will have the name of Sacha Sauda on his tongue', says the DSS website.[15]

When we first began research on the DSS in 2004 it claimed to have 1–2 million devotees; by 2018 it claimed 60 million.[16] Excess of all kinds: a ramping up of the celebrity status that other spiritual leaders have sought and achieved, frequently through adept harnessing of new media forms; and world record-breaking spectacles of 'service' inspired by, or achieved because of, the blessings of the guru. Many such events involve all-justifying *seva* (service) activities,[17] but others possess a more hallucinogenic, whimsical quality: the most blood pressure readings and diabetes screenings in a single day, the largest display of oil lamps (150,009), the largest finger painting (3,900m^2), the largest vegetable mosaic (185,807m^2), and even the highest number of people sanitising their hands simultaneously (Roy 2017). The latter is now taken as evidence that the DSS guru had foreknowledge of the COVID-19 pandemic, with the hand sanitisation spectacles he inspired evidence of his seeking to prepare and equip humanity for what would befall it.[18]

As will be clear, the DSS presents a devotion of and to the gigantic and the exaggerated. Its claim to possess 60 million devotees may be wildly inaccurate. But still, there is a story worth telling here. How does someone who 20 years ago was an obscure provincial guru come to achieve such an escalation of presence, devotees and national and international fame? We mentioned earlier a notion of a devotion of attractions, and we propose that this lies at the heart of the expansion. Famously, Tom Gunning (1990) coined the term 'cinema of attractions' to refer to the dominance of special effects and technological wonders over narrative coherence in early cinematography. Whatever the value or the coherence of DSS teachings may be, they have tended to be completely eclipsed – in devotional practice, reportage and scholarship – in part no doubt by the politics of caste and electoral alliances associated with the movement, but most of all by the sheer escalating spectacle of the guru himself. The message of his guruship progressively came to be overshadowed by the command 'See!', by devotional novelties, by his ability – like that of the cinema of attractions – to show, but far less to tell.

Yet the DSS's devotion of attractions does not exist in a vacuum, but within a larger burgeoning landscape of 'Disney divinity' (Srivastava 2009), replete with 'amusement park-like' ashrams (McKean 1996, 4) and multiple past and present instances of guru-focused excess and theatricality.[19] Certainly, other gurus have proliferated their roles and wider presences well beyond the bounds of the ashram. The DSS guru's embrace of Hindutva politics, likewise, is far from novel, with numerous gurus' increasing engagement in this area well documented.[20] In such cases a complementary relationship often quickly develops: 'while Hindutva extends state patronage to the gurus, on their part, the gurus facilitate Hindutva's entry among new social groups and into new geographical regions' (Kanungo 2012, 284). In the DSS's case, before Modi's ascent the organisation did not espouse a straightforwardly Hindu nationalist programme, but a more ecumenical vision with stronger links to Sikh than to Hindu traditions. To be sure, it harboured certain prototypical elements of a Hinduising agenda, for instance a strict approach to vegetarianism, a fascination with the Indian armed forces and an engagement with Adivasis as 'spiritual minors who required special supervision' (Roberts 2016, 8).[21] But such attitudes and understandings are passively accepted across the spectrum of mainstream national opinion, including, often, by those formally opposed to Hindutva ideology (Roberts 2016, 114). That is to say, there was nothing *especially* Hindu nationalist about these traits until they were sharpened and explicitly drawn into support of Modi's agenda in the *MSG* films. With the provisos just outlined, we can fairly say that the DSS guru's experiments in media spectacle were novel in their sheer profusion. Further, though on one level the DSS guru's turn to cinematic acting merely makes explicit a theatricality that already lay at the heart of public guruship, the fact of a guru acting in a movie as a version of himself nonetheless has never been done before and so introduces an unfamiliar and original element into not only the history of the DSS but also the broader world of guruship.

We highlight here how the DSS guru has sought to employ visual media to augment a sense of totality and embed himself across the various manifestations and scales of social life. Echoing and extending a formula laid down as early as the time of Emperor Akbar, who in the 1570s began to be depicted as a fusion of emperor, Sufi *pir* and Hindu guru (Pinch 2012), the DSS guru sought to become a kind of 'all-in-one' figure of totality, who bears comparison with Modi as described in Landau and Rageth's chapter, in his attempt to occupy subject positions beyond the conventional bounds of the category he formally occupies. The guru's own website declaims his remarkable 'versatility' and 'multi-talented' personality: he is 'Spiritual Saint; Writer; Musician; Director; Scientist; Feminist; Youth Icon; etc'.[22] But that is not all. Each category is further subdivided into a further array of subject positions, each of which he occupies. The trailer for one of his films highlights the '42 Spectacular Roles [performed in its realisation] by Dr. MSG Insan': direction, action, music, stunts, special effects, make-up, costume design and more: 'pitaji u are the only one who is all in one', as one devotee put it (Copeman and Duggal 2023). 'All in one' phraseology is, of course, inspired by commodity labelling and advertisements, and its use to describe the DSS guru is more than an analogy: 'all in one' is indeed his marketing strategy. The logic and phenomenon are not novel. The expansive, encompassing qualities of 'guru personhood' across time and space have been well documented. The 'all in one' phrase marks a quality of excessive subjecthood common to many a guru who contains many. For instance, the sense of totality it invokes and pays testament to recalls Lépinasse and Voix's (2011/12) discussion of Prabhat Ranjan Sarkar, the founder of the Hindu sect

Ananda Marga. Sarkar's 'teachings seem to be influenced by a totalising ambition to cover all fields of knowledge' (p. 65), from social treatises and works on health and history, to neo-humanism, and so on. Anandmurti Gurumaa, too, has been called an 'all-in-one' guru by her devotees on account of her multifacetedness and her ability to be everything they look for in a spiritual master (Rudert 2017, xvii). Just as Sarkar's followers find in this diversity evidence of his omniscience (p. 66), DSS followers locate in their guru's extraordinary 'versatility' and 'all-in-oneness' further suggestions of his supernatural ability. Omnipresence seems to stand in for omnipotence. To be sure, devotee comments that appreciatively call attention to his all-in-oneness are, in part, DSS-scripted 'talking points'. Despite this, it is evident that his all-in-oneness inspires awe in devotees: 'You, your voice, your music, your lyrics, your walk, your talk'; 'Never seen so many varieties in a single album'; 'HE is an all-rounder'; 'to have so much in one person is more than a miracle'; 'HE will be the only man in Bollywood who is so versatile'.[23]

In the case of Anandamayi Ma it is specifically the medium of photography that has the capacity to disclose the sublime multi-dimensionality of the guru persona. 'Ma', writes one devotee, 'famously incarnated Shiva, Krishna, Durga and Kali. When we see pictures of Ma in these *bhavas* (dispositions), we see her blazing with the wisdom virtues of Gods, but shining through a human lens. ... Ma left us with thousands upon thousands of images of herself. Each image is startlingly unique and expressive. There seems to be no aspect of human possibility that she did not embody. We can learn to appreciate the potentials of human life through contemplating these images.'[24] The DSS guru, too, is a prolific subject of the photographic image (Copeman and Duggal 2023), and, as for Ma, new media forms become apt instruments for not only conveying but instantiating his fullness. A key difference, however, is that Ma apparently embodies for her devotees every aspect of human possibility in the form of a kind of sublime prototype; she foreshadows an unrestrictive potential. The DSS guru's totalism, on the other hand, reduces the world to a single principle (himself). She may be a total guru to her followers, but he is a totalising one. Yet there remains, as we have stated, a strongly participatory element for devotees. Through their participation in the guru's extended personhood they too can traverse dimensions and subject positions – though always of course on his terms.

Celebration of the multifaceted, totalising nature of the guru's personality alongside his much-publicised accumulation of awards is of course reminiscent of a further distinctive mode of totality, that of the citizen's putative relation to the leader in totalitarian political regimes.

For instance, Lisa Wedeen's (1998, 504) description of how, 'On any given day', official discourse could extol the former Syrian President Hafiz al-Asad 'as the nation's "premier" pharmacist, teacher, lawyer, or doctor … the "father", the "combatant", the "savior of Lebanon", the "leader forever", or the "gallant knight", the modern-day Salah al-Din' [with] "complete understanding of all issues"' discloses a hagiography of versatility and encompassment similar to that used in reference to the DSS guru. Moreover, just as Syrian youth and others were 'ritualistically enlisted to assemble at "spontaneous" rallies orchestrated by "popular" organizations' to produce public spectacles in support of the leader, the emphasis on 'sheer chance' in DSS publications seeks to impose an a posteriori sense of 'as if spontaneity' (Ssorin-Chaikov 2006, 363) in order to draw a veil over the painstaking preparation required to mobilise the thousands of devotees required to achieve the world records attributed to their leader.[25] We discuss below the guru's award of a doctorate from 'world record university London' after which he became known as Dr MSG. Enumeration of distinctions such as this – especially those attained in Europe – is a key code of prestige in the authoritarian postcolony, notes Achille Mbembe (2001, 130); ruling-class citizens 'show off their titles – doctor, chief, president, and so on – with great affectation, as a way of claiming honor, glory, attention'. Indeed, from the guru's pronounced 'concern with rank', militaristic self-presentation, 'tendency to exaggerate and indulge systematically in superlatives' and ability to access and requisition devotee bodies in multiple ways[26] to his intimate address as Pita Ji (Father) and 'the almost invisible assumption [of] his right to enjoy everything' (114, 118, 125), we are confronted with a particularly vivid instance of what Mbembe calls *commandement* – an authoritarian modality of rule that is 'simultaneously a tone, an accoutrement, and an attitude' (2001, 32).[27] Further, and as we describe elsewhere,[28] the methods employed to enact dominion by certain gurus, the DSS guru chief among them, are strikingly in tune with key characteristics of totalitarian rule, namely 'their reliance on both premodern and modern forms of sovereignty, on both death cults and biopolitics, as well as a demand for subjective identification with the father' (Borneman 2004, 4). If our specific focus here is on forms of totalism connected with what we are calling the guru's excessive, or exorbitant, subjecthood, rather than on the mechanics of political totalitarianism, we nevertheless recognise the obvious entanglement and co-implication of the 'different' modalities in many instances, including this one.

In the first *MSG* instalment the guru turns other characters into visual likenesses of himself, an effect that is uncannily reminiscent of the

Modi mask-wearing phenomenon,[29] and which also demonstrates the reduction of everything to the guru – the totalisation that is the hallmark of DSS guruship. It is also visually emblematic of devotional participation in the collective personality of the guru (the guru's encompassment of multiplicity), which we discuss elsewhere.[30] Writing primarily of the figure of an ascetic rather than of that of a guru – though the line between them is of course frequently blurred – R. S. Khare (1984, 30) describes how they are often a 'multipurpose' figure: 'an operator, mediator, catalyst, bricolage', an 'all-worker'. They 'bridge' phenomena and 'pierce through tensions' (p. 22). Through special effects and the narrative possibilities it offers, cinema offered to the multipurpose guru new bridging powers that he utilised with a sense of relational abandon.

The heterogeneity of the associations he seeks to generate augments this sense of totality. As we shall see below, the dynamic is particularly visible in narrative terms in the guru's second film, *MSG 2: The Messenger* (2015), in which he stakes claims to both an Adivasi spiritual lineage and a Rajput inheritance. He entraps the auras of others through inhabitation of different forms and identities. A guru who never stands still, he seeks to encompass, or possess, all subject positions, enacting a kind of incorporative ungraspability. The different 'modes of exhibition' (Gunning 1990, 65) afforded by the polymedia landscape the DSS is alive to have facilitated the expression of the guru's persona(s) in more and more dimensions. At the heart of the DSS's devotion of attractions is an aesthetics of variety. We have written about his fashion and pop star roles elsewhere.[31] But why, specifically, did he make the move into film? The answer lies at least in part in cinema's mass appeal and the DSS's aspirations to massify its base further. The extraordinary reach and significance of cinema in India is often noted: it has been able to establish a mass public independent of literacy (Mazzarella 2013, 10). For the DSS, part of the promise of the enterprise lay precisely in the attempt to harness this reach in order to nurture a mass of devotees beyond its established constituencies in north India. Dubbing enables producers to 'tap new markets' for their movies 'beyond their [originating] linguistic region' (Ganti 2021, 77), and indeed, in addition to the expected Hindi and English, the DSS films were released in Tamil, Telugu and Malayalam.

Responses in Kerala to the guru's attempts to enter the local spiritual marketplace demonstrate the linguistic block on the reach of the DSS that prevailed until cinematic dubbing was to offer at least part of the solution.[32] A regular visitor to the southern state from 2012 onwards, in 2014 the DSS guru presided over a second *satsang* in the hills of Vagamon, Kerala, which was mostly attended by local tea estate workers. The guru,

386   GURUS AND MEDIA

writes Shahina (2014), 'makes a dramatic entry to the hall at 10:30am. ... He is accompanied by a large group of followers who have also come all the way from Sirsa, the headquarters of DSS in Haryana. ... Outside the hall, a team of percussion artistes perform the traditional Keralite orchestra, *Pancharimelam*.' Attendees, however, remain 'more curious than swayed. ... The speech he delivers ... is old rhetoric on the "good" and "evil" within oneself, and the quest for self knowledge. It is followed by Singh crooning a devotional rock number from his album *Love Charger*. It is a mellow performance accompanied by slow head and body movements. ... Many in the hall look bewildered.' A female attendant of the guru addresses the crowd in Hindi and Malayalam. She 'desperately tries to make them shout the [standard DSS] slogan, "*Dhan dhan Satguru, tera hi asra*" ("Glory of the Satguru, you are our shelter.") Except for a few children, no one responds to her exhortations.' Shahina, fluent in both languages, is asked by the event organisers to help them overcome the language barrier by collecting the names and addresses of the participants.

As the movement – always subject to a temporality of rush[33] – sought to accelerate a shift from a provincial to a national identity, it is not difficult to see how cinema's technology of dubbing might assist the guru's self-mythologisation in different regional languages, allowing it to retain its expansionist hopes in challenging linguistic circumstances. The feature film would afford a kind of 'pollination' (Moulier-Boutang 2011, 108) – 'to cast or scatter abroad over an area, as seed in sowing' (Thrift 2012, 155) – beyond 'home' territories. The guru, dubbed and thrust into criss-crossing media platforms, might become 'open to unknowns' and thereby able to catch 'nonlinear multiplier effects' (p. 150).

MSG 1: miracles and menace

What, then, of the guru's first film and its publicity? The *MSG* film still (Figure 12.1) strongly recalls that of the Indian superhero film *Krrish* (2006), which features lead actor Hrithik Roshan standing facing a darkening cityscape. This pose in turn borrowed from iconic images of Batman surveying Gotham City, with the saviour figure facing the city to be rescued during the film. On the *MSG* poster, the guru's muscular back faces the spectator in a concert setting as he looks towards his followers, hands folded. The film itself consists mainly of song and dance sequences followed by episodes of crisis in which the DSS faces threats on account of the guru's welfare measures, especially his crusade against drug mafias. The guru is addressed in the film by many terms including *sant*, fakir and guru; but

Figure 12.1 Still from *MSG: The Messenger* official trailer. Source: YouTube. https://www.youtube.com/watch?v=scuWiXG5bh8.

most frequently the term of address is *Pita Ji* (Father), and indeed the guru is presented as a larger-than-life paternal figure who is dedicated to his mission of the welfare and protection of his *dera*, 'the youth', and the nation. His enemies in the end are reformed by virtue of the main protagonist's charismatic appeal. A particular feature of this first instalment is the performance by the guru of many miraculous deeds. He brings bullets to a halt, as in the Hollywood action thriller *The Matrix* (1999), which he turns into a tiara that crowns his head. He turns swords into flowers and flies like Superman (sometimes on the back of a lion).

Here the DSS was following, but also cinematically reconfiguring, an established template in which miracle performances can serve as effective means of devotee recruitment (Babb 1983). For a proselytising guru, cinematic realisation and projection of an aura of the miraculous might advance the goal of further massifying his movement. But here the DSS faced a problem, at least initially. The lumpen Indian masses have long been thought by authorities and intelligentsia to require special censorial protection from cinematic provocations because of their excessive vulnerability to being influenced (Mazzarella 2013), and, in connection with this, the cinematic depiction of miracles has been frowned upon (Vasudevan 2005). So it was not unexpected when legal complaints were filed about the film's alleged promotion of superstition (its depiction of miracles being at odds with the duty to 'develop ... scientific temper' as per a 1976 amendment to India's constitution). The superhero's supernatural feats were considered all too likely to be taken as real by an 'underdeveloped public', and the government Censor Board duly banned the film for this reason. However, as we have noted, the guru had asked his devotees to vote for the current ruling political party, and had accrued some political power. The Board, in an obvious case of political interference, was overruled. Her authority undermined, the chair of the Board resigned, and a film director known to be sympathetic to the ruling party was appointed in her place. The film was then released, albeit with a lengthy condescending disclaimer explaining that the miracles depicted were not really miracles but simply special effects, though of course such a disclaimer assumes literacy. William Mazzarella (2013, 12) has described 'the attribution to Indian publics of an excessive permeability to affective appeals', and just such an attribution was seen in the initial ban. Indeed, presumably the non-elite (extra-permeable?) nature of the devotee fan base made it even more imperative to ban or add the lengthy disclaimer to the film: these spectators were judged perhaps especially incapable of the 'critical reflexivity' required to avoid being 'easily duped by any passing demagogue' (Mazzarella 2013, 17).

Some have argued that the Censor Board's stance was at the very least inconsistent, since plenty of other Indian feature films depict superhuman feats without generating calls for bans. Abhishek Sudhir, for instance, writes of the Censor Board's disquiet about a film that

> glorified Rahim as a 'messenger of God', and a miracle worker who had the ability to vanquish drug addiction, restore sight to the blind, cure terminally-ill patients and single-handedly destroy his opponents. The hypocrisy of the members of the [Censor Board] stands exposed when one compares their handling of the recent [uncensored] Aamir Khan blockbuster *PK*. In that film, Khan plays an alien who picks up the Bhojpuri language by holding hands with a prostitute for several hours.[34]

But of course Sudhir is not comparing like with like. Other films obviously do feature superhuman deeds and special-effect miracles, but the 'day job' of the actors who perform them is not usually that of a spiritual guru. One can take issue with the Board's initial decision on account of its belittling conception of an 'underdeveloped public' or on the grounds of freedom of expression (a point also raised by Sudhir) – but one can at least understand the logic the film board was following.

More interesting is how an ostensibly social reformist guru who previously debunked the signature miracles of other spiritual personalities has latterly sought to project his own miraculous capabilities with such fervour.[35] He previously called – at least rhetorically, and perhaps as an alibi – for his devotees to 'Please think!' about such feats.

We have previously described the DSS's particular order of the miraculous as 'secular-compatible', for instead of infringing the laws governing the universe, miracles consist of feats of remarkable speed and quantity – the most blood collected in a single day, the most bodies pledged for donation, the fastest-ever construction of a cricket stadium, etc.[36] The temporality of rush, time compression and *as if* spontaneity (but in fact meticulously planned nature) of these feats is 'inspired by the guru'. 'A miraculously huge "Ajooba" [miraculous or wonderful] washing machine' is described in a DSS publication with the heading 'What a wonder it is!': 'The washermen [in a Sacha Sauda students' hostel] urged [the guru], and He gave instructions about this wonderful washing machine [that] has the capacity of simultaneously washing 1,000 clothes within only half an hour.' The repeated use of the English word 'wonder' is apt in that it is wonderment inside the bounds of natural law that is the foundation of such miracles. They are not miracles, but equally they are not not-miracles. Rather, they are apparently compatible with the movement's professed social reformism; indeed, feats such as most hand sanitisations, most blood donations, etc. are precisely enacted in order to combat 'social evils' and 'contribute to society'. But they also evoke a narrative and atmosphere of the miraculous. As one doctor told us of the extraordinary blood donation exploits of the DSS: 'Baba Ji created a miracle. He made 16,000 people donate blood in one day – it's definitely a miracle. Nowhere in the world could anyone make 16,000 people give blood in one day. Jesus and other spiritual masters did miracles in their own times based on the needs of society at the time. Jesus had hungry devotees – all of them needed to be fed, and the food multiplied. Similarly, [DSS guru] Hazoor Maharaj created a miracle based on the needs of society.'[37] The doctor's argument reflects the guru's emphasis on social utility: unlike the 'useless' materialisations of ash or rings (characteristic of gurus such as Sathya Sai Baba) that he criticises so acerbically, the DSS guru's miracles are miracles that 'contribute to society'. The labour of such miracles is performed, of course, by devotees. The guru inspires the labour. That is to say, DSS followers are responsible for the miracles they attribute to him. The participatory production of such miracles is ideologically denied both by the movement's literature and by devotees themselves. The guru's followers fetishise the energy they have produced together as a power inherent to the 'magnetiser'-guru (Mazzarella 2010, 724).

Large-scale follower participation for the achievement of world records is obviously critical. A DSS website advertises world records such as most ever birthday greeting videos (2017), largest ever vegetable mosaic (2014), largest human droplet (2013), and most people tossing coins (2011).[38] In 2012 alone the DSS reportedly created six world records.[39] Under the guru's guidance, we learn, 'more than 115 humanitarian works are being conducted and also 55 world records are registered on his name'. In light of this, 'world record university London has decided to grant Him [a doctoral] degree'.[40] Therefore, 'from [25 January 2016] onwards Revered Saint Ji will be addressed as Saint Dr Gurmeet Ram Rahim Singh Ji Insan', says the guru's fittingly named personal website, https://www.saintdrmsginsan.me/. In this way it is the guru who is credited with the world-record miracles his devotees perform. Partaking of the miracle-records for which they praise their guru, devotees are struck by their own ability to be mobilised. Numbers are key: DSS numbers do not simply represent devotional-humanitarian achievements but are constitutive of the order itself; the DSS and its guru are a kind of composite of cumulated numbers. Numbers both carry and hide human endeavours (Verran 2014, 279). The work, the human devotional labour that generates these numbers, becomes invisible as an unrecorded background story: they are the guru's numbers. Numbers make more seamless the conflation of a project whose stated purpose is to provide resources for the stricken and needy with a project of aggrandising and extending the influence and gain of a singular entity.[41]

However, this requires immediate qualification. Though the guru is every inch a unique person – an individual who is not only at ease with but a vigorous contributor to the society of the exhibition (Harcourt 2014) – it is not quite right to describe him in terms of singular personhood. As we have explained elsewhere, a guru is frequently the form through which a plurality (of devotees) appears as a singularity to others, a collective that is constituted as a single image.[42] Such a model of inclusive singularity complicates any simplistic story of one-sided appropriation of devotional labour. The miracles are perfectly in tune with bhakti-devotion: they are participatory. Bhakts are participants in – co-generators of – miracles. The plaudits received by the guru – the world records writ large in the Guinness Book, doctorates, acceleration and magnification of personality – *they* receive too. They both produce and consume the effects of wonder generated by the DSS.[43] Thus, DSS miracles – not miracles, not not-miracles – embody a certain plausible deniability that allows the guru to bridge the anti-miracle social reformism of the movement's heritage and his own projection of miraculous capabilities (in which devotees participate). The full-palette guru occupies every subject position, here both social reformer and miracle man.

At least, this was the state of affairs before the release of *MSG* in 2015, which saw the guru's entry into the domain of special-effect miracles – a move that brought his miracles under the purview of the Censor Board. His adoption of them seemed to signal a step change: whereas previously atmospheres of the miraculous were achieved through exaggeration, exorbitance, and mass appropriation of devotional labour, they were now generated through digital manipulation. We would question this understanding, however. Certainly, their digital production was novel (for him at least), facilitating all sorts of previously unimaginable incarnations and extraordinary feats. Yet there remained key similarities to the prior order of miracles. In their digital production at least, if not in terms of the feats they depict, they do not infringe the laws governing the universe: they are simply special effects. If previously the miracle was reduced to time compression coupled with bigness, it was now reduced to the digital knowhow of the production team. Indeed, the lengthy disclaimer at the film's opening plays into DSS hands, allowing it to retain the same plausible deniability characteristic of the DSS's prior order of the miraculous ('Of course they are not miracles!'), while continuing to cultivate miraculous atmospheres. Similarly, the new miracles tend to be in the service of 'good causes' – combating the drug mafia, etc. – and so retain some legitimising suggestion of social commitment, even as they augment the guru's hyperbolic personality.

The previous mode of miraculous production, as we have seen, excised devotees even as they themselves generated the exorbitant feats that produced in them effects of wonder, and the simultaneous reliance on and erasure of devotee labour was a signal feature of the production of these films. Not just devotees but everyone involved in creating the film is subordinated to the totalising figure of the guru. Publicity seemed to deny almost any participatory sense of its production, instead again fetishising the energies and capacities of the many as a singular property of the magnetiser-guru. *MSG* was reportedly written and produced by the DSS guru. But not only that: 'He also is its co-director, co-costume designer, co-choreographer, co-editor, co-action director, stuntman, lyricist, singer, music director and of course, the lead actor' (Roy 2017), and yet devotees, necessarily, are ever present, too. They are the indispensable constituency that the superhero 'saves'; they form the large crowds in the many crowd scenes; they are the necessary primary witnesses of his special-effect miracles. Indeed, *MSG* holds the world record for the most ever – in excess of a million – film extras. They were necessary, too, if one is to believe the reports, for *MSG* to attain the feat of the highest-grossing opening week in Indian cinematic history – yet another record and proof of wonder. The simultaneous erasure of devotees and critical participation of and dependency on them is thus maintained in this modified digital order of the miraculous.

How were devotee understandings affected when the guru's miracles began to be conveyed cinematically? The devotee comments we have been drawing on, and our own interactions with devotees, suggest that while they remained fully aware that the miracles depicted are not real, the film nonetheless augments an atmosphere of miracles and wonder around the person of the guru. The guru, as we have noted, has railed in his discourses against showy miracles: 'Saints [such as he] hold *satsangs* in which they don't put on any spectacle [*tamasha*] where they touch a thing and it becomes a ring [*anguthi*], where rice will come, or ashes [*rakh*] materialise. This is the work of a magician, not of a saint. "I'll make you live. I'll kill you." The saints can do it, but they don't do it.'[44] Devotees see in *MSG* what the guru can or could do but holds back from doing in 'real life' contexts of devotion, even as a process of 'image transference, from screen-to-street' (Jacob 2009, 118) takes place, so that the digital miracle comes to augment an atmosphere of miracles in 'extra-cinematic space' (p. 3). Surpassing even the flamboyance of his singing and modelling, it is through the no-holds-barred miraculous spectacularism of the first *MSG* film that the guru gives freest reign to his id in the sense of 'an unruly crowd of instincts' (MacIntyre 2004, 10) that is incompatible with the constative dimension of DSS guruship but can be given performative expression within a cinematic space whose 'fictional' character is fully exploited by the guru.

We find a parallel in the work of Emmanuel Grimaud (2011), who describes how the stage-effect miracles of robotic Hindu deities – unreal though spectators know them to be – 'are treated as capable of producing a miraculous result', for 'one can legitimately use them to spread rumours of authentic miracles. People are quite capable of distinguishing a real miracle from a fake one, but ... a miracle, even if it is produced in a display powered by machines, is never alone. It awakens stories of other ambiguous events suitable for revealing the gods' unique presence' (p. 26). More pertinent still is the sense encountered by Grimaud that obviously machine-made miracles are incapable of lying; special effects 'are not acts of imagination or a fabrication of objects that do not exist. It is not a question of extrapolating something outside reality, but rather materialising an earlier possibility that has since become impossible, or creating something that is impossible today but could very well assume a concrete form in the future. Special effects crystallise a hidden existence or unexploited potentiality' (p. 215). Similarly, *MSG* is a presentation of what the guru otherwise holds back or keeps hidden, a demonstration of all that he keeps in reserve.

There is an important second sense in which *MSG 1* was able to present what the guru otherwise holds back and keeps in reserve that relates to the role of DSS devotee extras. The various dictionary meanings of 'extra' are pertinent here: as an amount 'added to an existing or usual amount or number'; 'excessive or extravagant'; 'to a greater extent than usual'; 'a person engaged temporarily to fill out a crowd scene in a film or play: *the film used an army of extras*'.[45] An army indeed. The devotee-crowd – whose mass body is put to performative work in the form of collective blood donor, hygienic exemplar or film extra – is controlled by the guru 'for now' but potentially uncontrollable, facts that the film vividly discloses.

This is particularly pertinent in respect of the criminal charges that the guru faced at the time. His arrest and conviction in 2017 were indeed followed by multiple casualties as devotees directed their violent anger against authorities.[46] As Piyush Roy (2017) wrote shortly afterwards, the film features the guru 'playing a larger-than-life version of himself, as the sat-guru, saviour and *"father"* of a million plus people on-screen, and another five-crore [50 million] hinted to be constantly lurking in the background. In an ominous forecast of the post-conviction mayhem in Panchkula, his followers in the film frequently hint at thwarting any challenge coming their *pitaji*'s way, through violence, if necessary.' The film thus also served as a demonstration of power: evidence, once more, of all that the guru keeps in reserve, of unexploited potentiality (at least, in the sense of an armed force; devotees' potentiality is also harnessed in other ways, of course). A peculiarity of the film is the literal (non-representational) place of its audience within it; the susceptibilities of the Censor Board's non-deliberative public, at once 'passive and hyperactive: easily duped by any passing demagogue and constantly on the brink of violence' (Mazzarella 2013, 17), are on display in the film itself. The tank of the guru's grand entry might as well have been real; police entering his *dera* after his imprisonment found an arsenal of weapons.[47] If the devotee-crowd of the film largely took the form of a spectacle spectating itself – benignly wondering at its own generation of wonder effects (arrogated to the figure of the guru), its potentiality remaining mediated (contained) by him – we are also shown that were he to be taken forcibly from it the result would likely be this potentiality's devastating uncontainment. Apart from anything else, then, the devotee-crowd formed a demonstration of power and warning to state authorities: stay back from the fiefdom. *MSG 1* thus formed a strident demonstration of the guru's power that hinted at the unrest and civil strife that would result if he were imprisoned. This shows how the otherwise powerful model in which gurus and politicians collaborate in the exercise of power (Jaffrelot 2012) can come under pressure, echoing Swami Ramdev's earlier, pre-Modi call for the establishment of a 'yoga army' to tackle political corruption and the accompanying demand that corrupt politicians be hanged.[48] William Pinch (2006, 2012), too, has shown how the notion of the guru as a military commander possesses deep historical antecedents.

But the films bear another, more poignant relationship to the guru's imprisonment. Watching the films after their guru's removal from their immediate lives is a deeply emotionally charged experience for devotees. Moreover, they come to appear prophetic in terms of the events that later unfolded.[49] In interviews conducted in 2021 devotees described to us the poignancy of seeing the films at a time of enforced separation from their guru:

> we used to go [to the cinema] to get the fruits of attending *naam charcha* [lit. 'discussion of the divine name'; akin to prayer]. Now, after Pita Ji's departure, in the present time we understand that he, through the medium [*zariya*] of movies, was telling [or showing] us the truth. We were unaware of that [before his imprisonment]. Pita Ji, in each and every scene, told that: '*Beta ji* [an affectionate way for an elder to address a child], I will return soon. You should not cry.' Earlier we went to see the movies ... for happiness. But now when we see them the feeling is different, because [we realise the] truth is unfolding before us.

Other followers emphasised to us the emotional effects on them of viewing the films after his imprisonment, now, of course, via TV sets or YouTube in intimate domestic spaces rather than on the big screen:[50]

> Now the point of view of seeing the films has changed. For example, in one film Pita Ji [shows us] he is going, and the followers are crying. ... Pita Ji tells them: 'Why are you crying? I will return soon. I have turned you into *Insan* (human). Now I need to reform others. I must go – this is my *seva* (service). In another movie, too – *Jattu Engineer* – Pita Ji leaves in the end. But the followers are crying. We are not enjoying happiness because our Guru Ji is not with us. Even at that time we felt like crying, wondering why Guru Ji made such a scene. But now when we see, we feel like crying because Pita Ji showed the truth beforehand that he will leave us.

There is thus a shift from warning what would happen were he to be imprisoned to a different kind of foreshadowing, with followers seeing his present imprisonment foretold in the films. Indeed, the prophetic film now reveals to devotees that his imprisonment was part of the guru's plan all along, a form of service to humanity:

> Whatever is shown in the movie is actually happening in the present. … It is shown in the movie that this society is reformed, [but] other people [now] need to be reformed. So, Guru Ji has gone [to prison] to do his work; he has gone to perform his *seva*. Whatever is happening is happening in accordance with his wish and we are with Guru Ji. He will return when his work is done.

MSG 2: arrogation of lineage and the Hindutva turn

The focus of the guru's next film, *MSG 2*, is the guru's attempts to civilise indigenous Adivasi communities through both force and love as an exemplary instance and promotion of DSS welfare activities. Strongly reflecting the tendency in representations of Indic indigeneity to reproduce colonial-era tropes of 'criminal tribes' and a 'series of stereotypes of adivasis as our "primitive other", with a propensity for violence and quick to take up arms' (Bates and Shah 2017, 2), the guru is able successfully to 'humanise the devils' (*in shaitano ko insan bananay keliye*), who then come to recognise him as their 'Adi Guru'. The primary encounter between the 'ferocious Adivasis' and the guru is depicted as a moment of iconic intervention: the guru is shown from behind standing on the top of a hill as the camera moves slowly upwards, registering the towering, authoritative figure who overlooks the Adivasis below. Distance is thereby established between the latter and the elevated figure of the guru. In the next sequence, the camera zooms in on the disc he holds in one hand, similar to a *chakra* (circular weapon with sharpened outer edge), and then his other hand, in which he holds a large sword (see Figures 12.2 and 12.3). In a dramatic zooming out of the frame, we now see depicted his standing frontal figure in what is a moment of 'divine revelation' for the Adivasis (also intended for the theatre audience of course). As the camera zooms onto his face, a shift takes place from a moment of divine revelation to one of 'photo op *darshan*' (Figure 12.4), thereby forming an instance of the cinematic transposition of traditional devotional visual exchange, in which the icon sees and is seen by the devotee, which is now fairly standard, with many precedents (Prasad 2021, 55).

Here, as elsewhere in the *MSG* franchise, the guru's bejewelled attire, headgear and stylised postures assimilate the iconographies of

Figure 12.2 Still from *MSG 2*. Source: YouTube https://www.youtube.com/watch?v=hzdcY5lBJ8I.

Figure 12.3 Still from *MSG 2*. Source: YouTube https://www.youtube.com/watch?v=hzdcY5lBJ8I.

Figure 12.4 Still from *MSG 2*. Source: YouTube https://www.youtube.com/watch?v=hzdcY5lBJ8I.

earlier devotional and Bollywood films and TV serials. The guru's still studio portraits and photographs in magazines and calendars enact similar assimilations (Copeman and Duggal 2023). The general absence of facial expression, but for the faint hint of a smile, recalls the portrayal of gods in devotional calendar art. The dialogue, meanwhile, consists of either one-liners or adages lifted from his *satsang* discourses.

The guru claims to seek to transform the Adivasis through the *hathyar* (weapon) of *pyar* (love), though there are also many fight sequences. His benevolence is highlighted in a scene in which he protects the child of an Adivasi character, Babru, one of his enemies, from attack by a wild elephant. His act of humanity and bravery depicts him as the saviour of the helpless. Babru realises his error: both the savage and the animal (which becomes the guru's pet) submit and are tamed. Babru not only realises his mistake in resisting the guru but also recognises his powers as signs (*nishaniyan*) that he is in fact their Adi Guru. A flashback of a conversation between him and a tribal elder describing the traits and image of Adi Guru reveals to him a match with the DSS guru – a sub-narrative demonstrating that the DSS guru is not an outside force come to colonise but the reincarnation of their own spiritual master. It is not clear if Adi Guru is based on a historical figure. Outside of the filmic space, 'Adi Guru' often refers to the primordial first guru of yoga, Lord Shiva. Another Adi Guru is Adi Shankara, the first in the line of Shankarcharyas. However, neither of these is a likely candidate for an Adivasi Adi Guru. The Bhil culture hero and spiritual leader, Govind Giri (1858–1931), is more likely. An ascetic from the *banjara* nomadic caste, he was also popularly known as Govind Guru and was a committed social reformer (Nilsen 2018). Pari Kupar Lingo, too, has been described as 'first philosopher and guru of the Gond religion' (Jothe 2017).

However, Adi Guru is not the only forebear brought into the DSS guru's orbit. For Ajgar, one of the Adivasis who fight with the guru, the guru represents or calls to mind Maharana Pratap Singh, a famous Rajput king of the medieval period who fought against the Mughals: 'his walk, his demeanour and his style of fighting was like Maharana's'. An exchange of dialogue between Babru and Ajgar spins the fiction of the guru character's direct descent from the Maharana, indicating the DSS guru's aspiration to claim warriorlike Rajput traits for himself and so underscore his hypermasculine power and fighting abilities. We noted earlier the preponderance of Dalits among the guru's devotees. In claiming an affinity with, and even direct descent from, the Rajput icon Maharana Pratap, the guru portrays himself as an upper-caste saviour of the Adivasis and other oppressed castes, an agent of social and spiritual transformation who, like the Buddha, will bring change and equality despite (because of?) hailing from a higher caste. Of further significance is that the Maharana died defending Hindu territory from Muslim invaders (Snodgrass 2002). He is thus very much a hero of the Hindu right, whose agenda, in this film, the DSS guru begins explicitly to embrace. Yet the associational matrix is complexified still further. Babru explains to Ajgar that 'Adi Guru is from the same lineage. ... [H]e is from the lineage of Maharana's son Man Singh.' 'Man Singh who went to Punjab to fight the holy war alongside Guru Hargobind?', asks Ajgar. Babru responds: 'Yes, Adi Guru is from the lineage of the same Man Singh.' Man Singh in fact was not Maharana Pratap's son; nor did he fight alongside the sixth Sikh Guru Hargobind. The 'uncontrolled relatedness' (da Col 2012) of the dialogue's entirely fictional lineage construction thereby seeks to forge a connection between the DSS guru and the line of Sikh gurus, repeating an earlier attempt that offended mainstream Sikhs and led to serious social unrest in north India in 2007 (see the Introduction in this volume, on the 'unauthorised copying' of the Sikh guru and its intermediality).[51]

Guruship, in the mode of of religious semiosis, entails an array of associative registers.[52] What singles out the DSS guru is his attempt – and his use of the cinema – to grasp at totality across different scales and dimensions as he seeks to craft and take possession of relations by proving they were already there. The guru seeks to create authority and selfhood (Brosius 2005, 99) by means of imitation and alteration, prompting and circulating 'semiotic arousal' (Landes 2011, 14) and 'ancestry effects' (Albert 2001) as means of inscribing himself into the histories and moral landscapes of given communities (Gayer and Therwath 2010). Such practices of relational suggestion form a parallel with conspiracy theory logics, which see (and claim) connectedness across unrelated phenomena. Of course, the connections are primed. Previously he dressed up as Guru Gobind Singh. In *MSG* 2 his kinesics – 'systematic use of facial and body gesture to communicate meaning' (Crystal 1983, 200) – prompt characters to make certain connections. He seeks to induce states of semiotic arousal that fire devotees' imaginations, suggesting divine and historical parallels that take on deep meaning for devotees and soon become established facts of devotion.

We have mentioned Maharana Pratap's status among Hindu nationalists. The guru's claim of a connection with him was consonant with his increasing endorsement of Hindutva politics, which became particularly pronounced from *MSG 2* onwards. Promoting vegetarianism and 'proper' attitudes towards the cow through motifs of civilisational progress and purification, *MSG 2* Hinduises not only Adivasis but the DSS as well. Its narrative thereby dovetailed with the wider context of the time in which it was released, which was one of Hindutva political dominance and drastic increases in the lynching of Muslims and Dalits by 'cow protection' vigilantes after Modi became prime minister (Pinney 2019; Mohammad-Arif and Naudet 2020; Bouillier 2020). The film shows how Adivasis, having eventually submitted to the guru's civilising overtures, are escorted by members of his 'welfare force' back to their huts to cover their obscenely naked bodies and trim their nails. Meanwhile, the guru is shown showering water on bare-bodied men. The sequence recalls the *shuddhi* (purification) ceremonies performed by the proto-Hindutva Arya Samaj[53] socio-religious organisation that brought converts back into the Hindu fold (Jones 1976), symbolised by the transformation of the Adivasis into 'clean' villagers.[54] After being made to stop drinking *mahua* (local fruit-based liquor) and to enter the structure of north Indian kinship relations, Adivasi men and women are shown marrying before the guru. They are forced, as well, to give up hunting and instead to cultivate crops, and strikingly, change their attitude towards the cow. The guru's real-life interest in 'civilising' Adivasis and promoting vegetarianism preceded his entry into film.[55] Such priorities were already congruent with upper-caste Hindutva attempts to 'purify', 'uplift' and 'return' Adivasis to the Hindu fold (Bhatt 2001, 61). It was in his 'reel life' (Pandian 2015), however, that he made the connection explicit and took it further.

These connections and the mutual support between the DSS and the Modi agenda continued when the BJP Chief Minister of Rajasthan Vasundhara Raje exempted the guru's next film – *MSG: The Warrior Lion Heart* – from entertainment duty in the state.[56] Released in October 2016, it is a historical sci-fi fantasy picture that switches back and forth between an alien-threatened space age and a Rajput kingdom of 300 years earlier, with much of the narrative relayed in flashback. Five planetary alien battalions conspire to attack Planet Earth. The main bulwark against the attack is the guru, who had previously defended his kingdom (*rashtra*) from alien attack some 300 years earlier. The guru is now a kind of secret agent with advanced gadgets and weapons reminiscent of James Bond.[57] The film unremittingly asserts a hyper-masculine superhero image for the guru, with spectacular slow-motion action sequences featuring monsters, elephants and the guru running, leaping and flying. The film ends with the aliens' defeat and the guru's coronation as emperor of the entire earth. Before this we see that 300 years earlier he had been senapati (military commander) of a Rajput kingdom, and its protector guru. The film, like *MSG 2*, valorises Rajput lineage and tradition, the senapati's being traced back to the *Suryavanshi kul* (royal Rajput clan). The sets are reminiscent of the wildly popular and influential Ramayana and Mahabharata TV serials (see Introduction), with the guru's weaponry borrowing elements of the iconography of Hindu gods as conveyed in those series, in particular his carrying of weapons such as *gadas* (clubs), swords, axes and bows and arrows. Unlike in previous films in the franchise, the chanting of Om features as much as the standard DSS '*Dhan dhan Satguru*' chant. The film thus presents an elaborate construction for the DSS guru of a Hindu past that simultaneously thrusts the guru and the movement on a trajectory towards Hinduisation and Hindutva politics.

This is particularly seen within sub-narratives that depict evil forces as not only aliens but also Muslims. Of course, in Hindutva politics, the categories frequently imply each other: Muslims are considered 'foreign' to the land of India. The opening crisis in the film depicts Muslims as child-kidnappers. One flashback to the era of Rajput rule depicts a battle with the Muslim leader Zalim Khan, who has abducted Rajput women for the purpose of forceful conversion by *nikah* (marriage). The guru not only defeats Zalim Khan – in so doing saving the honour of Rajput women – but also warns him: 'You have a great desire to marry [Rajput women]; shall I marry you with death?' ('*Zyada nikah karne ka ka shauq hai. Maut se nikah karvau tera*') (see Figure 12.5). Such depiction of Muslim invaders' lustful desire for Hindu Rajput women readily connects with present-day moral panics and slurs that centre on so-called 'Love Jihad', 'a moral panic against the alleged seduction, marriage, forced conversion and trafficking of young Hindu girls by Muslim men' (Tyagi and Sen 2020, 104; see also Strohl 2019), a controversy that other saffron holy men have stoked, with Mahant Bajrang Muni, for instance, alleged to have issued rape threats against Muslim women: 'If you commit atrocities on one Hindu girl by trapping her into love jihad, I will trap 10 Muslim girls into love *sanatan* and persecute them. You will dupe them but I want to say this openly that I will abduct them in broad daylight.'[58]

Another sequence in the film extends beyond the promotion of vegetarianism and cow protection, as depicted in *MSG 2*, to active cow vigilantism, with the guru the chief vigilante (see Figure 12.6). The issue of cow smuggling – the 'transportation of sacred cattle for slaughter in Muslim meat markets' (Cons 2016, 126–7) – has been communally charged for centuries; however, emotive viral images of cow slaughter enabled by widespread smartphone access, coupled with the BJP's political domination, have led to a 'resurgence of anti-cow slaughter sentiment' (Pinney 2019, 201–2) and an upsurge in violence against

Figure 12.5 Guru as 'saviour' of Rajput women held captive by Muslim ruler Zalim Khan in *MSG: Warrior Lion Heart*. Source: YouTube channel MSGians. https://www.youtube.com/watch?v=kDo9pza6R9U&t=5248s.

alleged perpetrators. Witnessing a group of skullcapped men smuggling cows, the guru intervenes:

MSG:	Why are you beating these speechless creatures?
Muslim man:	The people [Hindus] have this problem. They call cow their mother. OK, we won't beat them with sticks, but we will butcher them.
MSG:	Do you drink their milk?
Muslim man:	Yes.
MSG:	We drink the milk of our mother. Therefore, this cow is also your mother.
Muslim man:	Along with milk, we also relish their meat. We will butcher them.

Conflict ensues. The smugglers bring out sticks. The guru brandishes his sword. Awed by the guru's strength, the men quickly disperse, the cows are freed. With the guru now the very embodiment of Hindutva politics, *MSG: The Warrior Lion Heart* makes even more explicit than *MSG 2* the guru's shift towards Hindu majoritarianism.

Hind ka Napak Ko Jawab: MSG Lion Heart 2 and *Jattu Engineer*

The film's sequel and the guru's fourth film overall, *Hind ka Napak Ko Jawab: MSG Lion Heart 2*, was released in February 2017, the guru

Figure 12.6 Guru as 'cow vigilante' confronting Muslim men depicted as cow smugglers in *MSG: Warrior Lion Heart*. Source: YouTube channel MSGians. https://www.youtube.com/watch?v=kDo9pza6R9U&t=5248s.

playing the role of Sher-e-Hind ('Tiger of India'). Its plot is loosely based on the real-life Uri attack in September 2016, when insurgents from Pakistan, rumoured to be supported by its government, attacked the Indian army in Indian-administered areas of Jammu and Kashmir. India retaliated with a much-debated 'surgical strike' across the Line of Control in Pakistan-administered Kashmir. Subverting 'Pakistan' (land of the pure) by naming it 'Napak' (unholy or unhallowed), the film depicts India and Pakistan in binary terms of good and evil. Aliens again touch down on earth, this time in Pakistan, disguised as jihadis with the aim of becoming allies of Pakistan's army and terrorist groups in a plot to defeat India and Sher-e-Hind. The enemy thus takes three forms in the film: aliens, Pakistan army, and jihadis. The guru, as Sher-e-Hind, is the nation's only weapon against Napak. Stereotypes of the Islamist terrorist abound, in their clothing, their beards, and their gun-toting ways. Recruitment to jihadi terrorist groups is repeatedly shown to be motivated by God's gift of '72 *houris* [virgins] to the one who dies fighting *jihad*'. Jihadis are thereby presented as perverted, lustful and exploitative. In one subplot, Honeypreet Insan, the guru's real-life adopted daughter – who is co-director of as well as an actor in the film – embarks on a secret mission to Balochistan to destroy a Pakistani terrorist base located there and liberate the Balochi people. Terrorists are shown torturing and sexually exploiting their Balochi captives. Her rhetoric particularly focuses on the Pakistani army's alleged sexual exploitation of Balochis as she seeks to mobilise the latter to fight for their self-determination: 'I have killed the biggest enemy of Balochistan.

Now entire India is with you. Tear out those eyes that look at your mothers and sisters. Who will fight for this freedom?'

Numerous asides and subplots display the guru's ever more vehement support for Modi. For instance, Indian opposition politicians are depicted as cowardly 'anti-nationals' simply for asking the Modi government for evidence about the origin of the Uri attack that would justify the 'surgical strike' retaliation. It is a character resembling Modi's National Security Adviser Ajit Doval who instructs Sher-e-Hind to go to Pakistan, emphasising the sense of mutual endorsement between the BJP government and the guru. The film also ventriloquises the Modi government's justification of its heavily criticised 2016 policy of demonetisation as an effective counter-terrorism measure, as disclosed in a conversation between the head of a terrorist group and the Pakistani prime minister: 'Prime Minister, do something! They have banned the use of 500 and 1,000 rupee notes. We used to print fake [Indian] currency and give 500 to each Kashmiri to pelt stones at [Indian] policemen. Now [since demonetisation] the entire scheme has stopped.'

Jattu Engineer, the final film released before the guru's imprisonment, appeared in May 2017. As a comedy it breaks from the action thriller genre of the previous films, yet it remains centrally concerned with 'reform' and 'transformation', in this case of a village, Tatiya Kar ('Defecation'), and its inhabitants. This time the guru takes the role of a school headmaster, Shakti Singh Sisodiya. Mostly told in flashback, it tells us of the village's filthy past: lacking a proper sewage system, local governance and school, its dirty, uneducated inhabitants are shown consuming drugs and engaging in other 'anti-social activities'. The dysfunctional local school has no schoolteacher, previous ones having been chased away by the student *kala kaccha* gang (black shorts gang) organised by a school *chaprasi* (junior office worker who carries messages) who is disinclined to have a teacher at the school and so be subject to supervision. Similarly, the dysfunctional state of the village is epitomised by the figure of the corrupt *sarpanch* (village head).

All this changes after the arrival of Shakti Singh Sisodiya, who begins to bring change to the lives of every individual in the village through instilling self-respect. The second change concerns village infrastructure. Here the developmental vision of the guru comes to the fore as he tackles the problems of open defecation, lack of drainage, and failing agriculture. As in the preceding films, these improvements are effected through both fear and benevolence. The guru's caste status again is accentuated, here as the Jat he really is rather than as a Rajput, although both are dominant north Indian castes. In one scene, after Shakti Singh Sisodiya has humiliated and beaten the *sarpanch*, he declares that an 'illiterate Jat is like an educated person and an educated Jat is like god. And if a Jat is in the form of a headmaster, then he is the father of the village head.'[59] If such a muscular, authoritarian development crusade is entirely in keeping with Modi's own strong-arm tactics in support of development (Cohen 2008), so too is the film's assertion of dominant-caste-initiated social reform, which tallies with recent Hindi films in which this template is normatively posited. As the media commentator Bhavya Dore put it in reference to recent roles played by Punjab and Bollywood icon Akshay Kumar, 'Most mainstream Bollywood films feature upper-caste heroes; Kumar himself has played several of them. Non-upper-caste characters are rare, especially as protagonists. ... Historical dramas – such as *Panipat, Padmavat* and *Tanhaji*, two of which made more than Rs 200 crore – amplify the achievements of various upper-caste rulers.'[60]

The DSS guru not only models his films partly on Akshay Kumar's, but also models Kumar's obsequious attitude towards Modi via these Modi-flattering films. Consider the parallel between *Jattu Engineer* and Akshay Kumar's recent 'political' films, in particular the latter's 2017 movie *Toilet: Ek Prem Katha*, which promoted Modi's *Swacch Bharat Abhiyan* initiative, launched in 2014. Both centre on village-based hygiene initiatives (in *Toilet*, Kumar's character opines, 'When our prime minister can stop currency notes, why can't we stop our bowels?'), and were praised by BJP ministers and officials and granted tax exemptions. Modi tweeted his support for the DSS guru's cleanliness initiatives.[61] But as *Toilet* shows, the guru's films were far from alone in promoting the ruling regime with which they enjoyed a mutually beneficial relationship.[62] Rather, the films formed part of a network of Bollywood films that aspired to expand audience reach via contributing to a form of national myth-making that preserved and enhanced their own status. In this process, as with Akshay Kumar and other film stars, if the government had a message, it seemed that the DSS guru was its messenger.[63]

Reflection: the guru as an unstable totality

Collectively the *MSG* narratives constitute what Ashish Rajadhyaksha has called 'self-validating accounts' (2009, 4). Censor Board members objected to the first film's flagrant auto-hagiographic self-promotion, suggesting they resembled feature-length advertisements for the DSS, a point also repeatedly made by film critics. The miracles they depict were a particular source of anxiety for the Board. Its intervention – later overruled – invoked the figure of the credulous viewer (S. V. Srinivas 2009), who would meld together 'reel life' miracles and the real-life guru. The guru's performance of miracles brings him into the compass of those gurus for whom miracles are an important means of recruitment (Babb 1983), gurus he otherwise criticises. Since they are evidently generated by special effects, they do not constitute a direct claim to supernatural powers, but they augment a sense of the guru's miraculous capabilities nonetheless, thereby mediating between the guru's exhibitory self and the founding social reformist message of the DSS.

The films' umbrella narrative projects a new mythology of the guru based on mixing fictional plots and settings with depictions of actually existing DSS welfare activities (blood donation, cleanliness, anti-drugs campaigns, etc.). Surpassing world records, they seem to cover a lack: 'The charismatic leader tries to repair their own wounded self-regard by seeking attention and adulation through outsized public gestures' (Mazzarella 2022). That the throbbing guru id is dressed up as exaggerated social service in this way apparently combines with the semi-fictional nature of the guru's cinematic persona to grant the ego permission to be less committed to supressing its attachment to 'this impersonal, this bestial layer like [the relationship of] the centaur to his equestrian underpinnings' (Erikson 1963, 192). However, the films function in various registers. Their accounts are not only *self*-validating; external mechanisms also played a role in their narrative construction. The imbrication of cinema and the state functions at several levels. If state apparatuses have been known to invest in film productions that map 'storytelling upon systems that validate and authorize modern states', here the 'spectatorial presence' was mapped onto 'the structures by which modern states produce and authorize their self-image' (Rajadhyaksha 2009, 12). We have seen how the Modi government bypassed the objections of its own regulator by allowing the release of *MSG* in 2015, demonstrating its keen interest in the *MSG* franchise and its presiding guru. The Modi-fronted state, quite correctly, saw the guru's spectacular narratives of self-promotion as entirely congruent with its own agenda – indeed, as logical extensions of its own ideology – and hence legitimate. Ideological synchronisation between the films and Modi's agenda is notably visible in their promotion of cleanliness initiatives, echoing Modi's *Swachh Bharat* (Clean India) mission, while their praise for demonetisation ventriloquised the BJP's own rationale for it. Tropes of cleanliness cross-cut the films, from suggestions of the ethnic cleansing of Muslims, to 'civilising missions' in the form of Adivasi Hinduisation, and the promotion of vegetarianism and cow protection. In the form of a Rajput warrior, the guru fights Muslim invaders and protects the honour of Rajput women. As a secret agent, he combats Pakistani terrorists and protects Indian territory. While this is similar to other mainstream Bollywood films, such as *Bajirao Mastani* (2015), *Padmaavat* (2018), *Tanhaji* (2020) and *Uri* (2019), whose narratives also legitimise Indian state operations, those films don't feature a 'real-life guru' as the lead actor offering such an endorsement.

In her discussion of the 1936 film *Sant Tukaram* on the life of the low-caste saint of the same name, Geeta Kapur highlights significant cross-referencing between the film and 'outside' political history in the making, which was dominated at the time by the spiritual hegemony of Mahatma Gandhi. The presence of Vishnupant Pagnis, the actor playing Tukaram, 'extends beyond his fine, nearly beatific countenance, beyond his actor's reverie, beyond even his being, into becoming through discourse a reflective symbol within a political situation already conditioned by a contemporary "saint", Mahatma Gandhi' (Kapur 2000, 242). DSS narratives, with their emphasis on muscular welfarism, both complement and collude with Modi government messaging, extending beyond the film and into the political situation. The DSS guru – as teacher and preacher reforming uncivilised Adivasis and degraded villagers through a bhakti-fied agenda of cleanliness, purification and vegetarianism – performs like a *pracharak* (full-time RSS worker), just as Modi was before his entry into BJP politics and ascension to Chief Minister of Gujarat. Both portray themselves as hard-working, simple-living, celibate *faqir*s (ascetics).[64] If, as portrayed in the Tukaram film, 'Gandhi is in a sense the actor-pedagogue on the nationalist stage' on which the representation of Tukaram draws (Kapur 2000, 242), the DSS guru similarly draws on elements of Modi's persona. Just as Modi transcended the regional space of Gujarat to become the national leader, the *MSG* enterprise displays and instantiates the guru's desire to do the same, that is, to transcend the provincial and ascend to spaces of the national and supranational imagination.

This points to his pursuit of what we have called total guruship. Totality is sought here through the attempt to occupy 'every' subject position. He forms a mirror image of Modi in this respect, who has himself sought to embody a kind of totalism by uniting the kingly and Raj Guru spheres, drawing on the reservoirs of authority associated with each to create 'a new and all-powerful position' (Landau and Rageth in this volume). In turn, the DSS guru augments his own vision of totality by forming an association with Modi that might 'abduct' a part of his authority and so extend his own selfhood. Both figures exhibit a certain categorial restiveness. Imitation is capable of eroding the authority of the source (Lempert 2014, 388). This was the concern voiced by mainstream Sikhs when the DSS guru mimicked Guru Gobind Singh, with an association between their revered tenth guru and one whom they viewed as a criminal imposter potentially undermining the former's 'power to be a model' (Bhabha 1994, 128). But, as when the DSS guru became a 'reflective symbol' of Modi, the point was more to tap into the final living Sikh guru's power and authority than to seek to undermine it.

The guru, then, is an *unstable totality*. Bergson employs a musical analogy to explain how our perception of a 'now', which simultaneously involves the recollection of a 'before', is 'like a musical phrase which is constantly on the point of ending and constantly altered in its totality by the addition of some new note' (1991, 106). The guru, likewise, is total and yet continually added to – an unstable totality. Lifting the auras of others, he quickly moves on, continually remixing himself. The temporariness of the inhabitation allows for deniability, while begging the question 'What next?' and enhancing the acceleration effects of the movement. Writing of commodity trends, Thrift (2012, 151) points to the

> art of building attachments, of continually restarting the work of association. The overall goal is to produce, often for only the briefest of moments, … temporary gestalts to use Merleau-Ponty's filmic description, which have pull through their 'whatever singularity', an internally plural collectivity…, 'a solidarity that in no way concerns an essence'.

The filmic nature of Merleau-Ponty's description is apt, for film affords the guru's diverse images a flickering momentariness that contributes to generating these sorts of (non-)association. If the guru is a totality of entities, he is so in the form of 'an open whole' (Evens 2012, 8). The guru seeks to be a kind of personified cosmogram in Tresch's (2007, 92–3) sense: a person-image that discloses the world of events in history and poetically materialises connections between them, thereby mustering a totality of heterogeneous things as one (Oustinova-Stjepanovic 2023, 97).

Ram Rahim's enactment of a guruship of constant semiosis and accrual of resonances tapped into multiple forms of visual media even before his adventures in cinema. However, cinema offered three further means for augmenting his semiological expansiveness, providing: (1) an efficient method for staging and amplifying multiple associations and accruing 'ancestry effects' (Albert 2001), from Adi Guru to Maharana Pratap Singh and beyond, (2) an array of production positions – direction, action, music, stunts, special effects, make-up, costume design, etc. – for him to occupy, thereby advertising his 'versatility' as an 'all-in-one' figure of ultimacy, omnipresence standing (in) for omnipotence, and (3) special effects that transform other characters into likenesses of himself. Each method allows the guru intentionally to self-multiply, with everything becoming a celebrative expression of the guru's fullness (Diller 2021, 23). However, the third method, as a totalising effect, differs from the others in that it renders others into his likeness and under his authority rather than drawing on the likenesses and authority of others. That is because symbolically it is the culmination of the totalising process that the other two methods inaugurate. The guru makes the world into a continually evolving and involving store through increasing what is appropriable to be 'sold' to prospective devotees in a process of mutual appropriation (the formation of the guru–devotee relationship).[65]

The three methods also connect back, once more, to Modi. This is not only because methods (1) and (2) reflect the categorial restiveness of Modi's aspiration to be a guru beyond guruship and a politician beyond the political (see Introduction) and because the special effects of method (3) replicate the Modi mask-wearing phenomenon. Before he assumed his guru avatar, the 'image events' (DeLuca 1999) of Modi's early years as prime minister were fully consonant with 'the expository society' (Harcourt 2014), perfectly encapsulated by the occasion on which he received President Barack Obama wearing a luxury suit embroidered with pinstripes made up of hundreds of iterations of his own name. Modi's attire stood in stark contrast with the modest dress of his predecessor Manmohan Singh. As one article stated, 'by spelling his name out over and over again, Modi has turned Narendra Damodardas Modi into a mantra, a *namabali* in pinstripes'.[66] *Namabali* is a reference to the 108 names of God, and closely linked to the *namamala* (garland of names), that is to say, the worshipper's repetition of the names of god, the name being both means and object of worship. Such is the devotion of Hanuman that Ram's name suffuses and composes his body. But Modi's suit was of course not made up of the name of another but of his own name, hence the accusation of self-worship.[67] Similarly, Ram Rahim, in seeing himself wherever he looks – and, if he doesn't see himself, employing media machinery to insert himself actively into a multitude of visual settings across time and space – initiates a guruship of the exhibition, the guru an 'exposing subject' (Harcourt 2014, 17). Exposing himself in more and more dimensions, he continually generates associations that can, in turn, continually restock the guru's semiological store. It is guruship as semiological laboratory, feasting on media.[68]

But then, as we know, he went to prison. Images of the guru subsequently took on a different kind of importance as a means of preserving his presence in his physical absence (see also the chapters by Chowdhuri, Lucia and Srinivas in this volume). Rewatching his films, as we have shown, became extremely emotionally charged experiences for devotees. In July 2022 the guru was released on parole for a limited time. The fact was probably not unconnected to that year's Haryana state elections. Required to uphold restraint under the terms of his parole, he nevertheless conducted virtual *naam charchas* and *satsangs* from his temporary base in an ashram in Baghpat. If such restraint was something new for him, it is perhaps not surprising that devotees wondered if it was really their guru who had been released. His gestures didn't look right; the performance had changed. Had he been substituted with a body double? Whether he had or not, the very suggestion of a body double performing the role of the DSS guru continues the cinematic spectacle of his guruship. Electoral politics mean it is impossible to write off the DSS guru. There may yet be another instalment of the *MSG* franchise that will 'cast believers as spectators' and 'spectacles as miracles' (Meyer and Moors 2006, 9), once more dividing into opposing camps the horrified critic and the enraptured devotee.

Acknowledgements

Our thanks to Nina Rageth, Lindsay Graham and Arkotong Longkumer for very helpful feedback on this chapter. Its authors contributed equally to writing it.

Notes

1 'Exorbitant magnitude' is borrowed from Alberto Corsín Jiménez's (2010, 125) characterisation of the descriptive language employed by Gabriel Tarde, which likewise is preoccupied with size and scale at their 'highest', 'widest', 'profoundest', and so on.
2 *Dera* – the extended residential site of an influential figure – usually has similar connotations to 'ashram'.
3 On his criminality, see the book-length work of investigative journalism by Anurag Tripathi (2018). See Lucia (this volume; 2018) on other guru-related criminality.
4 *Mumbai Mirror*, 14 October 2015. See Copeman (2009), Beckerlegge (2016) and Bhattacharya (2019) on gurus and *seva*.
5 Devotional gathering.
6 See Introduction (this volume) and Copeman and Ikegame (2012, 307–8).
7 On guruship and mimesis, see Landau and Rageth (this volume) and the Introduction.
8 That the guru ended up in jail suggests his strategy failed. But in fact Modi did support the guru so far as was possible: the Censor Board was overruled; the films received tax breaks; he wrote

laudatory tweets about the guru's good works, and so on. If the gravity of the guru's criminal activity and sentence demonstrated the limits of this support, there remains the possibility that the guru will have his sentence commuted, and there is therefore still good reason for the guru to continue to instruct his followers to vote for Modi.

9   On which see Copeman and Duggal (2023).
10 This chapter draws on intermittent fieldwork in Sirsa, Delhi and Chandigarh by both authors from 2004 to 2021 and on analysis of DSS films and other elements of public culture.
11 See also Parciack (2023) on the close relations between film stardom and the religious domain in India.
12 http://www.derasachasauda.in/index.html (accessed 4 April 2008).
13 http://www.derasachasauda.org (accessed 10 March 2023).
14 Copeman (2012).
15 http://www.sachasauda.com (accessed 4 April 2008).
16 https://www.prnewswire.com/in/news-releases/millions-visit-dera-sacha-sauda-sirsa-to-commemorate-incarnation-day-of-its-founder-shah-mastana-ji-701319251.html, 27 November 2018 (accessed 7 July 2022).
17 See Copeman 2009, chapter 5.
18 Ajay Sura, 'Sirsa dera claims its chief had known about Covid-19 outbreak 8 years back', *Times of India*, 5 April 2020. See T. Srinivas (2010) and Copeman (2009) on gurus and prophecies.
19 Copeman and Ikegame (2012).
20 Lise McKean pioneered the study of Hindutva-oriented guru movements (1996). See also Introduction, and Landau and Rageth (both this volume), Gupta and Copeman (2018), Copeman and Banerjee (2019, chapter 2), and Bouillier (2020).
21 See Copeman (2008) on DSS donation of blood for the Indian armed forces and Copeman (2009) on DSS vegetarianism and Adivasi welfare initiatives.
22 https://www.saintdrmsginsan.me/ (accessed 7 July 2022).
23 Comments on the YouTube video *Saint Gurmeet Ram Rahim Singh Ji Insan – Love Charger* (https://www.youtube.com/watch?v=Q48tagwurUw), and comments on the YouTube video: *Never Ever (Remix) – Full Video Song – MSG* (https://www.youtube.com/watch?v=lN5YXmIz2QI) (both accessed 10 March 2023).
24 Shambhavi Sarasvati, 'Anandamayi Ma: "I am not an alien"', 1 December 2009. https://jayakula.org/anandamayi-not-alien/ (accessed 10 March 2023).
25 See account in Copeman (2009, 115–22).
26 See Introduction (this volume); Copeman and Ikegame (2012, 320–4).
27 Mbembe explains that he uses the term 'as it was used to denote colonial authority – that is, in so far as it embraces the images and structures of power and coercion, the instruments and agents of their enactment, and a degree of rapport between those who give orders and those who are supposed to obey (without, of course, discussing) them'. Hence it denotes 'the authoritarian modality par excellence' (Mbembe 2001, 135 n. 8).
28 See Copeman and Ikegame (2012, 318–22) and Copeman and Duggal (2023); also Ikegame (2019) on guru sovereignty and Mandair (this volume) on 'highly exploitable proto-fascist tendencies under the veil of unquestioning "devotion" to a charismatic master'.
29 'The Modi mask, as much as any other merchandise, symbolised Brand Modi during the 2014 general election. Along with selfies and holograms, it was an element of his mythology and iconography. ... At BJP rallies, hundreds of supporters would be seen donning the mask, reiterating the narrative that the contest was between Modi and the rest. ... His face was everywhere – on billboards, Metro stations, buses and in the newspaper' (Chaudhuri 2016).
30 See Copeman and Duggal (2023).
31 Copeman and Duggal (2023).
32 Shahina KK, 'Godman's own country', *Open*, 26 June 2014. https://openthemagazine.com/features/india/godmans-own-country/ (accessed 10 March 2023).
33 Copeman (2009, 118).
34 Abhishek Sudhir, 'If Aamir Khan could be given his right to free expression with PK, why not godman Ram Rahim?', Scroll.in, 19 January 2015. https://scroll.in/article/701159/if-aamir-khan-could-be-given-his-right-to-free-expression-with-pk-why-not-godman-ram-rahim (accessed 10 March 2023).
35 Copeman (2009, 116).

36 Copeman (2009, chapter 5).

37 Copeman (2009, chapter 5).

38 https://www.derasachasauda.org/welfare-world-records/guinness-world-records/ (accessed 20 July 2023).

39 On 24 January 2012, the DSS created three world records. These were for the most blood pressure readings, cholesterol readings and Doppler ultrasounds. On 23 September in the same year it achieved two further world records: for the largest finger painting and the most people hand sanitising.

40 https://www.saintdrmsginsan.me/degree-of-doctorate/#:~:text=On%20the%20auspicious%20 occasion%20of,Ram%20Rahim%20Singh%20Ji%20Insan (accessed 7 July 2022). Little public information is available about the World Records University. It describes itself as 'an autonomous university formed by the conglomeration of Record Books around the World. Its associates include Asia Book of Records, Vietnam Book of Records, Indo-China Book of Records, India Book of Records, Nepal Book of Records, World Records Union, World Creativity Science Academy, and Indo-Vietnam Medical Board. World Records University is the only university offering an honorary Doctorate to Record Holder's/breaker's Community. The degree is awarded to those who have demonstrated an Honoris Causa, or cause to be honored. This program is offered only to a select group of highly accomplished individuals specially who have made a world or a national record.' https://worldrecordsuniversity.co.uk/ (accessed 10 March 2023).

41 This draws on Verran (2014, 280).

42 See Copeman and Ikegame (2012).

43 Compare with the Ford Motor Company's production in the 1910s of the Model T, the world's first affordable automobile. A production landmark – with assembly-line production instead of individual handcrafting – it was ground-breaking also from a consumer perspective, with workers now paid a wage proportionate to the cost of the car, which provided a ready-made market.

44 Dera Sacha Sauda. n.d. *Dhan Dhan Satguru Tera Hi Aasra, The Truth*. Vol. 1. DSS Video CD.

45 These definitions are from Oxford Dictionaries (online).

46 More than 40 were killed, with devotees bearing the brunt. See https://en.wikipedia.org/ wiki/2017_Northern_India_riots (accessed 11 March 2023).

47 Compare with other militarised guru fiefdoms: see Pinch (2012) and Chatterjee (1999). See also the 2014 case of Sant Rampal: Annie Gowen, 'Deadly showdown at Indian guru's compound reveals dubious side of the country's "godmen"', *Washington Post*, 19 November 2014 (accessed 11 March 2023). https://www.washingtonpost.com/news/worldviews/ wp/2014/11/19/deadly-showdown-at-indian-gurus-compound-reveals-dubious-side-of-the-countrys-godmen/

48 Copeman and Ikegame (2012, 318).

49 On cinematic prophecies, see Meyer (2003); see also Pinney (2010) on photographic prophecies.

50 Most DSS followers subscribe to the Sach private TV network run by the DSS, which also has a YouTube channel with 151,000 subscribers. Much of their content consists of daily morning *satsangs* and *naam charcha*. Though described as 'live', the morning *satsangs* feature footage from before the guru's imprisonment (cf. Lucia, this volume).

51 See Copeman and Banerjee (2019, chapter 6).

52 See Introduction.

53 The Arya Samaj has engaged in Hindu reformist activity since its inception in 1875 by Swami Dayananda, pursuing campaigns against idolatry and caste. Its teachings 'exalt rationality, restraint and austerity. The movement is radically monotheistic, abhorring priestly authority and elaborate ritual. Its experience of Hinduism is action-centered, soldierlike, and explicitly masculinized' (Bayly 2004, 130).

54 On Sangh Parivar attempts to recruit local indigenous traditions into their vision of a greater Hindu nation, see Longkumer (2017).

55 See Copeman (2009, 136).

56 Rohit Parihar, 'Punjab election move? BJP's Vasundhara Raje makes Gurmeet Ram Rahim's *MSG – The Warrior* tax-free in Rajasthan', *India Today*, 7 October 2016. https://www. indiatoday.in/india/story/vasundhara-raje-gurmeet-ram-rahim-msg-tax-free-rajasthan-punjab-elections-345341-2016-10-06 (accessed 11 March 2023).

57 See Copeman and Ikegame (2012, 315) on archetypal holy men secret agents.

58 'Hate speech: what Bajrang Muni, Yati Narsinghanand, Anand Swaroop said in the past', BOOM, 8 July 2022. https://www.boomlive.in/news/bajrang-muni-das-rape-threat-muslim-women-hate-speech-mohammed-zubair-supreme-court-18453 (accessed 11 March 2023); 'Zubair gets 14 more days in custody for calling Hindutva leaders facing hate charges "hatemonger"', *Hindutva Watch*, 5 July 2022. https://hindutvawatch.org/zubair-gets-14-more-days-in-custody-for-calling-hindutva-leaders-facing-hate-charges-hatemongers/ (accessed 22 May 2023).

59 'The Jat insistence on marking caste over religious, linguistic, regional, or other identities' (Mooney 2013, 315) is an utterly mainstream element of popular culture in both Punjab and in the Sikh diaspora; for instance, it is a central ingredient of its pop music (Dhanda 2009).

60 Bhavya Dore, 'The player', *The Caravan*, 1 February 2021. https://caravanmagazine.in/reportage/akshay-kumar-role-hindutva-poster-boy (accessed 22 May 2023).

61 Modi launched the Clean India Mission on Mahatma Gandhi's birthday (2 October) to promote cleanliness and hygiene in the country. On 2 October 2014 he tweeted, 'Appreciable effort by Baba Ram Rahimji and his team. Will motivate people across India to join Swachh Bharat Mission!' (*Hindustan Times*, 14 October 2014). The tweet can be found at https://twitter.com/narendramodi/status/527699386013196289?lang=en (accessed 22 May 2023).

62 See Dore again: 'The beginning of 2019, leading up to a general election, saw a slew of politically charged films, including *PM Narendra Modi*, *The Accidental Prime Minister* and *Uri*, which drew on the government's 2016 claim of having conducted "surgical strikes" on militant bases in Pakistan-administered Kashmir. That phrase crept into the promotion of *Tanhaji*, a period drama, described as "the surgical strike that shook the Mughal empire"' (*The Caravan*, 1 February 2021).

63 *The Caravan*, 1 February 2021.

64 Though Modi is married, like Mahatma Gandhi and the DSS guru, laudatory narratives convey the prime minister's transcendence of the familial form and dedication to working towards the societal common good. See also Landau and Rageth (this volume).

65 This formulation draws inspiration from Thrift (2012, 142).

66 Sandip Roy, 'Narendra Damodardas Modi suit was a PM sized fail: Here's why', *Firstpost*, 28 January 2015. https://www.firstpost.com/living/narendra-damodardas-modi-suit-was-a-pm-sized-fail-heres-why-2067815.html (accessed 22 May 2023).

67 Far from the tradition of small business owners modestly using their fathers' names as business names (Pinney 2004), Shukla (2013) sees evidence in support of Nandy's (2013) thesis concerning a present-day exaltation of the self that operates to cover up spiralling self-doubt in the inauguration of a new era of business names that proclaim their owners' personal names loudly and in neon. Modi's *namamala* suit seemed of a piece with such a regime of narcissism, in which tattoos of the names of gods are replaced with tattoos of one's own name.

68 We again draw inspiration from Thrift's work on the value of innovation (2012, 142).

References

Abreu, Maria José Alves de. 2005. 'Breathing in the heart of the matter: Why Padre Marcelo needs no wings', *Postscripts* 1 (2/3): 325–49. https://doi.org/10.1558/post.v1i2_3.325.

Albert, Jean-Pierre. 2001. 'Sens et enjeux du martyre: De la religion à la politique', in *Saints, sainteté et martyre: La fabrication de l'exemplarité*, edited by Pierre Centlivres, 17–25. Neuchâtel/Paris: Editions de l'Institut d'ethnologie/Editions de la Maison des sciences de l'homme.

Babb, Lawrence A. 1983. 'Sathya Sai Baba's magic', *Anthropological Quarterly* 56 (3): 116–24. https://doi.org/10.2307/3317305.

Babb, Lawrence A. 1986. *Redemptive Encounters: Three modern styles in the Hindu tradition*. Berkeley: University of California Press.

Bates, Crispin and Alpa Shah. 2017. 'Introduction: Savage attack: Adivasis and insurgency in India', in *Savage Attack: Tribal insurgency in India*, edited by Crispin Bates and Alpa Shah, 1–34. Abingdon: Routledge.

Bayly, Susan. 2004. 'Conceptualizing from within: Divergent religious modes from Asian modernist perspectives', in *Ritual and Memory: Toward a comparative anthropology of religion*, edited by Harvey Whitehouse and James Laidlaw, 111–34. Walnut Creek, CA: Altamira Press.

Beckerlegge, Gwilym. 2016. 'Seva: The focus of a fragmented but gradually coalescing field of study', *Religions of South Asia* 9 (2): 208–39. https://doi.org/10.1558/rosa.v9i2.31070.

Bergson, Henri. 1991. *Matter and Memory* (trans. N. M. Paul and W. S. Palmer). New York: Zone Books.

Bhabha, Homi K. 1994. *The Location of Culture*. London: Routledge.

Bhatt, Chetan. 2001. *Hindu Nationalism: Origins, ideologies and modern myths*. Oxford: Berg.

Bhattacharya, Srirupa. 2019. 'Groundwater, gurus, and governmentality: *Seva* in the neo-liberal development regime in India', *Economic & Political Weekly* 54 (32): 51–9.

Borneman, John. 2004. 'Introduction: Theorizing regime ends', in *Death of the Father: An anthropology of the end in political authority*, edited by John Borneman, 1–31. Oxford: Berghahn Books.

Bouillier, Véronique. 2020. 'Yogi Adityanath's background and rise to power', *South Asia Multidisciplinary Academic Journal* 24/25. https://doi.org/10.4000/samaj.6778.

Brosius, Christiane. 2005. *Empowering Visions: The politics of representation in Hindu nationalism*. London: Anthem Press.

Chatterjee, Partha. 1999. 'Modernity, democracy and a political negotiation of death', *South Asia Research* 19 (2): 103–19. https://doi.org/10.1177/026272809901900201.

Chaudhuri, Zinnia Ray. 2016. 'Why the Modi mask is no longer in fashion in Delhi's iconic Sadar Bazaar', Scroll.in, 26 May. https://scroll.in/article/807888/why-the-modi-mask-is-no-longer-in-fashion-in-delhis-iconic-sadar-bazaar (accessed 10 March 2023).

Cohen, Lawrence. 2008. 'Science, politics, and dancing boys: Propositions and accounts', *Parallax* 14 (3): 35–47. https://doi.org/10.1080/13534640802159112.

Cons, Jason. 2016. *Sensitive Space: Fragmented territory at the India-Bangladesh border*. Seattle: University of Washington Press.

Copeman, Jacob. 2008. 'Violence, non-violence, and blood donation in India', *Journal of the Royal Anthropological Institute* NS 14 (2): 278–96. https://doi.org/10.1111/j.1467-9655.2008.00501.x.

Copeman, Jacob. 2009. *Veins of Devotion: Blood donation and religious experience in north India*. New Brunswick, NJ: Rutgers University Press.

Copeman, Jacob. 2012. 'The mimetic guru: Tracing the real in Sikh–Dera Sacha Sauda relations', in *The Guru in South Asia: New interdisciplinary perspectives*, edited by Jacob Copeman and Aya Ikegame, 156–80. Abingdon: Routledge.

Copeman, Jacob and Dwaipayan Banerjee. 2019. *Hematologies: The political life of blood in India*. Ithaca, NY: Cornell University Press.

Copeman, Jacob and Koonal Duggal. 2023. '"Guruji Rocked … Duniya Shocked": Wondertraps and the full-palette guruship of Dera Sacha Sauda guru Dr Saint Gurmeet Ram Rahim Singh Ji Insan', in *Wonder in South Asia: Politics, aesthetics, ethics*, edited by Tulasi Srinivas. New York: SUNY Press.

Copeman, Jacob and Aya Ikegame. 2012. 'Guru logics', *HAU: Journal of Ethnographic Theory* 2 (1): 289–336. https://doi.org/10.14318/hau2.1.014.

Corsín Jiménez, Alberto. 2010. 'The height, length and width of social theory', in *The Social after Gabriel Tarde: Debates and assessments*, edited by Matei Candea, 110–28. Abingdon: Routledge.

Crystal, David. 1983. *A First Dictionary of Linguistics and Phonetics*. London: André Deutsch.

Da Col, Giovanni. 2012. 'Introduction: Natural philosophies of fortune – luck, vitality, and uncontrolled relatedness', *Social Analysis* 56 (1): 1–23. https://doi.org/10.3167/sa.2012.560102.

Das, Veena. 1981. 'The mythological film and its framework of meaning: An analysis of "Jai Santoshi Ma"', *India International Centre Quarterly* 8 (1): 43–56.

DeLuca, Kevin Michael. 1999. *Image Politics: The new rhetoric of environmental activism*. New York: Guilford Press.

De Vries, Hent. 2001. 'Of miracles and special effects', *International Journal for Philosophy of Religion* 50 (1/3): 41–56.

Dhanda, Meena. 2009. 'Punjabi *dalit* youth: Social dynamics of transitions in identity', *Contemporary South Asia* 17 (1): 47–64. https://doi.org/10.1080/09584930802624661.

Diller, Jeanine. 2021. 'God and other ultimates', in *The Stanford Encyclopedia of Philosophy* (Winter 2021 edn), edited by Edward N. Zalta. https://plato.stanford.edu/archives/win2021/entries/god-ultimates (accessed 11 March).

Erikson, Erik H. 1963. *Childhood and Society*, 2nd edn. New York: W. W. Norton.

Evens, T. M. S. 2012. 'Twins are birds and a whale is a fish, a mammal, a submarine: Revisiting "primitive mentality" as a question of ontology', *Social Analysis* 56 (3): 1–11. https://doi.org/10.3167/sa.2012.560301.

Fattelal, Vishnupant Govind and Damle (dirs). 1936. *Sant Tukaram*, film, Prabhat Film Company.

Ganti, Tejaswini. 2021. 'Dubbing', *BioScope: South Asian Screen Studies* 12 (1–2): 75–8. https://doi.org/10.1177/09749276211026066.

Gayer, Laurent and Ingrid Therwath. 2010. 'Introduction: Modelling exemplarity in South Asia', *South Asia Multidisciplinary Academic Journal* 4. https://doi.org/10.4000/samaj.3011.

Gell, Alfred. 1997. 'Exalting the king and obstructing the state: A political interpretation of royal ritual in Bastar District, Central India', *Journal of the Royal Anthropological Institute* 3 (3): 433–50. https://doi.org/10.2307/3034761.

Grimaud, Emmanuel. 2011. 'Gods and robots.' Unpublished manuscript.

Gunning, Tom. 1990. 'The cinema of attractions: Early film, its spectator and the avant-garde', in *Early Cinema: Space, frame, narrative*, edited by Thomas Elsaesser, 56–62. London: British Film Institute.

Gupta, Bhuvi and Jacob Copeman. 2019. 'Awakening Hindu nationalism through yoga: Swami Ramdev and the Bharat Swabhiman movement', *Contemporary South Asia* 27 (3): 313–29. https://doi.org/10.1080/09584935.2019.1587386.

Harcourt, Bernard E. 2014. 'Digital security in the expository society: Spectacle, surveillance, and exhibition in the neoliberal age of big data'/ 'Spectacle, surveillance, exposition: Relire Foucault à l'ère numérique'. Columbia Public Law Research Paper no. 14-404: 1–23/1–21. https://scholarship.law.columbia.edu/faculty_scholarship/1865/ (accessed 12 March 2023).

Hughes, Stephen. 2005. 'Mythologicals and modernity', *Postscripts* 1: 207–35.

Hughes, Stephen and Birgit Meyer. 2005. 'Introduction: Mediating religion and film in a post-secular world', *Postscripts* 1 (2/3): 149–53.

Ikegame, Aya. 2019. 'The guru as legislator: Religious leadership and informal legal space in rural South India', in *South Asian Sovereignty: The conundrum of worldly power*, edited by David Gilmartin, Pamela Price and Arild Engelsen Ruud, 58–77. Delhi: Routledge.

Jacob, Preminda. 2009. *Celluloid Deities: The visual culture of cinema and politics in South India*. Plymouth: Lexington Books.

Jaffrelot, Christophe. 2012. 'The political guru: The guru as éminence grise', in *The Guru in South Asia: New interdisciplinary perspectives*, edited by Jacob Copeman and Aya Ikegame, 80–96. Abingdon: Routledge.

Jaffrelot, Christophe. 2021. *Modi's India: Hindu nationalism and the rise of ethnic democracy* (trans. Cynthia Schoch). Princeton, NJ: Princeton University Press.

Jones, Kenneth W. 1976. *Arya Dharm: Hindu consciousness in nineteenth-century Punjab*. Berkeley and Los Angeles: University of California Press.

Jothe, Sanjay Shraman. 2017. 'Gond Punem philosophy and Mahishasur', *Forward Press*, 3 July.

Kanungo, Pralay. 2012. 'Fusing the ideals of the Math with the ideology of the Sangh? Vivekananda Kendra, ecumenical Hinduism and Hindu nationalism', in *Public Hinduisms*, edited by John Zavos, Pralay Kanungo, Deepa S. Reddy, Maya Warrier and Raymond Brady Williams, 119–40. New Delhi: Sage.

Kapur, Geeta. 2000. *When Was Modernism: Essays on contemporary cultural practice in India*. New Delhi: Tulika.

Khare, R. S. 1984. *The Untouchable as Himself: Ideology, identity and pragmatism among the Lucknow Chamars*. Cambridge: Cambridge University Press.

Landes, Richard. 2011. *Heaven on Earth: The varieties of the millennial experience*. New York: Oxford University Press.

Lasch, Christopher. 1991. *The Culture of Narcissism: American life in an age of diminishing expectations*. New York: W. W. Norton.

Lempert, Michael. 2014. 'Imitation', *Annual Review of Anthropology* 43: 379–95. https://doi.org/10.1146/annurev-anthro-102313-030008.

Lépinasse, Pascale and Raphaël Voix. 2011/12. 'Learn nothing, know all: Anti-intellectualism and practi[c]es of erudition in two modern Hindu sects', *Archives de sciences sociales des religions* 154 (2): 61–78.

Longkumer, Arkotong. 2017. 'The power of persuasion: Hindutva, Christianity, and the discourse of religion and culture in Northeast India', *Religion* 47 (2): 203–27. https://doi.org/10.1080/0048721X.2016.1256845.

Lucia, Amanda. 2018. 'Guru sex: Charisma, proxemic desire, and the haptic logics of the guru–disciple relationship', *Journal of the American Academy of Religion* 86 (4): 953–88. https://doi.org/10.1093/jaarel/lfy025.

MacIntyre, Alasdair. 2004. *The Unconscious: A conceptual analysis*, rev. edn. New York: Routledge.

Mazzarella, William. 2010. 'The myth of the multitude, or, Who's afraid of the crowd?' *Critical Inquiry* 36 (4): 697–727. https://doi.org/10.1086/655209.

Mazzarella, William. 2013. *Censorium: Cinema and the open edge of mass publicity*. Durham, NC: Duke University Press.

Mazzarella, William. 2022. 'Charisma in the age of Trumpism', *E-flux*, 22 September. https://www.e-flux.com/notes/492472/charisma-in-the-age-of-trumpism (accessed 12 March 2023).

Mbembe, Achille. 2001. *On the Postcolony*. Berkeley: University of California Press.

McKean, Lise. 1996. *Divine Enterprise: Gurus and the Hindu nationalist movement*. Chicago, IL: University of Chicago Press.

Meyer, Birgit. 2003. 'Visions of blood, sex and money: Fantasy spaces in popular Ghanaian cinema', *Visual Anthropology* 16 (1): 15–41. https://doi.org/10.1080/08949460309595097.

Meyer, Birgit and Annelise Moors. 2006. 'Introduction', in *Religion, Media, and the Public Sphere*, edited by Birgit Meyer and Annelies Moors, 1–25. Bloomington: Indiana University Press.

Mohammad-Arif, Aminah and Jules Naudet. 2020. 'Introduction: Academia, scholarship and the challenge of Hindutvaism: Making sense of India's authoritarian turn', *South Asia Multidisciplinary Academic Journal* 24/25. https://doi.org/10.4000/samaj.6982.

Mooney, Nicola. 2013. 'Dancing in diaspora space: Bhangra, caste, and gender among Jat Sikhs', in *Sikh Diaspora: Theory, agency, and experience*, edited by Michael Hawley, 279–318. Leiden: Brill.

Moulier Boutang, Yann. 2011. *Cognitive Capitalism* (trans. Ed Emery). Cambridge: Polity.

Nandy, Ashis. 2013. *Regimes of Narcissism, Regimes of Despair*. New Delhi: Oxford University Press.

Nilsen, Alf Gunvald. 2018. *Adivasis and the State: Subalternity and citizenship in India's Bhil heartland*. Cambridge: Cambridge University Press.

Oustinova-Stjepanovic, Galina. 2023. *Monumental Names: Archival aesthetics and the conjuration of history in Moscow*. Abingdon: Routledge.

Pandian, Anand. 2015. *Reel World: An anthropology of creation*. Durham, NC: Duke University Press.

Parciack, Ronie. 2023. 'Defeat and glory: Social media, neoliberalism and the transnational tragedy of a divinized *baba*', *Religions* 14 (1): art. no. 123, 1–15. https://doi.org/10.3390/rel14010123.

Pinch, William R. 2006. *Warrior Ascetics and Indian Empires*. Cambridge: Cambridge University Press.

Pinch, William. 2012. 'The slave guru: Masters, commanders, and disciples in early modern South Asia', in *The Guru in South Asia: New interdisciplinary perspectives*, edited by Jacob Copeman and Aya Ikegame, 64–79. Abingdon: Routledge.

Pinney, Christopher. 2004. *Photos of the Gods: The printed image and political struggle in India*. London: Reaktion Books.

Pinney, Christopher. 2010. '"It is a different nature which speaks to the camera": Observations on screen culture, prophecy, and politics', *BioScope: South Asian Screen Studies* 1 (2): 111–17. https://doi.org/10.1177/097492761000100203.

Pinney, Christopher. 2019. 'Digital cows: Flesh and code', in *Photo-Objects: On the materiality of photographs and photo archives*, edited by Julia Bärnighausen, Costanza Caraffa, Stefanie Klamm, Franka Schneider and Petra Wodtke, 199–210. Online version at http://mprl-series.mpg.de/studies/12/ (accessed 12 March 2023).

Prasad, M. Madhava. 2021. 'Darshan(a)', *BioScope: South Asian Screen Studies* 12 (1–2): 53–6. https://doi.org/10.1177/09749276211026138.

Rajadhyaksha, Ashish. 2009. *Indian Cinema in the Time of Celluloid: From Bollywood to the emergency*. Bloomington: Indiana University Press.

Ramnath, Nandini, 'MSG 2: The Messenger', Scroll.in, 18 September 2015. https://scroll.in/article/756336/msg-2-the-messenger-sees-the-return-of-the-guru-of-bad-cinema (accessed 10 March 2023).

Roberts, Nathaniel. 2016. *To Be Cared For: The power of conversion and foreignness of belonging in an Indian slum*. Oakland: University of California Press.

Roy, Piyush. 2017. 'The barred baba of bling', *Orissa Post*, 3 September.

Rudert, Angela. 2017. *Shakti's New Voice: Guru devotion in a woman-led spiritual movement*. Lanham, MD: Lexington Books.

Shukla, Rakesh. 2013. 'Agent provocateur par excellence [Review of Ashis Nandy, *Regimes of Narcissism, Regimes of Despair*]', *Himal South Asia*, 4 December.

Singh, Santosh K. 2017. 'Deras as "little fiefdoms": Understanding the Dera Sacha Sauda phenomenon', *Economic and Political Weekly* 52 (37): 20–3.

Singh, Surinder. 2019. 'Social cleavages, Deras and politics in Eastern Punjab: A study of Dera Sacha Sauda', *Journal of Social and Administrative Sciences* 6 (1): 47–65.

Snodgrass, Jeffrey. 2002. 'Imitation is far more than the sincerest of flattery: The mimetic power of spirit possession in Rajasthan, India', *Cultural Anthropology* 17 (1): 32–64. https://doi.org/10.1525/can.2002.17.1.32.

Srinivas, S. V. 1996. 'Devotion and defiance in fan activity', *Journal of Arts and Ideas* 29 (1): 67–83.

Srinivas, S. V. 2009. *Megastar: Chiranjeevi and Telugu cinema after N. T. Rama Rao*. New Delhi: Oxford University Press.

Srinivas, Tulasi. 2010. *Winged Faith: Rethinking globalization and religious pluralism through the Sathya Sai movement*. New York: Columbia University Press.

Srinivas, Tulasi. 2012. 'Articles of faith: Material piety, devotional aesthetics and the construction of a moral economy in the transnational Sathya Sai movement', *Visual Anthropology* 25 (4): 270–302. https://doi.org/10.1080/08949468.2012.687959.

Srivastava, Sanjay. 2009. 'Urban spaces, Disney-divinity and moral middle classes in Delhi', *Economic and Political Weekly* 44 (26/27): 338–45. http://dx.doi.org/10.2307/40279794.

Ssorin-Chaikov, Nikolai. 2006. 'On heterochrony: Birthday gifts to Stalin, 1949', *Journal of the Royal Anthropological Institute* NS 12 (2): 355–75. https://doi.org/10.1111/j.1467-9655.2006.00295.x.

Strohl, David James. 2019. 'Love jihad in India's moral imaginaries: Religion, kinship, and citizenship in late liberalism', *Contemporary South Asia* 27 (1): 27–39. https://doi.org/10.1080/09584935.2018.1528209.

Thrift, Nigel. 2012. 'The insubstantial pageant: Producing an untoward land', *Cultural Geographies* 19 (2): 141–68. https://doi.org/10.1177/1474474011427268.

Tresch, John. 2007. 'Technological world-pictures', *Isis* 98 (1): 84–99. http://dx.doi.org/10.1086/512833.

Tripathi, Anurag. 2018. *Dera Sacha Sauda and Gurmeet Ram Rahim: A decade-long investigation*. Gurgaon: Penguin Books.

Tyagi, Aastha and Atreyee Sen. 2020. '*Love-jihad* (Muslim sexual seduction) and *ched-chad* (sexual harassment): Hindu nationalist discourses and the ideal/deviant urban citizen in India', *Gender, Place and Culture* 27 (1): 104–25. https://doi.org/10.1080/0966369X.2018.1557602.

Vanita, Ruth. 2002. '*Dosti* and *Tamanna*: Male-male love, difference, and normativity in Hindi cinema', in *Everyday Life in South Asia*, edited by Diane Mines and Sarah Lamb, 146–58. Bloomington: Indiana University Press.

Vasudevan, Ravi. 2005. 'Devotional transformation: Miracles, mechanical artifice, and spectatorship in Indian cinema', *Postscripts* 1 (2–3): 237–57. https://doi.org/10.1558/post.v1i2_3.237.

Verran, Helen. 2014. 'Number', in *Globalization in Practice*, edited by Nigel Thrift, Adam Tickell, Steve Woolgar and William H. Rupp, 277–80. Oxford: Oxford University Press.

Wedeen, Lisa. 1998. 'Acting "as if": Symbolic politics and social control in Syria', *Comparative Studies in Society and History* 40 (3): 503–23. https://doi.org/10.1017/S0010417598001388.

13
Doing seeing: televised yoga, consumption and religious nationalism in neoliberal India

Srirupa Bhattacharya

Some say that the idea of holding yoga lessons on television was not Baba Ramdev's own. It came to him in 2002 from a top executive of Aastha (meaning 'faith'), a religious television channel in India, and even though they could not convince the Chief Executive Officer of the company, the idea never left Baba Ramdev (see for example Pathak-Narain 2017, 55–6[1]). What happened after that is widely reported: Baba Ramdev took this idea to Sanskar (which means 'values'), a rival religious television channel, and successfully bargained for a 20-minute morning slot in 2003. The programme was so popular that within months television channels were fighting for the yoga guru to appear in their programmes. A long way from these boardroom negotiations and tussles, I had finished school and started going to college in Calcutta. My father had suffered a stroke and was hospitalised for a couple of days. When he came home, he tried to give up smoking, and began to wake up at 6.30 a.m. to watch Baba Ramdev's show. I was baffled that a person who I had never seen entering a temple, performing a religious ritual, praying, or practising yoga, would now *religiously* watch a saffron-clad and bearded sannyasi every day. Walking round a predominantly CPM-para (Communist Party of India (Marxist) neighbourhood, or a neighbourhood that mostly votes for the Left), I was surprised to hear the sound of spiritual healing coming out of television sets in several *secular* homes, especially in the morning. After a few months my father went back to smoking and waking up at 8.00 a.m., and I forgot about Baba Ramdev's meteoric rise to fame and wealth through teaching yoga on television, till the time came for me to write an initial proposal for my MPhil in 2008.

By this time Baba Ramdev had expanded the scope of his sermons on television, from yoga to promoting Ayurveda, critiquing Western medicine and enterprises, and upholding swadeshi or home-grown products, lifestyle and values. His hundred-acre ashram Patanjali Yogpeeth near Haridwar had been launched, and he owned the religious television channel Aastha. In 2010 Baba Ramdev's discourse became more aggressively religious-nationalist through his new political platform Bharat Swabhimaan ('India self-respect').[2] Even in this phase television remained an important aspect of his dissemination. His own success was not driven only by his tele-proselytising; in fact, many commentators believe that the boom in the religious television business in India hinged on Baba Ramdev's entry (see for example Pathak-Narain 2017, 49–61; Dubey 2019). Feeding into each other's success, it is no surprise that in another 10 years Baba Ramdev owned or had controlling stakes in 10 religious television channels in India (Dubey 2019).

This chapter has two main objectives. First, it looks at Patanjali Yogpeeth's discourse on health and religious nationalism and how it sits within the politics of television watching in India since the late 1980s. Drawing on media theory, it sets out to show how the medium of religious television channels influences the presentation of yoga and Ayurveda in front of a twenty-first-century audience. Baba Ramdev's method of dissemination commanded a certain unity in watching television: a person watching his live *shivirs* (camps) on a personal television set would not just see the guru doing yoga, but follow his instructions at the same time. Simultaneously the viewer saw thousands of people in the live *shivir* practising what the guru asks, each day in a different city or town. Similarly, when an Ayurvedic product was endorsed during the *shivir*, the viewer could see people in a large audience shouting out that they had benefited from it. While conspicuous consumption has been seen as a characteristic of the new middle class, Baba Ramdev's shows gave a public or mass appeal to the act of buying or consuming through television watching. Viewers and consumers could see their own experience of healing within the nation's healing. The act of watching, then, was no longer solitary or passive.

Secondly, the chapter traces the making of the religious nationalist activist through the experiences of 'doing seeing' of volunteers who joined Baba Ramdev's cause, be it taking yoga to the masses as a national healthcare programme, as envisioned in Patanjali Yogpeeth, or participating in political cleansing and nation-building, as envisioned in Bharat Swabhimaan. This data is drawn from interviews with volunteers and from ethnography in and around the Haridwar ashram (which is the headquarters for both Patanjali Yogpeeth and Bharat Swabhimaan), as well as in New Delhi between 2010 and 2013. The journeys were different for different people, some starting with watching Baba Ramdev on television and being cured, others being influenced by his teachings and finally accepting him as their guru. It tries to show how a community is formed around the vision of religious nationalism in the midst of the different trajectories of followers. While the first section deals with the medium, popularity and content of the programmes, the second section discusses the act of seeing and the relationship between the seer and the seen, via Foucault.

The term 'doing seeing' is a play on the art historian W. J. T. Mitchell's term 'showing seeing' (2002), which he uses to describe a pedagogical practice he introduced into his classroom while teaching visual studies courses. In this exercise he would ask his students to assume that they were ethnographers interacting with an audience which had no visual culture, who did not know what 'seeing' means. The exercise was to demonstrate, or 'show', to the class what seeing means, through a show-and-tell performance.[3] In this chapter I use 'doing seeing' to emphasise that, in Baba Ramdev's method of proselytising, seeing acquired meaning only in praxis, or in doing, and doing acquired meaning in being seen. Thousands of people were copying the exercises Baba Ramdev was doing on stage, listening to his discourse, asking questions about their illnesses, while seeing others doing the same, in a *shivir* or during its live telecast on television. The audience shared their experiences of miraculous healing through yoga and Ayurveda, promising to teach yoga in their localities and pledging themselves to the nationalist cause. Just as, for Mitchell, showing seeing was a tool for classroom teaching, for Baba Ramdev doing seeing was a tool for teaching a large audience through television. In fact this method defined his *guruship*, his pedagogy, since the word 'guru' literally means teacher. His followers repeat his pedagogical method of doing seeing when they take the yoga courses to their neighbourhoods and localities, after receiving teacher training through Patanjali Yogpeeth. The role of the television here is more than just a medium transmitting a programme: people participating in the *shivir* are doing yoga with the intention of being seen live by the television audience; they, along with the guru, are instructing the television audience, embodying and demonstrating a visual call for united action or doing of yoga, and becoming a nation in the process. The television audience follow the programme with the knowledge that in doing what they are seeing, they are becoming not only an ideal devotee or student but a self-reliant, healthy and patriotic citizen.

Message qua medium: Indian television and Baba Ramdev's shows

When Baba Ramdev's shows were first aired on Sanskar in 2003, they were pre-recorded, 20-minute sessions in which he would be seen teaching yoga sitting on a plain carpeted floor, with a plain blue background on which was the emblem of Divya Yog Mandir[4] (which later became the emblem of Patanjali Yogpeeth). On the logo was a vermilion Om symbol with a yogi on one side and herbs in a mortar on the other. Baba Ramdev himself appeared in a saffron dhoti (an unstitched cloth tied in a particular way to cover the lower part of the body) and *chaadar* (unstitched cloth to cover the upper portion of the body) with thick, black, long hair and a beard. The visual was austere and the tone of the show very matter-of-fact. There were no idols or pictures of gods or gurus, no garlands or incense sticks, no pleas for prayers or donations. All attention was focused on the orange and red at the centre of a blue screen. Baba Ramdev did not offer a panacea for all the problems of humanity; he did not promise he would be there for his followers in their time of need; he did not talk about rituals to appease God or philosophise about life or the afterlife. Each day he would choose a particular physical disorder and prescribe asanas (yogic postures) and pranayama (breathing techniques) which could cure it. The disorders included obesity, high blood pressure, diabetes, hernia, piles, hair loss, high cholesterol, asthma, difficulties during pregnancy, and kidney or gall bladder stones. He would also suggest herbs, vegetables and fruits which are beneficial for these ailments. He advocated vegetarianism, teetotalism, a simple diet, and some breathing exercises which were not specific for disorders but suitable for everyone.

On the one hand, the novelty of the message was that yoga had a practical use as never before, as it had never been projected as a public health system. On the other hand, the style and visuality of his teaching was also unique. Although yoga was taught in almost every school in India for a general fitness of mind and body, and some neighbourhoods had yoga clubs, the teacher or instructor hardly ever claimed to be an ascetic, or donned saffron clothes. Gurus who claimed to live ascetic lives and taught yoga did so for a Western audience, or a very niche Indian audience, and their lessons were more concerned with lifestyle changes than with public health. Baba Ramdev's message and style, then, were secular, national and religious all at the same time. The message also demanded that one did what one saw, as one saw it, and promised short- and long-term benefits which made the programme more absorbing than other television shows. It is also important to note that this television show was a perfect fit with (1) the fact that television viewership was at its peak in India at the time, in both urban and rural settings, (2) the constraint of being crisp and precise given that it had a tight morning slot before people leave for work, school or college, or go about their chores, (3) the middle-class, upper-caste belief that exercise is particularly effective if done in the morning, (4) the general belief that starting the day by going to a temple or listening to an enlightened ascetic is auspicious, (5) the predominant feeling of loss of values, health and community in modern living, especially among the middle class. The message, the medium and the format of the programme were meant for each other, it would seem.

With television rating points (TRPs) for the programme, as well as numbers on the Sanskar channel, going through the roof, another religious TV channel, Aastha, poached Baba Ramdev within a few months and gave him a 40-minute slot. In the new format, which first aired in January 2004, Acharya Balakrishna spoke about Ayurveda, herbs and diet in the last 10 to 15 minutes of the show. Soon the 40-minute slot increased to an hour and included coverage of live mass yoga *shivirs*, which gave a new vitality to the message and brand of Baba Ramdev. Baba Ramdev's style with a live audience was completely different. He was not only interactive about the exercises but joked with the audience, appealed emotionally to people to join the cause of public health by spreading yoga, shun foreign products, especially allopathic medicine, to turn to faith and contribute to nation building. Whereas these aspects brought out his human side, the stories of miraculous healing that were shared in the *shivir* bestowed a touch of the superhuman or divine in Baba Ramdev. He never claimed enlightenment, or that he had discovered something new; rather he emphasised that he had researched what was already in the Indian 'civilisational knowledge'. The programme now combined the spontaneity and interactivity of a reality TV show, the simplicity and playfulness of a rustic host, and the authenticity and authority of symbols of saffron robes, Om, yoga, Ayurveda and Sanskrit chants. Flushed with the success of the television programmes, the huge Patanjali Yogpeeth ashram and the Divya Yog Pharmacy factory were inaugurated in 2006. Advertisements for the various services and products of these bodies began to fill the gaps between religious television programmes.

Hindu religious television programmes in India have been an area of interest among several scholars of South Asia. Rajagopal's work (2001) on the serialised version of the epic Ramayana is probably the most relevant to this chapter. He shows how a state-sponsored programme on the state-run television channel Doordarshan actually formed public opinion against Congress, which was then the party in power. The right-wing Bharatiya Janata Party (BJP) capitalised on this moment and built a religious nationalist Ram Janmabhoomi (birthplace of Ram, the god/avatar) movement around it that attracted popular support. The serial ran from 1987 to 1990, when Doordarshan was the only television channel available to the Indian audience. Congress had in fact decided to shed its shell of religious neutrality in public dissemination and shape a new modern Indian identity by appealing to the sentiments of the majority community. Although Rajagopal's work principally delineated how 'prime time religion' influenced audiences, it also traced how other media, such as print with its readership 'split' between local/vernacular and 'national' Hindi and English dailies, contributed to the communal turmoil before and after the telecast. While devotional films existed as a genre, this show brought the devotional into the weekly routine of the masses, and de-secularised television as a medium. By doing so it brought performative politics to the fore, especially that of the BJP, in the form of fairs and *rathyatras*,[5] *karseva*,[6] and speeches about *dharmayuddha* ('religious war', which was a common motif in epics). In the midst of ambiguities of identity, exasperation with unfulfilled promises of state development, and the apparent exigency of privatisation and liberalisation, a restless hegemony in public opinion could be seen forming.

With the opening of the Indian market to foreign consumer products, and the availability of more highly paid jobs in multinational corporations, television viewing in the 1990s became more directly guided by consumption, entertainment and ideas of 'choice'. Myriad channels, in regional languages as well as in Hindi and English, that catered to a more diverse audience with different kinds of programmes and increased television advertisements, changed the very habit of watching into choosing and buying. The national plan of an Indian identity formation through television was replaced by the market's agenda of capitalising on a more fragmented consumer-driven citizenship. Although Rajagopal's fieldwork continued through the 1990s he does not take these changes into account. Television programmes became more interactive with the audience, and although they alluded to the cultural diversity and unity of India through music contest shows and talk shows, they shied away from the political agenda of identity assertion. Doordarshan broadcast a number of new religious serials in an attempt to repeat the success of the drama series *Ramayan* and *Mahabharat*. But these failed to woo audiences, given the desire of the Indian audience to 'become' cosmopolitan and the range of channels exclusively telecasting films, sports events, music and news. A host of sitcoms featured for the first time on Indian television and were very successful. Some of them parodied the Indian state and politics, including a popular talk show. These, along with televised international beauty contests, in which Indian models were consistently recognised and declared winners in the 1990s, expose a patterned promotion of pure entertainment in a changed amoral mediascape.

While recognising the changes in the supply side of television business since liberalisation, it is also important to keep in mind socio-political shifts, or the demand side. Jaffrelot (2008), for example, in a study of changing attitudes towards voting, observes strong anti-parliamentarianism and an apolitical stance among the upper-caste, middle- and upper-class category, along with the rise of regional subaltern politics. A Dalit respondent in Jaffrelot's study remarks that because of the increased political participation of hitherto excluded groups in the 1990s, middle-class upper-caste Indians began to articulate their aspirations in media and NGOs, which became arenas aimed at tarnishing, or denying the importance of, politics (2008, 50). The correspondence of middle-class upper-caste aspirations and television shows becomes clearer in the 2000s, as I show below.

The 2000s in India witnessed a consolidation of a new middle-class identity riding on the 'IT boom' wave. Though the IT sector still employed only a minuscule percentage of the Indian working population, their numbers increased from 0.3 million in 1995–6 to 1.3 million by 2005–6. The IT sector in India generated total earnings of almost US$18 billion that year, while Information Technology Enabled Services (ITES: business process outsourcing, call centres and customer service) generated more than US$7 billion (National Association of Software and Service Companies (NASSCOM) 2007, cited in Upadhya and Vasavi 2008, 13). Moreover, one could observe a declining trend in public sector employment after 2000, whereas private sector employment grew steadily through the 1990s and 2000s (Ministry of Labour and Employment 2010–11). Although liberalisation and privatisation were touted as great equalisers, members of the new middle class, especially those in the IT and ITES sectors, came from remarkably homogeneous caste and educational backgrounds (see for example Ilavarasan 2008), and their social values were strongly reflected in television programmes.

It was the decade of the mega family dramas produced by the *tika*-and *dhaga*-sporting,[7] god-fearing, Blackberry-using upper-caste single woman entrepreneur Ekta Kapoor who, it was rumoured, had been assured success by her astrologer if the title of her shows began with the letter 'K'. The shows, popularly known as the K-serials, ran for between five and eight years, with plots revolving around characters of 'traditional', ever sacrificing, motherly housewives trapped in upper-middle-class joint-family politics discussing the dichotomies of chastity and promiscuity, humility and over-ambition. The 1980s secular-moral portrayals of Indian problems like poverty, bureaucratic red tape, unemployment, illiteracy, dowry, disease, lack of family planning, and gender inequality in serials like *Hum Log* and *Buniyaad*, had found their spiritual-moral heirs. Neither genre needed gods like Ram or mythological figures like Pandavas, but revolved around humans. However, the K-serials, rather than highlighting structural problems, narrated stories of moral characters dealing with daily domestic spiritual-moral battles, with their 'victory' or 'defeat' depending on how 'traditional'/'moral' the actions were. Mazzarella (2003, 138–45), while discussing contemporary advertising strategies in India, termed this phenomena auto-orientalism, by which the post-colonial subject internalises orientalist stereotypes and celebrates them. In a context in which the Indian middle class is trying to define itself in global terms, Indian leaders, advertisers and companies are adopting Western signifiers of Indian 'tradition' to woo this class. Yoga, especially its commodified televised form, is one such auto-orientalist trope.

Reality shows became a popular genre of the 2000s, and they too showed a pattern of auto-orientalist tropes, with contestants and hosts constantly referring to Indianness, as well as to family values, patriotism, love for one's language, and respect for gurus (here it means music mentors). While music and dance contests began to be televised in the 1990s, it was in the new millennium that they became consumer-oriented. The decisions on elimination from or selection for the next round now depended in large part on audience voting. Although many authors have highlighted the uniqueness of Baba Ramdev's message and method, what I am trying to show is how television programming guided the content. His shows, for example, had an interactive nature whereby audience narratives bring a sense of empowerment, which is similar to reality shows. It was the decade when internet 'infotainment' had taken off in India, but it was irregular and its reach was limited, mostly to the upper and upper-middle classes.

With the BJP-led coalition at the centre of power for the first time (1999–2004), slogans of religious nationalism, demands for jobs in multinational corporations, and political strategies to establish India as a superpower were louder than ever. It is in this context that Baba Ramdev's yoga shows are situated. Upadhya and Vasavi (2008, 35) refer to this cultural consequence of IT work in India in the new millennium, where there is 'a process of reaffirmation of "tradition"'. The authors argue that a 'sense of loss and nostalgia for an earlier form of sociality, dense with networks of family, kin and friends, pervades the self-reflective narratives of IT workers', alongside their projection of India as an economic superpower in the making. Srivastava (2009) brings out brilliantly the relationship between visuality, religiosity and the new middle-class identity in the Akshardham temple in Delhi, inaugurated in 2005. He notes that the space, spread over an area of 100 acres, is surrounded by slums, and yet its own plush premises play host exclusively to middle-class devotees. The space is also highly mediated, in that the temple complex presents a host of shows, tableaux and rides, presenting themes such as the life of Swaminaraya (an early nineteenth-century saint), India's beautiful landscapes, statues of religious and nationalist icons, gods and avatars, with background narratives of the greatness of Hinduism, and India's achievements in scientific disciplines, warfare and governance. Technologically modern in appearance, but traditionalist in perspective, it represents 'surplus and moral consumption' (p. 341), which is part of the 'new' middle-class Indian identity assertion. Srivastava sketches the blurred boundaries between the things one sees and consumes inside the temple – opulence, efficiency, devotion, righteousness, educational achievement – and the things that one does and consumes outside it. The car one drives, the mall one shops in, the college one goes to, or one's job, reflect the same values as one's attachment to a temple. At the same time all these activities assert one's membership of the middle class. In a similar way, in the case of television shows on yoga by Baba Ramdev, what is seen on television has to be done, consumed and taught, to prove one's belonging to a class, religion and nation.

While mediated religiosity of the new millennium has characteristics of a substratum for identity (re)creation, another aspect is its commodity form, as a provider of innovative solutions to new problems. Several authors, including Goldberg and Singleton (2014), Lewis (2016) and Gooptu (2016), note that new spirituality has become a tool or technique of self-management, wellness, healing, and achieving educational and economic success in India. While yoga has existed in this commodity form in the West, it was not a mass capitalist product until recently. The popularity of Baba Ramdev's televised yoga is an excellent example of such a commodity providing solutions to health problems for the masses. Yoga has become a way of making one's way in the world, rather than a means of critiquing or rejecting it, which may have been the quest of some of the early twentieth-century practitioners and religious reformers. For example, when Gandhi was exhorting Indians to exercise, maintain a simple diet and reject allopathy, it was a call to establish an Indian system in opposition to the Western system, not to compete in it (Alter 2000, 7–27). On the other hand, the strong public health motivation, the respect for tradition and the nationalism one could see in Gandhi's endorsement of yoga made a comeback with Baba Ramdev. But this comeback is not a simple replication. Yoga's journey through niche audiences in the Western world in the second half of the twentieth century has stereotyped and re-aestheticised it; its aura has been (re)activated in the twenty-first century through the medium of television, especially Indian religious channels. Walter Benjamin ([1936] 1969) introduced the idea of aura and its reproduction or 'reactivation' in art, and it has been highly influential in media theory ever since. Dasgupta (2006), for example, applies the theory in order to understand television in contemporary India and to argue that technology can add a magical value to an older form of art (say a musical genre), by virtue of easy replicability, which changes the nature of its authority. Similarly, the aura of yoga, before its technological mediation through television, signified 'authority in that its distanciation from its audience confers a socially recognized privilege on those sanctioned to maintain this distance' (Dasgupta 2006, 255). When this aura is 'reactivated' through contemporary technology, the authority of yoga overcomes its distant nature, and becomes magically accessible. However, in both cases, the aura justifies meanings of authority in the socio-economic structures they are born in.

From 2009, Baba Ramdev's discourse shifted its focus towards nationalism, although yoga and pranayama remained important as well. He launched a new political platform, Bharat Swabhimaan, through which he wanted to transform the very body politic of the nation into something new. Whereas the commonly held belief is that a deity or a guru takes care of the troubles of a devotee who truly surrenders, Baba Ramdev (through Bharat Swabhimaan) exhorted devotees to do their duty to the nation. The relationship of dependence thus shifted to one of empowerment. There were repeated calls for a people's movement to right the wrongs committed by corrupt politicians, to purge Indian society of Western education, which had allegedly caused dilution of Indian values and neglect of Indian medical systems, to ensure punishment of terrorists and tax evaders, to rid the country of multinational corporations, and to reinstate India's economic power. Bharat Swabhimaan openly critiqued the party in power at the time (Congress) and threatened that Bharat Swabhimaan, or rather the youth of the country, would contest elections in order to reinstate the just and moral society that India had been in its ancient past. The images of India's glorious past, her current decrepit state and a path to an ideal future were presented as factual, scientific and rational.

Summing up this section, I reiterate that Congress developed the national broadcasting policy in the 1970s and 1980s, while making sure that more Indian consumers have access to television. Reeves (1994) argued that the national identity Congress sought to create depended as much on the content of the programmes as on the medium through which it could reach the masses. He gives the example of the Doordarshan's introduction of colour broadcasting during the Asian Games (Asiad, a multi-sport event in which Asian countries participate) in 1982, arguing that colour images, being more *real*, have the potential to instil national pride and a sense of integration in the audience. With the privatisation of television broadcasting since the 1990s, the method of wooing audiences changed, and programmes changed too, as I have tried to show. It is to be noted that Baba Ramdev has a presence on the internet, on his official website as well as on his YouTube channel, which also have visual aspects. However, my fieldwork suggests that his followers were influenced by his television programmes or by participating in live *shivirs*.

Further, I have sought, first, to show that Baba Ramdev's morning shows on television used auto-orientalist tropes like yoga, Ayurveda and swadeshi, around which the aura of Indian tradition was modernised and reactivated to fit the needs of an audience who are becoming part of the global capitalist order in new ways. Secondly, I have argued that the medium of the television gave the programme a pedagogical and yet very practical everyman quality that made it successful, among not only the middle class but also those who aspired to be part of it. Removed from intellectuality and theory, it had all the ingredients of a popular movement. Thirdly, the everydayness and interactive nature of the show made people feel empowered and motivated, which was made possible by the medium. Audiences sitting in front of a television could now see people asking the guru about their ailments, and he would answer their questions immediately, not only in terms of time, but in terms of giving an appearance of being unmediated, as if there was nothing between the message of the guru and the learning of the devotee. This particular quality of modern media like television, of vanishing in the act of mediation, is discussed by Eisenlohr (2011). The disappearing quality of live television as a medium made a message (in this case a religious message in a particular show) seem unmediated, and therefore *real*. The format makes it look as if there is no editing or scripting or deliberate visual design. Furthermore, the answers given by Baba Ramdev to the queries of devotees, whether about ailments or politics, were precise and confident and therefore had qualities of a modern scientific discipline. Eisenlohr (2011) argues that this quality of modern media can 'sell' any idea or product and maximise economic turnover for an investor, and is particularly used by religious and political figures as a potent tool of mass mobilisation and identity assertion. How far Baba Ramdev was able to do this will be further explored through the narratives of his followers and their journeys to become activists, delineated in the next section.

Doing seeing: narratives from the other side of the television

When I interviewed her in December 2010, N. A., a 58-year-old woman from rural Madhya Pradesh, was visiting the Patanjali Yogpeeth ashram in Haridwar, looking for a cure for her respiratory problems. She said she had been suffering for years and the problem had not been properly diagnosed by her doctors, and while she had spent thousands of rupees on allopathic medicine, it had not helped. Coming from a backward-caste peasant background, she felt that Baba Ramdev, who she had seen on television, was her last refuge. 'He is a *mahapurush* ['great man', a term usually used of prophet-like figures] and has cured millions of people of difficult diseases. He has the knowledge of *rishi-munis* [sages]', she said, further explaining that ancient sages had the ability to cure the sick by merely touching them. Although she could not meet Baba Ramdev personally during her visit, she hoped that *vaids* (Ayurvedic doctors) and yoga instructors in the ashram would be able to cure her. K. K., a 39-year-old woman from urban West Bengal, had travelled 1,700km to attend the teacher training programme at the ashram (interview December 2010). She had been diagnosed with high blood pressure and was saddled with a lot of medicines at a young age. Once she started watching Baba Ramdev's shows on television, she decided to give yoga a chance. She said that by watching and practising the suggested asanas and pranayama exercises suggested on television, she was cured within a year. Even though she came from a lower-caste, lower-middle-class background she felt that she owed it to the mission to spend money to come here to attend the teacher training programme so that she can take Baba Ramdev's mission forward by teaching people in her neighbourhood. She did not want to make money out of it, she told me, as she was inspired by Baba Ramdev, who helped the poor free of cost.

Narratives like these were common during my fieldwork in the ashram in 2010, which points to the fact that, for people who watched Baba

Ramdev's shows and those who visited the ashram, darshan (seeing and being seen by the divine) was important, but not the primary motivation. The primary motivations were being cured of physical ailments and being able to take forward the message and praxis of Patanjali Yogeeth. In recent years darshan has been identified by several anthropologists as a key motif in Hinduism, especially for understanding moments when devotees visit ashrams to see the guru (Srinivas 2010, 156–90; Warrier 2005), worship an image of God (Pinney 2004, 180–95), worship online (Karapanagiotis 2013; Scheifinger 2010), or view religious films (Brosius 2002) or serials (Rajagopal 2001, 75–120). Brosius (2002, 275), however, goes beyond the idea of darshan as seeing, and draws on Foucault's conception of panopticon to theorise it as 'a means of creating worldly knowledge and power ... where vision is ... a tool of social discipline and order'.[8] People who came to the Patanjali Yogpeeth ashram, and those who watched Baba Ramdev on television, did so to learn, to become part of a knowledge system, and to encourage others to do the same. They wanted to create a different social order and envisioned their own roles in a system of power. Fifty-one-year-old P. P. U., who was in charge of Patanjali Yogpeeth's activities in a remote *upkhand* (subdivision of a district) of Almora district, echoed this ideal when I interviewed him in his village (name withheld) in January 2012. As we talked in the tiny, dark grocer's shop he ran in the village, I observed that many of the goods he sold were Patanjali products. He was an upper-caste man and had retired from the army and joined Patanjali Yogpeeth and then Bharat Swabhimaan because he wanted to continue working for the nation. He was particularly anguished by the fact that the government had not developed the hilly areas of the state of Uttarakhand, as a result of which there were no jobs and the young people were migrating to other states. P. P. U. was a fit and healthy man, used to physical exercise, but what drew him to the mission of Baba Ramdev was its ability to motivate people to collectivise, which, he hoped, would force the government to develop the state. P. P. U. claimed that he hardly ever visited the main ashram in Haridwar and that Baba Ramdev hardly ever visited remote villages like his, although they were in the same state. But the important thing was that the organisational structure made it possible for people to communicate their problems and aspirations to the guru and plan campaigns in a participatory manner.

This apparent sharing of power is not so easy for many gurus; for example, the experience of *kriya* (praxis, doing) is considered non-transferable, which is why videography of Sudarshan Kriya (a technique of breathing exercises or pranayama pioneered by Sri Sri Ravi Shankar) or Isha Yoga (yoga and pranayama pioneered by Jaggi Vasudev) is not allowed. Similarly, *unauthorised* teaching of these techniques is not allowed; even images of the gurus, to remain potent, have to be sacralised from time to time with special rituals like *guru puja*. On the contrary, Baba Ramdev's public pedagogy of doing seeing encouraged people to record videos, practise on their own, and show and teach others the techniques they had learnt. Most respondents felt empowered, as if their fate was in their own hands. Very few of the people who came to the Patanjali Yogpeeth ashram took away photos of Baba Ramdev; they would rather go back with medicines, ghee, honey or even clothes bought from the ashram shops as a token of their faith in him. This is unusual, given that devotees of Sri Sri Ravi Shankar, Sathya Sai Baba and Mata Amritanandamayi prefer to carry images of their gurus. If one visited their ashrams one would see the significance of the darshan of the living guru in the daily routine, whereas Baba Ramdev does not give darshan in his ashram or anywhere else. He only appears on television every day, doing yoga, teaching, conversing and politicising. He does not appear in any forum sitting or philosophising.

Even volunteers I interviewed in their homes did not display Baba Ramdev's portrait on the walls, except one. In another house, the ground floor had been turned into a Divya Pharmacy shop, where there was a photograph of Baba Ramdev sitting on a rather lavish chair, with many people standing on both sides. The devotee whose house I was visiting was also in the photograph, kneeling on the ground, with his hands touching Baba Ramdev's feet. It looked more like a family photograph than one meant for darshan and worship. Most of the authors cited above speak of the significance of images in which the divine figures seem to be directly and benevolently looking at the devotee, while the latter seeks their blessings through prayer and ritual worship. In many idols of deities in Indian temples, prominent open eyes are common, as are devotees gazing into them as an act of surrender. The underlying belief in this practice is that the deity or guru can judge the soul of the devotee, or even cleanse it, when their eyes meet. Baba Ramdev does not claim such sacred sight. Although hoardings and shop banners of Patanjali Yogpeeth and Divya Pharmacy have photographs of Baba Ramdev, most of the packaging of yoga/pranayama videos sold by the organisations show only his silhouette, or images in which his eyes are closed in meditation. These images or their absence go against the understanding of a divine figure *giving* darshan to devotees.

Baba Ramdev's serving of generous helpings of yoga and Ayurveda to the public through TV, and his impersonal relationship with devotees, do create a kind of panopticon of knowledge. He sees and listens to the masses, he knows what ails them and how to cure them with his religious-scientific expertise, yet he is dispassionate and distant from them, a distance shaped by the medium of television. He assures them that his knowledge can be learnt and passed on, with people's participation, just like any modern scientific panoptical system. Foucault did not talk about the panopticon as a method of mobilisation or collectivisation, but about how its power of surveillance becomes accepted or normalised in society. He talks about the shift of responsibility from the seer to the seen: 'He who is subjected to a field of visibility, and who knows it, assumes responsibility for the constraints of power; he makes them play spontaneously upon himself; ... he becomes the principle of his own subjection' (Foucault 1977, 202–3). What I am trying to draw attention to here is the politics of seeing/showing/teaching/doing the sacred that has turned into a site of reclamation, where people are submitting themselves as subjects, to be seen. The reason for this is that people feel they are finally being heard, that they will be reformed into better human beings and activists who can influence others. The reciprocal will of the panopticon to reform and its subjects' will to be reformed, according to Foucault, is the reason it becomes constant and generalisable (1977, 204–5) in contemporary society. However, Ramdev's followers come from a feeling of being neglected by an absentee state for decades, a situation they seek to change. The reclamation of being visible/audible is reflected in the wide demographic that Baba Ramdev is able to draw, which is not restricted to the typical English-speaking urban middle-class clientele, but extends to Hindi-speaking middle classes from smaller cities, lower-middle classes from across northern India, and people from different caste backgrounds as well. During ethnography in 2010, I could see the difference in accommodation and treatment of patients in the ashram, depending on their social and economic capital. My interactions with visitors in the ashram also betrayed the more transactional attitude of the English-speaking urban middle-class clientele, and their association with the organisation was shorter than other classes. Despite these differences, devotees expressed a predominant sentiment of finally being seen, heard and enabled to act where the *vyavastha* (the system, including state education and health, private hospitals and political parties) had failed them. The feeling that Baba Ramdev's mission had a place for everyone brought with it a sense of evenness and participation.

The seeming evenness of power among followers and clients of Patanjali Yogpeeth, again, did not go uncriticised by religious authority. Walking down the streets of Haridwar, I encountered more conservative practitioners of yoga, Ayurveda and pranayama, affiliated to several monastic orders, who were rather displeased with Baba Ramdev's desacralising of the 'pure ways'. One questioned whether Baba Ramdev can be called a guru at all, since he 'was nothing before his TV show', and 'he went door to door on the streets of Haridwar on a bicycle, distributing Ayurvedic medicine and teaching yoga' (field notes from December 2010, Haridwar city). He felt that it was not a guru's job to take the ancient knowledge to the people, but rather the devotee's job to come seeking. Another felt that teaching and showing yoga on television was *wrong* in itself, because without a long and personal association with a guru such knowledge cannot be passed on. Baba Ramdev, therefore, had, in his view, plebeianised religious authority. It is important here to keep in mind that Baba Ramdev came from an illiterate backward-caste background, and his claim to religious authority went against conservative Hindu attitudes about the reservation of sacred knowledge to the upper castes. Similarly, any vehicle one propels oneself, especially a bicycle, is traditionally considered to be a means of mobility for non-upper castes, and Baba Ramdev used that very means. To make matters worse, Baba Ramdev's use of the medium of television made his endeavour a profit-making enterprise, which debased the ideas of renunciation promoted by monastic orders.

As mentioned earlier, from 2009 onwards Baba Ramdev addressed the question of Hindu nationalism more directly than before, which added a different kind of follower base to his newly launched platform Bharat Swabhimaan. Starting with the discourse of rejecting the goods and services of foreign corporations in favour of swadeshi (home-grown), Baba Ramdev spoke about a range of issues afflicting Indian society, and mobilised masses to launch a battle for reform, once again using television as the broadcast medium. In addition, the internet, smartphones and computers were becoming more common, which contributed to the popularity of his messages on YouTube channels. In January 2012 I interviewed K. A., a student activist, in his college in Haridwar. He said that he used to be a member of Akhil Bharatiya Vidyarthi Parishad (ABVP), which is a students' organisation affiliated to the Rashtriya Swayamsevak Sangh (RSS), a right-wing umbrella organisation in India. K. A., from an upper-caste, middle-class family in Haridwar, said he was disgusted with the top-down approach of political parties. For this reason, he resigned from ABVP, and in 2010 formed his own organisation, which by 2012 had student cadres in four colleges in Haridwar. He had no interest in yoga, but became associated with Bharat Swabhimaan because he felt that Baba Ramdev had a vision of changing the nation and was especially concerned about young people in small towns and villages.

K. A. said that the right-wing political party Bharatiya Janata Party (also affiliated to the RSS) was in power in the state of Uttarakhand with single (absolute) majority from 2007 to 2012. But in its term it was unable to fulfil the expectations of the people, who then vented their frustrations on activists on the ground like himself. This was another reason why he disassociated himself from known RSS organisations; he felt he could work better with new faces that people trusted. Because of his participation in the Haridwar chapter of the anti-corruption movement led by Baba Ramdev (2010–12), he was arrested in 2011, but he claimed that it was Baba Ramdev who saw to it that he got out. When I asked him what he felt about the commercial interests of Patanjali Yogpeeth, he said that it would give jobs to the youth of Uttarakhand (the state being the headquarters of the organisation), which he was all for.

While Bharat Swabhimaan drew non-members to its cause, it also appealed to a very different group of full-time volunteers, especially young people, to surrender their lives to the mission. Baba Ramdev called them the *jeevandani* (life donor) when he announced his Bharat Swabhimaan plans on television. When I interviewed two young female *jeevandanis* in the Haridwar ashram in December 2010, they explained that anyone who had completed school education was eligible to become a *jeevandani*, but a bachelor's degree and being between 20 and 40 years old was preferable. These volunteers would have to renounce their families, homes, caste identities and material assets, and adopt teetotalism, vegetarianism, white khadi clothes and celibacy. The ashram took responsibility for their welfare, although their lifestyles were austere and highly regimented. Once they were in the ashram, volunteers would be given different tasks. Some had been sent to state-level committees to supervise the formation of *gram samitis* (village-level bodies) or *zilla samitis* (district-level bodies) of Bharat Swabhimaan. Female volunteers were mostly given responsibilities in the headquarters of the Haridwar ashram, including the two I spoke to. According to them, at the time of interview, there were around 120 *jeevandanis*. None of the *jeevandanis* I met came from a metropolis and none of them had been to an English-medium school, although many of them had English as one of the subjects in their curriculum. Some of the young men had been secluded in the gurukul within the ashram, and once their scriptural and religious training was over they would take the scholarly knowledge to the masses. Interestingly, although most *jeevandanis* had come to know about Bharat Swabhimaan through television, once they became volunteers, they were not allowed to watch entertainment or even the news. The use of phones was also restricted.

R. *behen*, a 25-year-old *jeevandani* (*behen* means 'sister'; *jeevandanis* do not use their family or caste names: they are referred to as *behen* or *bhai* ('brother')), was interested in continuing her education. Although all the *jeevandanis* in the ashram could take some philosophy classes on the Upanishads and the Shaastras, she was particularly interested in ancient Indian history, which was not available to her. She was distrustful of what had been taught in her school and college. When I asked if she felt it was unfair that the gurukul was only for men, she said she was sure that Swamiji (Baba Ramdev) would create similar opportunities for women in the future. During my conversation with *jeevandanis* after an Upanishad class in the ashram in December 2010, I asked if they found it paradoxical that Baba Ramdev was prescribing renunciation for the *jeevandanis*, while promoting commercial products for the masses. A male *jeevandani* defended the guru, saying that in any monastic order the expectations of householders and monks are different. Another male *jeevandani* quipped, 'If more people contribute to Baba Ramdev's mission by buying skin creams of Patanjali Yogpeeth they will be serving his motto of swadeshi instead of buying foreign goods.' A female *jeevandani* said, 'Who knows? … We might have a gurukul for women if his business does well. After all someone is at last looking out for women's health.' The fact that half the *jeevandanis* were women gave them hope of equality.

As can be seen from the narratives above, the mission means different things to different people. Whereas for K. A. it brings a sense of independence, allowing him to work among the masses apart from the organisational structure, for the *jeevandanis* it gives a structure to contribute in the work of nation building. Among the patients too, we can see that for some it is the last resort to regain their health, while for some it is a platform to give back to society. For the metropolitan middle classes I interviewed in the ashram, it is an experiment, a question of choice for their health. Some felt that their monetary contributions to the organisation when they availed themselves of yoga, Ayurveda or naturopathy courses, or by way of donation, went towards charitable causes. In the midst of these various motivations, can we still find a community feeling necessary for the identity assertion of majoritarian Hindu nationalism? Even in the diversity of aspirations, social locations and roles of the Baba Ramdev's followers, one can observe a strong sense of solidarity and community, which is not pre-existing, but is being created, embodied and lived by the practitioners themselves. For example, the *jeevandanis* were accommodative of the householder followers, and the activist was happy that others would get jobs at Patanjali's ever-expanding empire. The question of circulation and mediation is also important: a strong sense of becoming examples for their society or to prove themselves is palpable. Respondents encouraged me to record our interviews, they were eager to talk to me, and they kept pointing me towards internet links where I could follow the story of the mission or the lives of followers. At the same time they warned me about negative publicity from some media sources. I was asked if I was from Congress or if I worked for a newspaper or news channel, which did not stem from a sense of self-preservation but from a sense of loyalty to and protection of their *community*.

In the creation of this community, unequal social relations and underlying structures are invisibilised. However, their invisibility does not mean that they are absent. Rather, they are couched in an innovative message presented through a newly available media. It is the coming together of these factors that obliterates differences of caste, gender, urban/rural/diasporic location, and language, to create seemingly homogeneous identities. Brosius (2002) calls this 'tickling and teaching' in her essay on a film called *God Manifests Himself*, through which right-wing organisations evoke nationalism in the minds of spectators. The images and narrative of the film are like a documentary, as if it were presenting facts and history, not a story, while stereotyping self (Hindus) and other (Muslims), and finally creating the possibility of a utopic future, which the audience is invited to build. The experience of being healed through yoga prescribed by Baba Ramdev on television is accompanied by similar techniques of 'tickling' by appealing to the audience's emotions and senses and imploring them to join the cause of nation building. Brosius also points to the fact that this appeal to the senses has the potential of creating a kind of unity in the utopic past and future, even though the present is fraught with differences of class, caste, gender, nationality, political leanings, and so forth. While talking to the followers of Baba Ramdev in and outside the ashram I found that this sense of building unity was strong. In the previous section, I drew attention to the fact that most television shows of the 1990s targeted the cosmopolitan urban middle class and portrayed their consumerist, apolitical lifestyles, whereas the 2000s brought the backlash of more conservative upper-caste sections into public view. What I have tried to show in this section is how this portrayal subsumed aspirations of other sections within it, and was able to create uniformity and pride in the *traditional Hindu-Indian* identity. Munshi (2008), for example, shows how working-class women in Delhi emulate the *traditional* women in the Ekta Kapoor serials in their clothes, make-up and even festivals and fasts. Eisenlohr (2011) traces the emergent diasporic Hindu identity in Mauritius, which is consolidating through the use of religious media, stereotyping 'people you want to resemble' (Hindus) and 'those you don't want to be like' (Muslims). While Rajagopal (2001) portrayed a tenuous hegemony of the Hindu nationalist leadership swaying the emotions and differences of opinion of a fragmented public for electoral gain, what we see in the new millennium is much more organised and embedded in the daily lives of people.

Hindi-speaking women from the town of Dehradun were extremely active in spreading not only yoga but also the message of Bharat Swabhimaan. Unlike the *jeevandanis*, they were part-time volunteers and householders. D. S., a 48-year-old upper-caste middle-class woman and *rajya prabhari* (person in charge at the state level) of Patanjali Yogpeeth Yog Samiti, as well as Bharat Swabhimaan for the state of Uttarakhand, was an epitome of matriarchal poise and administrative acumen. She became a member after a cyst in her ovary miraculously vanished after she started practising yoga and taking Ayurvedic medicine prescribed by *vaids* of Patanjali Yogpeeth. She believed that it was her duty to realise the dream of Baba Ramdev, who had unlocked her potential to be more than a housewife, to serve her nation actively. N. U., the *upkhand* (division) in-charge of a part of Dehradun city West, came from a similar background and age group as D. S., but her volunteer work stemmed from bhakti (devotion). She had worshipped gods all her life and now she worshipped the guru as well. So this was not a change for her, she told me. She had not suffered or recovered from any serious illness, but felt that after one's children are grown up one should serve society. Unlike D. S., N. U. did not have much decision-making power within the organisation, but she was happy to do what was expected of her. She distributed the pamphlets of the organisation, set up stalls that sold Patanjali products on festival days, and taught yoga. Both these interviews took place in January 2012, at the homes of the volunteers.

Even when I was doing fieldwork at Ramlila Maidan in Delhi, at the site of Baba Ramdev's hunger strike to end political corruption in 2011, I found this strong sense of community, despite the diversity of people and opinion represented. There were militant Hindu organisations, monastic orders, reformist organisations, women's organisations, school groups, university students' organisations, all ready to fast with Baba Ramdev and even face state backlash from Congress. They came from different parts of north India, and television and social media at the time were saturated with images and news of this event.

Baba Ramdev's campaign to end political corruption and thereby build India's future continued after the hunger strike was over. Many of Baba Ramdev's followers were not keen on Bharat Swabhimaan directly entering electoral politics and felt that they could influence the results more radically by taking the message of political change to the people. But nevertheless they felt that political intervention by a spiritual leader had become necessary. This was not common in religious organisations in India before Baba Ramdev; most kept their political beliefs covert or left it to personal decisions. However, in Baba Ramdev's discourse, good health and political responsibility were fused and overt. The medium of television added a quality of transparency which helped create the doing seeing, empowered subject. The relationship between the guru and the devotee became more active, and seemingly democratic. It is this relationship that makes the utopia of India's glorious past, combined with its strong military and economic future, seem realisable.

Conclusion

In this chapter I have tried to show how the visuality of religious nationalism has become gradually acceptable, by tracing the rise of the Hindu guru Baba Ramdev through televised yoga and Ayurvedic treatment. In the first section I traced the continuities and innovations brought by the guru into the existing content of television programmes in India, especially in terms of religious and nationalist tropes. I have also shown Baba Ramdev's clever capture of the technology available to woo the strident middle-class audience of the new millennium. In the second section I followed the experiences of members and activists of Patanjali Yogpeeth and Bharat Shabhimaan, all of whom started out by watching the yoga show. Baba Ramdev's show was able to break the wall between seeing and passively consuming, and doing yoga and nationalist politics. Viewers were implored to take the message of the programme forward to their localities. This helped establish a panopticon of sorts, in which surveillance of bodies was diffused through society, in the name of health or righteous politics. Even though the journeys of the activists were different from those of the organisation, a unity in action and the path to building a new nation was clear. The generous use of religious nationalist tropes, visible Hindu symbols, body regimes and popular festivals made it easier to profile or discipline 'others' in this panopticon. What I have tried to show in this chapter is how the combination of a potent message and a proliferating medium imbues consumer-citizens with a strong sense of participation and empowerment, personally and communally.

The argument that medium and message influence, create and maintain each other is not new, especially in the study of the relationship between religion and popular media. Meyer (2011) goes to the extent of arguing that, rather than studying 'religion and media', we must turn our attention to 'religious mediation'. The moment a religious figure presents his discourse to the public, he becomes a medium between a scripture, a philosophical school or a ritual on the one hand, and the public on the other. To add to this, in contemporary times the use of media technology (television, internet, camera, cassette or even a microphone) becomes inevitable for religious dissemination. Meyer also suggests that certain media technologies are developed by and for religious actors (a horoscope-making application comes to mind). In a way, it can be said that media is also constantly in a mode either of *becoming*, or of *being* made by religion. While this method of exploring the relationship between religion and media is important, it cannot fully explain Baba Ramdev's televangelism. The investigation has to turn towards the specifics of why and how a particular (religious) message becomes immensely popular when disseminated through a particular medium, i.e., television, and why and how the medium moulds the message, for example, by fitting it into the morning time slot. Needless to say, not every medium fits every religious message. In the case of Patanjali Yogpeeth's website divyayoga.com, no learning or actual engagement or religious act (such as darshan or worship) takes place through this medium.[9] Similarly, on Patanjali Yogpeeth's YouTube channel one can see some of the recordings of Baba Ramdev's televised yoga camps, but nothing specifically made for internet users. Even during my ethnography, I found that followers did not rely on the internet for their engagement with the organisation. In fact, in 2018 a television serial based on the life of Baba Ramdev came out, but it was not very popular, even though the biographical tele-serial as a genre is popular in India.

My main contribution to this body of knowledge on religious mediation is the portrayal of subjectivities that grow out of the process. Gupta and Copeman (2019) argued that Baba Ramdev's yoga must be theorised beyond commodification as well as beyond religious nationalism encased in a health regime or body discipline. They showed that yoga provides a suitable form of physical cultural enterprise, which is often combined with more direct religious nationalist campaigning. To add to this, Patanjali Yogpeeth was able to prove yoga's efficacy as a public health policy, and provide the public with low-cost cures for serious illnesses, and thereby win the trust of different classes, especially the poorer sections of society, in the context of the lack or inadequacy of government healthcare in India. The authors also note that, although Bharat Swabhimaan's discourse shifted to religious nationalism as a political programme more directly than Patanjali Yogpeeth's, it is yoga's centrality in Hindutva that continues to make Baba Ramdev relevant. But then, yoga has been used by Hindutva forces or has played this role for a long time within the Hindutva project. The popularity of many gurus and their organisations has hinged on the projection of yoga's importance within organised Hinduism. The argument of this chapter is not simply that Baba Ramdev's innovation was his use of television, nor that it was a fortunate coincidence of his finding capital investment for his TV show idea. The chapter's emphasis is, rather, the new, everyday sense of community created by his followers doing seeing yoga, talking about their problems, being seen on TV, seeing others, who are suffering, being healed, sharing experiences of becoming a yoga teacher, and making public commitments on live television to join the cause of the organisation. The guruship thus created is, at the same time, about a figurehead and not about him, and that is the uniqueness of this collective enterprise. It is an enterprise that comprises the personal journeys of the audience, but also their coming together to create a formidable narrative of unity. The immediacy created by a live television show of a *shivir* allows the everyman to 'see' the whole nation at once, speak to them through a live 'Q and A', and actively expand the horizon of religious nationalism, every day. And this was not possible in previous media formats. It had an advantage over soaps, which were scripted and therefore not interactive, while internet religiosity was yet to take off in India. However, lessons of the power of visual media combined with the miracle of the live-feed have, since Baba Ramdev, not only transformed religious nationalist dissemination in Indian television, but exploded in social media and internet use in India.

Notes

1   Pathak-Narain's biographical book on Baba Ramdev titled *Godman to Tycoon* was banned in India in 2017 as soon as it was released, as the result of a defamation case filed on behalf of Baba Ramdev. However, the injunction was removed the following year.

2   Bharat Swabhimaan was initially launched as a political party that would contest the 2014 Lok Sabha elections to remove the corrupt Congress Party from power and instate a new political order and just society in India. Baba Ramdev claimed that the already existing organisational support for Patanjali Yogpeeth across the country would ensure his victory. However, soon after its launch Baba Ramdev declared his support for the Bharatiya Janata Party in the 2014 election, and campaigned extensively for the right-wing party.

3   Mitchell's argument in the paper was that perspectives in visual studies look at seeing either as natural or given, or as completely cultural or constructed. Mitchell was trying to say that both aspects exist in one's experience. Secondly, he critiques the argument that the visual had come to dominate our lives only in contemporary times. According to him it was a predominant sensory mode, even when we did not have so-called visual media.

4   The Divya Yog Mandir ('divine yoga temple') Trust was founded by the guru Shankar Dev in Haridwar in 1995, after Baba Ramdev became his disciple. Baba Ramdev was also a trustee, along with Shankar Dev and his other disciple Acharya Karamveer.

5   Chariot processions. In Indian epics and myths a *rath* or chariot is a recurrent motif and is also ritualistic in certain festivals, for example in the worship of the deity Jagannath. Certain *shuddhi* (reconversion to Hinduism) campaigns in India have used *rathyatras* as a symbol since colonial times, during which religious or political leaders on a modern vehicle, representing a chariot, would go from place to place (re)converting people or 'bringing them back' to Hinduism. In the 1990s *rathyatra* was used by the BJP to garner support for the Ram Janmabhoomi (birthplace of Ram) movement.

6   Voluntary labour for a spiritual-humanitarian cause. During the Ram Janmabhoomi movement, however, it specifically came to mean contributing to the construction of a Ram temple in Ayodhya, at a legally disputed site on which an early sixteenth-century mosque stood. The unsubstantiated claim of BJP and certain Hindu religious groups was that the Mughal ruler Babur had demolished a temple built in honour of the deity Ram before commissioning the construction of a mosque at that very site. The Ram Janmabhoomi movement sought to right this alleged wrong.

7   *Tika* is a Hindu religious mark worn on the forehead, usually made of vermilion paste, but it can also be made of turmeric or sandalwood paste. *Dhaga* is a thread usually sacralised during specific Hindu rituals and then worn on the wrist for protection by a deity or as a mark of devotion to a deity. It must be noted here that Ekta Kapoor has changed her look and strategy of naming serials in the last decade.

8   Elsewhere, Brosius (2005) cites Sophie Hawkins as having come up with this definition while discussing visualisation of devotion on the internet.

9   There are religious websites on which one can offer online pujas, or worship online, or have darshan, or access videos of festivals and sermons, or even go on a pilgrimage (see for example Scheifinger 2010; Karapanagiotis 2013). Such religious acts are not possible through the divyayoga website.

References

Alter, Joseph S. 2000. *Gandhi's Body: Sex, diet, and the politics of nationalism*. Philadelphia: University of Pennsylvania Press.

Benjamin, Walter. [1936] 1969. 'The work of art in the age of mechanical reproduction', in *Illuminations* (ed. Hannah Arendt, trans. Harry Zohn), 217–51. New York: Schocken Books.

Brosius, Christiane. 2002. 'Hindutva intervisuality: Videos and politics of representation', *Contributions to Indian Sociology* 36 (1–2): 264–95. https://doi.org/10.1177/006996 670203600109.

Brosius, Christiane. 2005. *Empowering Visions: The politics of representation in Hindu nationalism*. London: Anthem Press.

Dasgupta, Sudeep. 2006. 'Gods in the sacred marketplace: Hindu nationalism and the return of the aura in the public sphere', in *Religion, Media and the Public Sphere*, edited by Birgit Meyer and Annelies Moors, 251–76. Bloomington: Indiana University Press.

Dubey, Jyotindra. 2019. 'Owned by corporates, run by babas – the economics behind India's devotional television', *The Wire*, 14 April. https://thewire.in/media/owned-by-corporates-run-by-babas-the-economics-behind-indias-devotional-television (accessed 13 March 2023).

Eisenlohr, Patrick. 2011. 'The anthropology of media and the question of ethnic and religious pluralism', *Social Anthropology* 19 (1): 40–55. https://doi.org/10.1111/j.1469-8676.2010. 00136.x.

Foucault, Michel. [1977] 1995. *Discipline and Punish: The birth of the prison* (trans. Alan Sheridan), 2nd Vintage Books edn. New York: Vintage Books.

Goldberg, Ellen and Mark Singleton. 2014. 'Introduction', in *Gurus of Modern Yoga*, edited by Mark Singleton and Ellen Goldberg, 1–14. New York: Oxford University Press.

Gooptu, Nandini. 2016. 'New spirituality, politics of self-empowerment, citizenship, and democracy in contemporary India', *Modern Asian Studies* 50 (3): 934–74. https://doi. org/10.1017/S0026749X14000171.

Gupta, Bhuvi and Jacob Copeman. 2019. 'Awakening Hindu nationalism through yoga: Swami Ramdev and the Bharat Swabhiman movement', *Contemporary South Asia* 27 (3): 313–29. https://doi.org/10.1080/09584935.2019.1587386.

Ilavarasan, P. Vigneswara. 2008. 'Software work in India: A labour process view', in *In an Outpost of the Global Information Economy: Work and workers in India's information technology industry*, edited by Carol Upadhya and A. R. Vasavi, 162–89. New Delhi: Routledge.

Jaffrelot, Christophe. 2008. 'Why should we vote? The Indian middle class and the functioning of the world's largest democracy', in *Patterns of Middle Class Consumption in India and China*, edited by Christophe Jaffrelot and Peter van der Veer, 35–54. New Delhi: Sage.

Karapanagiotis, Nicole. 2013. 'Cyber forms, *"worshipable forms"*: Hindu devotional viewpoints on the ontology of cyber-gods and -goddesses', *International Journal of Hindu Studies* 17 (1): 57–82. https://doi.org/10.1007/s11407-013-9136-4.

Lewis, Tania. 2016. 'Spirited publics? Post-secularism, enchantment and enterprise on Indian television', in *Contemporary Publics: Shifting boundaries in new media, technology and culture*, edited by P. David Marshall, Glenn D'Cruz, Sharyn McDonald and Katja Lee, 283–300. London: Palgrave Macmillan.

Mazzarella, William. 2003. *Shoveling Smoke: Advertising and globalization in contemporary India*. Durham, NC: Duke University Press.

McLuhan, Marshall. 1964. *Understanding Media: The extensions of man*. New York: Signet Books.

Meyer, Birgit. 2011. 'Mediation and immediacy: Sensational forms, semiotic ideologies and the question of the medium', *Social Anthropology* 19 (1): 23–39. https://doi.org/10.1111/j.1469-8676.2010.00137.x.

Ministry of Labour and Employment. 2011. *Economic Survey of India 2010–11*. Government of India.

Mitchell, W. J. T. 2002. 'Showing seeing: A critique of visual culture', *Journal of Visual Culture* 1 (2): 165–81. https://doi.org/10.1177/147041290200100202.

Munshi, Shoma. 2008. 'Yeh dil maange more: Television and consumer choices in a global city', in *Patterns of Middle Class Consumption in India and China*, edited by Christophe Jaffrelot and Peter van der Veer, 263–76. New Delhi: Sage.

Pathak-Narain, Priyanka. 2017. *Godman to Tycoon: The untold story of Baba Ramdev*. New Delhi: Juggernaut Books.

Pinney, Christopher. 2004. *Photos of Gods: The printed image and political struggle in India*. London: Reaktion Books.

Rajagopal, Arvind. 2001. *Politics after Television: Hindu nationalism and the reshaping of the public in India*. Cambridge: Cambridge University Press.

Reeves, Geoffrey W. 1994. 'Indian television: The state, privatisation and the struggle for media autonomy', Centre of Asian Communication, Media Studies and Cultural Studies, Edith Cowan University, Occasional Paper no. 3. Perth: Research Online. https://ro.ecu.edu.au/cgi/viewcontent.cgi?article=7853&context=ecuworks (accessed 13 March 2023).

Scheifinger, Heinz. 2010. 'Internet threats to Hindu authority: Puja-ordering websites and the Kalighat Temple', *Asian Journal of Social Science* 38 (4): 636–56. https://doi.org/10.1163/156853110X517818.

Srinivas, Tulasi. 2010. *Winged Faith: Rethinking globalization and religious pluralism through the Sathys Sai movement*. New York: Columbia University Press.

Srivastava, Sanjay. 2009. 'Urban spaces, Disney-divinity and moral middle classes in Delhi', *Economic and Political Weekly* 44 (26–27): 338–45.

Upadhya, Carol and A. R. Vasavi. 2008. 'Outposts of the global information economy: Work and workers in India's outsourcing industry', in *In an Outpost of the Global Information Economy: Work and workers in India's information technology industry*, edited by Carol Upadhya and A. R. Vasavi, 9–49. New Delhi: Routledge.

Warrier, Maya. 2005. *Hindu Selves in a Modern World: Guru faith in the Mata Amritanandamayi Mission*. Abingdon: RoutledgeCurzon.

Index

References to images are in *italics*; references to notes are indicated by n.

Aastha 419, 420, 423
ABAP (Akhil Bharatiya Akhara Parishad) 46, 271–2
abduction 30, 47, 401, 407
absent-present guruship 29–37, 272–5, 288–91
abuse 2–3; *see also* child sex abuse
ABVP (Akhil Bharatiya Vidyarthi Parishad) 434
accidental guruship 38, 44, 325
Acharya, Satish 11
activism 17–19, 62, 73, 77, 235, 262, 420, 430, 433–436, 439
Adi Granth 214–15, 226–7
Adityanath, Yogi 130, 134
adultery 6
Advaita 329–30, 331–2, 340–7, 347n3
Africa 61, 350
afterlife 300, 336, 422
Agneepath (film) 377
Agni (band) 87
agriculture 79, 137, 404
Akali Dal 217
Akbar, Emperor 383
AKJ (Akhand Kirtani Jatha) 222, 223, 224
Akshardham temple (Delhi) 427
Alfassa, Mirra 168, 169
Amaladoss, Michael: *The Asian Jesus* 354–5
Ambedkar, Dr 18, 19
Amritanandamayi, Mata 14, 101–2, 314, 316
Amritsar 222
Ananda Marga 383–4
Anandamayi Ma 14, 35, 168, 384
Anandmurti Gurumaa 384
Anderson, Ian 72
Andrews, Charles Freer 183, 184, 185, 186–8, 203–4
    and Gandhi 192–5
    and Tagore 196–7, 198–9
Angkang, Stephen 70, 79, 80
Appadurai, Arjun 4, 29, 156
Appar 13
archaeology 99
Arjuna 14, 15, 16
Armed Forces Special Powers Act (AFSPA) 77
art 13–14, 15, 37–8
    and Christ 27–8, 349–51, 355–7, *358*, 359–70
Arunachala mountain 328–9, 331, 338, 345

al-Asad, Hafiz 385
Asaram Bapu 3, 8, 49n14
Asaram Bapu 3, 8
ascetics 5–6, 22, 44, 173
Ashutosh Maharaj 31
Attar Singh Mastuana-wale 221
Auerbach, Erich 326
aura 428
aural traditions 1
Aurobindo, Sri 39, 127–8, 133, 168, 169
authoritarianism 2–3, 21, 34, 49n, 222, 385, 405
avatars 25, 37, 101, 105–6, 110, 175n, 238, 264–5, 304, 352, 427, 431–4, 438–9
Aymard, Orianne 29, 313, 316
Ayurveda 25, 420, 421, 423, 430, 432
AZ I AM doll 114–17

Baba-sects 211, 213, 222–5
Baez, Joan 76
Bajirao Mastani (film) 407
Bajpai, Shailaja 302–3, 307
Balan, V. 356, 357, *358*, 359
Bama Ksepa 171
Banerjee, Mamta 130
banyan trees 364, 368
Bappa 36, 47; *see also* Ganesh Yourself
BAPS 24
Barbie doll 100, *101*, 106–7, *108*, 109, 113–14, 116–17
Barthes, Roland: *Camera Lucida* 334–6
'Basti ki masti' (song) 86–7
Basu, Amrita 7, 49n14
Basu, Anustup 21
Baudrillard, Jean 272, 286, 287–8
Bayly, Susan 318–19
beards 125, 127, 128, 129–30
Beckerlegge, Gwilym 334
Bellamy, Carla 318
Beltramini, Enrico 354
Bengaluru 350, 351, 356
Benjamin, Walter 87, 286, 428
    'Dream kitsch' 317
Berlant, Lauren 5, 29
Bhagwat Gita 16
Bhairavi Brahmani 168
Bharat Swabhimaan ('India self-respect') 420–1, 428–9, 434–6, 438–9, 440–1
bhārata 153–4

INDEX   **445**

Bharati, Uma 134
Bhatti, Shaila 337–8
Bhindranwale, Jarnail Singh 222
BJP (Bharatiya Janata Party) 8, 20, 21, 132–4,
    139–40
    and guru branding 41
    and television 424
    and yoga 105–6
    see also Modi, Narendra
BJS (Bharatiya Jana Sangh) 139
'Blowin' in the wind' (song) 74–5
blues music 61–2, 64, 86
Bollywood 327–8, 375–6
books 95
Boomarang (band) 77–8
Bose, Nandalal 15, 16–17
Bouillier, Véronique 19–20, 29
Brahma Kumaris 24, 168
Brahmachari, Balak 31, 321n14
Brahmananda 166, 167
Brahmanism 40n35
Brahmasutrabhasya 4
branding 5, 21, 41–3, 97, 131–2, 143n1
Brazil 95, 116
breathing gurus 25
bribery see corruption
bricolage 63–4
Bridges, Robert 204
Brihadeshwara temple (Thanjavur) 14
British colonial government 24, 83, 133,
    134
    and letters 183, 184–5, 196–7
Brunton, Paul 329
Buddha 157, 177n19, 364
Buddhism 13, 37, 39
Bull, Sara 183, 185, 189
Burma see Myanmar

Cadava, Eduardo 336
Caitanya 155, 157, 160, 164–5
capitalism 85
capitivation 44–8
Cartier-Bresson, Henri 329, 340–2, 347n7
caste 4, 15, 310; see also Dalits
castration 11, 18
Cave, Nick: 'Red Right Hand' 2
Celebrity Big Brother (TV show) 10
celibacy 6, 22, 41, 130, 132, 153, 194, 200,
    201, 203, 274, 290, 407, 435
Censor Board 377–8, 388–9, 392,
    405–6
censorship 7
Chamroy, Ngachonmi 66, 76, 78–9
'Chankhom philava' (song) 69–70, 85
Chattampi Swamikal 163
Chaudhary, Zahid 344
Chaurasia, Hariprasad 72
child sex abuse 7, 305–6
children 96–7, 99, 277–9; see also toys
China 87, 104, 105, 116, 137
Choithar 67–8
Chola bronzes 13, 31
Christ see Jesus Christ
Christ the Guru (Manoj) 349, 350, 351
Christian Musicological Society of India 349,
    356

Christianity 27–8, 174, 279–81; see also
    Jesus Christ; Mashangva, Rewben;
    missionaries
cinema see films
Clifford, James 326
clothing 11, 14, 22, 38, 45, 51n, 64, 71, 82,
    106–7, 278, 338, 341, 409
    and Modi 126, 1289–30, 131–2, 136–7, 143n5
Cole, W. Owen 211–12
Colston, Edward 19
Comaroff, John and Jean: Ethnicity, Inc. 38,
    40, 41, 85
comedy 9–11
commodification 43–4
comportment 38
conceptual art 367–8
Copeman, Jacob 62, 96, 126, 129, 207n, 292,
    326, 347n1
    The Guru in South Asia 352
Corbin, Henri 165
corruption 7, 10, 246–52
COVID-19 pandemic 12, 22, 24–5, 66
    and Modi 125, 128–30, 135–6, 137–9
cow protection 23, 400, 401–2, 406–7
criminality 6–8, 10–11
crypto-futurity 301, 317–19

Dalits 17–19, 29, 224–5, 357
dargahs 317–19
darshan 3, 26, 45, 49n4, 129, 273–5, 304–5,
    316, 319, 396, 430, 432
Dasgupta, Koushiki 41
De Man, Paul 337
death 31–2, 34
    and Sai Baba 299–304, 306–10, 319–20
deceased gurus 31–2, 34
deep play 5, 23, 38, 46
deindividuation 102
Deleuze, Gilles 327
Dera Sacha Sauda (DSS) 3, 10–11, 23–4,
    47–8, 223–4, 375–6, 378, 380–5; see
    also MSG: Messenger of God (film series)
Dera Sachkhand Ballan 224–5
Derrida, Jacques 286–7
    Specters of Marx 309–10, 311, 320
Desai, Mahadev 185
Deseriis, Marco 34
Desi Toys 107
désika images 150, 151, 152–6; see also
    'Immortal Gurus of Bhārata'
devata images 150
Devi, Indra 47
Devi Ma 169
Devi, Phoolan 18
devotion 2, 376–7, 381–2
Dick, Philip K. 237
didactic death 300, 320n3
digital media see social media; video
Dinkar, Niharika 26
disciples see Indophile disciples
disintermediation 301
distributed guruship 5, 30–7
Divya Yog Pharmacy 423
'doing seeing' 420–1, 430–9
dolls 30, 98–9; see also yoga dolls
Doordarshan 424–5, 429

Doval, Ajit 404
dreams 314–17, 317, 322n24
Dronacharya 15, 16–18
DT (Damdami Taksaal) 222, 223
Duchamp, Marcel 37–8
Durga 14
Dyal Singh, Baba 220
Dylan, Bob 39, 64, 72, 74–7

ecologies of creation 63, 70–2, 89–90
ecumenism 28–9
education 17–18
egalitarian pluralism 149, 170–5
Ekalavya 16–18, 20, 31
Ekanatha, Sri Sant 28
Elamkunnapuzha, Fr Joy 356, 357, *358*
Elaridi, Frank 278, 280
Elmhirst, Leonard 185, 204
Elsewhere 301–2, 312–14, 315–16
encryption 301, 310–12, 320
ethnocracy 140–1, 144n15
exoticism 85–6

fashion dolls 100
Fateh Singh 221–2
Featherheads (band) 82, 84–5, 88
figures 325–8
films 9–10, 11, 376–7; *see also* Bollywood;
 MSG: Messenger of God (film series)
F.I.R. (TV show) 10
FirstCry 106–7
Fisher-Price 111–12
Flipkart 107
flooding 272, 281–8, 291–2
folk music 39–40, 61–2, 70–2, 86
 and definitions 90n2
 and Dylan 74–6
 and preservation 80–3
 and survival 87–9
Fonseca, Angelo da 355
Foucault, Michel 10, 26, 80, 431, 433
fusion 63–4, 69–70, 89–90

Gaidinliu, Rani 40
gaming 36–7; *see also* Ganesh Yourself
Gandhi, M. K. 12–13, 35, 202–4, 428
 and assassination 139
 and branding 41–2
 and Cartier-Bresson 341, 342
 and clothing 136
 and films 407
 and image 131
 and love letters 191–6
 and neo-Hinduism 127–8, 133
 and Western disciples 183, 185–6, 188–9,
  190, 199–200, 201
Gandhi, Rajiv 222
Gandhi, Vikram 46
Ganesh 25, 37
Ganesh Yourself 235–9, 266–8
 and dynamics 259–60
 and first interaction 239–46
 and parameters 260–6
 and second interaction 246–58
Gaytri Parivar 24
Gell, Alfred 30, 31

gender 15
Genette, Gérard 326
ghosts 311–12
Girard, René 14
Gleason, Benjamin 287
Goa 28
God Manifests Himself (film) 437
Godman, David 329
Gokhale, Gopal Krishna 186
Golwalkar, Guruji 20
Goodwin, Josiah 190, 207n10
Gopalan, Lalitha: *Cinema of Interruptions* 328
Goraknāth 158
gosains 6
graffiti 17, 18
Gretter, Sarah 287
Grewal, J. S. 226
Grimaud, Emmanuel 393
Guide (film) 38–9, 46
Gunning, Tom 382
gurmat (teaching) 211, 217, 219, 226–7
Guru Arjan 34, 213–15
Guru Gobind Singh 11, 34, 213, 215
 and succession 219–20, 221, 226
Guru Granth Sahib 33, 34, 95, 215, 217–18
Guru Hargobind 214
Guru Nanak 157, 213, 215, 230
 and Siddhas 228–9
 and succession 227
'Guru, Inc.' 5, 41–3
guru-tattva ('teacher's principle') 96
guru trope 126, 352–5, 370–2
 Jesus Christ 356–7, 359–60
Gurumata 226

habitus 97
Hacker, Paul 170–1
hairstyles 85, 113, 130, 136
Haridāsa 157
Harimandir 214, 227
Haryana 16
healthcare 24–5, 420, 422–3; *see also*
 Ayurveda; yoga
Hedgewar, K. B. 134, 139
Heehs, Peter: *The Lives of Sri Aurobindo* 39
Henn, Alexander 28
hidden cameras 3, 10, 49n3
Himalaya 165
Hindu deities 104
Hindu Janajagruti Samiti (Society for Hindu
 Awakening) 21
Hindu nationalism 14–15, 133–4, 420–1,
 426–8, 437–41
 and Modi 125
 and Tagore 187
 and television 424
 and Western disciples 201–2
 see also Hindutva
Hindu symbols 164–5
Hindutva 4–5, 6–9, 19–29
 and DSS 382–3
 and Manu 18–19
 and Modi 127–8, 142
 and *MSG* 396, 398–405, 406–7
 and RSS 139–40
Hirschkind, Charles 62

Ikegame, Aya 15, 62, 326, 347n1
The Guru in South Asia 352
'Immortal Gurus of *Bhārata*' 26–7, 150, *151*,
   152–6
   and cultural biography 156–61
   and pluralism 170–5
   and variants 161, *162*, 163–70
Imphal 66
incarnations 47
incorporeal Word (*anhad sabda*) 212, 230
Indian Constitution 20–1, 153–4
Indian government 103–7; *see also* Modi,
   Narendra
Indophile disciples 184–90, 191–207
International Yoga Day 21, 105
intimidation 3, 7
Isha Foundation 43–4
ISKCON 42
Islam 7, 174, 175n8; *see also* Muslims;
   Sufism
IT sector 425, 427

Jackson, Michael 375
Jai Santoshi Maa (film) 377
Jainism 13
Jajo, Grace 66
Jammu and Kashmir 403–4
jeevandanis (life donors) 435–6
Jesuits 28
Jesus Christ 27–8, 349–51
   artworks 355–7, *358*, 359–70
   and guru trope 352–5, 370–2
Jina Mahāvīra 157
Joshi, Bahiyyaji 24

K-serials 426, 437
Kabir 27, 40, 158, 171, 174
Kalam, A. P. J. Abdul 276
Kali 14
Kallenbach, Hermann 191–2,
   207n15
Kapoor, Ekta 425–6, 437
Kapur, Geeta 407
Karapanagiotis, Nicole 42
Kaviraj, Gopinath: *Jñānaganja* 164–5
Kerala 349–50, 351, 356, 386–7
Kerrigan, William 319
Khan, Shah Rukh 377
Khattar, Manohar Lal 16
killings 3, 21–2
knowledge 84–5, 95
Kripalani, Lekhraj K. 168
Krishna 13, 14
Krishna Consciousness 42
Krishnaswami, T. N. 342, 343–4, 345
Krrish (film) 387
Kumaré (documentary) 46

Landry, Sarah 279, 293n2
language 86, 88, 135–6, 140–1
Lannoy, Richard 352, 353–4, 359–60
Lasch, Christopher 378
Lederle, Fr Matthew 366
legitimacy 4
LEGO 104–5
Lenin, Vladimir 311, 321n21

letters 34–5, 183, 184–5, 200–7
   and communities 185–6
   and Gandhi 188–9
   and longing 196–200
   and love 190–6
   and Tagore 187–8
   and Vivekananda 189–90
Lévi-Strauss, Claude 63–4
lifestyle 100–3, 106
Lokenath Bahmachari 172
longing 196–200
Longkumer, Anungla Zoe 73–4
Longkumer, Arkotong 15–16
Longowal, Harchand Singh 222
Lott, Dr Eric 364–5
Love Guru, The (film) 9
Lucia, Amanda 3, 8, 31, 32–3, 43, 143n,
   313–4, 316

McCartney, Patrick 21
McDowell, Andrew 311–12
McKean, Lise 20, 21
MacLeod, Josephine 183, 185, 191
McLeod, W. H. 213, 216
Madhusūdana Sarasvatī 158
Madhvas 4
Mahabharata 15, 19, 20
Mahabharata (TV series) 377, 401
Maharaj, Sakshi 6, 134
Mahendravarman I 13
Mahesh Yogi 130
Malreddy, Pavan Kumar 9–10
Mani, P. R. S. 334
Manipur 39–40, 66, 67–8, 77
Mann Ki Baat (radio programme) 135
Manoj, M. P.: *Christ the Guru* 350, 351, 356,
   357, *358*, 359–61
Manu 18–19
marketing 45–6, 85–7; *see also* branding
Marley, Bob 39, 64, 72–3, 76
Marshall, John 99
masculinity 114, 127, 132, 194, 201, 376, 398,
   400
Mashangva, Guru Rewben 16, 39–41, 48,
   61–4, 89–90
   and Christianity 78–80
   and guruship 80–3
   and influences 72–4
   and knowledge 84–5
   and marketing 85–7
   and sound 64, *65*, 66–70, 71–2
   and survival 87–9
Masoji, Vinayak 355
   The Last Supper 356
'Matek chim' (song) 71
Mathew, Fr Saji 350
   St Anthony's Shrine 356–7, 361–4, 371–2
Mathias, Fr 350
Matrix, The (film) 388
Mattel 109–11
Maugham, W. Somerset: *The Razor's Edge*
   331–2, 347n5
mausolea 32, 312–19
Mazzarella, William 10, 87, 308, 378, 389,
   426
Mbembe, Achille 385

meditation 43, 111–12
militarism 114
mimesis 11–14, 16, 38, 87
Mira Behn *see* Slade, Madeleine
Mīrābāī 168
miracles 244, 266, 292, 304–5, 377
   and *MSG* 387–96, 405–6
Missio Germany 350, 357, 364–70
missionaries 186–7, 197
Mitchell, W. J. T. 421
Mittermaier, Amira 301–2
Miyazaki, Hirokazu 29
Modi, Narendra 11–12, 24, 133, 137–8
   and clothing 136–7
   and guru persona 21–3, 38, 125–32, 138–9,
     140–3
   and language 135–6
   and *MSG* films 379, 383, 404, 406, 407–8,
     409
   and yoga 105–6
Modi Toys 104
money laundering 10
monks of India *151*, *162–3*, 175n5
MSG: Messenger of God (film series) 3, 23–4,
     51n66, 376, 377–80, 385–6
   and *Hind ka Napak Ko Jawab: MSG Lion
     Heart 2* 402–4
   and *Jattu Engineer* 404–5
   and lineage 396, *397*, 398–402
   and miracles 387–96
   and totality 405–10
multi-mediation 300–1
Mumbai 45
murder 7, 11; *see also* killings
music *see* folk music; sound
music festivals 73–4
musical instruments 70
Muslims:
   and killings 21–2
   and Modi 127, 143n1
   and *MSG* 401, 403–4, 406–7
   and saints' tombs 301
Myanmar 69, 87
Mysore 15

Nābhādās: *Bhaktamāla* 170
Naga, Alobo 64, 71, 79–80, 82–3, 86, 88
Naga community 67–8, 79–80
Naga Students' Federation (NSF) 76
Nambudiri, Guruvayur Surya 10
Namdharis 219–20
Narayan, R. K.: *Guide* 38–9
Narayana Guru 163
narratives 97–8, 103, 213–18
Nataraja Guru 163
National Highway 39 69
nationalism *see* Hindu nationalism
nature 39, 70–1
Nehru, Jawaharlal 341, 342
Nesbitt, Eleanor 221
'Ngahuirot haoki kachi thali' (song) 70
Nirankaris 213, 219, 220, 222–4
Nirmala sect 226
Nitaichaitanya Paramhansadev, Sri Sri 161,
   162
Nithyananda, Swami 8, 10, 32–3, 275–7

and flooding 281–4, 285–6, 292
   and message 277–81
   and scandal 271–5, 288–91
Nityānanda 157
Nivedita, Sister *see* Noble, Margaret
Niyananda, Bhagawan 163
Nobili, Roberto de 352
Noble, Margaret 183, 184, 185, 188–91,
   200–1
non-absent guruship 34
North East Zone Cultural Centre (NEZCC)
   15–16, 80–1
Northeast India 61, 62, 64, 66

Obama, Barack 131, 143n5, 409
Ohm, Britta 138
Om 20
oral traditions 1, 63, 70
Osborne, Arthur 329
Osho né Rajneesh 37, 39, 46, 164
outrage politics 6–7

Padmaavat (film) 407
Padmapādācārya 157
Padoux, André 1, 165
Pagnis, Vishnupant 407
Pakistan 403–4
Palmer, Norris 306
pandemic *see* COVID-19 pandemic
paramparā 81, 95, 96
Paré, Zaven 36, 235
Parliament of Religions 155
Patañjalayoga 115–16
Patanjali Yogpeeth 26, 420–1, 423, 430–9,
   440–1
patronage 62
Pearson, William 183, 184, 185, 186–8
   and Tagore 197–8, 205–6
Pechilis, Karen 5
performance 5, 14, 22–3, 31, 37–41, 46, 47,
   125–7, 129, 137, 140, 185, 201, 230,
   235, 243, 273, 377, 409, 424
perfume 315–16
persecution 7–8
phenomenology 212–13
philanthropy 305
photography 30, 35–6, 41, 158–9
   and Anandamayi Ma 384
   and Ramana Maharshi 329–30, 332–47
   and retouching 39
pilgrimage 318–19, 322n24
Pilot Baba 10
Pinney, Christopher 337–8
PK (film) 10
pluralism 170–5
poet-saints 13
Polak, Henry 191
politics 131–5, 428–9
   and Sikhism 216, 217, 221–2, 223–4
   see also Hindutva; Modi, Narendra
pop music 375–6
portrait groups *151–2*, 154–5; see also
   'Immortal Gurus of *Bhārata*'
postal communication *see* letters
Prakashmani 168
Prem Sai 47, 52n82

INDEX   **449**

presence 29–33
prosperity gospel 279–81
protest 18–19, 25, 77–8, 137, 222–3
public gifting 5
public gurus 6, 10, 23–6, 40, 42, 43–4, 383
Punjab 99, 221–2, 223–5
pushtimarg sex scandal 3, 6
Puttaparthi 299–300, 302, 304, 305, 319
Pyarelal 185

Radhe Maa 45–6
Raghu Dixit Project 86
Rahm, Alaya 305–6
Rai, Amit 327–8
Raj, Solomon 355
   Padmasana 356
Rajadhyaksha, Ashish 405
Rajaraja I, King 14
Raje, Vasundhara 400
Rajneesh *see* Osho né Rajneesh
Rajputs 400–1, 406–7
Ram, Munshi 186, 194
Ram Rahim Singh Ji Insan, Gurmeet 10–11,
   223, 375–6, 384–7; see also *MSG:*
   Messenger of God (film series)
Ramakrishna 28–9, 41, 158
Ramana Maharshi 35–6, 44, 325, 328–32,
   347n2
   and photography 332–47
Rāmānujā 157
Ramayana (TV serial) 14–15
Ramdas Ramdas 163
Ramdev, Baba 3, 24, 25–6, 42, 130
   and doing seeing 430–9
   and Hindu slogan 143n6
   and politics 133, 134
   and televised yoga 419–23, 426–8, 429–30,
   440–1
Ramakrishna 28, 41, 158, 167, 168,
   176n11
Ramakrishna Mission 24, 132, 158, 167,
   175n3, 176n11, 178n26, 207n2
Ranjitha 289
rape 7, 11
rationalists 25
Ratnakar, J. 302
Ravidas, Bhagat 224–5
Ravidas, Sant 40
Razor's Edge, The (film) 330–2
readymades 37, 38, 39–40, 45–6
Reddy, Gita 303
'Redemption song' (song) 73
religious nationalism *see* Hindu nationalism
remediation 14–19
resistance 77–8
Revill, George 87
Rikhang, Matbam 74
robots 30, 36–7, 47; *see also* Ganesh Yourself
Rolland, Romain 185, 186, 188
roots 72–4
Roshan, Hrithik 387
Rothenstein, William 204
Roy, Arundhati 137
Roy, Rammohan 173
RSS (Rashtriya Swayamsevak Sangh) 16, 20,
   21, 134

and ideology 139–40
and Mashangva 86–7
and Modi 142
and students 434–5
Rudra, S. K. 186, 194
Rungsung, Apen 69

Sabavala, Jehangir 359
sabda-guru (Guru as Word) 1, 33–4, 212–13,
   230–2
   and functions 215–16, 225–7
Sadhguru (Jaggi Vasudev) 16, 42, 43–4, 130,
   133
Safaya, Dr N. 303
Sahi, Jyoti 350, 351, 355, 357, 364–70
Sai Baba 174, 376, 321n19
   and darshan 304–5
   and death 299–304, 319–20
   and encryption 310–12
   and funeral 306–10
   and mausoleum 312–17
   and scandal 305–6
Sai Baba, Shirdi 151, 162, 304, 306, 310, 313,
   318, 319, 321n17
Sai Gayathri chant 310
saints of India *152*, 153–6, 175n5, 380–1
Saivism 13
samadhi 301
   and Brahmachari 321n14
   and crypto-futurity 317–19
   and Sai Baba 312–14, 315–17, 320
Sangh Parivar 20, 21, 140, 142
Śankara 157, 171
Sanskar 419, 422–3
Sant Tukaram (film) 376, 377, 407
Santan Dal 321n14
Sants 220–2
'Sapsa runglo sapsa' (song) 72
Sarada Devi 168
Sarasvati, Jagadamba 168
Sarkar, Prabhat Ranjan 383–4
satguru 227–30
satire 9–11
Scheer, Monique 202
Schouten, Jan 353
Scientology, Church of 284
screen presences 30
sectarianism 149, 154–5, 159–61, 171–2
   and Sikhism 218–19
semiotics 47–8
Sen, Keshubchandra 173, 174
service spectacles 381–2
sexual assault 6, 18
   and DSS 376, 394–6
   and Nithyananda 272–3
   and Sai Baba 305–5
   see also child sex abuse
SGPC (Shiromani Gurdwara Parbhandhak
   Committee) 217, 218
Shankar, Sri Sri Ravi 24, 42, 130, 143n8
Shankaracharya 27
Shantiniketan 183, 187, 192–3, 197, 198–9
Sharda, Kiku 11, *12*, 47
Sharma, Maya 306–7, 310
Sharmila, Irom 77
shishyas (students) 81

Shital, B. K. 168
Shiva 13, 14
Shonen Knife (band) 86
Shri Sathya Sai Foundation 24
Shubhananda Swami 163
Siddhas 228–9
Sikhism 1, 11, 211–12, 213–14
    and distributed guru-ship 33–4
    and Namdharis 219–20
    and Sants 220–2
    and *satguru* 227–30
    and violence 222–5
    see also Guru Granth Sahib; *sabda-guru*
        (Guru as Word)
Silber, Illana 5
Singh, Gurbachan 222–3
Singh, Maharaja Ranjit 220, 226
Singh, Sobha 11
Singh Mastuana-wale, Sant Attar 221
Sivananda 164
Slade, Madeleine 183, 184, 186, 188–9
    and Gandhi 195–6, 199–200, 202–3
    and Hindu nationalism 201–2
slavery 19, 61, 73, 191, 203–4
Sloterdijk, Peter 37, 39
Smith, Daniel 150
Smith, Joseph 319
social media 7, 44, 127, 136, 281–4
socioculture 97
Sorcar, P. C. 305
sound 62–4
South Africa 191, 192–4
South Korea 87
Souza, Francis Newton 355
sovereignty 32, 34, 73–4, 212, 215, 218, 221,
    225–6, 228, 274–5, 385, 411n
Soviet Union 311
spectacle 10, 45–6, 129, 142, 200, 222, 307,
    375, 377, 381–3, 385, 393–4, 410
spiderweb guruship 5, 43–8
sport 16
SRM (Sikh Rahi Maryada) 218–19
states 15–16
statuary 19
sterilisation 18
Sterne, Jonathan 62
subscription 43–4
Sudhir, Abhishek 389
Sufism 317–19, 321n23
surveillance 7, 10
Swamy, Subramaniam 8
Sword of the Chosen One (documentary) 77
Syria 385

Tagore, Debendranath 173
Tagore, Rabindranath 12–13, 35, 205–6
    and Andrews 193, 194, 203–4
    and Modi 130
    and neo-Hinduism 133
    and Western disciples 183, 185–6, 187–8,
        196–9
Taiwan 105
Tambiah, Stanley 316
Taneja, Anand 301
Tangkhul culture 40, 61, 64, 71, 86
Tanhaji (film) 407

Tanner, Jeremy 32
Taussig, Michael 313
television 3, 10, 14–15, 423–6
    and Sai Baba 299–300, 302–4,
        306–11
    and yoga 25–6, 419–23, 426–8, 429–30,
        440
Tendulkar, Sachin 307
texts and sayings 30
Thayil, Jeet: *Names of the Women* 351
Thompson, Edward J. 186, 204
Tiruvannamalai 328–9, 330, 332–3
Tiwari 10
tombs 30, 32, 317–19
totality 161, 383–6, 399, 405–10
Toy Association of India 104
toys 42–3, 96–7, 103–7; *see also* dolls
Trindade, Angela: *Christ and the Woman of
    Samaria* 355–6
Trump, Donald 284–5
Tulsīdās 158

Übelmesser, Fr Joe 366
Udasi sect 226
Ukhrul 67, 68
United States of America (USA) 61, 276,
    289–91
    and toys 107, 109, 114–15
unstable totality 408–10
Uri (film) 407
Uri attack 403–4

Vardhman Seva Kendra 24
Vasudev, Jaggi *see* Sadhguru
Vedanti Maharaj 10
vegetarianism 383, 399, 400, 401–2,
    406–7
Vemula, Rohith 17, 18
verbal traditions 1
VHP (Vishva Hindu Parishad) 19, 20, 26–7,
    134, 139
    and College of Holy Men 21
video 3, 43–4
Vienna 224–5
violence 18, 216–17, 218–19, 222–5
Vishnu 13
Visvanathan, Susan 35–6, 336–7
    The Christians of Kerala 349–50
Vivekananda Kendra 20, 35, 41, 200–1
    and Advaita 330
    and neo-Hinduism 127–8, 133
    and portrait 158, 166–7, 176n11
    and Western disciples 183, 185–6,
        189–91
Volunteer Village Force (VVF) 67
Voss Roberts, M 350–1, 371

Wallang, Keith 73
Warrier, Maya 6, 126
Weber, Max 138
Wedeen, Lisa 385
Welling, G. G. 333
WhatsApp 61, 66, 282, 332
women 7, 112–13, 168–70, 436–8
Word *see* incorporeal Word; *sabda-guru*
world gurus 21

Yadav, Aman 287
YEGO 104–5
Yiftachel, Oren 144n15
yoga 21, 42, 95, 103–7
  and Modi 22, 127
  and television 26, 419–23, 426–8, 429–30, 440
yoga dolls 6, 42, 96–7, 117–19
  and AZ I AM 114–17
  and history 99–100
  and lifestyle 100–3
and meditation 111–12
and narratives 112–14
and USA 107, *108*, 109–11
Yoga Joes 114
Young Mizo Association (YMA) 77–8
YouTube 10, 33, 66, 106, 273, 277–8, 282, 395, 429
Yurchak, Alexei 311, 321n21
Yusuf Khan 318–19

Zubair, Mohammed 3, 6–7

Milton Keynes UK
Ingram Content Group UK Ltd.
UKHW051513070224
437437UK00026B/322